To my wife, Hannelore,
who died shortly after this book was completed;
and to my brothers Michael, Adrian and John.

The Brothers Mann

The Brothers Mann

The Lives of Heinrich and Thomas Mann
1871-1950 and 1875-1955

NIGEL HAMILTON

SECKER & WARBURG
LONDON

First published in England 1978 by
Martin Secker & Warburg Limited
14 Carlisle Street, London W1V 6NN

Copyright © 1978 Nigel Hamilton

SBN: 436 19103 2

c

Printed in Great Britain by
REDWOOD BURN LIMITED
Trowbridge and Esher

CONTENTS

AUTHOR'S NOTE AND ACKNOWLEDGMENTS

The Brothers Mann was intended to provide a historical portrait of un-doubtedly the most distinguished and representative literary brotherhood in modern history. Curiously, neither life has hitherto attracted a biographer in English, but by attempting the life-story of both the Manns I have had to omit many names and influences which properly belong to their individual lives. Despite its limitations, I hope nevertheless that this account will be of interest and value both to general reader and to the specialist.

I am indebted to numerous individuals and institutions for their help and material. The two primary archives, the Heinrich Mann Archiv in East Berlin and the Thomas Mann Archiv in Zurich, were more than generous in their assistance; to the Lübeck Stadtbibliothek and Stadt Archiv, the Schiller-National-Museum in Marbach a. Neckar, the British Museum, the German Institute Library, the Institute of Germanic Studies, London, and the Greenwich Public Libraries and their staffs I owe a great debt of gratitude. Dr Hans Bürgin, Ida Herz, Professors Alfred Kantorowicz and Golo Mann, Mrs C. Bloch-Zavrel, Dr E. Plessen, Professor Pierre Bertaux and Dr and Mrs G.B. Fischer all helped me personally. Thanks to a grant from the Inter Nationes department of the Federal Republic I was able to make an extended visit to West Germany, as well as further trips made possible by the generosity of my English and American publishers. Lastly, but in fact firstly, I must thank my German-born wife Hannelore who first introduced me to the subject and assisted me throughout the writing of this book.

I wish also to thank the owners, copyright-holders and publishers of the numerous letters, works and writings quoted in this volume. Wherever possible I have used English translations where they exist (see bibliography), only very occasionally retranslating where the sense is not made clear in such short extracts; otherwise I have had to make my own translations from the German, and frequently in the case of Heinrich Mann from the French. Here I must crave the indulgence of the reader for my ineptitude — for only a professional can really do justice to the linguistic skills both of Heinrich and Thomas Mann — and even professional translators have never managed to convey the essentially poetic diction of Heinrich Mann. If the poetry and delight of the original has therefore been lost, I hope at least that the story itself of their unique careers has not suffered.

PART ONE

CHAPTER ONE

Genesis

The little town of Lübeck stands today as a forgotten testament to Hanseatic greatness; a city founded by Henry the Lion in 1158 that came to rule the Baltic for almost seven centuries; a republic whose laws and constitution were exported as later were those of Great Britain; a city built on the North-German peninsular between the Trave and the Wakenitz, some seventy miles from Hamburg, on the instep of what was known as the Eastern Sea.

The Mann family arrived relatively late in Lübeck's history, shortly before the Napoleonic Wars ended its once world-wide reputation forever. From Jena General Bernadotte chased the Prussian Blücher to Lübeck's gates, and the town was persuaded to give him shelter. Overnight Lübeck's neutrality, which had preserved its independence — and wealth — for more than half a millennium, was broken. Bernadotte was able to infiltrate troops from behind. Blücher was shelled, and fled; and the French made mincemeat of a population quite unaccustomed to the reality of war.

The city had been built, planned to avoid this, with a circle of moats and fortifications thrown about it and high, imposing gatehouses to fend off the attacker. Its warehouses within looked out over the quays; and scarcely a house in the city did not have floors that served as storerooms, granaries, or cellars for the rich produce of the north, east and south. Even the churches — vast, towering cathedrals in plain red brick — gave the impression of giant storage houses of God.

But the Senate's mistake could not be rectified. Blücher (future saviour of Waterloo) countered the Burgomaster's plea of neutrality with the despairing words: "I am a Mecklenburger and have not been able to preserve my own state." He added, however, the Burgomaster need not be alarmed. "I promise you," he assured him, "that if you give me and my troops only the bare necessities we need, no hair on your heads will be touched, nor dust soil your shoes."

It was an empty promise, and two days later Blücher surrendered, unable to prevent the pillaging of one of Europe's oldest Free cities.

Thus Lübeck was cut out of the European trading network in Napoleon's attempt to blockade Great Britain. The city became the prey of unscrupulous garrison commanders and army generals. All silver vanished — knives, forks, spoons, all linen was stolen and ransomed. The port was closed, the warehouses ransacked. The merchants of Lübeck never recovered.

The rise of the Mann family in Lübeck, therefore, must be seen against a century that opened disastrously for the city. Such tribulations were, however, not uncommon in a family whose ancestors traced wealth and good-standing, perseverance and piety beyond the Thirty Years' War.

2

It seems likely the Manns originated as peasants in Bavaria; then turned to tailoring in Nuremberg in the Middle Ages, and moved from Parchim to Grabow in the second half of the seventeenth century. It was there Johann Mann was elected to the Senate and town council; there that a fire broke out in the city and reduced the family's house and business to ashes.

According to Johann Mann's grandson, however, Almightly God looked after Johann's daily bread until, at the venerable age of eighty-seven, he was ready to move into "better accommodation".

The year was 1744. Johann's son, Siegmund, had in the meantime moved to Rostock on the Baltic Sea, where he became a Master of the Guild of Tailors. His first wife he chose from this circle, a Court Tailor's daughter by the name of Christina Richterin. His second was a pastor's widow.

Siegmund's son carried the name of both his father and Joachim; and it was he who, for reasons unknown, decided to set aside the family business and try his luck at sea.

Joachim Siegmund Mann's idea was to leave his home and not to reappear "for the space of ten years". He joined the Baltic seafarers, trading to Norway, Sweden and Russia, and finished life as a "brewer and shipowner".

As an apprentice young Joachim Siegmund almost drowned in Bergen, Norway; and the episode provides perhaps the first intimation of "literary" leanings in the Mann family: for in a white, sewn-bound copybook Joachim Siegmund continued what was known as the "family bible" — a record of family events, from his grandfather onwards: their moments of birth and death, of marriage and provenance, of tragedy and miraculous escape. This "family bible" was passed from father to son and never lost.[1]

Joachim Siegmund recorded his "near-death", however, not for literary purposes, nor to "reveal" his "passions", but to remind his descendants of the "glory of God".

It was evening in Bergen when the accident occurred. It was dark already and the boy was trying to guide his boat through the many moored yachts to the Rostock landing-stage. Suddenly the oak thole or rowlock on which he was standing snapped, and the boy fell headlong into the water. After surfacing twice, he did not reappear a third time; by good fortune one of the yachts broke its mooring; in the space it left the boy's hair was sighted; and amid bellowing and screaming the boy was rescued.

As had been the case with his father, only one of Joachim Siegmund's sons survived; and he too underwent a curious and distant apprenticeship. He was fourteen and at home during the annual Whitsun Fair at Rostock when a Lübeck merchant made his acquaintance and, taking a liking to the boy, offered to take him back to Lübeck and train him in his business. The boy was Johann Siegmund Mann; and at the age of twenty-eight, in 1790, he established, with the help of his benefactors, his own company: J.S. Mann, Grain Merchants, Commission and Shipping Agents. Four years later he was granted citizenship, the "Burgher's Letter", of the Free Hanseatic City of Lübeck.

Thus began the Mann dynasty in Lübeck: the beginning of a merchant house that would last for one hundred and one years.

In September 1790 Johann Siegmund Mann married. More than likely his wife was chosen for her dowry, for the match was made in Hamburg, on a special "visit" organized for him by the wife of a friend, Frau Bousset.

The bride, Anna Catherina Grotjan, was the daughter of a Hamburg merchant; even so Johann Siegmund can hardly have been greatly excited by her, for even fifty years later the author of a little ditty in local dialect could recollect that the bridegroom had failed to appear for the wedding:

But oh, no bridegroom shows his face
"Something terrible must have taken place"
Is what they whimper back in Höltigboom
Who will save us poor folks from this bad dream?[2]

In the end the marriage did, however, take place; a year later a daughter was born, and in 1797 a son, to be known as Johann Siegmund Mann junior.

At six the son was sent away to school. For his secondary education the boy returned to Lübeck and attended the famous town grammar school, the Katharineum.

These were the worst years in Lübeck's history, the years of French occupation; but in December 1813 the same general who had taken the city arrived with a Swedish army to relieve it: the Crown Prince of Sweden, ex-General Bernadotte. From the boom year of 1806 when the harbour could not handle the number of ships seeking entry, the yearly shipping figures had sunk to four hundred in 1807, fifty ships in 1808, and from 1811 no movement at all. For a township utterly dependent on its mercantile trade, coerced into paying penal sums in war-taxes to Napoleon, it had spelled almost universal bankruptcy.

Bernadotte's victorious army was thus ecstatically welcomed, as far as

Hanseatic uprightness allowed: candles in the windows — yet even there "only as many as scarcity, need and destitution allowed".

With the French had departed the Danish occupying forces; and the enmity between Lübeck and Denmark — ancient rivals in Baltic fishing and maritime history — was further fanned by the Danish collusion in Napoleon's bitter empire.

Johann Siegmund junior was destined for commercial rather than academic success. He was withdrawn from school at the age of sixteen and sent abroad to study the methods of Hanseatic trade. Here, despite repeated ill-health, he showed an astonishing talent for business. Johann Siegmund senior had "by unflagging industry, combined with thrifty domestic life" achieved a respectable position of bourgeois prosperity; now his son brought to bear his own ideas on the activities of the firm: namely the selection of those areas of commerce commonly neglected by Lübeck merchants, the rich produce of its Holstein and Mecklenburg hinterland — from grain to rape-seed, skins, hide, bones, oil and oil-cakes. As more and more of Lübeck's commission-trading fell into the hands of traders from outside the Baltic — Dutch, English, and even Hamburgers — so Johann Siegmund junior's specialization began to pay off. By 1823 his father was sufficiently impressed to take him as a partner in the firm, entitled to a third of all profits.

Assured — as far as could be foreseen — of a reasonable burgher's income, Johann Siegmund junior now tried for the hand of the daughter of Senator Wunderlich, who later became Burgomaster of Lübeck. The girl's name was Emily; and there followed five children and "nine of the most precious years of my life" with her. Delivery of the fifth child, however, resulted in Emily's death; all three daughters failed to survive; and the two sons, for unknown reasons, were sent away to school.

Despite this domestic misfortune, however, the young widower continued to play his part in Lübeck's politcal and social life. He joined the College of Bergen Voyagers, of which his father was an alderman. He was elected to the city's Bürgerschaft, or council of citizens (a form of lower house to the Senate), served on the city Finance Committee, on the board of the Commercial College, St Anne's Poor and Workhouse, the Commercial Rifle Club and Central Arms Deputation. He became a Captain in the City Militia and at length Brazilian Vice-Consul.

Consul Mann, despite personal misfortune, had therefore due cause to be proud. In 1827 he had made a "renewed" journey to Holland, Brabant and Ostend; and from there he sailed to England, "in order to make closer contacts for our merchant house in this country too". Notwithstanding several "useful" acquaintanceships he was forced to recognize the "dangerous character and great risk involved in exporting there, for which reason", he noted wisely, "further cultivation of the same did not take place, especially since my father had spoken the following words: 'My son, work hard by day, but be sure only to undertake such business as will allow us to sleep soundly at night!' "[3]

The partnership between father and son prospered; and in 1837 Consul

Mann remarried. He was now forty years old, and his choice was the daughter of a fellow business man, of Swiss origins, called Elizabeth Marty. It was this association with the Martys that introduced a new and opulent character to the hitherto thrifty Manns — as well as the beautiful rococo town house that would one day enter the annals of world literature.

3

J.H. Marty was also a Consul in Lübeck. He came from Glarus in Switzerland, where his family had been peasants and craftsmen. Born in 1778, he had moved to Pernau, near Riga, in Estonia, on the Baltic Sea where an elder cousin had begun a trading enterprise. His merchant activities brought him to Lübeck; and in 1805, at the age of twenty-seven, he tried for the hand of the daughter of a Lübeck merchant, Johann Wilhelm Croll. The marriage was permitted on condition that Marty settle in Lübeck. Whether his sudden rise to fortune arose from this marriage or, as tradition has it, he became a rich man overnight by supplying Napoleon's army with grain during the long years of French aggrandisement, no one knows. But in 1817, when news of terrible famine came from his home in Switzerland he was able immediately to despatch 3,000 Gulden from his own pocket to the Glarus pastor; and within five weeks, from friends in Lübeck, Hamburg, Kiel and various other Baltic cities he had collected 18,238 Marks in different currencies. In 1819 he was promoted to Major in the City Defence Regiment, and from 1823 to his death in 1844 he was the Royal Netherlands Consul in Lübeck.

Johann Marty's home was situated just outside the main city gate, "the most beautiful house" in the vicinity. However it was his father-in-law's house, a splendid three-storeyed town house with rococo-gabled façade overlooking the Marienkirche, that Elizabeth Marty set her heart upon.

The fanlit doors of this town house were framed by fluted, banded pillars and architraves in place of a stately portico on the steep and cobbled street. It was Number 4 in the Mengstrasse, a stone's throw from the city's market square, with access to the parallel street and the main city thoroughfare, the Breitestrasse, through the garden and annexe.

Two stone sculptured figures reclined on the scrolled gables, gazing at the Grecian urn that crowned the façade. A starred rose window and stone balustrade concealed the sharp V of the roof, and tall arched windows set in a rusticated parterre front rose to the first cornice of the building.

There were twenty-one rooms in the house, and like all Lübeck buildings, however stately, it doubled as a storehouse or granary, with company offices on the ground floor and trap-doors opening into the upper floors of the loft.

It was here that Johann Marty's wife had grown up, here that her two sons and two daughters visited and played with their grandparents. Behind the house was a large courtyard with a stone fountain and spacious garden. The hall was filled with old mahogany furniture and heavy folding tables for use in larger family or social gatherings. And for the amusement of the children, there stood a life-size rocking horse. Carved on the architrave of the front door, overlooking the street, were the words: Dominus Providebit.

Elizabeth Marty was Johann Marty's second daughter. She was twenty-six when her marriage with the wealthy, talented and widowed Consul Mann was arranged; and she lived with him for a further twenty-six years, during which time (her daughter later recalled) "nothing was ever seen or heard which might have offended our ears". Consul Mann purchased a "very pretty little house" on the Parade, south of the market square; and it was there that their first two children — including the future Senator — were born.

Then in 1841 Croll's son, who had inherited the rococo house in the Mengstrasse, decided to sell the building; and for the sum of 23,000 Marks, at an annual rateable value of 100 Marks, Consul Mann was able to purchase his wife's childhood dream. They moved in on the 15th June 1842; and the new life of what would one day be celebrated throughout Germany as the Buddenbrook-house had begun.

Their first child, Maria Elizabeth Amalia Hippolite Mann, was born on 26th August 1838; their second, Thomas Johann Heinrich Mann, the future Senator, on 22nd August 1840. A third son followed, born in the Mengstrasse, in 1844, but died at the age of two — a bitter blow for the Frau Consul. In 1845 a second daughter arrived, and in 1847 Friedrich Wilhelm Leberecht Mann, a second surviving son.

"Our childhood and youth together were indescribably happy," wrote Elizabeth later, telling of the games and adventures they enjoyed in the Mengstrasse. Outside, beyond the first courtyard behind the house was a path that led to the coach house and billiard room where the old family chests filled with pictures and books were stored. A fir-lined path led from there to the next street. Up in the granary lofts of the main house was a winch for raising sacks through trap-doors, and through holes in the roof the children could squeeze onto the guttering that joined the terraced roofs of the street and play to their heart's content.

The house was a children's paradise. They were allowed to run barefoot and were dressed in simple smocks. "Never were we 'taken for walks' as in modern times," Elizabeth recalled; and the boys were allowed to keep their own pets — rabbits. "*Absolute* obedience" however was demanded of the children, "*never* would we have gone to bed without a heartfelt plea for forgiveness if we had been naughty."[4]

This free-and-easy childhood was to have serious repercussions in the family, for the contrast between freedom and parental discipline ("*absolute*" obedience) was bound to make it difficult for the children to adjust to "outside" society. Friedrich Leberecht's wayward, eccentric life, Elizabeth's broken marriages, and even the Senator's later difficulty in bringing up his own children would owe much to this.

In the meantime the firm of J.S. Mann, Grain Merchants, Commission and Shipping Agents, prospered, undeterred by occasional hindrances and the jealousies of other merchants in the city. Johann Siegmund senior advanced towards his eighties in blooming health, rejuvenated by the companionship of his son, but long since widowed. Finally, at the age of eighty-six, the founding father died.

He was on his way to a party, was ready dressed, and his "lady companion" was waiting for him. He went into his room, seemingly to fetch something. When he did not reappear the lady grew anxious, entered the bedroom. The old man was sitting in his armchair with his eyes closed. He had suffered a heart attack.

Johann Siegmund junior was now the sole proprietor of the firm. The date was 19th March 1848; and its proximity to another, more harrowing experience gave rise to a family saying: that old Johann Siegmund had died of a heart attack at the news of the '48 Revolution breaking out in the town. The story went that he had gone to heaven "cursing the canaille" — the mob. It was a story totally without foundation.

4

The "Revolution" in Lübeck was in fact a curious affair. Elsewhere in Germany it took the form first of a mild Liberal explosion — an attempt to form a democratic Parliament in Frankfurt that would be answerable to all Germans — and of street riots in the major cities. The people mounted the barricades; the Junkers, landowners and conservatives trembled and gave temporary way in the end. It was, unfortunately, a tragic failure.

In the Free City of Lübeck, however, events were to take another form. Throughout the spring the Senate and Citizens' Council attempted to hammer out democratic reforms: proper public election of Senators and Representatives on the Bürgerschaft, the Citizens' Council. Instead of a self-elective Senate and a Citizens' Council made up from representatives from the twelve commercial corporations (dominated almost exclusively by merchants), there would now be a Senate of twenty persons, elected publicly and holding office for life, and a Bürgerschaft, or Citizens' Council of a hundred and twenty representatives, elected by the different — and specified — "estates" of the town — merchants, the professions (law, teaching, etc), guild craftsmen and so forth.

Thus the major elements of democratic reform had been effected in Lübeck by the summer of 1848, several months after Johann Siegmund Mann's death.

Unfortunately the reforms were not far-reaching enough. Married journeymen and workers had been given new "resident's rights", but these did not include voting. Political representation thus remained exclusively with the upper and middle classes.

Under the leadership of Herr Meyer, a town "intellectual" who had represented Lübeck's Liberals at the Frankfurt Parliament, pressure was put on the new Senate and Bürgerschaft to extend the electorate. Cautiously the lower house or Bürgerschaft agreed to appoint a Commission to look into this — but only on the understanding that the "estate" or professional system of voting be retained.

The Commission reported on 29th August 1848. It assented to the extension of the electorate, but recommended a new "estate" to cover them in terms of voting. Some of the residents were "deeply offended" by this and turned to the Senate. By 18th September the Senate had made its own proposal: complete abolition of distinction between "citizens" and "residents"; universal suffrage for married or "independent" men; abolition of religious restrictions; "open" election of the one hundred and twenty council representatives; and abolition of the "estate" system. It was this document, paradoxically, which was to cause the Lübeck "Revolution" of 1848.

Frau Consul Mann's daughter Elizabeth was standing with her mother in the drawing room of the house in the Mengstrasse when it began. Elizabeth was nine years old. Outside a great crowd had gathered, they could hear people shouting and screaming. When she asked her mother what it was all about, her mother broke into tears. Consul Mann had gone to the latest sitting of the Bürgerschaft, at which the Senate's proposals and the Bürgerschaft's own commission on the matter were to be discussed. It was evident there was going to be violence.

The commission again prevaricated. It reported that there were two choices before the Bürgerschaft: in extending the electorate they either retain the "estate" system, or they abolish it. The Bürgerschaft had assembled in the largest hall of the town, that of the Reformed Church in the Königstrasse.

The meeting went on into the afternoon. Outside an ever-larger crowd began to assemble, demanding entry. In the end a delegate from the sitting went out to speak to them. He returned with a veritable ultimatum. The people demanded that the council retain the "estates" principle in extending the electorate!

The reason was as reactionary as the Senate had proved revolutionary: the journeymen and guild members were afraid that universal suffrage would lead to the breakdown of the guild system. At a meeting of the unfranchised residents in August someone had asked a bellicose speaker what it was they really wanted.

"We demand a republic," the speaker had proclaimed.

"But we've already got one," the man replied.

"Then we demand another!"[5]

The Bürgerschaft, despite the growing din and violence outside, finally voted: fifty votes for the Senate proposal, twenty-six against. The motion was carried.

Outside the news was greeted with distinct signs of unpopularity. A hail of bricks and stones flew through the windows, the door began to break. Bricklayers and carpenters climbed onto the roof and began to tear off the roof tiles, hurling them to the ground. The church was surrounded, and a state of violent siege resulted. The town militia, many of those members belonged to the guilds, refused to muster and declined to interfere. Even the adjoining houses were broken into and the garden wall guarded so that no one might escape.

At length the doors of the church broke down and the mob entered. The lamp on the desk of the meeting's chairman was snatched up and smashed into smithereens against the table. The meeting was hastily concluded and further business adjourned; but the mob refused to let the representatives leave until they had rescinded their decision and restored the "estate" voting system. This continued for over five hours.

Meanwhile the Senate, finding that the militia would neither assemble nor act, rang the city alarm bells. Fifty to sixty men collected, and were led by Captain Grevsmühl of the 4th Company to the Katharinen church where a second company had formed under Captain von Bultzingslöwen. An attempt to clear the Königstrasse was made, but with little success. However a second lieutenant of the 4th Company did manage to get into the besieged building through a side window, and opening the front doors from inside, allowed Captain Grevsmühl to enter. Immediately a brick was thrown in the Captain's face, forcing him to retire; and the relief of the Bürgerschaft came to a bloody and unsuccessful end.

At last Captain Schütt arrived towards midnight from the town armoury. The bricklayers and carpenters on the roof were chased off with bullets, but it was only in the early hours of the morning that the beleaguered representatives finally managed to escape, mostly across the roofs of the neighbouring houses.

Such was Lübeck's curious skirmish with revolution in 1848. A number of demonstrators were arrested and charged, but when the heat of the affair had died down, the Senate ordered all proceedings to be dropped the following year. Democracy had come to Lübeck — but only by autocratic leadership.

5

Consul Mann thus became one of the "heroes of '48". The hair above his broad, high forehead began to thin a little at the temples and his wife, accustomed to opulent living in the Marty family, spent fairly lavishly. From morning to night the Consul laboured at his business, supervising the shipments, arranging the purchase of crops, detailing the warehouses to be used. The little business that had survived the Napoleonic wars now flourished as never before, and every year the Consul travelled south to the Rhineland, Bavaria, Austria and Switzerland to take a "cure" at one of the spas there.

Frau Consul Mann turned to religion.

Soon the house echoed with the conversations of missionaries and pastors. The Consul only appeared at mealtimes, frequently accompanied by unexpected business friends. Then he would be off again. The children — Elizabeth, Henry, Olga and Friedrich — amused themselves. In the summer months they would stay with their Marty relations whose beautiful villa lay just beyond the northern gate of the city, the Burgtor. Here there was an enormous garden; and if they were lucky, their mother would take them to Lübeck's pretty sea-front resort, Travemünde, at the mouth of the Trave.

Elizabeth's small, fine face was beginning to cause attention. She had ash-blond hair and grey-blue eyes, her upper lip protruded very slightly. Though clever at lessons, she had been sent from school to school, her temperament was undisciplined, lively; and she possessed a pronounced strain of self-righteousness.

Elizabeth and Henry were always up to something, mimicking the eccentric old ladies of the town or playing pranks at home. In the end Elizabeth was sent away to a small boarding school in the town. A hollow oak tree near the Burgtor was soon in use as a hiding place for letters. Elizabeth had fallen in love with a young Spaniard.

At seventeen, Elizabeth was confirmed. At eighteen she was married.

The story of Elizabeth's marriage need not detain us here. It was to provide Thomas Mann with one of the keys to *Buddenbrooks;* but its failure introduced a new strain on the Mann family.

It was Elizabeth's fault in many ways. Her vivacious temperament worried her parents; perhaps they imagined a nice, polite merchant from Hamburg, a pastor's son, older and experienced in the ways of life, would calm her down. If so they were spectacularly mistaken.

Elizabeth at first showed complete contempt for her suitor; he threatened suicide.

Such a gesture satisfied her vanity — as did the prospect of a fine establishment in Hamburg, her own servants, furniture, surroundings. She consented. They were married on 19th May 1857 and Elizabeth gave birth to a daughter the following year. It was said she did not care for children greatly.

Then suddenly her husband went bankrupt. Eighty-thousand Marks were lost in dowry — a small fortune in those days, enough to purchase the most expensive house in the city. Elizabeth withdrew with her daughter to an apartment on the Lüneburg heath. Consul Mann was deeply upset, particularly regarding the loss of so much money.

It was in this atmosphere that young Henry Mann left the Katharineum Grammar School and entered his father's business as an apprentice. He was fourteen, and four years later he was sent as a clerk to the firm of Hensleben and Vollenhoven in Amsterdam. Three years later his father was dead; and the twenty-two year old youth became head of a family firm about to celebrate its seventieth birthday. It was a tremendous challenge.

6

Lübeck in 1863 differed very little from its size and way of life at the previous turn of the century. True, it had, following — or in spite of — the momentous days of 1848, a new constitution. True, the city now possessed a railway: the Lübeck-Buchener Eisenbahn, completed in 1851. But that was virtually all.

The railway was intended to link Lübeck with Hamburg: and thus the Baltic with the North Sea and the Atlantic. Unfortunately for Lübeck, however, relations with Denmark had not improved since the days of Danish-

French occupation; and Denmark, through its royal title to the Duchy of Holstein, now controlled the territory between Lübeck and Hamburg. For years it levied heavy taxes on all overland traffic between the two cities. In 1848 the Holsteiners rose up against their masters and turned to Prussia for deliverance. The Danish appealed to the English and the Austrians; and in the interest of "European peace" the Holstein revolt was put down. Prussia, for the moment, remained dormant.

It was unlikely, in such circumstances, that the Danish crown would authorize a railway connecting Germany east and west across its own "border state". Plans had been presented as early as 1831, a prospectus prepared and shares drawn up. Nothing happened. Even the proposal for a railway between Lübeck and Kiel, a growing seaport further north on the Baltic, met with immutable Danish resistance. It seemed as if Lübeck, once the symbol of free trade in Europe, would slowly be strangled. The Danes allowed the overland route to Hamburg to decay and refused to repair the road. The only solution appeared to be a railway running directly south, eventually linking up with the Prussian railway network at Buchen. In this roundabout fashion the railway link between Lübeck and Hamburg was effected; the Danish stranglehold was loosened but not released.

The North Sea ports of Hamburg and Bremen had meanwhile doubled in population as the balance of world commerce shifted towards the Atlantic, and the growing trade with America. The survival of the little independent City of Lübeck came to depend more and more on the political development of North Germany: on the Danes and the Prussians.

In November 1863 the last male claimant to the Danish throne died, and the whole question of Germany's northern "neck" was once more thrown open. Troops of the Confederation of German States moved into Holstein; and in December Prussian troops arrived to a tumultuous welcome in Lübeck; it looked very much like war.

In February 1864 the struggle began. By August a preliminary peace was settled; and on 30th October 1864 Denmark finally gave up all pretensions to Holstein, Schleswig, and to Lauenburg. Administration was handed over to Prussia and Austria. Lübeck was free.

Lübeck had followed the progress of the war with a certain "profitable interest", however; and ugly rumours were heard in the corridors of Berlin that Lübeck had supplied arms and munitions to the Danes; namely sulphur and potassium nitrate. Senator Curtius replied on behalf of the Senate: Mr Bismarck should be informed that his Prussian horses had been fed with Danish oats and his Prussian soldiers nourished on Danish ox meat and pork — all imported through Lübeck's neutral harbour.

The rumours, however, were true; and at least one opportunist merchant had his windows smashed and house mobbed by irate crowds, intent on the freeing of the "German" duchies.

Three years later Prussia was at war with her confederate partner, Austria, and the balance of European power took a new turn. But if Lübeck had hoped to profit by the growing power of Prussia, it was to be disappointed.

Berlin's outlet to the Baltic was Stettin; and for strategic reasons it was Kiel, on the frontier with a withdrawn Denmark, that would attract Prussian investment and attention — culminating with the Kiel canal.

Lübeck was doomed. But among the city's population there were still men of integrity and foresight, dedicated to helping steer the famous Hanseatic seaport through its days of decline. Such a man was Johann Heinrich Mann.

Johann Heinrich, or Henry Mann as he was known, proved himself a man of exceptional character. He was popular with his employees, he impressed people with his decisive spirit. Within the space of ten years 'the firm of J.S. Mann was undoubtedly the foremost grain business in Lübeck, and one of the leading names in the Baltic. The young Consul — for he was made Royal Netherlands Consul a month after his father's death — travelled extensively, importing from Russia and the whole of Scandinavia, and shipping as far south as Frankfurt am Main. It was a trade which carried high risks and demanded a great deal of nerve. It was largely speculative, dependent on unknown quantities — weather, crop-yield, shortage or surplus on the market; and it involved considerable capital in stored produce around the town. To offset these risks, young Henry Mann began to spread his net. It was a move which, given the movement of trade in the little city, was very wise.

He bought shares in the Lübeck-Buchener Eisenbahn; and on 1st August 1865 a new direct line between Lübeck and Hamburg was opened. He invested money in property, took shares in life assurance, banking, and shipping. In 1836 Johann Siegmund Mann had travelled on an English steamship from Hamburg to Great Britain; how proud he would have been to think his grandson would one day be a steamship owner himself!

In December 1865 Georg Thorbahn, the chief clerk of the firm for twelve years, and a junior partner since the retirement and death of old Consul Mann, himself died. Henry Mann was left sole proprietor. He wore wide, checked trousers, in the fashion of Brunel, a frock coat and gold chain. His flat, slightly wavy hair was parted across a broad forehead, and the full moustache made him look a little older than he was. His eyes had a clear, perspicacious character; but there was sensitivity too in their setting, the lip of skin beneath the eyes, the soft, long-fingered hands. He could speak and read perfect Dutch and French as well as German, and was fairly fluent in English. His youth, his independence, strength of character and ambitious mien brought him as high regard among men as among women. Despite his work he enjoyed company; it was time, the aunts began to murmur, he found himself a wife.

7

The woman he chose was born under the same star as he, some eleven years later. Though she gradually forgot her Portuguese, the memory of her infant years in South America, of coloured servants, of exotic fruits and the cries of jungle monkeys and parrots never left her. Her grandparents had owned a large plantation on the Ilha Grande. It shocked them to see her playing with the Negro children. She was hauled in by the ear and made instead to watch her grandmother making lace. However she adored her father — her "splendid, solemn Pai", as she called him. Into her childish heart "flowed a great feeling, a mixture of respect, of love, and of wonder".[6]

Johann Ludwig Hermann Bruhns, her father, was in fact the younger son of a merchant family which had settled in Lübeck at the same time as the Manns, and which traced its descent back through Rostock to the merchant sailors of the Baltic and Scandinavia. The family had achieved considerable wealth in the wine trade, and owned a number of properties in Lübeck. But as younger brothers were once cast to the church, so the surviving younger brethren of a Lübeck merchant family were expected to go abroad and "seek their fortune across the seas".

Johann Ludwig thus emigrated to South America. He was sixteen. Before he was much older he had founded his own export company in São Paulo, specializing in coffee and sugar. Soon he had begun his own plantation near Paraty, on the coast, and owned sugarmills in Buona Vista and Augra des Reis, about seventy miles south of Rio. He was still in his twenties when the Emperor Dom Pedro II announced the opening up of the Interior. Because of an extraordinary physical resemblance to the Emperor, Johann Ludwig Bruhns became widely mistaken in the capital; the Emperor summoned him to an audience. Impressed by the young man's intelligence and ideas the Emperor gave him wide-reaching powers and the blond-bearded youth from Lübeck became Imperial Delegate of Dom Pedro to the Interior. He made the river Piracicaba navigable and achieved considerable renown as the "man of few words".

In the 1840s he married the fifteen-year-old daughter of a rich Portuguese planter, Manuel Caetano da Silva, whose family had settled in Brazil for three generations. The girl was slightly plump, beautiful skinned, with dark eyebrows, large eyes, and jet-black hair. She bore him five children before tragedy struck. One day Johann Ludwig came into Julia's room with a more serious face than usual, and led the little six-year-old into the next room where her mother was lying, "quite pale, quite motionless and cold, surrounded by tall, burning candles; her hair and body were decked with flowers, and in her arms there was a tiny dead baby".

After Julia's mother's death, Bruhns brought the surviving children to Lübeck to be brought up by relations. They made such a curious impression with their Nankin dresses and Panama hats that Herr Bruhns had to buy off the crowd of yelling children who collected behind them with buns and sweets. The Bruhns family assumed he had married a native girl in South America; and one of his sisters had even asked impatiently before their arrival: "Whenever is Ludwig going to get here with his little black ones?"

That little Julia never quite accustomed herself to the cold winters on the Baltic, the dull, Lutheran faith and stiff Lübeck manners is understandable. Though sent to the same private school as Henry Mann's sister Elizabeth, she only reluctantly assumed the values of Protestant, merchant society, and set aside her memories of colourful carnivals, of masks and coloured costumes, and the music of South America — the mandolins, guitars, harmonicas, trumpets, tubas and drums. She became intensely musical, and called herself not Julia Bruhns, but Julia da Silva Bruhns. By then she had grown into a very attractive young woman, "much in demand" at parties and balls, wearing pretty dresses with satin brocade and white sashes, silk petticoats and tulle skirts . . . It was at one such party, an eve-of-the-wedding party, that she saw her future husband. She was sixteen and a half years old, "and from that moment", she later wrote about herself, "her fate was sealed". On 4th February 1869 her father wrote to her from Rio de Janeiro:

My dear daughter Julia

This morning's post has just brought the happy news of your engagement to Mr Heinrich Mann. . .

    You have, dear Julia, now had ample opportunity to judge your fiancé and since you have already promised your hand to Heinrich, I may presume that you hope to find your happiness with him.

    Let my blessing be upon your betrothal to Heinrich, my dear child, let God protect you and ease your path through life.

    Uncle Edward and Aunt Emmy write that they are very pleased with the event and we all hope that you will have a happy marriage. Your fiancé has all the virtues with which to make a young woman content, and it will be your responsibility to ensure his faithful love is returned.

    You are very young and lack a certain experience and knowledge in the practical conduct of life without which no domestic happiness is to be found; but I am sure that your upright love towards the man of your choice will spur you to order, thrift and domesticity, things which every man prizes in a relationship. In marriage, dear daughter, there are sunshine and storms, but the latter disperse all the quicker if the wife is sensible and shows good character.

Your father, I Luiz G. Bruhns[7]

They were married in the summer, on 4th June 1869. The following month Consul Thomas Johann Heinrich Mann was elected to represent the Marienkirche district on the Bürgerschaft. He was twenty-eight. His young bride was still seventeen.

CHAPTER TWO

Childhood, Youth — and Death

Next year Prussia was yet again at war, this time with its partner in the dispute that had led to the Austrian war: France. Lübeck's own city battalion had been dissolved and incorporated in the Prussian army; it marched with a Hamburg contingent under the Grand Duke of Mecklenburg to stop the relief of Paris at Orleans. The city bard, a liberal poet called Emmanuel Geibel, cast an appropriately patriotic rhyme for the affair, and Lübeck's independent heritage sank a little further.

It was not alone. As soon as Prussia's highly trained army swept across the plains of northern France, the south German states announced allegiance with the North German Confederation and took immediate steps to participate in the war. Bavaria's monarch offered the Imperial Crown to King William of Prussia: the way to German Empire was paved. On 18th January 1871 the new German Reich began, its Emperor crowned at Versailles.

Two months later, ʼ7 March 1871, in an apartment on the Breitestrasse, in Lübeck, Frau Consul Julia Mann, née da Silva-Bruhns, was delivered of a first child, a boy. He was christened Luiz after his maternal grandfather, and Heinrich after his father.

Four years later, at midday on 6th June 1875, he was followed by a brother, named Paul Thomas after a maternal uncle and his father. In the shadow of the new Empire, Germany's fiercest critic and, for a time, her staunchest defender, had been born.

The Consul's fortunes meanwhile continued to prosper. In 1871 he was appointed to the board of the Lübeck-Buchener Eisenbahn, took an active part in the founding of the Lübecker Bank in the same year, and from 1873 to 1875 was a member of the town council's main committee. His sister Elizabeth's disastrous marriage had been eclipsed by the young Consul's success. He agreed to take his younger brother Friedrich Wilhelm into the business as chief clerk.

Friedrich Wilhelm did not look unlike his elder brother, the Consul. He too had a broad, high forehead and clear eyes. But nowhere in them could be traced ambition, nor even caution. To the children of the Consul he became a figure of fun, a favourite uncle who would one day furnish Thomas with his most famous comic figure. For the moment, though, he was going prematurely bald; he drank heavily, led an irregular life and did little work. After a brief stay with the firm, he was quietly dismissed by the Consul.

The Consul's business was increasing in leaps and bounds. In 1875 the firm imported nearly 200,000 hundredweight of corn, rye and oats. By 1878 the figure had doubled; and in 1879 it passed the half-million mark. He was having to give securities in excess of 60,000 Marks against customs duties, and his warehousing arrangements involved more than a hundred floors in over thirty buildings of the city. Here, clearly, was a man to be reckoned with in Lübeck.

"We're not rich, but we're very well off," the Frau Consul once whispered in little Heinrich's ear. The child's hair was fair and close-cropped, his forehead high and wide like his father's. "A very young, innocent woman," Heinrich later described his mother in one of his autobiographical stories.[1] "She must have just learned of it, in fact in those very words." They were staying in one of the villas outside the town, beyond the Burgtor. "My father in those days was a handsome and proud young man. Whether in good spirits or in fury, he always seemed to me to be on the crest of life. He wore suits of soft cloth, low collars and had tufts of hair combed forwards on the temples, in the manner of Napoleon III. He walked with a firm stride and as confidently as a Captain on his own ship. The moment he entered, a room became alive, a place in which something was happening." But one day he came in silent and grave:

> We hardly noticed, already he was in his chair, his head in his hands. He moaned, and I was terrified. He who only conducted light and lively discussions now groaned the names of people whose firms had crashed, and his money with them. I looked at my mother, I remembered the words she had once spoken. She seemed to have forgotten them; she was anxious now, not with regard to the money, but about her husband . . . This was my earliest impression of a change in fortune. It took the rest of my father's life to make up what was lost in a couple of days. You couldn't earn money any faster in those peaceful days, and by the beginning of the nineties he was already dead. Perhaps it was not a complete change of fortune I witnessed here, so much as the changeability of life's faces.

It is not possible to verify the incident. Thomas Mann transposed it into an ill-advised investment recommended by the jonah-sister, Tony Buddenbrook, in *Buddenbrooks;* but it is likely that Heinrich's version is the more accurate.

At any rate a certain earnestness now entered the young Consul's striding gait. His thick waxed moustache concealed his mouth, but the eyes looked sadder, heavier. And then in 1877 Senator Minlos died after only six years in office. At the ensuing election, on 19th February of that year, Consul Henry Mann was elected in his place. He was still not yet thirty-seven. He had two healthy sons, his wife was pregnant again. The financial set-back he had sustained he met full-face. By 1880 he was depositing securities of over 70,000 Marks per annum against customs duties. The following year he felt sufficiently confident to purchase an old house in the Beckergrube, parallel to his offices and his mother's house in the Mengstrasse. The price was 30,000 Marks and for a similar sum he demolished the building and built a new three-storeyed town house which, for almost the first time in the city's history, dispensed with granaries. Before long he owned his own steamship, the *Alpha*, and his interests in Baltic shipping lines became numerous. He was addressed as "Your Excellency" by the older citizens, and everywhere people doffed their hats to him. His English suits and Russian cigars made him unmistakable.

2

Senator "Henry" Mann was not a self-made man. His was the third generation of the Manns in Lübeck, the firm of J.S. Mann was sound and well-established. But it was a city, as the local newspaper pointed out, in which fortunes were as quickly lost as made. The Senator had wisely covered himself in other areas of investment, in property, banking, railway shares, private loans, insurance and assurance companies. For the rest, he looked to his children.

Heinrich and Thomas were followed, for the moment, by two sisters: Julia, born in 1877, and Carla, in 1881. The Senator's hopes, naturally, rested upon his sons.

That they were gifted was not to be inferred so much from their performance at school, as from their precocious literary interest at home. The Senator's house had become one of the city's focal points for cultural and social gatherings. Every Thursday evening in the winter a group of friends and acquaintances, "from every walk of life", would assemble in the Beckergrube. Literature, music and art were the topics, with dancing to celebrate them. The "charming, beautiful lady of the house understood perfectly how to make her guests at home, as did the host who would sometimes relate interesting tales from his life . . . Heinrich and Thomas, timid and rather embarrassed little boys, watched everything minutely from the background", recalled an old Lübecker in the 1920s.[2]

The house was "spacious and dignified", and in the "parquetry ballroom the officers of the garrison" would court "the daughters of the patriciate".[3] Before long brothers and sisters would be performing little plays before their parents and aunts.

Despite her social and domestic duties the Frau Senator was able to spend at least a part of the day with her children. In the evenings she would read them fairy tales, Perrault and Grimm, and even the stories in local dialect by Fritz Reuter, which, despite her Portuguese background, she had mastered better than anyone in the house.

The children's upbringing became, perhaps, an opportunity to relive her own, broken childhood. She sang to them, incanting in the nasal tone and rhythm of the Negro slaves in the plantations, telling them of the poisonous snakes, and the boa constrictor which the houseservants came and beat to death with sticks. She was intensely musical, and her passion for the piano embraced all the great classical and romantic composers from Beethoven to Wagner. She was sensuous, artistic: but she avoided sentimentality or melodrama. Her passion was genuine, controlled. She was not self-righteous, neither bigoted nor falsly humble. She shared with her husband a certain pride; but for all her virtues she was never really "accepted" in Lübeck.

Some of this was bound to affect the children. Their father a Senator, universally respected, admired, their mother beautiful, musical, with her exotic past — it both stimulated them and made it more difficult for them to adjust to life, the town around them. Their sights, unconsciously, were raised to other things than the corn sacks and rye-bags they played with in the attic of the Mengstrasse. The old stuffed rocking-horse, with saddle and stirrups, glass eyes and pony fur, was given to little Thomas. He threw his arms about its neck, christened it Achilles, and loved it "not as a knight his horse, but out of sympathy for the creature, its furry coat, its hooves and nostrils".[4] It was the Trojan horse of later Homer reading, a tangible image for distant myths of Greece and beyond.

The Senator tried to engender an interest in the firm, the merchant spirit. But neither Heinrich nor Thomas could remember the names of his warehouses down on the quayside; and besides, the Senator's time was so taken with the business of the state — Senate meetings, committee work, the problems of Lübeck's declining importance in the Baltic, of integration within the monetary, fiscal and trading policies of the new Reich — he had little enough time for his business, let alone the children. In 1885 the Senator became the chairman of the Senate tax committee, as well as that of trade and shipping. He was forced to take his chief clerk now as partner in the firm. "Yes," Heinrich once heard him say, "I am always where there is nothing to be earned."[5] His power and authority in the little Hanseatic city increased, the future of Lübeck began to rest in his hands. That of his children, unfortunately did not.

3

We can only guess when the seeds of Heinrich's later rebelliousness were sown. Perhaps the birth of a younger brother was traumatic for the four-year-old. At any rate he was often ill, missed much school, and in the early years of adult life would spend long periods of the year in spas. Later he attributed this to his "fear of writing".

Yet there behind him, his entire life, was a brother who revered him, but stole the limelight. Perhaps illness brought a certain security, the attention of his mother. It was one way of winning her back. The other way was not to care. One day he left a book at his grandmother's in the Mengstrasse. It had songs, pictures and stories in it. "Grandmother Marty", as she was known, held a Sunday school for poorer children in the house and would lend them books from her library. Heinrich's book disappeared among them.

> I had loved it unusually deeply, yes, perhaps I had left it in my grand-mother's house so that I would find it there each time, like a newly-given present. After I had lost my book I dreamed of it, regretted ever having been given it, and even wept over its beauty in my sleep. But I never expressed the wish to be given a new one. I said nothing about it, as though it had never existed.[6]

In some ways he would do the same with people, particularly with Thomas. Literature, politics, the pursuit of humanity in an age of progressive barbarism would   he place of the "lost book". It was a conquest of grief, of "first sorrows", a brave face on bitter loss. It happened again with his violin:

> It was a little violin, nothing special, but russet coloured and varnished, and with the proper four strings of catgut. The bow was painted like all others with rosin, and in the little boy's hand it released sounds, perhaps which screeched. But didn't he listen to them with an inner ear, to which they seemed soft and pure?
>
> At certain points the sounds seemed to bless him like a self-initiated miracle. That's me! I can do it! The violin became an instrument of self-confidence. Of course sometimes it lost this property. Perhaps someone who was listening made a grimace, but not even this was necessary — he himself suddenly stopped hearing with his obliging inner ear. His two others, planted firmly on his head, informed him briefly and moodily that he was screeching horribly on his violin. He realized what he had hitherto suppressed with remarkable mental energy: that he had never learned to play the instrument; and that his violin was really only a children's toy, that he himself was only a child and powerless. The truth of this overpowered him.
>
> Nevertheless there was the promise to be happy which we make our-selves each day — in this case with respect to the violin. Before school in the morning he took it out once again from inside his nicely polished desk where it was safe. Whatever tragedy occurred in the mathematics lesson, the violin would be waiting for him!
>
> This he firmly believed. But in no way did it wait. It permitted itself to be played in the interval by his younger brother. The little one was still too young to go to school, he had time enough to play the violin. The violin didn't mind, it was all the same who played it, whoever it was, the violin made him into a famous virtuoso. The polished writing desk had no

lock. The little brother wasn't quite tall enough to reach it, but someone opened the lid for him and gave him the violin. Who? It was a hateful deed, injustice itself. The unknown person also put the violin back; but in any case at least one of the strings had broken. Who was it who had helped the little one?[7]

He never found out, because he didn't want to know, didn't want to have to show understanding, a little goodwill. He had some of his aunt's self-righteousness, her obstinacy. He preferred to say nothing, to savour at least the sanctity of knowing an injustice had been done to him. And Thomas?

The younger brother only became more impenitent. The maid lied about everything. But the mother of the boy turned away with a punishing look, wanted to hear no more of it. Her eyes, her posture punished — but whom? Not the one who had been responsible for the injustice, but the one who suffered it. Wasn't it enough to make one despair of everything?

So Heinrich gave up his violin.

He sat and fed his anger on the damage sustained by the instrument. Within a short time it was cracked. It had been his happiness — or at least the promise of it each day, the promise we need. At the time he had no other. Because of this he hated all who had anything to do with the piracy. Jealousy tormented him, for his mother did nothing to protect him, only his brother. His sense of justice was offended in his own person, the place where it is most vulnerable.

In addition he was a child. He couldn't know first that his own errors had contributed to his unhappiness. Moreover he could not know justice is no normal fact of life and that not even a mother's love is always equally divided. So he stopped playing the violin and saw no way out in any other direction either.

A few days later he returned from school to find the violin in pieces — and at last he burst into tears. "Until then he had not cried because a younger brother cannot be allowed to make his elder brother cry: it would be too much of an honour."

Now finally, at the moment when he neither stamped in fury nor demanded his rights, he felt a "cool arm around his heated neck". It was his mother. Now she was with him, comforting him. She said consolingly: "You see. Whether it had belonged only to you or to you both, it's broken now."

Perhaps her words were not completely logical, but they helped him. He felt, as his tears gradually changed from tears of sorrow to tears of shame and finally to tears of joy, that what he had done was childish. It was childish, it was pointless and led to no happiness to want only to possess and not to share it. He put his trust more in grown ups. They recognized this and treated him differently.

It was, as the tale was titled, a salutary lesson. But was the lesson completely learned? It is impossible not to see in this memory an uncanny foretaste of what was yet to come in the relationship between the two brothers. Thus the infants' quarrel foreshadowed one far larger in the years ahead: a quarrel which centred not on the strings of a child's toy, but the "flower of Europe's manhood".

4

Thomas, we know, felt more secure in his mother's love. It was his father, if anyone, who presented a problem. He could be frightening when angry, even to Thomas' mother. Thomas felt an extra bond with her, an identity in the face of his father. "Of the five children, it was I, I think, who was closest to my mother," he asserted later. "I sat in a corner and watched my father and mother," he once recalled, "as though I were choosing between them, deciding whether life would best be spent in the dreamworld of the senses or in deed and power. And my eyes rested finally on the quiet features of my mother."

My father was a big, broad man dressed in fine black cloth and a white waistcoat, from which hung his gold eye-glasses. Between his short, ice-grey sideboards protruded his chin which, like his upper lip, was clean-shaven, round and masculine, and between his brows could always be seen two deep furrows. He was a powerful man in public affairs; I saw men leave him with beating heart and burning eyes, and others who were broken and utterly despairing. For it sometimes happened that I as well as my mother and two sisters were made to witness such scenes, perhaps because my father wished to instil the ambition into me to do as well as he in the world, or perhaps, as I suspect, because he wanted an audience.[8]

But a child who comes — or thinks he comes — between the love of mother and father is punished with guilt. More and more the child turns to his mother for protection.

So Thomas held to his mother. His attitude to school was his attitude to the establishment, his father's business:

I detested school and right to the end failed to satisfy its demands — out of an inborn and crippling resistance to all demands from outside, something I learned to correct only later and with great pain.[9]

The one brother revolted overtly, full of righteousness and conquered tears; the other inwardly, indolent and with little sign of outward ambition. Both turned to the arts.

Relations between the two brothers, however, remained difficult. They shared the same bedroom in the Breitestrasse and then the Beckergrube, but seldom played together. For one year of their childhood (we know from Thomas Mann's wife and also his daughter), the brothers refused to speak a word to each other; and Heinrich, whose facility with paint and pencil suggested a possible career as an artist, developed a savage tongue. "Heinrich could be so hurtful," Thomas later told his daughter.[10]

In the meantime, though, there were compensations. The Senator's wealth permitted a standard of living both rich and varied. In the summer they would rent a villa outside the town, and for several weeks the family would take their holiday at Travemünde.

Here the sand was white, wicker beach cabins faced the sea, and the air was bracing. You could row across the Trave to Prival, look for amber, or stroll along the beach to the "Sea-temple" overlooking the Baltic. There was a warm-water spa, casino and stage. A spa-band gave a morning concert every day, and out on the sea the ships would pass within waving distance. "The brightest hours of my youth were those holidays at Travemünde," recorded Thomas later, "and when the four weeks, which had seemed a little eternity when they began, were over and we returned to daily life, my breast was torn with tender, self-pitying pangs."[11]

The boys grew older. There was the question of their future.

5

At what point the Senator must have realized Heinrich would not follow him into the family business we do not know. According to Thomas he then transferred his expectations onto him. Neither son responded.

The boys were sent to Dr Bussenius' private preparatory school. Here they were trained for the Grammar School, the Katharineum. Heinrich's reports were generally good, he moved steadily towards the top class. Then, at the end of his penultimate year, he left.

For his father, this was galling. The boy had long since indicated his unwillingness to go into commerce. He was determined to be a writer. For years he had been writing poetry and short stories, his notebooks were full of them. Then in the spring and summer of 1889 the local newspaper, the *Lübecker Zeitung*, had printed two of his stories, the first of his works ever to be published. They were *Beppo as Best Man*, in May, and *The Frau Baron's Birthday* in July. Both appeared anonymously, but to the eighteen-year-old schoolboy it was the first taste of success. He refused to go back to school; his father refused to contemplate such an idea. In the end a compromise was reached. He would go as a bookseller's apprentice to Dresden.

It was a curious arrangement, really — a merchant's idea of a solid grounding in the field for his son, if he really wished to be a writer. The Senator had left school at fourteen, he could not relinquish the value he attached to a proper practical preparation for life, one's career.

So the boy was sent to Dresden, four hundred miles away. Naturally he detested the work. But at least it was a chance to leave Lübeck. In May he had written a short article about the city, *Fantasies about my Hometown L.*[12] It was filled with loathing and bitter sarcasm for the side of the town no one seemed aware of: its money-grabbing materialism: the "stink of millions". It was unpublishable and remained unpublished. But its reeling sense of social injustice was reminiscent of an earlier experience, not without its humour, when Heinrich was a small child: the Masked Ball.[13]

It was a winter afternoon in Lübeck in the Seventies. I see a street falling away steeply. It is covered in ice and almost dark. Each gas-lamp lights only the house in front of it. A distant house-bell noisily announces someone leaving the building. A girl leads the boy, who is me.

I pulled myself free, however, the street was such a perfect slipway. I started sliding down it, faster and faster I went. The crossroad approached. In the moment before I reached it, a muffled woman stepped out, carrying something under a cloth. I could not stop, I went straight into her, she was in no way prepared for the crash. Because it was icy, she fell. Because it was dark, I escaped.

But I heard the breaking of china. The woman was carrying china under her cloth. What had I done! I stood there, my heart beating. At last the maid arrived. I said:

"I couldn't help it."

"The woman has nothing to eat now," said the maid.

"Do you know her, Stine?"

"She knows you," Stine claimed.

"Will she come and tell my parents?"

Stine said a threatening yes; I was terrified.

We did our shopping, for the next day there was going to be a party at our house, quite different from any other party: a masked ball.

The boy goes to bed. He cannot forget the woman he has knocked down, the likelihood she will come and tell his parents. The next day when Stine fetches him from school it is the first question. Did she come? But she hasn't — yet.

The ball takes place, the little seven-year-old is allowed to "admire" his mother in her costume, as Queen of Hearts. There is the smell of flowers, of unusual dishes.

The little boy goes to bed; but unnoticed, steals down later to peep at the gathering: the "naked shoulders, suffused with the mellow light, people's hair shimmering like jewelry, sparkling with life, turning effortlessly in dance. My father was an officer from abroad, powdered, with a sword, I was very proud of him. Mother, Queen of Hearts, paid court to him more than ever . . . I stood aged seven behind the door of the ballroom, helplessly swayed by the happiness which they all dance after . . ."

Suddenly the door was wrenched from me, someone had discovered me. It was one of the servants, he shouted to me that downstairs there was a woman asking for me. He took no notice of my pale shocked face, his coat tails hurried on. I was left alone to my decision. Was it me? If I didn't go down to the woman, who knows, perhaps she would force her way into the ballroom. Public catastrophe. Rather than that I would sacrifice myself.

The woman was standing by the front door, where the light was poor. Behind her a dark room. She was wrapped up like the day before, she did not move. She is the Statue of Conscience standing in the night. I went nearer, I was about to ask what she wanted, but my voice failed me. "You broke my china," she said, quite muffled: "My little boy hasn't got anything to eat now." I swallowed, stirred by the misfortunes of the other little boy as well as my own, which had brought us here.

Should I have got her something from the kitchen?

But the kitchen was full of maids and servants, I would have aroused too much attention. "Wait," I stammered and rushed into the room behind her. It was full of guests' coats. I forced my way through and finally reached things which were mine.

So the little boy brings the woman his books, his soldiers, his treasures. All he takes her she packs into her bag, then goes. The little boy runs back to his bed.

He sleeps much better that night than the previous one; but the next day all his things are returned to their rightful places. He cannot understand it. Stine smiles when he tells her. Only much later does he realize it must have been her at the door, dressed up like the woman. "Probably no one went hungry in reality," Heinrich concluded.

Who knows even if the china was really broken? Stine, as a good actress, brought extra tragedy to the affair with the effect of her costume. But I have never forgotten how, at the age of seven, I was torn from contented reverie over the outward elegance of life to confront poverty and my own guilt.

Both remained. The *Fantasies about my Hometown L* were a mere prelude. to a power of indictment Germany had not known since Heine.

6

While Thomas stayed at home, learned the violin under one of the City Theatre musicians, set up his puppet theatre, dreamed he was an eighteen-year-old prince called Karl, staged imaginary plays and paid little or no attention in class, Heinrich took up his minion's appointment with Messrs von Zahn and Jaensch.

It was not his first trip abroad from the little Hanseatic city. At thirteen, in the summer of 1884, he had been sent on his own to relations in St Petersburg. The precision with which, as a thirteen-year-old, Heinrich described his journey and vacation suggest both more and less than literary talent. He wrote copious letters home to his parents as well as keeping a fully documented diary. They show precocity and the determination to encompass all that he experiences. Everything was recorded — his aunt's headaches, times of trains, times of visits. The accounts were so detailed, they suggest an almost troubled mind.

Dresden, if anything, was worse than home. Heinrich had his freedom from school: but was pursued by a stream of letters from his father attempting to instil a more serious attitude towards his apprenticeship: frugality in his expenditure, and better behaviour towards his relations, landlady, etc. Heinrich took this series of corrective missives with a mixture of patient refutation and bored indifference.

His father sent him a book; the eighteen-year-old son thanked him, denied he had been "disrespectful" to the "old-maidish" Miss Lincke, advised his father blandly to keep away from German classical authors such as Herder, Wieland and Klopstock who where "enormously high-minded and very great, but at the same time frightfully boring and terribly old-fashioned". But about his work — for which purpose the Senator had sent him — Heinrich wrote nothing. He simply wasn't interested: and the Senator was increasingly dissatisfied.

It was, however, but one of the problems besetting Heinrich's long-suffering father. The Senator's sister Elizabeth had divorced her first husband after his bankruptcy; but her daughter's choice of spouse showed alarming signs of going the same way. In February 1890 Guido Biermann, Director of the Lübeck Fire Insurance Company was tried for misrepresentation of the affairs of a limited company and attempted fraud. In order to improve the company's profit (of which he received five per cent) he had falsified the annual accounts, and declared non-existent gains. Worse, he had failed to re-insure with other insurance firms and on four occasions had attempted to defraud other companies by re-insuring *after* a fire had occurred. In 1888 there had been an investigation; the following year he was suspended and then dismissed. Finally in February 1890 he was sentenced to two years' imprisonment. The Senator informed Heinrich of the sad event.

Lübeck, 22nd Feb. 1890

My dear Heinrich
I am sending you today the latest newspaper reports on Biermann. The sentence to 2 years' imprisonment was passed yesterday. — The summing-up had taken from one o'clock to half past three and the news of the sentence was brought to me by Uncle Friedel, whom I had fetched from table at Grandmother's to break the sad news to Aunt Elizabeth and Alice. From outside I heard only a piercing cry and then I went into the drawing room and shared her misery myself. Biermann was arrested straight away and this afternoon wrote the first heart-rending letter to his wife — if B. did wrong, he is now paying for it dearly and with him above all little Alice. That we are all suffering goes without saying . . .

Again the family name had been besmirched. Meanwhile from a comfortable majority in the Reichstag in 1887, February 1890 had brought Bismarck a disastrous election result — a clear majority of seats against him. Heinrich's father called it "scandalous" and the prospect of a new election "deeply humiliating". "God knows where this will lead," he continued his letter.

The times are serious and the outlook more so. More than ever it is necessary to work towards personal efficiency, independence and personal frugality. God save the Kaiser and Bismarck. Plus or minus 60 socialists and some 90 centre-party members will be entering the Reichstag — it will be no joke to rule with that majority!
I will write in more detail next time, I am in a bit of a rush today.

With love, your father, H. Mann.

But neither God nor the new Kaiser were anxious to save Bismarck, and a few weeks later the grand old man tendered his resignation. He was seventy-five.

The new age had finally begun. For Lübeck, however, it spelled further economic problems, and for Senator Mann no release.

7

The shortest route between the Baltic and the Atlantic was between Hamburg and Lübeck: and by rights the new North Sea Canal should have run between them.

Unfortunately for Lübeck, it was not to be; and it was Kiel, further North, which was chosen by the Prussian government. Kiel was in Holstein, now a Prussian territory; whereas Lübeck, however honorary the title was becoming, was still an Independent City.

Kiel appealed to the government in Berlin for strategic reasons too. It was nearer the new border with Denmark, left the German part of the peninsula less vulnerable. There was a naval yard there, in which the new German fleet was swelling. So Lübeck lost the struggle; and in 1887 work began on the canal.

Senator Mann had long called for modernization of the Lübeck harbour and its installations. Modern cranes were needed, railways to the quayside, wider loading bays. But everything went so slowly. Only in 1894 would negotiations with Prussia over a smaller, barge-size canal between Hamburg's Elbe river and Lübeck be completed; and even when opened, the capital costs were never recovered.

Nevertheless the Senator's term of office did see an improvement in the river approach to the city, as well as in its railway connections; and his final years did see some recognition of the grave problems confronting the state, as well as possible solutions. Whatever scandal might attach to his righteous sister and her daughter, however great a failure his brother Friedrich had turned out to be, however little his sons seemed capable of following him, the city of Lübeck knew its debt to the Senator. When the centenary of his firm arrived in May 1890, the Senator could for once indulge in some restrained feelings of pride and achievement. Despite all the problems of these years the Senator had persevered. His wearier, sadder countenance still accompanied the perfect grooming of a twenty-year-old; the waxed moustache, the thinner, receding, but still well groomed hair, the well-cut suits, the gold watch, the diamond ring. His shield hung in the Senate, the telephone (number 150) rang at the office. "He was no longer a simple man," wrote Thomas later, "no longer robust, nervous and prone to ill health, but a man of self-control and success, who had achieved honour and reputation early in the world."[14] The hundredth anniversary came; soon it would also be the Senator's own fiftieth birthday. The city put out its flags, a holiday was declared for the employees, the harbour was festooned with colours, the Senator's own steamship *Alpha* lay at the quay below the Beckergrube, and a deputation bore congratulations from the Chamber of Commerce.

"Among the numerous business firms which represent commerce in a merchant city," the *Lübeckische Blätter* noted on 25th May, "there are those which for a short period draw all attention to themselves and become the focal point of the trading community. But only too often, when the seemingly firmly established business collapses, all trace of the firm as well as its name disappear. Few merchant concerns have the good fortune to look back not over a generation, or less, but over half or even a full century of blessed and respected activity.

"Last Friday, however, the Lübeck firm Joh. Sieg^{md}. Mann celebrated such a rare centenary."

The newspaper recorded the history of the firm and its current head. Exact cognizance of the nautical and commercial needs of the city and cautious but clear decisions had lead to his early election to Bürgerschaft and Senate. The firm enjoyed "universal respect and esteem", and, the paper concluded, merited "a long and prosperous future".

In Dresden, meanwhile, Heinrich had also prepared something for the centenary celebrations of the firm — but it was of a very different nature. In February he had heard that his first poem was to be published in *Die Gesellschaft*.

Heinrich was overjoyed. He wrote straightaway to his friend Ludwig Ewers to tell him the news. *Die Gesellschaft* was radically modern, dedicated to Zola and the new realism, and Heinrich had to explain: "There was no other possibility," he excused himself. "A 'family' paper would certainly have put it in the 'Letters' column, together with a moral lecture on the depravity of modern youth . . . Not even the *Deutsche Dichtung* did I dare approach, given the tone which speaks all too clearly out of the verses.

"I don't know whether I have succeeded in dispelling your doubts about the matter, but I hope so from the bottom of my heart. At all events I beg you to exercise *absolute discretion,*" he insisted. "At the beginning of May there will be the 100th anniversary of the firm Joh. Sieg^{md}. Mann (discretion about this too!) and I want to give my father a surprise, pleasant, I hope, with the publication of my poem."

Perhaps the Senator ought to have been delighted. But as his letter to Heinrich showed, he was the very opposite.

Lübeck, 26 May 1890

Dear Heinrich

My inquiry about you addressed to Messrs von Zahn & Jaensch has been answered in the most ungratifying terms possible. They have drawn sharp attention to your apathetic, indolent manner and after reading the whole account — I tremble for your future. If you do not recognize that even seemingly unimportant things not only have to be done, and done with proper thought and painstaking care, then you simply have not understood why you are there, nor have you reached the stage where you can sit back and contemplate what you are going to do with your life. This cannot be miraculously achieved with a vaccination, you know, and if you don't come to your senses soon, things are going to look pretty grim for you —

The only reason your employers will consider a fortnight's holiday is so that somewhat greater influence can be brought upon you at this end, for your employers make it quite clear: "from his whole manner and behaviour one can see he lacks the necessary qualities for this chosen profession, both in determination and desire". They also say that "he is so taciturn that it is very difficult for us to get close to him and exercise any influence at all".

This is very sad news, but completely to be expected, exactly what your teacher, Professor Hofman, said. But the time is coming when no one is going to bother with you any more, when you must prove yourself, and if you don't, you will be left behind and find yourself pushed aside in life.

Take heed, but quickly. Soon it will be too late! What will happen if you are dismissed from there after idly wasting your apprenticeship, and with a bad report? When that time comes you will have to stand on your own two feet. For goodness sake be reasonable, and make sure you heed the warnings of those who have your interests at heart. If you think these are just empty words then you are very foolish and blind to the realities of life. Life is hard in its demands. I am frankly too pained and depressed by the report of your employers to make any decision about whether you may come home or not. The 23rd May, the day so much was said about hopes for my sons, has certainly not been made more memorable by you —

Your father, H. Mann.

Both Heinrich and Thomas later chose to play down their father's disappointment in them — Thomas suggesting it was really his father's "Privatgeschäfte", his business affairs, which were worrying him. It is possible that business worries may have contributed to his parental dissatisfaction in these last years of his life, but the size of the fortune he left makes this appear very unlikely. Thomas' son Klaus even went so far as to say the Senator had frittered his wealth away in his extravagant life-style — an accusation which would have pained the Senator deeply.

His was simply the vexation of an ailing man, a merchant who by thrift and industry, by charm and ambition, by intelligence and integrity had achieved something in the world. That his two sons should defy their upbringing, should cast aside the advantages, the education and cultured background their parents had so painstakingly created for them — it was more than disheartening. In April, however, the Frau Senator had given birth to a fifth child, and it turned out to be a boy. In jubilation friends and relatives everywhere were informed.

Senator and Frau Mann, née Bruhns, have the honour of announcing the birth of a strong and healthy son.

The date was 12th April 1890. The Senator was forty-nine, his wife thirty-eight. The child was christened Carl Viktor; and there arose a faint chance that even if both Heinrich and Thomas proved unfit to take over the family firm, as appeared to be the case, this third son might grow up to confound them all.

8

The Senator believed, had always believed, in certain values: in loyalty and hard work, in foresight, careful preparation, and exemplary conduct.

But Heinrich was still only nineteen, and though he wanted to prove his worth to his father, it was evidently impossible as a bookseller's apprentice in Dresden. On 28th May 1890, Heinrich answered his father's reprimand:

Dear Papa

Your letter had understandably distressed me deeply. However I want to make it clear that I do not feel nearly as guilty as perhaps you imagine. What do Messrs von Zahn and Jaensch actually say about my *work*, which, after all, is the reason for which I am here at all? I don't think I carry out my duties worse than any other apprentice who has just entered the firm, and who also makes a few mistakes at the beginning. For a long time now I have avoided any inaccuracy in the till, which in my early days showed an occasional surplus, and for months I have heard no reproach.

It seems really not to come down so much to the performance of my duties: my "manner" I suppose must be the problem. Certainly I have no idea what is meant by my "apathy" and "indolence". I leap up the stairs whenever the boss calls, with a rapidity neither apathetic nor indolent, and answer every question addressed to me briefly and to the point. That there is rarely an opportunity for apprentice and principal to conduct long conversations is however quite natural; what is meant by "taciturn" I simply do not understand. However since this is not the first time these qualities of mine have been complained of here, I suppose they must be justified — but I simply do not understand them. One thing I do know however: that there are people who are more sympathetic to a person's individuality than Mr Jaensch, who in the first weeks made a scene because I did not wish him "Good Morning" loudly and gladly enough. Quite often there are noisy altercations between my colleagues (for instance Bruhn) and Mr Jaensch, whose principle seems to be to treat his apprentices as badly as possible (even resorting to swear words). The one argues and is called impudent, the other holds his tongue and is called — apathetic. If we were treated better things would be different, and in any case enthusiasm or lack of enthusiasm has *nothing* to do with the matter. I know that you will not approve of my criticizing my principal in this way. But I am old and sceptical enough not to have to take anything, anything at all, blindly as gospel — especially from a man like Mr Jaensch who has already given me proof enough of an inadequate education.

> . . . Your faithful son, L. Heinrich Mann

It was a splendid letter, but not one likely to endear him to his father. What else could he do? He wanted to be a writer, not a minion. He wanted to please his father, but could not — understandably — agree to deny his own individuality or sense of justice. To hold his tongue in Dresden was to be criticized for being "taciturn"; but to defend himself before his own father was to be arrogant, unfilial.

Heinrich's heart had never been in bookselling. Among his posthumous papers more than half a century later were found a hundred and three poems and ten fictional "attempts", all written between 1886 and 1891. Most of the poems date from this period in Dresden.

It was with the Muse that Heinrich was really serving his apprenticeship, not as a bookseller, but as an author. To Ludwig Ewers he poured out his soul, his ambitions and his literary loves. Heine obsessed him — "the only 'teacher' of mine for whom I have absolute respect and love."[15] Fontane, too fired his admiration. "He is my favourite among the moderns," he wrote in February 1890. "I know him as a brilliant critic without prejudices and as a novelist of pace and skill. But where he has really touched my heart is in his poems. Good God! Are they beautiful! Those ballads! Of stone and steel — compared with them the highly praised masterpieces of the late Ludwig Uhland are rubber!"[16]

He was reading most contemporary French writers in the original ("Half my existence consisted of French books," he wrote later of this time[17]), and however much he tried to satisfy the expectations of his father and Messrs Zahn and Jaensch, the arrangement was doomed.

The Senator kept up his critical assault, but it did no good. In November 1890 he travelled to Dresden with the Frau Senator to see Heinrich; a few weeks later "Grandmother Marty" died in the Mengstrasse at the age of seventy-nine, and the Senator was made executor of her estate. At the same time the Senator's own health began to deteriorate. In the spring of 1891 he received a letter from Messrs von Zahn and Jaensch to say they doubted whether they could continue to employ young Heinrich; and again the Senator decided to go to Dresden in person.

> Lübeck, 3rd April 1891

Dear Son,
At a time when pupils and other boys of your age, having finished their exams, are getting ready in high spirits to go out and prepare themselves for life by their studies, it befalls your mother and me to suffer the pain

of a son who once again frustrates our intentions by insubordination and lack of will-power, and who chooses paths which to my mind do not lead to happiness.

Your letter — undated — which arrived yesterday was very soon followed by a communication from Messrs von Zahn and Jaensch in which they doubt very much the possibility of your staying with them. Their reasons, as was to be expected, do not agree with your version of the matter.

I stayed up into the night to collect myself, so as not to undertake anything too rashly and to make up my mind in quiet. — I then wrote to Messrs Zahn & Jaensch that I would visit Mr Jaensch on Saturday, the day after tomorrow, when the rest can be discussed.

One thing, however, I warn you now: my son will leave an honourable firm neither as a fugitive nor as one dismissed. If we are going to negotiate, then I must have a definite not too distant date that we can agree upon for your remaining with Messrs von Z & J. And this will have to be on the express condition that, even if to nobody else, you acknowledge a responsibility towards us, your parents, and promise to behave properly with Herr Jaensch and your superiors . . .

I will expect to see you on Saturday morning at about 9 o'clock at the Hotel Bellevue. I would have preferred to see you again in different circumstances.

Your father, H. Mann.

9

The Senator must have realized, once in Dresden, that it was no use. Heinrich left the firm immediately; and it was agreed he might go to Berlin now to seek his fortune. One thing had emerged: he was never going to make a bookseller.

The Senator returned to Lübeck and his other problems. The young Kaiser had visited the city at the beginning of the month amidst great ceremony; a special audience and banquet in the Senate. But the Kiel Canal was half-finished, there was still the question of the modernization of Lübeck's docks and who would pay for it. The other Hanseatic cities like Bremen and Hamburg had installed the latest hydraulic machinery and equipment. The whole nature of trade, too, was changing — no longer was it necessary to unload goods and store them away in the multifarious granaries and warehouses of the city: the port was rapidly becoming a transit station in which everything possible — weighing, checking, repacking — was done on the quayside itself.

But modernization costs money, and not even the Kaiser's visit could help there. Bismarck had also been, but the Senator was not interested in sabre-rattling. Once, when reading Bismarck's latest speech, he had considered the phrase: "We Germans fear God, otherwise nothing on earth." "In reality," the Senator had sighed and remarked, "there are a number of things we fear."[18] The future for Lübeck, as well as his sons, looked sadly unpromising.

Thomas meantime had also caught the literary disease. Heinrich's departure from home, his life in Dresden, his theatre visits and his poem published in the *Gesellschaft*, seemed to him unbelievably heroic, romantic. He "bombarded" Heinrich with outbursts of "gushing admiration".[19] Thomas knew that there were unhappy exchanges between his parents and Heinrich, but he had little idea of Heinrich's daily torture running for Herr Jaensch or trying to make the till balance.

Life in Lübeck for the second-born was homely and sheltered. Thomas, too, began writing poetry, worshipped Schiller and was greatly attracted by the stage. In his first extant letter, soon after Heinrich left for Dresden, in 1889, Thomas was quoting from one of his own plays — *Aischa*. The quotation ("Still no news") was not very striking, and the letter, addressed to an old nanny, less than tactful. "Have you heard again from Friedele," he enquired, "who was supposed to have a life-or-death (?) operation, or from Herminele, who can be nice when she wants to — or from Grandmother? Oh, no, I suppose she's dead." The letter was signed: "Th. Mann. Lyric-dramatist."[20]

"How did you like the farewell scene at the station?" he asked. "Touching, wasn't it?" And three months later, in another letter to her:

I am now diligently reading Schiller's works which I got for Christmas, and when I came to the poem, "Hector's Parting from Andromache", I thought of the parting at your train the morning you left. That was really a dramatically touching scene, as though the good ladies wanted to say with Schiller: "Hector's love shall not be drowned in Lethe."[21]

A certain innocence that would pervade all Thomas Mann's work until his death was thus to be seen from the very beginning, a contented refusal to look at life except in literary terms. The farewell scene at the railway station: it was "touching" in a literary sense as much, or even more, than the personal: and becomes, after Christmas, an illustration for a line from Schiller.

Thomas had returned to school quite happily in January 1890. "School starts again on Saturday," he had remarked in his letter. "Think of it, Saturday! How dopey!! I think, though, that I can handle the work pretty well from here on." He was still not fifteen.

Already in the first form of the Katharineum (to which he was sent in October 1889), Thomas ran into problems with his pursuit of literature. As Heinrich aroused the wrath and indignation of his superiors in Dresden by his "manner", so Thomas now excited the suspicion and ill-will of his teachers by his behaviour in school. "Out of vanity" he showed a fellow pupil his latest romance "whose theme was the heroic death of Arria: 'Paete, non dolet!' " Both in admiration and to cause trouble the boy showed it to the form-master. It was obvious that the Senator's son had other horizons than the aping of his teachers.

"School I loathed . . . I despised it as a milieu, I was critical of the manners of its despots, and I soon found myself in a sort of literary opposition to its spirit, its discipline, and its methods of teaching," he wrote later. Together with the son of a Lübeck bookseller, who had gone bankrupt and died, Thomas refused to take school seriously, indulging in a "fantastical and macabre humoured mockery of the 'whole thing', but in particular the institution and its officials".[22]

It was during this literary revolt that Thomas' feelings for another school-boy introduced him to one of life's profoundest paradoxes: the pain of love. Though he never made any secret of the autobiographical nature of his novella, *Tonio Kröger*, it was only in a letter dating from the end of his life that we know the identity of the boy he fell in love with, and the in-tensity of their relationship. The boy was Armin Martens. "He was my first love," Thomas confessed to an old school friend, "him I *really* loved, and a more tender, blissful yet painful one I was never to experience the rest of my life."[23]

"He loved him in the first place," was the version in *Tonio Kröger*, "because he was in every respect his own opposite and foil . . . and ever since Tonio Kröger had known him, from the very minute he set eyes on him, he had burned inwardly with a heavy envious longing. 'Who else has blue eyes like yours, or lives in such friendliness and harmony with all the world? . . . To be like you . . .' "

In the midst of all this Senator Mann died.

10

An operation in the summer had caused the Senator to reconsider the future. And the more he thought about it the more he was convinced that neither Heinrich nor Thomas would ever be able to take over the responsibility of the firm, even with his able and experienced partner Consul Eschenburg at the practical helm. It was obvious Heinrich had no wish to return to Lübeck, and Thomas' idleness at school was matched by a complete lack of interest in the business at home. The Senator had made a will in 1879; he now decided to revise it completely.

Everything — houses, home, ships, stock, furniture — would be sold. The company would be liquidated.

It is difficult to avoid the inference that the Senator felt betrayed. Why otherwise would he give instructions for *all* his property to be sold — and within a year? He might well have liquidated the firm while leaving the houses in the possession of his family, so that his wife and the still dependent children could have lived on the income.

It is not difficult to sympathize with his feelings, however. Only a year before his firm had celebrated its hundredth anniversary. Its name had never stood higher. Yet for years now it was the Senator, alone, who had kept the name alive. His self-righteous sister Elizabeth wrote bad poetry and had two divorces to her credit; his sister Olga had died seven years ago, his mother the year before, and Friedrich — he could not be trusted to keep himself in shoes! And what of the five healthy children he had been "blessed" with? His wife had been little help; her temperament had never been that of a merchant's wife. He had loved her deeply, he knew she had done her best: but with what results? An eldest son who spent all his pocket-money on theatre tickets and books, who dreamed of literary success and fame when he did not know how to shave himself properly . . . The Senator tried to collect himself. On four folded sheets of paper he drafted his revised Last Will and Testament.

He was a careful, tidy man and had no debts except one for wine, and a small one with a firm in Bremen. His state papers he left in a special drawer, as well as those of the Lübeck-Büchener Railway. The last photograph that had been taken of him was to be enlarged and distributed among friends and colleagues. He attached no importance to the style of his funeral. He asked that Pastor Ranke should give the funeral address. God had always been good to him, he had prayed to Him. Joyful faith had always been an inheritance of the family, and he was confident God would know how to bring his children to Him — "I hope without much suffering!"

The guardians of his children were to be responsible for seeing that the children received a *"practical"* upbringing. As far as possible Heinrich's "leanings toward a literary career" were to be opposed, for he lacked the "necessary qualifications for successful activity in this direction": namely "sufficient education and experience". The background to his leanings, the Senator declared, was a "dreamy disposition" and "lack of consideration for others, perhaps from a failure to *reflect*".

It was a classic "headmaster's report". It showed neither the least sympathy nor recognition of his talent: only awareness of his failure as a bookseller's clerk.

Thomas, however, was characterized in the document as open to "gentler methods of persuasion": he had a good heart and "would find his way into a practical profession". He would be a great support to his mother.

Julia, the Senator's eldest daughter, had also shown signs of rebelliousness. Her "lively temperament" was to be "suppressed". Carla, his second daughter, was similar in character to Thomas, and would constitute a "quiet element" in the family.

As for Viktor, the youngest — God take care of him. Late children often turn out to be intelligent, and the child had "such good eyes".

The Senator warned his wife to be firm with the children and to keep them dependent on her. If ever she wavered she was to read King Lear![24]

The following day the Senator called the notaries to make out the final will. The last page of the draft contained a request that the Senator's brother Friedrich also do his best to ensure Heinrich did not tread a "false" path that would lead to his "eventual unhappiness". Heinrich was to keep the end in sight, not merely his present wishes. Thomas would weep for his father. Prayer, regard for his mother and hard work should never be neglected.

The children love each other and their mother dearly. I build all my hopes on that. They will be fulfilled if my wife does not weaken.[25]

The notaries arrived. The family was in Travemünde for a few weeks, including Heinrich. It was a sorry moment. Heinrich and Thomas both later wished their father could have lived to see their success. Yet, as much as anything, it was the Senator's death which would set the two boys on their path to greatness. With his death all further obstacles to their literary "inclinations" were removed, moral and financial. Their mother, dark-haired, Latin in temperament, ignorant of commerce, deeply and artistically muscial, "cared nothing about the reports", as Thomas put it in *Tonio Kröger*. She had read Heinrich's poems, she knew his ambition was no dream. It was she who would finance the publication of his first novel, she who would guide both Heinrich and Thomas to their first successes, who stood behind them and between them when they fought. Without her we may well wonder whether either would have achieved what they did.

11

My dear Heinrich

Your father is *very* ill. I think it best you come *right away*, so that, *if it proves necessary,* you can hold out your hand to him, and with us all be near him.

   Ask Fischer for a few days temporary leave.

With love
Your mother.

The date was 4th October 1891; since June Heinrich had been working at the publishing house of Samuel Fischer as an unpaid assistant on the *Freie Bühne* — an organ of the highly successful theatre club that was bringing the new "Naturalism" of Ibsen and Hauptmann uncensored to the Berlin stage. Fischer himself was only thirty-two, and his publishing company scarcely four years old. Heinrich's father cannot have been happy with the arrangement. "Naturalism" meant scandal in contemporary Berlin; when Heinrich had written to ask if he could have the money to join the Freie Bühne theatre club at the end of May, his father was still unwilling — "I have already written to you that this matter can be postponed until August." However the Senator had seemed more anxious to help generally, and had given Heinrich an introduction to someone "connected with the Press, who can be of use to us".[26] His opinion of Heinrich's domestic abilities, however, had not changed. He was furious that Heinrich had asked for more money — to be sent telegraphically — above the 120 Marks odd he was given a month. "Surely you have reached an age at which I don't have to send your money weekly?" Nor was he to remain silent at table with the Krebs family, with whom he was staying, but to "play his part in the conversation". Dr Krebs might also be useful to him in Berlin society.

   The Senator's letter remained unanswered, and again in June he was writing. Heinrich had told his mother he wanted to take six weeks holiday, but he hadn't told Dr Krebs' wife. Another 100 Marks and more would be wasted in rent. He bought too expensive seats at the theatre, he visited the barber instead of shaving himself.

Heinrich, however, had more "important" things to worry about than personal thrift. Berlin was alive, the long awaited literary revolution was coming. And at twenty, he was at the heart of it! He put his name down for a few lecture-courses at the university, and in August he sent his mother a new poem, dedicated to her: *Restingplace*. It was dressed in the cool romantic lines of Heine, but the theme was personal and genuine. The summer weeks by the sea at Travemünde with the family had given him courage again.

Then in October came his mother's note. Heinrich hurried back to Lübeck. The street was laid with straw. "The dying man said to the twenty-year-old what he had meant for a long time though had never spoken: 'I want to help you.' To become a writer: both of us knew it; the one kissed the other's hand, he kisses it still today," Heinrich wrote nearly sixty years later.[27] A reconciliation of sorts, thus took place, the boy "stretched out his hand" as his mother had asked. And the Senator closed his tired eyes for the last time.

Thomas, too, had been at hand. In a short contribution to a book on artists' religious beliefs[28] some forty years later, he too described the moment — though somewhat differently.

As the vicar of St Marien, Lübeck, kneeled in priest's clothes at my father's deathbed and launched loudly into prayers, the dying man made an uneasy motion with his head and interrupted the pious rhetoric with a vigorous "Amen". The holy man didn't allow himself to be disturbed by this and even commended it in his funeral oration — when it had been immediately obvious to me, a half grown up boy, that my father had meant nothing less than "Stop it!"

It was a slow and painful death, from blood poisoning. In the summer the Senator had had to undergo an operation; it was not a success.

The Senator's death came as a great surprise to the citizens of Lübeck; so much so that it was two days before the local newspaper, the *Eisenbahn-Zeitung* could furnish a proper obituary, which ran as follows:

Lübeck, 14 October. Senator Thomas Johann Heinrich Mann died last night, in the prime of his life. His death released him from great physical pain. Since 19 February 1877, the deceased had been a member of the Senate. For fifteen years this wise and experienced merchant was given a rich opportunity to serve his hometown, and the manner in which he did it is known to every man. Our trade and shipping has taken a new turn and Senator Mann, the proprietor of one of our oldest and most important firms, worked with rare tenacity and energy to achieve this. As Chairman of the tax department and the board of the Lübeck-Buchener Railway Company he found many ways of serving and helping all circles of our community. The city mourns today! On the ships and from the roofs, everywhere the flags are at half-mast. Lübeck will not forget him!

The *Lübeckische Blätter* had, however, followed the Senator's illness with increasing anxiety. Its obituary filled both front and second pages and paid tribute as much to the character and integrity of the Senator as to the extraordinary diversity of his public and private interests. His activities stretched from being churchwarden of the Marienkirche to chairmanship of numerous societies for the poor and needy, from insurance to banking, from commerce to the arts, from shipping to fiscal problems of the state. It would be difficult, if not impossible, to replace him:

And in the same way as he always made the welfare and honour of the people of Lübeck his greatest concern, so they will preserve his memory now.

On Friday 16th October 1891 the Senator's body was borne to its grave. He had specifically stated that he did not want an expensive funeral, but he underestimated his position and popularity in Lübeck. The funeral "surpassed anything that had been seen for many years" as Thomas later recalled. In their thousands the people lined the streets: from the Senator's house in the Beckergrube to the Breitestrasse, from the town hall to the city gate, "still and silent", as the *Eisenbahn-Zeitung* reported the following day.

At nine o'clock it had begun — the servants taking leave, then the dignitaries and relatives. "Everywhere the same topic, everywhere one heard the same thing: Senator Mann was the very best of men." At half-past nine the church bells began their peal, and the Senator's coffin was carried out of the house and laid on the hearse. The four-horse team began to pull, and the guard of honour presented arms. It was followed then by the guard of honour, employees of the firm with wreaths, the grain-porters, officials of the Lübeck railway, and then an "endless stream of carriages", beginning with the State Coach of the Senate, the representatives of the Bürgerschaft and then the next of kin. "Everyone who meant anything in Lübeck" was there to pay his last respects.

The procession turned into the Breitestrasse and made its way slowly towards the Burgtor and the cemetery: past the Fischergrube, the Engelsgrube, the great red-brick edifice of St Jakobi, past the Chamber of Commerce with its flags at half-mast, the tall, right-angle Renaissance gables of the Society of Seafarers. The town had scarcely altered since the Senator's youth. Pavements had come, the town gates were no longer closed at sunset, an attempt had been made at public drainage and sewers: but the bricks of the city were the same, the narrow lanes and alleys, the dark dancing-taverns by the quayside, the "world within a world" that was Lübeck. Since the 1860s shops had finally been permitted to display their goods in front windows, but the benches outside people's houses remained, the cobbled streets grew no wider. Above the town soared the steeples of the city's five "cathedrals", churches of plain red brick whose massive towers leaned towards and away from each other, whose bells had rung over centuries of prosperity and growth.

At the cemetery the family vault had been opened. The guard of honour again presented arms, the fifty and more carriages halted and the people of

Lübeck gathered round the grave.

The trees of the nearby wood rustled in the autumn breeze. They too had known the deceased, as a boy, as a man he had wandered among them. Today they deck the place with their last golden leaves, and now that he is buried they wish to say: as long as civic virtues count for anything in the ancient Hansa city, his name will never be forgotten.

Towards the family however, the people showed a different face. Even Heinrich was aware of the change. "The day came when my father died," he wrote in one of his autobiographical stories:[29]

I was twenty and I had to take the first steps of my own, not his. Outside the people were standing, my old teacher too. Without thinking, I expected the old warmth and sympathy, and I went up to him. What? The teacher turned his head away. He even left the group of people, went into his house, closed the door.

Others did the same, but the old teacher's behaviour hit me hardest. Yet I understood: they were sick of taking trouble over me, all at once they were sick and tired of it. Before, they had done too much, so now they didn't even do enough. It wasn't intentionally cruel, it was simply the giving up of an arrangement for which there was no longer any point.

That is the way it always happens when success is avenged. One of the waves of success, which every life has, runs back, people give up a man they have wooed all the faster the more they previously bothered about him. How good it feels for them at last to be able to put on another face. There is nothing more weary than to have to show a certain person only a happy face all the time. Success is over. The Senator for taxes is dead.

Heinrich stood alone. No longer did he have a father to fight, to convince. "The young person thinks he has seen and accomplished everything," he wrote in 1929, "he cannot see further. Then one day his father dies — a human being, not an intellectual model. The son is racked by pain, unexpected pain, like guilt. He realizes that till now he has only been anticipating pain, life, with harmless rehearsals. Reality is harder and without satisfaction. Now he must face the real world into which he will have to go, his career, the unknown!" He returned to Berlin.

CHAPTER THREE

First Steps

The death of his father must have hit Heinrich much harder than he imagined. Nine weeks after returning to Berlin he was admitted to a sanatorium there.

His illness was diagnosed as tubercular, a lung haemorrhage and in February 1892, when the Frau Senator managed to get away and visit him, she was sufficiently worried to have him transferred to Wiesbaden, and then, later in the spring, to Lausanne.

Heinrich's unpaid apprenticeship with Fischer thus came to an end, as also the lecture courses at Berlin University which he had begun to attend. He was rising twenty-one, and it was time, he felt, to concentrate on his real career. As the summer wore on in Switzerland and he began to recover both from illness and the psychological shock of his father's death, Heinrich felt a "new spiritual epoch" beginning for him. In August he was writing to Ludwig Ewers that he was beginning his first novel — "to find out what I can and cannot do".[1]

It took a year to write, was called *In einer Familie*, and was finished in Riva, on Lake Garda, in October 1893. Whether he offered it to his old boss, Samuel Fischer, we do not know, but apparently it was rejected by the publishing house of Cotta in January 1894; and in the end his mother paid for it to be privately printed in Munich — 500 Marks, as Heinrich bitterly recollected towards the end of his life, "when it can barely have cost 200 to produce".[2] But his real bitterness was over the work itself. When asked in a questionnaire in 1947, when and where the plan for his first novel "ripened", Heinrich entered the laconic reply:

In einer Familie did not ripen; its author was not mature enough to

write a novel at that time . . . There was no inner compulsion either —
only the will was there.[3]

The faults of the novel were indeed legion. It was a working out of his own
limbo in life, his own conflicting desire for order and rationality and at the
same time mystery, the grotesque. It was the conflict between father and
mother, between Lübeck Protestantism and the South-American exotic —
a conflict which was to remain with him throughout his life. Yet the most
curious thing is that with the death of his father, Heinrich actually became
more rather than less conservative — and any hope of *In einer Familie*
growing into a real human story broke down with Heinrich's insistent moral
straitjacket. It was as though Heinrich was determined to prove now a sense
of responsibility which he could not show his father during his lifetime. The
autobiographical hero of *In einer Familie* is a self-confessed "reactionary",
a follower of Paul Bourget's social theories (to whom Heinrich dedicated the
book), an unrepentant opposer of the "mob-rule of money", of the breakdown of the old social and religious order by sudden prosperity.

Heinrich returned to Germany at the end of spring 1894; but not to the
Hanseatic city of his childhood. His mother had first moved to a villa in the
Roeckstrasse outside Lübeck after the Senator's death, then decided to move
from the city altogether, leaving Thomas to finish his schooling at the
Katharineum. She had chosen Munich as the new home for the family: and
it was there, in May 1894, that she, Heinrich, Thomas, Julia, Carla and
baby Viktor reassembled for the first time since Senator Mann's funeral.

2

We sold the town house, as my grandmother's had been sold before,
and moved from that spacious home, where in the parquetry ballroom
the officers of the garrison had courted the daughters of the patriciate,
into a comparatively modest villa with a garden, outside the city gate. My
mother, however, soon left the town for good and all. She loved the
south, the mountains, Munich, to which she had once travelled with my
father; and to Munich she moved with my younger brothers and sisters,
leaving me to board with a professor's family. There I lived, with the
sons of some Mecklenburg and Holstein nobles and gentry, until my
school life gradually dwindled to an end.

Of this period I have most jovial memories. The "institution" had
given up all hope for me. It left me to my fate, and that was dark to me;
but, feeling myself quite hearty and clever, I was not cast down. I sat
away the hours.[4]

Thomas, then, does not appear to have been unduly perturbed by his
father's death — and it certainly shook him into no academic fever. The
last two years at school he failed to be promoted:

I was lazy, stubborn and full of disrespect and mockery. I was hated by the teachers who quite rightly — and in complete agreement with the established facts of the matter — prophesied my imminent downfall.[5]

Yet if his teachers gave up hope and even his mother grew angry at the continual reports of his idleness, Thomas seems to have had no doubts about himself. Ever since the city had celebrated the centenary of the founding of his father's firm, he had known he could never be the successor his father so dearly wished. Heinrich's departure from Fischer's and his work on his first novel only confirmed Thomas' own literary inclinations; and the Lyric-Dramatist, after the difficult friendship with Armin Martens came to an end, now addressed his poems to his partner at Herr Kroll's private dancing class. One of them Thomas included in the school arts magazine he and some "revolutionary" friends in the top form brought out. The poem was called *Zweimaliger Abschied* (Twice Times Farewell); like Heinrich's poem *Sleep,* it was also accepted by M.G. Conrad for publication in *Die Gesellschaft* — and with what pride Thomas walked the streets of Lübeck that day, he remembered later.[6]

The *Frühlingssturm* (Spring Storm), as the school magazine was called, was far from being sedate; and Thomas' "philosophic and revolutionary"[7] leading articles soon had the school buzzing. *"Spring Storm!"* he wrote in his opening editorial. "Yes, like the spring storm in the dusty country, we want to hurl ourselves against the mass of intellectual paralysis, ignorance and blinkered, pompous philistinism which confronts us." In another editorial he rose to defend his idol, Heine, from the current attempt by a Dr Scipio in the *Berliner Tageblatt* to represent the exiled Jew as a good, honest patriotic German Protestant. "How pathetic!" Thomas commented. "Does this little man really believe he is doing the late Harry Heine a post-humous favour by praising him with such drivel?! — And what proofs he has enlisted! Because Heine speaks with admiration of Martin Luther, he is a Protestant! Dr Scipio could equally claim that because Heine — I believe he was in Heligoland — read the Bible so avidly and liked the book so much, that he was a pietist! — Heinrich Heine, my dear Doctor, admired Napoleon, though by birth he was a German, and he also admired Luther, though he was *not* a Protestant!" Thomas completed the salvo with the acid remark: "Apart from that, the article was so dull and 'worthy' that the Doctor deserves to be made a professor."

Perhaps school, in this respect, had really taught Thomas something. It was after all, a microcosm of the world, as philistine at heart, as outside. The headmaster was an authoritarian tyrant but there was at least one teacher, a Dr Bäthke, whose progressive socialism and worship of Schiller, particularly the ballads, made a profound impression on Thomas. "This is not just *any* reading you are having, it is the very best reading you *could* have!" he would declare.[8] Bäthke was a die-hard freedom-fighter, spokesman of the Progressives on the Lübeck town council, and the only redoubtable opponent to the Senate's national-liberalism. In chorus the class would have to recite revolutionary French poems and songs, such as:

Le char de l'opulence
M'éclabousse en passant
J'éprouve l'insolense
Du riche et du puissant . . .

His speeches in the Bürgerschaft were much the same. " 'Qui s'excuse,
s'accuse' — that means in German, he who defends himself, accuses himself,
Herr Senator," he would finish. Against the prevalent mood of chauvinism
and fanatic fear of the Social Democrats — outlawed by Bismarck from
1878 to 1890 — his must indeed been a voice of freedom in the ancient
Hanseatic city.

So the hours were sat away. "Outside school I lived very much as I liked,
and stood well with my fellow boarders at Dr Timpe's" Thomas recalled,
"in those premature drinking bouts I gaily condescended to take part, now
and then."[9]

The one thing that really aroused Thomas' enthusiasm however, apart
from Schiller and his books, was music. From infancy he had listened to his
mother at the piano, to her playing the Etudes and Nocturnes of Chopin,
but even more to her singing. From Mozart and Beethoven, from Schubert,
Schumann, Robert Franz, Brahms and Liszt to Wagner she commanded a
range of Lieder which Thomas would never forget, arrangements of
Eichendorff and Heine's poems which became part of his being, his
property.[10] And if the new "Naturalism" that was scandalizing Berlin only
found a "faint echo" in Lübeck, the City Theatre was quick to perform the
work of Richard Wagner.

"I don't wish to be presumptuous," Thomas wrote forty years later, "but
I don't think the City Theatre ever harboured a more impressionable, a more
captive audience than in me . . . I was there whenever I could — permitted or
forbidden. I had a sort of 'reserved' seat in the Parterre . . . a seat which
unlike the others didn't have a number but the initial A."[11] In the orchestra
sat his violin-teacher; there were false notes, unfortunate falsettos in the
choir (a member of the Brabant gentry apparently) and the swan sometimes
swam backwards, but the young admirer was "transporté" by Lohengrin.
Wagner he adored; and until Heinrich introduced him to Nietzsche, Wagner
remained his idol. In time the composer would begin to appear suspect, but
his music always retained its hold. Before the gramophone it was the theatre
and the concert hall which drew the "captive audience". And beyond the
drama, the gigantic fusion of music, of stage, and human voice the eighteen
year old began to sense the structure behind it, the secret of epic narration.
As his son Klaus was later to say of Thomas' piano improvization:

It was always the same rhythm, at once drawing and violent; always that
swelling, weeping, jubilating song. It was always Tristan.[12]

Finally, in the Spring of 1894, he was permitted to leave school. With his
violin and case he made his way to the station. He had said goodbye to aunts
and uncles and remaining relatives. For ten years he would not see the town;
and when he did he would already have earned more than a "certain regard"
among the literary pundits of the nation. What Lübeck felt about his novel,

however, was something quite different.

3

Munich is one of the great paradoxes of modern Germany. A market town in Bavaria, a city of artists and coffee-house thinkers, the freest in the Empire — yet which was to see one of the only two soviet republics in Western Europe, and was subsequently to become the home of Hitler and the National Socialists.

Perhaps its very laxity was bound to make it one day the easiest target for social revolutionaries; but before the First World War it was simply the mecca of young painters, of struggling writers and poets. Its beer was renowned, its architecture and landscaping incomparable. It was a city of music, of theatre and opera, famous for its university. It was virtually classless and had been spared by the industrial explosion sweeping the Rhineland. It was solidly agricultural, a town of "petty officials, small traders, retired farmers, businessmen and craftsmen . . . There was no sharply circumscribed lower class. Apart from the Breweries the town had few large-scale industries, and its workers had neither class feelings nor class standards of living. No upper middle class was in evidence; among the leading citizens of Munich, in those days, scarcely anyone could be called a captain of industry . . . The only native plutocrats were the brewers; nearly all retained the features of their lower middle-class origin even after they were rolling in riches."[13]

It was also a very cheap town to live in. The Senator's estate on death had been worth almost a million Marks. After the sale of property, the business, and stock, it was worth barely 400,000 Marks, which were then invested in shares by the executor and from which the Frau Senator drew interest. Munich, then, was a town in which the Senator's talented and still youngish widow could live comfortably. She took a ground-floor apartment in a suburb to the north, called Schwabing. It was the cultural quarter of Munich — its "Montmartre" as the poet Erich Mühsam put it. Here she could live in comparative ease with her children without needing to touch the invested capital of the Senator's estate.

The apartment contained eight rooms, with a verandah and garden. The Frau Senator moved in in March 1893 while Thomas was left at school in Lübeck with Dr Timpe and Heinrich made preparations for a trip to Paris from Lausanne. Julia was by this time fifteen, Carla eleven, and little Viktor barely three.

Frau Senator Mann had other reasons for choosing Munich, though, besides its freedom and charm. In 1888 she had made her last trip "abroad" with her husband from Lübeck: and the centrepiece of it had been Munich.

They had stayed in the grandest hotel, the Vier Jahreszeiten, had enjoyed the native beer and been magnetized by the shops, by Wagner's *Siegfried* performed at the Court Opera House; and by the eighty-eight rooms of the city art exhibition. They had visited the famous lakes outside the town and gone up into the mountains. It was a journey the Frau Senator had never forgotten. "Met at the station by Heinrich, our beloved (17 year old) eldest son," she had ended her account of it.[14]

In Munich the Frau Senator arranged the family furniture she had brought from Lübeck, including her most important treasure: the grand piano. About this time she also began writing children's stories and novellas. The first was called *Vergeltung* (Requital). It was a heroic, sentimental sort of tale that finished with the tragic death of its hero, Colonel von Arras.

"Then Arras opened his eyes," it went, "and they grew larger as though to soak in the picture of his beloved and take it into eternity. His last words were disconnected, barely audible: 'My wife! My child. I wanted to take the place of your father. − Alice! Where are your beautiful eyes? Don't cry − oh, my children! − bring to them − last . . .' He became unconscious and after a few violent convulsions, Colonel von Arras had breathed his last. His wife held his hands in hers, gently closed his eyes which had, oh so often told her of his love . . . and touched his forehead with her lips. Then she stood up, utterly composed; she had made a firm decision which could be seen in her features . . . She turned her head a last time to the body of her husband. 'From now on I belong to your children,' she whispered."[15]

She did. She paid for publication of Heinrich's first novel in 1894, never put the least pressure on him financially, as the Senator had done.

Heinrich bore out so well her own conception of the "artist" − proud, fierce, prone to illness. In Munich she surrounded herself immediately with an entourage of musical and creative people, and with little of the formality that had characterized such gatherings in Lübeck. Perhaps it wasn't good for Heinrich; perhaps it imposed suddenly, after the absence of moral support from the Senator, an expectation of artistic prowess which related to the show of art, its bravura, rather than to the content.

Perhaps. It was certainly something which Heinrich would have to struggle against all his life, this awareness of talent, of artistic potential, of public expectation.

For Thomas it would be quite the reverse. At school no one expected anything, his reports were unsatisfactory, and his mother allowed him to join her in Munich in the spring of 1894 more out of resignation than anything else. Together with Herr Krafft Tesdorpf and Consul Alfred Mann, the eighteen-year-old boy's guardians, it was now decided that Thomas should enter the offices of a fire-insurance company in Munich, whose director was an old friend of the late Senator's, and who had once pursued a similar business in Lübeck.

"Curious," his mother admitted later to Ludwig Ewers, "it must have been my profound disappointment over Thomas' school reports which made me lose faith in his talent; or else, to try and encourage more zeal for learning, I wanted to discourage his poetic urge − at any rate the truth is that you were aware even then what was lurking in that 'idle' little Tommy."[16]

4

There was indeed something lurking; and it was not long before it began to surface. Beside the snuff-taking clerks copying out accounts after accounts the unpaid apprentice sat at his desk writing his first novella. It was called *Gefallen;* it opened with a bachelor's dinner party and proceeded to recount the story of a love affair. No one in the South German Fire Insurance Company knew of it; and the worst that little three-year-old Viktor — who was taken one day to see Thomas at work — suspected was that when nobody was looking "Uncle Ommo", as he was affectionately called, would start twirling himself up and down on his swivel chair.

Then, in the summer, came the news that M.G. Conrad had accepted the story for publication in *Die Gesellschaft.* It appeared in October 1894; and on that slim success Thomas tried to persuade his mother to let him leave the insurance company. He was only just nineteen.

It cannot have been an easy decision; but perhaps Heinrich's unhappy time at Messrs Zahn and Jaensch in Dresden may have convinced her. After all, Heinrich was home again, had written his first novel and was contributing sizeable articles to *Die Gesellschaft* and *Die Gegenwart.* She consented: but perhaps to placate his Lübeck guardian she made it a condition that Thomas enrol at the university for some lecture courses and at least prepare himself for a journalistic career.

So Thomas, with the help of the family lawyer, released himself from his apprenticeship in insurance, and on 4th November booked the following lecture courses at the Technical High School: Economics (four hours per week), Culture and World History (four hours), German Mythology (four hours), Foundations of Aesthetics (one hour) and, finally, Professor von Reinhardstöttner on Shakespeare's Tragedies. The next day came a letter from Richard Dehmel, the celebrated poet.

Dear Sir

I have just read your wonderful story *Gefallen* in the magazine *Die Gesellschaft.* I read it again to my wife and cannot refrain from telling you how delighted and moved by it I was. There are so few writers today who can relate an experience in simple, tender prose that you must forgive this rather importunate expression of my joy and admiration. In case you have any other stories of equal maturity, may I ask you if you would submit them to the arts magazine *Pan* which is being started, as you no doubt have heard, and on whose editorial committee I serve. (10—15 Marks per printed page.)

With best wishes, respectfully yours
Richard Dehmel

It was the letter every fledgling dreams of receiving; and evidently caught Thomas a little unawares. He thanked Dehmel profusely; made some heavy remarks about modern literature "wallowing in compromises with the *misera plebs*" (a reference no doubt to the Hauptmann style of social naturalism) and ended by confessing that "at the moment I have nothing finished". Three weeks later he managed to complete a new story *The Little Teacher*. Dehmel declined it with a "very kind" letter, and Thomas tried *Die Gesellschaft*, where it was accepted, but never published.

Dehmel's letter, he later told the poet, was his "discovery". It must have given him enormous encouragement since Dehmel was the name in every literary's man's mouth in those days. Yet the praise was by no means far-fetched. Undoubtedly, in its tale of disillusion in love, the story was tendentious: but the quality of the writing, the ability to set a scene, introduce characters and weave dialogue was not simply astounding for a nineteen-year-old — it revealed the precocious but utterly assured hand of a master. How surprised his publisher, Fischer, would one day be when Thomas tendered a novel more than a thousand pages long! He had seemed, from his first success with *Gefallen* to be earmarked for the short-story, the novella: deft, blessed with an extraordinary eye for detail, seemingly unweighted by the heavier manner of the novelist.

Thus Dehmel's letter appeared out of the blue, as if to confirm his move from the South German Fire Insurance Company. He joined the Academic Drama Group of the University, and in Munich coffee houses enjoyed a little prestige as the "author of *Gefallen*". There he met Hartleben, Panizza, Schaumberger, Ludwig-Scharf, von Reder and Kock-Weser. A world-première of Ibsen's *Wild Duck* was planned for the following year; in the meantime he attended his lectures with "fair regularity" and penned verses, including a children's fairy-play in verse. "All kinds of poetry I've been writing," he wrote in February to Otto Grautoff, his old class-mate from Lübeck — whose father, a bookseller, had gone bankrupt and been pointed out by Senator Mann with the terrible words "a crushed man". "Of course for poetry you need neither hard work nor tenacity," Thomas declared. "I usually write them while going to sleep."[17] In January *Die Gesellschaft* had published his poem *Child, you see, I love you,* but as he admitted later in his life, he understood very little about poetry, he lacked the necessary imagination. The few poems he published were somewhat sickly-sweet, a hang-over from German Romanticism. Here fortunately Heinrich came to his aid.

5

It was natural, at this time, that Thomas should look up to Heinrich, his elder brother — tall, shy, proud, reserved, and always meticulously dressed. Heinrich stayed in Munich for much of the year in 1894, leaving in January 1895 for his second trip to Italy.

For countless centuries Italy had drawn the literary and artistic talents of Europe to its cities, its ruins, its mountains and its shores; and Heinrich was no exception. For the next two decades he was to spend longer in Italy and the South Tyrol than he would in Germany. The climate suited him, the surroundings bewitched him — "the magic of the unknown, the new, is so heightened here that I feel as though I were one of the Arab sailors in 1001 Nights entering a mysterious town which so confuses and frightens me that I slow down before every street corner in order to prepare myself for what is coming." he wrote of Rome in his diary in January 1895. It was a revelation — "as though I were in wonderland," he wrote, for the difference between Italy and Germany overwhelmed him. At home — especially in Lübeck — everything must have a purpose; whereas in Rome beauty mushroomed seemingly regardless of function or order. Churches, palaces, cathedrals, gardens abounded; and for the second time he felt this "purposeless beauty", as he put it in his diary, acting as a salve to his feelings of containment, of frustration and dissatisfaction at home. His first trip to Italy had thrown up no less than eight short stories and novellas in 1894 after finishing his novel; his second would stimulate him even more. Except that, in the meantime, he had decided to edit a monthly magazine: *Das Zwanzigste Jahrhundert* (The Twentieth Century).

Quite how Heinrich came to be offered the post we do not know today; it was not an association Heinrich liked to be reminded of. The magazine, founded in 1890, was radically conservative, anti-Semitic and polemical. It was anti-monarchist because, it felt, Wilhelm II had "sold-out" to the capitalist and moneyed groups in German society at the expense of the solid, hard-working middle classes.

It was the only editorship Heinrich was to assume in his life, and he wrote prolifically for the magazine, apart from commissioning articles and reviews — including six from his brother Thomas. In fifteen months he covered every conceivable subject from militarism (which he deplored) to religion, from political reconstruction to rabid anti-semitism. He had begun to read Nietzsche deeply, and contributed two articles on the philosopher. Whether it was good journalism is questionable; but as experience it was invaluable; and it could be done from Italy. From Rome, in April, he moved up into the Sabine hills around Palestrina with his friend Heinrich Lehmann, whom he had first met in the Black Forest in 1892 — two of the "best and most important periods of my life", he confessed to Lehmann's mother in 1898 after Lehmann died.[18] From Palestrina he wrote asking if Thomas would join him; and in July, after the performance of Ibsen's *Wild Duck* — in which Thomas played, in the producer's fur coat and spectacles, old Werle the wholesale merchant — he made his first journey to Italy. "Poeta di Monaco" Thomas entered in the landlady's register in Palestrina; and returned to Munich in October for the winter term.

Yet Palestrina was not forgotten; it was to Palestrina Heinrich and Thomas would return some two years later for the "long hot summer" that would set both brothers on the road to literary fame as novelists; and provide the back-cloth, exactly half a century later, for Adrian Leverkühn's pact with the Devil in *Doctor Faustus*.

6

In April 1896 *Das Zwanzigste Jahrhundert* was taken over by a new publisher in Zurich and Leipzig, and Heinrich only figured as the Munich editor. By June he had written his last signed article (on Nietzsche), and in July he took his leave. August and September were spent in Munich — where Thomas' new novella *The Will to Happiness* was currently appearing in the columns of the New Munich satirical weekly, *Simplicissimus*.

Simplicissimus was the sensation of the 'Nineties. Its first edition had appeared on 1st April 1896, and 480,000 copies had been printed — a rather optimistic figure, since only 15,000 were sold. Nevertheless it soon became the sharpest satirical magazine in Germany, famous (or infamous) for its lawsuits and scandals. Its founder was Albert Langen, a failed painter and son of a wealthy Rhineland industrialist, who had gone to Paris and been advised by a Danish confidence trickster and fake-artist to start a "Gil Blas illustré". Strindberg's wife Frieda later claimed the idea originated from her husband; but whatever the origin, *Simplicissimus* did not happen overnight. Langen first decided to open a publishing house in December 1893. Only later did he move to Munich, where, in the anarchic atmosphere of the street cafés and teeming artists he became convinced the magazine would work.

"Ten pfennigs an issue. A weekly with colour-illustrations: *Simplicissimus* we'll call it," he announced to T.T. Heine one day as the artist sat sipping punch and "staring fixedly at Germany's dim future". Heine asked for 200 Marks in advance.

"Never!" cried Langen. "To give you less than 1,000 Marks in advance would be vulgar!"[19]

So *Simplicissimus* was born, with a two-colour cover and at the price of a newspaper. It tilted at everything, from imperialism to the threat of socialism and literary sentimentality. The illustrations were cartoons, more outrageous than *Punch* and considerably funnier. By its seventh week it had to answer a summons forbidding it to appear.

But Langen had chosen well in choosing Munich. The court at Munich was little interested in politics, still less in literature. While the Berlin establishment went wild with fury, Langen proceeded to make his reputation.

Above all he wanted good short stories — and was prepared to pay for them. He engaged the young Jakob Wassermann — then only twenty-two and one of the most talented young authors in Munich — as a member of his staff. And Wassermann soon found space in his columns for the twenty-one year old Thomas Mann.

Thomas was paid in gold for his story; and on the strength of it decided to follow Heinrich back to Italy. In its 22nd August number, *Simplicissimus* had drawn attention to the increasing number of manuscripts being offered in which sex played the major role. Out of 433 entries for its Novella and Humorous Short Story Prize more than half were simply "not to be taken seriously". Worse still the rest seemed almost entirely concerned with the depiction of sex — as though, the editor complained, their main concern was to provide *Simplicissimus* with "pornographic reading". Love was represented "always from the standpoint of the gourmand, the satiated man-of-the-world, the tired cocotte". It was never "pure, fresh, gracious love . . . the love of Gottfried Keller and Robert Burns . . . but a smutty, brusque, unhealthy, banal love, symptomatic somehow . . . Where is your humour, Germany," the magazine asked, "where is your youth and joy in struggle?" It offered a prize of 300 Marks "for the best novella in which sexual love plays no part."

Filled with curiosity as to who would take the prize, Thomas left Munich in October for Italy. For three weeks he stayed in Venice, sailed south to Ancona, travelling from there by train to Rome and Naples — "far too expensive, but with a wonderful view over the sea and Mount Vesuvius".[20] "Here I feel very much at ease. Only now do I really feel I am in the South; it's the distinct note of the Orient which mixes in the life here," he wrote to Korfiz Holm (his old co-editor of the Lübeck *Frühlingssturm*) who was now working on *Simplicissimus*.

"Has the decision been made on the story without love?" he inquired eagerly. "Who's received the golden laurel?"[21]

Well might Thomas ask, for his own short-story reservoir was beginning to brim again; as was Heinrich's. "Around 1895 I just missed winning a short-story prize," Heinrich once reminisced. "But the president of one jury, Ernst von Wolzogen, said: 'He can't have written this by himself!' "[22] Throughout the year 1894 while in Munich Heinrich had been hard at work on novellas: *The Lion* in March, *Abroad* in April, *Mistake, Is she the one?* and *The Hound* in August, *Contessina* in October, *The Marvel* and *Two New Year's Nights* in November. Apart from *The Mistake* none was published until now, almost two years later, when Heinrich abruptly cast off his *Twentieth Century* mantle and began to write creatively again.

In November 1896 *Pan* published his novella *The Marvel*; in December *Simplicissimus* brought out *The Hound*. A week later *The Stolen Document*, a novella he had written in Munich that September, appeared in *Simplicissimus*; and in the same month, January 1897, Thomas' three page diary-story *Death*.

It was Jakob Wassermann, however, who ran away with the non-sex story prize — for the appropriately titled *Here Lies the Little Ox*. Meanwhile Thomas returned with Heinrich from Naples to Rome.

7

It would have been surprising if the spate of Heinrich and Thomas' short stories in contemporary German magazines had not attracted at least one publisher's attention. It attracted two, almost simultaneously.

Albert Langen was just beginning to expand the publishing side of his business beyond *Simplicissimus*. Though short-story volumes seldom made money he was sufficiently struck by Heinrich's powerful, clear and poetic style to offer him a contract. Since the *Stolen Document* of September 1896

Heinrich had written *The Cameo* in November and two further novellas, *Stories from Rocca de' Fichi* and *Disillusion* in December. Langen wrote early in 1897 to say he would publish Heinrich's collection of novellas under the title of the main story *Das Wunderbare* (The Marvel).

A few weeks later Oscar Bie, editor of Fischer's Berlin arts magazine *Neue Deutsche Rundschau*, wrote to say they would accept Thomas' latest short story *Little Herr Friedemann* for publication in the magazine; moreover they would be interested in any other stories he had written. Thomas immediately collected his published and unpublished stories and sent them to Bie. By the end of May Fischer himself had read them.

"Esteemed Mr Mann!" Fischer wrote. "I will gladly publish your volume of novellas. I liked the stories very much indeed, I would like to put them in my 'Collection Fischer' series with an illustrated cover . . ." For the sum of one hundred and fifty Marks Fischer thus bought book publication rights in the volume, including the right to publish *Der Bajazzo* in his magazine *Neue Deutsche Rundschau* — a subtle way of covering his royalty expenses over the book. However to mitigate the apparent meanness of the royalty he went on to add: "nevertheless I would be very pleased if you would give me an opportunity to publish something larger in the way of prose, even if it is not very long."

Fischer concluded his letter to Thomas by saying a novel would bring a much higher royalty, especially if serialized beforehand. "I wish to do my best to further your writing," he ended, "though naturally on condition that you give all your works to my firm. Respectfully yours. S. Fischer Publisher."

It would be more than three years before Thomas completed his next book, but Fischer's letter was to pay off in a way no other publisher's letter can have done in the history of the German book trade. *Little Herr Friedemann* meanwhile, was a failure, and within a short time had disappeared, with the rest of the 'Collection Fischer' from Fischer's catalogues.

8

Spring in Rome had been delightful, and the news that they would both soon be fully-fledged "published" authors must have given the brothers Mann added confidence. Their mother sent them each their regular 160–180 Marks per month — "a remittance", as Thomas explained later, "which improved in the Italian exchange and to us meant a great deal: economic freedom, the power to bide our time." If they ran short of money, as Viktor later recorded, they would write humorous telegrams home, on Royal Italian Post Office stationery:

Taken a nasty fall on the back of the head —
Send thousand urgently H + T

— a play on their mother's extreme fear of street accidents on slippery roads.

They were together, but otherwise very much alone. "We made no friends," Thomas recalled; "if we heard German spoken, we fled."[23] Rome was a "refuge" from the world, from "regularity", from the fact that neither had a job. It was in this atmosphere that they spent their last months of freedom, before their life's work began in earnest.

They had made arrangements to spend the summer of 1897 outside Rome again, about thirty miles away in the Sabine Hills in the little town where Palestrina had been born.

"Most worthy Signora," Heinrich wrote to the landlady of the Albergo Casa Bernardini, "at last we can leave Rome. Please expect us *tomorrow*, Thursday, for supper in the evening, prepare the beds with insecticide, and send the cab to meet the 6 o'clock train."[24]

Anna Bernardini's hotel was a very "proper" establishment which had included ambassadors and distinguished authors among its guests, and in whose kitchen Signora Bernardini — or Manardi as Thomas altered her name in *Doctor Faustus* — "reigned".

She was a stately Roman matron, with arched upper lip, not very dark, the good eyes and hair were only chestnut brown, with at most a faint silver network on the smooth head. Her figure was full and well-proportioned, the impression she made both capable and rustically simple, as one saw her small hard-worked hands, the double widow's ring on the right one, poised on the firm strong hips, bound by their stiff apron-strings.

In fact Signor Bernardini, a painter by profession, had died in most unsavoury circumstances, having been escorting two of his pupils, Russian princes, back to Russia when in Constantinople he was murdered by a fellow Italian.

Here Heinrich and Thomas settled for the "long, scorching summer". They found a stray dog on a haystack which attached itself to Thomas. He christened it Titino and even took it home to Munich with him later.

Then "in a burst of energy" the two brothers set to work on the only collaboration of their lives. "Seventy-five works of art by the hand of Masters, among which twenty-eight coloured pictures and forty-eight engravings beside which sixteen accompanying works of poetic art, and many captions containing instructive and illuminating morals collected and published with care and especial regard for the moral mind of Germany's growing youth": *The Picture Book for Good Little Children.*

It was a kind of "classic *Simplicissimus*" Thomas later recounted, which Heinrich had begun in Rome. He had called the pictures — mainly finely-drawn caricatures — "The Social Order", but they referred to it usually as the "Life-Work". Thomas added his own wild drawings and they stuck them together in a long frieze representing the whole of human society, "from Kaiser to the Pope, from loutish worker to street-beggar — no one was left out in this fanfare of social classes".

They decided, to make the book into a Confirmation and birthday present for their younger sister and brother, Carla and Viktor. The editor was given as "Senior Teacher Dr Hugo Giese-Widerlich" — pictured as a fish-faced, be-spectacled gentleman with sparse beard and spiteful countenance. Poor Viktor, on the eve of going to school, was terrified.

Bourgeois life was mercilessly parodied, in heroic and ghostly verse;

violent murderers popped up, and a poor "Art-painter" related his sorrowful autobiography as best he could. The funniest, Viktor found, was the parody on Schiller — a poem entitled "Murderer Bittenfeld Overpowered by Sunset," together with the inane commentary of a pseudo German-teacher. There was even an illustration relating to Thomas' new novella *Little Luise* — "from the charming novella by the well-loved poet Thomas Mann, which is warmly recommended to the German public". Viktor, who at four had decided the family should go to the Baltic for their next summer holiday and had screamed in tears he would go alone when told to be quiet, was pictured at the window of a meandering train in the countryside. It was headed: 'Viko travels alone to Timmendorf". There was also a caricature of a duel with morality — with a note below, in which the artist explains how he was forced to cut down "Assistant-Administrator Dr X", who had "stolen his wife's affections". *Simplicissimus* would have been delighted.[25]

As Thomas later noted, the Picture Book was more than a simple distraction. For the two merchant's sons it was a last irreverent fling before their real careers as novelists finally began.

9

It was during the summer of 1897 in Palestrina that Thomas began innocently to assemble the information he needed for a new novel he had conceived. It was not intended to be anything very large: a short, "family saga" in the modern manner of Kielland and Jonas Lie. The idea had originally been mooted by Heinrich, who found certain aspects of their family history — such as Consul Marty's rise to wealth by supplying the Napoleonic armies — interesting. Thomas' concept, however, went much deeper. "I was the first to speak," Heinrich noted towards the end of his life, "but Thomas was prepared."

What Thomas intended was a book of "about two hundred and fifty pages", comprising roughly fifteen chapters. It would be a continuation of his autobiographical pre-occupation, a "novella of adolescence", drawn from experiences "still fresh in my mind" and a little "poetic introspection".[26] It would not have differed greatly, as Thomas later confessed in America, from any other similar books published in Germany at that time. But before he began, he was concerned to lay the groundwork for the book fully. From his uncle in Lübeck, Consul Wilhelm Marty, he requested as much information as possible on the city in the second half of the century: Lübeck currency, grain prices, harvests, political "atmosphere" vis à vis Prussia and so on. From his mother in Munich he wrote off for traditional Lübeck recipes. And from his sister Julia (then nineteen and very class-conscious) all the "personal" details on the members of the Mann family she could muster — their characters, marriages, scandals . . .

What stopped the book from becoming the introspective "novella of adolescence" Thomas originally intended we can only guess at: for

Buddenbrooks, as Thomas himself pointed out, was perhaps the only major work of Naturalism in the realm of the German novel. It achieved a fame and popularity among the most sophisticated readers as well as the least literate; and in time it went on to be translated into almost all the languages of the world. No other book Thomas afterwards attempted had its simple, classical structure, its effortlessly natural narration, its perfect balance of observation, imagination, detail, characterization and humour. It was a style and an approach to which he never returned, an extraordinary and singular monument to his abilities as a writer — begun at the age of twenty-two.

It seems likely that the "epic" construction of *Buddenbrooks* arose from a rare and unusual combination of factors. Thomas was lonely but ambitious, a late-developer who at the age of twenty had suffered "a late and violent outbreak of sexuality" as he later put it. And it was in this spirit of "psychological susceptibility" that he opened himself to the main-streams of European literary development. He absorbed his brother's favourites in French writing — Bourget, Goncourt, Zola — but he did not read happily in the original and it was to the German translations of English, Russian and Scandinavian authors that he increasingly turned. Ibsen, Thackeray, Dickens, Tolstoy, Turgenev, the Norwegians Kielland and Lie he "devoured", intoxicated too by the epic, "motivistic"[27] music of Wagner, and aware that he possessed a rare "power of vision",[28] a profound and unusual insight into epic artistic creativity.

Most of his philosophical and social ideas came from Nietzsche — an influence which, he later remarked, was "decisive for an intellect still in its formative stage".[29] The idea of dilettantism, of a generation that was too "refined" to remain in its traditional role, haunted him. *Buddenbrooks* became the story of a family's decline.

But here his "epic instinct", nurtured by classics still firmly imprinted on his mind, came into its own. His preparations, using the replies from his family, convinced him that the real story lay not in the "introspective character and experiences" of the autobiographical last descendant, Hanno Buddenbrook, but in the people and events which led up to Hanno. He began to read *Anna Karenina,* and marvelled at Tolstoy's ease of narration, noting the short chapters which read as though he were never out of breath. At the end of September he and Heinrich returned to Rome.

The first page of the *Buddenbrook* manuscript (as it was originally called, after a minor character in one of Fontane's novels) was dated Rome, October 1897. "After zealous preparations," he related, "I had begun. I had no great faith in the practical outcome of the exercise; yet with the patience which my native slowness laid upon me — a phlegm perhaps better described as restrained nervousness — I continued it in Via Torre Argentina." In the "reek of endless three centisimi cigarettes" he scribbled, while Heinrich "sketched a great deal" and breathed in the glories of the ancient capital of the world.[30]

The city, however, meant curiously little to Thomas, "At heart," he confessed, "I lived there not on account of the south, which I did not love, but quite simply because there was no room for me at home. I accepted respectfully the historical and aesthetic impressions the city had to offer, but scarcely with the feeling that they concerned me or had significance for me."[31] It was a strange confession from the man who later became famous also for his *Death in Venice.* Italy provided a contrast to his native land, a chance to "flee" Germans, to be alone. But it was the land in which Heinrich was "at home", whose language Heinrich spoke, whose monuments and art Heinrich loved, and whose spirit and society Heinrich would capture for posterity in his "Song of democracy", *The Little Town.*

10

"At the end of a hot summer day we walked down the main road of our little Italian hill-town. In front of us, around us, the sky had turned a massive gold. I said: 'Byzantine painting is based on gold. As we see, that is not imagery, it is an optical fact. All we need now is the small face of the Virgin with her crown, far too heavy, looking down at us from the plastic heavens, uninvolved," Heinrich once related.

"That is the eternal aspect," Thomas replied.[32]

It cannot have been easy for the younger brother. They did everything together, eating at a little restaurant in Rome named Genzano, drinking good wine and "capital crochette di pollo".[33] In the evenings they went to a café, played dominoes together, drank punch. Their large, stone-walled room was rented from an old woman half way up the Via Torre Argentina. It had wicker chairs and a piano, on which Thomas sometimes improvised.

" 'In imicos,' you said, 22 years old, sitting at the piano in via Argentina trento quattro, with your back towards me,"[34] Heinrich recollected with some bitterness at the height of their quarrel twenty years later. They must have argued again, about art, or themselves. They were inseparable and yet . . . how hard for a younger brother, shyer, less sure of himself, who wanted to prove himself, in his own way. It is a wonder they remained together till the spring.

Heinrich's collection of short stories had appeared — though without much critical attention. His next collection, published the following year, came out under a different publisher, Robert Baum Verlag, Leipzig. It was called *A Crime and other Stories.* Three had been written four years before in 1894; the novella *Rendezvous* had appeared in *Simplicissimus* on their return from Palestrina to Rome, *The Stolen Document* a year before. The title story, *A Crime,* was written in Rome in December 1897, *Doctor Bieber's Temptation* in February 1898. Shortly afterwards Thomas left for home.

While Thomas returned to Munich with his "fearsomely swollen bundle of manuscript",[35] Heinrich had, in the first month of 1898 begun his own magnum opus which in a single year in 1916 would outsell a decade-and-a-half's sales of *Buddenbrooks: In the Land of Cockaigne.*

He too had felt the "power of vision," but without the least concern for epic themes and construction. For here the brothers Mann divided; only in his sixties, almost forty years later, did Heinrich turn to history and attempt the arduous reproduction of the past. What inflamed Heinrich in Rome towards the end of 1897, as Thomas sat working on his family saga, was a feeling of strength, of having been chosen, been given special gifts of insight, perception, articulation. "1897 in Rome, Via Argentina 34, I was overcome by the feeling of talent, I didn't know what I was doing. I thought I would make a pencil draft, wrote instead almost the complete novel," he entered on a questionnaire at the end of his life. "My talent was born in Rome, after three years influence of the city."[36]

Thus arose perhaps the first completely "new" novel of the twentieth century in Germany. Like Thomas' *Buddenbrooks* it bore the traces of European literary development, from Balzac to Maupassant, from Daudet to Zola. "Half my being consisted at this time of French sentences," he wrote later;[37] and the contact with French thought and style gave him a new confidence in his own language, a power and dexterity he had not felt before.

His story was in outline simple, in practice involved. It concerned the "temptations" of an innocent young writer who wishes to make his mark in Berlin towards the end of the nineteenth century: and into this plot he poured his talent, his venomous eye for money, for deceit, and sham. He peopled it with characters in the manner of Balzac, he brought the cynical eye for social-climbing of Maupassant's *Bel-Ami*, he loosed Zola's savage portrayal of the effects of money from *L'Argent*. It was a style, an attitude, an "impudence" as his publisher put it, that had never existed before in the German novel. It had all the faults of a first novel, the casting overboard of structure for immediate effect, a breathless tour de force which is not quite certain where it is going. He wrote and wrote and wrote; and then in the spring of 1899 he seems to have broken down. He moved to Bad Brunnthal ("no cheerful place") and tried to rest. He had not been able to finish the book, and his confidence collapsed. He felt himself sinking into despair with the constant satire of his work, into nihilism. To try and show a more lively face he wrote to his sister Carla, then seventeen and staying in Lausanne, depicting a meeting between the Pope, the Kaiser and Dreyfus! Carla was beautiful, proud, determined already to become an actress, and utterly devoted to Heinrich.

But the book's uncertain ending was its own failing from the beginning; the fact that Heinrich had not thought it out. How else could he have brought to bear such satirical energy, such grotesque imagination? Berlin recognized itself in the book which was not destined to be popular among the "safe" middle classes. Towards the end of the year Heinrich decided to send the book as it stood to Korfiz Holm, the editor who had taken over *Simplicissimus* after the latest lèse majesté scandal; and Holm forwarded it to Albert Langen, the offending proprietor, in Norway.

"Esteemed Mr Mann," Langen wrote to Heinrich, who by this time (November) was staying in Berlin, "I read your manuscript *Im Schlaraffenland* with great pleasure up to the last two chapters, which Mr Holm has promised to forward when you are ready. But without having read them I have decided to publish your novel . . .". He found the book a trifle long but had no idea how to cut it. It was an "extremely talented" work which exploded from reality to burlesque with an impudence that appeals to me greatly".

So the fleeing publisher of *Simplicissimus* accepted Heinrich's second novel, at an agreed royalty of fifteen per cent, of which 600 Marks was payable on receipt of the completed manuscript. By March 1900 the book was finished. The contract gave Langen an option on "all future literary works" — a clause which was to vex Heinrich considerably in future years. But for the moment he was far from angry. He was twenty-nine years old, and in the summer of 1900 *In the Land of Cockaigne* could be found in all the major bookshops of the Reich. By February of the following year Langen had ordered a second edition — news which gave Heinrich, in Riva, such a shock he promptly contracted "Influenza of the Nerves".[38]

11

In the meantime at the end of April 1898 Thomas made his way back to Munich. For eighteen months he had spent nothing on clothes; and for a little while — even in the relaxed and relatively classless atmosphere of the Bavarian capital — he did not dare to be seen.

His book of short stories — *Little Herr Friedemann* — had appeared while he was in Rome ("I could see myself in the Roman bookshops"[39]) and he was anxious to show it to somebody at home "so that at least *one* person reads it", as he wrote to Korfiz Holm.[40]

The Frau Senator by this time was living in a Pension in the Theresien-strasse while looking for a new apartment, and for a short period Thomas stayed there. He had written almost immediately to Korfiz Holm, "eager" to see him. It was a friendship which was to prove useful; for when the Kaiser travelled to Palestine that summer, Frank Wedekind let loose a number of satirical verses in *Simplicissimus* and soon had the ceiling crashing on himself and Langen. Both fled via Switzerland to Paris while proceedings for lèse majesté were announced. Korfiz Holm was left to pick up the pieces and take over the publishing house as well. Holm engaged Ludwig Thoma — a magnificent Bavarian poet and storyteller, who became editor of *Simplicissimus* two years later. And meeting Thomas Mann "on the street one day", Holm offered him a position on the magazine, at 100 Marks per month.[41]

Thus arose Thomas' working connection with the country's foremost satirical paper — an occupation which, as Thomas later acknowledged, had "some sense". He was given an office of his own in the Schackstrasse, and there his particular task became the "first selection from incoming story-manuscripts". His recommendations were then submitted to Dr Geheeb, and a final choice made. In this way, Thomas came into contact with the most incisive humorists, caricaturists and writers of the day.

In the autumn he moved into rooms of his own in Schwabing, while the family moved to a new apartment not far from Thomas, in the Herzogstrasse. In November Thomas found a better lodging on the third floor of the Marktstrasse No. 5. Here he spread the extending table with green baize and painted the new wicker chairs he had bought with red enamel. The white walls he covered partly with green hessian, and the ceiling too was painted green. Then on the table he set his heavy silver candlestick, a vase with flowers, a portrait of Tolstoy, and a "pile of closely-written sheets of paper". "That will be *Buddenbrooks*", their mother whispered to little Viktor when they visited Thomas in his new abode.[42] The great mahogany bed his parents had slept in in Lübeck was now his own, as also the Senator's old cigar-case. Letters, papers, the family bible with events and recollections, all had been borrowed from his mother to further the book. In the corner was a hired piano, and on top Thomas' violin-case. Each day *Buddenbrooks* progressed a little further. He ate lunch usually in the Herzogstrasse with the family; but whether the book was a "protracted finger-exercise with no ulterior motive"[43] or something more ambitious, no one really knew. In November he turned out a new novella *The Wardrobe*, a phantasy about the backless wardrobe his landlady had supplied with the room, which was published the following year in Fischer's *Neue Deutsche Rundschau*. He nourished his appetite for epic on *Anna Karenina*, graced the Café Odéon occasionally with his quiet presence, attended every major concert of importance, and was enthralled by the talents of Herr Possart, the Intendant General of the Residence Theatre, whose mastery of stage diction, from tragedy to farce, appealed enormously to Thomas' linguistic sensitivity. "Of course," said Possart once cuttingly to an actor he found imitating him, "if one copies the Herr Intendant the whole morning, it is only natural one is a dead loss in the evening".[44] It was the polished, masterly talent of Possart Thomas admired; and which, with the caricaturing genius of *Simplicissimus*, would also find its way into the "swelling manuscript" — in the shape of Herr Permaneder, a caricature of the simple, plump, fun-loving, beer-adoring, South German businessman who "wants to be left in peace".

Since Julia sent her twenty-eight page letter to Thomas in Palestrina, the conception of the book, its centre of gravity, had in fact shifted. The "last descendant" Hanno was kept for the end; the grandfather and great grandfather served as introductory themes. And in the centre the story of Thomas Buddenbrook, a portrait of Thomas' father, began to steal the scene.

"Only he [Thomas] then understood the theme of decline" Heinrich wrote later; "experienced through his own successful rise what it is to fall, how a large family dwindles into a small one and never overcomes the loss of its last responsible male."[45] And to highlight the tragedy of the "last responsible" head of the family Thomas had given him a brother and sister to prefigure the fall: a comedian of a brother (Christian Buddenbrook), and a hopelessly self-willed, righteous sister (Tony Buddenbrook) who goes from one disastrous marriage to another. It was the Mann family story; but seen with such lucidity and humour it became an insight into humanity, into human frailty and strength.

"One thing I must beg you," Julia had written in her covering note: "to use this information very, very cautiously" since "many of the people are still alive".[46]

12

It was at this time, when Thomas was working for *Simplicissimus* in Munich and Heinrich remained in Italy, that their different attitudes to life and to their work began to crystallize. At heart, as Thomas confessed, Italy had only kept him because there was no room for him at home; once back, he slipped into a cultural and social milieu that both stimulated and protected him in its very conventionality. It was the very atmosphere he required for his precocious, lucid social observation, his amazing eye for character – and between his mother's salon, the irreverent humourists of *Simplicissimus* and his few intimate confidants and friends he managed to tread a rewarding if often cynical path.

By contrast Heinrich, reserved and austere, an expatriate who could never settle in one place for more than a few months, found life at home in Munich unsatisfying. The genius that impelled him was ambitious, urgent and un-comfortable, at once critical and idealistic – whereas for Thomas it was naturalistic. Nowhere was this difference better illustrated than in their attitude to the courtship and wedding of their sister Julia.

Julia Mann was by now twenty-one, and Carla seventeen. From an "anaemic emaciated teenager" Carla was now rapidly becoming a very attractive young woman who "practised her wiles on every male object who dared to come near".[47] But above all, apparently, it was the Frau Senator herself who exercised the greatest attraction. Though she dressed mainly in black, her apartment was filled with attentive admirers, from musicians to comedians, university teachers and solicitors, bankers and artists. It was from the ranks of the bankers that Julia's husband was selected.

In *Buddenbrooks*, Tony's first husband is chosen for her by her parents. She resists: but is overcome by the temptations of her vanity. It is likely Thomas' relevant chapters were written long before Josef Löhr began to pay court to Thomas' sister;[48] but the result was the same. Julia hesitated. Thomas' own wife later claimed that Löhr was torn between mother and daughter – we shall never know. Löhr was a very talented banker from Frankfurt who had raised himself from poorer circumstances and now had every prospect of a brilliant career. Under the "unmistakeable motto of 'Senator Mann's Daughter Marries'", as Viktor related, the wedding was finally announced.[49] "Lula and Löhr have come closer to one another in the most gratifying way," Thomas wrote to his friend Paul Ehrenberg. "Lula only recently told me how you virtually fell on your knees that time, imploring her to say No to him. Really, was that so sensible of you? In these matters one must not fetch up too much idealism. With all due respect for 'love'," remarked the twenty-four year old, "one does get further without it.

A truism by the way," he added, "that is rather repugnant to me personally. But what can one do on this inferior planet?"[50] Thomas gave her away the following year, at a white wedding with a magnificent reception in the Hotel Vier Jahreszeiten. But Heinrich would have nothing to do with such a match. Despite the exhortations of his mother, he stayed in Italy, refusing to attend. It was the first sign of division in the Mann family since the Senator had died. In the isolated, unyielding pride of Heinrich and the ironic, compromising nature of Thomas one can already trace the pattern of their latent conflict.

For the moment, however, Thomas took no part in the dispute, nor felt the least defensive about his way of life. His closest friends at this time were brothers, Paul and Carl Ehrenberg. Paul was a painter, Carl a musician and composer. Paul was a "capital violinist as well. My liking for him had originally something of my former feeling for my blond schoolmate," Thomas later confessed, "but thanks to our having much more in common mentally and spiritually, the relationship was happier."

While Paul painted my portrait, Carl in his admirably sustained and harmonious style would play to us out of "Tristan". Sometimes, as I played the violin too, we would play his trios. We bicycled together, went to the Schwabing "Peasant Balls", or had pleasant suppers at my place or theirs. Thanks to them I learned the pleasures of friendship, as without them I scarcely should have done: gently and tactfully they overcame my heaviness, shyness and irritability, by accepting them frankly as accompanying phenomena to gifts which they respected. These were precious days.

I was such an impassioned cyclist at that time that I hardly ever went on foot, but even in pouring rain made my way, in cloak and galoshes, on my machine. I carried it on my shoulder up the three flights of stairs to my flat, where it was parked in the kitchen. Mornings, after my work, I used to stand it on its saddle and clean it . . . Summer afternoons I rode into the Schleissheimer woods with a book on my handlebars. My supper I bought in a Schwabing grocers and washed it down with tea or beef-extract.[51]

These were days, in Munich, when the family was paramount in society. A visiting guest would be expected to sit out in the sitting room. He would be asked what he would like to eat and the maid sent out to get it. She would return with a stein of beer and some sausages, and the visitor was expected to pay for it. In the Bohemian atmosphere of Schwabing, however, Thomas suffered no such limitations. At the Café Odéon Ludwig Thoma would go to sleep with his pipe in his mouth and the sins of society were dissected and literary gossip exchanged.

If he took part in such society, Thomas did not neglect his work. He became acquainted with Kurt Martens, a successful young novelist and essayist, who has left us his recollection of Thomas at this time:

From the very start I had been struck by his early sketches and a poem of his in the *Gesellschaft*. It was less the still rather imperfect, groping form which had impressed and touched me than the desire to know the inner person who seemed to be, by background, feelings and inner experience, very similar to me. What this Thomas Mann had in him or where he even lived, I had no idea. I was therefore all the more surprised when one day I received a friendly note of receipt from the editorial department of *Simplicissimus*, to whom I had sent a novella, signed with the name Thomas Mann.

Immediately I asked him to visit me. And he came. Very cautious, almost shy and yet quite composed a serious, slim young man crossed the threshold. His clever, thoughtful, gently melancholic conversation captivated me as no other man's words had ever done before. He was living in a mean little room in a poor people's house in the Feilitzschstrasse. There he played the violin for me a few times and told me of his grand design for a two-volume, half-autobiographical novel, on which he laboured without much confidence.

When he showed me the first chapter I was on the point of gawping in admiration; for it was as though there was something here which surpassed the whole of contemporary fiction. But then, as an incorrigible sceptic and disillusionist, I said to myself I must be letting my feelings of inner sympathy and friendship run away with me. I said the novel, which was later to be called *Buddenbrooks* was a sound, solid piece of work, but I didn't want to overrate it . . .

But when Martens tried to "draw Thomas into society a little more" he found it impossible. For a time he had "won" his friendship "exclusively", "loved him from the first word," "subordinated myself willingly to the younger of us because he was the greater"; but "nothing which did not come from his inner self could hope to fetter him", as Martens perceived. He lived in the "greatest seclusion", and his motto was quite simple: "Genius," he claimed, "comes from a good night's sleep."[52] It was a phase redolent of Thomas' great grandfather, the founder of the family firm.

13

Thomas still worked on *Simplicissimus*, reserving two hours every day for *Buddenbrooks*. Sometimes he grew depressed about the book, feeling that he might never end it, or no one ever read it. It did him good, therefore, to read passages from it to the family and sometimes to his friends. It became a habit with him for life.

Martens invited him to the hills in the summer, but Thomas had "a lot of office work to complete in order to earn a small holiday in the autumn". His plan was to travel to Scandinavia in September and "lay myself on the beach somewhere".[53] It was this plan that was to give him the idea for his most autobiographical and to him the "dearest" of all his works: *Tonio Kröger*.

His route to Aalsgard am Sund led via Lübeck, where he booked in at the Hotel Stadt Hamburg. Almost immediately he was questioned by the police about a case of fraud just discovered in the town. It was one of the smaller disappointments of Thomas' life that he didn't in the least — however hard he posed for his photographs — resemble the public's idea of a poet or novelist. He was, as his wife Katja later recalled, most often mistaken for a commercial traveller.

The episode amused and frightened him a little, confirming the distinction between inner and outer reality. It was also symbolic of the "artist's problem", that he was not recognized in his own country, was an exile. What he could not know at that time was that the episode was prophetic of an even deeper misunderstanding between the author and his home town: the reception of *Buddenbrooks* among the God-fearing, Hanseatic families who would see in it a monstrous libel, an unpardonable caricature of the merchant virtues which had once brought fame and prosperity to the Baltic seaport.

The two-week sojourn in the north, however, rested Thomas' soul. He returned to Munich determined to complete *Buddenbrooks;* and "the hour came that made me read, and I read day and night, as perhaps one reads only once in a lifetime". It was a "spiritual experience of absolutely first rank and unforgettable in kind",[54] and it gave rise to serious thoughts of suicide — morbidity which was subtly transferred to the primary figure of Budden-brooks.

Thomas had brought the Brockhaus edition of Schopenhauer's works at a sale some time previously, "more to own it than to study it". The volumes had "stood a long time uncut on the shelves" when the day arrived. "The little, high-up room in the suburb sways before my eyes," Thomas wrote in 1916, "in which, sixteen years ago I lay stretched all day on the curiously-shaped chair or sofa reading *The World as Will and Idea.* Lonely, undisciplined youth, yearning for both life and death — how it swallowed the magical potion of this metaphysics, whose deepest being is eroticism, and in which I recognized the spiritual source of Wagner's Tristan music! One only reads once like that, it never recurs. And what a stroke of fortune that I did not have to contain such an experience but had an immediate opportunity of expressing it, of showing my gratitude: a chance to give it a poetic rendering! For two yards from my sofa lay the impossibly growing manuscript — burden, honour, home and blessing of that strange period of my youth, highly problematic in terms of its chances of publication — which had just come to the point where Thomas Buddenbrook must be brought to death. To him, who was to me a thrice-related figure — father, descendant, shadow of myself — I gave the precious experience, the great discovery in his life, shortly before his end; I wove it into the story for it seemed to belong to him — the suffering mortal who had bravely confronted life, the moralist and 'militarist' of my heart, the late and complex burgher whose nerves are no longer at home in this sphere of life, one of the rulers of an aristocratic town democracy, which, grown modern and dubious, obeying the needs of an industrializing Europe and without tradition of taste had begun to detach itself from its more healthy, genuine and tightly-knit surroundings — and to mock them."[55]

Thomas thus calmly brought his "thrice-related figure" to the summit and end of his life. It was the turning point of the book, for without the last, nervous strength of Thomas Buddenbrook, the family is doomed. Buddenbrook complains of toothache, visits the dentist. The dentist attempts to extract the tooth in question, but breaks it. There are four roots still to remove.

"Four. Then you must take hold and lift four times?"

"Yes — unfortunately."

"Well this is enough for today," said the Senator. He started to rise but remained seated and put his head back instead.

On his way home he collapses.

He fell upon his face, beneath which, presently, a little pool of blood began to form. His hat rolled a little way off down the road; his fur coat was wet with mud and slush; his hands, in their white kid gloves, lay outstretched in a puddle.

Thus he lay, and thus he remained, until some people came down the street and turned him over.

The Senator was dead.

There were now less than a hundred pages to go. On 30th May 1900 he wrote to Kurt Martens he was "at the end".

"It was an impossible manuscript, written on both sides,"[56] Thomas later recalled, and the habit of blacking out all corrections in thick black ink made it even less presentable. The first chapters were still not right, it seemed time to bid farewell to *Simplicissimus* and complete the book properly. Langen took the matter out of his hands by "abolishing the job I held", and on a warm day in August Thomas made his way to the main post office. "I still remember packing it," he wrote later, "clumsily dropping the hot wax on my hand and making a big blister which was to hurt for days . . . There was only one copy, so I registered it, and after the word 'manuscript' on the form put down a value of 1,000 Marks. The post-office clerk smiled."[57]

It was going to Fischer's in Berlin, "with whom, after *Little Herr Friedemann*, I felt I had a connection".[58] He had written to warn Fischer of its imminence in January, and Fischer had replied he was "very eager" to see it. What he did not realize was that it was over a thousand pages long.

CHAPTER FOUR

Buddenbrooks, Fame — and
First Conflict

"Hear now a pretty little tale," Thomas wrote to his friend Paul Ehrenberg in June 1900. "At the beginning of this month, on the 6th to be precise, their lordships of the Higher Reserve Commission, to whom I had the honour of presenting myself, classified me as fit for all branches of the army; whence it follows that on October 1, to the consternation of all enemies of the Fatherland, I shall shoulder a gun . . . What do you say to that?"[1]

A few weeks of military service was enough to provide the answer. It was unbearable.

"My determination to get out became deadly," he said later. "I suffered tortures from the noise, the enforced idleness, the iron compulsion to be smart."[2] His ankle began to swell on parade drill, the sinew was inflamed. He went on the sick-list, then into the garrison hospital. "Write to me again," he wrote from there to Kurt Martens, "but don't visit me — I wouldn't like it. I hope you never have to see me in uniform!"[3] To the absolute consternation of his guardian, Krafft Tesdorpf, he proceeded to try to obtain his release with the help of his mother's doctor, Hofrat May.

It is hard to understand why Thomas desired to serve in the first place. A "nervous heart" had been enough to disqualify him the previous occasion, but perhaps the long and weary labour on *Buddenbrooks* persuaded him a change would help. "I am sincerely glad that I have not been rejected again," he explained to Ehrenberg in his June letter. "I really felt humiliated the time I was rejected at the barracks on medical grounds, and the sense of satisfaction when I returned from the 'hot seat' with the certificate of fitness in my pocket is still with me. It is certainly providential. Only in this way can those nervous crotchets of mine be exorcised; and if I forfeit a year from my civilian work, it will undoubtedly add ten more to my life. Of course," he added prophetically, "it is possible that I won't be able to stand up to it, and that they will have to release me again after a few weeks; but I hope for the best."

By 1st October, relieved of the manuscript that had clung to him for three years, he was "blooming enough to deceive a staff-officer as to my fitness", and "reported at the infantry guards regiment, and had myself measured for a uniform".[4]

The regiment was the Royal Bavarian Infantry-Guards. In the bright-blue uniform with its red collar, polished buttons, silver braid, and gleaming black sword-belt he looked a very fine example of a soldier, little Viko thought. Viktor and the cook had slipped out secretly to the Borerstrasse to see the cadets drilling there. They peered through the iron railings and soon enough Tommy was to be seen presenting and shouldering arms like a professional. "Very good," remarked the cook, who ought to have known, for her boy-friend was a sergeant.

By November, however, the "romantically-attired, brutalized mercenary who drinks immodestly, spits on the floor and altogether behaves in the best style of a landsknecht" had become a role Thomas no longer enjoyed playing. The cadet-recruit which "the German army could not possibly manage without", the "arrogant *decadent*" who imagined it would be "extra-ordinarily refreshing to be bawled out ruthlessly and vigorously for a year" had tired of the sport.[5] He deliberately "exercised" the foot when he returned to duty, and was again incarcerated in the garrison hospital. As his mother's doctor was acquainted with both his Captain and the Regimental Chief Physician, it seemed possible he might be able to "stir the people into releasing me."[6] Hofrat May was consulted. He was of the opinion that Thomas could not possibly fulfil his service.

The junior battalion doctor, however, was the main obstacle. He was not in the least impressed by Thomas' swelling. "Who are you, what do you want?" was his tone, as Thomas later related to Heinrich. He was "shame-lessly rude — for instance explained that he would have first to light a cigar, as otherwise he would faint (from disgust)". He declared Thomas "fit for duty".

Meanwhile Hofrat May had spoken to the Chief Physician. The latter called Thomas to his surgery from parade, "seemed not to find a great deal wrong, but said I should only go on doing duty for the present, the rest would soon be arranged. With *that* foot . . . A few days later an impression was taken of my foot on charcoaled paper by an orderly." He had been treated in the garrison hospital for an "inflamed flat-foot," but the print showed quite clearly there could be no question of this.

Now, however, the Chief Physician stepped in. He stood in front of the junior doctor and stared angrily at his cap, which the latter, used to informal association as a colleague, had not removed. The junior doctor doffed his cap and stood to attention.

Thereupon the Chief Physician showed him the paper, spoke to him in a low voice, and instructed him to find something there which didn't exist. The junior doctor blinked alternately at his superior, then at me and the paper, and agreed with a click of his heels. From that moment on he was exceedingly polite to me and treated me as a gentleman. He knew I had higher connections.[7]

Krafft Tesdorpf, however, was not so easily persuaded. From Lübeck he wrote to the Frau Senator, calling it an obvious and scandalous case of fraud to get Thomas out of his proper military service; but by then Thomas was free. Whether it was a good thing that Thomas got off so lightly is another question. As with his fire-insurance apprenticeship, it was almost too easy. The rather shy twenty-four-year-old took one further step back from life.

2

It was now that Thomas began to get a little more anxious about the novel. He had sent it off in the second week of August. Three months had passed without news, except an acknowledgment of receipt, and a letter from Fischer to say he looked forward to reading it. Arthur Holitscher, a novelist-friend of Thomas', had "put in a good word" for it, but the relationship between Holitscher and Thomas was a little uneasy ever since Holitscher caught Thomas in the act of "spying on him".

It was a ridiculous incident really, but in Holitscher's mind the forerunner of much worse.

Holitscher played the piano; so they "musicked" together in Thomas' room with the manuscript of *Buddenbrooks* on the table and the portrait of Tolstoy. Thomas, Holitscher recalled, played the violin beautifully.

They had talked about life before playing, Holitscher's anxiety about his work and his consequent loneliness. Then Thomas had read him the chapter about the death of Thomas Buddenbrook from his manuscript. "A painful irony trembled behind his words," Holitscher recollected, "as it did whenever he spoke of his life, which seemed to contain some measure of sorrow and affliction." At least he didn't have to worry about his work, though, Holitscher maintained, he "knew its worth."

Holitscher felt they had drawn closer that summer afternoon, and he left with the "happy consciousness" that he had "made a friend".

Yet for some reason Holitscher suddenly felt compelled to stop in the street and turn round. He looked up, and there, framed in the window, he felt certain he could see Thomas staring after him through opera-glasses. "It only lasted a second, the next moment the head had disappeared from view."

A few mornings later Thomas appeared in Holitscher's rooms, and again Holitscher felt sure Thomas had come to "spy" on him, to get a glimpse of him, unwashed and half-asleep, in his unkempt student surroundings. Three years later, on the publication of Thomas' collection of novellas under the title *Tristan*, Holitscher found himself portrayed among a "grotesque band of caricatures, 'heroes' of everyday life who showed their inability to cope with life in situations of lamentable irony. I immediately recognized myself in one of these figures," he later wrote; but only after several months did he send Thomas a letter in which he called into question the morality of such behaviour. Thomas was "deeply hurt" by the letter, and put an immediate end to their friendship; "his melancholic irony," as Holitscher put it, "seemed suddenly to have become enormously bitter and sharp."[8]

Thomas later denied the incident with the opera-glasses. He was, as others have pointed out, gifted with an extraordinary ability to capture a person's likeness, his mannerisms, his personality: certainly without the need for opera-glasses.

But in the autumn of 1900 he had great need of Holitscher's friendship. For catastrophe seemed to have struck the ship he had steered for almost three years through storm and distress, struggle and personal privation. Fischer said *Buddenbrooks* would have to be cut by half. Holitscher bore the news in a letter from Berlin:

Esteemed Mr Mann!

I would have written to you some time ago, but with the amount of business I have to attend to it is no trifling matter to read a work of some 65 sections. I have got down to it however and have reached about half-way. Everything I can say is better said in my reader's report, which I enclose for your information. If you think you can shorten it by about half I am in principle quite prepared to publish the book. A novel of 65 printer's sections is by today's standards an impossibility; I doubt if many people have the time or the concentration to pick up a book of that size. I know it is an enormous demand to make of you, that it may require your re-writing the entire book, but as a publisher I can take no other course.[9]

It was a terrible blow; and the copy of Emil Strauss' *Der Engelwirt* which Fischer gave Holitscher to take to the invalid guardsman nursing his ankle in the regimental hospital was scant consolation. It was an insult. A cloud descended on the Herzogstrasse; even little Viko was told; and "was disposed to see Herr Fischer as a very bad man", as he recorded later; "for if we happened to have had such a long past then he had no right to remove any of it!"[10]

Half of three years' work! As Thomas wrote to Heinrich, then in Italy, "I know so clearly that there are chapters in the book which not every person could write, and yet I fear I will be left lumbered with the thing" — for in a moment of anger and intractable faith he had replied to Fischer, from the hospital, saying he would cut nothing. The letter was written in pencil, he later recalled. "I think it was a good letter — necessity made me eloquent."[11] He explained that the length of the book was one of its virtues, not its problems, that Fischer would botch it if he attempted to interfere. There were books, he declared, that were nothing without their richness, that entertainment had nothing to do with length.

In his letter to Heinrich, however, he revealed he had "otherwise shown himself resigned and open to compromise"[12] — particularly with regard to the financing of the book. He offered to do anything — to forgo an advance royalty, to repay any loss out of his royalties from future publications — but Fischer must publish the book as it stood. It was a strange plea from a young author whose last book had sold only 413 copies!

3

Heinrich's *In the Land of Cockaigne* meanwhile appeared with a fanfare of publicity. Ludwig Ewers had written a piece about the novel under the title of "A New Social Novel" — "a bit sloppily written," as Thomas put it, "but it certainly must have gained more buyers for your book."[13]

The buyers, Ewers recollected later,[14] were queuing up for copies in Bonn, where he was living. The drastic portrayal of Berlin society was something beyond even the columns of *Simplicissimus:* and the novel soon gained a certain notoriety — a fact which rather pleased Heinrich, stimulated him. Unlike Thomas he had no wish to be accepted: his intense, nervous style was the expression of a deeply-rooted urge to needle and to shock — a characteristic evident from his *Fantasies about my Hometown L,* written in 1889, and one which was to remain with him throughout his life.

In the Land of Cockaigne, at last established Heinrich as a novelist. It was high time; after eight years of apprenticeship he needed a sign from the gods — and they gave it. Langen ordered a second printing.

"The advertising was magnificent," Thomas wrote from Munich, barely subduing a note of envy. "I heard recently there were notices about the book on the Variété programmes — Does Langen mean to underwrite your studying in Paris? . . . How well looked after you are, and how brightly your star is beginning to shine."[15]

The reviews, too, were good — amounting certainly to "a *literary* success," as Heinrich wrote to his publisher.[16] M.G. Conrad in *Die Gesellschaft* had placed the work higher than Maupassant's *Bel-Ami* — to which it bore certain similarities. Heinrich Hart thought he detected the influence of D'Annunzio, the famous Italian poet — a source Heinrich denied, never having read D'Annunzio. Hart continued his review:

> However this German author is not simply imitator and successor, there is a good deal of originality in the book, and a pronounced artistic and poetic talent manifests itself in a hundred individual ways. The figures he draws have an unusual plasticity and definition . . . the language is lively, full of colour and vigour, even if the feuilletonist sometimes pushes the poet to one side.
>
> The best artistic elements in the book, however, are the social descriptions; they remind one of certain satires exposing Imperial Rome at

the height of its depravity: corruption and more corruption and nowhere a glimpse of sunlight, no point from which one might obtain relief, a view of the future. Mann has nothing of the Juvenal or a Tolstoy. He doesn't get angry or bellow like the Roman, nor does he contrast the common with the elevating as Tolstoy, who guides the reader through all evil and ugliness to a magnificent hallowed solemnity. Never does Mann play the judge of society, he trips gracefully through all the vulgarities he has summoned; and the only thing which makes his exhibition tolerable in the long run is a certain sense of humour. This however is not sufficient, whatever the book has to offer artistically, to give it the importance of idealism and human greatness.[17]

Hart's review, if incorrect about D'Annunzio, remains one of the more perceptive pieces of literary criticism on Heinrich's work. What Heinrich had brought to the German novel, as Ewers indicated in his own essay, was the topicality and penetration of the European social novel, exemplified in writers such as Zola and Maupassant. As Hart wrote, he had managed to transfer this lucidity and directness to the German tongue with a large measure of originality and individual artistry. For a first novel, this was a considerable achievement. What Heinrich had not achieved — "the importance of idealism and human greatness" — was perhaps what Thomas had to offer. And Fischer, having received Thomas' letter, vacillated. The year 1900 drew to its close. Still Thomas had no answer.

4

Every young author dreams he has written an international best-seller, or at least a work of seminal literary importance; trembles each morning when the postman calls. Military service had promised a somewhat coarse relief for such "nervous crotchets" as Thomas called them: but with the success of Hofrat May's efforts, the distraction of military service disappeared. Only Krafft Tesdorpf's indignation remained: and Thomas soon put paid to that. To Lübeck he sent Tesdorpf — his ex-guardian and executor of the Senator's estate — "the nastiest letter of my life" as he reported to Heinrich — "which worked so well (oh, what talent we have!) that the old ass is now threatening to sue me."[18]

What had come over the Manns, poor Tesdorpf must have wondered, that neither Heinrich nor Thomas could complete his apprenticeship and now Thomas had committed fraud rather than carry out his service to his Kaiser? But "the old ass's" reaction was only a foretaste of what the Hanseatic citizens would say when they read *Buddenbrooks*!

Thomas meanwhile went through what must have been one of the most trying periods of his life. After the success of *Buddenbrooks*, Heinrich once wrote,[19] Thomas never looked back. It is an exaggeration, but it contains a measure of truth. The success of *Buddenbrooks* was what Thomas dearly wanted. But until that success was achieved he lived in a difficult limbo, irresponsible, carefree: and yet always overshadowed by the question of *Buddenbrooks.* Heinrich had invited him to join him in Florence, but Thomas could not drag himself away from Munich. He loved the city in the winter, the concerts, the snow on the Frauenkirche; he was writing a story of "bitter, melancholic character",[20] too long for *Simplicissimus,* and which wouldn't be finished for "a long time".[21] In Munich he had his friends and his family. In any case, as he lamented to Heinrich, he was broke.

He was faced with a series of bills including that of his military tailor, which left him, in little Viko's words, "All-a-tremble", with 240 Marks to last the quarter. "The sheet of paper with its irrefutable sums lies beside me," he concluded in his letter to Heinrich, "and to repeat them sickens me. To try and travel on that would be insanity. Not only can I not come on the 15th or the 20th; I cannot come to Florence before April.

"Fischer is silent, as I said," he finished his letter, "and if I inquire after the novel, he'll probably shoot the changeling straight back at me. Suppose *nobody* wants the book? I think I would become a bank clerk . . ."[22]

But whether he seriously doubted his calling is unlikely. Behind the lamentation to Heinrich there was a certain joy he could not conceal: Richard Strauss was coming to Munich, and Wüllnow the singer; there were premières to be attended and the Literary Society had arranged for him to gave his first public reading from *The Way to the Churchyard* — which his old Lübeck schoolfriend, Otto Grautoff, subsequently gave a "wild write-up" in the Leipzig press.[23]

"What is true," Thomas reported to Heinrich, "is that with every sentence Piepsam (the Protagonist) aroused warm and lively approval and was continually being clapped. I am very pleased at having read so well, most of all because Stollberg (the Theatre director), who had turned up, gave me especial applause and even a bow. A Theatre director is such an important power!"[24]

He immediately sent the newspaper cuttings to Fischer — for he had begun to raise his hopes about *Buddenbrooks.* At a party Korfiz Holm had told him Langen would be only too pleased to consider the book, and in principle had nothing against a two-volume edition. Financially Holm had given a very "friendly and enticing" account of Langen — an assurance which encouraged Thomas to issue a warning, perhaps even "threaten" Fischer,[25] and for one moment it looked as if the Manns might yet appear under the same Langen imprint.

At last Fischer responded. He bade his editor read the manuscript again. He himself had reached the very last chapters. Obviously he had begun to realize what was at stake.

"Dear Herr Mann," he wrote on 4th February 1901, "I must ask you please to forgive me for taking so long over the question of your book . . . I am now prepared to publish it, despite its length."[26]

Thomas wrote proudly to Heinrich, "I shall have my picture taken, with my right hand inserted in the waistcoat of my evening dress and the left resting on the three volumes. Then I can go quite confidently to my grave."[27]

Ironically he might well have done so: for *Buddenbrooks* alone would establish his name in the annals of world literature. The grave, however, was by no means ready for such a young author. It had another half-century to wait.

5

Fischer was not, in fact, convinced he was doing the right thing. Samuel Fischer was a modern "city man" who was greatly overworked and could not imagine others having the time to read such a long book. But the literary instinct which had attracted him to Ibsen, Hauptmann, Hamsun and others forbade him to let Thomas go. As Thomas himself had pointed out, it was not only a question of this one novel, but of his future work as well. Thomas had appealed to Fischer to accept the book as a sign of faith in his talent; and Fischer finally did. He even offered to publish a new volume of Thomas' short stories in the meantime. It was a risk — but it paid off. Within days came Dr Heimann's reappraisal of the manuscript after a second reading.

"It is magnificent work", the report now ran, "honest, positive, rich . . . I am astonished that the book's satirical and grotesque elements not only do not disturb the epic form — but actually reinforce it."

This part of the report was particularly gratifying to Thomas. "So greatness despite the satire!" he wrote delightedly to Heinrich.

> For during the work my secret and painful ambition was always to achieve greatness you see. The more I wrote in this vein, the more I respected what I had done, and demanded an even better style of myself. It is good that it begins so modestly and by the end reveals not just an ordinary novel but something quite different, perhaps rather rare. Sometimes my heart really begins to pound at the thought.[28]

However, it was still months before the book could appear: there was the editing, correcting and typesetting still to be done. The recognition he sought — and would seek throughout his life — from his writing, he transferred now to his friend Paul Ehrenberg. Their friendship deepened into what Grautoff likened to an adolescent love-affair — an experience "which cannot be related in a letter, the very hinting of which is already a form of boast", Thomas wrote to Heinrich in March 1901.

> What it concerns is not a love-story, at least not in the normal sense of the word, but a friendship, a — wonder of wonders! — mutual, rewarding, understanding friendship which, frankly, takes on at certain times a somewhat too painful character, particularly at times of depression or loneliness; Grautoff even claimed I was in love like a schoolboy — but that is said as he understands it. My nervous constitution and philosophic nature have complicated the matter unbelievably: it has a hundred sides, from the simplest to the most spiritually exciting. But for the main part there remains a joyous amazement at a mutual feeling I had ceased to hope for in this life. That's enough. Perhaps I will let you know more when we see each other.[29]

Heinrich, in Riva and then Florence, must have found it difficult to follow the vacillations of his younger brother. "Congratulations on the news of *Cockaigne* being bought for translation into French!" Thomas had written in February. "What fun that must be for you! In short you are blossoming while at the moment I am failing miserably. What I could do with now is a good attack of Typhoid with the requisite, satisfactory end — although I suppose it is rather tactless to make you anxious with such remarks."[30]

Soon Thomas was having to reassure Heinrich he had no serious intention of committing suicide. "The whole thing," he confessed, "is metaphysics, music and adolescent eroticism. I am never going to emerge from puberty. Even Grautoff was very worried; but the matter is so unacute, it takes such slow root and at the moment there is such little practical reason for it, that you can rest assured on that point."[31]

He admitted Heinrich's presence would, at that juncture, be "precisely the one influence right for me at the moment", and prepared to leave for Florence. Then came Fischer's letter of acceptance, and the contract for *Buddenbrooks;* and for a while all was well. Paul Ehrenberg was painting his portrait and a late spring had suddenly warmed away the snow and brought the trees to bud. "I ironize and negate life at my desk," wrote Thomas, "but only out of habit, for otherwise I love, laud and live; and since, what is more, it is now Spring the whole thing has become quite simply a carnival."[32] He wanted to finish his latest novella in order to take up Fischer's offer, had the final author's corrections on *Buddenbrooks* to do, and asked now if Heinrich couldn't postpone or cancel his intended trip to southern Italy. But either his letter did not reach Heinrich in time, or Heinrich had tired of his younger brother's moods and indecision; for by the time Thomas finally set off for Florence, in April, Heinrich had gone.

6

Heinrich's own crisis had taken place almost a decade before, when Thomas was still at school and was all now in the past. Langen had accepted *In the Land of Cockaigne* before Heinrich had even finished the book; and though it could hardly be described as a best-seller, it had at last established him in the public eye as a social novelist of considerable talent — even notoriety.

What he had now begun, on completing *In the Land of Cockaigne*, was, however, a novel of a very different genre — a novel so utterly *un*social as to make a number of people question whether it was by the same author. It remains unique in the history of the German novel, is considered by many to be the first major foundation of German Expressionism; and became, curiously, of seminal importance to German poetry, from Rilke and Eric Mühsam to Gottfried Benn.

"The greatest undertaking a German novelist has ever attempted," wrote Mühsam some five years after it appeared;[33] and to Rilke it represented the very highest attainment in linguistic skill. "When did this great artist undergo his apprenticeship?" he asked later. "Here he exceeds even Flaubert: if the latter is somewhat of a collector, then Heinrich Mann is in contrast a linguistic spender, a spendthrift. Who has ever described scenery so brilliantly — simply to fling it into the pulse of the story? — Yes, to me that is the most wonderful part about it, that here an unceasing painter at the same time creates a current which tears his works from him."[34]

The book was in fact a trilogy: conceived in Riva in 1900, and written over a period of a year and a half. It was called *Die Göttinnen* (The Goddesses): *Diana, Minerva,* and *Venus.* It was as unconventional as it was contemporary. As Rilke alluded, Heinrich was like a painter: and the public gaped at his new work like the first exhibitions of the Futurists and later, Expressionists. It defied decorum, good taste, the established sense of proportion.

To Langen Heinrich described the book as "a modern fairy tale. Please don't be alarmed," he explained however, "I simply set figures in motion who despite their strangeness will I hope be no less lively than those of my first novel." The story was planned to take place in an imaginary kingdom and concern the life of a certain Duchess of Assy:

At the end I propose a whirlpool of hedonism, modern swindling, sensual refinements, classical mysticism, etc. At the same time, there will be a number of true facts and tales to underpin it: Viennese court gossip, Italian Corbellerie, etc.

"I am now in the first half," he ended his letter in February 1901. "In the middle of April I will have to break off to make a trip to Southern Italy which doesn't tempt me very much and will be very expensive. However the book requires it, as the heroine moves down there towards the end of her life. You see I am taking the project quite seriously."

This was the trip that took him away from Florence in the spring of 1901 just before Thomas arrived. And while Heinrich collected material for his goddesses in Naples, Thomas entertained the two English girls Heinrich had left behind at the pension in Florence: Edith and Mary Smith. Edith, the elder, was dark and friendly, knew enough German to wish to read Heinrich's *In the Land of Cockaigne,* though "inexplicably" she had waited vainly for him to give her a copy.[35] But Mary, or Molly, was blonde, "delightful" and clever. And Thomas, still emotionally at sixes and sevens, looked to her to "deliver" him. "There followed a tender relationship," he recalled later,[36] "and talk of marriage." Her birthday came, and he presented her with a basket of candied fruits. Writing of Paul Ehrenberg Thomas had only four weeks before revealed to Heinrich his own "sentimental need, a need for enthusiasm, devotion, trust, encouragement, faithfulness"; and now, perhaps for the first time in his life, there was a chance a woman might fulfil this longing.

Miss Mary's heart, however, was not to be bought with candied fruits; and though she made Thomas, on the surface, "very happy", the dream of marriage soon dispersed.

"She is so very clever, and I am stupid enough always to fall in love with those who are clever, though in the long run I simply can't keep up," Thomas wrote to Heinrich — deliberately using the English phrase — in May 1901. He begged Heinrich to return from the south. They could meet in Venice, he suggested, and Grautoff could join them. His old "melancholy" had reappeared, the emotional problems he thought he had left behind in Munich were reappearing: "again," he wrote, "I go through moments when I don't think I can continue."

Later Thomas put the failure of his "tender relationship" down to "certain misgivings" — that they were too young to marry, and that the "difference of nationality" might become a bar.[37] Perhaps the "talk of marriage"was just a childish dream; at any rate Thomas appealed to Heinrich now to help him in his hour of need. And Heinrich came. "The hostility of your mind," Heinrich wrote with some truth in the middle of their great quarrel in 1917, "I knew from long ago . . . this knowledge however did not stop me from comforting you as a younger brother whenever you lost faith in yourself . . ."[38]

They met in Venice, at the Casa Kirsch which Thomas had selected from his Baedecker. Molly, who had had "similar reservations" about matrimony, was left behind. Many years later she found her place among the figures of *The Magic Mountain*. In the meantime Thomas felt sufficiently grateful for the happiness she had brought him to dedicate his next short story, *Gladius Dei*, to her. It concerned a wild, idealistic and puritanical young man who makes an idiot of himself by demanding the removal of a nude portrait from a Munich art-dealer's window.

He returned briefly to Munich in June 1901, but most of the rest of the year he spent with Heinrich — first on holiday in the South Tyrol, then on Lake Garda where Heinrich's doctor ran his clinic for "nervous disorders". It was there Heinrich pushed ahead with his *Göttinnen* while Thomas attempted to continue his long postponed novella of "bitter melancholic character" — but without advancing "a single line".[39] His other novella, "a burlesque which I am working on and which will probably be called *Tristan*",[40] went more smoothly — indeed Thomas' clinical observations must have helped considerably in giving clarity and credibility to the tale.

So the year 1901 drew to its close with Heinrich and Thomas together. On 19th December Thomas returned to Munich to spend Christmas with the family.

Buddenbrooks had appeared on 1st October. With one celebrated exception it attracted little or no attention. The copies sold only very slowly — at 12 Marks it was an expensive purchase — and Thomas had to do his best to circulate them among friends and relations. For a while it looked as though Fischer's fears were going to be realized: people just didn't have the time to read such a large work. But then, almost side by side with *Buddenbrooks*, the Norwegian novelist Gustav Frenssen's *Jörn Uhl* achieved a sensational success. It was just as long but half the price and in a single volume. Book-sellers began to report there was no slackening in demand for *Buddenbrooks:* it was only its price which was damping sales.

Fischer watched his figures; the thousand copies of the first edition were moving, slowly but surely. To Thomas, the following summer, he confessed he might have sold five or six times the amount had the price been lower. At any rate, a reprint was now inevitable. Fischer gave Thomas 1,000 Marks on account and commissioned a new, single-volume cover from Wilhelm Schulz.

This was the turning point, the moment at which the melancholy young man filled with "metaphysics, music and adolescent eroticism" rose from obscurity to stardom. After a winter without literary output and a spring of intense musical activity he at last began to write once more. And while Heinrich slaved to finish the *Göttinnen* in Italy in time for Christmas publication in Germany, Thomas worked on the volume of short stories Fischer had promised to publish. They were virtually all typeset and due to appear under the title of *Tristan* when in the autumn of 1902 Thomas left again for Riva. The printer was waiting, Fischer was waiting; but *Tonio Kröger,* "the dearest" of all that Thomas wrote in his life, would not be hurried.

8

Tonio Kröger appeared in 1903 in the February number of Fischer's *Neue deutsche Rundschau;* and in book form early that spring, together with *Tristan* and other stories. Simultaneously Fischer published the second impression of *Buddenbrooks* — at 6 Marks, and in its new Biedermeier-style single-volume binding. Both were instantly successful

Tonio Kröger and *Tristan* were destined to become classics in the tradition of the German novella. For those who were curious about the author of the latest Hanseatic epic these stories gave new literary and autobiographical evidence. They took up where *Buddenbrooks* had finished; the lessons of Tolstoy and nineteenth-century Naturalism were now spurned, and what developed was a highly "melancholic style", intensely personal, full of a tortured "I" intricately and irrevocably bound up with the dilemma of the artist and society. "After two thick volumes of Hanseatic merchant life we finally got to Art," wrote Heinrich a trifle sarcastically the following year.

But Thomas had not made the transition so facilely. His tortured "I" had great representative and symbolic power for thousands of readers who found difficulty in adjusting to modern urban society. Also his work was prevented from becoming self-pitying or tendentious, not only by the unusual irony he managed to weave into his tales, but now by a musical style of composition that overwhelmed even his staunchest critics.

"Here perhaps for the first time" — in *Tonio Kröger* — "I learned to use music to mould my style and form," Thomas wrote later.[41] "Here for the first time I grasped the idea of epic prose composition as a thought-texture of different themes, as a musically related complex." As a consequence, the ideas within the story underwent a transformation. "The linguistic leit-motif in particular," Thomas explained, "was not handled, as in *Budden-brooks,* on a purely external and naturalistic basis, but was transformed to the more lucent realm of ideas and emotions, and thus lifted from the mechanical into the musical sphere."

In a country of great intellectual — and musical — tradition, this was a courageous but rewarding step. The simplicity and clarity of *Buddenbrooks* was strong enough to appeal even to the least literate; the musical structure of his post-*Buddenbrooks* writings seductive enough to magnetize the intellectual élite of the country. His experience with the great masters — Nietzsche, Schopenhauer, Wagner — and the epic novelists of the nineteenth century had given him an enormous confidence in himself. He did not imagine he was "clever"; but then cleverness alone creates neither great novels nor great art. What he had done was to penetrate the secrets of epic construction and now musical form in prose writing. Success swept him into its whirlpool. Thomas moved to a "very pretty little apartment" in the Konradstrasse. Already in March that year *Buddenbrooks* had entered its fourth impression; and by October, when Thomas made a second trip to Berlin, it had passed the 10,000 sales mark.

"No longer was I the entirely obscure young man of former days," he quietly recalled. "What I had been biding my time for, in my Schwabing and Italian retreats, was now — I will not say attained, but begun. No longer did it embarrass me to be questioned about my daily life . . . I had justified my position, justified my complete resistance to the demands for a con-ventional career made upon me by the world; society took me up . . . and I began to frequent the drawing rooms of Munich where there was an artistic and literary atmosphere." The press "grew louder in its praise . . . the printings began to tread on one another's heels. It was fame."[42]

The money "flowed in streams." Only in Lübeck was Thomas' name proving more scandalous than popular.

9

What had happened was not difficult to understand. The older citizens of the town had begun to write out by hand and disseminate among the burghers of the city keys to the characters in the books.

Key to Buddenbrooks by Thomas Mann

The time of the events in the novel is set back about twelve years:

Family Buddenbrook = Family Mann
Old Buddenbrook = Consul Johann Siegmund Mann
His wife Betty, née Kröger = the same, née Marty
Thomas Buddenbrook = Senator Heinrich Mann
Gerda, his wife, née Arnoldsen = Frau Senator Mann, née Julia Bruhns

Christian = Friedel Mann
Tony = Elizabeth Mann . . .
And so on. Every character in the book found a Lübeck home: and many of
the homes were outraged.

Seen in this light the book became little more than a cruel defamation of
the little Hanseatic city and its virtuous people; and an insult to privacy. It
did not seem as if Thomas had made the least attempt to disguise his
characters, and the clarity of his depiction only made the matter worse; for
they stepped out of the pages as though they could be touched, every
mannerism and eccentricity captured for posterity. What Thomas' had brought
to bear on his subject-matter was precisely the quality the Baltic seaport with
its pious traders had *never* possessed: a sense of humour, a wry, unintimidated
irony which, as Dr Heimann had noted, did not detract from the book's epic
stature, but seemed actually to enhance it.

So the citizens of Lübeck declined to share the general felicitation of
Germany's youngest literary star.

Otto Anthes, for instance, moved to Lübeck at about this time:

I found the town in great agitation over the book, which for some
appeared just the treacherous revenge of a malcontent, for others the
expression of disrespectful impudence; but to everyone it seemed a nasty
concoction with which an ill-bred son had disgraced his hometown.

For a while I did not know what to say. I attempted to speak of the
artistic and literary qualities of the work; but I was looked at as though
I had gone out of my mind. A teacher at the Katharineum who had
taught Thomas Mann screamed at me in disgust: "So you think he is an
'important' writer? I took him in German. He was incapable of writing a
proper essay!"

But Munich, where Thomas had settled, could not have cared less, however
insulting the portrait of Herr Permaneder, the Bavarian beer-drinker. There
Thomas was soon entered in the *Visitor's Guide* and *Who's Who* as the
author of *Buddenbrooks*.

At the Herzogstrasse the Frau Senator was flushed with pride. The "idle
little Tommy" of Lübeck schooldays was suddenly a famous writer; and even
Aunt Elizabeth — now nicknamed "Tony" by all her friends — quite forgave
her nephew. For in a strange way Thomas' triumph had dispelled the sorrow
and sudden obscurity caused by the Senator's early death. And as Tony
Buddenbrook warmed to the rising prestige of her brother Thomas Buddenbrook in the novel, so Aunt Elizabeth basked a little now in the way Thomas'
name seemed on every tongue.

Thomas was now twenty-eight: the age at which his father had paused to
choose a bride.

10

Meanwhile Heinrich's stays at Dr von Harungen's clinic became longer as

Heinrich also battled for recognition. The last volume of the *Göttinnen* was startlingly erotic for the times, but it never stood a chance of competing with *Buddenbrooks*. It was undoubtedly Thomas' hour.

Success and fame, however, are not always helpful to the creative artist. While Thomas' efforts, after *Buddenbrooks*, became more removed from real life, Heinrich seemed spurred by some inner demon. Hardly had he finished one novel than he was writing the next. Where Thomas, after his long years of writing *Buddenbrooks*, turned back to society with a renewed desire to belong, Heinrich seemed with each new work to draw further away. He had almost no friends, invested all his feelings and desires in his writing. In the autobiographical sketches he wrote for Langen's publishing catalogue in 1904 he revealed some of the motives behind his work:

One knows my background, from my brother's celebrated novel. After having been Hanseatic merchants for two thick volumes, with the help of latin blood we finally got to Art — according to Nietzsche this always produces nervous disorders and artists. As soon as I could, then, I "returned" to Italy. Yes, for a time I thought I was "home". But even there I found I was not; and from the moment I realized this, I began to produce something worthwhile. Being caught between two races strengthens the weak, makes him single-minded, difficult to influence, obsessed with creating for himself a little world, a homeland which he cannot find elsewhere. Since nowhere he meets compatriots he withdraws politely from the usual framework of responsibilities. Since he nowhere finds a readership with the same instincts he finally reduces his need to communicate to an audience of one; by which at least it gains in intensity. He treads shocking paths, puts the bestial beside beautiful dreams, ideals beside satire, couples tenderness with hostility. The aim is not to amuse others: where would others come from? No, he creates sensations for a single being. He is out to make his own life richer, to improve the bitter task of his own loneliness . . .

To illustrate this remarkable self-analysis the *Simplicissimus* cartoonist Olaf Gulbransson contributed a caricature of Heinrich as telling as Heinrich's words: a three-quarter length line drawing of a tall, stiff figure with long, fine fingers drumming his thigh as he sits, and a high white collar stretching up to the pointed black beard, the heavy black moustache with its ends turned, the chiselled, almost broken nose and distant, heavy-lidded eyes. His contempt for bourgeois values is self-evident; his features betray only a studied, harsh wisdom, stark and upright, and a nervous constitution. A man of extraordinary reserve and self-control, one would say: a little frightening even; uncompromising, unyielding. A revolutionary.

Die Göttinnen appeared under the Langen imprint in three volumes in January 1903; but Heinrich remained in Italy where he had already conceived a new novel. This he began in February.

Die Göttinnen or the *Three Novels of the Duchess of Assy* were not a commercial success. That Heinrich must have been deeply disappointed one can sense from the optimism of the suggested blurb he had sent to Langen.

The novels provoked very differing responses from the critics, though not all were negative.

Here was a "renaissance recklessness" — but one that defied belief: erotic, sensuous, cultural and utterly outspoken: a trilogy which, as one reviewer wrote, was "above all a work of our time. Not of eternal merit, to be sure; but for all that, a book which could only be written in our age."

"It restores," as the reviewer more pointedly remarked, "a feeling of our culture; and at last, instead of endless psychological analyses of the 'artist', it throws up an abundance of new life."[43] Richard Wengraf was even more specific:

> Heinrich Mann's trilogy is a work of unbelievable energy that towers alone above contemporary epic literature. It is an art without precedent ... a masterpiece by a great writer; and perhaps, because of that, spared the often treacherous fame of commercial success. Some will lay aside the first of those three novels, perplexed and exhausted by the strange mixture of true circumstances and bold imagination. For so many the Duchess of Assy has never lived, her author never written.[44]

Others, however, were shocked by Heinrich's "licence"; and little Viko, now thirteen and boarding at a school in Augsburg, began to discover the embarrassment two famous older brothers can cause. "Most of the parents of my friends," he recalled, "were unsure as to whether they should honour me as brother of the author of *Buddenbrooks* or mistrust me as next-of-kin to the writer of the *Duchess of Assy*."

One person alone remained the staunch defender of both Heinrich and Thomas: their mother. She had moved into a new block of flats in Munich, and then to Augsburg to be near Viktor. She "checked the windows of the Augsburger bookshop", as Viktor related, and if there were no books by Heinrich and Thomas, she would go in and buttonhole the Manager.

On one occasion, when the proprietor of a new bookshop declared he had no books by either author, the Frau Senator lost her self-control and began to wave a pair of large scissors which she had in her hand. The bookseller retreated behind his table: and only then did the Frau Senator burst out laughing, as the man began to put his hands above his head! It became one of the historic anecdotes of the family.

"He thought I was going to stab him to death!" she chuckled with tears of laughter as she walked home with Viktor.

11

For the protagonists themselves, however, it was becoming increasingly hard. Here were two brothers, from an identical background, bidding for the same stakes, yet in unmistakably different styles, their conceptions of art, epic and the novel so radically distinct from one another it seemed hard to credit their relationship. Little by little — particularly after publication of such a deeply autobiographical work as *Tonio Kröger* — the literary critics and commentators began to take sides. By September 1903 Thomas was having to reassure his brother he was not behind Richard Schaukal's August piece in the *Rheinisch-Westfälische Zeitung.*

Schaukal was a young poet of the same age as Thomas. He had entered the lives of both brothers a few years before, preceded by a photograph of himself and a set of his published works. Thomas had even dedicated his short-story *Little Louise* to Schaukal. Now, in an article entitled "Thomas Mann", Schaukal chose to squeeze in an attack on the *Göttinnen.*

"Since I can't be sure whether you might one day come across the piece, I want to make it quite clear to you now that I have never given the author the slightest grounds to suppose that, particularly where I am the subject of discussion, I could either listen or agree in any way to a disparagement of your works," Thomas was at pains to reassure Heinrich.[45] Publicly he wanted no hint of disagreement between them.

But privately Thomas was racked with doubts and awkward feelings. Throughout the summer and autumn of 1903 he ran a "very serious and profound correspondence" with Heinrich about *Die Göttinnen,* which left him more confused than before. "Do you know it?" he wrote to Kurt Martens in December. "What do you think of it? I am at a loss over it."[46]

It was now that the whole edifice of brotherly love and affection began to creak, from this moment that tempers became frayed, unhappy criticisms were made; and Heinrich withdrew more and more from the family. On 23rd December Thomas was restraining himself from his natural reaction to Heinrich's latest missive:

Thank you very much for your letter! Again there is a great deal I would like to take up with you, but the devil with it! We are both at best when we are friends — I am, certainly. My worst moments are when I am feeling hostile towards you. Certain points in my small review in the *Freistatt* were quite consciously aimed at you; this I must in all honesty confess . . .

The "small review" had appeared in March that year. Phrases like "the breathlessness of certain novels" which mount "wild and desperate attacks on the reader's interest", the "bellows-type of poetry which has been introduced in recent years from the beautiful land of Italy", were hardly calculated to reinforce brotherly affection. Above all, it was his brief analysis of love, emphasizing the importance of humility, that was too close for Heinrich's comfort. "For he who knows love," Thomas proposed, "knows also suffering" ("Whoever does not know it," he qualified, "knows only 'Beauty' "). He summed up:

To us plebeians and outcasts, who beneath the contemptuous smile of Renaissance man honour the womanly ideals in culture and art, we who as artists believe in pain, experience, profundity, and sorrowful love and who stand somewhat ironically in relation to the beautiful surface of life: to us it must appear likely that women, as artists, promise the most extraordinary and interesting things, yes, that one day they will become the leaders and greatest artists among us . . . which is nothing to do with what cold and stiff hearts call "Beauty".

What Thomas was seeking was the revelation of something within himself; and after *Buddenbrooks* this came more and more to obsess and isolate him. Heinrich's glittering world of free-fancy, of linguistic and thematic out-rageousness simply defeated his understanding, even threatened him. Thomas began to draw a protective wall about himself and his writing: and it was this defensiveness, perhaps, which finally convinced him he must marry.

The bride he chose was both a chance to extend his inward search — this honouring of woman as symbol of "pain, experience, profundity and sorrow-ful love" — and to evade the challenge of the new world in which as an artist he was living. Beneath Heinrich's "contemptuous" smile Thomas pursued his course; and, curiously, it was largely in their attitude towards women, their own and each other's, that the growing conflict between the brothers became manifest — a conflict whose fuse was already lit by Thomas' success and by Heinrich's disturbing intellectual and artistic progress, but which would not explode until, like the strained situation of Europe itself, relations finally broke down in world war.

CHAPTER FIVE

Tyrant, Tenderness — and a Marriage

Katja Pringsheim was nineteen; and as the Manns had once been one of the most influential and esteemed families in Lübeck, the Pringsheims were the talk of Munich. They lived in a magnificent neo-Renaissance house in the Arcisstrasse; Frau Pringsheim was one of the town's great beauties, the daughter of the celebrated Dohms of Berlin — Ernst Dohm, the founder and editor of *Kladderdatsch,* the famous pre-*Simplicissimus* satirical broadsheet, and Hedwig Dohm, feminist and novelist.

Herr Pringsheim was even more imposing. He was the Professor of Mathematics at the University of Munich, heir to one of the largest fortunes in Germany, a collector of distinction (his collection of Renaissance silver and faience unrivalled in Germany), an ardent musician (whose enthusiasm and friendship with Wagner had resulted in a duel and had only sobered on experiencing Wagner's anti-semitism). The Pringsheims kept the most lively cultural and academic house in the city, a haven of music (with two grand pianos), art (paintings and tapestries) and literature (each of the five children had his own beautifully bound library). Katja, the youngest child and only daughter, had become the first girl in Bavaria to take — and pass — the matriculation exam for university entrance, the Abitur.

It was Hedwig Dohm, Katja's grandmother, who had first suggested she go to Grammar School; but as there was no such institution for girls in Bavaria, Katja had been tutored at home. At seventeen she had passed the Abitur examination and put her name down for science at the University. She read physics and experimental physics under the celebrated Röntgen; mathematics under her father.

She attended most major concerts; and it was at one in the new Kaimsaal in Munich that Thomas first caught sight of her, with her brothers.

Like Thomas she was an ardent cyclist; but it was in the tram, on the way to the University a few days later, that Thomas got his second chance to observe her. The tram was trundling up the Ludwigstrasse when a ticket-inspector asked Miss Pringsheim for her ticket. She said she had thrown it away as she was nearing her stop. The ticket collector began to argue. The tram stopped; Katja stuck her tongue out, opened the door, and leaped out to her physics class.

Thomas, however, was not Miss Pringsheim's only suitor. She was the Tania of the Arcisstrasse, the only female student at the university, and studying science and mathematics! She soon numbered a professor among competitors for her hand — who naturally found favour with her father. Katja, however, had no intention of getting married.

Thomas felt differently. Not only was he smitten by love for the tomboy student on her bicycle, he began to dream of marriage straight away. Through an acquaintance, the painter Stuck, he managed to get an invitation to the Pringsheims' house. At the end of August 1903, he was writing to his friend Otto Grautoff:

> If you knew what wonders and wild tales I have dreamed up these past few days — and nights . . . What a fool I am! What a nitwit! Better to stand up and do some proper work instead of dwelling on such fairy-tales. Never mind! One has to be someone already to come up with such dreams, and since the days when the classical garden with the international public was just a bare flagstone-court (in those days you were also with me — extra-ordinary how it always remains the same), both I *and* the "object" of my dreams have established ourselves.
>
> And what if it was only the cut of my suit which attracted all the attention? But I don't think it was. I don't have to think it.[1]

Thomas, chronicler of the Buddenbrooks had realized the key to little Miss Katja's hand — her mother.

The atmosphere of the Pringsheim home recalled Thomas' own childhood in Lübeck.

> I had known the traditional elegance that belonged to the great families; here I found it transformed and intellectualized in this stately society compact of art and literature . . . The head of the house, one of the first Wagnerians, was personally acquainted with the Master. Only by a sort of intelligent self-compulsion did he devote himself to mathematics instead of wholly to music. The lady of the house came of a Berlin literary family . . . My existence and my youthful performance were not lost upon her, nor did she oppose the passionate feeling that soon grew up in me for the only daughter of the house — a feeling which my solitary youth had not taught me any need to dissimulate. There was a ball in the gilded High Renaissance salons of the Pringsheim House, a brilliant and heavily attended gathering, where for the first time I was conscious of basking in the full sunshine of public favour and regard; it ripened in me the feelings upon which I hoped

to base the happiness of my life.[2]

Thomas' intuition paid off handsomely. Professor Pringsheim was unlikely to be impressed by the attentions of the rather solitary young novelist, but Frau Pringsheim was evidently delighted. A few days later she went to her bookseller, Herr Buchholz, and asked about Thomas' literary reputation.

"Thomas Mann?" the bookseller said. "Now him! He'll go at least as far as Gottfried Keller,[3] I can tell you!"

Frau Pringsheim returned home rather pleased. From that moment she put no obstacle in Thomas' path.

2

The earning of Katja's own affection, however, was another matter. She was still barely nineteen, and she had no desire to get married. She was not even particularly literary. But then that perhaps was the challenge.

Meanwhile the literary front was commercially good but creatively bleak. A sort of paralysis seems to have overtaken Thomas. He avoided literary companions like Kurt Martens, and when, in October on a public-reading trip to Königsberg and Berlin, he was introduced to Gerhart Hauptmann and other celebrities, he came away convinced he had made a terrible impression. "A momentous experience," he called the meeting with Hauptmann in a letter to Samuel Fischer, who had arranged it. "I only wish I had been able to make a somewhat more favourable impression than the one he probably got of me. He, the Conqueror, will have gained an impression of confusion, conflict, tension and great weariness — and he would be right."[4]

Thomas' letters of this period all confirm a dwindling sense of creativity, the impotence wrought by public success. For the first time he began to see art as a symbolic confessional in which his "moustachioed personality" could be rendered "less uninteresting".[5] He began, in other words, to hide behind the literary mask he had created — "the diligently forged symbols of my life" as he put it in his letter to Fischer.

To Walter Opitz, a fellow author who had departed from Munich disappointed with Thomas' "coldness", Thomas replied:

O time of 3—5 page long letters, O time when one gave of oneself, lived out one's life in letters, tested one's talents in correspondence, and in correspondence overcame one's experiences and depicted them — where, must I ask, have you gone! No longer does one sit lonely, free and without responsibilities in one's little chamber and write innocently away, art for art's sake. Now one finds onself in the full beam of the great spotlight, the whole of one's being exposed to the public, weighed down with responsibility for the use of one's talents, which one has been unwise enough to betray to the world . . .

You complain that you were not able to come into closer "contact" with me . . . but no-one can come closer to me than he, like you, who reads *Tonio Kröger*. And if you found me personally very reserved, that may be because one loses the taste for personal communication when one is used to expressing oneself symbolically — that is to say, in works of art. One leads, I would like to put it, a symbolic, a representative existence, similar to a prince — and see! In this idea lies the core to the most wonderful thing I am considering writing, a novel of a prince, a counterpiece to *Tonio Kröger,* which will be called "Royal Highness" . . .[6]

Royal Highness did in fact come into being — after another five years of "representative existence". And it was this weak-kneed withdrawal into "symbolic" existence, his denial of the actual realities of life, that had begun to grate on Heinrich's nerves. Thomas had become razor-sensitive to the slightest criticism of his work; and when Heinrich repeated the words of one critic, Thomas was consumed with rage. "I would also like to know," he wrote to Heinrich in December 1903, "who wrote you that with such fanaticism and intensity. If I am acquainted with him (or her) even only distantly, I demand you tell me who it is. I must know who is against me."[7]

But after Thomas' criticism of the *Göttinnen* and his review in the *Freistatt,* it would not have been all that surprising if the culprit was none other than Heinrich himself.

3

"Your reproach about my absence and my silence finds its mark and I am most contrite," Thomas apologized to Kurt Martens at the end of the year 1903. "But it stems from the fact that I am so terribly poor at managing my time. I save and spend it in the wrong places, and am full of nervous anxiety that — despite all my seclusion — I am producing so little . . ."[8] He was receiving invitations to give readings the length and breadth of Germany, even abroad, newspapers were telegraphing for short stories from his "prized pen" as he put it. He ended up by producing "unbelievable trash shamelessly produced for the money" as he confessed to Heinrich.[9]

Meanwhile Heinrich continued writing without pause. No sooner had *Die Göttinnen* been published in January 1903, than Langen was announcing a new Heinrich Mann novel to appear that autumn, *Die Jagd nach Liebe* (The Hunt for Love), a five hundred page work written in six months. Side by side with his novels, Heinrich had been producing a stream of short stories and novellas which, despite his apparently cloistered seclusion from the outside world, teemed with life and ideas. By February 1904, when Thomas had read Heinrich's latest novella *Fulvia* he was moved to write:

> I have read it twice with great involvement . . . It is a brilliant little piece, strong, gem-like, masterly, and told with that Italian intensity of style which is so much your own. Again it occurred to me that you are actually the only writer left today who can still write stories, adventures, real "novellas", who still has anything "new" to tell . . .[10]

However one thing worried Thomas, having enthusiastically greeted the story. "What is much more curious, strangely interesting, and for me still a

little implausible is the development of your Weltanschauung towards Liberalism which is shown in this work. Strange, as I have said, and interesting! You
must feel incredibly young and strong now, I suppose," he added somewhat
sarcastically for with his customary intuition he had recognized — even if he
could not accept — the importance of a positive, identifiable attitude to life:
it was, in the midst of such sudden celebrity, precisely the quality he lacked.

"Really, I would put your 'liberalism' down to a sort of self-conscious
mastering of youth if it didn't more probably indicate simply 'maturity'.
Maturity! will I ever reach it?" he asked in a spasm of despair.

Firstly I understand little about so-called freedom. To me it is a moral
and intellectual concept, meaning the same as "Truthfulness". (Some
critics call it "coldness" in my work.) I have absolutely no interest, however, in political freedom. The great works of Russian literature were
written under enormous oppression, weren't they? Would they have been
produced without this oppression? If nothing else, this proves that the
fight for freedom is better than freedom itself. What is "freedom" anyway?
Perhaps because so much blood has been spilled for the word it has something strangely un-free for me, something quite medieval about it . . .
But I suppose I'm not qualified to talk about it.

I have hardly done anything recently and have a very guilty conscience,
since there was so much to do! . . . It is a new and turbulent period in my
life, not well suited to work. *Buddenbrooks* has just reached the 18
thousand mark, and even *Tristan* is up to three thousand now. I first
have to get used to my role of "famous man" — it is very exhausting . . .

I have been "introduced", socially, at Bernsteins and Pringsheims.
The visit to Pringsheims gave me plenty to think about — a grandiose
environment with genuine culture. The father a university Professor with
a gold cigarette-case, the mother a painter's delight, the youngest son a
musician and his twin-sister Katja (her name really is Katja) a miracle,
indescribably rare and precious, a creation whose simple existence out-
weighs the cultural activities of fifteen writers or thirty painters . . .

This will give the atmosphere; but it is one which, if I continue to
move in it, could have the most immeasurable and diverse consequences.
One day I found myself in the Renaissance salon with its Gobelins, its
Lenbachs, its door carvings in antique gold, and accepted an invitation to
the big ball that was to take place there. It was on the next night — 150
people, from literature and art . . .

That evening I at last met the daughter of the house, after only having
been able to see her from afar, long and insatiable gazes; only once when
I first visited had I spoken a word of greeting to her. Eight days later I was
there again, to tea this time, ostensibly to return a book to the mother
which she had lent me. I saw her alone. She . . . she called Katja down,
and the three of us chatted for an hour . . . An invitation to lunch was
dangled before me. Was I misguided in thinking I had sensed a mutual
feeling? No! Two days later the youngest son, Klaus, the musician, sat at
my place, reciprocating my visit . . . .

You have no impression of Jewishness with these people; only culture. We gossiped about art, his music, his sister . . . That was six days ago. Since then nothing has happened. In fact nothing has actually *taken place* since the beginning: it is all in my imagination — but it is too bold, too new, too colourful, too much of an adventure to be dismissed at present. The *possibility* has presented itself — and makes me feverish. I cannot think of other things. Humpty Dumpty fell down the stairs and yet still got a princess for a wife.[11] And I, let's face it, I am more than Humpty Dumpty! The whole thing is so terribly complicated, I would give anything to be able to talk it all over with you in some quiet corner. But one thing I tell you: it is pointless to ask if she will bring me "happiness". Am I striving for happiness? I strive — after life; and *in that sense,* I suppose, I strive "to write". And another thing: I am not afraid of wealth . . .

But all this is looking too far ahead. I have to await events, and there is no point in asking your advice, because I am letting myself be borne along by these events. Frau Professor Pringsheim is going to Berlin to visit her family for a fortnight. In the meantime I hope to meet Katja at Bernsteins, where I am due to give a reading. What will happen? As I have said, I have the distinct impression that I would be a welcome suitor to the family. I am a Christian, of good family, have achieved something which precisely these people are in a position to understand . . . What will happen? Nothing probably. But isn't the possibility already a tumultuous experience?

It was a long letter to Heinrich, deeply conservative in its rejection of Liberalism, of political ideals such as freedom — even the personal ideal of "happiness".

But what could Heinrich answer when it was so obvious Thomas was in love? Thomas would not even take Grautoff's and Martens' on-the spot advice. His sights were fixed; and to the credit of the rather melancholic young celebrity, he stuck firmly to his guns.

4

Kurt Martens now became chief confidant; he was addressed in the intimate "Du" or *tu*. On 2nd April 1904, Thomas revealed the affair with Katja had made "gigantic strides". He had arranged to meet Heinrich in Riva for a rest and a chance to "discuss a world of things",[12] but everything depended on the outcome of his suit — or pursuit as Katja later saw it.

"Waiting and wondering" was how he characterized the moment to Martens. The Bernsteins threw generous dinner parties at which the pair could meet; but otherwise the only way to Katja's hand was through the somewhat frightening doors of Professor Pringsheim's home. Frau Pringsheim was now on his side — "she smiles encouragingly when I speak simply of 'Katja' to her" he had told Heinrich at the end of March.[13] Somehow he had to win over the Professor; and at this juncture fate brought a headache to his aid. Triumphantly he reported it to Katja who was lying in hospital recovering from an operation.

My headache recently, when I had supper with your family after the theatre, was trivial; it was only a side-effect of my sore throat, which I've now cured beautifully, thanks to your father. Naturally you don't understand that, being unaware how deeply concerned your father is for my welfare. You see, I let it be known that I had a sore throat, that I was all swollen up. "Then you must make a damp compress," your mother said. "Yes, I suppose I must," I said in my conciliatory fashion. "Do you have gutta percha?" your father asked . . . "No," I replied in my decisive manner. Whereupon your father stood up — he stood up, I say, although because of his ailing stomach he was lying on the sofa, went to the closet, and brought me his last and only piece of gutta percha, which was in fact already somewhat brittle. He gave it to me and carefully instructed me how I must use it in order to benefit from it — What do you say to that? What conclusion can we draw? *At least* that he doesn't want my death. But *more* follows from it. You will say again that your father knows how to control his feelings. But this is more than self-control, whatever you say. You're always telling me of your father's tigerish temper only because you don't like me . . .[14]

Thus Thomas hoped he had beaten the last external obstacle. It was a little like the story of the Trojan horse. Because of his small, rather pale features he was nicknamed the "liverish riding-master" among Katja's brothers. But Klaus, her twin, was resolutely behind Thomas' bid, her mother and father were now more or less "unopposed". It remained to win Katja's own consent, which was by no means easy.

5

Perhaps, like his own character Life, in *The Way to the Churchyard,* the bicycle made Thomas bolder. At any rate he rolled up at the Arcisstrasse one morning on his bicycle and announced he had arranged to go for a ride with Katja.

Katja recollected no such arrangement; but with the sun shining and the university closed for the Easter vacation she accepted the offer. And the cycle-ride, transposed to horse-back, eventually was to find its way into *Royal Highness.*

On Saturday 9th April, Thomas recorded a "big discuss. with K.P." A few days later he left for Riva, as arranged. He hoped Katja would write to him. But weeks went by and there was no letter. When it did arrive, late in April, he had almost given up hope.

"You must not make me wait like that again, Katja. Waiting is horrible," he wrote back. "One must not abet fate in its evil propensity for letting all good things arrive only after we are so benumbed from sheer waiting that we can scarcely rejoice in them.

"I also wholly approve of your not giving too much attention to your tomes on mathematics," he added. "For although I usually don't like to admit it, I will confess to you just this once that underneath I am a little jealous of the sciences and secretly experience a diabolic joy when you thoroughly neglect them. That is old-fashioned, sentimental, and base, I know, and I promise that I'll never again voice such feelings . . ."

He returned to Munich in the first week of May. Whether Heinrich had been able to "drill any sense" into him is doubtful. As we shall see, it was a difficult time for Heinrich too.

In mid-May Katja confessed to being "perplexed" about Thomas: an admission which strengthened, not weakened, Thomas' case.

"I am quite conscious of not being the sort of man to arouse plain and uncomplicated feelings," he wrote, "I add today that I do not regard this as an objection to myself. To prompt mixed emotions, perplexity, is after all, if you will forgive me, a sign of personality. The man who never awakens doubt," he warned, "never causes troubled surprise, never, *sit venia verbo,* excites a touch of *horror,* the man who is always simply loved, is a fool, a phantom, a ridiculous figure. I have no ambitions in that direction —"

His letters became more intimate, tender — "I see you, Katja, I really see you so luminously, so vividly alive, in magically fine detail," he wrote to her at the end of May, "such as the most successful portrait could not attain. At such times I am shaken with joy. Curiously enough, it is almost always in the Kaimsaal that I see you, for I often watched you there through my opera-glasses before we knew each other. I see you coming in from the left, up front, with your mother and your brothers, see you going to your seat in one of the front rows, see the silver shawl around your shoulders, your black hair, the pearly pallor of your face, your expression as you try to seem unaware that people's eyes are on you — it is impossible to say how perfectly and how wonderfully in detail I see you!"

And in this mood, this obsession that seemed to paralyse him creatively ("of course I am completely deranged," he had written in March to Henrich, "and lack the necessary peace of mind to work, that egotistical single-mindedness one needs in order to write"), he made do with a short-story. He called it *At the Prophet's*[15]; a trivial tale which he sent, as a "harmless tribute"[16] to Katja's mother. In it he pictured her as a "rich woman" with satin-lined coupé and an interest in genius. By portraying the prophet as a passionate radical he was able to contrast his own more human, "normal" being — as well as his feelings for the rich woman's daughter, Sonia.

On 16th May Thomas at last formally asked Katja for her hand in marriage. Three days later a "waiting period" began.

6

Meanwhile, as Thomas courted the "rich woman's daughter", Heinrich was becoming progressively more lonely, more "nomadic" as his mother put it to him; and less successful.

The Hunt for Love had appeared in the late autumn of 1903; but despite its racy title, contemporary plot and first printing of 3,000 copies, it did not fulfil its promise. In his long letter to Heinrich the following February, Thomas related how he had met Langen at the Pringsheims' ball:

Langen had himself introduced to me, I who had once worked in his office; and he behaved almost obsequiously. We spoke of you. "If," I said, "I may take the liberty of giving you some advice, it would be this: hold on to my brother and make sure you never drop him! *One* day he *will* have a big success."

"I wouldn't dream of it!" said he. "I know why you say this. I have been guilty of big mistakes of this kind, I know it. But I have no intention of dropping your brother!" He sounded very zealous and convincing, and I tell you this because you once expressed anxiety on the subject. You can rest assured. Best wishes!17

It must indeed have been galling for Heinrich, particularly since *The Hunt for Love* had indeed been written in the hope of success. He had taken his younger sister Carla, who was just beginning her career on the stage, and portrayed her as a fundamentally untalented actress who sacrifices all hope of happiness and genuine love to her "art". In the story Heinrich had also included a number of Munich people he had met at his sister Julia's: and had aroused considerable ill-will in the family because of it. Relations between Heinrich and the Löhrs came to breaking point.

Thomas made no bones of not liking the book, despite his continued "respect" for Heinrich as a writer. Perhaps Heinrich's exposure, in the novel, of *fin de siècle* land speculation in Munich, the city's excessive attention to art, and his personal caricatures offended Thomas at a time when he was making such a supreme effort to win the daughter of such an important household; or perhaps the extreme ease and speed with which Heinrich finished the novel (he also managed to write a celebrated novella, *Pippo Spano,* in the midst of it) irritated Thomas in his paralysed creative state; but these were small objections. What Thomas had said to Langen, however condescending it sounded in the letter, was meant genuinely. Thomas sensed, all the more so at a time when he himself was so creatively inhibited, the growing power and authority behind Heinrich's language: but he felt it was being misdirected, was failing to find truly epic, lasting expression. *His* expression.

Here there could be no agreement: and the developments within the family — Julia's shallow bourgeois pretensions (that would one day end disastrously), Thomas' attentions to the Pringsheim house, Carla's dedicated but controversial and doomed pursuit of theatrical success, and Heinrich's lonely and nomadic artistry — only served to make matters worse. Thomas was determined to find his way back into society, while Heinrich — proud, shy, denied popular success — was determined now to remain outside. His neo-romantic conservatism and even the outburst of individualism in the *Göttinnen* were giving way now to what Thomas identified in his letter as

Liberalism. Heinrich was now thirty-three, it had taken a long time; but the development was far from being "implausible" as Thomas had suggested. In other countries — such as France or Britain — Heinrich's conversion would have been considered tardy; yet among the creative voices of Germany Heinrich was one of the first.

In his stark, pungent prose Heinrich now began to espouse the causes of equality and justice, of democracy and freedom. The nervous, Quixote-like author of the *Göttinnen* now became a warrior. And Thomas mistrusted this, it came at the wrong time. Their rift — evident from the piece in the *Freistatt* the previous year — deepened. On the political and social front Heinrich now openly contested the anti-democratic forces that were shaping Germany's destiny in the twentieth century. In October 1904 he refuted Karl Jentsch's allegations about the French republic in the columns of the Berlin magazine *Die Zukunft*. It was the first shot — employing almost the same vocabulary — in a tirade that was to culminate, in 1914, with his epic satire on the doomed empire.

But first, in Florence, the curious idea came to him that, thirty years later, would make him more famous than all his political and social writings combined: the story of *The Blue Angel*.

I was sitting as usual in the Teatro Alfieri, an old-style Florentine playhouse with five-high tiers of narrow boxes, and always empty . . .

In the interval newspapers were sold, and it was there I read the story which would one day be called the "Blue Angel".

In fact something quite different appeared in the paper, had been mis-reported, and dated from Berlin. Nevertheless the story ran through my head so fast that I barely reached the theatre-bar. I sat paralysed, noticed then that the curtain had gone up; and not often can a play have received so much applause from a single spectator.[18]

The Blue Angel was the title Sternberg gave his film; but the novel, when it appeared early in 1905, bore the unusual name *Professor Unrat*. It concerned the story of a small town secondary-school teacher, Professor Rat, who is so hated by his pupils that they nickname him "Unrat" — a negative that changes his name from meaning "counsel" or "advice" to "excrement". Even the other teaching staff accept the name.

Professor Unrat, lonely and tyrannical, follows a group of his most hated pupils to one of the shady nightclubs of the little seaport-town — the Blue Angel — where he intends to discredit them and ruin their future careers. But there he himself becomes corrupted by the charms of Künstlerin Frölich, the night-club singer. Forced into a "pact" with his pupils, Professor Unrat transforms his obsessional, almost psychopathic hatred for his pupils into an equally obsessional self-abasement to Künstlerin Frölich. He sinks deeper and deeper, is dismissed finally from the school, marries the singer, and takes her into society; where with her charms and the lure of gambling, he proceeds to corrupt the whole town.

The book, short and dramatic, was published in a cautious edition of 2,200 copies. Although a reprint of the same number was later made, it was again a comparative failure: a book which, when republished in 1916, sold over 50,000 copies!

It was indeed "before its time". The style was uncomfortably modern; its very "breathlessness", as Thomas had once called it in his *Freistatt* article, was now to the author's advantage, tore the reader into a story hardly credible yet which, by the very intensity of the language, was as actual and direct as a newspaper report. It left Thomas utterly overwhelmed at the time.

"I consider it immoral to write one bad book after another out of fear of idleness," he entered in his notebook under the heading "Anti-Heinrich":

"Artistic Entertainment" — All well and good — if it were not a contradiction in terms!

The whole thing is the most amusing and superficial stuff that has appeared in Germany for a long time.

And what a jumble! One of the pupils, Erztum, gives in an essay — after having been put in the corner before they begin to write the essay! Tobacconists and café-owners are erstwhile pupils of the Grammar-School professor: such instances are hardly to be ascribed to the "higher concerns of the artist" but to something else, namely the belletrist in full swing. The book doesn't seem written with any idea of permanence.

In short, eating groats must make one very frivolous — and very productive. But perhaps productivity is simply another form of frivolity.[19]

These were strong words from someone whose collected works would total twelve thick volumes! Later he was to prize *Professor Unrat* as linguistically one of Heinrich's most important contributions to the modern German novel;[20] but for the moment it haunted him with its "ungodly impressionistic style", its insults to credibility and convention ("Impossible things where one does not believe one's eyes. Unrat shouts in the middle of the concert-hall: 'Into the corner' ").[21] It seemed to slap the face of "permanence", of literary posterity. And yet Thomas seemed blinded by its faults, unable to recognize its almost revolutionary stylistic import. Here at last was the most "German" of Heinrich's novels to date, not only because of its extraordinary descriptions and feel for the seamy side of the unnamed Baltic seaport (Lübeck without question) and its rendering of the German classroom, but for the depiction of its central character, Unrat himself.

"My head and Marlene Dietrich's legs," Heinrich said once, later, after the film had become a world box-office success. He said it sardonically, and yet the truth was there. Not only did Emil Jannings play a part whose features — the pointed beard and broad head — resembled Heinrich, but the character of Unrat *was* Heinrich: and this Thomas seems to have ignored. Tyrannical in his isolation, his inner loneliness, desperate for love, venting his spleen on his pupils: and then when singer Fröhlich shows her charms, he collapses. All his disillusionment and hostility to the world is transformed into a fantastic demonstration of love, of tenderness for her: but always in the ridiculous, heart-breaking strait-jacket of the person he has become: the man the world despises.

Professor Unrat was a tour-de-force in a number of ways, not least the autobiographical. As a stylized self-portrait it went beyond belief — until the following year, in the spring, when Heinrich *did* meet a singer: a girl not yet twenty-one, of Argentinian birth, who captured his heart as unexpectedly, as wildly and uncontrollably as Künstlerin Fröhlich had Professor Unrat's the summer before.

7

Thomas, meanwhile, was having a struggle to win the girl he had set his heart on. "Dear Martens, Rest assured I am grateful for your friendly comments," he wrote on 13th June, 1904:

> The way you see the matter is the way every impartial person must see it, and those who are most concerned about me have been urging the same thing. Nevertheless you are not right. To manifest manly strength by confronting the girl with the decision would mean forcing her to say No, to the sorrow of us both; for right now, due to the unusual nature of her whole development, she cannot persuade herself to say Yes. To play the vexed lord and master on that account and with dignity throw the whole up strikes me as the height of folly as long as I have reason to believe that it would be doing her an ill-service. And she has given me every reason for believing that.

Thomas and Katja had cycled again into the countryside; had flirted at the Bernsteins. Her eyes had "flashed with such artfulness . . ." and yet all this was torture to Thomas:

> all these little amusements that fill the evening mean wasted time, an almost wicked waste of time, while we — you and I — should have so many more important things to talk about. You must know, must see from my face how intensely, how painfully that keeps coming to my mind. If only we were alone more! Or if I knew how better to make use of the brief minutes that are sometimes given to me! I've already told you with what gladness I read what you wrote about "coming closer" — and how poignantly it affected me at the same time. I know, know only too well how guilty *I* am of causing that "kind of awkwardness or something" (this touching "or something"!) which you feel towards me, how my "lack of innocuousness", of unconstraint, of unselfconsciousness, all the nervousness, artificiality, and difficulty of my nature, hampers everyone, even those who are most well-meaning, from coming closer to me or in fact from dealing with me in any tolerably comfortable way . . .

> So it is my fault; and that is the reason for my incessant craving to analyse, to explain, to justify myself to you. It may be that this craving is altogether superfluous. You are intelligent, after all; you are perceptive, out of kindness — and out of just a little fondness. You know that I could not develop myself personally, humanly, as other young people do; that a talent can act as a vampire: bloodsucking, absorbing. You know what a cold, impoverished existence mine has been, organized purely to display art,

to represent life; you know that for many years, *important* years, I regarded myself as nothing, humanly speaking, and wished to be considered only as an artist . . . You know also that this is no easy life, no merry life, and, even given strong sympathy from the outside world, cannot lead to any relaxed and bold self-confidence.

"Only one thing can cure me of the disease of representation and art that clings to me, of my lack of trust in my personal and human side," he finished his letter to Katja; "Only happiness can cure me; only *you*, my clever, sweet, kind, beloved little queen! . . . What I beg of you, hope for, long for, is trust, is for you to stay by me without doubting me — it is something like faith — in short, is *love* . . . This plea and this longing . . . Be my affirmation, my justification, my fulfilment, my saviour, my wife! And never let yourself be put off by that 'awkwardness or something'! Laugh at me and yourself if I awaken such a feeling in you, and stay by me!"[22]

So finally he had said it: not that he loved her, but that he needed her, which must only have made it more difficult for the little science student from the cultured home. She had four brothers and had been surrounded from infancy by wealth and love: she cannot ever have known "need" in this sense.

But Katja had clumsily upset an instrument in the physics laboratory and incurred the wrath of Röntgen. And what should it all lead to, this integral and differential calculus, the tomes of experiments and mathematical theories for a girl? Her mother was a Lenbach-beauty indeed, and had omitted ever to tell her daughter she too was remarkably pretty. Everyone was gossiping about the relationship, Thomas was so desperate . . .

Katja tried to explain in a letter to Thomas that he was expecting too much of her, had made her into an ideal, that she could not possibly fulfil his expectations . . .

But her letter was tender, unsure; and Thomas, driven to "a desperate ride at an insane pace" into the country, having barely survived a "skirmish with a butcher's dog that obviously thirsted for my young life," answered it with all the frenzied tenderness, all the love he could muster:

Silly little Katja, still going on with that nonsense about "overestimating" and still maintaining that she cannot "be" to me what I "expect" of her. But I love you — good Lord, don't you understand what that means? What more is there to expect and to be? I want you to "be" my wife and by being so make me madly proud and happy . . . What I "make of you," the meaning I attribute to you, which you have and will have for my life, is my affair, after all, and imposes no trouble and obligation on you. Silly little Katja! Babbling on quite seriously as if she — now really! — were not worthy of me — of me who asks timorously each time after we see each other: "Do I come up to her? Can she possibly want me? Am I not too clumsy for her, too unworldly, too much 'a poet'?"[23]

But though they began to see each other every other day, Katja still resisted.

Thomas' literary efforts had come to a full stop with *At the Prophet's*. "Two whole months" had passed since he had told her "in plain words how much I love you",[24] but to no apparent avail.

At this juncture Katja's father fell seriously ill. "How do I feel? Thomas answered a postcard from Martens:

> Thoroughly miserable. She is gone, departed to join her gravely ill father in Bad Kissingen, where her mother is too. These last days have been wonderful. I saw her every other day. Then, on the afternoon before her departure, her good little twin brother actually left me alone with her for half an hour. There was an inexplicably sweet and painful parting which has left all my nerves and senses still quivering, but again without any definite result. Impossible. She cannot, cannot "imagine it", cannot decide. As long as the decision does not directly confront her, she feels that everything — in her own words — is easy, natural and uncomplicated, but when the issue comes up, she looks at me like a hunted doe and is incapable . . . Dr Seif, a neurologist and good psychologist who knows all about the affair, like everybody else, has discussed the matter in detail with me. He confirmed (what I have long suspected) that this fear of coming to a decision has a decidedly morbid element. If I do not proceed with much more tact and restraint, he said, he would predict from experience that nothing would come of the engagement.

The relationship, therefore, had reached crisis point. But without knowing it, this enforced separation was perhaps the very best thing that could have happened. Katja left by train, Thomas was there with a bunch of flowers, Klaus took long enough to pay the porter for Thomas to exchange a few words alone with her:

> Did she, too, feel a little sadness? A little, yes. Very careful. But at any rate she pressed my hand for a long time, and looked only at me while the train pulled out of the station. I feel like death. This is a parting for an almost indefinite time. She will stay three weeks in Kissingen, then stop only briefly in Munich on her way back, and she is going to Switzerland with her mother for the rest of the summer. In the autumn she will be with relatives in north Germany. Isn't it enough to drive one to despair?

Enough certainly to miss *Parsifal* at Bayreuth for "fifteen minutes with her . . . You cannot imagine how I love this creature. I dream of her every night, and wake with my heart all sore. I have tasted too much of her to be able to surrender now. Death seems to me far less a surrender than living without her."[25]

What Martens made of these confessions we do not know. He himself had married a plain middle-class girl who promised him not romantic love or excitement but a comfortable home in which to write. If Miss Pringsheim played so difficult to get, what would she be like in marriage?

But nothing Martens may have said could dissuade Thomas from his choice. Working was "still absolutely impossible"[26] for him; he was possessed with the idea of marrying Katja, and his "need" of her bordered, as he had said, on despair. All his writing since *Buddenbrooks* had centred, as in *Tonio Kröger,* on the dichotomy between "art" and "life". But here was the solution! Here was a girl he was convinced he loved, as he had loved no other person before: and characteristically he could not imagine, so strong was his feeling, that it might not be so for her.

Curiously enough he had "known" her even before seeing her that evening at the Kaimsaal — a strange coincidence which added to the fairy-tale element in the whole relationship. For when Katja had been quite young she had been seen by the painter Kaulbach at a children's masked ball in Munich. She was with her four brothers: and they were all dressed as pierrots, or clowns.

Kaulbach was a court portrait-painter and his eye was riveted by the five. He asked their parents if he might do a portrait of them at home; and when finished the picture became a succès-fou, exhibited throughout Germany and reproduced in magazines as far as St Petersburg. Thomas, at the age of fourteen, had seen one such reproduction in Lübeck. Because it appealed to him, he cut it out and pinned it above his desk. The picture was called "Kinder Karneval" (Children's carnival). What a stroke of fate, therefore, which fourteen years later brought the celebrated Lübeck novelist into the hall of the Pringsheim house in Munich — and there was the painting itself on the wall.

Coincidence? Predestination? Thomas reluctantly made his way into the Bavarian alps, to Berchtesgaden. Suddenly a sort of peace descended on him.

8

The summer of 1904 was a turning point for Heinrich, too. He completed *Professor Unrat* and sent it to Langen. His sympathy with "things French" had been evident for years; it now began to take a midly anti-German form which contributed to the strained relationship with Thomas.

Thomas had correctly sensed the "development" of Heinrich's "Weltanschauung towards Liberalism" that February. In late summer Heinrich's translation of Anatole France's *Histoire Comique* appeared under the Langen imprint, and in October his letter to Maximilian Harden, the Editor of *Die Zukunft*.

"In reality," Heinrich retorted to Harden's anti-French opponent, Karl Jentsch, "France is just beginning to settle down now that it has a republic: a republic which it has achieved not by way of 'superficial civilization', but to which it has struggled hard, by dint of its innermost will, its intransigent sense of justice, its critical-literary intellectualism, its absolute intellectual honesty; for it was this that stopped it from separating the practical from the spiritual and from putting up with a poor political system in life just because it might be more comfortable or useful."

Certainly the social democrats had won much for German Labour by compromise and settlement: but at what cost? They were "hypnotised" by the question of money, they overlooked the disadvantages of imperial monarchy because they thought it could be "useful": colonial enterprise promising higher wages for the exploiting countries. Because their concern was exclusively financial, they rejected support from the intellectuals; they were as uninterested in equality as they were in freedom.

Against this Heinrich saw French "workers' democracy" as a part of its greater, national democracy, based on a long and hard-won past; foundations of life, not the question of money. "The workers in France also want tax-reform: but not out of the hands of the oppressors who are exploiting them." If threatened they too would disregard their class interests and fight to defend the republic; "for they know," Heinrich concluded: "a clever tyranny can have fat subjects; but always as underdogs."

To Thomas this was mere word-play; at best a form of "maturity" for which he did not yet seem ready. As he had put it, he knew little of freedom — it was a "spiritual and moral term" like the word "honesty" for him. But political freedom? He had no use for it — and had quoted Russian literature to support the thesis that great works grow out of great oppression.

With that Thomas had tried to dismiss the subject. But as Heinrich was becoming more and more aware, it was a subject one could less and less *afford* to ignore in this "chauvinist and reactionary period which Germany has still to finish with". While Thomas culled literary and financial rewards and threw himself towards a marriage he felt vital for his personality and future happiness, Heinrich began to assume the conscience of a country which seemed not to know where it was going.

But while Heinrich studied the exemplary virtues of France, Thomas had eyes and ears, heart and soul for only one mortal. With her departure he had begun to work; begun to feel the strength she gave him. Berchtesgaden was "magnificent". In the mornings before breakfast "when the snow-covered peaks of the Watzmann sway above the mists against the blue sky — you should be with me", he wrote to her in mid-July. He was "living without a shirt" and reading . . . Rousseau!

But what Heinrich had found in Rousseau, Thomas, in his blissful state, dismissed with scepticism. Let Heinrich ten years later recite the *Social Contract,* "with one hand on heart, the other outstretched". Such an attitude struck Thomas as ridiculous. The summer took its course, Rousseau was discarded. Only the "rich woman's daughter" counted.

9

Katja Pringsheim visited her father in Bad Kissingen; and then went to the north coast, to the Baltic, with her twin brother for the rest of the summer. It was the place to which she was always sent when her parents and elder brothers made their European bicycle tours.

And now, at last, Thomas' literary genius began to pay dividends. Katja began to feel where he was strong, to take him seriously as a writer with a richness and subtlety of mind which set him quite apart from the rest of humanity. His letters "rained" on the Baltic seaside town, she began to long for them. They were filled with tenderness and love . . . and confidence now. In mid-August he wrote:

Katja, dear beloved little Katja, never have I been more filled with you than in these past few days. I imagine I hear the strange and elusive sound of your voice, see before me the dark gleam of your eyes, the pearly pallor of your sweet, clever, mutable face — and a burning admiration seizes me, a tenderness wells up in me, for which there are no signs and symbols! And you? And you?

"In you I saw a small miracle of harmonious education," he confessed later that month:

a realized cultural ideal, an altogether rare and lucky chance of a creature, artistic and demure, free and full of grace. But what was my delight in all this by comparison with my rapture at the knowledge granted me gradually, and which I could not have acquired at first sight. For you were *good,* were *kind.* If you understood what that meant to me! The feeling for you, which until then had stirred only hesitantly and uncertainly in me, was suddenly released; I took heart, saw wonderful hopes. Up to then, where I had loved I had always at the same time despised. The mingling of longing and contempt, ironic love, had been my most characteristic emotion. Tonio Kröger loved "life", blue-eyed commonness, nostalgically, mockingly, and hopelessly. And now? A being sweet as the world — and also good, and also uncommon, and also able (though perhaps not willing) to meet me with intelligence and kindness: something absolutely and incredibly new! This love, the strongest there can be, is from this point of view — *whatever may happen* — my first and only *happy* love.

He had started work again on his epic Florentine play *Fiorenza* that had already pre-occupied him for almost four years. "My work is causing me much trouble," he wrote to Katja. "But this is quite in order and not in itself a bad sign. It has never 'effervesced' and would make me suspicious if it did. It effervesces only for ladies and dilettantes, for the easily satisfied and the ignorant who do not live under the pressure and the discipline of talent."

For talent is not easy, is nothing playful; it is not an ability to perform without hesitation. At heart it is a *necessity,* a critical awareness of the ideal, an insatiability which creates and intensifies the ability it requires, and does so at the cost of some torment. For the greatest, the most insatiable, their talent is the hardest scourge. Once when I was much younger I came on an inconspicuous sentence in Flaubert's letters that I lingered over a long time. He wrote to a friend, at the time he was working on *Salammbô,* I think: "Mon livre me fait beaucoup de douleurs!" Beaucoup de douleurs! Even then I understood that, and since then I have done nothing without repeating this sentence to myself a hundred times, for consolation . . .[27]

Katja sensed how Thomas was now incorporating her within his own creative world, and felt at once frightened and excited. Here no differential calculus could help, nor Röntgen's discoveries. She wrote that she was stupid, felt stupid . . .

"Stupid?" Thomas answered immediately:

If you like. You are so utterly enchanting a creature, my Katja, that for all I care you could be a little stupid. That you aren't, you yourself know best. But if by "stupid" you mean the opposite of "clever" (and I suppose that is it), by all means be so. I am the same way and am pleased to be so. For "cleverness" is something deeply nasty. The "clever" person confines himself to eating no more than two rolls every day, lives cautiously, loves cautiously, and is too cautious to resolutely bind his life to his love. Everything naive, noble, and devout is "stupid", all intrepid devotion on this earth. *Let us be* "stupid", my Katja!

Your letter, your last letter, those few deliciously shy, evasive, promising, ambiguous phrases — can you really guess what a Grail miracle and sign of salvation this little sheet of paper covered with its somewhat childlike scrawl was for me? . . . A store of rapture! And then, by way of reaction, an almost sluggish sinking down in happiness . . .[28]

Behind the "merriment" of his letter, that late August, Thomas was leading up to the great question.

Once, in the good old days, when you still had great respect for me, when you were simply my reader and, who knows, perhaps even "admirer", I told you that in associating with people I was almost never consciously aware of my own worth. That is true. But if I do not have this awareness, I have instead the confidence *that others have it for me*. And arrogant as it may sound, I regard a person's conduct towards me as a criterion of his inner cultivation... People say that a strong emotion elevates and animates a man, must make him bold, joyous, and active; but that is only what people say, though it may be true enough for the common run. Not for me. I am distracted, derailed, alienated from myself . . . But you must not be misled by this, but keep in mind that I am, by my origins and personal merit, fully entitled to hope for you. No matter what kind of faces I may make, you should never forget that you absolutely will not be stooping, absolutely will not be performing an act of condescension, if some day you publicly take the hand I so beseechingly extend.

So the Senator's son made again his lightly-veiled proposal, bearing in mind the warning Dr Seif, the neurologist, had given him. Don't force the girl! Don't press too hard!

September opened with a "festive blue" sky that had been hidden for weeks. "With your letter in my hand I wept like a child," Thomas confessed.

No doubt I would damage myself by this candour if I were dealing with an ordinary girl; but you are not ordinary. If you were, the joys — and sorrows — you give me would be less extraordinary.

Do you remember what I once wrote you: A primitive and vital instinct tells me, in a kind of colloquial and unsophisticated language, that emotions of the sort I have for you cannot be in vain? They cannot!

By mid-September he felt bold enough to write:

Do you know why we suit each other so well? Because you belong to neither bourgeois nor the Junker class. Because you, in your way, are something extraordinary — because you are, as I understand the word, a *princess*. And I — you may laugh now, but you must understand me — I have always seen myself as a kind of prince, and in you I have found, with absolute certainty, my predestined bride and companion.

These were bold assertions indeed, forgetful of all the little details of environment and situation which Thomas, a German Tolstoy, had illumined and recorded for the world: the gossiping friends, the wealthy and — in so many ways — decidedly bourgeois background, however cultured.

But this was love, as he had written in August, something which coloured all things. By late September he was writing:

I think you feel as well as I that it is high time this interim state was ended. Once we belong together publicly . . . won't that be a much cleaner and cozier relationship?

The excitement came to a climax; with the prospect of real matrimony, even sensual arousal:

Oh you amazing, painfully sweet, painfully tangy creature! Longing — *Sehnsucht!* You don't know how I love the word. It is my favourite word, my holy word, my magic formula, my key to the mystery of the world . . .

On 3rd October 1904, Thomas Mann and Katja Pringsheim were officially engaged.

"Along with expressing regret for having missed you," Thomas apologized to Martens, "I can now inform you that *I became engaged to Katja Pringsheim* yesterday. I would be delighted to see you soon." By November he was far advanced enough with the completion of *Fiorenza* to agree to read from the new play in Lübeck and Berlin.

10

Viktor Mann records in his autobiography how pleased their mother, the Frau Senator, was with the match.

Viktor however was still too young to know the envy and ill-will which go hand in hand with a marriage. Julia's, or Lula's, marriage had brought its share of problems, being a marriage without love. But here it was all too obvious how deeply Thomas had fallen for Katja; and this, paradoxically, made the marriage all the more difficult for his family to accept. Heinrich's relations with Thomas were in any case severely strained; the news of Thomas' engagement did nothing to help and Heinrich made no plans to return from Italy for the wedding. Correspondence between the brothers had virtually ceased and their mother became more and more hysterical trying to keep the family peace.

If the matter rested with T. and L's, like the majority of the reading public, criticizing your last novels — but that you turn away from your brother and sister completely makes me *very sad* for you. Hold to them, my dear Heinrich, send them now and then a few friendly lines, and do not let them see that you feel less appreciated by the literary world than Thomas is at the moment — or if you do, then that it does not affect you. You wanted to show a mirror to the world, have earned in places ingratitude and ill-will (admittedly, because people felt personally offended) — but at the same time (to my mind) you have written enough in this vein, and will move in another direction now, won't you? ...

When I told Tommy, by the way, that you had sent me good reviews, he answered roughly: Be grateful that H. sends them to you, the Löhrs and I receive nothing like that from him any more. — H. must know how highly I respect him, even though there was much in his latest novels which I didn't exactly delight in — well that is very reasonable isn't it?

That you brought known people into the *Hunt for Love* in too obvious a fashion is somewhat uncomfortable for Löhr at his job . . . Once again, though, my dear Heinrich, the *next* thing you do after this translation[29] won't disclose such immoral practices, will it? *With all my soul* I would like you also to have success and recognition, for unfortunately no writer can do without them, and as your mother I am pained through and through whenever I have to read a bad review; just as appreciative reviews and judgements, both printed and verbal, and news of financial successes, fill me every time with joy. The translation is going very well, isn't it? — and is something not everyone can do. You are *both* god-gifted boys, dear Heinrich — don't let your relations with T. and L's deteriorate; how can 1½ years have changed everything just because your last books didn't satisfy throughout? It has *nothing to do* with fraternal problems! I will say nothing to them about your letter to me, *you yourself* can best restore relations — that is to say, only if you want me to explain to T. *why* you are staying away the whole winter, or to Löhrs that you feel inwardly alienated from Tommy — then perhaps I would do it; but I feel that would again be underhand on your part, and it would be so much better if you did as I suggest.[30]

Meanwhile Thomas departed to Berlin with his fiancée and her mother. Thomas' reading was due to take place on 29th November before the "Verein für Kunst", the Berlin Art Society.

The newspaper reports mocked his Lübeck accent, the rich Rosenbergs gave a dinner and found them a "pretty little couple"; then Katja's paternal grandfather summoned the jeweller and presented Thomas with the best watch money could buy.

"The vengeful asses in Lübeck worry me less," confessed the Frau Senator to Heinrich after Christmas, "than (between us, please) *T's marriage!*"

By now Thomas' mother had met the Pringsheims: and was sickened by the moneyed heartlessness of it all. She felt Thomas was just a pawn in a rich people's game, she found Katja's parents placing ridiculous expectations on Thomas while expecting nothing of themselves. They understood neither his need to work, to write, nor the Frau Senator's wish that it be a church wedding. "Wedding!" she burst out in her letter to her eldest son. "I, Heinrich, I was *never* in favour of this choice." Though Katja had behaved very sweetly in her presence, she had omitted to send a New Year's card, and her general deference to her parents' wishes made the Frau Senator wonder whether she really loved Thomas as was claimed. The Frau Senator was under the impression that because her New Year's wishes and letter had not been answered, she was being "provoked". "So much money," she wrote, "makes people cold and exacting, makes hard heads, and demands consideration from others which they themselves do not give. I often wonder how Papa would have handled all this. Lula was somewhat upset when I told them my fears, and my concern over T.: she said she believed in Katja's love for T.: oh, God, if only it were so! How many other dear, sweet girls, and less spoilt ones, would have loved him deeper and more faithfully — and tended to him!" And; "Forgive me for making such a fuss, but *if* Tommy were free again (for example his heart!) I think it would relieve me of a great weight."[31]

The Frau Senator need not have worried for Katja was to dedicate herself to Thomas and their children through wealth and poverty, peace and war, as few great writers' wives have ever done.

In the meantime Katja spent her last Christmas holiday with her parents, and Thomas retreated to the country at Polling, in Bavaria, where he hoped to finish *Fiorenza.* There too the Frau Senator foresaw disaster — a play too literary and rarefied for the "general" public. Heinrich moved from Florence back to Dr Hartungen in Riva, finished his translation of *Les liaisons dangereuses* and promptly completed — in a fortnight — his most important essay to date, *Gustave Flaubert and George Sand* — the prototype for the moral literary and political essays which were to establish Heinrich Mann as one of the boldest and most powerful German essayists of the twentieth century.

Heinrich remained in Riva. On 11th February after one postponement, his younger brother Thomas entered the long-awaited, long striven-for state of matrimony: and the relationship between the brothers Mann moved into a new phase.

CHAPTER SIX

Heinrich's Doomed Affair

Neither Carla nor Heinrich attended Thomas' wedding; and as it was a civil affair, the Frau Senator was not even permitted to be present at the ceremony. At breakfast, before Thomas left, she wept.

She had begged Heinrich to come: for Thomas' sake; for her own; and apparently, to dispel the impression created by his novels at the Pringsheims. But Carla was away acting, and Heinrich, in Riva, declined to come. Heinrich felt Thomas had "changed" over the past year — a remark which bitterly hurt Thomas when the Frau Senator told him; but worst of all he detected the aura of wealth and bourgeois arrogance that surrounded the wedding. The Frau Senator's letter describing the event came as no surprise:

Even my cutlery is for everyday use; for the grandparents in Berlin gave them a *commode* with silver for *24 people.* There are things in it you have never seen the like of. *Those* characters must have money!

Professor Pringsheim is furnishing the apartment very nicely and hardly permits any involvement from T., who would be quite able to do it himself . . . The father has already had a telephone installed. I assume he will use it every morning to ask how his daughter is feeling . . . The farewell is of course mere illusion in fact, for K. is staying in Munich and will go as often as she can and wishes to her parents, and they to her; I also *believe* that K. will stay the same, *belonging totally* to them, and in the same dutifully domestic way — though Tommy will be blamed if he so much as once longs for his mother or brothers and sisters.

The honeymoon was in Switzerland, on Lake Zurich, one day to be their refuge against the Nazis and later, when they left America, a home for the twilight of their lives. For the moment, however, it was simply an expensive beginning to marriage: in the Hotel Baur am Zee, with dinner jackets and waiters in livery in the evenings. It was as one such waiter at the hotel that Felix Krull, the protagonist of Thomas' last great novel before he died, was originally intended to appear.

The waiters "rushed about and opened doors".[1] It was the opposite of comfortable, in a spiritual sense. A week after the wedding Thomas was writing to Heinrich that his stomach was suffering, as well as his conscience. He likened the life to Heinrich's *In the Land of Cockaigne,* an "idle and luxurious life"; "and I not infrequently long for a bit more cloistered peace and . . . spirituality." He was unhappy with *Fiorenza,* which he had now completed and despatched to Fischer, convinced it would be rejected.

I resigned myself. It would be a great defeat, but salutary. Ever since *Tonio Kröger* the terms "mind" and "art" had run too close to one another. I had confused the two and set them against one another in the play. It was this that led to the catastrophe, this fiasco in which I attempted to fill an intellectual concept with life. About turn! Back to the Buddenbrook-naiveté!

However, Fischer liked the manuscript. His editor, Oscar Bie, found it "quite exquisite", and it looked as though an "outward success" would result.

"This made me childishly happy," Thomas continued his letter to Heinrich, "but even so, I want to steel myself bravely against public opinion and continue to see the work as an artistic failure." Which brought him to Heinrich's work: "And you? You seem to be brimming over. You seem to have found yourself completely and not to know what it means to lose one's way, or to suffer these inner defeats . . . You realize, of course," came the ominous remark, "that you have lost yourself in the opposite extreme, inasmuch as you are now no more than an artist − whereas a creative artist, a poet, God help me, must be more than just an artist . . ."[2]

Did Thomas really imagine his elder brother was innocent and free of "inner defeats", that his life as a self-imposed exile (for that is what it was becoming) in Italy was calculated to spare him all inner discomfort? Evidently Thomas read in Heinrich's work only self-indulgent artistry and failed to recognize the lonely heart behind the satirical outbursts; considered it correct that he, Thomas, should "submit" to the rigours of happiness; but wrong, or "curious," that Heinrich submit to the ideals of justice, equality and political freedom. It was this misunderstanding that led, inevitably, to their quarrel; and the intervening years appear but a doomed and irregular attempt to maintain contact, to prove basic affection and loyalty. There arose a terrible paradox: that as Thomas "found himself" inwardly in his love for Katja and his marriage, he began to lose himself socio-politically, became more and more reactionary, defensive; while the opposite seems true of Heinrich: that while he "found himself" at last in his dedication to humanitarian and progressive ideals in man, he became further and further estranged from the lonely figure inside like Professor Unrat who longed for tenderness and love;

and finding none, vents his anger upon a world both corrupt and bankrupt in ideals. Nowhere was this more tragically shown than in his affair with the beautiful and self-willed Ines Schmied whom he met with her mother, in Milan, in the spring of 1905.

2

Before he met Ines, there had been only one woman in Heinrich's life, he later confessed[3]: Carla. So close did he feel to her that when she committed suicide, in 1910, Heinrich claimed to have experienced a form of psychic warning, some two hundred miles away.

Carla was the model for the heroine of *The Hunt for Love:* a girl not naturally endowed with theatrical talent who seeks to develop it by the strength of her dedication to the profession.

Carla's decision to become an actress had caused considerable difficulty in the Mann family. Julia was concerned at what people would say; Heinrich felt she should follow her inclination regardless of what people said. Thomas was divided, all too aware that she would never achieve "greatness"; while the Frau Senator sympathized with Carla's desire but dreaded the consequences for her.

The Hunt for Love followed the fortunes — or misfortunes — of an actress, Ute Ende; but also of a weak and conscience-stricken young man called Claude Marehn. Claude loves Ute, but has not the strength of will or character to match her single-minded drive for success and recognition as an actress. In the novella *Schauspielerin* (Actress) Heinrich attempted to delve yet deeper into the problem, involving a near incestuous relationship between an actress and her cousin (a choirmaster). But the actress rejects her cousin's advances and falls in love with a wealthy Jew.

"I am reading your novella with the greatest interest," the Frau Senator wrote to Heinrich in January 1905, "and I find it so psychologically exact that one senses you have studied the three protagonists closely . . . but for my personal taste, the story is sometimes gruelling, because you confided to me last summer — about which I have told *no-one* — that Carla was attached to a Jewish man in Düsseldorf, only his parents were too orthodox. Naturally I involuntarily think of Carla when reading the story, and find myself continually sighing at the thought that she can have suffered in the same way. The choirmaster thus consoles me somewhat — if it isn't Ehrenberg! For that ape did follow Carla around at the time and upset her in Polling; he isn't staying in her neighbourhood now is he?"[4]

Whichever Ehrenberg was meant, the Frau Senator little supposed the choirmaster to be a self-portrait by Heinrich: which undoubtedly it was. Like Professor Unrat, the choirmaster longs for trust and affection, tenderness and proximity. Like Heinrich, the choirmaster uses — and needs — his cousin as the theme of an operatic composition. But his love is doomed to failure; while through her *own* defeat, the actress first achieves success on the stage.

Heinrich, at this time, knew little of stage life, only what his sister had told him. Both *The Hunt for Love* and *Schauspielerin,* therefore, were one-sided. And yet the portrayal of women in them is unusual and remarkable, prefiguring German Expressionism by a decade. The women stand desperate, stripped of gentleness and natural confidence, determined to be more than mothers and wives. The stage promises an escape from domestic slavery, a chance for self-expression, self-realization; but the promise — as in Carla's life — is as destructive as it is enticing.

"Life isn't like that," the literary pundits protested, and either rejected or ignored Heinrich's work. But life all too evidently *was* like that when stripped to essentials, as the Emancipation and Suffragette movements proved. What perhaps most disturbed and distressed readers was the absence of hope. It was what Heinrich Hart had once written about the *Land of Cockaigne:* "nowhere a glimpse of sunlight, no point from which one might obtain relief, a view of the future . . ."

Heinrich felt more and more misunderstood, especially by his family. His new-found Liberalism, his espousal of humanitarian ideals can be seen (as Thomas sensed, but could not fathom) almost as the conquest of private despair.

"Flaubert completes his whole work in a struggle against himself," Heinrich wrote in his celebrated essay, written in January and February 1905.[5] "This final master of realism is no lover of reality; this modernist hates the bourgeois world; this founder of the impersonal novel-style has lyricism he must conceal."

3

Heinrich first met Ines Schmied six weeks after Thomas and Katja were married. Like Thomas, he fell in love at first sight. Like Thomas, his first thoughts were of marriage.

But there, sadly, all similarity ended. Thomas in the end won Katja; Heinrich failed to win Ines.

Like Katja, Ines Schmied was twenty-one when it happened; strikingly pretty, with a spirited temperament, bird-like gestures and the ambition of becoming a singer.

Her father, like Heinrich's maternal grandfather, had emigrated from Germany and become a wealthy merchant, planter, landowner and even explorer, with property in Brazil, Argentina, Paraguay and Bolivia. Two of his sons stayed with him in South America, helping the government to "open up" the interior, while his wife, his son Rudolf, and his only daughter Ines went on a prolonged tour of Europe. Heinrich met them in Milan at the end of March, 1905. A surviving post-card, dated 2.4.1905, in Ines' hand, suggests a rendez-vous outside the post office, in the afternoon.

Heinrich must have been on his way to Florence, for the next communication came from him there on 11th April. It stated he would be passing through Milan on his way to meet his sister and hoped he might be permitted to take Ines for a walk at half-past three. The Schmieds then came to stay in Florence for a while.

"My dear friend," Ines was writing on 19th April, "I cannot tell you how much I look forward to seeing you again tomorrow. I feel such longing for you, and yet I don't wish to be sentimental, it is not my style . . ." The handwriting was wild and uncontrolled.

An American, with whom she now broke, had been courting Ines. The Schmieds then moved away from Florence; on 28th May, however, Heinrich met Ines in Spezia, in Ines' hotel-room, out of earshot of her mother. Then Ines departed to Fiesole, outside Florence, Heinrich, Ines' mother and her brother Rudolf to Dr von Hartungen's clinic at Riva. For the next two months Ines and Heinrich corresponded, Heinrich writing almost every day, Ines more irregularly, but equally emotionally. She read his latest novella and was "almost proud" of Heinrich. "I don't know why I need you so much" — she turned now to the intimate "Du" — "whilst you make no demands on me and seem, I think, to like me, despite my weaknesses. I long for you, but you mustn't come here. It would attract too much attention."[6]

They tried, then, to keep their love a secret. Why, it is impossible to say, unless they were afraid Ines' mother would disapprove. As Thomas had once done with Frau Pringsheim, Heinrich now made every effort to appease Ines' mother at Riva, befriending Rudolf and reading his work to them.

"I have the feeling that if I were now to say to her, 'I love your daughter,' she would not have any objections to me," Heinrich wrote at the end of June,[7]

I was very pleased to hear that she wrote nice things about me. I court the affection of your mother not because I need it, but because I like her and do not wish to be guilty of dishonesty. My conscience plagues me whenever I come to her with a letter of yours in my wallet. Some queer moments arise through this secret of ours. Recently Rudolf was talking with me about the engagement of Dr Hartungen's daughter, which was quite obvious though nothing was said about it. Rudolf exclaimed: — "the doctor hasn't told you! If my sister were to get engaged, I would surely feel obliged to tell you!"

Secretly they had in fact become engaged, on the understanding they would marry as soon as Ines had completed her voice-training. But the days became long, she didn't like going out into "the crowd", and though she had asked Heinrich not to come to Fiesole, she eventually broke down. She was ashamed of ever having felt attracted by a man of "such un-fine character" as the American, whereas Heinrich appeared to be "faultless"; indeed he probably kept a list of her "failings", she wrote, because he himself had "so few", and she "felt a real fear of that".[8]

It was Heinrich's pride, his stiffness and haughtiness which made even Thomas afraid, that was the problem. Heinrich had written to say he was now on poor terms with Carla, who was staying with him in Riva, and again Ines felt guilty. "I can't tell you how sorry I am," she apologized, "and that I am the cause of it."[9] Surely one could "love two people at the same time", she wrote on the 25th June. "Naturally I want to remain the more important one to you. You write that you love your sister so dearly. Her trust and intimacy cannot suddenly cease — perhaps for a while, but not for ever."

"You know," she went on, "I think your affection for your sister is not so much because of the person she is, but more your need to care for someone, to be able to think of someone, to show her your tenderness."

Some historians have hinted at an abnormally close relationship between Heinrich and his sister Carla, but there is no shred of evidence pointing to incestuous love. As in so many distinguished families, birth had given Heinrich a pride which made it difficult for him to bend. By reason of her sister-relationship, her devotion to Heinrich as her "big" brother, and her passion for art rather than social pretensions, Heinrich had indeed grown to feel a special bond with Carla — quite in contrast to his contempt for Lula's hypocritical bourgeois world in Munich. That Carla should feel threatened by Ines was only natural, but it never seriously affected Heinrich's feelings for Ines. Ines at last had breached the thirty-four-year-old novelist's defensive pride, his apparent coldness and hostility to the world. But did she love him enough to build a whole life on this?

"Tomorrow I shall be going to Venice for the Whitsun holiday," Heinrich wrote to Ines on 9th June 1905;

> but before I go I must talk to you once more. Do you remember when we thought we might meet each other again in Venice? I didn't tell you then that I loved you, I pressed for this meeting in Venice simply out of fear of losing you. How things have changed! This morning I was out walking, alone, up a hill planted with olives, and again I became aware of now belonging to those who with confidence may think of someone lovingly. I remember exactly how impossible a really intimate relationship with a woman used to seem to me. That it has happened with you! That I was able to tell you this! That you liked everything about me and felt, feature by feature, as I did! (As far as one can with another person one loves. Complete equality would not be desirable, I think; it would reduce the excitement of being close to a young woman.) To have come closer with every meeting, and almost without my doing anything, simply — as it seems to me — through the force of our inner attraction! That is something which I still cannot explain to you, something so incomprehensive, so magical. That is to say, the incomprehensible, the enchanting is you, my sweet Nena!

On the strength of this new affection Heinrich had written another novella, *Der Unbekannte* (The Stranger), which was published in book form the following year.[10] It was an autobiographical tale, set in Lübeck, about the passionate but unrequited love of an adolescent schoolboy for the wife of one of the city consuls, Frau Vermühlen. It wonderfully recaptures the torment of precocious but inarticulate youth, and the climate is masterly. In his desperate and secret love for the Frau Consul, Raffael, the boy, imagines she is being poisoned by her husband. "I love her, I love her,"

Raffael repeats. His friend, Albert Bishop, the son of an English merchant, finds his concern ridiculous:

Bishop remarked curtly: "Love means nothing to me. Have you kissed the woman yet?"

"What do you think?" stammered Raffael.

"Hm, all the better. I shall never kiss anybody, except my parents and my sister. I find it unmanly."

Raffael excused his feelings.

"She is very, very unhappy. She is either being beaten by her husband or poisoned, I'm not sure. She used to walk so quickly; now she goes so terribly slowly. Her hands, her whole body I think are swollen — she can hardly move."

Raffael arranges to rescue and elope with her, intending to use one of his father's steamships whose Captain he knows. In the end, of course, all becomes clear. Raffael rushes to his father when Frau Vermühlen faints at the ball, telling him she has been poisoned; but she is not poisoned, and Raffael's mother's remark, "Well, it's happened, who would have thought him capable of it," on returning one day from the Vermühlens is at last understood in the correct light. She is merely expecting a child.

This was the novella which made Ines so "proud" of Heinrich. "Have you read it to my mother?" she wrote on 14th June. "How much . . . oh for how much must I thank you, I don't know where to begin. Your novella delighted me, I find it very, very sensitive."

But now Heinrich found it difficult to think clearly, and work was impossible:

Whatever stimulates my imagination leads inevitably to thoughts of you. Today I finished reading a wonderful novel by Jean Bertheroy . . . It is the story of a woman who never gets beyond longing. She cannot reach love because she wants too much to control her own destiny and will not give herself to love. But we have given ourselves, haven't we? It is stronger than our will; it binds us to another person; — but I get panic-stricken when I think I might ever be untied, without bonds again. You must remain my law, my standard; I want to live with you and for you, always. This decision I have come to, quite firmly, now that we are apart. The only thing that worries me, is the fear of ever disappointing you, of not satisfying you, of sometimes appearing dull or feeble, or letting you see my bad moods. Do you think that possible? Am I right in all respects? Tell me, now that you are far away from me, what you think about us: whether, after consideration, you still feel so deeply attached to me as I to you.[11]

He wanted Ines to declare her love, he was anxious at the news from her mother that they were going to London for the summer, her singing instruction would have to be shelved, and thus their marriage "postponed even further".

Ines had written hardly at all. Heinrich became nervous and agitated, especially at the news — again from her mother — that Ines was not well.

He enclosed pills and prescriptions with his letters, chided her for not writing, insisted she give up tea, approved her mother's suggestion she come to Riva in September for a cure.

We can go for wonderful walks alone through the olive groves and in the rowing boat on the lake I can tell my little Nena how much I love her . . .

His words sounded perhaps too desperately avuncular for a twenty-one-year-old, particularly his mention of Ines' mother, the fact that he felt she suspected something now — "and is not in the least bit less friendly towards me!"

"Be good and answer me quickly," he finished his letter of 24th June. But Ines answered she felt miserable and depressed, was losing faith in her voice, and wondered whether life was really worth living. It was the first indication of her extreme morbidity which seemed to go with bouts of great wilfulness and ambition. Heinrich answered with wise words about the nature of talent and happiness, encouragement over her singing, and more suggestions for gargling and headache relief. A few days later Ines put an end to this tame and sentimental correspondence. She asked Heinrich to do what he should already have done had he not been so concerned to placate Ines' mother: abduct her!

4

My dearest Nena,

Without a moment's hesitation I tell you I will come wherever you wish! From my last letter you will be aware of the hard struggle I was having with reason. But now you give me the signal, discarding reason: let us throw it to the winds then!

Heinrich suggested they meet on Wednesday 5th July.

Tell me please, immediately, if this is all right. I look forward to it very, very much. It will be as unplanned as that time in Spezia. That is the best way: le divin imprévu. Who would have thought we would be seeing each other again so soon . . .[12]

Ines replied by return of post[13] that she agreed with "everything". Her letter was necessarily short: "I am so excited at the prospect of seeing you soon that I cannot write . . ."

The arrangement meant a complicated series of explanations by Heinrich to his sister, Ines' brother Rudolf — with whom he had intended to go to Munich — and most important of all, Ines' mother. But for good or for bad Heinrich managed to do this. He persuaded the doctor his catarrh was better, and he and Ines met in the Tuscan hills.

It was a doomed relationship, of course. In his heart of hearts the Senator's son wanted to be married, with the security and intimacy which only marriage could bring. It was the dream behind his novella *The Marvel* in 1897, the matrix of idealistic longing. But it was to be another eight years before he found the woman to fulfil this dream.

The elopement lasted six days. On 13th July Heinrich wrote from Munich:

My dear, dear little Nena,

It is no fun without you, you can believe me! After my departure the day before yesterday, I felt only gloomy and depressed. Then, thinking of what we had last talked about, I was overcome by a kind of mild anxiety.

From others to whom I had once been close, I said to myself, I withdrew because they rejected my books, because they didn't understand that the man and the artist in the end are one person, or at least that books issue from certain, perhaps unhappy experiences of a man. To reject his work, therefore, means only to want the happy side of him, the superficial side, means not basically to be interested in him . . .

That is the way others act; — and that is the way those I love are behaving (I said to myself) and with whom I want to be one! It is horrible! For one moment I set your memory aside and foresaw only complete and final solitude, loneliness. This I must tell you, you must realize what I have gone through, perhaps as a penance for the all-too-wonderful days — and nights — in Abetone! But then, as I travelled through the sensuous Italian night, your being came back to me, my dear, dear Nena, and your love rested once more with me and I knew in all the world only this: "I love her, and I never, never want to lose her! Even if she understands nothing of that which I write. But the truth is that since I have got to know her, I am no longer the same person, nor do I write the same. What I write now I hope she will understand (she is so clever!) that in a certain nervous and spiritual state it would be dishonest to reproduce nature as the simple mind sees it; that the violence, the feverish and the grotesque are sometimes the only right and proper manner. And whether she likes this or not: the most important thing is that she likes him who simply takes her in his arms and calls her his dear, dear Nena. The best thing about me is probably this: that I love her. And she recognizes this . . ." When once I had made this clear to myself, I travelled much happier through the night.

Here was Heinrich's self-revelation. It showed how different he was from Thomas, and proved how deeply he was hurt by Thomas' rejection of his work, and the rejection of the rest of his family. In rejecting his work, he felt, they were rejecting him.

Heinrich hoped that in accepting him, in loving him, Ines would also accept and exercise understanding towards his work. But his anxiety on this point proved well-founded; for when Ines now began to read his earlier novels she too was distressed. She could find no excuse for their immorality, their lapses of taste and decorum. They seemed to drive a new wedge between the two rather than bind them closer. The question of marriage was put off still further. And though Heinrich tried for the next four years, Ines would not agree. They met, they stayed (to the anger of her father in the Argentine who was concerned about her reputation) in the same towns and in the same places; but for two years their engagement remained secret, and for a further two, once public, it teetered between on and off. From wanting to be a singer, Ines changed to wanting to be an actress and then a writer or playwright too. She tortured her father (who thought the match with Heinrich a good one) and she eventually drove Heinrich to despair. She was unstable perhaps. But like Heinrich's sister Carla she wanted to achieve something individual, and neither contemporary society nor her own nature augured for her success.

But whether his relationship with Ines fail or prosper it had gone further and deeper than any Heinrich had known before. "This founder of the impersonal novel-style has lyricism he must conceal," were the words Heinrich had written of Flaubert. Now he too, master of the grotesque in the modern European novel, had a lyricism he must hide.

5

A "family gathering" had been arranged for the weekend following Heinrich's arrival in Munich; but as Heinrich put in a postscript to his letter of 13th July to Ines: "without you I have no family".

No one but Carla was told about their engagement; and Carla, too, felt estranged from the family.

Heinrich then moved out to the country, to Rossholzen on the Inn; and from there he wrote to try and reassure his now doubting fiancée:

My delightful little Nena!

No, I know you don't simply reject what doesn't appeal to you or seem comprehensible: you are too serious, too genuine a being for that. But it hurts me to think you are now less clear and content than you used to be. Is it my fault with my novels? You already knew a number of awful things in literature — think of the story of the peasant-farmer and his mother. But there one was able to rise again with the great power of the work, I suppose; and one cannot do that with the Duchess of Assy.

I'd like to tell you my own opinion about what is dissatisfying in the book: the fact that the great pagan sensuality which is celebrated in the work is not acutally the real ideal. It is just a substitute for something higher, but in which no-one believes. You must remember: I had never experienced love, had never encountered anything worthy of love. I claimed that everything depended on sensuality because I lacked nourishment for my tenderness: and the louder I claimed it, the less I believed inwardly in it.

I was not exactly lying; one can convince oneself of many things. But the time had really come to make an end of youthful sensuality; and yet at the same time my need for real love became stronger and stronger; and it is just this that gives the *Hunt for Love* its passionate streak. (The book has been completely misunderstood. It has been taken as an effusion of sensuality: it goes much deeper.) Now it follows that you like *Unrat* more than the *Duchess.* That which is closer to *you* in time, to the time that I met you, must also be closer to you in person; inwardly I was slowly maturing, preparing for the moment when I would meet you . . . *Unrat,* that laughable old monster, does at least feel love for Künstlerin Fröhlich, defends her before the whole world, heaps on her all his wounded tenderness. For that reason he is more human than the Duchess, and that is why you understand him better. He has (don't take fright!) some similarities with me: and him, who loves you; whilst with everyone that stands in the *Göttinnen* I feel hardly any relationship . . .

What I now intend to write brings the whole story into focus. I am changing my sex (as an artist one is bisexual); and the servant who at length asks for 50,000 marks, represents the period of sensuality. At the end tenderness at last is permitted to break out; and everyone will be happy. One is no longer innocent, no longer so young; but with a little melancholy and plenty of knowledge in one's heart, one reaches happiness. Does the idea appeal to you, my dear, dear Nena?[14]

This was the conception behind *Zwischen den Rassen* (Between the Races).

Curiously, like Thomas' *Royal Highness* which was also written at this time, with the same theme in mind, *Zwischen den Rassen* was commercially more successful than Heinrich's previous novels (Langen printed a first edition of 2,000 copies, rising to 4,000 the same year), but artistically a failure. It had pace, character, dialogue and range. But love is the hardest thing of all to render directly; and both *Royal Highness* and *Zwischen den Rassen* were products of the will to write about love rather than products of artistic inspiration. "It was a novel of high-life, with a happy ending," Thomas later characterized his *Royal Highness,*[15] "almost suitable for a serial in a magazine." The style, as he admitted, was nothing more than "dignified journalese". It could "not compare with *Buddenbrooks*", it was "a pen-trial", the "work of a young married man". It was, as he said, "a stage of progress . . . without which neither *The Magic Mountain* nor *Joseph and His Brothers* could have been written".

Nevertheless, the brothers had found at least the love and confidence they sought. *"I am filled with the conviction that we must keep together,"* Thomas added to his letter of mid-October 1905; and underlined the sentence. It was as though he had sensed the change in Heinrich without having been told of Ines. Heinrich's private qualms about Katja's family he kept to himself and Carla; towards Thomas he now re-assumed the role of the elder, wiser, protecting brother. When Thomas wrote in November 1905 to voice his misgivings over the publication of his play *Fiorenza*, Heinrich wrote him a letter which brought him "to tears".[16] Thomas read it to Katja, and had it read to his sister Julia by her husband Löhr. "I always thought *Fiorenza* would bring you two together again," said Lula with characteristic blindness.

Fiorenza was merely the outward sign. They were brothers now in love as well as birth and upbringing. When *Blood of the Walsungs* — Thomas' latest novella — threatened to create a scandal in the family, Thomas again wrote to Heinrich for his advice. Heinrich recommended he should go ahead with the story, despite its anti-semitic or potentially anti-semitic overtones. He also dedicated to Thomas his new short-story *Abdankung* (Abdication), in which a clever school bully suddenly abdicates and makes himself utterly servile, obeying each command an idle, fat schoolboy gives him, finally to the point of drowning.

Thomas was overjoyed. He called it a "strangely strange, profound thing", a tale of "the perverse tragedy of genius in the form of a schoolboy-story, to my mind the most personal and extraordinary piece you have ever written".[17]

But was it just a tale of genius, the desire to be rid of one's own power over others, to show ordinary people their own strength? With its dedication to Thomas, was it not also a form of confession: the lonely being who at heart wishes to *belong,* not be leader: and thus finally humiliates himself?

At any rate a new spirit had entered their relationship. Past jealousies and misunderstandings were set aside. Thomas felt that at last he had been "accepted" as the successful younger brother; and in his *Royal Highness* he also introduced the theme of abdication by making the Grand Duke Albrecht abdicate in favour of his younger brother, who is healthier, more popular with the people, and enjoys the role of representation. "The artist is like a prince," Thomas later explained to Hilde Distel,[18] "in so far as, like the latter, he conducts a *representative* existence."

Royal Highness was a simple allegory on Thomas' life and love. As long as he was able to think of Heinrich as the elder brother he had always admired since childhood, there was no problem: and *Royal Highness* is an interesting reflection of the mythology Thomas had concocted and wished to preserve in relation to his elder brother.

Albrecht is portrayed as sickly, wise and shy — whereas Klaus Heinrich, the younger brother is a "Sunday child" for whom "everything turns up trumps". "I've always looked up to you because I've always known that you are the superior and higher of us two," confesses Klaus Heinrich at one point to his elder brother, "and that I am only a plebeian compared with you. But if you think me worthy to stand at your side and to bear your title and to represent you to the people . . . then I thank you and put myself at your feet."

There was a mildly democratic flavour to the novel — a spirit which Heinrich would be amongst the first to welcome. But how deep did it really go: and could Thomas really pretend to respect the convictions Heinrich now held?

Because of his family, because of his literary problems Thomas was anxious that there be no split. He needed Heinrich's support, and without hesitation Heinrich gave it. Yet artistically, politically and even personally it was only a papering of the cracks: just as the nations of Europe itself made diplomatic and military agreements which in time were bound to fail.

CHAPTER SEVEN

The Brink of Exhaustion

"I know very well there are people in Lübeck who see in me the infamous bird who defiles his own nest," Thomas wrote to the *Lübecker General-Anzeiger* in November 1905. It was the opening salvo of a self-defence that became known, when rewritten for the *Münchner Neueste Nachrichten*, as *Bilse and I.*

The circumstances were trivial in the extreme. A Lübeck novelist had been sued for libel, and in his defence a slighting reference to *Buddenbrooks* had been made, putting Thomas' masterpiece in the category of "Bilse-type" novels (Bilse had written a scandalous milieu-novel, *Aus einer kleinen Garnison* in 1903).

"These people do me an injustice," Thomas complained:

— I don't know by what I can swear this, for they don't believe anything is sacred to me. But if I may speak as a Lübecker, a member of a Lübeck family, then permit me to say: I have done just as much for the honour of my family and my hometown in my own way as my father, who is perhaps not completely forgotten in Lübeck, in *his* own way. In a hundred thousand Germans I have awakened interest in Lübeck life and being, I have drawn the attention of a hundred thousand people to the old gabled house in the Mengstrasse, have ensured that a hundred thousand people would consider it an interesting recollection to have met the original models for the characters in my book, and it is not impossible that in times to come people will still enjoy reading about them when we are all long since resting in our graves.

Without notion of family and hometown, without love for them, such books as *Buddenbrooks* cannot be written; and whoever knows me, whoever has followed my subsequent works, will know how deeply despite all artistic licence, I have remained a citizen of Lübeck.

Throughout his life Thomas remained anxious to win the recognition of his home town; but his plea in the winter of 1905 was motivated by more than righteous indignation over Bilse. The courtship of Katja, the necessity to tailor himself to the wishes and expectations of the Arcisstrasse, had required enormous will and tenacity. For a while, amid the presents, the literary readings and the visits to Berlin, he had been able to relax. But now *Blood of the Walsungs* had affronted the Pringsheims, the editor of the *Rundschau* wanted him to rephrase some of the more obviously semitic expressions, and Thomas began to feel his entire artistic being on trial. It was this, more than anything, which prompted his self-defence in Lübeck and Munich; and it was in this situation that he turned, as in years before, to his brother Heinrich. And Heinrich, struggling to win the hand of Ines, gave Thomas the support he needed, both privately and, where necessary, publicly. This period of renewed trust and understanding between the brothers was heralded publicly by Heinrich's knightly defence of Thomas' *Fiorenza* in *Die Zukunft* in March 1906 — a demonstration of faith that would be broken publicly only nine years later by the publication of Heinrich's bitter allegorical essay *Zola*.

2

Despite Thomas' letter to the *Lübecker General-Anzeiger* defending the privilege of the artist, and Heinrich's encouragement to stand firm over his new novella, Thomas' *Blood of the Walsungs* did *not* appear.

It was intended to be a parody of Wagner-worship, and a play on the incestuous emotions and themes behind such music. Unfortunately the protagonists — Siegmund and Siegelinde — were too reminiscent of Katja and her twin Klaus, as was the Aarenhold household of the Pringsheim "palace" in the Arcisstrasse in Munich. Perhaps unconsciously Thomas was giving vent to feelings he had otherwise had to suppress, of impotence amidst such wealth. At any rate he did not send the story to Frau Pringsheim as he had *At the Prophet's;* word only filtered through to the Pringsheims after the story was already set in type for the *Neue Rundschau* — and the first real crisis of Thomas' married life blazed up.

There was only one thing for Thomas to do. To affront the Pringsheims publicly when he had married their daughter, had been set up by them in a new flat and had accepted a regular allowance from them would have been worse than tactless. Thomas telegraphed Berlin; and such was his standing already — and Fischer's integrity — that the whole edition of the *Rundschau* was pulped and reprinted without Thomas' tale. It was not a very good novella, in fact, and even though not intended maliciously, its racialist tone was incontrovertible. Its publication might well have exploded Thomas'

Bilse and I thesis, quite apart from the ill-will it would have caused within Katja's family. It was better so. But every artist needs the reminder of a grateful audience, however irregular, and the suppression of *Blood of the Walsungs* can only have made Thomas feel more defensive, more misunderstood, less "humanly and socially free"; "a feeling of lack of freedom which," Thomas wrote in his letter to Heinrich, "becomes extremely oppressive in moments of hypochondria, and you will no doubt call me a cowardly bourgeois. But you can talk. You are absolute. In contrast I have at least submitted to a constitution.[1]"

Amid this "dearth of fresh fame" caused by the suppression of his novella, Thomas was pleased, then, to note how well his cultured, polished Renaissance drama *Fiorenza* was beginning to do. Fischer had ordered a second impression which, as he pointed out to its author, was the equivalent of "ten printings of a novel". However the good news turned out to be only a lull before the next attack on his honour. And this time it was delivered by none other than Richard Schaukal — the "friend" who had already indirectly tilted at Heinrich and been dropped recently from Thomas' circle on account of his continuous "boorishness". Thomas was mortified by the piece Schaukal wrote. It appeared in the *Berliner Tageblatt* on 5th March 1906, began with laudatory words about Thomas and his well-deserved literary reputation; and then proceeded to tear his play *Fiorenza* apart as no one had ever done before, adding as many gratuitous slights as Schaukal could bring to bear.

Against this form of personal envious attack Thomas, strangely, was almost defenceless. The writer who conceals his self in his work has a shield against personal criticism; and perhaps that was what had saved *Buddenbrooks* from worse treatment among those who were offended by it. But all Thomas' subsequent work had borne a deeply subjective and autobiographical character. He had exposed his heart — however "cold" critics might call it — and in the hands of the unscrupulous this became a dangerous thing. Schaukal's character assassination, in the guise of a review, of *Fiorenza*, was only a foretaste of what was to come. "A frosty coldness emanates from the work," Schaukal wrote,[2] " . . . a complete failure . . . Mann is not at ease, he seems embarrassed and conceals it behind the drapery of his words . . . One thing becomes clear: Mann is not the kind of writer who is going to surprise us, he is no Proteus, no many-sided author. Where he cannot be his worthy comfortable self, he will inevitably disappoint us."

Small wonder Thomas felt stricken. Yet he found he could not reply to this attack since to do so, he wrote to Heinrich, would reduce him to a nervous wreck. "You cannot imagine how gruelling the thought of a polemic is to me, how tortured I am by inner conflict," he explained — while deploring the fact that none of his friends or admirers seemed willing to put Schaukal, the "small-minded and righteous fool" in his place, either publicly or privately.[3]

So Heinrich now rose, sword in hand, to defend his younger brother. His piece *Mache* (Shame) was published in the March issue of Maximilian Harden's

radical magazine *Die Zukunft*. He turned the tables on Schaukal, exposed
the critic's own infinitely more disappointing novels, and defended Thomas'
right to use history, the effect of famous names and the distance of past
centuries to tell "all the more colourfully his own, always his own destiny".

It was a sparkling rejoinder, a thousand words long, as stylistically entertaining as it was effective. The Frau Senator wept to see her sons at last under
the same colours again; and for Thomas it was like their childhood years:
"someone does something to me, and my elder brother comes and avenges
me," he thanked Heinrich.[4]

Samuel Lublinski, the Berlin critic, had said to Thomas on a visit to
Munich that there was a "fanatical group of admirers" of Heinrich among
the "rising generation" in Berlin.[5] It seemed as if, slowly, the recognition
that had been denied Heinrich for so long was also beginning to take root.

But were they really fighting on the same side now? Or had personal
circumstances merely brought them together for a while — only to tear
them apart with a vengeance when the time came?

Simultaneously with Heinrich's article in *Die Zukunft* appeared an article
on the brothers Mann by none other than Kurt Martens. It was published in
the *Leipziger Tageblatt*,[6] and the idea had appealed to Thomas. "You are the
right person to do it," he had told Martens, "for you know how to do *both*
of us justice. Every other writer would play the one against the other."[7]
But when Martens' article came out, dressing Thomas in the same colours as
Heinrich — both "at odds with their people", both likely "like Heine, Grill-
parzer and Platen" to arouse "more respect than love" — Thomas was the
first to put the record straight. Their dedication to their profession, Martens
claimed, made both Heinrich and Thomas "exclusive", made them haughty
towards anything of "flesh and blood", gave them an "icy hostility towards
human beings", a "hot and imperious passion for all creative things, in
particular for their own art, their own talents, their own world". Heinrich —
"this most repulsive of all German writers to the average reader" — was
a "master of caricature, the fiercest enemy of the German bourgeoisie from
which he comes", a man who made "no bones of his contempt for Germans
and their way of life". Thomas, however, was of a "much softer nature",
stood somewhat "helpless" before his youth and school experiences —
whereas Heinrich overcame the latter with "biting scorn". If Heinrich were
to be found behind any of his own characters, you could be sure it would
be one of the less "sympathetic" ones, which made him more objective than
his brother.

"Never before in German fiction," Martens claimed, had the human
psyche been "so closely and sensitively observed to its last, most delicate
fibres", nor its motives laid bare.

He regretted their tendency to portray friends and colleagues in their
works, descriptions as "unmistakeable as they are artistically without point".
"*Bilse and I,*" Martens wrote, "would convince no one." "The proud rejection of all human considerations," as he put it, "in favour of the purely
artistic may be the only criterion for him [Thomas] as an artist, but human

society — to which, whether voluntarily or not, he belongs — will always find the consequences of social recklessness unpleasant."

"But this much can be said now," Martens concluded, "that Heinrich has the stronger temperament, the more open mind, the more wide-reaching education; while Thomas has the more tender feelings and the deeper knowledge of man."

With these words the article ended; and incited Thomas to yet another self-defence, this time in a personal letter to Martens:

It won't do to attribute to me "icy misanthropy" and "lovelessness toward everything of flesh and blood", which is "replaced" by a fanatic worship of art. Both *Tonio Kröger* and *Fiorenza* are full or irony for life which verges on the inartistic in its overtones and directness. It won't do to call *Buddenbrooks* a "destructive" book. "Critical" and "sardonic" it may be — but not destructive. Must one write dithyrambs to establish oneself as an affirmer of life? Every good book that is written against life is actually tempting its readers on behalf of life . . .[8]

On the question of whether he lacked imagination Thomas' indignation boiled.

It won't do to say that I "would like to put creative imagination on a par with cheap-novel ingenuity". In fact, I simply do not regard the gift of inventing characters and plots as the essence of the art of writing. Every lyric poet who can do nothing but express his own soul proves that I am right. And I am, after all, a lyric poet (at heart). I maintain that writers who have nothing but inventiveness are not far from cheap novelty. I maintain that there are very great writers who invented nothing throughout their whole lives but merely poured their souls into traditional casts and created anew. I maintain that Tolstoy's work is at least as strictly autobiographical as my own tiny contribution. "Fantasy"? You must admit that I have some gift for detail, some liveliness and modernity, one or two shafts of perception and *power of vision*. And what does this all amount to if not fantasy? (To say nothing of linguistic fantasy and invention.) "*Creative* imagination"? But I *have* created, you know! Terribly little as yet — four medium-good books — but they do *exist*. What more do you people want?

The attempt to put him on an ascetic, humanly-hostile pedestal, opposed to all pleasures of the flesh, Thomas utterly disdained:

I am ascetic only insofar as my *conscience* directs me to achievement rather than pleasure or "happiness" . . .

"I don't believe," he added, "that anyone today can be a *bon vivant* and at the same time an artist . . . man is not strong or perfect enough to do so. One must decide, and my conscience decides for achievement . . ."

"And now just one more thing," he finished:

You say that one of these days, if I am ever to become somebody, I will receive more cool respect than heartfelt affection. Dear friend, that is simply not true . . . *Buddenbrooks* and *Tonio Kröger*, these expressions of my self, are *loved*, believe me, and to such an extent that I might well feel disturbed. "Am I so soft, so insipid, so mediocre," I have more than once asked myself, "that I should be loved like this?" No matter. Since I am neither frivolous nor whimsical nor tart nor stiff I do not see why, if my work should prove lasting, Germans should refuse to love me in the future. What aspects of my humanity would they take exception to?

"These are the sorts of things I objected to in your essay," Thomas wound up his letter to Martens in March 1906. "I am pretty sure that my brother too would have similar reservations," he added, "this Heinrich Mann whom you describe as so egoistically solitary and who, right now, in the most expansive way, is doing battle in the newspapers for Professor Murri."

For once again, in the columns of *Die Zukunft* Heinrich had turned advocate for the defence, this time in connection with a murder trial. The "fiercest enemy of the German bourgeoisie", who "made no bones of his contempt for German being", the man with an "icy hostility toward human beings" was showing himself to be remarkably human.

3

Thomas was saying to Kurt Martens in the spring of 1906 that he was neither haughty nor exclusive, neither anti-German nor anti-life. He was merely shy; and compelled by his conscience to choose the path of achievement rather than pleasure.

But instinctively Thomas also felt the epithets to be unfair on Heinrich; and eight weeks later, at the beginning of June 1906, his suspicions about Heinrich were confirmed. Heinrich wrote in confidence and told him of his engagement to Ines.

A few days previously Thomas had returned from a fourteen-day visit to Dresden and a nearby sanatorium. There he had been reading Heinrich's latest volume of novellas *Stürmische Morgen;* and for almost the first time Thomas complimented Heinrich without reserve. He had read the novellas "eagerly and in one go as I have hardly ever done with another book".[9]

For several months rumours of Heinrich's secret engagement had been circulating in the family and among friends: and Thomas, whose wife was four months pregnant, looked at the novellas with curious eyes, anxious to know if love had in any way altered Heinrich's style and preoccupations; and conversely what the stories might reveal of this love itself.

There was *Jungfrauen,* which he had already read ("it showed too obviously the traces of hastiness", he had written to Heinrich at the time, October 1905), *Abdankung* — the story Heinrich had dedicated to Thomas — and now *Der Unbekannte,* Heinrich's tale of Lübeck adolescence.

"I admire *Der Unbekannte* very much," Thomas wrote, "and imagine that there are few who can appreciate it as deeply as I, who know and feel its most personal symbolism . . ." It was a "brilliant book", he summarized, "which shows all your best qualities, your terrific pace, your famous 'lash', the delightful pregnancy of your words, your quite astounding virtuosity to which one surrenders because without doubt it arises directly from passion. These four stories will foster your growing fame."[10]

Thomas had already somewhat "disgraced" himself at the *Neue Rundschau* for recommending "the most frightful rubbish out of simple goodwill". But his praise of Heinrich's work was now genuine enough, and his response to Heinrich's revelatory letter carried the same enthusiasm.

"It seems," he wrote back to Heinrich on 11th June 1906, "to be a similar relationship to the one between me and Katja before we married, despite the difference in the kind of women and the external circumstances. You are united, you are sure of yourselves (sure of one another and sure of your own selves) — and that already is a more favourable position than the one I was in. Outward problems of any permanence do not appear to bar your way. I see in this so much happiness — for me as well; for it is not out of the question that you might spend part of the year in Munich with your wife, and that could provide a wonderful and comfortably stimulating life together . . ."

"But you say your fiancée is a singer?" Thomas queried with inevitable anxiety, "Professionally? Won't that entail a life of travelling? I'm not sure if I should actually wish you that! For as much as I approve of a certain movement, freedom, restlessness, uncertainty, nevertheless I seem to remember from earlier days that you also have a distinct need for settling down and 'bourgeois' regularity . . . Well, that must all be solved in one way or another."

But it was not. Ines still concealed the engagement from her parents and her brother Rudolf, all letters had to be addressed in an unidentifiable hand and, where possible, the postman had to be warned. Heinrich's novel, *Zwischen dan Rassen,* begun so eagerly in Rossholzen in the summer of 1905, had begun to slow down now — as had Thomas' *Royal Highness.* Heinrich had asked his mother for her recollections of infancy in South America. He now changed his sex, as he explained to Ines, and proceeded to chronicle the fortunes of Lola, a South-American girl who is seduced by a sensual fake, and only at the end aspires to real love. It was really an allegory on Heinrich's own life.

4

Royal Highness meanwhile took up most of Thomas' working time from the summer of 1906 until spring 1909. However, there is evidence that Thomas — though he was mortified by the contempt of Heinrich's friends for the book — did not himself take it seriously as a work of art or literature. It was important to him because of the love-story it contained — for which Katja had loaned Thomas his old love-letters to her; when Kurt Martens published a review referring to the "lower race" of the heroine, Thomas was so insulted that he called an end to their friendship. Yet in truth the writing of the book "bored" him. It was a "child's game", as he called it.[11]

What he really wished to do was write a novel of greatness, about Frederick of Prussia. "My 'Frederick' — now that is something quite different," he wrote proudly to Heinrich at the beginning of 1906.[12] Heinrich had questioned his "historical instinct;" but as Thomas made clear, his aim was not history but the representation of something timeless: namely greatness:

> The real presumption in the undertaking seems to me not so much that I, so subjectively unhistorical, intend to write a historical novel, as that I, as a poet, am undertaking to portray *greatness* — because for that one needs knowledge of greatness, experience, personal experience *in* greatness . . . Do I have that?

Such thoughts put him into a "mood of feverish exaltation":

> if I could achieve in large what I am told I have done in small: namely making greatness tangible, intimate, alive — then my pride will know no bounds.

But though he made copious notes, he was too easily distracted, and the project never came to being. It was too ambitious, demanded a strength the "liverish riding-master" did not possess. His digestion gave him trouble, he needed constant medical attention. "What will distinguish my book," he wrote in his notebook in 1906, "is a radical, honest and naturalistic psychology of greatness. My justice and psychological freedom shall border on malice." And to Heinrich he wrote:

> To portray a hero humanly, all too humanly, with scepticism, with *malice,* with psychological radicalism; and yet positively, lyrically, out of my own experience: it seems to me no one has ever done this before . . . The counter-figure would be his brother, the Prince of Prussia *(the fraternal problem still preoccupies me),* a dreamer, who goes to bits because of his "feelings" . . . Am I up to such a task? I am thirty now. It is time to start thinking of a masterpiece."

Did Heinrich think he could do it, he asked?

We have no record of Heinrich's answer, save the indication that Thomas lacked sufficient "historical instinct". Yet history teaches; and if, in 1906, the thirty-year-old author of the best-selling *Buddenbrooks* lacked sufficient historical insight, then the next twelve years would provide it: both for him and millions of others.

5

Heinrich's revelation about his engagement to Ines meanwhile brought the two brothers together again. They agreed to meet in the summer of 1906 in Oberammergau, where Thomas hoped to pick up sufficient strength to continue work on *Royal Highness.*

The following year, in 1907, they again holidayed together, in Venice in the spring and in August by the Starnberger See outside Munich. By this time *Fiorenza* had received its first stage production in Frankfurt ("The production, despite being to a large extent rather awkward, did prove that the play isn't nearly as impossible as almost everyone claimed"[13]), but Thomas' literary productivity had almost ceased. "I eat and sleep well," he wrote to Heinrich, "only the good soul is as empty as death." He struggled on with *Royal Highness;* and for relief turned to Heinrich's *Zwischen den Rassen* which had just appeared in the spring of 1907.

"My God," he reported to Heinrich, "when I compare this with what else is being produced in Germany in the way of the novel today! — my feelings of family ambition are very satisifed. What will Busse, Hesse and Simpel say now!"[14]

Carl Busse had already indicated what he would say, in words Heinrich never forgot or forgave. "Trumped-up imaginings based on a coldness of heart," Busse had written the previous November, " . . . and the works that arise out of this, whether they are called *Die Göttinnen* or *The Hunt for Love, Flöten und Dolche* or *Professor Unrat, Stürmische Morgen* or any other name, and no matter how much they contain, — they belong to the category of works which I will fight to my dying breath."[15]

But where Thomas had once been torn and distressed by the revolutionary and seemingly reckless style of his brother's work, he was now, as with the collection of Heinrich's novellas in 1906, more than enthusiastic about the new novel. And before Thomas could recover from it, Heinrich had sent him his new novella *Branzilla*.

"Great God," Thomas wrote to him from Munich on 7th June 1907, "you've finished yet another — and I'm not even through with your last — that is to say, I've already finished reading it, but it hasn't stopped there, it continues to engage me and seems to grow with distance — as a work of art that is, for in forgiveable manner I read it primarily as a personal document and confession: read it tremendously fast and was often very moved by it. I'd like just to give you a brief idea of my impressions. The lasting one is that *Zwischen den Rassen* is — at least at present — my favourite among your works — Why? To begin with, as I have said, as confession, creed. Never have you *shown* such involvement, and despite all the discipline behind its beauty, this book has something gentle, human, devoted that at times held me in irrepressible emotion. But the real grounds for its unusual effect on me lie deeper I think. It lies in the fact that this book is, of all your works, the most just, the most deeply experienced, the gentlest, most free. Here is no tendentiousness, no limitation, no glorification or derision, no trumpery and no contempt, no taking of sides in spiritual, moral, or aesthetic matters:— but on all sides recognition; and art. This rests naturally in the material, the subject. But the subject is you! *Zwischen den Rassen* [Between the Races] is really *'Above* the Races'; and since 'race' in the end is simply a symbol, it becomes 'Above the *World'.*"

Thomas was reacting over-generously, for *Zwischen den Rassen* was by no means Heinrich's highest achievement from a literary or artistic standpoint; and Heinrich soon replied, saying how "very, very difficult"[16] it was to re-read.

But Thomas was judging it primarily, as he indicated, from a personal point of view; and to him it was obvious a great change had taken place in Heinrich.

It was Heinrich's positive, suddenly more human, understanding spirit which now drew Thomas; he even asked whether Heinrich would allow Katja a try at translating one of Flaubert's novels for the new German collected edition Müller was negotiating with Heinrich to bring out. They spent the summer of 1907 together, and Thomas begged Heinrich to attend the Munich staging of *Fiorenza* due to take place that winter.

Then Fischer arrived in October from Berlin to arrange the royalty question of *Royal Highness*. Thomas read him a chapter. Fischer listened intently, offered 6,000 Marks for pre-publication serialization rights, and 10,000 Marks advance royalty on the book. It seemed as though *Royal Highness*, despite its frivolous nature as compared with Thomas' other projected "masterpieces", would turn out to be a highly lucrative undertaking.

Heinrich, however, had no such luck. Though *Zwischen den Rassen* had sold 3,000 copies by July of 1907, Heinrich received only 3,000 Marks. It was enough to take a thermal cure in Munich, however, and August he spent with Thomas and Katja. Ines had returned meanwhile with her mother to Argentina.

In February 1907 she had written,

Dear Heinrich,
Papa now knows I am engaged. I never dared to tell him, because he places great importance on marriage. But he is glad it is you . . .
Papa will send me approximately 600 marks a month . . . At any rate it is now settled that we shall marry when I return to Europe; that is to say, if you want to.
I long to be with you; when will we see each other again?[17]

But February's tender longing soon dispersed; and Ines' primary objective in returning to Europe became not marriage but the stage. All year Heinrich waited for her to come; all year she remained in South America. Heinrich was reduced to writing to her father; and her father's attitude to Ines' ideas of a "public" career were no different from Thomas'. It was an "illusion" he declared in a letter to Heinrich from Buenos Aires in September. Ines' artistic nature was "far too fine-feeling to allow her to appear on the stage". A theatrical career required a roughness she simply didn't possess, he pointed out; nor was she a very able housewife, he added.[18]

Ines, however, was not so easily dissuaded; and by November she had informed her father she now had no intention of marrying "until she had achieved something in Art".[19]

She had, Ines' father noted however, wept a little in telling him this; Herr Schmied had tried to comfort her, and he and his wife had attempted to point out the disagreeable aspect of a failed career.

She must have been a very difficult girl. She "revelled" in the idea of Art, Herr Schmied wrote to Heinrich, "perhaps also in the idea of fame".[20] Heinrich must have known it all too well. As with Carla, it was not simply emancipation ("It is too stupid being a woman" Ines had written to Heinrich in August 1905. "It is beginning to bore me. At heart I feel like a man dressed up as a woman. Uncomfortable."),[21] it was also a way of overcoming her own personal problems. Fame! Neither Carla nor Ines had the talent a stage career requires; yet both blindly dedicated themselves to the theatre: and the one drove herself to suicide, the other wrecked her life over it.

"You cannot imagine how much I suffer by our being separated," Ines had written at the end of August 1905.[22] "I have made the firm resolution that when we are married we shall never be parted . . ." Yet three days later their engagement felt "very odd" to her. She was, as Heinrich's mother later put it, "like a reed in the wind".[23]

But Heinrich loved this small, beautiful, bird-like creature. He wrote to Ines' father with "indestructible optimism";[24] and it was in this frame of mind, in the autumn of 1907, that Heinrich gave up work on his latest idea for a satirical social novel to write a novella which, in Thomas' eyes at least, outclassed his own *Royal Highness*.

6

Heinrich's course, in fact, was the very opposite to Thomas', however much the two brothers attempted to overcome their differences. Against the background of his awkward and tormenting affair with Ines, Heinrich's "Liberalism" was quickly turning to something more extreme.

"What makes me an exception in today's Germany," Heinrich wrote to his solicitor and friend Maximilian Brantl in October 1907,[25] "is my radicalism; I am a Radical in spirit, in soul and in form. That reviewer [Wilhelm Michel, who had criticized *Zwischen den Rassen* in the *Münchner Neueste Nachrichten*] thought he would be clever and confine himself to the linguistic nature of my book; but rest assured what is so foreign and hostile to him is its world, its passions and movements. The pace of dialogue is a function of one's feelings: that he knows. These poor people must be terrible liars to remain patriotic artists and politicians today, when European democracy is on the rise . . ."

For over a decade Heinrich had developed his style until it was unmistakable: a sharpness and cogency unequalled in his own language. Slowly he was overcoming the private torment of his individuality, had met and become friends with a number of other contemporaries — Wedekind, Schnitzler, Schickele. His writing began now to fill with power and authority. He began to give readings — like Thomas — across Germany and Austria. And already in 1906 he had begun to make notes for the most important satirical novel of his life: *The Man of Straw*.

"The name *Untertan* [literally: underdog or slave-like subject] for your book I like very much," Ines wrote to Heinrich in September 1906, "but please don't call Diderich Hessling [the protagonist] 'Demmling'. Demmling sounds false, one thinks of dumm [stupid]; but Hessling sounds just right, so philistinically hateful and fusty. I look forward to the novel!!"[26]

"My ambition is becoming more and more spiritual," Heinrich wrote to Ludwig Ewers the following month:

I want to create heroes, real heroes, generous, gay and loving humanity in contrast to the hostile race of today, given completely to reaction. Since living in Berlin I find myself oppressed by this slave-like man without ideals. To the old contemptuous Prussian-officer spirit has been added the modern mechanical mass-response of the metropolis: and the result is a sinking of human dignity beyond all known measure.

I am making notes. How an unimportant member of this mass is treated when he or she buys a slice of bread. How at almost every opportunity each acts as the superior and enemy of the other: openly and brutally as nowhere else in the world. On the station platforms, in the sweaty cafes I sometimes have the feeling: if suddenly a police troop were to burst in and cut down ten or twenty of those present with their swords, the others would neither miss their train nor let their pudding get cold.

All this I want to include; but I must first feel it in my bones before I can allow my characters to touch on this . . . The chief character shall be the average New-German, one who takes the Berlin spirit to the provinces; above all a Byzantine down to his toes. My idea is to make him into a paper manufacturer who slowly graduates to printing patriotic postcards which show the Kaiser in battle-scenes and apotheoses . . .[27]

He began the first sentence the following summer, in 1907, after visiting a Munich paper-factory. "All for the 'hero' of my new novel," he wrote again to Ewers, "and once again a great burden on my back for goodness knows how long."[28] *Der Untertan*, as it was called, carried the subtitle: "A history of the public soul under Wilhelm II": and it was the slide towards "national inhumanity" to which the new spirit was leading which concerned Heinrich so deeply.

"The idea of *personal immortality* is so much the dream of the frustrated nationalist," Heinrich had entered in his notebook to *Zwischen den Rassen* in Florence, 1905.

But infinity at least provides an answer for those of us who belong to no people. We shall, I am certain, return to nature, we shall disappear in her arms. That tree, that hill will no longer have us to adorn it. What egoism, what uninvolvement in the whole, the idea of personal immortality presupposes! Even after death to want to stand selfishly aside as a restless single entity from the whole — that is revolting!

Heinrich's Weltanschauung had travelled a long way since the days on the *Zwanzigste Jahrhundert*. No sooner had he begun work on the *Untertan*, though, than he realized he would not be able to write it as he first intended. "Only someone who is convinced of the eventual triumph of democracy can create real beauty today," he wrote to a Dutch newspaper editor in October 1907. And who in Germany believed in genuine democracy?

So the novel he wished to write with "real heroes, generous, gay and loving humanity" was lifted out of Germany and *Der Untertan* to make a work of its own, transposed to Italy: *Die Kleine Stadt* (The Little Town).

It grew out of a story intended for *Simplicissimus* in 1907 to become perhaps Heinrich's most masterly literary achievement to date. It was a "hymn to democracy"[29] as Thomas first called it, the inverse of that other, north-German, seaport town in which Professor Unrat had been driven to dissolution and tyranny. This time Heinrich was concerned to show the creative, life-stimulating richness of a community bent not on chauvinism but toleration, the celebration of the variety of human motivations which true democracy allows. Among later literary pundits it came to be considered Heinrich's most classic literary work, stylistically brilliant but without the extremes of the grotesque that marred so much of his other writings. It took Heinrich two years to write; but by the time it was finished the mood of Germany was so hostile to democracy that the word had to be omitted from all advertising and publicity: and the book, written with such love, wit and sagacity, sank like an unwanted litter in the dark waters of the empire.

7

Thomas, at this time, was certainly no nationalist; but unlike Heinrich, he had nothing against contemporary Germany. "I was a quiet, well-behaved person who won a measure of prosperity by the work of his hands, took a wife, begot children, attended first nights, and was so good a German that I could not stand being abroad for more than four weeks," he had corrected Kurt Martens' portrait.

Thomas was exaggerating over "children": he had in fact only begotten one child by then, a daughter named Erika born in November 1905; but the following November a second child arrived, this time a boy, named Klaus Heinrich like the prince in *Royal Highness*. In 1908 they built a new summer-house in Bad Tölz on the Inn; in March 1909 a third child was born (Golo), the following year a fourth (Monika). The family moved into a new apartment in the Mauerkircherstrasse; and by 1912 Thomas was looking for a site to build a new town-house for the family in Munich.

He was striving to emulate his father, to be worthy of him not only in literary distinction but also in bourgeois terms (he and Katja even considered taking a house in Lübeck to which Thomas had a right by inheritance at this time). There was no particular reason why he should seek a change of political structure in Germany.

"How can cultured people, how can the intellect support a system which contradicts all intellect?" one of the characters of Heinrich's *Zwischen den Rassen* had declared. But Thomas' attitude was the attitude of virtually all established German writers: that the artist had no business to interfere with politics. *Royal Highness* was democratic in that the spirit which underlies the little princedom of the novel was one of love and dedication to the good of the "people"; but those who saw anything "political" in this Thomas was quick to set aright. Part of the reason for the commercial success of *Royal*

Highness, in fact, was that it soothed the public demand for monarchy and "things royal".

Thus the renewed intimacy and trust Thomas felt towards Heinrich in the spring and summer of 1906 was made possible and lasting only by an identity of *personal* circumstances, of personal emotions. And as soon as that identity broke: as soon as Ines entered the family as bride-to-be and touched off old jealousies and disagreements, their relationship was doomed.

Ines, then when finally she returned from Argentina early in 1908, was forced into a new role. Sensitive, neurotic, she could not fail to be aware of the pressure this put onto her. She arrived in Munich in March 1908 with Heinrich, pursued by her father's exhortations to marry the good gentleman.

The first encounters went well, and the Frau Senator — who, unlike Thomas, had not been informed of the engagement in 1906 — was pleasantly, if somewhat overwhelmingly surprised.

"Heinrich," she wrote in a letter to Ludwig Ewers, "the curious creature he is, got himself engaged in Florence some 1½ years ago without telling us, and three weeks ago he suddenly introduced his bride to me in Munich, Ines Schmied from Buenos Aires, medium height, pretty, golden-haired, gold-brown eyes, a skin like milk-and-blood, rather lovable, like a fairy. A few days ago they drove off to Meran, Hotel-Pension Windsor. It won't be long before they get married — as silently as they seem to have met one another!"[30]

But Ines' letter home brought her father no joy. It was not dated, she said nothing of her meetings with the Mann family. And her desire still to become an actress roused the anxious Herr Schmied to his most articulated disapproval:

> Dear child, you simply lack the qualities which lead to success: energy, fight, strength, tenacity, shamelessness, recklessness, lack of self-consciousness, and finally most important of all, good health. Your voice is neither strong enough for singing nor for declaiming in large halls. You are simply not made for theatrical life. You can't force it. And what sort of life, virtually without exception, is that of the theatre?
>
> I have the feeling I am talking to the wind. Well, then you will have to learn by harsh and bitter experience. Sadly, sadly!

"The right thing to do," he urged, "is to marry the distinguished Dr Enrique Mann;" but on no account was she to be "seen travelling and so forth" with him at a time when they were not even "officially engaged".

"Write to me, please, immediately, and take heed of this advice your rather anxious but most loving father gives you," he finished. "I am not at all pleased that you and Mann are living in the same place, that is to say in Munich. I fear you will not listen to your father's words. Perhaps you think you have more experience than I?"[31]

But Ines wouldn't listen. Thomas innocently suggested they all meet in Venice, where he and Katja were intending to spend the first fortnight in May. He left the hotel-booking to Heinrich because, as he put it, he wasn't sure "how you want your rooms".[32] It was hoped Carla would be there too.

The meeting in Venice was not the cosy and enjoyable family gathering Thomas had intended, however. Ines took a dislike to Thomas and quarrelled so loudly and openly with Heinrich that even eight months later the incident had not been forgotten. Heinrich became very ill and went to Riva while the others returned to Munich. Ines remained there, having been forbidden to spend the summer with Heinrich "as we are not married. Should you want marriage," she wrote in an unusual note of submission, "I suppose the best thing would be for us to get married as soon as possible so that I can stay at your side."[33] Heinrich answered with alacrity, offering to come immediately to Munich, but Ines, confronted now by the prospect of Heinrich's tender affections, begged him not to. "To tell you the truth," she wrote on 15th June 1908, "I fear your arrival as much as I look forward to it. You are bound to come with all sorts of medicines which you want me to take, and torture me with them till I am completely ruined."[34]

So Heinrich stayed in Riva, and Ines in and around Munich. She visited Heinrich's mother in Polling at the end of June ("c'était la troisième fois que j'avais le plaisir de voir Ines. Elle me plaît toujours meilleur, chaque fois mieux," the Frau Senator wrote to Heinrich), and met Thomas there a second time — a meeting she recorded in a letter to Heinrich with the laconic words: "I don't like your brother very much." She then left for Dachau, and a few days later took up Thomas' invitation to Bad Tölz. Months later she was still having nightmares about it.

"Sometimes still I wake up in the night because of a sort of nightmare," she confessed to Heinrich. "But it is I who am at fault, not your relations. Sometimes I re-live the day in Tölz and try to make an 'idyll' out of it . . ." But the thought of the day soon brought back the bitterness. "I still see your brother's face," she added in the same letter, "as he looked up so coldly, so indifferently, and yet with a kind of unease. And in the background that sober countryside, devoid of all poetry . . . Nothing big, nothing beautiful . . . a touch of woods here, a touch of meadows there . . . a bit of everything . . . That your relations cannot stand me is no wonder, but that I can't stand them either is also none."[35]

Heinrich was deeply perturbed by what had happened in Tölz. He suggested meeting Ines in the country and travelling back to Munich with her. Ines declined, in deference to her father's wishes suddenly, adding that she had now come "much closer"[36] to Wilhelm Herzog, a young friend of Heinrich's staying in the same place. By September 1908 the three-year-old engagement between Ines and Heinrich was broken and Thomas was inviting his elder brother to supper in the Franz-Joseph-Strasse — alone.

8

Dear Heinrich

Having read your dear card I went straight away to send you my maternal consolation; and here I must openly confess that it is *better* for you so, my dear boy, however much you may have looked forward to a permanent life together with the dear Ines. But see, it would have been far worse if you had had at your side from the very beginning such a tender, defence-less, nervous wife, in whose sight you would have brought torment in every way . . .

How much I would like you to have a *healthy* wife, my dear Heinrich, who would keep a beautiful home for you. But if not, better to be a bachelor![37]

Thus the fifty-seven-year-old Frau Senator consoled her eldest son in September. But Heinrich was inconsolable. He had put an end to the engage-ment with Ines in Munich; he then packed his manuscript of *The Little Town* and fled to the French Riviera. The news of the break-up quickly passed around the family, and Ines was quietly dropped. Her previous visits to Lula and Thomas were not returned. Thomas was working on the last chapters of *Royal Highness* which was meant to have begun serialization in the October 1908 issue of Fischer's *Rundschau*. But he could not finish the book: and with Katja he set off for his first visit to Vienna. There he met Heinrich's friend Arthur Schnitzler and also Jakob Wassermann; and in early December he visited Hugo von Hofmannsthal, who was also working on a comedy in the style of *Royal Highness:* "The high point in the trip," Thomas wrote to Heinrich, "was a half-day in Rodaun with Hofmannstahl, with whom I am still very taken. When he read to me from his comedy he put on a pair of glasses, exactly like you do."[38]

Meanwhile, however, came the first indication of problems over *The Little Town*. Heinrich had hoped that Fischer's *Rundschau* would serialize it after *Royal Highness,* and sent the unfinished manuscript to Thomas. But Fischer and his editors Bie and Heimann all agreed it was not "suitable" for multiple-part serialization.[39] Fischer did offer to publish the book, though, on condition Heinrich give all future works to Fischer Verlag — a condition the ex-apprentice could not accept.

He was not well, felt continually feverish, and was deeply unhappy over Ines. He wrote to his mother from Nice to say he still wanted to marry Ines, and still hoped she might give up her ideas of becoming an actress.

But Ines, whom the Frau Senator continued to see in Munich, denied that she had any such intentions. "I pointed out," Heinrich's mother reported on 11th November 1908, "that in time you would perhaps desire a regular domestic life: to which she replied, being alone and undisturbed were your primary requirements. I am again of the opinion that she has, *fundamentally,* a good heart, but that she sometimes overreaches herself and gets into compromising situations," the Frau Senator summarized. "I understand that," and she felt it was up to Heinrich to make sure that no scandal or disrepute arise from their relationship or separation.

Heinrich agreed to meet Ines for a few days in Milan — a meeting which for Ines "wiped out the very sad impression the days in Munich had left of you". But about her theatrical career they still could not see eye to eye.

"I am glad everything is clear between us now," Ines wrote on 7th December:

> There is only one thing I wish to ask. It occurs to me again that you haven't been quite honest with me. Why did you make promises which you then did not consider important to keep? You know that I am not just saying this, but I can tell you that in certain respects you have made me very unhappy, for I shall never be able to love another man. You can believe this or not. But had you not told me you would marry me despite the theatre, I would never have become engaged to you and wouldn't be as depressed as I am now. I could in fact be very happy. To be an actress no longer satisfies me, it belongs to me now like my nose to my face, as surely as breathing. I cannot live without it. Please write and tell me what you were thinking of when you made such promises . . . You know I love truth almost to gruesomeness, as somebody once remarked of me.

In the circumstances it was not possible to remain engaged. Ines felt betrayed, Heinrich disappointed. Thomas had written to say he had had tea with Katja, Ines and their mother — a meeting the Frau Senator had insisted on, so that no injustice be done to Ines. But Lula declined the invitation; and three weeks later Ines wrote to Heinrich to say her mother had agreed they publicly end their engagement.

"It is extraordinary how all the best writers seem to be writing on the brink of exhaustion," Thomas wrote innocently. "Hofmannsthal was similarly completely run-down and unable to work when I saw him in Vienna. But I hope you can soon finish your novel, whose importance and value I *firmly believe in*. I wish I could believe half so firmly in *Royal Highness*. Still, I have other irons in the fire."[40]

Thus, as "silently as they met one another", Heinrich and Ines broke up. But their affair had been too profound, too tortuous and too tormenting simply to cease. They continued to correspond; and only now did the real recrimination begin.

9

In January 1909 Fischer's *Rundschau* began serialization of *Royal Highness;* and in February Thomas finally completed the novel. For Heinrich's birthday in March Thomas sent the new edition of his first volume of short stories, *Little Herr Friedemann*. He was still having stomach trouble, but the completion of *Royal Highness* had brought him tremendous relief. "Altogether," he wrote in his birthday-letter, "I feel as if a new 'period' was beginning now, as Schaukal would say." The third baby was awaited "daily and hourly", and Katja sent her best birthday wishes and congratulations.[41] The very last thing Thomas expected was what Heinrich now sent: a vituperative rebuke.

Thomas answered it on 1st April 1909:

Dear Heinrich

Your letter both grieved and astonished me — especially as I am in no position to defend myself at the moment. The seventeen hours with Katja were very wearing for me as well, and even today I am still not really capable of going into the Ines-Lula matter in writing, however deeply I have thought about it since reading your letter. Let me tell you first and foremost that you treat the matter in the shrill and dramatic manner which accords with your genius but which is simply too passionate, too high-minded for the small, human reality of Lula's case. For the sake of your own health and nervous energy, which is much too important to be wasted on such trifles, I beg you to consider the subject much, much more quietly. If Lula and Ines cannot stand one another it is not really so astounding, for they are very different kinds of women, and clever people surely need not grow grey hairs over such female antipathies. Lula can claim that when she declined Ines' invitation, she no longer considered her your bride-to-be. She had heard that nothing was going to come of the relationship and so she said: "Either-or. If she is not his fiancée, then she is a stranger and has nothing to do with me." She does not understand anything less simple. And as regards the invitation to Ines' pension room, Lula can rightly claim that Katja did not visit Ines either. Evidently it is not really the done thing, and nobody thought of it, myself included. But who is going to be so punctilious? Start at your own door and ask yourself if in matters of etiquette you have always only done those things which you wanted to — for example, towards my parents-in-law! And Ines herself! Lula is full of weaknesses and faults, but that she is five times more disciplined than Ines there can be — forgive me! — no question! No one took exception to Ines' behaviour in Venice, in Munich and in Tölz; Katja and I at least accepted her always for the person she is. But that she has assumed the right to be, on her side, particularly critical, I find that really unacceptable. Be reasonable and do not confuse shadow and sunlight. And how did you find out that Lula would not come to the tea at Mama's? You need never, ought never, to have learned about that. Did Ines denounce Lula to you (as she denounced me to Mama, saying I was horrible to her in Venice!). I could consider that as unseemly as Lula's refusal of the invitation. Nor has Ines the right, if she is no longer your fiancée, to cause ill-feeling between you and your sister. Or did she believe there was nothing more to be destroyed? I have the impression that Ines was prejudiced against Lula, that you had drilled all too much about bourgeoisie and narrowness into her head from the start. Much of the blame lies with poor, mad Mama, who has behaved as crow-footedly as possible throughout. It is not her doing if things do not stand as badly between Ines and us as between Ines and Lula.

The Frau Senator had sent Ines a birthday present, and Ines, thinking it was a "peace-offering" from Lula, returned it. "I hope at least you felt a small tremble of amusement at the misunderstanding." Thomas added.

But if Mama now hears of the return of the present, there will be terrible trouble, there will be weeping and gnashing-of-teeth and two crazy letters to me and you each day. Remember, she is getting weaker and more troubled from year to year. In your place I would write extremely comfortingly.

I am not happy at the news that you are reading *R.H.* in the *Rundschau.* I fear you are not in the right frame of mind to take the play on our brotherly relationship in the way it ought to be taken. If only the tone I adopted in the book weren't so accurate! What if you had said to Lula at the time: "Listen, Lula, Ines expects you to return her visit, you must go over"? Don't you think she would have gone? A little less stiffness and distance! A little more robustness and brotherly feeling. I always feel brothers and sisters should not allow themselves to be knocked down. They can laugh at each other or scream at each other, but they should not take shuddering leave of one another.

Farewell, dear Heinrich, I hope to hear from you soon, in friendly terms: also about *The Little Town.*

How Heinrich must have sighed. His mother had written in December, upset at reports that Ines was receiving "visitors, both male and female", in her pension room late in the evening, and apparently in "the best of spirits". "Since both you and Miss Ines have explained to me the engagement is as good as finished and will continue from now on as friendship only," the Frau Senator wrote, "let me speak openly to you and confess that I hope you do *not* marry her. If one day you want a woman to share your *whole life* other than your mother, then let it be one who is *wholly* worthy of you and makes you completely happy; then I will gladly cede my place."[42]

Heinrich left Nice and went to Meran, begging Ines to meet him there; but her telegram arrived from Bolzano to say she could not. The reason "you are so sad," she had written to him in January,[43] "is because you shy away from people so much. Your relations are right actually," she had added, "I am not good enough for marriage. You cannot imagine what horror I have of families etc . . .!!! For me it is just like being put into a feeding stall . . ." On 17th January she had written: "If only you could force your-self to be more sociable. The less one sees people, the less one can stand them; but the reason is, one no longer understands them and is oneself unbearable."

Thomas' letter thus confronted Heinrich with a choice. Thomas had no idea how much in love with Ines Heinrich had been, and underneath still was. Yet it was obvious now that marriage at least was out of the question. A few days later, in April 1909 Heinrich replied to Thomas, asking him to think no more of the subject, and sent flowers for Katja. Thomas breathed a sigh of relief.

CHAPTER EIGHT

Death in Venice — and the Rise of the Man of Straw

Serialization of *Royal Highness* finished in September 1909. In October the book finally appeared. Fischer had printed 10,000 copies — ten times the first printing of *Buddenbrooks* — but even this figure was too low; and by December he was giving orders for a third impression: bringing the total to 25,000. The appeal of monarchy and a love-story was too great for it to be otherwise.

Heinrich, however, now found himself confronted by commercial disaster. Once Fischer had declined serialization Heinrich found it impossible to place *The Little Town* with any other magazine. He was certain Langen had ceased to take interest in his work and began to look for an alternative publisher. For almost six months he found none: and in April 1909 Langen was killed in a car crash. When finally, in the late summer of 1909, the famous Insel Verlag accepted *The Little Town* they insisted the word "democracy" be removed from any placard or publicity material. The novel was brought out in October, simultaneously with *Royal Highness:* but by spring of the following year its sales had not even reached 1,000 copies. "Never in my years with Langen," Heinrich wrote to his friend and solicitor Maximilian Brantl in January 1910[1] "has my lack of success sunk so low."

"The direction in which Germany is heading is too intellectually hostile to hope for wide success," he lamented to Ludwig Ewers five weeks later.[2]

The Little Town, Heinrich explained to his friend René Schickele at this time, represented "the triumph of love. Translated into larger terms: as democracy, as abdication even of the individual spirit in favour of mankind."[3] In a suggested prospectus for the book, Heinrich declared readers "will find that the residents of this little town lack none of the weaknesses, from vanity to intrigue, one calls 'human'; but they will also find something of that gentleness, the urge to help, that brotherliness emerging from the characters which one calls 'humanity' ''.

It was indeed his most positive work to date, and for that reason, in Thomas' eyes, unquestionably Heinrich's best. "The whole thing reads like a hymn to democracy," Thomas wrote in a letter to Heinrich at the end of September 1909, "and one gains the impression that only in a democracy are great men possible. It isn't so, but the impact of your writing makes it believable." He doubted whether, in fact, the time was ripe for such a progressive work or whether in fact the "people" would approve of it. "Who knows, though?" he asked. "Perhaps the time has already come . . . I am very curious to know how well it does — actually far more curious than about R.H."

They met in Nice for a short holiday in October 1909. Heinrich had written almost nothing since finishing *The Little Town* in March, he looked unwell, spoke of financial problems, Ines had not written to him for months, and when he wrote to her in November, her answer gave him no hope:

Dear Heinrich, I see from your letter that you must really be very ill. I didn't think my silence would upset you so much. I hoped you would forget me.

It is better you marry a woman who fits into your family, best of all German, any other would not fit into your family. When you are older you will see that I am right. You are so much closer to your brother now, that is a sign that you agree with him. And will continue to do so even more.

You must understand, you were born in Lübeck, in *North Germany*, and I in *South America*. How can these two go together? I have always had this guilty conscience, the feeling that real identity and belonging doesn't exist between us. Don't confuse this with tenderness. You feel tenderness towards me, I have no doubt, but it is not sufficient for me. That we are, at heart, complete strangers to one another has often occurred to me. Why ruin the whole of one's life through a mistake?[4]

She offered still to write to him, but this was, as it turned out, the last of her letters. Already she had indicated, at the end of it, that she would probably not become an actress after all, she had not the stamina to wait for parts.

Heinrich stayed in Nice until the following February. He had lost the woman "without whom I have no family" as he had once written. His novel had met first with rejection among editors and publishers, and now with the public. "May Heinrich's happiness rest still in the lap of the future," the Frau Senator wrote to his friend Ewers, "but may he at least have his share of the experience."[5]

2

Thomas had now begun a curious novella not destined to be finished until a year before his death, over forty years later: *Confessions of Felix Krull, Confidence Man*, inspired by the memoirs of Georges Manolescu *(Ein Fürst der Diebe)*.

"I collect, make notes, and study for the Confessions of the Confidence Trickster," Thomas informed Heinrich in January 1910, "which will be the most singular thing I have done. I am sometimes surprized at what I manage to produce. It is an unhealthy piece of work and not at all good for my nerves . . ."6

He was interrupted, however, by another attack on his "honour" — this time by Alfred Kerr, a well-known critic who had already disparaged *Royal Highness* in October 1909, and now, in Fischer's *Neue Rundschau* in January 1910, slipped a slighting reference to Thomas into an article about Bernard Shaw. " 'He doesn't brag like *mediocre novelists,* ' " Thomas quoted the sentence in question to Heinrich, " 'Every laughable neurotic clerk and erstwhile sanatorium patient who one day starts to write novels will portray himself in high society and fictionally click his Achilles heels . . .' How do you like that? Of course no one but me notices it, but that is the great thing about it . . . I must confess I was very upset for days afterwards. I have no use for such enemies inwardly, especially such a repulsive kind of enemy, I am not made that way."7

So Felix Krull was set aside; and a few weeks later Thomas launched into yet another polemic, this time against a Dr Theodor Lessing, attached to the Polytechnic at Hanover. "Again I can't start my book," he wrote to Heinrich, "and find a hundred distractions."8

The "distraction" with Dr Lessing was more ridiculous than serious, but Thomas' personal invective showed perhaps a disturbing intensity — particularly since the argument, in its first stage, began over a satire Lessing had written not about Thomas, but about Lublinski, the critic who had once greeted *Buddenbrooks* so enthusiastically. It indicated something more than a lapse of judgment or temper. Ever since the previous summer Thomas had been hard at work on "something critical, a treatise over which I run down my nerves so much every morning that I find myself nearer rubbish than epistolography":9 *Der Literat und der Künstler* (The Littérateur and the Creative Artist). Though he continued to praise and console Heinrich after publication of *The Little Town* ("I have the feeling that the success of your book — in the higher sense — is greater than of mine"10), and even encouraged him to link with René Schickele in producing a new magazine "so that one can hear directly from you in politics,"11 his own feelings about life, art and society had reached the point almost of desperation. The reason for his polemic against the "miserable wretch" Lessing, as he confided to Heinrich, "was at heart a blind urge to *do* something. The secret is: I couldn't get started with the *Confidence Man;* out of painful inactivity I let fly, I know that now, I suppose; and merely reduced my strength still further in doing so."12

Ines' brother Rudolf had been heard in Berlin to say how much he admired Heinrich, but what an "uncommonly poor and shallow novel" *Royal Highness* was. "Our friends were never the best about us," Thomas reported to Heinrich.[13] Yet to Kurt Martens Thomas called Heinrich "a passionate democrat of the newest stamp," one of the "sword-swallowers". Heinrich had referred to the "democratic" or "anti-individualistic" element in *Royal Highness* — a "misunderstanding" Thomas pointed out. "You are perfectly right in saying that henceforth 'democratic' books cannot seriously be expected from me," he wrote to Martens. "As you know, an artist can give certain trends of the times their due in one work and then show himself entirely independent of them afterwards. Insofar as I can foresee my future work, it will certainly have nothing to do with democracy."[14]

Electoral reform in Prussia had become the great political issue of contemporary Germany. At the 1908 elections the Conservatives had obtained a mere 14 per cent of the Prussian electoral vote; for this they were given 152 seats in the Prussian Landtag while the Social Democrats, having polled· 24 per cent of the entire vote, had won the sum total of a single seat. While most of the major men of letters in the country had signed the *Berliner Tageblatt* appeal for reform, Thomas had remained aloof. In *Der Literat und der Künstler* he now distinguished between the Man of Letters and the Poet: between Heinrich and himself. It was a fine essay, profoundly perceptive, and by no means unsympathetic to the literary men who scorned popular success and pleaded the cause of humanity.

He [the Littérateur] is radical, because radicalism means purity, nobility and profundity. He despises half-way thinking, cowardice in logic, compromise; he lives in protest against the corruption of the idea through reality . . . The Littérateur is upright to the point of absurdity, he is honourable to the point of saintliness, yes, as wise man and judge he is related to the prophets of old, in fact he represents the category of the saint more completely in its highest level of development than any Anachoret of simpler times. His feeling for beauty, his sensitivity over anything common, ridiculous, unworthy leads to the destruction of all inferior passions, of ill-will, of envy, of the lust for power, of vengeance, of jealousy . . . Yes, if he is by birth a judge, called upon and gifted with the ability to penetrate things with sharp words, then it is, when all said and done, his "cleverness" that proves stronger than his "love of virtue": his knowledge of the heart, his knowledge of the many-sidedness and the profound injustice of human behaviour which enables him to understand, to forgive, which lead him to *goodness* . . .

It was almost an appeal. But where had the "gentleness", "allsidedness", "understanding" of *The Little Town* led to, other than commercial failure? Who in Germany was interested in such "virtues" when "democracy" was a forbidden word even among independent private publishers? In October 1908 the "Daily-Telegraph-Affair" — in which the Kaiser declared that his friendship towards England was only shared by a "Minority" of the German people — caused a storm of political protest; yet nothing was altered. Parliamentary government was not strengthened, and the ever-increasing level of military and naval preparation for eventual war was not halted or even slowed. In the uneasy truce between modern industrial capitalism and the autocratic tradition of Prussian obedience and *Realpolitik,* the ship of Europe began to creak more and more ominously.

Thomas had identified some of the motives for the bitter radicalism of writers such as Heinrich. What he refused to take seriously was the disastrous direction in which Germany was heading. It was a naïveté for which he was to pay very dearly in years to come. In the meantime Heinrich emerged from the failure of *The Little Town* and the end of his relationship with Ines to produce two of the finest essays of his life: *Geist und Tat* and *Voltaire-Goethe.*

"For my own part I remember firstly," Heinrich recollected over forty years later, "how difficult one or two — in fact very modest — essays became; and then how immodestly they worked. Never before had I written so slowly, struggled so hard over words. He who always portrays and never speaks in his own name would certainly have given up at every attempt, no matter what the problem. It was my most responsible work. It was a matter of life and death. If nothing else, I was betrayed by the resistance of language, I was pitting myself against a nation's destiny; and naturally in vain."[15]

Voltaire-Goethe had been begun the previous winter in Nice. "I am trying to draw together the threads of an essay about France," he wrote to René Schickele in December 1909: "I suppose the most outspoken that I can bring to bear in this respect. If I were not ill I would have finished it long ago; and would be in Paris now. As it is, it means writing and hoping."[16]

Voltaire-Goethe — originally published under the title of *Französischer Geist* — first appeared in issue 11 of *Der Sozialist* in Berlin in June 1910. It was a call to commitment to the social and political responsibilities of literature. In it Heinrich made clear how Goethe had become a cultural façade for inhumanity, for the rule of injustice and inequality. It ended:

For freedom: that is the sum of all the aims of the spirit, of all human ideals. Freedom is dynamic, is the casting off of slime and rising above the animal: is progress and humanity. To be free is to be just and honest: is to be just and honest to the point where one can no longer tolerate inequality. Yes, freedom *is* equality. Inequality binds even him to whose advantage it exists. Whoever exercises power is no less the serf of power than he who must endure it . . . For freedom is the will to truth, even if dishonesty were to one's advantage. Freedom is the love of life, including death. Freedom is the totem dance of reason. Freedom is the absolute human being.

This indeed was the absolutism which Thomas characterized as the "saintliness", the "absurdity" of the Littérateur.

But was it so absurd in an age of militarism, of surging nationalsim, where reason was a second-class citizen and the Reserve Officer a symbol of right? When the critic Julius Bab sent a copy of his latest work on Bernard Shaw to Thomas in February 1910, even Thomas was sufficiently concerned about the mood of the times to object. "Thank you very much for your rich, clever, thoughtful book," he wrote. "I will not conceal from you that I dislike your sharp antithesis between the 'poet' and the 'writer'. In the land of Wagner, in a country of alienation and hostility towards literature, where every Littérateur who writes rather than stammers is scorned and where every intellectual insight is mocked as 'unpoetic', the emphasis of your not-always tenable antithesis is likely to be more confusing than helpful."[17] Already, at a production of *Parsifal* in Bayreuth the previous summer, Thomas had become sceptical about Wagner — not with his enjoyment of the music, and the operatic drama, but over its relation to modern civilization. "Does it have a future?" he asked Walter Opitz in a letter.[18] "Hasn't it already become, in its atmosphere, its direction and taste, some-what historical? I believe Walt Whitman exercises more influence on young people today than Wagner . . ."

But Whitman didn't; and ironically it was to be over a critical lecture Thomas gave on Wagner some thirty-four years later that he would be hounded out of Germany by his compatriots. In likening Heinrich and the literati of modern Germany to the prophets of old, Thomas can have had little idea that their prophecies would one day come true. The Kaiser's Germany was still too pleasant for those with a good income and a house in the country to take such warnings seriously. In December 1909 Thomas offered Heinrich a loan of 2,000 Marks to enable him to travel to the south of Italy or even Africa. "I have done so well this year in financial terms," he wrote to Heinrich in Nice, "that I can part with a couple of thousand quite painlessly. You could spend them at your leisure without having to worry about re-paying me. Please, if this is any help to you, let me know."[19]

But money loaned between brethren is always a dangerous affair; and Thomas was the first to chide literary men who spout about humanity and do not repay their debts.

Meanwhile, however, as Heinrich prepared the sequel to *Voltaire-Goethe* and began to make further studies for the satirical novel he had set aside in 1907, while Thomas belaboured the neurotic Dr Lessing and continued the adventures of *Felix Krull,* their sister Carla had reached the end of her brief life. Her career on the stage had never borne fruit and she had compromised herself with man after man. In Polling, in the apartment her mother rented every year, she had now had a quarrel with her fiancé, a rich and somewhat innocent industrialist's son from Alsace. The Frau Senator heard her gargling in her room: but to the mortification of both mother and brothers it was to cool the lethal dose of cyanide she had taken.

3

Carla's death, on 31st July 1910, shook the family as only the death of Senator Mann had done almost twenty years before. According to Viktor Mann, the Frau Senator never really recovered from the blow. She had devoted herself to her children, and spurned the kind of social life which in Munich, as the still beautiful young widow of a Lübeck senator, she could have pursued. She watched the progress of her sons and daughters with apprehension and delight, she remained impartial in their quarrels and reassured them when they needed her support. When Carla took her life she felt it was a reflection upon her failure as a mother. Her grief never really lifted; thereafter she could not remain for more than a few weeks in one place but lived the last thirteen years of her life wandering and mourning.

"We are all very distressed," Thomas wrote to Heinrich from Bad Tölz four days later:

It is the bitterest thing that could have happened to me. My sense of fraternal solidarity makes it seem as though Carla's act has put our existence into question, has broken the bonds between us. At first I kept saying to myself: "One of us!" What I mean by that I am only beginning to understand now. Carla thought of no one else. You will say, "as though she didn't have enough on her mind!" And yet I cannot help feeling that she had no right to leave us. In doing as she did she showed no sense of family solidarity, no feeling for the common destiny of our family. She acted as it were *against an unspoken agreement*. It is unspeakably bitter. Towards Mama I control myself. Otherwise I find myself crying almost continually.

The main object of this letter, however, is to beg you, before you come to us, to visit Lula. You are doing her an injustice and to my mind you are guilty of a lack of self-respect if you consider *one of us* a common philistine. None of us can be that. If you allow this opportunity to pass then the danger arises that the break between you and Lula becomes as definitive as Carla's death, yes, becomes somewhat similar to it. I appeal to your reason and your heart, and will be deeply disappointed if you come without having spoken to Lula.

But if Thomas was distressed by Carla's suicide and his sense of family solidarity shattered, how much more so was Heinrich. He was staying with Dr von Hartungen in the Tyrol at the time. He had been out for a walk when suddenly he heard a woman's voice calling him, quite clearly and urgently, and using his forename — which no one there would do. He was sitting in the house thinking about this strange phenomenon when the telegram arrived.

PLEASE INFORM MANN CAUTIOUSLY THAT KARLA HAS MET WITH AN ACCIDENT HE SHOULD COME.

On top of his broken engagement to Ines and the comparative failure of his novel *The Little Town* it was more than he could bear. Carla had worshipped him as her elder brother. In her eyes he could do no wrong. With his fine, delicate features, his penetrating wit and mastery of language he was for her the epitome of the artist. Her dedication to the theatre, her ruthlessness with herself were perhaps modelled upon him. And now she had taken her own life.

Small wonder Heinrich was consumed by self-reproach — a feeling of guilt that persisted throughout his life. He blamed himself for not having been there in Polling to help her. He looked at Thomas and particularly at Lula, and he blamed them for having been insensitive to Carla's struggle, for not having supported her enough. But underneath it was himself he could not forgive.

"Dear Heinrich," Thomas wrote to him on 7th August 1910:

> After writing you a long letter I have decided to scrap it, for I see that in your present state of nerves it would cause more harm than help, and so I want to tell you simply that we expect you at any time. Your letter contains much that is feverish and reprehensible, much that ought to be firmly and strictly rejected. But I hope that we can sort it out when we meet rather than in continued correspondence — which in our case has always somewhat of a literary character.

Carla had taken enough cyanide "to kill a whole company of soldiers."[20] She had left a note for her fiancé, in French: "Je t'aime. Une fois je t'ai trompé, mais je t'aime."

The bonds between the members of the family, the perception of which had given rise to *Buddenbrooks* itself, the sense of destiny behind them: it was this lyrical simplification which Thomas now had to relinquish. "In truth there was no justice in my grievance. For had not I too grown greatly 'down to earth' by dint of work and dignities, wife and child and home and all the serious and humanly pleasant things of this life whatever they are called? And if in my case 'reality' bore an ironic and benignant face, still it was made of the same stuff as my sister's deed and involved the same breach of faith," Thomas acknowledged. "All reality is deadly earnest; and it is morality itself that, one with life, forbids us be true to the innocence of youth."[21]

Carla's suicide had spoiled the notion of the Mann family moving from commerce into the untarnished realms of literary greatness. The dynasty — in its lyrical aspect — had been sundered. Though Thomas still dreamed as late as 1913 of writing a sequel to *Buddenbrooks,* the innocence of his youth, an innocence which had pervaded *Royal Highness,* was now in pieces. His next great work — which began the move to award him the Nobel Prize — was unequivocably bound up with the idea of death; a book whose greatest admirer would be Heinrich; a book which was to become perhaps the most famous of all novellas in modern European literature: *Death in Venice.*

4

"About *The Little Town* I hear nothing but enthusiasm," Thomas had written to Heinrich in February 1910. "Everyone says it is your best book — and the last you will write."[22]

For a time it looked as if it might be. It had been his eighth novel in nine years, and its failure gave little promise for the future. "Soon, well rested, you will start again," Thomas had added. But then Carla's death had come, and Heinrich yet again shelved his notes and manuscript for *Man of Straw.* He felt the urge to be heard directly. He turned playwright not because he possessed a feeling for the stage, but because the time demanded it. As luck would have it, a wealthy art patron, Paul Cassirer, had taken an interest in Heinrich's earlier works, and in 1909 had republished his first four novels in a Collected Edition. Cassirer had married a beautiful and celebrated actress, Tilla Durieux, and in June 1910, in return for a "considerable" guaranteed monthly advance royalty,[23] Heinrich agreed to put all his future work — with a minimum of seventy printer's sheets every five years — in the hands of Cassirer's publishing company. His first three one-act plays were produced in 1910; and each succeeding year he turned out a new three-act drama: *Schauspielerin* in 1911, *Die grosse Liebe* in 1912 and *Madame Legros* in 1913. All were radical, outspoken, humanitarian. But it was his essay *Geist und Tat,* published in Cassirer's new periodical *Pan* in January 1911, that became one of the seminal essays of pre-war German humanitarianism. It was the sequel to *Voltaire-Goethe,* an appeal to Germany to take heed. A nation in which all thinking people avoided politics; a nation in which intellectual matters, by tradition, were considered to belong to a realm of their own, divorced from every-day considerations; a nation which — save for a brief liberal moment in 1848 — had never had to *fight* for its ideals, was bound to go adrift. "No one has seen to it that here, where so much profound thinking is done, the strength of the nation be marshalled to translate word into deed," Heinrich protested in *Geist und Tat.* "The dissolution of unjust power has found no support. We think further and more deeply than in any other nation, we think to the ends of reason, we think to a standstill, to nothing: and in the country it is God's grace and the fist that rule."

A nation has to learn to *act* in defence of its beliefs, as France in the Revolution, or England in the Civil War, even if it lead to bloodshed: for the loss of life, the lowering of the quality of life will only be worse in succeeding years if it does not. A nation which willingly sacrifices its rights and representation to its monarchs and great men — to the Kaiser and to Bismarck — is doing itself the greatest injustice, however temporarily advantageous the result. Without true and active democracy people will always project themselves in the figures of their leaders, "will talk themselves into the idea of supermen," Heinrich wrote prophetically, "when their own human growth is dangerously retarded."

But the element which worried Heinrich most in his essay, and which was the source of its title and its imperative appeal, was the inactivity of literary men, the literati: those journalists, critics, essayists and writers who define the cultural awareness of an epoch. For the literary men would be the last to be forgiven for not recognizing the state of affairs, or not acting to alter them. What was God's gift of intellect and reason if not to be used — and to the common, not only personal, good? Who else could better distinguish principle from practice if not the educated?

But it is precisely they who for centuries have worked to beautify the practical, sophisticatedly to justify injustice, and its deadly enemy, might. What strange corruption is responsible? What can explain this Nietzsche — who has lent his genius to the type — and all those who have followed him? Is it the overwhelming success of might which people in this country and this period saw? . . . From tragic ambition to wretched vanity, from the pathetic search to be someone special down to the panic-stricken fear of loneliness and aversion to nihilism: the faithless literati have many excuses. Above all they have one in the enormous distance that has grown and which separates — after such long ineffectiveness — German intellectuals from their people.

But what have they done to diminish this? They took the life of the people merely as a symbol for their own lofty experience. They gave the world only a numerical role to play, never mixed their beautiful passions with those of the people, they have never known what democracy is and they have despised it.

They despise parliamentary government before it is even reached, public opinion before it is heard. They act as though they had behind them that for which others have had to bleed, and wear the face of tiredness and saturation, though they have never fought nor enjoyed such things.

. . . The time has come, honour demands that now, finally, finally, they fulfil the demands of reason and the intellect, that they devote the strength of the word to this struggle, which is the struggle of the word. Their distinction should not be the cult of self: the German overestimation of the exception is directed daily more against reason and truth; their distinction should be in their ability to give a standard, a model which others can follow . . . The man who uses might and authority must be our enemy. An intellectual who attaches himself to the master-caste is committing treason against the mind today. For the mind, the spirit, reason gives no privilege, keeps no one. It destroys, it levels, it makes equal. And over the ruins of a hundred tyrant's castles it drives towards the fulfilment of truth and of justice, their perfection: even if it be death.

The *Berliner Tageblatt* carried a large extract from *Geist und Tat*, together with congratulation and assent, as Thomas reported to Heinrich. But the nationalist *Deutsche Tageszeitung* abhorred it, and the general reception was hostile. The hundred academics, philosophers and distinguished men of letters who before long would be declaring in the press their total support for the Kaiser's march into Belgium and the Declaration of War were unperturbed. Even Thomas, when the time came, could not forgive some of the tone and penetration behind Heinrich's invective. But for the moment, with the death of their sister and the precarious health of their mother, it seemed important to remain friends. Heinrich sent a beautiful illustrated book of fairy tales for his young nephews and nieces (with the birth of Monika in

June 1910 there were now four), and Thomas brought good news for the success of Heinrich's one-act plays in Berlin. In October 1910 Thomas and Katja had moved into their new apartment in the Mauerkircherstrasse in Munich, and in November Thomas visited Weimar — an experience which almost thirty years later would give rise to his famous Goethe-novel *Lotte in Weimar*. Heinrich had wanted to meet him there, but two important newspaper pieces had to be finished by December, neither of which Thomas had started. The one, an article on Chamisso's famous novella *Peter Schlemihl*, appeared in the *Berliner Tageblatt* on Christmas Day 1910; but the other, *The Fight Between Jappe and Do Escobar,* he had finished before the second week in December.

It was as entertaining as Chamisso's famous tale, very short and perfectly executed. Apart from his distracted work on *Felix Krull, The Fight Between Jappe and Do Escobar* was the first work of narration Thomas had attempted since *Royal Highness*. And for those who read it in the *Süddeutsche Monatsheften* in February 1911 it must have come as a considerable surprise. Here was no "terrible weak-kneed lack of heroism" as Dr Lessing was still busy maintaining. Here in eight pages was a tale, a school-boy memory, whose depiction had brevity, directness, humour and exquisite subtlety. Here was the finest narrator in modern German letters beginning to flex his talents again. All he required now was a story he could stick to and finish. And in May 1911, on the Lido in Venice, the story began.

5

"In May we are planning a Dalmatian holiday — all being well. When are you coming to Germany?" Thomas wrote to Heinrich towards the end of March 1911. Heinrich answered that he would be glad to accompany Thomas and Katja. The idea was to start in Brioni.

So the fateful spring visit to Italy began. But the island had no sandy beaches and the Archduchess of Austria was staying at the same resort. She had the habit of coming to table two minutes after all the assembled guests had sat down; everyone — foreigners included — had to rise for her. Then two minutes before the end of the meal the Archduchess would get up again; and the same performance was repeated. So it was decided to have done with Brioni and travel by sea to Venice. However, during the stay in Brioni alarming reports had come from Vienna that Gustav Mahler was seriously ill. Because of Mahler's international fame bulletins were issued every two hours or so; and on 18th May the great composer and conductor died.

The Pringsheims had been on very friendly terms with Mahler, and Thomas had met him for the first time a few years before, when Mahler was invited to tea in Franz-Joseph-Strasse. The previous summer when conducting his own Eighth Symphony, Mahler had again come to Munich, and Thomas and Katja had attended the dress-rehearsal. Mahler was by no means popular among all music-lovers, and when he sent for some small and unusual instrument needed for the symphony the Musical Director returned the message with the words that he himself would unfortunately be requiring the instrument that evening.

"Give the Herr Musical Director my best wishes," retorted Mahler; "and tell him one way or another I will still perform my symphony." But Thomas himself had no doubts about Mahler's genius. To Katja he confessed it was the first time he had ever had the feeling of meeting a great man — "devouringly intense" as he later called him.

The little party of Manns steamed into Venice in the third week of May 1911. It was the first time they had entered by water — usually they travelled there by train — and on the ship was an old "queen", hideously made up and surrounded by young people romping about in high spirits. At the pier the Manns looked for someone to take them to the Lido. Immediately a gondolier presented himself; but hardly had they got out at the Lido and paid than someone came up and warned them the gondolier had no licence to make the trip across to the Lido. They were lucky nothing untoward had occurred, he added.

It was a curious beginning. A porter carried their bags to the Hotel des Bains; and at table the first day they caught sight of a striking Polish family — the girls rather austerely dressed, and beside them a wildly beautiful thirteen-year old boy in a blue sailor suit. The boy fascinated Thomas — his serenity, his Grecian head, his little, supple movements and delicate grace. On the beach Thomas found himself studying the boy, how he played with his friends, the utterly unconscious way he carried his beauty — and yet at the same time was aware of it!

But Heinrich, whether bored by the beach or finding the weather too sultry for comfort, soon begged that they should go up to the hills where it would be cooler and they could take long walks. So, unwillingly, Thomas and Katja agreed.

But in Bolzano the villa they wanted was occupied by an English couple and the hotel itself without modern conveniences. And Heinrich's trunk had gone astray. Triumphantly they returned to Venice and the Lido. The Polish family was still there — to Thomas' great satisfaction; and on Hotel des Bains notepaper, he wrote an article on the 1909 production of Wagner's *Parsifal* he had promised the Viennese *Merkur* to write. *Auseinandersetzung mit Wagner* (Quarrel with Wagner) it was called. "To build temples to his work, I thought in my bitterness," he told Ernst Bertram, "is something only a barbaric and half-blind nation could do."[24]

However, on the beach and in the luxurious rooms of the Hotel des Bains it was the beautiful image of the thirteen-year-old Polish boy which continued to exercise its strange fascination. It took Thomas back to the moods and amours of his youth, to *Tonio Kröger*, to Lübeck and Travemünde, the sea-front orchestra. Now the whole edifice of German romantic opera was beginning to come down. "I believe I can say," he wrote in his article, "that Wagner's star in the firmament of German culture is now beginning to sink."

If so, then "Tadzio", the Polish boy, seemed unaware of it. His star ruled over the Lido, over the Hotel and its special beach, the deckchairs and cabins, the slight lapping of the sea. He ran barefoot through the sand in his striped swimming costume, presided over dinner in the Grand Salon with his raging good looks and water-blue eyes.

One evening an "obscene" Neapolitan singer entered the grounds of the hotel, his face leering and yellow. People began to leave the hotel and a rumour circulated that there was cholera in the city. When "Tadzio" left and Thomas and Katja went to book their return to Munich by sleeping car, the man at Cook's advised them not to stay their intended further week but to travel the following day, for there had been a disturbing number of cholera-cases, hushed up by the authorities.

Without "Tadzio" there seemed little point in staying. They packed their bags. It was the last time they would see Venice before the War; and yet its features — the sultry sirocco heat, the beauty of a once powerful maritime state hiding the disease which could now ruin its tourist season, the sumptuousness and rumour of death — were not forgotten. Having finished his essay on Wagner Thomas set about the "quick little improvisation" which would "serve as an interlude to my work on the Krull novel"; in material and scope it was to be something that "might do for *Simplicissimus*".[25]

But the improvisation was not to be so quickly finished. "I am working at the moment," Thomas wrote to Philipp Witkop on 11th July 1911: "a very strange thing that I brought with me from Venice, a novella, serious and clear in tone, concerning the case of an ageing artist who falls in love with a boy."

It was indeed a strange and perverse story for the man who had so recently criticized Dr Lessing for his debauchery. But the truth was, as Thomas later reflected:

Every piece of work is a realization, fragmentary but complete in itself, of our individuality; and this kind of realization is the sole and painful way we have of getting the particular experience.

As inwardly, so outwardly, all the elements of the fable fell into the picture in the most singular way. Nothing is invented in *Death in Venice*. The "pilgrim" at the North Cemetery, the dreary Pola boat, the grey-haired rake, the sinister gondolier, Tadzio and his family, the journey interrupted by a mistake about the luggage, the cholera, the honest clerk in the travel bureau, the rascally ballad-singer, all that, and anything else you like, they were all there. I had only to arrange them, when they showed at once and in the oddest way their capacity as elements of composition.[26]

But this time he knew he had found his mark.

As I worked on the story I had at moments the clearest feeling of transcendence, a sovereign sense of being borne up, such as I had never before experienced.

In the figure of the hero, Gustav von Aschenbach, he invested the profile, the physical characteristics of Mahler; but the soul, the conscience and the spirit were his own.

It took almost a year to finish. Katja was unwell and in September she went with the children to Sils Maria. Thomas remained in Bad Tölz, and to friends in the evening — and to Heinrich when he visited — he read aloud the developing tale.

"The German public really only likes serious and significant stuff," Thomas wrote after its publication. "It does not care for light reading: and despite its questionable subject, *Death in Venice* was taken as a sort of moral rehabilitation of the author of *Royal Highness.*"[27]

The homosexual element proved no barrier, it merely added to the strange and powerful symbolism of the fable. In a Europe that had reached the culmination of civilization and culture, the fatal attraction of a celebrated and ageing man to a young boy proved a theme that stunned the literary world:

The day will come when a master, a guardian of noble form, a paragon for youth and the voice of the nation will sit ruined by the edge of an over-grown fountain in the centre of that decaying square in Venice, washed over by the lukewarm smell of carbolic in the diseased city, and whispering through made-up lips depraved and wonderful words to the boy he desires.

This man has gambled away what once seemed to him most worthy of attaining: a fruitful evening of life, the pursuit of art at the final period of life, in wisdom and perfection. No more will he write; he will not climb the watchtower of old age from which one can only first truly encompass one's work and life — and in which one grows cold. His years will be curtailed, the hours of departure rotted and rendered magical by un-disciplined outbursts of the senses. And so these hours will at least be human, will release him once again through love, a wordless, impossible love from his austere loneliness, unexpectedly; and his last heartbeats will·swell his breast as though they were his first. Should he regret them? He doesn't even ask. Around him the city is sick, and like the courtesan that she is, Venice conceals it out of greed. She is beauty, beauty that entices — and which kills. From afar, through faces in a dream and enigmatic messengers in the uncertain masks of death she has drawn to herself a being who was ready to die in her bosom. The sweet and suspicious sultriness of her air, the holy colours of her rottenness, her voluptuous depravity: this is identity, fraternal destiny. The soul of a man mixes its last colourful moments with that of the world outside; and through the interplay of desire and fear arise events of great depth and meaning, of held breath, yet filled with voices, the cries of the stormbirds, the plague, of sweet humanity and the voices of greatness and ruin. They echo through a city and a man's heart: echo and die away in death, Death in Venice.

Heinrich had been there, had witnessed this strange affection, knew the perverse beauty of this once mighty citadel, had heard Thomas' first gropings towards the form and sinister fable, had seen perhaps even more closely — because he was outside — its historical significance. In the first edition of *März* for 1913 appeared his review, perhaps the most moving the novella received.

But now it was not the rumours of disease which began to spread in Germany but of the highest accolade in the literary world: the Nobel Prize for Literature.

6

But the rumours were not substantiated; and within a year Germany was at war. How sinister the parallel with *Death in Venice:* the tired, cultured man who is inexorably drawn towards death, a last "wild and wanton outburst" of the senses — the gambling away of what once "seemed most worthy of attaining". Death draws to itself a being "who was ready to die," the great and ancient city conceals the danger out of greed . . .

Almost as though trying to rule out, subconsciously, such a terrible parallel Thomas became — and remained — dissatisifed with the quality of the work. Having finished *Death in Venice* in the summer of 1912 he felt it was "not good enough" for publication in Fischer's *Neue Rundschau.* Only at Katja's insistence did he submit the novella.

But Fischer and his editor, Oscar Bie, were of quite a different opinion. It appeared in the October and November issues of the magazine in 1912, and in April 1913 the first 8,000 copies of the book edition rolled off the presses.[28] Before the year was out another 10,000 were in print.

Fischer spoke of its "enrolment into the history of humanity". Bruno Frank, the novelist, wrote of "a new nobility, with a new level of honour."[29] Heinrich, as we have seen, paid it perhaps the most moving tribute he had ever written to a work of Thomas'. Yet to Fischer in November 1912 Thomas lamented the "errors and weaknesses" of the novella, and a year later — long after Heinrich's review — he still castigated himself to Heinrich, saying the book was "full of half-baked ideas and falsehood".[30]

The prospect of the Nobel Prize slipped away and Thomas began to lose faith in himself. "I believe I am played out," he avowed to Heinrich, "and should probably never have become a novelist. *Buddenbrooks* was a bourgeois book and not fitted for the twentieth century. *Tonio Kröger* was merely maudlin, *Royal Highness* vain, *Death in Venice* full of half-baked ideas and falsehood." He complained of his "inability to orientate myself, politically and spiritually, as you have done, Heinrich." His "growing sympathy with death" was, he felt, a sign of his inability to cope with modern times and with "progress". And yet even this explanation was unsatisfactory, he wrote. "It is awful to feel the whole misery of the time and the fatherland oppressing one and yet not have the power to portray it . . . Or will it be portrayed in *Der Untertan?* I look forward to your work more than to my own" — for since the summer of 1912 Heinrich had taken up his original manuscript and notes and was now hard at work on his great satire of Imperial Germany — *Man of Straw.*

Naturally Heinrich wrote back reassuringly, "For your clever, tender letter I thank you from the bottom of my heart." Thomas answered three days later[31] — and confessed his desire now to write a sequel to *Budden-brooks:* "a great and faithful chronicle, a continuation of *Buddenbrooks,* the story of us five brothers and sisters. We are worth it. All of us."

But *Buddenbrooks* itself, ironically, had still not been forgiven in certain quarters — as an unusual notice, reported in newspapers throughout Germany testified.

Over the past 12 years, thanks to publication of the BUDDENBROCKS written by my nephew, Herr *Thomas Mann* of Munich, I have suffered such unpleasantnesses, and of such sorry consequences for me, to which are now added the publication of Wilhelm Albert's book *Thomas Mann and his Duty.*

For this reason I see myself forced to turn to the reading public of Lübeck and to ask them to treat the book as it deserves.

If the author of the *Buddenbrocks* drags his closest relatives into the mire, in the worst kind of caricature, and exposes their lives in the most blatant manner, then every right-minded person will find it dishonourable — a sorry bird who defiles his own nest.

The statement, issued as a display advertisement, appeared in the *Lübeck-ische Anzeigen* on 28th October 1913. It was signed "Friedrich Mann, Hamburg" — the model for perhaps Thomas' most comic figure — Christian Buddenbrook.

Yet it was not Uncle Friedrich's public stricture which caused Thomas to discard his dream of a sequel to *Buddenbrooks,* but his own, disquieted mind. Already in 1911 Germany had come to the brink of war with the Agadir crisis; and in 1912 the Social Democrats triumphed at the General Election, taking 110 seats against the Centre- Party's 91 and the Conservatives' 57. Yet still, by coalition, the Conservatives held power and it was clear the country, with its statutory and traditional allegiance to the Kaiser, was bound to suffer an upheaval.

Like so many of his fellow countrymen Thomas felt divided, afraid of disorder, sceptical of "progress", indifferent towards politics: and yet bound by his conscience to the demands for justice and humanity. He yearned to "portray" the times: yet found he could not. Instead he began a small novella which would take a further twelve years to complete: a work which would grow from innocent beginnings to become the great Bildungsroman, at once literary and philosophical, of the new century: *The Magic Mountain.*

7

The Magic Mountain was originally intended to be another "interlude" in the work on the arch-imposter Felix Krull; but more than that, as Thomas later recollected, it was an antidote to the "tragic novella of decay", *Death in Venice.* It was a way of "resting from" the "rigours" of the latter — a "humorous" work that would be "easy and amusing and not take much space". And like *Death in Venice* it drew its theme from a curious experience.

Katja's health over the past two years had given cause for increasing anxiety, her chest was repeatedly inflamed and her doctor urged her to go up to the mountains for a lung-cure. From March to September 1912 she had stayed in Dr Jessen's "Forest Sanatorium" in Davos. There Thomas had visited her for four weeks in May and June; and suffering a slight fever for a few days Thomas had been somewhat irresponsibly diagnosed as tubercular by the consultant: a diagnosis Thomas' doctor in Munich ridiculed. The idea for the *Magic Mountain* had been sown.

In the following year Katja had to go for a further stay at a sanatorium in Meran, and in January 1914 to Arosa. Her letters — and Thomas' own observations — were to prove of greater literary value than perhaps any other spa-correspondence in the annals of literature: even, as has been professionally maintained, to lead to a significant alteration in the treatment of tuberculosis.

But however he worked on both *Felix Krull* and the antidote to *Death in Venice,* Thomas could finish neither. Both showed epic rather than epitomic qualities; required time and faith. He was often "very melancholy and weighed-down by cares".[32] Katja coughed, little Klaus seemed to have inherited her "disposition", and the new town-house they were building across the Isar involved a mortgage loan of 70,000 Marks, in addition to the deposit and the cost of the land.

"If only the will to work could make up for this," he complained to Heinrich. "But inside: the constant threat of exhaustion, my scruples, tiredness, doubts, a sensitivity and weakness that lay me open to every attack and leave me prostrate." Heinrich, he felt, was "spiritually more attuned" to the times, that was the "decisive factor".

"Attuned"? Twenty years of loneliness and isolation, twenty years of self-exile and the opportunity of comparing his mother country with the other nations of Europe. If Thomas only knew the sense of bitterness and betrayal that went into satire! *Man of Straw* was Heinrich's first truly epic work, for only now did he seek to encompass the misfortunes of an era, the sham and deceit of four decades of authoritarian, nationalist, militarist, anti-democratic rule. What Thomas saw as Heinrich's enviable spiritual orientation to the times was in truth born of despair and suffering.

Heinrich had first made notes and begun the manuscript of *Man of Straw* in 1906, then set it aside for his "hymn to democracy", *The Little Town.* "In Germany there seems room for only one educated person in politics," he had written to René Schickele in January 1907;[33] "Harden already says everything which literature has to say on such matters. And naturally in vain. How stupid that everything depends on the fate of Bülow! 'This people is doomed' (Motto of my 'Untertan', but unwritten motto)," he added. In December 1907 he had hoped to finish *The Little Town* in order to continue work on *Man of Straw:* "the novel of the German [Diedrich Hessling] has got to be written," he again wrote to Schickele, "the time is more than ripe for it."

But it was only in 1912 that he felt sufficiently strong — or disillusioned — to set to work again on the novel in earnest. It had no precedent in German literature, was more akin to the great satires of Swift and Defoe than to the works of his own country. Unlike *Land of Cockaigne* events were not viewed through the innocent eyes of an outsider, but from the heart of evil itself, the "hero" Hessling. From childhood to university in Berlin and from there to his fortunes as the owner of a paper manufacturing company Heinrich charted the career of a bombastic coward whose patriotism is based on opportunism, his aggressiveness on spite and inferiority.

It was indeed an anti-German novel; and yet it could only have been written by someone who loved his country, like the great exiled political and social critics of the past — Voltaire, Herzen, Mazzini, Heine, Hugo, Zola. It was the opposite of Thomas' *Buddenbrooks* and yet stemmed from a matrix that was not essentially different.

And as with *Buddenbrooks* Heinrich did not have far to look for his material. The Zabern affair in 1913, in which the insolent behaviour of a young officer was followed up with the declaration of martial law by his commanding officer in Savergne, Alsace, bayonet charges on the demonstrating crowd and — despite a successful vote of no confidence in the Reichstag against the Chancellor — a decoration for the young officer from Wilhelm II soon afterwards, actually *followed* Heinrich's famous shooting scene outside the Governor's residence (written in the autumn of 1912) in which the guard shoots an unarmed demonstrator and is decorated by the Kaiser. It was not the first time such incidents had happened; and Heinrich's protracted study of the major trials of the era now bore fruit with a vengeance when it came to the climax of the book: the trial for lèse-majesté brought against the liberal newspaper owner of Netzig.

Once again Heinrich's satire verged on the grotesque; and yet its power, its authority, came from its veracity. He was penetrating in his analysis of the good as well as the bad, he painted the gradual emasculation of traditional German liberalism with devastating accuracy. Life had indeed become a war of materialistic survival, in which trade unionists were as hypnotized by prestige and power as the most extreme industrialists of the right.

Heinrich was now forty-one; and in the literary cafés of Germany and Austria he had become a symbol of humanitarian progress; there he was hailed as an uncompromising defender of justice and truth; the "father" of German Expressionism; and, after the two extracts from *Der Untertan* in *Simplicissimus* in April and September 1912, a satirist without peer.

8

Thomas' reputation meanwhile soared among the respectable and sank among the radicals of both left wing and right wing. To the nationalists and anti-semites he was now a Jew — mutated to "representative of Jewish interests" when he protested against the epithet. To revolutionaries like Erich Mühsam on the other hand his presence on the Munich Board of Censorship — though undertaken to protect art from the ignorant — was considered an act of artistic betrayal.

> If people really knew
> The sort of man
> Who is Thomas Mann
> They might show more respect
> For Heinrich Mann

was a popular ditty in the Café Grössenwahn in Berlin.[34]

In May 1913 Thomas resigned from the censorship committee. Yet, as Thomas' article on Fritz Behn in the *Lübecker Nachrichten* several weeks before showed, his sense of being misunderstood and of his motives being impugned stretched far beyond the activities of the censorship board. Behind his support for the Lübeck sculptor was something akin to a *cri de coeur.* "This traditional old town," he wrote, "is completely indifferent to the development, distinctions and success of its hardworking artistic sons. If a Lübeck artist becomes important in the world, achieves fame and honours and wins the respectful recognition of the entire fatherland, in its widest sense. Lübeck will not exactly take countermeasures — that it cannot do, nor does it wish to. It merely stands aside — it never occurs to it to do anything else. Yes, from this distance it appears almost as though Lübeck follows the careers of such sons not only without pride, satisfaction or pleasure, but even with a certain shamed annoyance . . ."

Lübeck had declined to commission Behn with the sculpture of its new monument of Kaiser Wilhelm I — a commission which Behn did not need and which would provide a further case-study for Heinrich's *Man of Straw* that year. "Lübeck seems incapable," Thomas pursued his theme "of believing that from within its walls exceptional minds can arise, men who are forbidden by nature and fortune from taking the customary Lübeck path, yet who are by no means inferior or born scoundrels, but who have been called and are entitled to aim for honours in the outside world of which the average Lübeck citizen is not even aware. Because their youth is almost necessarily problematic, because they alienate people and give offence by an irregularity of being that is difficult to define, because they are dreamily stubborn and decline to recognize as their teachers those who 'do not know what to make of them', people's judgement of them is confused from the start. Because they do not conceal their impatience to get away, to turn their back on the hated hometown and in fact in time — or even before time — break away and leave the city, its people are insulted, see in them worthless beings, drop-outs, failures; and find them contemptible."

But as Thomas pointed out, if the worthless wretch should "achieve something" in the outside world, the Lübecker is shamed; and in order not to have to confront this he invents and disseminates "scandalous rumours" — "gossip, misrepresentation and defamation".

His article finished with a warning: Lübeck should cease to pursue its sons with "unclean slanders," but should learn to "believe" in those who appeared such ne'er-do-wells at home and had now won "fame and reputation in the world".

Like his *Bilse and I* article, Thomas' plea for Fritz Behn was an appeal which came all too obviously from the heart. As Heinrich later pointed out, Thomas had a lot to learn about Germans: and the longer it took for him to discover, the more betrayed he felt.[35]

In the years of dedication to his art, in his choice of the path directed by conscience, not pleasure, he felt he had, if only symbolically, followed in his father's footsteps.

But in his heart of hearts he was tormented confronting the battle of the twentieth century. He was inwardly divided — as *The Magic Mountain* was soon to demonstrate. It " 'thought of itself' quite differently from the way I had to think in order to embark upon it". It grew larger and larger, and was evidently going to prove more than a novella — and take considerably longer.

But the problems dealt with in the narrative were all present and alive in me before the war; everything was there before the war — it was only actualized and bathed in the lurid and desolate light of the conflagration.[36]

But if Thomas was finding it difficult, despite outward success, to attain the peace of mind he longed for, Heinrich suddenly began to find life more rewarding than it had ever been for him before. In February 1913 he set aside the swelling manuscript of *Der Untertan* and travelled to Berlin to attend the Première of his latest play *Die grosse Liebe*. Tilla Durieux was playing the leading role; and in the hope of obtaining a part a small and strikingly pretty Czechoslovak actress had asked Heinrich for an interview. Heinrich went to her hotel; and after the painful years of solitude, the hopelessness of his affair with Ines, Heinrich at last found a woman who would love him without reserve, who cherished him both as man and as artist; and who was willing to sacrifice her career for him.

Her name was Maria Kanova. She was twenty-seven, Heinrich now forty-two. Though Heinrich left her at the end of February to negotiate serialization of *Man of Straw* in *Zeit im Bild*, a Munich weekly periodical, he wrote to her every day and even did his best to obtain her a role through the theatre director Robert.

"My dear little Mimi, it is nice to know that my letter made you happy," he wrote on 25th February from Partenkirchen in Bavaria.

I wish I could make you happy forever. You cannot imagine how much I long for permanence. Until now everything has broken in my hands. But perhaps it is the great intentions and promises which become dangerous as soon as they are fulfilled. For the moment you must not take me too seriously: perhaps I would only disappoint you. But perhaps, too, you are the one who will have patience with me and we are destined to share a happy life in love with one another . . . For happily we can talk to one another, our interests meet one another. For me that is something quite new: a woman who really appeals to me and to whom I also feel an inner bond. You cannot imagine how difficult (for me) that is.

Yet disaster still seemed to go with success. Michalski, the editor of

Zeit im Bild, offered Heinrich 10,000 Marks for full serialization rights of the *Man of Straw* — a princely sum for a novelist whose last work had fallen on such stony ground. But simultaneously Maria, or Mimi, was called home to Prague where she was told her brother was dying of a brain disease. Mimi could barely pluck up courage to visit him in the hospital, and only Heinrich's stern letter from Munich made her stay and give him comfort. Then on 22nd March she wrote to say there was no "little Heini" on the way as she had hoped.

The death of her brother at the end of that month was a bitter blow. Each had now lost one of their next-of-kin, and Heinrich took the little Czech girl more and more under his wing: to Venice and Italy in the spring, and in the summer they rented a villa in the Bavarian hills. For eight days Heinrich went over to Tölz to stay with Thomas; and like those years before when Heinrich first revealed his engagement to Ines, they seemed as close to one another as they had ever been: conversing till midnight and reading to one another from their latest work.

For Heinrich it was impossible to continue *Man of Straw* in this mood of contentment and affection, despite the contract with Michalski who intended to begin serialization that autumn. Unknown to Michalski Heinrich had in fact embarked on a new play, based on the French Revolution: *Madame Legros.* "I am writing one of the most beautiful scenes of my life," he wrote to Mimi on 9th June 1913; and by the 14th the draft of the first act was complete. "It has not overtaxed me," he wrote to Mimi, "and I am only sorry now to have to leave Mme Legros and return to the wretched Diederich." By October the new play was ready: but was considered too radical and anti-monarchic to be performed. Only in 1917, in a climate of growing war-weariness, did any theatrical director have the courage to put it on. However, Cassirer published the play in book form in November 1913; and Thomas was full of praise for it.

"It is a very beautiful work," he wrote after reading it in January 1914, "of wonderful economy in composition and dialogue . . . I cannot think but that it will have a great, yes inspiring effect on the theatre."

"I am often asked these days," Thomas continued: " 'Is your brother actually married now?' I answer 'I don't think so, for if he was I suppose I should know it.' "

In fact getting married was to prove rather more difficult than Heinrich imagined. When the following spring he asked his solicitor to make the preliminary arrangements he was told that no Jew could marry a Christian according to Paragraph 64 of the Austrian civil code. In the end Heinrich had to "leave" the Protestant Church. It was an extraordinary — and expensive — business: but one that proved only a distressing hint of what was to come.

In the meantime, with the unlikelihood of *Madame Legros* being staged in the near future and Michalski threatening to begin serialization of the first chapter of *Man of Straw* in October 1913, Heinrich returned to his satire. On 13th October he drove with Brantl to Augsburg for a performance of

Lohengrin — "in the interests of *Der Untertan*," as he informed Mimi the day before. He "observed" it through the eyes of Diederich and Guste (Hessling's wife), "noted everything down and will perhaps make one or two pretty pages from it. So much stupidity in such a Wagner hero, in the choir, in it all! Today Diederich has an earthy scene with the pastor's daughter, but they are interrupted," he wrote to Mimi on the 15th. "So you see, everything is going very properly here!"

What had been begun as a satire was becoming horribly prophetic. *Zeit im Bild* finally began serialization on 1st January 1914; and at the beginning of July Heinrich completed the manuscript, just four weeks before the outbreak of the hostilities it predicted. On 4th August 1914, Europe plunged irrevocably into war.

CHAPTER NINE

The Great War ·

So many of Germany's most distinguished thinkers, academics and artists responded "patriotically" to the outbreak of the First World War that it would be a mistake to see in Thomas' reaction anything extraordinary. He had not wanted or expected the war: yet it came as an almost physical release to him and permitted him to feel at one again with the destiny of his country. The fatherland was surrounded by countries who despised it and were only too anxious to see its fragmentation and downfall. Well then, Germany would fight! Thomas stepped forward as quasi-cultural spokesman for the Reich, for the German literary heritage under siege. Only months before he had resigned from the Board of Censorship and turned down the chairmanship of a new Arts Society on the grounds that he was not fitted for political activity, even in art, and that in any case such responsibilities conflicted too much with his work. But when he heard that Richard Dehmel, the poet who had first "discovered" him almost twenty years before, had enlisted and was fighting at the front, he sat down in August 1914 to write his first work of German "propaganda": *Thoughts in Wartime,* published eight weeks later in Fischer's *Neue Rundschau'*

Heinrich's reaction, on the other hand, was almost unique in Germany. While writers as radical even as Mühsam allowed themselves to be swept up by the war hysteria that accompanied the early days of August 1914, Heinrich's response was merely a stunned disbelief − followed by disgust. *Man of Straw* was coming true before his eyes − already on 1st August the new editor of *Zeit im Bild* had written to say serialization of the novel could not possibly continue.

At this moment a great public organ cannot criticize German conditions in the form of satire. Only very few readers would, in such anxious times, either notice or accept the distinction between art and life: they would hold the contents of *Der Untertan* as matters of fact. In this light certain parts of the novel might easily give offence among the general public in the present critical situation. But apart from this we might face the most severe censorship problems were we to publish anything of the least political intent, particularly regarding the person of the Kaiser.

We confidently expect that you will share our view completely and will do your utmost with us to find a satisfactory solution to this disagreeable matter.

Thus, on 13th August, serialization was suspended: and with it any hope that the novel might yet appear in book form.

Only days before the announcement of war, on 30th July Thomas had written from Tölz to congratulate Heinrich on finishing the book. "Above all, congratulations on completing your great work. Even despite the threatening situation of the world the news could not fail to impress me." Telephone communications with Munich were to be closed down, following the order to commandeer the network for military use. "In our whole lives it has never come to this," Thomas commented. "I would like to know how you feel about it. I must say that I feel shaken and shamed by the terrible force of reality. Until today I was optimistic and disbelieving — one is too civilly tempered to consider the enormity possible. And to some extent I am still inclined to believe they will only push the matter to a certain point and no further. But who knows what madness Europe can aspire to once precipitated!" He added he would be glad to act as best man and witness at Heinrich's wedding planned for the 12th August in Munich.

However events moved too quickly. Viktor, mobilized on the first day, wished also to be married before he left for the front, and then had to be seen off at the station, as well as Katja's brother Heinz. By the time he returned to Tölz at the end of the first week in August Thomas felt little desire to travel four hours again to the city for Heinrich's wedding, and asked if Heinrich would not postpone it a while or seek a substitute for him.

"I feel still as though in a dream — and yet one ought to be ashamed for not having considered it possible or seen that the catastrophe must come. What an affliction!" he wrote:

How will Europe look, inwardly and outwardly, when it is over? Personally, I shall have to prepare myself for a complete change in my standard of living. If the war goes on for long I shall without doubt be what one calls "a ruined man". In God's name! What significance has this against the revolution, the spiritual revolution which such great events must bring with them! Shouldn't one be thankful for such a completely unexpected opportunity to witness such great things? My main feeling is one of enormous curiosity — and, I admit, the deepest feeling of sympathy for this detested, enigmatic and fated Germany, which, if it didn't exactly rate "civilization" as man's highest estate, at least has taken upon itself to destroy the most depraved police-state in the world.[1]

Within days their relationship was under strain. Did Thomas really expect Heinrich to welcome a war with France, whose culture and painful political growth towards democracy Heinrich revered?

By November Thomas was pressing Heinrich to pay back some of the money he owed him, for Fischer could not now produce the advances on *Felix Krull* and *The Magic Mountain* he had promised, and Katja's father had halved the allowance he normally gave them. With the coming of war any chance of selling the villa at Tölz had disappeared.

But Heinrich was no better off. Cassirer, who was "almost ruined", had reduced his guaranteed royalty to a "tiny sum" on which — now that *Man of Straw* could not be published — Heinrich would have to manage for the duration of the war.

But as long as their disagreements remained political and financial they could at least continue a semblance of brotherly relations. Heinrich's pessimism about his work ("my work will be as impossible to place after the war as now," he had written on 13th November 1914) Thomas utterly refuted. "I think you do Germany an injustice by such pessimism," he answered. "Can you really believe that Germany will be so retarded in its culture or civilization by this great, deeply-honest, yes festive war of the people that it could reject your talents permanently?"[2]

Yet in a strange way — bar a brief surge of war-weary yearning for change towards socialism in 1918 — this is what did happen. A huge, powerful and still inexperienced young nation was seething at the heart of Europe, humiliated but far from humble. The war was the very worst introduction to democracy or even socialism — but then socialists and democrats had already betrayed their dearest ideals when the Reichstag put itself unitedly behind the army and the Kaiser. What should, according to Schlieffen, have been a six-week campaign in the West dragged on for four years: and the decades of righteous, nationalist and imperialist fervour swept aside the centuries of traditional caution. Diederich Hessling had been tragically truly drawn. And while Thomas embarked on his new role as self-appointed spiritual and cultural spokesman for the "detested" nation, Heinrich watched the débâcle with pain and despair.

2

"Extremely rewarding talk with Heinrich Mann, who judges the war very pessimistically" — such was Erich Mühsam's diary entry for 27th August 1914 — having erased his earlier, enthusiastic entries.

"Heinrich Mann also told me of his visit to his brother Thomas," Mühsam recorded the following day. "He somewhat mockingly quoted Thomas' admiration for the general enthusiasm for the war. 'My brother enjoys it, as he does everything, aesthetically,' Heinrich commented."[3]

" 'What do successful battles mean?' " Mühsam quoted Heinrich on

20th September three weeks later, after the battle of Tannenberg. " 'Victory and defeat are only concepts. How can a people be victorious when it is hated throughout the world?' "

But for Thomas the war was a chance to assume the laurels and literary-cultural leadership Gustav von Aschenbach had so movingly discarded in Venice. For a moment, but "for no more than a moment",[4] he was tempted to enlist.

"The nerve-racking days before the mobilization, the outbreak of the international catastrophe, we spent in our retreat in Tölz," Thomas recorded later:

> But we got an idea of how things stood in the country and in the world when we drove into town to take leave of my youngest brother, who was in the artillery reserve and left at once for the front. We saw the hot August hurly-burly of the railroad stations, choked with a host of distracted humanity shaken and torn by anguish and enthusiasm. The fatality took its course. I shared to the full the pangs of intellectual Germany in the clutch of destiny; which had so much faith in so much that was true and so much that was false, so much that was right and so much that was wrong . . .[5]

These words were written many years after the events, and Thomas was too aware of the integral part the war had played in his development as a writer ever outrightly to condemn his response. As the soldiers marched to their death "there was nothing in my tastes or cultural traditions to hold me aloof, as others were held . . . yet on the other hand I knew myself, in my physical essence, not made for a soldier and fighting man". He set aside his manuscripts and began his essay, *Thoughts in Wartime:* "a war service with the weapon of thought".

The theme of *Thoughts in Wartime* was the antithesis between "culture" and "civilization". "Culture" implied an almost "tribal sense of unity, of strength, form, energy", however "adventurous, scurrilous, wild, bloody and fearful" — whereas "civilization" on the other hand indicated "reason, enlightment, softening, good-breeding, scepticism, dissolution — the conquest of the mind". Germany was a culture; the "western powers" civilization.

Having defined the two categories Thomas launched into a panegyric on the moral rehabilitating effects of such a war: the cleansing of the spirit, the complete overthrow of peacetime corruption, "service" to a higher cause. It was the misguided enthusiasm almost of a schoolboy: and yet, through its profoundly artistic and autobiographical nature, its mixture of naïveté and wisdom worked movingly and winningly — so much so that soldiers and officers all across the German front wrote to say how much strength, courage and pride it had given them in their task.

> War! It was cleansing, it was freedom we felt, and a profound sense of hope . . .
>
> All inner hate, which the comforts of peace had turned poisonous — where was that now? A utopia of misfortune arose . . .

War as a way of bring unity and collective ambition was what characterized Thomas' essay. It was considerably more subtle than simple "hurrah-patriotism" and the triumph of victory and conquest. He recalled the days of Frederick the Great, forging a nation through adversity and struggle: and the thought delighted him. Thomas quoted the case of Frederick and his court-guest Voltaire: Voltaire who had listed all the wrongs of war in his *Questions encyclopédiques;* Frederick who had merely smiled on reading them, and given the order to march upon Saxony. "That is reason against demon," Thomas declared ecstatically, "intellect against genius, dry lucidity against clouded destiny, bourgeois good-breeding against heroic duty. Voltaire and the King: there stand the great civilian and the great warrior of all time."

It was a flouting of Heinrich's essay *Voltaire-Goethe.* Small wonder Heinrich was upset! "German militarism," Thomas went on, "is in truth the expression of German *morality* . . . and is not peace that element of civil corruption which appears frivolous and contemptible to it? Germany is warlike out of morality — not out of vanity or glory-seeking or imperialism . . . Germany's whole virtue and beauty — we have now witnessed it — first flowers in war. Peace does not always suit it — one might forget in peacetime how beautiful Germany is. Who can fear that in this festive struggle which Germany is conducting as its great right to live, it could be retarded in its way of life, its culture? It will emerge freer and better than it was."

There followed a bitter condemnation of France and her conduct of the war and of England's arrogance in wanting to "teach Germany democracy" by striving for her military defeat. Thomas, of course, was ignorant of the chain of events, diplomatic and military, that had led so inexorably to the war; but his refutation of the possibility that Germany could be educated in such a manner had more than a touch of prophecy. "Robert Dell," he wrote, "believes honestly and truly that Germany is to be revolutionized, democratized through her defeat — he does not see that the political expression of bourgeois freedom, already paved, already on its way, can only be achieved in peacetime, after victory, after certain and historically preordained German victory; that is to say in Germanic — not gallic-radical-fashion; that a German defeat would be only the way to defeat us *and* Europe in the progress towards civilization; and that after such a defeat Europe would never have peace or rest from German 'militarism' until Germany were back where it stood before the war; that on the contrary only Germany's victory can guarantee the peace of Europe."

It was a bold assertion, and one that was to be proved horrifically accurate in a certain respect.

"It is true," Thomas could not refrain from adding, "the German soul has something deep and irrational which makes it appear disturbing, worrying, alien, yes offensive and wild to the feeling and judgement of other, less profound peoples. It is its 'militarism', its moral conservatism, its military morality — an element of the demonic and the heroic which strives to attain civil 'spirit' only as the last and most humanly worthy ideal.

Germany is great also in respect of civilization — only the ridiculously ignorant could deny it. But *decline* into civilization Germany will not, and it goes against its grain to make a hypocritical or vain fuss about civilization. It is truly the most unknown people of Europe, whether because it is so difficult to get to know or because comfort and arrogance hinder its neighbours from attempting to learn about Germany. But Germany must be understood, life and history demand it, they will prove it impracticable to deny out of rude ignorance the indispensable and missionary qualities of this people. You wanted to surround us, tie us up, exploit us; but Germany, as you can already see, will defend its deep and hated 'I', its self, like a gull, and the result of your attack will be that, astonished, you are forced to study us."

The article appeared in the *Neue Rundschau* in November. And if that was not enough "in the service of" his country, Thomas immediately collated his notes on Frederick the Great to write a further essay, over sixty pages long, entitled *Frederick and the Grand Coalition, An Abstract for the Day and Hour.*

3

On the 14th November 1914, meanwhile, Mühsam recorded another meeting with Heinrich: "Yesterday morning went to coffee at Heinrich Mann's. At last a man who condemns the war without embarrassment — in other words, who hates it beyond measure."

Wilhelm Herzog was another of the few intellectuals who were bitterly opposed to the war: and Thomas' *Rundschau* article aroused Herzog to a distressed reply in the December issue of his magazine *Forum.* "One must read it twice," Herzog wrote, quoting Thomas' remarks about peace seeming too "frivolous and contemptible" to the German "soul":

One has to repeat the words of one of our most distinguished poets several times before calling for absolute denial of such manicured and erroneous literary teaching about the German soul . . .

We need no stylized *Thoughts in Wartime.* We want to get ourselves out of the enormous confusion into which mankind has stumbled. That our poets and artists have failed us as leaders, we have had to experience painfully.

But Thomas went on undeterred; nor was he alone. Who but a madman could protest when there was such undeniable popular support for the war, when every man of note or standing had declared himself behind the Kaiser? It was not a question of "civilized" Western countries teaching Germany, but of their being forced to learn from — and about — Germany as she really was.

Frederick and the Grand Coalition was completed by December 1914 and first published in *Der Neue Merkur* in January and February the following year. It was to be followed in May by his "letter" to the Swedish newspaper *Svenska Dagbladet.*

But despite the general acclaim for his patriotic work, Thomas could not fail to be aware of his growing unpopularity among the few intellectuals still capable of dispassionate thought. He was not afraid to part company with them now however — "that radical-humanitarian group of political litterateurs belonging to the French order, with whom I have inwardly been in conflict for a long time and who have now, after the appearance of my *Thoughts in Wartime,* banished me completely," as he wrote to his academic friend Ernst Bertram in February 1915. "My brother, for whom the Rhine border was a welcome state of affairs ('in those days we had a great literature,' he says), is not really tolerable at the moment" — and invited Bertram to come and visit him in Munich.

"My *Thoughts in Wartime,*" Thomas explained in the letter to Bertram, "are in fact an *action,* fought out of anger, out of the heartfelt wish to come to the help of my affronted nation whose mighty musical soul is as yet still little cultivated and somewhat inarticulate in comparison with the western powers. My heart is German; but a stronger stream of Latin-American blood enables me to see that what the Paris orators and advocates can do, *I can do also.*

"What justice is I do not know," he added ominously;

I believe however that justice can grow old and die, and that out of necessity and enthusiasm new justice can be born. What *truth* is I know better; but truth is three or four-dimensional and can at most be portrayed, but never said. So my little action, as such, has succeeded. I read the article publicly here recently, and the gratitude it engendered (and which probably stemmed from agreement) was most touching.

Yes, it is almost eerie, and from the beginning I was surprised how inwardly ready and prepared I was for the events (and certainly I was not alone in this) — without politically having had the least notion about it all . . . But that European unity has been so outwardly shaken by this (inwardly it had already happened) is the fault of those other nations who would not accept Germany, who wished neither to recognize her nor treat her as an equal, even though she came a little late. But for the political development of the Reich, for its inner consolidation and its final outward legitimisation, the war will undoubtedly do a great deal. My publications will look as though they have been inspired by the war — whereas in fact they were conceived in all their detail long before.

The Littérateur and the Creative Artist; the appeals to Lübeck citizens over the years to recognize and accept him; his political differences with Heinrich: all now appeared to Thomas as an inward preparation for this moment. That Heinrich should sit out the war silently in Munich without making public his objection to the catastrophe and the people who were inflaming it can hardly have seemed likely to Thomas; and yet, Heinrich's essay, when it came, seems to have caught Thomas completely unawares. Thomas was thrown into the greatest and profoundest turmoil of his life by it; he shut himself away for almost three years, he worked at times night and day to defend himself, to produce his monumental *Reflections of a Non-Political Man.*

But in the meantime, in the early months of 1915 it was still a gentleman-ly relationship, with Heinrich publicly silent, Thomas prolific in the service of the warring state. "My brother is not really tolerable at the moment – as important as he could become to me at any time," Thomas had written to Bertram. Relations between Heinrich's apartment in the Leopoldstrasse and Thomas' new house by the Isar were definitely becoming more and more difficult – but as yet they had not broken. Thomas continued his cultural flag-waving; but their mother now pursued Heinrich with unhappy letters deploring his unpatriotic response to the war.

My dear, good Heinrich, don't speak out against your fatherland because it now defends itself with *all its might;* – it only wanted to demonstrate its loyalty to its own allies and was forced into this struggle which will cost its life – or so the enemy would like. Some distinguished diplomats had seen the war coming even *earlier* because Germany was growing too large and powerful; hence the Entente between the Allies. We would have been their good friends perhaps if, like Switzerland, Denmark, Holland or Scandinavia, we had been willing to remain neutral – but always in fear of the more powerful. No, it would be nice now if the whole world belonged to the Germanic peoples – and if England mends her ways she could join us. Understand me, Heinrich, and don't speak ill of Germany to others!

4

In February 1915 Heinrich's wife Mimi returned to Prague to stay with her parents for a while; she was very anxious about Heinrich and there were sure to be telegrams unless he wrote every day.

She worried about his health; about the growing likelihood he would be called up; and about an action for obscenity the Munich police were attempt-ing to take against him. "Don't worry yourself about *Flöten und Dolche,*" Heinrich reassured her on 7th February 1915; "the book appeared I believe in 1904!"[6] Proceedings were soon squashed.

His health, however, gave genuine cause for anxiety: and in May he went to a sanatorium in Bad Kissingen. The cure was expensive but he continued to follow the course of the war as closely as he could, asking Mimi to send him two copies each of the main newspaper of Munich and where possible of Berlin. But already the call-up papers for men in their forties had gone out, the sanatorium consultant was only able to get an eight-week stay of execution; after that he was to report in Munich.

"Now they are bombarding Venice!" he wrote to Mimi on 26th May 1915:

Hurra! Tell Herzog he should publish an advance report of the shelling of San Marco: "San Marco, as is well known, belonged to the most interesting monuments in the world. The mosaics outside covered some 15,000 square metres, those inside some 160,000, and thus offered a perfect target for us to bombard," etc.

But the mood in Bad Kissingen offered an even better target for Heinrich's sarcasm and disgust. He continued his letter to Mimi,

Since Italy has joined the scoundrels who will soon populate the whole world, Kissingen has broken out into vain victory-celebration. The streets are beflagged. Yesterday in the spa grounds a well-dressed Jewish gentleman was reading aloud the report about the 21,000 Russian casualties and gave a sharp three-times harra. Such is the way the spa-guests spend their time.

At the Berliners' tables Italy is going to get a greater pounding than England as you will see from the following table. Punishment for the use of following words: for French: 5 pfennigs; for Russian: 10 pfennigs; for English: 15; Italian: 20. But if America once joins there will be a difficult problem for they have no language of their own. To my mind the English fine will have to be doubled.[7]

But if Heinrich only gave vent to his disgust privately, Thomas had now begun publicly to defend Germany's war aims abroad — for although Fischer arranged to print his ten-page letter to the *Svenska Dagbladet* in the *Neue Rundschau* Thomas felt it was "superfluous for Germany" as he told Ernst Bertram.[8]

As Thomas' letter to the Swedish daily in May 1915 showed, he saw Germany more and more as a culture under siege:

You are worried about the unity of Europe? But Europe *is* united you know — more than that, the *world* is united (or was during the first months after outbreak of the catastrophe): namely against Germany. What this people — let us try to be as calm as possible — has had to put up with and listen to since the beginning of the war, has been . . . to put it mildly, it was enough to make the most untrustworthy German take up sides.

I will give you an example. A Senegalese negro, guarding German prisoners, an animal with lips as thick as cushions, passes his grey paw across his throat and gabbles: "They ought to be executed. They are barbarians."

I hope my little illustration amuses you? Perhaps you will understand it if we Germans look at "humanity" for a while in the light of this pleasant representative.

Briefly, what is wrong with Germany? What are her sins? — She wanted the war, it is said, and started it. And she has also revealed other barbaric principles — May I today write a couple of words in answer to this?

Above all Europe, proud of its refinement, should not lower its mask of psychological civilization quite so venomously — that is to say at the first worthwhile opportunity; it ought not to sermonize quite so juvenilely about "guilt" and "ill-will" when it well knows that the question of whether Germany wanted the war leads right into the muddy — and never resolved — question of the freedom of will, and that it says a great deal for the courage and human pride of a people that it freely chooses what fate has ordained for it. Whoever knows and loves the history of Frederick the Great is astounded and almost delighted by the astonishing parallel between the inward state of affairs in the summer of 1914 and that of 1756. How deeply the King must have despised the diligence with which his gang of opponents strove to make themselves appear innocent, to appear as the "defenders" and transfer the odium of the aggressor onto him — he who was above hypocrisy or that simple psychology which distinguishes clearly between "offensive" and "defensive", Frederick who was not in the least afraid of either guilt or odium! What sneaking hypocrisy not to be guilty at all, not to *want* to be guilty!

Good! Given — for the sake of argument — that Germany was completely responsible for this war — was the state of Europe *before* the war so wonderful, was it so worth preserving that it merits the title of abominable to have brought about its fall? Was this state of affairs not much more recognized everywhere to be impossible, unmaintainable, intolerable? The balance of European power — but it was the European impotence. It had been more than once its disgrace; and if this impotence of the Continent, swaying in jealous and strained balance, had for long been in the interest of one politically outer-European, yes anti-European world-power, it was nowhere written that the said interest should remain like that forever. Have a little courage to think clearly, gentlemen!

Thus the letter started — written by the artist who had always criticized his brother for his radical, political outspokenness, who had tried to emulate the bourgeois (in the best sense) strivings of his distinguished father, to accept a "constitution" in life, the responsibilities of everyday living like any other man: a wife, children, house . . . a writer who had seemed a model for the Artist in peacetime. At best his letter was in bad taste but at worst it inevitably became — as his *Frederick and the Grand Coalition* had been — a disingenuous argument for *Machtpolitik,* the power of the sword. When the few responsible intellects in Europe — Bertrand Russell, Romain Rolland, his own brother Heinrich — were arguing that the nations of Europe were too big, too potentially destructive to engage one another in war, Thomas was returning to the morals of a century and a half before.

It was this refusal of Thomas to open his eyes and see beyond the pettiness of international rivalry that most distressed Heinrich. *"Germany is in the right,"* Thomas rounded off yet another article, entitled *Thoughts on the War,* this time in the *Frankfurter Zeitung* on 3rd August 1915.

Physical resistance seemed idle as long as the majority of Germans were convinced they were still "in the right", and Mühsam's attempts to organize a revolt Heinrich felt untimely. "The good Mühsam is becoming, it would appear, a little dangerous," he wrote to Mimi at the end of May 1915[9]; but the atmosphere in Kissingen drove him to despair. "You cannot imagine what torture it is for me to live in a 'patriotic household'," he confided to Mimi on 5th June 1915, "and to have to submit to the conversations they conduct with one another. You hear nothing but madness and criminal statements. If the feeble Russians allow themselves to be beaten and the Italians don't quickly change their tempo, we will one day find ourselves in the position of being able to overrun France with terrible ease. Miracles will then be superfluous, and the world which we know will take on a simply intolerable aspect. Perhaps we will have to look for another? Today I find myself making plans of despairing phantasy." Nevertheless he thanked Mimi for looking after his mother in Munich — though he raised the cynical question of why the Frau Senator bothered to go in to town from Polling "when she could just as well enjoy the victorious news in the country".

Yet still Heinrich didn't break with Thomas. "Give me all the news, please, regularly about Eissi" (the nickname for Klaus, Thomas' eldest son, who had been in grave danger after appendicitis, requiring four operations) he finished his letter to Mimi.

"My darling," Heinrich wrote to her on 8th June "today they are shooting out the war like every other day. For them there could be no finer existence . . ."

More than ever he was grateful for having a wife who loved and supported him. The consultant at the sanatorium had now diagnosed the symptoms of a "weak heart," and any prospect of having to serve finally disappeared. But the Germans had now begun to bombard his beloved Riva, and he heard that his old doctor Christoph von Hartungen, had arrived in Munich.

Should he continue to remain silent? For months Heinrich had been making notes for a new essay similar to his article on Flaubert, this time evaluating the life and significance of Emile Zola who had died thirteen years before, in 1902. Like Thomas' *Frederick and the Grand Coalition* this would be more than a historical treatise. Like Thomas' essay it was an abstract for the day and hour; but an allegory that would look not for precedents and excuses for the present-day military actions, but which would put the whole ethic of the war into question. Like Zola's famous letters to *L'Aurore* it was, as Thomas himself later acknowledged,[10] a "J'accuse against the imperialistic war": a cry of conscience, of passionate humanity.

5

First warning of Heinrich's essay came in the July 1915 edition of Herzog's *Das Forum: Preface to an essay on Zola.* But in September 1915 the periodical was banned by the Bavarian ministry of war on account of its "unpatriotic aestheticism and Europeanism"; and it was only in November 1915 in René Schickele's *Die Weissen Blätter* that the essay finally became public.

The writer, who was destined to embrace reality more than any other, was for years only a dreamer and reveller. A creator only reaches manhood relatively late in life — it is those who appear natural and worldly-wise in their early twenties who are destined soon to dry up.

Thus the essay began. It was the second sentence which upset Thomas —

for he felt it was aimed directly at him.

It seems difficult today to understand why Thomas was so profoundly hurt by this passage — "the truly French spitefulness, the defamations and slanders of this glittering piece of sham whose second sentence was already an inhuman excess,"[11] as Thomas wrote two years later, at the height of their quarrel. "A little more sturdiness and brotherliness," Thomas had exhorted in 1909 when Heinrich felt he must break with their sister Lula. "I always think that brothers and sisters should not be able to knock each other down. They laugh or shout at each other, but they do not take shuddering leave of one another."

But Thomas was too fraught, too inextricably bound up with the "destiny" of his country in the winter of 1915 to observe his old rules of "brotherliness". The war itself, as he had noted in his letter to Bertram in February that year, had changed everything. Justice could grow old and be outdated by the times, by "necessity". The sentence in *Zola* rankled because it was only the opening of a blistering attack.

The similarity between Zola's life and Heinrich's was all too obvious. Both had begun as lonely and ambitious artists, both became convinced of the necessity to relate art to social reality, to the theme of democracy. Both had written works which predicted catastrophe — and catastrophe had proved them right.

With searching insight Heinrich framed the life of Zola against this personal identity: the scorn and derision, the years of comparative failure, a growing certainty 'within. As Zola reaches the peak and end of his life he hears of Dreyfus' wrongful imprisonment and with his famous letter sets in motion the seminal trial of the Republic. Convicted in open court for his assertions in the letter Zola has to flee France, and returns from exile only to hear his own assertions proven but Dreyfus again found guilty. Behind Dreyfus assembled those few who were prepared to withstand insult, conspiracy and even imprisonment in the pursuit of justice and truth; behind the judges congregated the army, the government, an array of frenzied patriotic Frenchmen who believed the honour of France and its military caste were too important to be sacrificed to justice for a Jew.

It is surprising that *Die Weissen Blätter* was permitted to publish the article: within months in fact Schickele was forced to flee Germany and continue publication of the periodical in Switzerland.

But Heinrich felt too betrayed at the time by his fellow "intellects" in Germany who had sprung to support the war rather than question it to mince words. His essay was no less courageous and historic than Zola's *J'accuse;* and though Thomas would one day come to prize it, he could never quite bring himself to forgive it.

For as much as Heinrich identified himself with the "banned and silenced" figure of Zola, so he was bound to see Thomas, whose inner anxieties before the war he had come to know all too well, as an archetype of this betrayal. Thomas who scorned democracy on aesthetic grounds and who now excused slaughter on a scale never hitherto experienced by mankind, excused it as, in the parallel of King Frederick, "the right of the rising power". As Frederick had shown — and Hitler would show again all too soon — the rising power needs no intellectual justification, it is founded on fact, on the power of the sword. It is not military power which requires the "service" of its intellectuals but the oppressed who cry out for recognition and intellectual championing. It is significant that Heinrich's only major work of fiction to be written in the war — however disappointing as a literary work — was called *Die Armen* (The Poor).

But Thomas was away on a cloud of his own, fighting as he believed for his own and his country's survival — a Germany whom even a village simpleton could testify had armed and prepared for war since the setting down of the "pilot" Bismarck. Yet Thomas' defence was not simplistic, in many ways it showed a radical and bitter self-understanding. "Germany came late into being," he had written to the *Svenska Dagbladet,*

and when it began to look around it was evident that Might did in fact signify Right. In recent times we find this brutal, but to be intellectually fair one ought to know that it is a case here of conscious brutality, of a considered will to worldly reality, to worldly ability . . . Does one understand that? a case of brutality which in no way signifies primitiveness, but self-correction, resignation. Germany, highly radical in the spiritual sphere, never wished to be that in real life. That is its lack of generosity, of childishness. In reality we lack the generous and courteous gestures to which the French hold so fast. Bismarck's positivism, his "Realpolitik", his idea of justice — that corresponds in a deep and characteristic way with Kant's practical mind in contrast to the "pure" — and the categorical imperative beyond wretched scepticism is something very German. The German love of reality, real and passionate as any, is ironic and melancholic, somewhat gloomy and, in the final analysis, not without contempt for it . . .

This war for which Germany had prepared conscientiously and out of distrust, but which it would not have wanted if one had not forced it to want it: why did Germany recognize and welcome it when it broke upon us? — Because she recognized in it the herald of her *Third* Reich. — What is her Third Reich then? — It is the synthesis of *might* and *mind,* of might and spirit — it is her dream and her demand, her highest war aim — and not Calais or the "enslavement of peoples" or the Congo.

But Heinrich — the man whose *Man of Straw* had taken eight painful years to formulate and complete, was sickened by this sub-Hegelian propaganda. Heinrich was not anti-German or blindly pro-French as Thomas took pains to make him appear in his next book: he was much more a profound and passionate European, an artist who could so easily have elected to pursue the "individual" path of his early career, and go down in the history of German literature as the pioneer of twentieth-century German prose.

"Those were often the more enticing ways," he wrote of Zola's contemporaries:

Their talent seemed modern, their taste was often of the most sensitive kind. They made themselves out to be pessimists, they denied in the most ingenious manner ideas of progress and even humanity without ever thinking to deny what actually existed in the country and was dangerous . . .

But like Zola, Heinrich had felt the real responsibility of the artist to his society, above all in a country without parliamentary tradition, whose artists and philosophers had all too often shunned the "contemptuous realities" of the practical world.

For now it didn't matter if they [Zola's contemporaries] stood ranged in fine gear against truth and justice; they stood against them and thus belonged to the common herd, the herd that will one day disappear. They had chosen between history and the moment and had shown that with all their talents they were but entertaining parasites. And even their talents seemed now to have failed them, Zola saw the most distinguished writers and poets suddenly indulging in the most windy journalism.

Heinrich's strictures — as far as they applied to his own contemporaries in the war — were true of a whole host of artists and academics, for scarcely an important name had refrained from eager support of the Kaiser — the same. figure who for many of them had been the most execrable and untrustworthy of leaders only months before. But in German Heinrich used the third-person singular for this paragraph ("man"): and with deep pencil marks Thomas scored and underlined the copy of the essay he had obtained. It seemed a personal attack on him: and so public!

It was, of course, unkind of Heinrich not to warn Thomas of the piece, or even show him it in manuscript: but communications between the two had already deteriorated, and contact was made through the indirect channel of their wives,[12] — and Thomas had certainly not deigned to discuss his own "windy journalism" with Heinrich before allowing it to appear.

The *Zola* essay thus marked the end of an already strained relationship. Their correspondence, when they were upset, always assumed a "somewhat literary character" Thomas had noted in an earlier quarrel: now it had become a literary exchange.

The November edition of *Die Weissen Blätter* sold out instantly; it became the talk of all literary, intellectual and informed circles in Germany. Word soon reached the Poschingerstrasse that Thomas was implicated. On the 31st December 1915 Thomas wrote a short note to Maximilian Brantl, Heinrich's solicitor, whom he had seen during the day.

"Dear Herr Doctor," it ran, "I forgot to ask you for something today. You have a copy of the 'Weissen Blätter' which contains my brother's essay on Zola. Would you lend it to me for a while? If you can, could you please send it — before you join up if possible. Best wishes, yours, Thomas Mann." Brantl said he had loaned his copy to Ernst Bertram, and on 5th January 1916 Thomas wrote a similar card to Bertram. Bertram duly despatched the copy; and the rift between Heinrich and Thomas that had widened both above and beneath the surface for over fifteen years finally became unbridgeable.

6

The *Zola* essay was Heinrich's first major statement since the beginning of the war: and its challenge echoed across the Reich. It was, for instance, undoubtedly this essay which attracted the young publisher Kurt Wolff's attention to Heinrich, for it was Wolff himself who had helped to found the periodical *Die Weissen Blätter* in 1913 with E.E. Schwabach.

Frank Wedekind had written already on 1st December 1915, to congratulate Heinrich.

If France can be proud of Zola, then in my opinion we can be even prouder that this work has been written by a German in such times as these. Your essay personifies the superiority of German thinking not over nations but over the state of the world today. Besides this it seems to me your work is an act of peace for which everyone who believes in the happiness of his fellow men cannot be grateful enough.

Kurt Wolff went further. From his service post as an officer in the Balkans he instructed his chief editor G.H. Meyer to try to secure the publishing rights to all Heinrich's works. From the Balkans he then wrote on 1st February 1916:

Dear Herr Mann,

I didn't wish to write to you myself until I knew for certain from G.H. Meyer that my long-standing and earnest desire to be able to publish your work could be fulfilled in full agreement with your erstwhile publishers and yourself. Now I have received the good news and would like to express to you my great, great joy which I feel before this new, difficult and wonderful task. For the assumption of this responsibility, the signing of the contract with you, is for me the greatest undertaking I have ever entered . . .

Wolff decided to publish a 10-volume Collected Edition of Heinrich's works — but simultaneously to issue them individually in his new series entitled 'The New Novel' at 3.50 Marks each. Within twelve months the seven of Heinrich's novels in the series had sold collectively over 250,000 copies — not one of which had exceeded 5,000 with its original publisher — and by 1918 the figure had risen to 750,000.

But it was Heinrich's still unpublished *Der Untertan*, which seemed to Wolff the most important responsibility of all. On 4th April 1916, he wrote to Meyer:

I have just finished reading the book and am overwhelmed. Here is the start of what I have always been searching for: the German novel of the post-1871 period. (If *Land of Cockaigne* is a small contribution, then this is enormous). Here is the start of an analysis of German conditions which — since Fontane at least — has been entirely missing. Here suddenly is a work, unique and great, which, when enlarged, could be for German history and literature what Balzac's was for the first French empire and Zola for the second . . .

That *Der Untertan* cannot be published during the war, both author and publisher are agreed. But after the war it will definitely appear, boldly announced with kettledrums and trumpets . . . It is precisely at a time when we shall be flooded by a deluge of field-grey books that *Der Untertan* must appear."

Even without *Der Untertan*, however, Wolff's revolutionary techniques of publicity and advertising gave the impetus that had always been lacking in the marketing of Heinrich's works. From obscurity and near-penury (in February 1916 he had tried to raise 5,000 Marks from his inheritance, still held in Lübeck), Heinrich's name suddenly became a household word and with this fame came the financial security he had striven for over twenty years to achieve. Mimi was expecting a baby and in 1916 she gave birth to a girl. They moved into a new apartment in the Leopoldstrasse, and letters from readers poured in from all over Germany and the German front. The apartment, as Heinrich's brother Viktor noted,[13] became one of the centres of pacifist thought and post-war ideas in the Bavarian capital. Heinrich meanwhile set to work on a sequel to *Der Untertan*, covering the same period, to be entitled *Die Armen*.

But on the far bank of the Isar, in the Bogenhausen villa at the beginning of the Poschingerstrasse, Thomas found all hope of continuing his novels, *The Magic Mountain* and *Felix Krull*, impossible. Shortly after his *Thoughts on the War* essay he had begun what he hoped would be a brief but enlarged essay on the same subject, covering all the spiritual and artistic ramifications of the great European struggle. It was this essay which, after reading Heinrich's *Zola*, Thomas now attempted to revise and refine. Its vitriolic sallies against Heinrich and the muddled, superficial effect it had on Ernst Bertram, when Bertram read it in February 1916, convinced Thomas, however, that he would have to rewrite the whole piece. He can have had little idea it would take almost two more years to complete; and that the war would be lost by the time it appeared.

But clear his name of the "slanders and defamations" he would. "Que diable allait-il faire dans cette galère?" was the motto he chose from Molière's *Les Fourberies de Scapin:* "Compare yourself! Discover what you are!" that from Goethe's *Tasso*.

"I am writing a little self-critical and topical book which concerns art and politics and is aimed above all at the detestable category I call 'Civilisationsliteraten'. I think it will find your approval," he wrote on 17th June 1916 to his ex-employer at *Simplicissimus,* Korfiz Holm.

"Civilisation-Littérateur", "Rhetorical-bourgeois", "political new-waver", "Boulevard moralist", "oaf-psychologist", "German Western-ally", "the German belles-lettres activist" — there could be no doubt who the perfidious felon of the *Reflections of a Non-Political Man* might be. Bertram and Thomas' old friend Kurt Martens tried to moderate some of the more hysterical passages; but as Thomas' son Klaus later recorded, it was like Don Quixote tilting at the windmill.[14]

Heinrich's words had penetrated Thomas' deepest artistic and human identity. Thomas' aim was now to expose the detested "Civilisation-Littérateur", to rehabilitate himself — and through doing so, to rehabilitate Germany.

7

As news of the rift between Heinrich and Thomas began to penetrate literary and intellectual circles of Germany and even France, it gradually became a *cause célèbre*. And the more public, the more representative ·their quarrel, the less chance there was that a personal reconciliation could take place. It developed into a struggle of honour.

In Thomas' case the need to justify himself in the eyes of Heinrich and the world became obsessive: even though, as victory in the West moved inexorably away from the grasp of Germany's generals, not even his wife believed in a successful outcome.

"Our mother's opinions with regard to the war and its probable outcome dissented from what our father obstinately believed," Klaus Mann later recalled:[15]

They never argued: there was no loud word at table. But we were keen and observant enough to notice the divergence of their views. Mother had lost faith in the cause and the winning chance of the Reich, whereas the Magician [the children's nickname for their father] remained grimly confident.

This wartime father seems estranged and distant, essentially different from the father I have known before and after those years of struggle and bitterness. The paternal physiognomy that looms up when I recall this period seems devoid of the kindness and irony which both inseparably belong to his character. The face I visualize looks severe and sombre — a proud and nervous brow with sensitive temples and sunken cheeks. Curiously enough it is a bearded face, a long haggard oval framed by a hard prickly beard . . . His features, at once proud and worried, resemble those of a Spanish Knight and nobleman — the errant hero and dreamer called Don Quixote.

The origin of Thomas' family nickname, the Magician, seems to lie in a fancy-dress costume Thomas wore for a party to which Erika and Klaus insisted he accompany them, and which caused a sensation — rather like his impersonation of an imbecile that Viktor witnessed almost twenty years before. But, as Klaus also recalled, it was his father's supernatural powers which earned him the real title. Klaus suffered from a frightening nightmare about a "pallid gentleman who carried his head under his arm as if it were a pot or a cylinder"; and his nurse Anna told Thomas of it.

"He came to see us at bedtime," Klaus remembered,

— a rare event in itself! — and developed his proposed strategy. The decapitated guest, he suggested, wasn't really so frightful. He tried to get the better of us by sheer bluff. "Just don't look at him when he comes again!'' he advised us. "Then he'll probably vanish. If he still annoys you ask him politely to beat it. Tell him that a children's bedroom is no place for a decent phantom to hang out and that he should be ashamed of himself. This may be enough to get rid of him, but if he still hesitates, you may warn him that your father is very irritable and just doesn't like to have ugly spooks in his house. At this point he'll disappear without making any more fuss. For it is a well-known fact in ghostly circles that I can make myself very unpleasant indeed."

We followed his advice and the spook presently dissolved. It was an imposing proof of father's almost superhuman insight and influence. From that time on we began to call him "Zauberer" — magician.

But Heinrich's ghost would not dissolve so obediently. "Struggling to become national poets for half a lifetime if they should live so long," Heinrich had written of Zola's contemporaries; "but always following the band, always enflaming the lofty feelings of the senses, responsible for the oncoming catastrophe, and yet as ignorant of it as the dimmest fool!" So, with "anger and sorrow" Zola parts company from his fellows who, "despite everything", he had held to be his equals. "Toleration or further delay were no longer permissible. The greatest test of all had arisen and committed the intellects of the age firmly to step out, unjustly divided, the ones on the side of the victors of the day, the others on the side of those who struggle for eternal values."

"With sorrow and anger he turned away from me," Thomas remembered in his *Reflections of a Non-Political Man*, "which sorrow, however, didn't prevent his anger from allowing him to say half-public double-edged things which from a political standpoint might be excellent, but from a personal and human point of view were acts of mean vulgarity . . ."

Nothing the citizens of Lübeck, Richard Schaukal, Dr Lessing or Thomas' meanest critics — from Alfred Kerr to Adolf Bartels — had said or written had ever struck Thomas as deeply as Heinrich's essay. On 18th June 1916 he returned Brantl's copy of the infamous work:

I am at last returning your Weissen Blätter and beg a thousand times forgiveness for the pencil marks. I started to rub them out, but felt it would only make them worse. Actually, pencil marks almost belong to this article; it seems most readers will not notice the most outrageous ambiguities. Auf Wiedersehen.

In August 1916 he suffered a "nervous breakdown" which forced him to set aside his mammoth defence; but after eight days he was again back at work, disappearing after an early breakfast and seen only fleetingly again at lunch.

"What you say about the fate of Germany is only too true," he wrote to Bertram on 25th November.

It is not megalomania but only the need to see things in intimate terms which long ago made me see this fate symbolized and personified in my brother and myself. I have long believed that, for inner more than external reasons, it is impossible to create an authentic political life in Germany. I

feel deeply that like my brother I have no chance of influencing contemporary German events, but in a different way. It all comes down to
the fact that we are not a nation. Rather we are something like the
quintessence of Europe, so that we are subject to the clash of Europe's
spiritual contradictions without having a national synthesis. There is no
German solidarity and ultimate unity. European wars will no longer be
waged on German soil you say? Oh yes, they will be! There will always
be German civil wars in fact.

Time is swift, and I am slow. I must think out everything minutely and
pedantically, and I fear I am growing old and tired in the process.

But what was really happening was that, by confronting so deeply the
truths about German and European civilization, Thomas was gaining the
profundity and insight that would one day make him the acknowledged
spokesman of Western civilization.

8

Meanwhile the toll of lives on the Western front mounted and mounted:
Ypres, Loos, Verdun, the Somme — it was a savage price to pay for the
"cleansing" of Europe.

"Sometimes (for a long time now) I dream that I am in Italy during the
war and wander about in a town full of fear of capture and arrest," Heinrich
confessed to Mimi in a letter of 21st July 1916, while the Battle of the
Somme continued. He was asked to give a lecture on Zola in Prague, to speak
in Dresden, Leipzig, Hamburg and Northern Germany. But always his views
must be veiled in the allegory of the French Second Empire. Rosa Luxemburg
started the Spartacus League, and on 1st May 1916 Karl Liebknecht had led
the first workers' demonstration against the war, in the Potsdamer Platz,
Berlin. He distributed leaflets and shouted "Down with the war! Down with
the government!" Heinrich witnessed the scene, which inevitably ended in
bloodshed as police descended upon the 20,000-strong crowd with swords
and truncheons and then began firing into the mêlée. After this Heinrich
agreed to take part in a meeting of anti-war socialists in Munich: the future
"Council of Intellectual Workers" which heralded the Munich Revolution in
1918. In his notebook in 1916 he drafted an article addressed to the youth
of twenty years later: *To the twenty-year olds of 1936*. It was never — could
never be — published, but its analysis of the war and those who pursued it was
devastating.

"The war was not, was in no way what your history teachers will lie to
you," he noted prophetically.

War is nothing to enthuse over, it does not civilize, it does not cleanse, it
does not make anything true or just. And it does not make people more
brotherly.

It does the opposite of all this — anyone could verify this today,
but they wish to forget it, they don't even *want* to recognize it . . .

Brotherliness. Democratic: One million dead: very sad, says someone, as though waving away a flag. And the same man: "I got out of military service by corruption." — *The indifference of human beings towards one another as final effect* of the war. No belief in humanity. Late Darwinism: we are animals. Intellect, ideas: fooleries. Hostile to men and to the mind. *Trashy feeling of loneliness,* hangover from romantic literature. *Even we* are responsible for that.

The Lies. Who was a patriot in the war? Not those who in peacetime most loved their people. Never those who in their hearts wished to see it greater and more beautiful. But mainly the individualists, the sceptics about humanity, the worshippers of the State, the enemies of the *people.*

Definition. Who is a traitor? He who thinks only of his people and relates his ideas — freedom, truth, justice, well-being — all to his own people (but wishes other people well) . . .

One by one Heinrich recorded the lies of war, the inhumanities perpetrated against women and children, the boasting of "heroes' deeds".

Putting their entire hope in terrorism — and then denying it! And yet at the beginning they openly admitted to it as a way of "shortening" the war, and therefore making it more "humane". — Well it has not been shortened, terrorism no longer has this excuse. It has only made the war more inhuman. But they do not give up. They bite their lips furiously and throw themselves into the erroneous psychology which first brought such terrorism, and which is the final reason for war.

They no longer know human beings, let alone civilized human beings. They are wanting in literature, the feeling of human things. They blindly strike out when they attempt to condemn the enemy — the very enemy they want to influence! The last resort of the stupid is force: and when it brings the opposite of what was expected they just stand there stunned — and go on lying! . . .

What sort of idea is it that sees war as an educator, a creator, a father against the millions of dead who now surround us? Certain military men have lived out the ideology of war, long before it was formulated by so-called thinkers. The "realists" who thought they could see beyond the Littérateurs were ideologists! The war — again and again one comes to this realization — is the final consequence of unrealistic — because inhuman — unpsychological thought: the penalty for lack of literature.

It was obvious against whom many of these strictures were aimed: but the sincerity of Heinrich's distress and sense of betrayal is evident in every line. His analysis of how it had come about — a synthesis of the themes in his own *Man of Straw* — which followed, were no less telling:

The earlier ideals of Germans, their romantic nature, the honesty of their thinking and the genuineness of their feelings, their will to truth, their will to goodness: all were undermined in 43 years of empire; on the surface only beautiful phrases, no belief any more, underneath was the mine, death. And one day all erupts. It becomes clear that force here, only here, is everything, is the only thing anyone really respects, the only thing anyone has respected for a long, long time. In truth Germany has been made barbarous again by the continual pressure of the "Reich".

Meanwhile Thomas laboured to complete his *Reflections of a Non-Political Man*. He had hoped to finish them early in 1917, but more and more themes ("Virtue", "Humanity", "Aestheticizing Politics", "Radicalism", "Irony" and "Conservatism"[16]) presented themselves. This was certainly going to be the most comprehensive literary campaign of the Kaiser's war — and one for which, ironically, Thomas would be awarded the title of Honorary Doctor of Philosophy shortly after the founding of the Weimar Republic in 1919.

But neither the work on his titanic essay nor Heinrich's strictures could halt the flow of Thomas' war propaganda in the newspapers. Following his letter to the *Svenska Dagbladet* and his article *Thoughts on the War* came yet another article in the *Frankfurter Zeitung,* in the spring of 1917, in the form of an open letter. This time however Thomas' emphasis had shifted from the positive aims of the war to its possible negative results for European peace: if Germany were beaten it would give rise, he threatened, to even greater nationalism in the country.

I at any rate believe this would happen; for I can *not* imagine that the German people can ever bring itself to accept world-historical teachings about English virtue.

Already the course of the war had begun to swing against Germany, despite her victories in the East; and already since the end of 1916 Thomas had begun to have misgivings about the "cleansing" effect of the war, and was thinking more and more about the future. "I hate democracy," he wrote in November 1916 to Paul Amman who was serving at the front, "and I hate politics, for they are one and the same to me." He was caught, as he had been before the war, between two stools. Reason told him that democracy *must* come; yet his heart, his soul, told him that Germany was not suited to it. "We are not a nation like the others," he continued his letter to Amman.

We are more something like Europe in the abstract. In our souls, yes in the soul of every individual German, the contradictions of Europe are borne out. There is no national German solidarity and synthesis — only perhaps in music, our homeland, but never, never in the intellect and in politics: which is why it is a mad and un-national undertaking to substitute a literary-political atmosphere in Germany for that of the musical, as the "Civilisation-Littérateur" wishes to do. We are no nation. National feeling is only spiritually possible with us when we are at rock bottom, when things are going very badly . . . otherwise it is not possible . . . Today there is no longer pride, nor dignity, or hatred: there is only admiration for the enemy, duty to oneself, and egoistic corruption; *chacun pour soi* and *sauve qui peut*. The future looks terrible. Nothing will ever come of us . . .

A year later Thomas had already begun the slow and painful reconciliation between the demands of democracy and the Germanness of his soul. His response to the *Berliner Tageblatt's* request in December 1917 for the view of distinguished intellectuals and writers on the theme of "World Peace" gave the first glimpse of hope. But to Heinrich it came like a letter addressed to him: and Heinrich reached out for what he interpreted, after three years of rift, as an olive branch of peace.

9

"Even the greatest feeling is made small if it trumps itself with big words; a little goodness between one man and another is better than all the love one may feel for humanity," Thomas quoted Richard Dehmel in his article for the *Berliner Tageblatt*.

That is it, believe me! The politico-rehetorical love of humanity is a very peripheral kind of love and is usually expressed most melodiously when there is something amiss at the core of it. He who plays the philanthropist should first become better himself, less hard, less arrogantly dogmatic, less aggressively self-righteous . . . The man who knows how to annouce beautifully "I love God" may have great success. If in doing so, however "he should hate his brother", then, according to St John's Gospel, his love of God is nothing more than fine literature and sacrificial smoke which doesn't rise.

World peace . . . Not even in deepest national bitterness have I ever stopped thinking that the hate and hostility between the peoples of Europe is, in the final analysis, a deception, an error — that the sides which are tearing at each other's throats at heart are no sides, but are working together, according to God's will, in brotherly torment towards a resurrection of the world. Yes, it is permissible to dream of a reconciled and quietened Europe . . . For the refinement through suffering is higher and more human than that which derives from happiness and prosperity; I believe in this and in good moments also in a future Europe which, having reached a religious humanity and spiritual tolerance, will look back upon today's unwholesome quarrels with shame and derision . . .

I fear the "European intellectual" will deny my right to such dreams. It is true I found myself more German than I thought I was; but I was never a nationalist, a "patriotic artist". I found it impossible to pretend the war "had nothing to do" with me — on the grounds perhaps that war has nothing to do with culture, an assertion I find altogether too bold. Shaken, up-rooted, provoked to screaming point, I threw myself into the tumult and disputatiously defended my country. But God knows I will feel much better when my soul, cleansed of politics, can once again look at life and humanity, my being will be much more capable of proving itself when the peoples of Europe return to peaceful borders and live with one another in dignity and honour and exchange their most valued possessions: the fine Englishman, the polished Frenchman, the humane Russian and the knowledgeable German.

Thus ran Thomas' article in the *Berliner Tageblatt* on 27th December 1917. It was still hopelessly idealistic in its refusal to accept politics as the only way a people can live out — as it must — the sometimes frustrating path towards national maturity. Yet it was phrased in obviously quieter, more reconciled tones that were not lost on Heinrich.

America had entered the war, the Reichstag had already voted for a "peace without annexations", and though the Brest-Litovsk treaty had released a large number of German troops from the Eastern front, it was unlikely that Germany could win any crushing victories in the West. The blockade had begun to starve the country, there was no longer the blind belief in the Kaiser that had once prevailed.

Heinrich's hour was approaching. Kurt Wolff had published a private edition of *Der Untertan* in 1916, some ten copies that were sent to selected political and diplomatic names; but the type was now standing ready for the moment when the war would end — and the Russian translation, published in Moscow in 1915, had achieved a phenomenal success for a German author. The sequel to *Der Untertan, Die Armen,* had appeared in Wolff's "New Novel" series in 1917, as well as a new three-act play by Heinrich, *Brabach,* and a further collection of short stories, *Bunte Gesellschaft. Madame Legros* was now being staged in Munich and Berlin — the first "revolutionary" play to be staged in Germany since the beginning of the war.

But though many parts of the *Zola* essay were consciously aimed at his own contemporaries, Heinrich had never seen the war itself as a convenient event for the expression of his personal or political views. Every sentence in his letters and diaries at this time confirms his abhorrence for the war; as his prophecies came true, one after another, he was filled not with false pride but humility. He felt Wolff was wrong to issue his novels at such a low price, and begged him to take them out of the "Neuer Roman" series. He had worked for eighteen years without real success and he did not want to "throw away" the results of so much pain and suffering on the tide of temporary interest.[17]

"The struggle for eternal values" he had written in his *Zola* essay. When a friend read out to him Thomas' *Berliner Tageblatt* article he was deeply moved — the account that later reached Thomas was that he sat down and wept at the accusation of brotherly hate behind melodious calls to humanity.[18]

Three days later Heinrich wrote his first letter to Thomas since the early months of the war, of which the original draft has survived. It was headed "Attempt at Reconciliation" and dated 30.12.1917; but sadly it was to no avail.

10

Dear Tommy,

Your article in the B.T. has just been read aloud in my presence. I do not know if it struck the other listeners, but to me in certain passages it sounded as though addressed to me, almost as a letter. For this reason I feel I must answer, even if it is done without recourse to the roundabout way of the press, and with the sole intent of telling you how misguided is your reproach of brotherly hate. — There is no "I" in my public utterances, and for that reason also no brother. They are directed — at least I intend it so — beyond myself, my middle-class position, my advantage or disadvantage, and relate solely to an idea or theme. Love of humanity (in political terms: European democracy) is of course love of an ideal; but whosoever can lift his heart that far into the distance will also have proved his goodness in the particular . . . I know that in the course of the years I have shown some of this goodness, and can remember cases where I showed more than I received. I have read all your work with the best will in the world to try and understand and sympathize with it. But I have known your intellectual hostility from the beginning, and if your extreme response to the war came as a surprise to you it was for me quite predictable. This knowledge however did not stop me from often loving your work, even more frequently from studying it and time after time from publicly acclaiming it or defending it; and consoling you, when you doubted yourself, as a younger brother. Though I received almost nothing in return from this, I did not let myself be defeated. I knew that, in order to stand secure, you needed to hold yourself back, even to shun people, — and because of this I always got over your attacks — they stem as far back as an article in a magazine called the "Freistatt" up to your latest book — without great difficulty. Overcame them and did not reply to them — or only on one occasion when it was no longer a case of personal views, no longer literary preference or spiritual justifications at stake, but a case of the very greatest emergency and danger. It was in my protest, entitled *Zola,* that I took issue with those who, as I saw it, were rushing forward to do damage. It was not aimed against you but against a legion. And today, instead of a legion, there are only a few desperate ones; you yourself write sadly; — and your final argument should only be the reproach of brotherly hate? I can assure you, if not prove to you, that it is not true. I have never acted on that emotion — and have, on the contrary, tried to act *against* it when I tried to get us together again at a time when it looked hopeless. Our letter about the birth of our child was not well received. Perhaps my efforts today will get a better reception. This would be possible if your latest claim against me is dictated by sorrow: for then you would see that you do not have to look upon my words as those of an enemy.

Heinrich

Perhaps Heinrich modified the letter in the version he sent, but from Thomas' reply this would seem unlikely. For Thomas, having seen his "great, festive war of the people" turn into a European bloodbath without equal in the history of the world, having given up his calling as a poet of fiction to defend the fatherland, having spent two years of his life formulating his titanic self-justification in his *Reflections of a Non-Political Man,* was not going to give in to such a stiff and self-righteous offer of reconciliation – no more than President Wilson's Peace Proposals could be taken seriously in a Europe that had invested so much in this struggle. He answered Heinrich's letter the day after receiving it, on 3rd January 1918.

If Heinrich had predicted Thomas' response to the war he cannot have been surprised by Thomas' reply to his letter. It was pained, emotional, a trifle melodramatic (a "separation forever"); and yet was not this obstinacy a sign of more than pride? Was it not much more a statement finally of his independence, an indication that he had at last broken the fraternal bond which, he felt, was preventing him from finding himself, his freedom?

11

Munich 3 Jan. 18

Dear Heinrich:

Your letter comes at a moment when it is physically impossible for me to reply properly . . . However I wonder whether there is any sense in trying to compress the mental torment of two years into a letter which would have to be much longer than yours. I believe you implicitly when you say that you feel no hatred towards me. After the unleashing outburst of the Zola essay and considering the way everything stands with you and for you at the moment, you have no reason to. The phrase about fraternal hate was in any case rather a symbol for more general discrepancies in the psychology of the Rousseauiste.

If you have found me a difficult brother, I naturally have found you even more so; that was in the nature of things; and I too did my honest best. To this day I praise at least two of your books in the teeth of everyone else as masterpieces. You forget or are silent about the way you so often mishandled my simplest and strongest feelings with your justification of passion, before I could react with as much as a sentence. Of course my claim was as little *personally* directed at you as any of yours. Our fraternal experience of life and the world is bound to colour things personally. But things which you allowed yourself to say in your Zola essay and expected me to take – no, I have never allowed myself such liberties or expected any man to put up with such. That you believed, after the truly French spitefulness, the defamations and slanders of this glittering piece of sham whose second sentence was already an inhuman excess, you could "seek a rapprochement" although it seemed "hopeless" – this demonstrates the frivolity of a man who has "lifted his heart far into the distance." Incidentally my wife wrote at length at the time to yours, delicately and warmly, and received effronteries in reply.

It is not true that my conduct in the war has been "extreme". Yours was, and in fact to the point of being utterly detestable. But I have not suffered and struggled for two years, neglected my dearest projects, sentenced myself to silence as an artist, probed, compared and asserted myself just to answer a letter which — understandably — exudes triumph, sees me at the head of a "few desperate men" searching for last-ditch arguments, and concludes that I need not regard you as an enemy. Every line of your letter was dictated by moral smugness and self-righteousness. Don't expect me to fall sobbing on your breast. What lies behind me was like starving in a galley; all the same I thank you for the knowledge that I stand less helplessly exposed to your zealot's tongue today than in the days when you could hurt me to the quick with it.

You and your sort can call me a parasite if you like. The truth, *my* truth, is that I am none. A great bourgeois artist, Adalbert Stifter, once said in a letter: "My books are not simply poetic creations, but as moral revelations, as human dignity preserved with great seriousness, they have a value which will last longer than the poetic." I have a right to repeat those words, and thousands who I have helped to live — although without reciting the Social Contract, one hand on my heart and the other outstretched — *see* it, this right.

Not you. You cannot see the right and ethos of my life, because you are my brother. How was it that no one else . . . referred the invectives of the Zola article to himself? Why was it all, in its savage polemic, aimed at me? Fraternal experience drove you to it. Take Dehmel, who sent me thanks and congratulations from the trenches for my war articles in the "Neue Rundschau". You can show the greatest warmth to him at the dress-rehearsals and he can do likewise, for though you are radically different intellectually you are not brothers and therefore there's room for you both in the world. — Let the tragedy of our brotherhood take its course to the bitter end.

Sorrow? It is bearable. One grows hard and blunt. Ever since Carla killed herself and you broke with Lula for life such separations for all time are nothing new in our family circle. I have not enjoyed this life. I despise it. But one must live one's life to the end as best one can.

Farewell
T

Heinrich, less than a mile away in the Leopoldstrasse, must have fingered the reply to his appeal with a mixture of distress and yet understanding. He formulated his reply to Thomas' reply: but he must have known there was no point, for the letter bears the legend "Not sent" across the top. Yet as the concluding speech in a case which, after publication first of the *Zola* essay, then of the *Reflections,* became the intellectual *cause célèbre* of the war it is a very moving document.

Dear Tommy,
In the face of such bitterness I ought to keep silent and accept the "separation for all time" in the way you present it. But I want to try every

channel. I want to help you as far as possible to see things later, when all this is over, more justly. To a letter which betrayed not tenderness or suchlike but only arrogance I had to dictate to my wife the appropriate reply. But I never deliberately part for ever. I wait until the other party makes some effort towards rapprochement. That is the nature of my zealot's frivolity.

I did not seek an argument, not even over four pages — and it is with great regret I learn that one single statement of opinion on my part has caused you to spend two years formulating a reply. I think it better — as long as consideration of my reputation does not oblige me to do otherwise — if I do *not* read your book — not out of disregard but because I prefer a normal, natural relationship to you to a polemical one. As far as I can see you have underestimated your importance in my life as far as feelings are concerned, and overestimated it as far as intellectual influence is concerned. You have suffered from the latter. You must accept the truth of this, it is not meant abusively like the style of your letter, which shows more pathos than ethos. As far as I am concerned I see myself as an independent human being, and my "experience of life and the world" is not fraternal but simply my own. You do not get in my way. For instance I would be truly gladdened if you were to write something other than absurdities about French actions and virtues; whereas you — if it ever occurred to me to acknowledge Frederick of Prussia, do you know what you would do? You would throw all your notes to your *Frederick* in the fire.

"In inimicos" you once said, a 22 year old sitting at the piano in the via Argentina trento quattro, with your back turned to me. That is the way it has remained for you. But you are still young, I can still dissuade you from it before it is too late, for it wasn't good for you then, nor is it now. Stop relating my life and actions always to yourself, it has nothing to do with you, would be precisely the same if you did not exist. The 2nd sentence of the *Zola* article has nothing to do with you and the few pages that do would still stand almost word for word if only other people were at fault. But some of these others have thought better of their attitudes, and I am again on friendly terms with them. I never separate deliberately for ever.

Self-righteousness? Oh no — rather a feeling of combined guilt with those who, like me, know how much we who led the art and intellect of our generation were responsible for allowing the catastrophe to take place. Self-probing, struggle is something others, perhaps more modest minds than you, have gone through, but after it came regret and renewed energy — not only "self-assertion" (which does not warrant such pains), not only "suffering" for the sake of oneself, this furious passion for your own "I". You owe several narrow but private works to this passion. You also owe your complete lack of respect for anything which doesn't suit you to it, your "contempt" which is more unreliable in you than any other person I know; in short your inability ever to grasp the real seriousness of anyone's life but your own.

Around you are irrelevant extras who signify "the people" to you, as in your hymns of *Royal Highness*. Extras have their own destiny, or even ethos? — Your own ethos, who says I did not acknowledge it? I have always known it, I respected it as your subjective experience, and where portrayed in your works I did not long molest you with my reservations about its value for other people. But if I too consider myself in such a way, how does it appear to you? As the picture of a play-acting braggart and glittering hack. You poor fool!

The inability to take another person's life seriously in the end leads to monstrous things — and so you find my letter which was an act of simple friendliness — "exuding triumph". Triumph over what? That everything "stands" well with and for me, namely the world in ruins and 10 million corpses rotting. That is some kind of justification! That is satisfaction to the ideologist! But I am not the kind of person to cut the misery and death of whole peoples according to the fancies of my spirit, not I. I do not believe the success or victory of any matter is worth discussing where we human beings perish. Every bit of better humanity that can be won will taste bitter and sad after the last, most terrible things that are still in store for us. I do not know if anyone can actually help his fellow-men "to live"; but for God's sake don't ever allow our literature to help them to die!

And they still go on dying; — you, however, who applauded the war and continue to do so, who considers my conduct as utterly abominable — I who put on a play that became no small mirror of our present situation and was the very first to give some hope for the future to the tormented — if God wills you will have another 40 years to prove yourself, if not to "assert" yourself. The hour will come, I hope, in which you will see people, not shadows; and then perhaps me.

H.

PART TWO

CHAPTER TEN

The Brothers Reconciled

"And they still go on dying."

No human conflict had ever brought such casualties: yet among Thomas' writings of this period one may search in vain for any recognition of the realities of the war. His sole means of identity was through his own ego: and as Heinrich trenchantly observed, Thomas was too ready to use this "raging I" as a buffer to the "real seriousness of another person's life".

Here perhaps was the whole paradox of the German personality which Thomas felt he represented — "the problem of the German nation was beyond a doubt my own," he later wrote of his *Reflections of a Non-Political Man* "therein lay the national character of the book."[1]

The story of Thomas Mann's development after the First World War, then, is the story not only of his relationship with Heinrich — in literary and personal terms — but of gradual acknowledgment of the ideals which Heinrich stood for — ideals which Thomas found initially so abhorrent. This "conversion" was perhaps unique in German literary history — and the symbolic importance of their fraternal relationship was not lost on Thomas. It provided the structural tension for *The Magic Mountain*, Thomas' first major novel since *Buddenbrooks* in 1901; and the resolution of their fraternal conflict became the most profound and positive impetus of his whole life. The notion of "representing" his brother Heinrich that had lain behind *Royal Highness*, in other words, could only really become possible once the conflict of their personalities had been fully expressed — and overcome.

It is in this sense, perhaps, that one may see in the brothers Mann the most significant literary brotherhood of all time. Theirs was not the collaboration of the brothers Grimm or Goncourt, or even the complementary creativities of the Rossettis or the Brontë sisters. In the brotherhood of Heinrich and Thomas Mann German history was mirrored — and borne out — in all its agony. The tragedy was that history itself could not simply be reconciled, that the Weimar republic was only paper thin: and the two sons whose quarrel and rapprochement had suggested such high hope for the destiny of Germany, were exiled, dispossessed and reviled as "un-German".

This too, however, was reflective of the German epos, and would find its way into the two great works of Heinrich and Thomas Mann's maturity: *Henri IV* and *Doctor Faustus*. They took the German literary tradition with them into exile until the mad genius of German politics had fully played out the "raging I" of his people; and if greatness is understood to be more than the corpus of a writer's work, to include his "representative" self in the determination of a nation's culture, and the courage with which he stands for certain human principles, then the brothers Mann must qualify among the greatest names in German twentieth-century history. From outright mutual hostility in the First World War they became reconciled, stood with consistent courage for democracy in an age of rising fascism, and presided over the German émigré movement in exile. How proud the Senator would have been — the very father who despaired of Heinrich and could hold out no commercial hopes for either of them!

But if, in retrospect, their path seems straightforward, it was not so at the time. It was, if anything, more demanding, more threatened and dramatic than all the years that had preceded the Great War. Whatever social and political injustices Heinrich pilloried in his *Man of Straw*, they could have no comparison with what was to come to Germany. Within the ruins of the Kaiser's empire the people of Germany had to face up to defeat, a new republic, inflation, unemployment — and the growing threat of civil war. It was in this context that the brothers Mann had now to write, as the Great War came to its end. In this context they should be judged, as artists and as the conscience of a nation.

2

For the moment, however, having rejected Heinrich's offer of reconciliation in January 1918, Thomas set about the final chapter of his titanic self-defence, the *Reflections of a Non-Political Man*. To have acceded to Heinrich's offer would undoubtedly have meant rewriting — perhaps even, as Paul Amman begged him, scrapping the work entirely. This Thomas could not do, any more than he could contemplate a renewed intimacy with a brother whose existence and attitude to life and humanity tormented him. The *Reflections of a Non-Political Man* were vital to him in his development as a writer — and no one was more aware of this than Thomas himself.

"I still find it curious how even before the war — which I didn't believe would come — I seemed to have politics, in fact the politics of the war, both on my mind and in my blood," he had written to Amman in March 1917. "The novel I was interrupted in writing had a pedagogic-political theme: a young man finds himself caught between a disciple of Carducci, a Latin-speaking advocate of 'work and progress', and a cynical but clever reactionary — in Davos where he is held by an unvirtuous sympathy with death . . . Do you see? And I have to write the *Reflections* now for the simple reason that the novel would have otherwise been intolerably intellectually overloaded after the war."

The *Reflections* must therefore clear the way for *The Magic Mountain,* the essayist prepare the ground for the poet. Already in 1916, at the beginning of his work on the *Reflections,* Thomas had given Amman an insight into his artistic nature. "I am as little an intellectual," he wrote on 25th February 1916, "as Rolland himself. I will never be the slave of my thoughts, for I know that nothing which is only thought and said is true; the only unimpeachable truth is the *image.* Whenever I am engaged on essayistic work my motto is: 'You must not seek to confuse me with my contradictions. The moment one speaks one starts to err.'[2] My second is: 'As soon as our thoughts have found their way into words, they are no longer heart-felt, *nor are they, at heart, serious any more.'* (Schopenhauer). Far from being a way of stating my position in my écrits, the essayistic expression of my thoughts is much more the only safe way of getting rid of them, of getting beyond them to other, new, better and where possible completely oppositional ones — sans remords!"

As he approached the end of the *Reflections* in 1917/18 Thomas steeped himself in romantic music, literature, philosophy and lecture-tours — almost as though to drown the cries of the dying and the ogre of coming politcal revolution. He read *War and Peace* again for the first time since youth, attended Pfitzner's late-Wagnerian opera *Palestrina* five times, and went on a lecture-tour to Essen, Hamburg, Rostock, Lübeck, as well as watching a performance of his play, *Fiorenza,* in German-occupied Brussels in January 1918 — where he found himself fêted as a war-comrade:

> I breakfasted with the Commandant of the town, the Bavarian General Hurt, surrounded by his officers, all dapper and affable people, and one and all — for what service I do not know — decorated with the Iron Cross First Class.[3]

But was this not an indulgence? "My nature in truth was always more intellectually European than poetically German, but there are still one or two things to protest about from the standpoint of individual freedom," he had explained to Amman in February 1916. The "one or two things" had grown into a titanic essay, a tirade of unique proportions, "une mer à boire" as Thomas called his *Reflections* at the time,[4] or "a last great retreat-action, fought not without gallantry, of a romantic bourgeoisie in face of the triumphant new", as he described it later.[5]

Thomas still believed Germany would win the war — as it almost did — with its Spring offensive in the west under Ludendorff; but by now he was becoming anxious that the massive tome should *not* appear as "war propaganda" as at least one Council minister had acclaimed it after a reading in Munich. To both Bertram and his friend of earlier years, Paul Ehrenberg, he expressed the hope that the book would appear after hostilities had ended;[6] and to Kurt Martens he even asked that it be read as a novel, not to be taken too literally.[7] In the Preface which he wrote in March 1918 he then admitted most of the errors of the book, thus depriving critics of their most effective ammunition — as Amman bitterly pointed out in his review.[8]

At last on 16th March 1918, the 650-page manifesto was sent by post to Berlin. "I am continually racked with impatience to be story-telling, to be able to create freely again," he had said in his letter to Amman almost a year before. At last the moment had come. In yielding to "my tendency to essay" he wrote later, "I am more conscious of sharing Goethe's awareness of being a 'born writer' than when I am spinning a tale."[9] So, from the "passionate truancy" of essay writing he turned at last to the happier pastures of creative fiction — after an absence of nearly four years.

But before taking up the reins of *The Magic Mountain* again, he felt an urge to write something more intimate, more directly personal: a finger-exercise in narration that would prepare him for the work that would one day bring the award of the Nobel Prize.

The result was *A Man and His Dog,* written in the spring and summer of 1918: the first of Thomas' stories to gain widespread acclaim in English translation — though paradoxically *Royal Highness* had already been translated and published in Britain in 1916, half-way through the war.

3

Dear Heinrich!

That was a bitter disappointment! Your letter to Thomas was my last hope.

Ask Mimi not to inquire any more how the rest of the family is faring, which usually gives rise to discussions on the subject.

I no longer now believe that my death will bring you all together again, since not even Carla's could do it. You and I will have to be satisifed that what you did was the last unmistakably good act. From now on I beg you — *in your writings as well* — to let the matter rest, and not to utter a *hint* of criticism which, in the hands of evil people, would only lead to sensationalism over the rift between two great brothers. With *you* I have not talked *at length* over this sorry subject, with T. however *no more,* however much I love him. I had *really* hoped that a reconciliation, after mutual apologies, would have been welcome . . .

The Frau Senator's letter of 7th January 1918 was filled with pessimism and broken hopes. She had seen her two eldest sons rise to great literary distinction in Germany — only to fall foul of one another.

Only once after their New Year's correspondence did Heinrich and Thomas see one another. They were both present at Wedekind's burial in the Munich Waldfriedhof cemetery on 13th March 1918 when Heinrich delivered the funeral oration; Thomas listened quietly and added another scornful passage to his manuscript of the *Reflections* before it went off three days later.

Meanwhile in March Ludendorff launched the great German offensive on the Western front between Arras and Rheims. Though Rheims held out, German troops were soon pushing past as far as Château-Thierry on the Marne, only 56 miles from Paris. It was a last, vain effort to force a military solution, in spite of the Reichstag's vote for a "peace without annexations" the previous July; and it failed. By late July there were no German troops in reserve; it only needed a determined Allied offensive and the war was lost for Germany.

Ludendorff had gambled, ruthlessly; and with his defeat came a wave of war revulsion which now swept the Reich. It was evident the Kaiser could no longer remain on the throne. The Kaiser abdicated as revolution broke out; and it was a new Republic of Germany which, under the Chancellorship of Friedrich Ebert, accepted the Armistice terms on 11th November 1918.

It was the moment Heinrich had longed for. Two days later he wrote the original document setting up the Council of Intellectual Workers in Munich, whose ideal was the binding together of artists and intellectuals as a body capable of influencing the future of a new socialist-democratic Germany. Kurt Wolff immediately issued some 100,000 copies of *Man of Straw* — and by December over 75,000 of these had been sold.

It was Heinrich's hour. In 1917 his revolutionary play *Madame Legros* — written in 1913 — was finally performed — "a powerful throw of the dice", as even Thomas acknowledged in a letter to Paul Amman at the time. "Its counterpart would be, say a drama on Luther performed today in Paris. How would that be greeted?"[10] In 1917 had also come publication of *Die Armen* (The Poor) and another revolutionary play *Brabach* (first performed in 1919), in 1918 his play *Der Weg zur Macht* (The Way to Power) (first performed in 1920) and finally the long-awaited *Man of Straw*. Despite Thomas' effulgent patriotic support of the war and his huge *Reflections,* there could be no doubt now who had been proved the more far-seeing, the more courageous, the more honest — and, in the end, more correct. Or could there be?

The German revolution of November 1918 was not so very different from the Lübeck "revolution" of 1848. Prince Max of Baden — not under pressure from the Social Democrats or left-wing parties, but from the now despairing Ludendorff — had already, as Chancellor of a new coalition government in October 1918, prepared and passed the changeover to a new system of parliamentary government. Ebert, the man who then became Chancellor in November, only did so in fact because Scheidemann forced his hand; and his programme of reforms was trivial. It was Ebert who gave credence to the later "stab in the back" legend by greeting returning soldiers from the front with the words "Undefeated in the Field".

The changeover to a parliamentary republic, therefore, was scarcely the triumph of socialism it might have been. In January 1918 elections were held at which, for the first time, women had the vote. The Social Democrats won: yet not even in this, their strongest moment, could they form a clear majority. Government by coalition was to become the unhappy lot of Germany until the advent of Hitler. Even the new constitution — based on the great parliamentary democracies of the world from Switzerland to the USA — was in practice impotent. The Weimar Republic thus stumbled into existence on the tide of war-revulsion but without sinew or security.

Nowhere was this more clearly protrayed than in Munich — which called its own "revolution" some two days before that of Scheidemann in Berlin. It was in Munich that the future of Germany was now rehearsed — and decided. And both Heinrich and Thomas bore witness to the tragic comedy.

4

"On Monday we discussed it," its originator later told a visiting American diplomat, "and on Thursday we had done it."[11]

Kurt Eisner was a friend of Heinrich Mann and, like Heinrich, of North German descent, a pacifist and littérateur. He had no experience of politics; but when he called the revolution the armistice had still not been signed and it was easy to persuade the Munich garrison to join his revolution rather than go to the front. He then went to the offices of the leading German newspaper, occupied it in the name of the revolution, and thus took over the means with which to print decrees and proclamations. To the astonishment of most of the Bavarian population, King Luitpold packed his bags and vacated the throne.

But running a state as large as Bavaria was more difficult than simply issuing decrees. Having no parliamentary experience, Eisner was only able to remain in power with the help of the Majority Socialist Party once he had been defeated in the elections; and on 21st February 1919 he was murdered by a right-wing Jewish assassin, Count Arco. Heinrich Mann delivered the funeral oration, as he had for Wedekind in the previous year.

Fearing that Eisner's death would mean the end of socialist endeavour, the communists now staged a real revolution: the only Soviet Revolution ever to take place in Germany. Elsewhere in Germany the communists had tried to subvert the move towards a National Assembly rather than their own soviet model of government, and had been mercilessly put down by Ebert's orders. Karl Liebknecht and Rosa Luxemburg were both murdered — only two of the many hundreds of idealists and left-wing intellectuals who would be assassinated in the following three years. Their bodies were found in the Landwehr-canal in Berlin, on 16th January 1919. The soviet coup in Munich in April of that year thus took place against an inauspicious background. The legal government fled to Bamberg, and the new communist dynasty never in fact controlled more than a small perimeter around the city. From the gates of the old Turkish Palace the communist orators now spoke to the people.

"The age of bourgeois corruption has gone!"

"And that of proletarian corruption has begun," one voice called back from the crowd.[12]

The soviet republic was doomed from the start; some 75 per cent of the population was Roman Catholic, the soviet's ideals were alien, its organization and preparation in no way comparable to its Russian counterpart. Heinrich Mann would have nothing to do with it, but his poetic disciples Erich Mühsam and Ernst Toller both joined — Toller even becoming at one stage Prime Minister.

The farce could not last long. The farmers outside Munich refused to deliver up any produce and the town began to starve. The inhabitants, who had tolerated the revolution with typical Bavarian humour, waited; it would only have been a matter of time before the soviet negotiated some settlement with the government in Bamberg.

But in Berlin Ebert could not take such a passive view, and the Minister for the Interior, Noske, gave instructions for Munich to be besieged by regular army troops. When it was found there were not enough regulars and that their loyalty was also divided, the infamous Freikorps under Captain Erhard were sent in — and the bloodbath began.

Panic-stricken the communists now tried to take hostages from middle-class families — and Thomas Mann, incarcerated in the Poschingerstrasse, was only spared by a personal directive from Ernst Toller. Then, as the Free Corps began to storm the outskirts of the town, communist guards shot a group of 12 hostages. News of the murder soon reached the Freikorps commander — and the "white" troops went beserk, killing trade-unionists, their wives and children quite indiscriminately. As Heinrich Mann later put it, it was as though the triggers that had been silenced on the Western front had now been licensed to fire on their own people.[13] No final figure has ever been published of the extent of the slaughter, but it ran into thousands. It was the beginning of a reign of terror in the Bavarian capital that would lead inexorably to Hitler's triumph some fourteen years later.

5

What happened in Munich was soon mirrored in Berlin as the nationalists sensed their own power. In March 1920 Kapp's right-wing putsch put the parliamentary government of Germany to flight (first to Dresden, then to Stuttgart); but when the situation was restored the red workers of the Ruhr who had risen against Kapp's supporters were bloodily suppressed, while Kapp's brigade of Free Corps Marines received no punishment at all. Thus even in its infancy the Weimar Republic's impotence before paramilitary pressure was exposed.

A new age had dawned — an age of drastic and unpredictable change, the chaotic aftermath of imperialism and war as well as the confusion before a new and democratic future. In such circumstances it was hardly surprising that the impact of Heinrich's *Man of Straw* should lessen and sales fall. By 1920 sales, in fact, had almost ceased. Wolff published one further collection of Heinrich's essays *Macht und Mensch* in 1919 — containing not only his famous essays *Geist und Tat, Voltaire-Goethe* and *Zola,* but also the essay no German newspaper would accept after the signing of the Versailles treaty: *Kaisserreich und Republik.* But with this book Wolff's interest in publishing Heinrich's works expired. He had had enough of politics — and turned his attention now to art books.

"I have the impression that people didn't always read these critiques of our time voluntarily and from inner necessity," Heinrich wrote reflectively to his French friend Felix Bertaux in October 1922.

They were widely read at the time because circumstances demanded it: it was the order of the day. But people were glad when the hour was past, and returned more happily to books of other kinds.

That doesn't mean that I consider them to be ineffective. Even the opposition which they aroused continues; and if I am hated by young nationalists, the young republicans are fond of quoting me in their manifestos. The young republicans are just beginning to arise as a movement, and to declare themselves for or against particular writers. I have reason to believe that precisely those of my books which have been the most disliked in these last years of counter-revolution and have harmed my reputation, will in time have the deepest influence, an influence they could not have at the moment of their first success. In those days it was success through surprise, it hit helpless readers incapable of their own judgement. I hope the distant future of my country will witness the growth of a generation which does not stand far behind the ideas of *Macht und Mensch* any more.

But for the moment one cannot give people a fully-developed democracy — not even economically. One is barely reaching them when one seeks to win their support for a political, if highly Capitalist Republic. This I leave to others, while recognizing it is necessary. Even in 1919, when the radical socialists were full of wild hopes, I pointed out to them that history jumps no stages. We shall have to — as others have had to — undergo the epoch of purely capitalist democracy. I hope it will not last as long in our case; the recklessness of present-day capitalism seems to confirm this. But for the moment the nationalization of the coal mines slumbers in the Constitution of the Republic, and Herr Stinnes draws up state contracts. We have to come to terms with these facts, even my present standpoint is moulded by them.

Not far away, on the far bank of the Isar, Thomas was also trying to come to terms with them.

6

Though Thomas was not willing to be reconciled with Heinrich at New Year 1918, he had in fact reached the final limit of his conservative, self-justificatory self. Thereafter he wrote no further war propaganda. Even the giant *Reflections* he wished to be read as fiction — a writing out of a self which, as younger brother, he had never been able to express freely beneath the shadow of Heinrich's perceptive and sometimes cruelly sharp intellect.

But once this self had been turned over in all its contradictions, nuances and subtleties: once Thomas had proved himself as an independent personality, a mind distant from Heinrich, there was no threat: and the way to eventual reconciliation was open. "I should have added a third motto," Thomas wrote later of the *Reflections,* "if I had found it sooner. 'No one remains precisely what he is when he knows himself.' "[14] After all the hysterical proclamations of German right, of German destiny Thomas had finally found the self-understanding and confidence he was seeking — achievements which were not slow to come out in his work.

From the virtual artistic bankruptcy of his pre-war years Thomas now moved into a new creative phase. *A Man and his Dog* — perhaps one of the most quietly moving animal stories of this century — was completed in October 1918: and the symbol of the German pointer who is tempted to follow a hunter when out walking and then realizes he was not intended for that profession was self-evident. When Kurt Martens declined the story for the literary section of the *Münchner Neueste Nachrichten* and asked Thomas instead for an article on the current German situation, Thomas wisely refused. "What could I possibly say?" he wrote. "Fellows, cheer up, it isn't so bad?' I can't, for I find it as bad and repulsive as it could possibly be. In short don't be angry with me," Thomas concluded, "I am simply in no state to comfort and encourage people; I don't feel very much like the man of the hour who is called upon to speak, and will decidedly do better to tend quietly to my own affairs."[15]

Nor was this some post-war weariness, as it was for so many of Thomas' contemporaries. Shortly after finishing *A Man and his Dog* Thomas began an extended poem, the only long work of this kind he was to write in his life, completed in March 1920.

Gesang vom Kindchen (Song of the Child) has never been translated into English. Written in blank verse it celebrated the birth of a new child in the family: Elizabeth Veronika Mann, born on 24th April 1918.

> Last-born, and yet for me in truth
> Firstborn! — for important years
> Had passed since I, maturing as a man,
> Last became a father . . .
>   . . . All the reality which surrounded me
> Did it not stem more from dream than from life? . . .
>
> Thus I took heart in that which had once confused me.

Was this not the casting off of the "shadows", the final acceptance of "another person's" reality as Heinrich had written in his unsent letter in

January 1918? For the first time the birth of a new child in his life had been, as the poem recounted, an event with its own reality, not simply the romantic fulfilment of his love for his "princess' bride. Exactly a year later, on 21st April 1919, Katja gave birth to their sixth child, a boy they named Michael Thomas Mann; and in 1924 Thomas updated his *Gesang vom Kindchen* into a small novella, *Disorder and Early Sorrow,* considered by many to be the most "human" of all Thomas' short-stories.

It was this human awareness that was mirrored both in Thomas' work, and in his political views. Neither Martens' entreaty nor his mother's painful correspondence on the iniquities of the Versailles Treaty would rouse him to his former idealistic patriotism. The award by the University of Bonn of an Honorary Doctorate in Philosophy, news of which was telegraphed to him while staying with Fischer on the Baltic in the summer of 1919, pleased him deeply — Dr Cornelius, the autobiographical father-figure of *Disorder and Early Sorrow* is made a Professor of History at the university — but Thomas was careful to point out, in his acceptance, that the *Reflections of a Non-Political Man* was a personal document, and that any help it gave to others was merely an "accident".[16]

To Karl Strecker, a writer who had praised the *Reflections* in the Berlin *Monatschaften,* however, Thomas was more specific. "I cannot thank you without embarrassment," he wrote on 18th April 1919.

You judge between my brother and myself, placing the one above the other. As a critic you have the right to do so. But this is neither the intention nor the meaning of the book, and the antithesis itself strikes me as too important and symbolic for me really to welcome the intrusion of this question of rank and worth; I believe only in differences of temperament, character, morality and experience which have led to an antagonism that may be regarded as "significant" in the Goethean sense, an opposition of principles — but based upon a deeply-felt brotherliness. In me the nordic-Protestant element is uppermost, in my brother the Roman-Catholic element. With me, accordingly, the emphasis is more on conscience, with him more on the activistic will. I am an ethical individual-ist, he is a socialist. However, this antithesis might be further defined and formulated, it reveals itself in the realms of intellect, art, politics — in short, in every relationship. Any assignment of rank must be purely sub-jective, depending on personal affinity and sympathy. Indeed, in the end I think I get off lightly when I declare that the matter cannot be decided objectively.

This was indeed a far cry from the bitterness of the *Reflections.* He was not immune to the ultimately anti-European nature of the Versailles Treaty, but this emphasis had shifted from a refusal to accept the realities of life to a new awareness of them. "The venomous man who concocted this peace in the insomniac nights of old age has slant eyes," was all he would say privately of Clemenceau and the Peace Treaty.[17]

His heart was now in creating, not decrying. Despite his own acknowledged conservatism he welcomed democracy not only because he felt it historically inevitable, but because he discovered — to his own surprise — that democracy was really no more than a new word for classical humanitarianism.[18] "What's coming now," he wrote to Gustav Blume on 5th July 1919, "is the Anglo-Saxon dominance of the world, that is, perfected civilization. Why not? We will discover that it is quite comfortable to live under."

"One must take a contemplative, even a resignedly cheerful view," Thomas wrote in the same letter. He was soon appointed German literary correspondent of the American magazine *The Dial,* and his Anglo-Saxon sympathies — having sounded his last "retreat action"[19] of German romanticism — began now to deepen: a salutary preparation for the trials still in store for him.

7

On 27th March 1921, Heinrich celebrated his fiftieth birthday. Letters and telegrams came from all over Germany — even from the fortresses of Bavaria where Toller, Mühsam and others were serving out their sentences for their part in the Munich Revolution. Articles appeared in the newspapers and magazines reviewing Heinrich's life's work. Only one voice was missing: that of Thomas.

But if he could not yet bring himself to restore their friendship Thomas seems nevertheless to have celebrated the event, if only inwardly — and still with some bitterness. To Ludwig Ewers he wrote on 4th April 1921:

Your fine article on Heinrich's 50th birthday moved me deeply, as I am sure it did him. Heinrich is now being compensated by innumerable honours for all that was denied him in earlier years, denials which hurt him more than I could ever have imagined. It was there, I am certain, that the poison grew which once threatened to destroy his creative artistry. But if neglect made his response predictable then the homages of today will do likewise. I consider him now to be someone who, reconciled with both the world and his fatherland, will perhaps prefer your friendship at the bottom of his heart to that of those Jewish radicals and towncriers of his.

How things stand between us as brothers, I am sure you are well aware. The war simply brought our differences to a head. As for me, you know me well enough to believe me when I say I would have done anything on earth to prolong our brotherly relationship. But Heinrich, in a highly literary manner, in his Zola Essay — the reading of which rendered me ill for weeks — proudly announced his utter dissociation and separation from me and cannot have had much respect for me if he expected me frivolously and joyfully to accept the recent self-conscious attempt at rapprochement which he made, at a time when all his boldest wishes about Germany had been realized.

When all is said and done, one ought to treat a rift like ours with respect, one ought not to try and take away its deadly seriousness. Perhaps separated we are *more* brothers to one another than we would be at the same table, celebrating this occasion.

Thomas was now picking up the threads of *The Magic Mountain* and, however callous it may seem, had recognized even more clearly the creative potential of their brotherly relationship — in fact it is difficult to imagine *The Magic Mountain* taking the shape it did without their acute differences of mind and temperament.

In January 1921 Thomas had visited Davos again, staying some four days at the Sanatorium. "In the very place!" he wrote to Bertram on 1st February. "You can imagine, I am all agog. It is more than curious to see reality before your eyes after having kept it in the mind for so long."

Yet even now, in the middle of what he must have known was his most important work of fiction since *Buddenbrooks,* Thomas could not resist the attractions of a new essay. Bertram had called the *Reflections of a Non-Political Man* a sort of "intellectual Buddenbrooks",[20] and the phrase pleased Thomas greatly: not because it had any truth in it, but because he objected to the conventional German distinction between creative work and journalism or essayism. "Surely the dividing line does not run outwardly between the manifestations, but within the personality," he wrote later, "and even there is fluid."[21]

The object of this new bout of essay writing was, however, no less concerned underneath with the differences between himself and his brother than was his current work on *The Magic Mountain. Goethe and Tolstoy* sounded like an essay on classical literary art; but it was not. Its theme was pedagogic; and its impact came not from the comparison between Goethe and Tolstoy, but between Goethe and Schiller, and between Tolstoy and Dostoievsky. It was, as more than one German schoolmaster would point out to his pupils, a classic description of the differences between Heinrich and Thomas Mann.

It started as a speech — to be given as part of a celebration in Lübeck planned for September 1921. "As regards my lecture," Thomas wrote to Bertram at the end of July, "I am sitting right in the ink, literally. Without the slightest preparation or experience I began writing, possessed with the idea of saying everything, and recently read it aloud to my wife for two hours without getting anywhere near the end."

Here at last was an opportunity to explore the difference between his own and Heinrich's art — transposed into the antitheses between the four greatest Russian and German writers. What was different from the days of their rivalry, open or concealed, was that Thomas now accepted the antithesis. His letter to Karl Strecker had hinted at this; now, in the summer of 1921 he prepared for public utterance. "And to all eternity," he wrote, "the truth, power, calm and humility of nature will be in conflict with the disproportionate, fevered and dogmatic presumption of spirit."

This was Schiller's famous essay on "Naive and Sentimental" creation, the dichotomy between "natural" and "spiritual" genius, in different words. And as in his letter to Strecker, Thomas refused to judge which course was right, which the greater.

"Which is finer," Thomas asked in *Goethe and Tolstoy,* "which worthier of humanity: freedom or bondage, self-will or submission, the moral or the natural? . . . Which is greater? Which is more aristocratic? I shall not answer either of these questions. I will let the reader come to his own conclusion in the matter of value, according to his own taste. Or less glibly put: according to the reader's conception of humanity — which, I must add *sotte voce,* will have to be one-sided and incomplete to admit of his coming to any decision at all."

But Thomas had come too far since the days when great art appeared to have no relation to progress to view Goethe's artistic amorality without irony: and that was why he chose a pedagogic theme for the essay — originally titled *The Idea of Education in Goethe and Tolstoy.* Contrasted against the Goethean "sons of nature" and "children of God" he sketched the heroic world of the "saintly" figures, Schiller and Dostoievsky, their "nobility sharply distinguished from that love of self and the autobiographical pride of birth which is part of its consummate sense of its own ego."

" 'Natural nobility' is not the only nobility," Thomas wrote: "There does exist another kind of nobility besides that conferred by nature on her favoured sons. Clearly there are two ways of heightening and enhancing human values: one exalts them up to the god-like, and is a gift of nature's grace; the other exalts them up to the saintly, by grace of another power, which stands opposed to her and means emancipation from her, eternal revolt from her. That other power is the power of the spirit." "But well we know," Thomas concluded the essay, "that there is no deciding the question which of these two lofty types is called to contribute more and better to the highly cherished idea of a perfected humanity."

It was indeed, in 1921, an open question. But as Thomas also pointed out, disease appeared to be an "aristocratic attribute", a necessary concomitant to Schiller and Dostoievsky's world. Neither writer survived to old age: as though their spiritual "disjunction from nature" was destined to pay its own, natural penalty.

The *Goethe and Tolstoy* lecture was delivered in Lübeck to great applause, was repeated in Berlin and in the following month, October 1921, in Munich to a "packed and attentive audience", and yet again in Zurich. However, as if to confirm Thomas' theory of illness as the penalty of spiritual "disjunction from nature", Heinrich was taken to hospital with acute appendicitis in January 1922. Peritonitis developed; and for a while it looked as though the Schiller of modern Germany, nearing fifty-one — the same age as that at which his father, Senator Mann, had died — must succumb.

It was time for past differences to be cast aside; and after a rift which dated back to the early months of 1914, the brothers Mann were at last reunited.

8

Munich, January 28, 1922: The novelist Heinrich Mann who had been unwell for several days with a severe attack of influenza, underwent a successful operation for appendicitis and peritonitis on Thursday. His condition is described by doctors as serious, but by *no means hopeless*.[22]

Apparently Heinrich's wife Mimi was partly to blame, for in her concern over Heinrich's health she had so often misled the doctor as to the gravity of her husband's ailments that when appendicitis did occur, the doctor, Dr Lampe, decided not to call that evening, but only the following day.

The news was soon in every newspaper in the German-speaking world; telegrams poured into the Leopoldstrasse; and when Mimi finally rang the Poschingerstrasse, Katja immediately went round to be with her.

Dear Heinrich,

Accept with these flowers my dearest wishes — I was not permitted to send them any earlier.

Those were difficult days that lie behind us, but now we are over the hill and will get better — together if in your heart you feel as I do.

T

The card was dated 31.1.1922; and a week later Thomas was permitted to be at his brother's bedside.

To Ernst Bertram Thomas described what had happened. "How much I would like to have you here," he wrote on 2nd February.

Matters of life and death have happened and I miss you sorely. My brother (in the higher sense I have only one; the other is a good lad with whom no enmity could be possible) became seriously ill a few days ago; 'flu, appendicitis, peritonitis, an operation which, with bronchial-catarrh gave rise to fears of lung complications. Also there were heart-dangers, and for three or four days the situation looked very grave. My wife visited him. He was informed of my concern, my daily enquiries, and I was told how pleased he was — a joy which reached its peak when, as soon as it could do no harm, I was allowed to send flowers and a note . . . He thanked me and wanted me to know that from now on — whatever differences of opinion — we should "never lose each other again".

And yet even at this juncture Thomas was not entirely won over.

As moved, as overwhelmed as I am, I have no illusions about the fragility and difficulty of the revived relationship. A decent, human *modus vivendi* will be about all it can come to. The monuments of our rift still stand — incidentally, I am assured he has never read the *Reflections*. That is a help — and yet it is not, for of all that I went through he can have no idea. It wrenches my heart to hear that after reading a few sentences in the "Berliner Tageblatt" — in which I spoke of those who proclaim their love of God while hating their brother — he sat down and wept. But the years of struggle for everything I believe in, which I had to conduct half-starving, left me no time for tears. Of that, of how the times made me into a man, how I grew and became a leader and shepherd for others, of all that he knows nothing. Perhaps he will sense it somehow when we meet — for the moment he is allowed to see no one.

He is said to have become gentler, kindlier in these past years. It is impossible that his views should not also have changed or modified. Perhaps after all one can speak of a certain evolution towards one another: I certainly feel this when I consider that the dominating idea in my mind at the moment is that of a new, personal fulfilment of the idea of humanity — in contrast of course, to the humanitarian world of Rousseau. I shall speak about it at the end of this month at the Frankfurt Opera House, before the performance of *The Magic Flute* . . . The Reichspresident has said he is coming.

The speech was duly delivered — an excerpt from the *Goethe and Tolstoy* essay — but with the assassination of Rathenau on 24th June 1922 Thomas felt impelled to state his new position more clearly. Reviewing the new German translation of Walt Whitman's works in the *Frankfurter Zeitung* two months before, Thomas had already made public his conviction that democracy was "nothing other than that which we call, in our old-fashioned way, 'humanity'." "For me personally," Thomas had written, "I am convinced that there is no more pressing task for Germany today than to fulfil this word — which had been debased to a hollow shell, a mere schoolboy's phrase — anew . . ." Now, in his speech *The German Republic,* written to honour Gerhart Hauptmann's forthcoming fiftieth birthday, he gave vent to his new political standpoint: an incontrovertible "Yes" to the Republic.

Heinrich and Thomas had spent several days together on the Baltic that summer ("For me it was best part of the summer," Heinrich wrote to his solicitor and friend Maximilian Brantl on 20th September 1922), and on 6th October back in Munich, Thomas read his speech to Heinrich and a small gathering of friends. It was delivered nine days later in the Beethovensaal in Berlin to great applause — and consternation among readers of the *Reflections of a Non-Political Man.*

When later that year Fischer published the speech in book form Thomas felt the need to explain this apparent "volte-face of surprising, confusing and even frivolous kind":

But this view is wrong. I know of no change of mind. My ideas have perhaps altered — not my intention. Thoughts are always — however sophistic this may sound — only a means to an end, a tool in the service of an intention . . . If the author is found to pursue different thoughts in these pages than in the book of the *Non-Political Man,* then one simply accepts a contradiction in thoughts, but not a contradiction of the author and his self.

For this self has stayed the same, at one in both being and intention, in fact so much so that he can answer both those who praise him for the "change of tack" as well as those who accuse him of betraying his

Germanness with the words: This republican acceptance is a direct continuation of the *Reflections*, without a gap, into contemporary times and its concern is unchanged, is exactly the same as in the *Reflections*: namely that of German humanity.

If the rift between Heinrich and Thomas Mann had been, symbolically, a struggle for democratic, mature and socially responsible humanity, it was now over: and Thomas' speech in the Beethovensaal in November 1922 its monument. From now on it would be a struggle not with Heinrich, but with Germany itself.

CHAPTER ELEVEN

Ambassadors of Weimar

The German Republic in fact was about to undergo its worst crisis since the shaky beginnings of 1919/20: only this time it was financial. On 11th January 1923 France invaded the Ruhr, and by April the Reichsbank was unable to back the Mark with its gold reserves.

At the end of May a dollar cost 70,000 Marks, at the end of June 150,000, by mid-August 3½ million Marks, by late September 160 million. The Fascists had triumphed in Italy the previous October, and England to all intents and purposes now withdrew from Europe. The future looked bleak.

"Our French friends are behaving well," Thomas wrote sarcastically to Heinrich in February 1923:

They seem to have taken it into their heads to ruin the intentions of any-one who speaks moderately in Germany . . . The anger is terrible — deeper and more unified than even that which brought Napoleon's fall. It is impossible to see where the future leads. And the worst thing is that a French fiasco, however welcome it might be, would mean the triumph of nationalism in Germany. Must the better part of Germany really be forced into this dilemma? Germany was in a mess in 1918, but the others who thought themselves so much better have shown little educational talent.

Then on 11th March their mother died. She was seventy-seven, had watched over the fortunes of her children like a matriarch. How pleased she had been to know her eldest sons were at last reconciled. She had disobeyed the Senator in encouraging their artistic ambitions; but time had proved her right. "I don't believe," Thomas wrote to Bertram on 16th March, "that I have ever in my life been so sad."

However the sadder and more ominous the times, the more both Heinrich and Thomas now rose to the challenge — as did perhaps no other comparable German authors of the time. *Ihr müsst wollen* (You must be willing) was the title of Heinrich's front page article in April 1923 in the *Berliner Tageblatt*. Germany had reached a new point in her history, he claimed, when it was possible to overcome its own nationalism and thus "disarm foreign nationalism": a chance to "spread humanity in our own country and across the world. That would be something to work for, would denote progress. We can contribute to the co-existence of nations and the peaceful exchange of goods. Progress also — and perfectly possible. Only we must desire the means; and the best means is undoubtedly the handling of the economy according to ethical purposes. Not as at the moment: economy first; and then when once it is blooming perhaps by gathering all the scraps leading to a spiritual renewal, something to wait for — you may have to wait a long time," he warned. What was happening at the moment was the economic destruction of the middle class; and it was not likely to go "without a murmur", Heinrich pointed out prophetically. "They will become the most dangerous enemies of the Republic," he warned; "incomparably more dangerous than discharged officers." To Felix Bertaux in Paris he wrote how difficult it was to instil a sense of humanitarian purpose into the Republic.

For us it is so much more difficult than for the forces of evil, whose propaganda stems from their selves. It costs us great personal sacrifice. How much more happily would I sit now at my novel than continually have to interrupt it with articles. But if people like me do not do their duty, who will be left?

"How do I define it?" wrote Thomas of the concept of Republic to Ida Boy-Ed in December 1922:

Approximately as the opposite of what *exists* today. But for that very reason the attempt to infuse something like an idea, a soul, a vital spirit into this grievous state without citizens seemed to me no mean undertaking; it seemed to me something approaching a good deed . . . Today I take arms against the reactionary wave which is sweeping over Europe, just as one did after the Napoleonic wars (for I am not thinking of Germany alone), and which seems to me not a whit more agreeable where it takes a fascist-expressionistic form. I fear that the great danger and fascination for a human race weary of relativism, craving for absolutes, is obscurantism of one form or another (see the successes of the Roman Catholic Church).

It was now, in 1923, that both Heinrich and Thomas began their work as unofficial cultural ambassadors of the Republic: Heinrich to Pontigny in August as the guest of writers such as Gide and Fabre-Luce; Thomas to Switzerland, Austria, Hungary, Czechoslovakia and then Spain. In June the *Vossische Zeitung* in Berlin and the *Frankfurter Zeitung* carried Thomas' latest republican speech, addressed to students in Munich at a remembrance gathering for Walter Rathenau and entitled *Spirit and Being of the German Republic*.

And yet it was hopeless. It was useless to appeal to man's better humanitarian, European spirit when the facts of life screamed with injustice, shame and international hatred. An entire social class went bankrupt in the course of this fateful year; Poincaré had used the miserable excuse of the non-delivery of telegraph-poles to seize the still-unoccupied part of the Ruhr; in Munich Hitler was calling for the overthrow not of the French but of the German "traitors" who had allowed the shambles to take place.

Heinrich's appeal bcame more practical. On 11th August he addressed a celebration in Dresden for the Weimar Constitution: and he bitterly related how it had been abused.

The spirit of the constitution has in the meantime been ignored, deceived, cancelled out, it has almost been driven from it. War-crazy nationalism is as rife as it ever was and already clutches at the seat of power, which now however stems from the people and is responsible to it. Capitalism has only now become overwhelming, it is only now beginning to control every one of us, as it does the state itself. For this reason we celebrate now the constitution which was to avoid this, which was to free us and spread humanity. Up until now it has not been able to do it; but one day it must.

But above all in post-war Germany, the economy had become the new God. "The economic conception of life has become our ruin," Heinrich had lamented in March 1923. "I recognize this more and more, and would like to say it publicly — if only I knew who in Germany would listen. More than ever before we believe in making ourselves holy by economic means, already the word economy has become sacred."[1]

With the catastrophe of inflation, the God tumbled. It was the ideal moment for dictatorship, as both Hitler and Ludendorff in Munich realized; and Heinrich warned. In October 1923 came Heinrich's famous open letter to Stresemann, the Reich's Chancellor,[2] published with his other articles, speeches and essays of 1923 as *The Dictatorship of Reason*.

"Herr Reich's Chancellor, whoever believes there are half-way houses is mistaken," it ran. "The tragedy of Germany continues in the wake of missed opportunities. But I fear not even the tardiest people could forgive itself or you this time unless you act." Heinrich spelled out the dangers confronting nascent German democracy: and called for much firmer methods to protect the principles laid down in the Weimar Constitution.

Within weeks Hitler staged his beer-hall putsch; the Munich police, however, refused to join him or be intimidated — and Hitler failed.

In November too the introduction of the Rentenmark finally halted the ruinous national inflation by tying the Mark to the most fundamental German asset: its agriculture.

It was a dramatic month, watched all over the world with apprehension. As the months passed it seemed as though the Republic had weathered the storm — and a new era of stability and prosperity began.

Foreign observers breathed a sigh of relief. But had the ghost of dictatorship really been laid — and was the German economy really saved? When

Hitler came to trial he was merely confined to the Fortress of Landsberg for six months and not even exiled from Bavaria; nor could the new Rentenmark ever restore the faith of millions of dispossessed middle-class people: and these would form the backbone of German fascism.

For the moment, however, the crisis was over. Reason had dictated: and in its wake appeared perhaps the most seminal work of the Weimar epoch: *The Magic Mountain.*

2

The Magic Mountain was Thomas' first serious full-length novel — if *Royal Highness* be considered at best a comedy — since *Buddenbrooks.* Even before it appeared in late November 1924, Thomas had been tipped by a number of newspapers as next-in-line for the Nobel Prize. Reuters in Stockholm predicted the award would fall to Thomas Mann or W.B. Yeats; and perhaps if Thomas had finished the novel earlier, he might indeed have received the prize that year. By December 1923 the complete existing manuscript had been set — Fischer had decided on two volumes, despite the lesson of *Buddenbrooks,* and had already announced its forthcoming publication in an advertisement the year before, in 1922; but by the spring of 1924 Thomas realized he was still far from finished — and that Fischer might well end up ordering a third volume![3]

In the event Fischer stuck by two; and by October 1924 the last of the "rag-bag novel-creature", dating in manuscript as far back as the summer of 1913, finally went off to the printers in Leipzig.

Thomas himself was chary about the reception *The Magic Mountain* would receive. "Would anyone expect that a harassed public, economically oppressed, would take it upon itself to peruse through twelve-hundred pages of the dream-like ramification of this figment of thought?" he wrote later, looking back.[4] "Altogether obstinacy seems to have played such a large part in these crabbed, years-long preoccupations, I regard them so much as a highly dubious private enjoyment, that I question the likelihood of anyone caring to follow the track of my curious morning occupations."

But, as with *Buddenbrooks,* they did. Fischer had ordered a first edition of 20,000 copies based on the 5,000 advance orders from bookshops; by 6th December he had increased the printing to 30,000; and in the course of 1925 the figure went up to 50,000 — no mean sum for a two-volume novel costing 21 Marks. By February 1925 Thomas had earned enough — 70,000 Marks he reckoned in a letter to Bertram — to buy himself an automobile, "a handsome 6-seater Fiat. Our windbag Ludwig has already been trained as a chauffeur, so from now on I shall be able to drive — 33-horse-powered — into town affably acknowledging the people on every side".

However the success of *The Magic Mountain* was not simply commercial: against the background of his peculiar political metamorphosis *The Magic Mountain* restored Thomas to his rightful standing: the master novelist of his age.

The literary reviews and periodicals of all Germany were full of it. it was a conscious attempt to revive the Bildungsroman, the pedagogic novel, taking — as did E.M. Forster's *Longest Journey* — a rather weak and simple young man as its hero. In the mountainous surroundings of the sanatorium where he visits his cousin, Hans Castorp goes through, in microcosm, the extraordinary education to which Thomas himself had had to submit. "You found the section too long," Thomas wrote to Josef Ponten in February 1925,

> but it is not an arbitrary digression. Rather, it shows how there grows in the young man, out of the experience of sickness, death, and decay, the idea of man, the "sublime structure" of original life, whose destiny then becomes a real concern of his simple heart. Castorp is sensuously and intellectually infatuated with death (mysticism, romanticism); but his dire love is purified, at least in moments of illumination, into an inkling of a new humanity whose germ he bears in his heart as the bayonet attack carried him along. His author, who there takes leave of him, is the same who emerged from the novel to write the manifesto *The German Republic*. He is no Settembrini in his heart. But he desires to be free, reasonable, kindly in all his thoughts. That is what I would like to call goodwill — and do not like to hear it branded as hostility to life.

Settembrini was the Heinrich-like figure, the Carducci-follower, who advocates the cause of "humanity". Against him Thomas invented the character of Naphta, the all-too clever sceptic; and it is Castorp's growth ·between the two extremes which gives the book its tension and drama.

But towards the end of his epic Thomas began to feel the need for another primary figure, a symbol not of intellectual extremes as represented by Settembrini and Naphta but of nature in man. And in the autumn of 1923, while on holiday in Bolzano, he found him. He was a man whose work and physiognomy had given him something of the fame and stature which Bernard Shaw enjoyed in Britain: Gerhart Hauptmann.

For two weeks in the Hotel Austria, Hauptmann had regaled and entertained Thomas, in the autumn of 1923; and the following year they met again in Hauptmann's annual summer "retreat" on the Hiddensee. Hauptmann read — and sang — from his still unpublished *Eulenspiegel;* then asked that Thomas read him something from *The Magic Mountain*. Thomas declined — an unusual shyness in this respect — saying that he was too overwhelmed by Hauptmann's own reading; and Hauptmann admonished him. "You are wrong," he said. "In my father's house are many mansions."

So Thomas read to him from *The Magic Mountain* his latest chapter — "By the Ocean of Time", at the beginning of Chapter Seven. Hauptmann was enthralled; but Thomas was perturbed, and his unwillingness to read from it stemmed as much from conscience as from embarrassment; for the next sub-chapter was none other than "Mynheer Peeperkorn". "We might round out Hans Castorp's description by a few notes," the narrator of the Magic Mountain relates:

as that the Dutchman's nose was large and fleshy, his mouth large too, and bare of moustaches, the lips of irregular shape, as though chapped. His hands were fairly broad, with long, pointed nails; he used them freely as he talked, and he talked almost continuously, though Hans Castorp failed to get the drift. Those adequate, compelling, cleanly attitudes of the hands — so varied, so full of subtle nuances — possessed a technique like that of an orchestral conductor. He would curve forefinger and thumb to a circle; extend the palm, that was so broad, with nails so pointed, to hush, to caution, to enjoin attention — and then, having by such means led up to some stupendous utterance, produce an anti-climax by saying something his audience could not quite grasp . . .

He had said absolutely nothing. But look, manner, and gestures were so peremptory, perfervid, pregnant, that all, even Hans Castorp, were convinced they had heard something of high moment; or, if aware of the total lack of matter and sequence in the speech, certainly never missed it. We wonder how it might appear to a deaf person.

It was a damning as well as a creative portrait — but then that went for all the characters: — the hero Castorp, Settembrini, Naphta, the object of Castorp's affections Madame Chauchat — who so mindlessly bangs doors — the chief physician Hofrat Behrens . . .

Hauptmann was not really offended — at least in the first instance. As with the wagging tongues of Lübeck's citizens, so it was Hauptmann's friends who first caught on to the parody. By January 1925 Thomas was writing to Herbert Eulenberg begging him not to stir things up.

What do you want to do: write about the Peeperkorn case? Cry it from the rooftops? Rub the public's nose in it? Create a scandal? For whose benefit? Hauptmann's? Impossible! For the public's benefit? But you will only be providing it with a sensation, a false, outrageous sensation; and I should have to defend myself indignantly against the charge of having portrayed Gerhart Hauptmann in the character of the Dutchman, Pieter Peeperkorn. I did nothing of the kind. But in saying this I certainly want to tell the truth. At the time the character became a matter of urgency for me, in the autumn a year ago, in Bolzano, I was under the impress of the great writer's powerful and touching personality. This experience gave a certain stamp to the characterization of Peeperkorn, to some of his outward features. I cannot and would not deny it. But I won't go a step further in my concessions. What other similarity is there between Hauptmann's life and that of the former coffee trader from Java who comes to Davos with his malaria and his mistress and by way of abdication kills himself with Asiatic drugs?

Of course there were similarities. Hauptmann had married his mistress, he drank heavily, lived like a king and wrapped Fischer, among others, so tight around his little finger that Fischer had paid — and went on paying — Hauptmann a fortune in advance royalties, none of which were ever, unfortunately, met by sales.

But this was not what distressed Hauptmann when, in the end, the windbags and courtiers told their king how he had been libelled. What upset

Hauptmann was his own naïveté — for Hauptmann had read the advance copy Fischer had sent him without, at first, recognizing himself. Though Thomas' letter to Eulenberg avoided a public scandal, it was too late to stop him "informing" Hauptmann — and soon Fischer was having to claim — perhaps pretend — he had not had time to read the second volume of *The Magic Mountain* before it went to press — otherwise he "would have been able to convince Mann that the use of your physical features and gestures would lead to misunderstanding and ill-will".[5]

The "Peeperkorn Affair" fortunately never came to public light; Fischer soon persuaded Eulenberg to drop the idea of his article. Thomas and Hauptmann met in Munich three weeks after Thomas had sent a long letter of apology, and shook hands. In June 1925, in the *Vossische Zeitung* Hauptmann reviewed *The Magic Mountain:* and lauded it without reserve, both for its intellectual and for its creative brilliance.

But there their relationship halted. They missed one another by a few weeks when on holiday that year; and when, during the Nazi period, much later, they were both recognized by a sales assistant in the London-House department store in Zurich, the meeting came to nought. "Do you know who is downstairs?" the assistant said to Thomas — "Gerhart Hauptmann. Would you like to speak to him?" "Well, perhaps another time would be better," answered Thomas a little hesitantly. "That's exactly what Herr Hauptmann said!" exclaimed the salesman. By then Hauptmann had chosen to remain in Germany. "What do you expect?" he said to Fischer's son-in-law who took over the firm in 1933. "I am, after all, no Jew!"[6]

"I have sinned against you," Thomas' apology in 1925 ran, meanwhile.

I was in need, was led into temptation, and yielded to it. The need was artistic. I was seeking a character vital to my novel and long since provided for in its scheme, but whom I did not see, did not hear, did not hold. Uneasy, anxious and perplexed I came to Bolzano — and there, over wine, was unwittingly offered what I should never, never have allowed myself to accept, speaking in human and personal terms, but which, in a state of lowered human responsibility I did accept, I had the right to accept. I did so blinded by the passionate conviction, foreknowledge, certainty, that in my transmutation (for of course, it was not a question of a portrait but of a transmutation and stylization into a totally foreign element, in which even the externals were barely akin to reality) I should be able to create the most remarkable character of a book which, I no longer doubt, is itself remarkable.[7]

The Lübeck nest-besmircher had dared to parody Germany's Nobel-Prize-winning playwright, Gerhart Hauptmann. In the relative freedom and stability of the mid 'Twenties the matter went unnoticed. Nine years later when Thomas painted a realistic portrait of Richard Wagner the response was to be very different.

3

"He who has written this great work and now sees it finished, must indeed be happy and relieved," Heinrich wrote meanwhile to Thomas in December 1924. "I am still deeply enmeshed in my own, but the next few months should see it through."

Heinrich had begun *Der Kopf* (The Head) in the summer of 1918; but unlike *Die Armen* which was finished within a year, *Der Kopf* took almost seven to complete. Between 1919 and 1925 Heinrich published five collections of short stories,[8] two volumes of essays and speeches,[9] and two three-act plays;[10] but the novel resolutely refused to be completed. In the Heinrich Mann Archiv in Berlin are more than 800 pages of notes to the book; yet when it was finished it was a failure. From 1919 Wolff had ceased to publish any of Heinrich's works; and it was Paul Zsolnay who eventually took on publication of *Der Kopf*, as well as a new 13-volume collected edition of Heinrich's works.

Der Kopf, like *The Magic Mountain*, was an analysis of the pre-war German intelligentsia. But where Thomas' characters were painted against a backcloth of tuberculosis and disease, high in the Swiss Alps, Heinrich had attempted a more historical portrait — in microcosm — of the part the intelligentsia had actually played in the German catastrophe. Where Thomas' sources were medical and philosophical, Heinrich's were diplomatic, political and economic. Bülow the Reich's Chancellor, Wedekind the playwright, Harden the political publicist: all were sewn into the "tragedy", as Heinrich called it.[11]

Yet *The Magic Mountain* was a triumph, without doubt the touchstone of Thomas' expanding international reputation; whereas *Der Kopf*, like its subject, was a disaster. To the French literary historian Felix Bertaux, who had prompted Heinrich's invitation to the 1923 Entretiens de Pontigny and was now trying to promote his works in France, Heinrich explained the course he had chosen.

You see my critical spirit, I think, as a reaction to (still) current Teutonicism; however I hope, even if I cannot prove this to you, that my works represent the beginning of the social novel in German literature. We have none, as you state; but do you think that democracy can grow without portrayal of society? In terms of the future it is the only thing that has any significance or meaning: not "timelessness" which is still today the highest aim. (Ernst Barlach has just been given the Kleist-Prize by the Munich Professor Strich for pretended timelessness, "above time" or whatever rubbish it is called.) But Goethe's novels were not timeless. Those of Stendhal still are not, that is why they have lasted. They portrayed their time with such absolute critical sensitivity that I am sometimes astounded, in the midst of utterly modern views and technique the figures begin to speak the language of that older society — as though a contemporary of ours who had been there then were speaking the words (viz the love-scenes in the Chasseur vert). It is very discomforting, it tells one more about permanence than those fatuous attempts to reach it by being unspecific.[12]

Heinrich was right; but *Der Kopf* failed not because it was specific but because it was so willed, so forced, had none of the humour, satire and organic flow of *Man of Straw*.

Curiously, it was Thomas who best understood Heinrich's social concern. In his article for the New York *Dial* in October 1925 he gave a brief sketch of contemporary German letters. "Of all German writers," he noted, "Heinrich Mann is the most social-minded, a man whose interests are social and political to an extent which, while not unusual in west-European and especially Latin countries, is unheard-of among us . . ." To Julius Bab, Thomas explained the difference between his own and Heinrich's aims, no longer as mutually hostile or even exclusive attitudes to life and art, but as a *"division of labour"*, "I must thank you for your magnificent essay," he wrote on 23rd April 1925:

I have read it with deep emotion. I am very much aware that social problems are my weak point and I also know that this puts me to some extent at odds with my art form itself, the novel, which is propitious to the examination of social problems. But the lure — I put it frivolously — of individuality and metaphysics simply happens to be ever so much stronger for me. Certainly the very concept of the novel implies "novel of society", and *The Magic Mountain* did become this to a certain extent, quite of its own accord. Some criticism of pre-war capitalism comes into it, along with other things. But I grant you that the other things, such as music and the meaningful interweaving of life and death, were much, much more important to me. I am German — don't think I use the word in the sense of unreserved self-praise and without some national self-doubt. The Zola-esque streak in me is feeble, and that I should have to discuss the eight-hour day strikes me as almost a parody of the social view-point. But there you are; that's the crux of it. I am starting to dabble in such matters now, but suspect in advance that the principle of division of labour will be preserved between my brother and myself.

Thus Heinrich and Thomas agreed on their respective territories. Thomas' path — like that of Proust, Eliot, Joyce, and to some extent Musil — was a search, an expedition into the realms of the intellectual, musical, and most profoundly artistic world, yet without losing a critical relationship to everyday reality. Of these five great names in the history of modern literature it was Thomas who became — and remained — the most accessible, whose works were translated not only into every major tongue on earth, but also sold in their hundreds of thousands. It was, as he himself was aware, an extraordinary feat, one that he could only confront, in the long-run, by his own mixture of irony, humility, work; and responsibility.

"We both know the solemn misunderstanding, the fakery of fame, the shallowness of those who make it for us," Thomas replied to a letter from the strongly nationalist composer Hans Pfitzner on 23rd June 1925. "Of course I realize that my recent intellectual stand must be repugnant to you. Do believe at least that it sprang from goodwill — and from a sense of responsibility which may be sharper than that which a musician needs to feel. 'You rapturously obeyed the power of love,' " he quoted from Wagner's *Walküre*, " . . . Not everyone may do so, and there are cases of a conscious and by no means painless self-disciplining which earn a man the name of Judas . . . Whatever the romantic licence of the musician may be, a literary artist who in such a moment of European history as the present did not choose the party of life and the future as against the fascination of death would truly be an unprofitable servant."

Heinrich's attitude was the same. "Literature cannot be loved as simply as music," he wrote in *Sieben Jahre*, "For it is man's conscience: it works and influences always."

Heinrich's ambition was, as it had been since the first decade of the century, to storm the barriers between art and practical, political existence. But art — as Thomas knew — does not always favour intention. *Royal Highness*, in which Thomas had once hoped to sanctify his love for Katja, cannot really be said to have succeeded, despite its temporary popularity. Perhaps art requires time and suffering before she will grant her grace. Now, in his *Disorder and Early Sorrow*, sixteen years after *Royal Highness*, Thomas found the words and form with which to portray his own domestic joy. It wrote itself more "quickly and easily than almost any other" of his works, Thomas noted a year later.[13] But *Der Kopf*, over which Heinrich had slaved as over no other work in his life, found neither critical nor popular acclaim. Linguistically it contained passages which anticipate the unique impact of his late style; but as a work of literature and social criticism it was almost unreadable. Its failure came as a shock to Heinrich, particularly after the extraordinary success of *The Magic Mountain*, in itself a much more complex and profound challenge to the average reader.

Something had gone strangely wrong; but for the moment Heinrich allowed nothing to show. When Thomas' fiftieth birthday came on 6th June 1925, it was Heinrich who "stole the show"[14] by his speech in the Munich Rathaus, at the end of which Thomas went up to embrace his brother. In the newspapers of the Republic the great literary feud of the age was now publicly relegated to the past.

4

The sensation of the evening, however, and undoubtedly its peak moment came when Geheimrat Litzmann, lately Professor of Literature at the University of Bonn, rose with his Wilhelmenian decorations still gleaming and prayed silence for — *Heinrich Mann*. Every one of the guests was aware of the political dissension between the two brothers . . . the feud had been settled for years now, but the excitement of those days still rippled, as much in the two authors as in their avowed supporters.

So Heinrich Mann now got to his feet, his brother's most distinguished rival, even in the field of the novel, a few seats away from him at the table of honour and spoke with cool, clear voice his words of congratulation, words whose redeeming warmth seemed to be struggling slowly from a choked pit towards the open air, freedom. He recalled their child-hood, the birthdays they celebrated in their parents' house and never afterwards — until today, when he was ready to rejoice in his brother's fame. Thomas rushed over then and embraced him.

It was, as Kurt Martens noted in this report to the *Neue Badische Landeszeitung,* an almost theatrical moment, witnessed by distinguished guests of every political persuasion — in itself a unique event in Munich. Even the nationalist Munich press greeted it as "an act of human greatness". As Kurt Martens put it, the banquet had something historic about it which gave strength to the hope that a new age might be coming, in which reconciliation, not recalcitrant hostility might prevail.

But Ebert, the President of the Republic, was dead. Like Heinrich he had suffered appendicitis and then peritonitis, and a few days after the operation he died, at the age of fifty-four. In his stead, after a stalemate first election, the right-wing parties persuaded the seventy-eight-year-old Field Marshal von Hindenburg to stand; and the German people elected him!

It was a cruel blow to the Republic, and one which, ironically, Stresemann could have stopped. What point was there, amid a storm of international outrage, in putting forward as candidate a royalist military leader in his late seventies? Thomas, who had publicly supported Ebert as a well-meaning Republican, was beside himself. In the *Neue Freie Presse* he "denounced this shameful exploitation of the German people's romantic impulses," as he explained to Julius Bab on 23rd April 1925. "In it I say that I 'shall be proud of our nation's political discipline and instinct for life and for the future if on Sunday it refrains from electing an antediluvian valiant as its chief of state.'" "Little Hans has come that far!" he added ironically.

But Hindenburg won the election by almost a million votes, and the damage was done. Beneath the stony eyes of a man who took pride in not having read a non-military book since childhood, the socialists, centrists and nationalists began to tear at one another's throats. Worst of all Chamberlain and Gobineau's theories of race began to find more and more purchase among both young and old. Anti-semitism had always featured in European history, but now it was given the added stimulus of German self-righteousness. Hindenburg confirmed, as President of the Republic, the gathering legend of the "stab in the back"; and the first to suffer the back-lash of the German defeat were the Jews.

Ernst Bertram, already over-sensitive in Cologne to the national affront of French occupation of the Ruhr, began now to try and interest Thomas in Chamberlain's doctrine of race. Katja was naturally personally insulted and threatened to withdraw Bertram's godfathership to their daughter Elizabeth. Thomas tried gently to point out how important differences in culture and geography were to him. "I am simply more an artist, a melancholic, an enjoyer of contrasts and distinctions, than a judge and prophet who idolizes the one and damns the other," he wrote in April to Bertram.

One of the most tragic aspects of German anti-semitism was, however, that the Republic itself depended so profoundly on Jewish liberal thought and culture: "the critico-literary spirit of European democracy which is represented in Germany chiefly by Judaism," as Thomas put it in his letter to the New York *Dial* in October 1923. To seek to cast out the Jews was in fact to pass a death sentence on the Republic.

Yet despite the threat to the Republic the Communists insisted on re-proposing their own candidate Ernst Thälmann, notwithstanding the result of the first ballot; and by doing so they ensured the election of Hindenburg. Not even in the dying light of democracy in 1933 would they join the Social Democrats; and all too many were to die in concentration camps as a result.

But behind the ominous swastikas and symbols of racial and political hatred there lay an even more galling truth: that the democracy for which Heinrich had risked both his reputation and his life was rotten. Paradoxically it had been the French, with their insistence on punitive reparations and the march into the Ruhr, who had sealed its fate; but that it could not survive all this, the most catastrophic inflation ever known in the world, and the unwillingness of its *Untertanen* to face the responsibilities of self-government, was obvious to every intellectual in the Republic. There arose, as Heinrich later wrote, the conflict of having to support a government in which one did not believe: corrupt, incompetent, forever in coalition, at the mercy of reparation overseers and its own ruling industrialists, chasing a popular support which the radical nationalist parties were much better placed to receive . . . There is, therefore, something both moving and sad about the stand of Heinrich and Thomas in this era: the writer who, more than any other, had fought for democracy in Germany, yet paralysed, creatively, by its obvious ineffectiveness once it had come; and the novelist who, having achieved an outstanding position in European letters by his slow and painful growth towards humanitarian democracy, is denounced as a Judas by his own people. The years from 1925 to 1933 seem, in retrospect, to show a tragic inevitability.

And yet, as if to disprove the prophets of doom, the Republic now entered its "Golden Age". From having been the "Babylon of sin" for Hitler in 1923,[15] Berlin became the undoubted centre — economic, political and artistic — of the Weimar Republic; and while Hindenburg proudly announced the glory of Germany's "unbeaten" armies at the unveiling of the Tannenberg memorial in East Prussia, the central government got on with the task of rebuilding the country. Foreign loans more than made up for reparations, old machinery was scrapped, industry by 1928 had already reached record 1914 levels of output. Unemployment was stabilized at roughly one million, social insurance schemes and tribunals for resolving industrial disputes were introduced. Those who had been relieved of their mortgage debts by inflation were now made to pay special taxes to help build new homes for the unhoused. The eight-hour working day was retrieved by the introduction of over-time rates of pay. Germany joined — and became an important working member of — the League of Nations, her relations with Russia becoming vital to peace in Europe. Only the refusal of Germany

genuinely to disarm caused anxiety, making the French reluctant to withdraw from the Ruhr and putting Western European countries' decisions to
reduce their own arms expenditure in doubt.

But if the nationalists were permitted to cause international concern over
their statements and claims, the freedom of speech in Weimar Germany made
it the cultural mecca of Europe. Berlin alone published more than 1300
newspapers and periodicals, book production soared, the Bauhaus burst into
fashion, post-Expressionism — from having been a radical coffee-house
genre — became the order of the day. Beckmann, Dix, Grosz, Kollwitz, all
became, suddenly, almost pillars of the establishment, with state honours
and studios at their disposal. Almost overnight Thomas' son Klaus became
a well-known novelist and playwright. Thomas found his *Von dem Leben*
"remarkable"[16] in parts, and his play *Anja and Esther* "unbelievably fragile
and corrupt".[17] "Should I, can I forbid it?" he asked Bertram and himself.

But that would be madness in the new world we live in; a world which
of course is itself madness, but I cannot help that. Let us look on with
our very best wishes, but at a distance. For not even ten horses would
bring me to the Première.

To the founder of the Pan-Europa Movement, Coudenhove-Kalergi,
Thomas explained his attitude more fully:

Hasty thinkers too easily forget all the obstacles still ranged against this
victory [the idea of life]. They tend to regard the hatred and resistance
of those who adhere with godforsaken loyalty to traditional ways as
merely pitiable. That would be dangerous,

he noted prophetically,

for the power of this hatred and resistance, this godforsaken piety, is
terrible indeed, and it may prove the victor. If thinking men do not arm
themselves with that patience which a great philosopher equated with
fortitude; if, surrendering to their aesthetic impulse and repelled by the
intransigence of the material world, they grow prematurely bored with the
idea and choose to discard reality, all would be lost and what is needed will
not be achieved — which would mean death. Thinking men must understand
that what matters today is the realization of the dream — or else they
themselves will no longer matter. They must not grow bored. Let their
freedom of thought be inalienable, but,

Thomas continued, aware of the many writers and artists who had ceased to
concern themselves with present social reality,

this freedom demands that they resist boredom until the conditions for
life are fulfilled. That is what "politicalization" means.

What is at stake are the conditions of life for our children. It is hardly
likely that we men of fifty will see the Europe in which our children ought
to live, would want to live. But we can foresee it, and by the pressure of
our wills and words help to bring it about. That is a question of solicitude,
and also in a way a question of honour. We owe something to our
children, taken as a generation; to some degree we stand guilty before
them. May they recognize that they are not entirely alone, and that the

gulf between generations is not quite so deep and hopeless as they imagine. May they see that we, although less free of dogmas than they, have not entirely lost contact with present and future, are not without sympathy for life, are not without love.[18]

5

If Thomas' new-found republicanism was abhorrent to the German nationalists it was still, however, far from radical — in literary as much as political terms. If he praised Heinrich's social concern he was still far from sympathetic to the revolutionary innovations in German theatre — as for instance in the case of Brecht, whose new play *Leben Eduard des Zweiten von England* he reviewed for the *Dial* in November 1924.

"He is a strong but somewhat careless talent who has been pampered by the public in Germany,"[19] Thomas said about Brecht, but about the play itself he was less polite:

The performance was one of the most unpleasant sights I have ever witnessed. Brecht himself had superintended the staging of the play. He is a passionate director, and the Deutsche Theater in Berlin has employed him in this capacity. In the producing of this history of Edward he was especially determined to eschew all princely display and to disregard, with an ascetic malice, even historic spectacle. The scene was dominated by a deliberate niggardliness, a demonstrably proletarian shabbiness, all done with the code of Expressionism. A fellow in a kind of dirty painter's frock would appear before the curtain as announced and would say in a woebegone manner: "December 14, 1307, return of the minion Piers Gaveston on the occasion of Edward the Second's coronation, London." — "Mismanagement during the reign of King Edward in the years 1307— 1312. London." The view of the British capital was in the style of the most impoverished suburban theatre; a dilapidated Whitechapel and the dais on which Edward took his place with his "two women" were the last word in greasy makeshifts.

About Gaveston, Edward's "whore", Thomas felt he need not "dwell", the case being "generally and painfully well-known".

The part of the favourite, whom we must certainly imagine as a winsome, if somewhat loose and immoral chap, was — obviously here again out of sheer malice — taken by an actor whose personal tediousness placed the King's unhealthy passion beyond all human comprehension, no matter how well-disposed one might have been. And when the dear "Gav" was already loaded with honours and dignities, when he was Lord High Chamberlain, Chief Secretary, Earl of Cornwall, Lord of Man, he still wore the abominable and unhistoric sack coat in which he had returned from Ireland. He did not need to be ashamed before his deadly enemies, the "sumptuous" peers, for they were successfully engaged in justifying by their appearance the expression of an opponent who called them "rowdies" and "bums". They all had yellowish and green faces; and these were the brave troupe who fought the battle at Killingworth and who looked like inanimate firemen!

Thus Thomas introduced the most important German dramatist of the twentieth century to American readers. Somewhat later when Therese Giehse — a friend of both Thomas and Brecht — showed Thomas a new play by Brecht, Thomas expressed great surprise: "The monster has talent." When Giehse reported the remark to Brecht, Brecht affected to be moved: "Actually I always quite liked his short-stories," he said.

Thomas' short-stories and novellas were certainly proving popular in America. *Death in Venice* was serialized in *Dial* between March and May 1924, and the editor reported it as causing "quite a stir". Helen Lowe-Porter's translation of *Buddenbrooks* had also appeared in 1924, at first to a poor reception, then — as had happened in Germany — becoming a popular classic before the very eyes of the literary critics and reviewers who had damned it as "boring".[20] After initial hesitation Knopf commissioned a translation of *The Magic Mountain* and Thomas' American fame was secure.

Yet even while Thomas was having a success in *Dial* alongside other distinguished contributors such as Yeats, Bertrand Russell and E.M. Forster, he did not forget Heinrich. In February 1924 *Dial* had carried a translation of Heinrich's short story *Virgins*; and in October 1925 Thomas devoted most of his German letter to honouring Heinrich and his novel *Der Kopf:* "This author's development is almost without parallel," he wrote;

and when such artistic brilliance is taken into account, it *is* without parallel: from the beginning, the moral element in him manifested itself not as "innerworldly askesis" (to borrow a term from religious philosophy) but as political and socio-critical expansion. It was he who, while we still lived in splendour, suffered most deeply from the basic stagnation of our political life; and, in literary manifestos the fulminant injustice of which sprang from a higher justice, he dragged our leaders into the forum of the intellect. At the end of that novel in which he savagely caricatures the German "Patrioteer",[21] he prophesied symbolically the collapse of imperial Germany. And he tells us now, in a free artistic arrangement, the story of this decline — tells it in a prose which is neither more nor less than a German counterpart of Zola's *La Débâcle.*

But Thomas' generous words could not really help, though they moved Heinrich deeply. "My brother was kind enough to say some very complimentary things about *Der Kopf* in the American 'Dial'," he wrote to Felix Bertaux in October 1925, "whereupon a publisher over there immediately wishes to bring out a translation."[22] Any ideas of translation must have ceased when the American publisher read the book, for none ever appeared.

It was obvious Heinrich had tried to do something new here; but where *Man of Straw* had become a veritable document of the Imperial era, however grotesque and satirical, *Der Kopf* — despite its extensively researched background — failed completely. What gave *Man of Straw* its strength — its merciless exposé of middle-class chauvinism — was simply lacking in *Der Kopf*. Where once he had written with the gusto of passionate contempt, Heinrich found himself now in a much more complex situation: post-war events in Germany gave him a much deeper understanding and sympathetic insight into the problems of pre-war society. "There is much fighting in the book," he explained to Bertaux in March 1925; "but for me it is hardly a fighting book as the *Man of Straw* once was. You will see. What once seemed, before it collapsed, to be unbearable, is seen here sometimes as mild and sympathetic in comparison with the rising forces which have now grown powerful. Had I been able to finish the book by 1919 or 1920 I would not have known a number of things. Inflation and plutocracy have helped me in fact to write a more mature, more comprehensive book."[23]

In fact these things only served to make it more difficult to read. It was the very opposite of what had happened with Thomas. From political innocence and indifference Thomas had grown — like his hero Hans Castorp in *The Magic Mountain* — to find a new epoch of idealism in his life; whereas Heinrich was witnessing the destruction of a dream of democracy he himself had fought so fiercely to introduce in Germany. The ending of *Der Kopf* — the suicide, side by side, of its two protagonists — indicated a measure of the hopelessness of the book — "the saddest I have ever written," as he put it to Bertaux.[24] Though ostensibly it portrayed the decline and fall of the intellectual class in Germany, it could similarly be read as an indictment of the longed-for Republic. "Where is it written that we have to enrich a literature that is hardly read?" Heinrich lamented to Kurt Tucholsky before *Der Kopf* was even finished.

> To have to stand by and watch while it remains a private matter, that cannot change anything! One illiterate period of reaction follows the other, without pause — revolutions are only breathing spaces for the next period. During the whole of the Imperial era I waited for a chink of light. But after the revolution it is clear that a fifty year old will never live to see it.[25]

A crisis point had been reached in Heinrich's life. Like Thomas he had rapidly become one of the outstanding literary and cultural figures in Weimar Germany, an acknowledged leader; but a leader without a sword. To criticize conditions in the Republic — as he did in his famous novella *Kobes*, written in 1924 — was to attack the Republic he himself had striven for, a Republic already ominously threatened by renascent militarism and nationalism. He was proud his brother had reached such literary pre-eminence, but his own creative powers were rendered impotent by the conflict. He had nowhere to turn: too old, too austere and distinguished to join the proletariat, too conscientious yet to play satirist to the Republic. His marriage began to fail, he lowered his literary sights, his novels became thrillers. And Thomas, almost unruffled by the enormous success of *The Magic Mountain* began meanwhile the greatest work of his life — his tetralogy on the life of the biblical hero: *Joseph and his Brothers*.

6

The seed of *Joseph and his Brothers* had been planted as early as 1923. In the winter of that year "a Munich artist, an old friend of my wife, showed me a portfolio of illustrations of his, depicting quite prettily the story of Joseph, the son of Jacob," Thomas later recalled:

The artist wanted me to write a word or so of introduction to his work, and it was partly with his friendly service in mind that I looked up in my old family Bible — with its many underlinings in faded ink bearing witness to the study of long-dead pious forbears — the graceful fable of which Goethe said: "This natural narrative is most charming, only it seems too short, and one feels inclined to put in the detail." I did not know then how much the phrase, out of *Dichtung und Wahrheit,* was to mean to me as a motto in the years of work before me. But the evening hour was full of meditation, of tentative, groping speculation and the forecast of an entirely new thing; I felt an indescribable fascination of the mind and senses at this idea of leaving the modern bourgeois sphere so far behind and making my narrative pierce deep, deep into the human."[26]

Shortly after publication of *The Magic Mountain,* Thomas was offered free passage on the *General San Martin,* one of Hugo Stinnes' ships making a tour of the Mediterranean. He joined the steamer in Venice — "my God, how moved I was to see the beloved city again after bearing it 13 years in my heart!" he wrote in his article for the *Vossiche Zeitung,* in April 1925.[27] He occupied the doctor's cabin and watched the 160 passengers enjoying themselves in considerable luxury. "I don't wish to go into great detail," he wrote, "for it might well appear provocative, an approving portrait of an orgy of post-war capitalists with *nouveaux riches* in gleaming luxury cabins. It is like that, it has something of that," but he added how dour and upstanding the Hamburg Captain and his crew were.

However, it was neither the sea air nor the fellow travellers that had enticed Thomas; it was, as he wrote to Bertram on 4th February 1925, "primarily a question of Egypt. I will be able to cast an eye over the desert, the pyramids and the sphinx — it is for this reason I have accepted the invitation, for it may be of great help to certain still somewhat shadowy plans which I secretly have in mind."

In the spring of 1923 Thomas had visited Spain for the first time (by ship, avoiding France) and been impressed by the Mass held on Ascension Day in Seville, "the glorious organ music, and the *corrida* in the afternoon," and the "classic Spanish domain: Castile, Toledo, Aranjuez . . ."[28] His first plan was to write a series of three historico-religious novellas: one on Spain, one on Germany, and the other on Egypt. But, as Thomas put it, it was "the old story".[29] As soon as he got his teeth into the Biblical story he found its ancestral and epic quality defied the limits of a novella. More than he could have believed possible the story took him away from contemporary German problems: and yet became an inverted commentary on them: an opportunity to defy the "anti-intellectual bigots", the "exorcizing of the mind", the "ultra-romantic denial of the development of the cerebrum", the mythological clap-trap of racists "which seems to be the order of the day". He refused to part myth from psychology, and "by means of a mythical psychology", as he wrote, he attempted now a "psychology of the myth".

"The fascination grew. It was strengthened by another thought, the idea of assimilation, of continuation, continuity, of contributing to human tradition — again an idea which gains in power of attraction at the age which I have now reached," he wrote in 1930. For centuries artists had interpreted the story "in picture and poetic creation. My work, for good or for bad, would take its historic place in the line, in the tradition, bearing the stamp of its own time and place."

The very vastness of the undertaking called for time and dedication — elements no longer at hand to the fêted spokesman and cultural ambassador of the Republic. "What Christ meant by the 'world' I understand more and more," he wrote to Bertram in August 1925. "Truly one really has to be a man to come 'to God' despite it . . . Life has become so turbulent, so distracting; I am continually being kept from preparing for the future, above all from the plan for *Joseph.*"

But Bertram was hardly the best confidant for Thomas' psychological treatment of mythology. The Cologne Professor was now imbued with the Aryan ideal, one of the thousands of intellectuals who were suddenly willing to betray centuries of humanitarian education to live out the Wagnerian legends of the North.

In the meantime Thomas caught up on his numerous journalistic obligations with articles on cosmopolitanism, marriage, the spirit of medicine, his last German Letter to *Dial:*[30]

No wonder that in these times of turbulence and spiritual impoverishment the prose-epic has become the really modern, prevailing form of literary self-expression — even in Germany, where theoretically and thanks to the propaganda of two imposing and triumphant theatrical geniuses (Schiller and Wagner) drama has passed until recently for the leading literary art;

concluding with a sally on Wagner's *Tristan and Isolde:*

This is the pinnacle, the consummation, of romanticism, its furthest artistic expansion, the imperialism of a world-conquering oblivion — of an intoxicating self-annihilation. And all of this is uncongenial to the soul of Europe which, if it is still to be saved for life and reason, requires some hard work and some of that self-conquest which Nietzsche upheld with heroism and exemplariness.

But even Nietzsche's words were perverted into primitive mythological ideology. To the strains of Wagner's music the German superman was preparing for his own battle with reason. And as Heinrich had shown in his letter to Stresemann in 1923, reason needed stronger safeguards than those the government was willing to use if it were not to be toppled by the forces of evil.

7

In February 1924, on a visit to Prague to see a production of his play *Madame Legros,* Heinrich had been invited to breakfast with the Czechoslovak President, Thomas Masaryk; the following year, at the international PEN conference in Paris, the whole assembly rose to its feet when Heinrich was called to speak as the German representative. To people abroad he gave as optimistic an account of the Republic as possible, quoting the German love of order and conservatism as the chief reason why the Republic was not in danger of collapsing. After all, it had withstood disasters never experienced abroad and had survived: why should it not now grow stronger?[31]

But in his memoirs, Heinrich claimed that "even in its best years from 1925 to 1927, the Republic enjoyed no one's confidence".[32] Not even by incorporating Nationalists in the coalition cabinets could the government quieten the general hostility to France, the unwillingness to accept the new Eastern boundaries of Germany. "The Republicans are continually frightened of being excelled in nationalism, so they cannot find the courage to openly pursue a policy of internationalism," Heinrich wrote to Felix Bertaux in November 1924; a year later he was even more distressed. "Parliamentarianism is losing ground daily," he wrote to Bertaux on 27th December 1925. "We watch astounded as our own terms are misused. What does 'the freedom of the press' mean, when for instance every second word of mine is censored. It is strange and curious how the century-old system of liberalism is dying before our eyes."[33]

But how many people cared? The "hard work" Thomas considered necessary to save "the soul of Europe" was not easy in a country unwilling to accept the facts and lessons of the past. Though the Treaty of Locarno seemed a triumph of international accord, it was denounced inside Germany as a betrayal of the Fatherland. A fantastic and blindly hypocritical self-righteousness that had developed in Germany since 1871 grew stronger and stronger, a spirit which would continue even after the catastrophe of the Second World War: "We are right to use any means to gain our own ends," it maintained, "but it is wrong for others to condemn us when we have failed." Thus the War-Guilt clause of the Versailles Treaty was never accepted in Germany, even by the Republic after 1919, just as the Nuremberg Trials were considered immoral by the very people who, months before, had considered legality and justice a fiction of degenerates. No French soldier had fired a shot on German soil during the Great War; yet a fanatical arrogance insisted that Germany could not have been guilty.

The secret re-armament fooled no one in Germany, not even the Allied Control Commission; but England and France had had enough of war, there were economic and social issues of far greater magnitude to be confronted at home. America poured money into Germany under the Dawes plan: much of this, under government direction, went to offsetting German industrialists' losses: industrialists who promptly financed Hitler and the gathering tribes of uniformed "labour battalions".

To younger people the situation did not appear so serious. It was over ten years since the comparative calm of pre-war Germany, they accepted the new era with a spirit of adventure. "There were so many directions, so many promises, so many dangers," wrote Klaus Mann later of this period:

We could not make up our minds. We toyed with the most divergent formulas. We tried to reconcile and to fuse the most contradictory experiences. Our attitude was moulded by an abundance of incongruous devices. We tried to be urbane and seditious, sacerdotal and flippant, progressive and romantic. We were mystic and cynical. We wanted everybody to be happy, but were appallingly lacking in social consciousness. We pretended to be "good Europeans" but neglected or ignored the fundamental problems of our own country. Our light-minded chorus accompanied the gradual disintegration of the continent. We enjoyed the colourful scenery about us and failed to notice that, in reality, our devout dance was taking place in the midst of a social and moral vacuum.[34]

Heinrich, however, could not fail to notice. The dream of a genuine socialist future receded as the middle classes recovered from the blow of inflation — "like someone who was out for the count, but who gets up, adjusts his clothes and behaves as though nothing has happened", as Heinrich put it in a letter to Felix Bertaux.[35] Benevolent dictatorship would not help, because, as Heinrich went on, one could not hope to find a benevolent German dictator:

Particularly in Germany I can only expect evil men to become dictators, and that will hardly be to the advantage of greater spiritual ideals.

Why do I concern myself with all this? It is just that the novelty (retarded, and everywhere worn out) of parliamentary "democracy" has demonstrated a quite impermissable number of evil qualities as soon as Germany begins to use it. In this situation dictatorship is no longer terrifying — it cannot be any more corrupt, less just or less lawful, more rapacious or murderous. If dictatorship comes, then it will be because there is nothing more to be lost. But perhaps I am wrong, and it will find a way of doing even more evil.

For the moment Heinrich remained publicly loyal to the Republic, whatever his misgivings. He had noted in Berlin and Munich a movement towards Catholicism — another sign of evading democratic responsibility, as he perceived it — and in November 1925 had planned a new novel on the theme. It took eight months, of which only four and a half were spent writing. Events, he claimed in an essay at this time, were moving too fast for the writer to hide away and spend "years" over a book. Society was changing too rapidly, such a book could not be "organic, it could not live."[36] The disaster of the *Der Kopf* had proved this for him. "At least this one is all of a piece," Heinrich wrote to Bertaux in August, on completing the new novel, "and I believe it has life in it. One or two important characteristic types of today are in it . . ."[37]

Ten years before Heinrich and Thomas might have disputed such an attitude, and argued bitterly over the roles and aims of literature; yet curiously now they did not. If Heinrich had reservations about Thomas' somewhat Olympian stance in literature, he did not show it, nor did Thomas question Heinrich's approach. The "division of labour" to which Thomas had once referred still operated: between them they ruled the literary scene — as Heinrich ironically quoted in a letter to Thomas in August 1927. " 'German literature is under the absolute rule of the Mann family' I read in the 'Comoedia'."[38] And in 1926, with the founding of a literary section of the Prussian Academy of Arts in Berlin, they were both accorded the honours they had earned as writers and cultural ambassadors of the Republic.

Yet it was in the Academy itself, screened from public gaze, that their differing attitudes were most clearly demonstrated. Thomas was appointed a founding member by the president of the Academy, Max Liebermann, and Heinrich soon followed as one of the twenty-four senators.

But once a literary Academy had been created — over two centuries after its musical and visual arts counterpart — the question of its role arose. Was it to symbolize the status of literature in the new Republic: or ought it actively to promote and defend the spiritual and literary ideals of republicanism?

Gerhart Hauptmann caused the first scandal by resigning his founder-membership two days before the official inauguration ceremony. No sooner was the section established than its anachronistic position was revealed — a Prussian, not a national institution, in which the Prussian Minister of Education and the Arts controlled the appointment of new senators and the existing statutes of the old Academy precluded anything more than an advisory capacity in matters of literature.

The following year, in August 1927, the question of Chairmanship of the Literary Senate again arose, and Thomas agreed to his own nomination by Josef Ponten and Wilhelm Schäfer. But to Heinrich the question of Chairmanship signified the very purpose of the Literary Academy.

To obtain money for the academy, more and more money, to fight for its position in the public mind, to make it if possible into a power within the state — only someone prepared to invest great energy, practical energy, can do this. When I consider your candidacy, I cannot however believe that you would be prepared to allow your work to suffer under so many responsibilities . . .

The matter is of enormous importance. German literature has perhaps its sole opportunity to achieve its rightful social rank — and this is only possible if the Academy is aware of itself as the highest active organ of the literary spirit . . .[39]

It was, of course, a zealous ambition in the 'Thirties, akin to the concept of the Arts Council of Great Britain which would only come into being more than a quarter century later. But Thomas was entirely won over. He asked Ponten to withdraw his nomination. "You would be the right person," he wrote back to Heinrich from Sylt, on the Baltic, "if you had the time."[40]

Writers, by nature, do not form the most homogeneous of pressure groups, and Heinrich had instinctively realized the need for an active and dynamic

Chairman who would only require the support of the Senators.

There was, however no one with the qualities such a post demanded. Only in 1931, after moving to Berlin, did Heinrich himself accept the position: and by then the fate of the Republic was well-nigh sealed. Heinrich's expulsion (as will be seen) was one of the very first demands made by the Nazis, even before the Reichstag fire of February 1933 and the subsequent election which was to give the Nazis complete control of Germany.

8

It was the winter of 1926 before Thomas actually began writing the story of Joseph after a year of frenetic activity: a semi-official visit to Paris in January; the celebration of Lübeck's 700th anniversary in June; a holiday in Italy which would give rise — like that of 1911 — to another of his best known novellas; the inauguration of the Literary Section of the Prussian Academy of Arts in Berlin; and, together with Heinrich and several literary colleagues, a "political-cultural" manifesto delivered in Munich in November.

"I am very glad that I am writing again. I really feel myself and know something about myself only when I am writing something; the intervals are gruesome," Thomas wrote to Erika, his daughter, just before Christmas 1926:

> *Joseph* is growing, page by page, although for the present it is only a kind of sketch or humorously pseudoscientific layout of the foundation, just for my own amusement. For the thing is more fun than anything else I have ever done. It is for once something new and quite remarkable in spirit, in that with these people, meaning and being, myth and reality, are constantly passing into one another. And Joseph is a kind of mythic confidence man.

It would be a mistake, though, to assume that Thomas' withdrawal into the realms of Egyptian mythology signified a retreat from social reality. While Hesse withdrew to his little house in Montagnola, Hofmannsthal to Rodaun, Hauptmann to Agnetendorf, Thomas refused to budge from Munich, despite constant rumours and agitation from the nationalists. In an interview with *La Stampa* in Florence, 1925, he had expressed his feeling that the novel "like everything else today, has reached a state of crisis". "The novel is searching for a new form, just as life is searching for a new ideal," he declared. Expressionism was over. "I myself am searching for a new form, one that is tough, precise and self-contained, one which thus shows itself capable of embodying the new reality of things." The *Hamburger Fremdenblatt*, which carried the interview, added its own note:

> Thomas Mann is now at work on a new novel, whose hero will be utterly different from that of *The Magic Mountain.* It concerns an industrialist, a type of modern adventurer in large format and with the deepest conscience. The work is said to be far advanced.[41]

Where the *Hamburger Fremdenblatt* obtained this idea no one knows; possibly someone in the editorial department had heard talk of Heinrich's latest novella *Kobes,* with its illustrations by George Grosz, modelled on the German industrialist Hugo Stinnes.

But that Thomas questioned the very basis of the traditional middle-class epic was now evident. In discussing Freud's influence in his *Stampa* interview, Thomas remarked:

We are in fact suffering from an over-abundance of knowledge today. Our overwrought and overactive brains receive too great an inflow of information. That is why we find it so difficult to believe consistently, to forge straight paths and to grasp the world and life with erstwhile simplicity.

Our task is . . . to find a way of synthesizing knowledge and action . . . we must reach the wonder of original man on the shoulders of knowledge, innocence without losing the power of experience.

It was a return to the ideas Heinrich had put forward in his famous essay of 1910, *Geist und Tat* (Intellect and Action).[42] And the only way, as Heinrich was certain, was by a fusion of intellect with the principles of socialist endeavour.

It was Heinrich who urged Thomas along this path, and it says a great deal for their mutual respect that despite a chorus of protest from right and left, through Naziism and McCarthyism, they both came to retain their conviction that socialism was the only rightful course for modern man.

It was here that the tradition of Lübeck as an independent state, a republic, responsible and self-governing, came full circle. Heinrich and Thomas had gone out into the world, had established themselves not only as artists but as statesmen of culture. *Lübeck als geistige Lebensform* (Lübeck as a spiritual concept of life) was Thomas' grateful homage to the city which had educated him. In 1926 his speech was received with tremendous applause, and gained him the honorary title of Professor. Yet within ten years the same city would be celebrating the announcement that Thomas Mann had been deprived of his German citizenship for publishing "hostile views" towards the Fatherland.

In the great hall of the Lübeck Stadttheater on 5th June 1926, though, Thomas recounted the motives and genesis of his works, how their roots went back — even in *Death in Venice* — to the historic little Baltic seaport, its summer beaches at Travemünde, its spirit of patient, honourable, unflagging commerce, a burgher-form of society, not bourgeois in the parvenu, capitalist sense.

"When we say 'German' and 'burgher', " Thomas told his audience, "we are not using political jargon, nor are we referring to the international capitalist bourgeoisie. Here in Lübeck the word 'German' itself signifies world-burgherdom, being at the centre of life, maintaining a world-conscience, world-consideration, attributes which do not allow a man to be drawn towards violence, which cause him to defend the principles of humanity, of being human, of man and his upbringing, education against all extremists, both right and left. The German, placed between the extremes of the world, cannot be himself an extremist: it is a spiritual fact, a question of his soul which no radicalism can alter."

In truth, of course, Thomas well knew that this idealistic view of burgherdom was fated:

There is a tremendous wave of change which we all feel and experience, rolling over Europe today, a wave we call the "world-revolution," a fundamentally explosive movement which is altering our whole conception of life in all ways — moral, scientific, economic, political, technical, and artistic; a progress so fast that our children, whether born before or after the war, really inhabit a new world, which has little knowledge of our old one. But the world-revolution is a fact. To deny it is to deny life and evolution; to stand conservatively against it means to deny oneself life and development.

What then was the answer? For him personally it was, as *Buddenbrooks* had suggested almost a quarter of a century before, the path of art — ironic, watchful, recording, faintly heralding the striving for freedom. But the 700th anniversary of the city of Lübeck made him hope that there, too, a middle-stance, accepting the direction of history but without denying the past, would be possible.

Time was to prove Thomas wrong, and in a way which would offend him more deeply than Heinrich was to be offended. "I would like to have success in Germany only for the sake of the money," Heinrich had confided bitterly to Maximilian Brantl in 1910, "not for myself: my feeling of kinship to this people is not strong enough for that."[43] When persecution and exile finally came it was too inevitable to strike Heinrich as treachery. For over three decades he had been cast in the role of Francophile, of alien; Germany was only fulfilling a destiny Heinrich had foreseen and warned against for the major part of his adult life.

For Thomas it was different. He had tried always to identify with what was best in German culture and tradition, and the depth and understanding of this identification had brought him international as well as national fame: "cette postérité contemporaine", as he quoted the critic Emile Faguet.[44] That the country which he had honoured with such loyalty and affection should reject him was the greatest insult of his life: and many of Thomas' bitterly resentful statements in exile, never forgiven or forgotten in Germany, can be related to this. When Klaus and Erika telephoned to Switzerland in March 1933 to warn him of "bad weather" at home in Germany, it was some time before the "magician" could be made to understand. The man who had never been able to "stand being abroad for more than four weeks", who even in the early 1920s found it "best, after all, in chaotic Germany", had gone too far, had spoken with insufficient reverence for the national musical idol Richard Wagner; and was cast out. It was to be Thomas' first major change of home since he had left Lübeck nearly forty years before as a precocious but hardly successful schoolboy; an eviction that smarted for the rest of his life.

But first the Republic was to run to its final curtain; *The Magic Mountain* to storm the English-speaking world; and in 1929 the Nobel Prize Committee to honour at last one of the great masters of modern European letters.

9

"Have no fear — I have no intention of doing this again," Heinrich wrote to his friend Maximilian Brantl in May 1925. He was referring to the publication of *Der Kopf.* "I shall not write anything like that again. It was the most complete, the highest I had to offer."[45]

After *Der Kopf* Heinrich confined himself to a series of social novels, beginning with *Mutter Marie,* published in 1927, which demonstrated again his old command of pace and character, but could hardly be considered as more than entertainments: sometimes grotesque, always lively, but without the qualities which had made — despite all their faults — his initial works so important in the history of early twentieth-century German literature — namely their stylistic originality, their search for a new form, a new manner in which to expose social reality. When Paul Zsolnay issued his new edition of the Collected Works of Heinrich Mann, beginning in 1925, it was these early novels — *In the Land of Cockaigne* and the three separate volumes of *Die Göttinnen* — which, despite first printings of only 5,000 copies, went on to reach sales of more than 50,000 each in the following seven years; whereas the latter day novels of the Weimar Republic — *Mutter Marie, Eugenie oder die Bürgerzeit* (translated into English in 1930 as *Royal Woman), Die grosse Sache* and *Ein ernstes Leben* — though issued in first editions of 25,000 to 30,000 copies, did not achieve any comparable success.

Perhaps, as many critics have said, Heinrich was born to oppose: from his schoolboy denunciation of Lübeck to his leadership of the anti-fascists in the 'Thirties. And yet, from a human standpoint, this is too simple a view; for if he failed in the 'Twenties to produce the quality of literary works his earlier years had heralded, he became infinitely more active and effective in public terms. His articles appeared regularly on the front page of the *Berliner Tageblatt,* lecture tours took him across the whole of German-speaking Europe; and among friends and foe he enjoyed a reputation in Germany which far outshone any contemporary social writer. Döblin, Werfel, and the young Bertolt Brecht stole the limelight as modern authors; but in the end there was only one major voice in the Republic which became the embodiment of honesty, integrity, of consistency, of caring. Where even Thomas was regularly attacked in the nationalist press for being a turncoat and was still viewed among socialists with great mistrust, Heinrich's consistent struggle for clear, unmistakable and unchanging goals won him the respect, if not the affection, of a far wider public than the readership of his novels. Though he would find the "Weltbühne's" call that he stand for President of the German Republic against Hindenburg in 1932 ridiculous, it indicated a measure of his standing: and there would be many who would bewail the fact that he declined.

He became, like Shaw, and in modern times Sartre and Malraux, a public figure, a symbol. And though in many ways he enjoyed this fame — which would increase dramatically with the filming of his novel *Professor Unrat* in 1931 — though it fulfilled his call for action on the part of the intellects of Germany, it was also a yoke, a limitation of his freedom both as a writer and — which is no different really — as a human being.

He fought like a bull to oppose the government's Censorship bill of 1926 — the so-called Filth and Shame Law — and was called to Berlin by the *Berliner Tabeglatt* to direct operations. Thomas read out Heinrich's memorandum on the subject to the sitting of the Academy in Berlin which adopted it unanimously. Then in the autumn he combined with Thomas and four other writers in Munich to wage a "cultural war" against nationalism "in intellectual spheres". "It is a 'great period'," he wrote to Felix Bertaux in December 1926. "Much is being done which had been left to stagnate, out of cowardice and indifference. The reactionary spirit of the day no longer instils automatic fear, is itself aware that its absolute power will no longer be patiently tolerated."[46] The speeches, given before a "gigantic audience"[47] in the Tonhalle in Munich, were a tremendous success, "an explosion"[48] — yet against the force of the oncoming catastrophe the success was destined to be short-lived.

In May 1928 the National Socialists obtained their first tentative hold on the Reichstag, with 12 seats won (or obtained by coalition) — returning, among others, Goebbels, Göring, Gregor Strasser and Gottfried Feder. The election was considered a triumph for the Social Democrats, whose poll increased by over a million votes; but with the 6th Comintern ban on a Communist alliance or collaboration with the Social Democrats, and Alfred Hugenberg's new "agreement" with Hitler, any hope of a united social front to withstand the effects of an economic collapse or recession began to recede.

Der tieferer Sinn der Republik — (The Deeper Meaning of the Republic) — had been the title of Heinrich's address to the Hamburg conference of the German Democratic Party in April 1927. In it he warned of the dangers of re-militarization: not only for the political future of the Republic, but also its disastrous long-term threat to the worker. Re-armament might mean more work — but with what result? It was always the worker who would suffer most in war.

Yet another film is being shown throughout the country which morally defends re-armament: one ought not to deprive the worker of his bread. Bread! Hard, sour bread — so that, in return for his own consent, he may be gassed on behalf of his honest bread-givers! Thus the be-all and end-all of this "republican" business: thus its morality, thus its spirit and thus its heart![49]

It was Heinrich's first major public dissociation from the Republic: the forerunner of Thomas'*Appeal to Reason* speech of 1930. Yet the Communists were adamant: history after all, they claimed, was on their side. Into the divided ranks of the Communists and Social Democrats, Hitler began to drive his wedge.

10

It was in 1927 that Heinrich accepted the invitation of Felix Bertaux to stay with him in the Pyrenees, in the village of Lescun. The day after his arrival they descended to the plains of Béarn — once the scene of the great French wars of religion — and visited the famous castle of Pau, almost unaltered after four hundred years. In the dry, parched countryside Bertaux pointed out the great distance between the farms, and the occasional groups of three pine-trees at their entrances — a signal of refuge for hunted Protestants centuries before.

It was here, where so much persecution and suffering had taken place, that Heinrich first absorbed the impressions which would one day form the basis of *Henri IV*, one of the most important twentieth-century German historical novels. On it he lavished all the lessons of his life: and in the same way that *Joseph and his Brothers* reflected modern man's "search for his essence, his origin, his goal", so too *Henri IV* mirrored all too tragically modern Europe's wars of religion, of wild barbarism: and the struggle of one man to bring unity and humanitarian greatness to his country.

But for the moment, in the attempt to stave off the national madness threatening the Republic, any such plans were set aside. Both Heinrich and Thomas were asked to give lecture tour after lecture tour. In the course of 1927 Thomas managed to speak in Warsaw, Danzig, Essen, Heidelberg, Munich, Berlin, Stettin, Frankfurt, Karlsruhe, Wiesbaden, Aix-la-Chapelle, Mönchen-Gladbach, Krefeld and Düsseldorf. It was small wonder that the Joseph novel grew but slowly — with the first part completed in mid-June, and then left to rest.

Heinrich's itinerary was scarcely less exacting. "What have I done since last autumn except write speeches and travel with them?" he wrote to Felix Bertaux in May.[50] He had been invited to address the PEN club in Brussels in June, but was so exhausted he decided to spend five weeks in the sanatorium at Bad Gastein — preparing yet further talks for a "tournée de conférences" in the Rhineland that October, as he told Bertaux.[51] He was concerned about the high price of books and "mauvaise volonté" of those who published them, which had served to limit the literary market rather than increase it, as the age demanded; nor were publishers anxious to put out literature which reflected the times and conditions with social and economic honesty. Though Heinrich's Weimar novels were without great literary pretension, they did at least stem from a genuine concern with contemporary problems. In Bad Gastein, in July 1927, Heinrich began to plan a sequel to *Mutter Marie*, analysing this time the irresponsibility of the young. In the meantime, in spare moments he had already more than half-completed a new novel. "It is called Eugenie (this only between our-selves — it is the original Eugenie, but played by someone else, in 1873)."[52] It was a smallish novel, "easy to read" and containing "its own moral, if no great spirituality" as he later put it[53] — but even this was impossible to complete that year in the wake of his Rhineland lecture tour, a big speech in

Berlin entitled *A Spiritual Locarno* — calling for greater exchange of under-standing with both Russia and France and the avoidance of isolationist nationalism — followed by a further round of lectures in Paris in November, beginning at the League of Human Rights.

It was an exhausting year publicly for both Thomas and Heinrich; privately within the Mann family, too, the pressure of the Republic began to take its toll. Their sister Julia's husband had died shortly after the great inflation, leaving very little on which to bring up two daughters. Lula had always set great store on social appearances, and had found life difficult in such reduced circumstances. She began to take drugs; and when her lover left her, she hanged herself.

It was an especially bitter blow for Thomas, with his strong sense of family destiny. Of the family which had once gathered in the Beckergrube in Lübeck, only Heinrich, Thomas and "little Viko" — now an agriculturalist — were left. "Her grave is too new," Thomas wrote of Julia in his *A Sketch of My Life,* published three years later. "I will leave the story to a later narrative in a larger frame." By the time he found sufficient emotional distance to record it, the Republic had fallen, Hitler had launched his 1,000 year Reich, which itself was in ruins: and the death of Julia had come to represent not only a personal loss, but an important thread in a new tapestry whose theme was the fate of an entire nation: *Doctor Faustus.*

11

One reason for the increasing number of engagements which Heinrich and Thomas accepted away from Munich was the declining cultural level of the city. Already in June 1923 Heinrich had remarked on this decline: "You would not believe how desolate Munich has become in spiritual and artistic matters," he wrote to Felix Bertaux. "I remain here for outward reasons, but otherwise my relations are all with Berlin. Centralization is inevitable. It had begun even before the catastrophe; now it is picking up speed in the same measure as democracy."[54] By 1928 Heinrich was not only a Senator of the Berlin Academy of Arts, but also the Chairman of the *Volksverband für Filmkunst* in Berlin, a newly founded film group designed to combat the increasingly nationalist bias of the German film industry. It was only in April that he managed to finish *Eugenie und die Bürgerzeit* (Royal Woman); in the meantime both he and Thomas had come under severe fire from the nationalist and Nazi press for their conciliatory attitude towards France. Heinrich's speech in the Paris Trocadéro on the 150th anniversary of Victor Hugo's birth had brought a standing ovation from the 5,000 strong audience in 1927; but when Thomas welcomed this and the struggle for better Franco-German relations in an interview with the Paris *Comoedia* he was bitterly attacked at home. "Thomas Mann's kow-tow to Paris" ran the headline in the *Berliner Nachtausgabe.* "The Man who speaks on behalf of traitors to the fatherland and defames his people!"

Thomas' reply, in the columns of the *Literarische Welt,* was filled with scorn for the smear tactics and irresponsible journalism of such attacks. As Heinrich had noted in the war, nationalism betrays its humanity by its language: and the language of the Nazis was savage with hate and manipulated half-truths, with envy and fanatical self-righteousness. With justice Thomas could point out how much more he had done for the "fatherland" and its international literary rank than the "hollow, unproven, negative, paid party street-patriotism" that the *Berliner Nachtausgabe* was busy "megaphoning" to the masses.[55] "Does this so-called nationalism have anything to do with patriotism or any idea of real patriotism?" he asked Willy Haas, the then editor of *Literarische Welt* — a few weeks later. "It seems to me it does not. It is pure dynamistic romanticism, pure glorification of catastrophe for its own sake."[56]

By referring to the "two flying dunces" currently receiving a "nationalistic headstand in their honour" in Munich in June 1928,[57] Thomas unwittingly brought down another furious barrage from the nationalist press. Thomas' remark was contained in a private letter, and it "sprang from a fleeting annoyance at the fashionably extreme and anti-cultural overvaluation of sports records and the nationalistic exploitation of the same" — but it was enough for the *Suddeutsche Monatshefte* to use in a special pamphlet they prepared to castigate their most distinguished Munich author:

> Thus they printed the pamphlet, which I shall be the last to see, but which the "Münchner Zeitung" promptly received, whereupon it informed me that I had finally separated myself from the German people, from their love and their pride.[58]

The situation would have been laughable if it had not been so serious; for the scandal over Munich's "flying dunces" was only a foretaste of what was in store for Thomas.

In Berlin, though, Heinrich was unsure whether it was not better temporarily to spare the Republic further criticism, given its growing fragility. More than a year before, a Berlin theatre had commissioned him to write a new play. This time it was a musical, *Bibi.* The title role was written with a young actress, Trude Hesterberg, in mind. She had appeared in a comedy by Ernst Toller and Walter Hasenclever, which had been set to music by Friedrich Hollaender; and Heinrich had been very struck by her.

Bibi opened in Berlin on 20th October 1928. "The author of the revue was almost always to be seen in the company of the star of his play, Trude Hesterberg," one Berlin evening paper was quick to notice. Heinrich remained in Berlin, even over Christmas. Only on New Year's Eve did he at last reveal to his friend Felix Bertaux the nature of his relationship with Miss Hesterberg.

Dear Friend,

Your letter is the most moving sign of friendship I have received in this difficult affair. I feel deeply indebted to you for your sympathy, as for so much else.

You will believe me, I think, when I say that what I did came from inward necessity as well as the pressure of circumstances. My marriage had died a long time ago, only our daughter kept us together; otherwise all that remained were patience and resignation, and even with them one cannot go on for ever. One's work is no longer happy, one's anxieties weigh more heavily. Over and above this my wife showed her dissatisfaction too often, too vehemently, and I lost the sense of calm I need. On the other hand I noticed my own silence in all domestic matters. This puts me in the wrong. The factual blame for the separation lies beyond question with me, and I shall never blame my wife. Despite everything she remained loyal to me, and I know what I am losing there. For that reason she was right to fight tooth and nail when she saw the danger; but in doing so she only accentuated it probably.

But that was not the cause. First of all our marriage became unsatisfactory, and then came a love I had never known in my whole life. I am almost an old man now, but such torment and fear, this sense of unquestionable fate I had never experienced before. For a time I acted against my own will, let everything happen, could not do otherwise. Now that it has happened I must face the consequences. But I do not wish to appear without conscience.

The woman I am living with is one of the top actresses in Berlin. She had considered her steps better than I, but since what happened she wishes a permanent relationship. My wife refuses to countenance divorce . . . The whole situation is one of abeyance and unrest. The final decisions are not mine to make, they are, as Gide puts it, adjourned. I can of course see no possible way back to a wife who is drawing away from me in the meantime; and the new ties become only stronger. I have no legal right to the child, that is the worst part. I can only hope that in time this will settle down on all sides, perhaps then there might come indulgence and agreement. But I cannot foretell which ways the various parties will choose. I only begin to understand that for me and in my relationship every happiness gained must bring with it a penalty.[59]

Mimi had done everything in her power to halt the "relationship" — even hiring detectives to report on Heinrich's movements in Berlin. Temperamentally they had always been potentially at odds; and Mimi's expensive tastes, her penchant for rich foods and subsequent trips to dietary establishments had led to frequent quarrels. But above all, the circumstances which had brought them together — Heinrich's lonely struggle for recognition and success — no longer obtained; Mimi no longer promised the essential private solace, the excitement she once had done. Success — as once it had with Thomas — made demands on Heinrich he was not equipped to bear. He was perhaps too much an artist, and an eccentric, to accept either a false relationship or the exacting demands of a real marriage. Berlin had beckoned; and he had been powerless to resist.

The relationship with Trude Hesterberg was, however, itself fated. It lasted scarcely a year. But in its wake came the greatest success, ironically of Heinrich's life: the filming of his novel *Professor Unrat* — as Josef von Sternberg's legendary *The Blue Angel*.

After a summer cure at Bad Gastein with Thomas in 1929, Heinrich had intended to begin work on his new novel *(Die gross Sache)* which was "ready to set down".[60]

However the summer was interrupted by an urgent appeal from the UFA film studios in Berlin. On Trude Hesterberg's instigation — and with her in mind for the leading role — Heinrich had given permission for *Professor Unrat* to be screened. Carl Zuckmayer, after an unsuccessful stint with Brecht at Reinhardt's famous Deutsche Theater, had become a well-known humorous and colourful dramatist, and was asked to prepare a film script. Hollaender was enlisted for the music, Karl Vollmöller and Robert Liebmann helped write the songs and finalize the shooting script. Then the director, Josef von Sternberg, was appointed.

Sternberg, however, had other ideas. He had just discovered a young actress, Marlene Dietrich, who had trained with Reinhardt: and to the mortification of both Trude Hesterberg and Heinrich himself, Sternberg insisted that Dietrich take the main role as Lola-Lola. Heinrich threatened to withdraw permission: and only Trude Hesterberg herself saved the day by agreeing to the arrangement.

At the end of October the script was ready, having kept Heinrich in Berlin since August; and shooting began. Only one last hurdle remained: the rabidly-nationalist owner of the studios, Alfred Hugenberg. When Hugenberg discovered the film's story was not — as he had believed — by Thomas Mann, but by Heinrich, he immediately decided to scrap the venture. Only by showing Hugenberg a letter from Heinrich disagreeing with the finished filmscript could Hugenberg be persuaded to allow the film to be completed.

The Blue Angel was one of the first sound-films to be made in Germany. It was released there and in Austria in April 1930. With the ravishingly well-proportioned legs of Marlene Dietrich and the brilliant acting of Emil Jannings as the lonely and frustrated small-town schoolmaster the film became a sensation — before long in Paris, London and New York as well. Ironically it was no longer as author of the great satire *Der Untertan* that Heinrich now became popularly known, but as the writer of a dazzlingly perverse celluloid love-story whose original social satire had been excised: *The Blue Angel*. New editions of the book appeared immediately in Germany and abroad under the the the new title: but it was Sternberg's extraordinary film which went storming into cinematic history.

In the meantime the world's most coveted literary award had fallen at last to Thomas; and, by a similar irony, for a novel he too had written almost three decades before. Heinrich was among the first to congratulate him — on the era's new medium, radio.

12

The example of Thomas Mann shows how love and knowledge work together. Here is someone who began primarily as an observer, and who has grown to become involved with his people, a writer who in spirit serves and strives consciously for his whole people.

He himself knows, each day he is more certain that he does not stand for himself, does not live and write in isolation, but according to the needs of a vast number, who in turn represent every level of a people. If his work has become famous in the world, then his fame rests also on his people, and ought to. Every new work of his expresses the being of this people as well as its fortunes. *Buddenbrooks* showed first the German burgher family, its fortunes, its dangers. *Reflections of a Non-Political Man* also arose from dangers with which he identified himself, the fortunes and dangers of a whole nation in its most serious and distressing moments. But *The Magic Mountain* is a German textbook based on personal development. This novel above all confirms the long and responsible path of Thomas Mann from the burgher's son who wrote the memoirs of a house in Lübeck to the master who today speaks for his people . . .

Thomas Mann today received the Nobel Prize for Literature.[61]

Heinrich's radio speech in Berlin on 12th November 1929 moved Thomas deeply — "a simple, splendid gesture, intelligent and seemly" as Thomas wrote to Maximilian Brantl.[62] In his own acceptance speech, Thomas too stressed the wider significance of the award — the first time a German author had been honoured by the prize for almost twenty years. It seemed to set a seal on unhappy memories of the war, congratulations poured in from every corner of the globe.

"I am pleased," Thomas declared in Stockholm before King Gustav and the Academy, "to lay this prize, a world prize, which is made out more or less by chance in my name, at the feet of my country and people, this country and people with whom I and those like me feel more closely bound now than even at the time of its greatest imperial expansion. The Stockholm Nobel Prize honours this year the German mind, in particular German prose . . . Through its creative art Germany has proved its courage in this period of agony. It has preserved its honour . . ."

But the Swedish Academy, ironically, was not interested in Thomas' "development" or humanitarian maturity. It was honouring simply a novel of youth which had proved enduring: *Buddenbrooks*.

"The most amusing part of it," Thomas wrote to André Gide about *The Magic Mountain*, "is that the Stockholm critic and professor of literature Böök, who usually has a decisive influence upon the choice of the Nobel Prize winner, publicly proclaimed the book an artistic monstrosity and said I was receiving the prize exclusively, or at any rate chiefly, for my early novel *Buddenbrooks*"[63] — and this was confirmed in the "beautifully executed document which King Gustav gave me, that I owe the award primarily to the affection of the Northern people for my youthful novel of family life in Lübeck", as Thomas wrote in his *A Sketch of My Life* in 1930.

But however ironical the grounds for the Swedish choice, the award itself came as no surprise to the world. However much the Swedish Academy disliked the complex reasoning and extended ironies of *The Magic Mountain* there was little doubt that Thomas had confirmed his world-stature as a novelist with the work. Against the sordid simplicities of the National-Socialist theories of race and Aryan supremacy *The Magic Mountain* symbolized the cultural richness of Europe — doomed perhaps, but still great in its dissolution. In its English translation by H.T. Lowe-Porter the book became much more than a German novel of intellectual brilliance. It was the European parallel to Scott Fitzgerald's supple, winsome portrait of the Jazz Age, an insight into the European heritage of modern Western man on the brink of ruin — or salvation.

Germany itself, meanwhile, uninterested in the honour being done to the German mind, was busy voting on Alfred Hugenberg's new referendum: a national vote on the question of whether Germany should reject the war-guilt clause (and thus the reparation clauses too) of the Versailles treaty — and henceforward condemn all members of its own government and administrators who signed international agreements as "traitors to the fatherland".

The 'Thirties had begun.

CHAPTER TWELVE

The End of Weimar

The Nobel Prize was worth 200,000 Marks; and amid the banqueting in Stockholm in December 1929 more than one voice cautioned Thomas and Katja to keep the money outside Germany.

On 22nd December 1929, while Thomas was still in Stockholm, Hugenberg's referendum was defeated. But almost 6 million Germans had voted for Hugenberg's "freedom law": small cheer for the Allied Governments who had agreed to evacuate the Rhineland the following spring. Under the new Young Plan, reparations were to be spread over the next thirty years in order to safeguard the rebuilding and expansion of the German economy: but no provision was made about action to be taken if Germany were at any future time to refuse to pay, other than referring the matter to the Permanent Court of International Justice at the Hague.

Already in October 1929, Wall Street had crashed and the American economic miracle turned to vapour. During the winter unemployment in Germany doubled, to the point where the government's unemployment insurance scheme could no longer afford to pay benefits. Although the Prussian Government had banned the *Stahlhelm* (a group of uniformed nationalists), the President of the Republic continued to pronounce his membership and allegiance to the organization. Yet more ominous, Hugenberg had formed an alliance with Hitler to fight the Young Plan, thus uniting nationalists and Nazis: and giving Hitler both the publicity machine and social rank which until then he had in no way attained. Money too was now flowing into Hitler's coffers; sales of *Mein Kampf* had risen to 50,000 per annum, and when Emil Kirdorf, the iron and steel magnate, attended the 1929 Nuremberg Congress of the Nazi Party as guest of honour, the movement gathered momentum. The dream of a Germany which accepted the tragedy and lessons of the past began to dissolve and with it the Republic. Hitler's paid-up following doubled between 1929 and 1930 — and would quadruple again by the following year. The Social Democrat coalition broke down at the end of March 1930 over the question of unemployment insurance budgeting, and the Centre Party chairman, Brüning, was appointed Chancellor of Germany by Hindenburg — without a parliamentary majority to support him, and contrary to the Constitution. The Golden Age of Weimar was over.

It was a disastrous turn of events for the Social Democrats, who had bowed to Trade Union pressure rather than considering the national interest; and one from which they never recovered. Brüning had no option but to rule by *Diktat* (Article 4d of the Weimar Constitution). By July Brüning was forced to dissolve the Reichstag — which had voted against the new national aid programme — and when the new Elections took place on 14th September, the world was shocked to hear that the Nazis had rocketed from 12 to 107 seats — a landslide unparalleled in German history — and one that would be repeated yet again in 1932.

After his work with Zuckmayer on *The Blue Angel* filmscript, Heinrich had completed his Rhineland lecture-tour in the autumn of 1929, and begun work on the third of his "morality" novels ("celui qui veut encourager la joie modeste" as he wrote to Bertaux[1]). In Nice in March 1930, Erich Pommer, the producer of *The Blue Angel* brought the finished film for Heinrich to see, before its triumphant première in Berlin. "It was in a large and empty cinema on the seafront," Heinrich later recalled, "in the morning while the women cleaned. The projectionist was confused to begin with, for the sound-film has made such startling progress . . . we were an audience of three in a foreign cinema, and we watched the amazing Jannings smile — the tender, child-like smile of late and dangerous happiness, which seems to rise and gleam out of a luckless face . . ."[2]

By July 1930, Heinrich was back in Berlin, alarmed and upset by events. The major part of his newspaper piece *Wir Wählen* (We vote) was devoted to the threat of Naziism.

From the very start it is dishonest, the Nazi party in reality has nothing to do with what it pretends to be, is neither national nor socialist, and particularly not a party of the workers. Since it was founded it has worked with the financial support of one or two rich patrons and for the interests of large-scale capitalists. This entails both betrayal and exploitation. One hundred and fifty thousand poor souls contribute 300,000 Marks a month to their leaders. They do not know what they are doing, they are the victims of hard economic times and their distressed feelings. A better Republic would be able to cure them. As it is, they are exploited by their Party, are betrayed to their natural enemies, and added to all this they are made a mockery of. In Hitler's rubbishy statements they are told that the workers must obey only force and that a master race must be brought into being. For this these pitiable souls give their money and their faith! The erstwhile house-decorator betrays and makes a mockery not only of them, but himself. What is he? A master? . . . He was most a master when he pasted wallpaper with his own hands — a true and honest labour.

Given that this Party is against the workers and the opposite of socialist, let us be clear that it calls itself "national" only in the most patent misuse of the word. Above all, no one can call himself national who intends to start a great bloodbath within the nation. The National-Socialists have no idea how many people they would have to kill once they took power and wished to keep it. They underestimate their own bloodbath. In their newspapers they content themselves with quoting some of the better-known names, for instance Büchner, Gutzkow and myself — the dead and the living, they are not concerned who they put up against the wall. But if in fact this came to pass, they would certainly not stop at the big names. Can that be called, by any stretch of the imagination, national?

Despite the hysterical denunciations with which the Nazi press replied, Heinrich was not a communist or even a communist sympathizer. Their aims he found admirable — "they are not a Party of criminals," he wrote:

They want something which is honest, respectable and consistent; it is unfortunately, however, neither something for them nor for us, but for the time being something entirely Russian. History and geography cannot be changed; we lie too far to the west, and too many western facts of life have merged in us. Whether we say it with pride or resignation, that is the way things are. The great and admirable Russian experiment appeals to our intellect, but not to our core, and we feel that it would not be successful on the foundations of our being such as it is.

The Nazis and the nationalists were doing their best to frighten the people, harping on the nightmares of inflation and unemployment in order to portray themselves as saviours. "It is not true," Heinrich concluded his article,

that there was only peace before the last war. Now, now there is a better peace, because it could be free of menaces, ready to ripen. We must repudiate this pointless and, despite all its frenzy, ineffective, radicalism.

We must vote for those who think justly, not dictatorially. We must work, be patient and show ourselves far too proud to allow ourselves or our state to be "saved" by anyone. That is something only we ourselves can do.

The election results finished such hopes. Overnight Germany's financial credibility was ruined, her securities tumbled. The German government was no longer able to find a market for its treasury bills, and the gold and foreign exchange withdrawals from the Reichsbank rose to more than a billion marks. Not only were foreign countries calling in their loans, but German businessmen were placing their fortunes abroad; yet, paradoxically, nothing suited Hitler and the national "saviours" more than that the financial crisis deteriorate still further.

It was at this anxious and menacing moment that Thomas weighed in.

An Appeal to Reason, delivered in the Beethovensaal in Berlin on 17th October 1930, caused a sensation; not least because the Nazis found it sufficiently important to warrant a planned disruption in the hall. In the end it was only the intervention of the police which avoided bloodshed; and Thomas was hurried away through back passages to Bruno Walter's car which, with great foresight, he had kept waiting in a side street.

2

It was a demanding year for Thomas after the strenuous round of banquets, speeches and interviews that accompanied the Nobel Prize. In January 1930 he set down his seventy-page *A Sketch of My Life,* on 11th February he celebrated with Katja their Silver Wedding anniversary, and a few days later they set off, via Genoa, for Egypt and Palestine. "I expect to find the sky above and much of the earth beneath unchanged after three thousand five hundred years," he wrote concluding *A Sketch of My Life:* and so it was. They took the steamer to Nubia, and returned to Cairo past Aswan and Luxor. Katja fell ill, and Thomas travelled alone across the canal towards Asia. "How I took note!" he wrote on a postcard to Maximilian Brantl.[3] *"The Tales of Jacob* were finished and a part of *Young Joseph* had been written when I made my tour of the Middle East, to Egypt and Palestine, early in 1930," Thomas wrote in a foreword to the combined edition of the Joseph novels later.[4] "It could hardly be called a trip for the purpose of study; it rather served for verifying on the spot the things with which I had been concerned at a distance. At any rate, with my physical eyes I saw the Nile country from the Delta up (or down) to Nubia and the memorable places of the Holy Land" — impressions which did in fact help in the growing biblical tapestry: for what had once been conceived as a "fairly long short story of religious tinge",[5] one of a triptych of historical novellas, was growing into a multi-volume work, larger even than *Buddenbrooks,* the *Reflections of a Non-Politcal Man* or *The Magic Mountain.*

In Nidden, near the Baltic, Thomas had built a summer-house with a thatched roof.

> We were so thrilled by the indescribable and unique beauty of nature in this place — the fantastic world of sandy dunes mile on mile, the birch and pine groves full of elk between the Haff and the Baltic, the wild splendour of the beach — that we decided to acquire a dwelling-place in this remote spot, a pendant as it were, to our South German home.[6]

It was there he had written *Mario and the Magician,* a strange and prophetic tale of sorcery, the previous year (published in *Velhagen und Klasings Monatshefte* in April 1930 and in book form later that year); there that he spent the summer of 1930 continuing his mythological epic, from which he was invited to give a public reading in October.

But the rise in unemployment — to 3 million — and the result of the September elections had shaken him too much for him to ignore them. In

Geneva, at a visit to the League of Nations, he had heard the news and witnessed the consternation they had produced among the delegates of other nations. It was time to protest, publicly: "There are hours," Thomas declared in his *Appeal to Reason,*

> there are moments of our common life when art fails to justify itself in practice; when the inner urgency of the artist fails him; when the more immediate necessities of our existence choke back his own thought, when the general distress and crisis shake him too, in such a way that what we call art, the happy and impassioned preoccupation with eternally human values, comes to seem idle, ephemeral, a superfluous thing, a mental impossibility . . .

> What can the government's plan to set its house in order for the coming budget year give to those who are facing unemployment, lockouts, hunger, and ruin, months that threaten to fill the cup of misery for millions and display all the phenomena and all the consequences of a people's despair? Every person with any feeling is conscious of the state of things. Heavy as lead — as in the darkest years of the war — the weight lies on every breast and will not let us breathe.

The September election result, was, Thomas declared amidst the first Nazi cat-calls in the audience, "a storm signal, a warning that one can at no time demand of a people which has as much ground for self-esteem as any other, all that has in fact been demanded of Germany, without producing in it a state of feeling which may become a world menace".

The Imperial system of government, the war, the Treaty of Versailles, the lack of European disarmament, the Eastern frontier regulations and treatment of German minorities — all these Thomas denounced and gave as political reasons for the disturbing election results.

At this point in the speech Arnolt Bronnen and his SA men started their demonstration. But Thomas went on:

> When one thinks what it has cost humanity, through the ages, to rise from orgiastic nature-cults, from the service of Moloch, Baal and Astarte, with the barbaric refinements of its gnosticism and the sexual excesses of its divinities, to the plane of a more spiritual worship, one stands amazed at the light-hearted way in which today we repudiate our gains and liberations.

German nationalism was not confined to the simple-minded; it pervaded — and was "strengthened" — by "philological, academic and professiorial" circles — as Thomas had found all too distressingly in the case of his once nearest confidant and godfather to his daughter, Ernst Bertram, Professor at Cologne.

> It addresses the Germany of 1930 in a high-flown, wishy-washy jargon, full of mystical good feeling, with hyphenated prefixes like race- and folk- and fellowship-, and lends to the movement a concomitant of fanatical cult barbarism, more dangerous and estranging, with more power to clog and stupefy the brain, than even the lack of contact and the political romanticism which led us into the war . . .

This fantastic state of mind, of a humanity that has outrun its ideas, is matched by a political scene in the grotesque style, with Salvation Army methods, hallelujahs and bell-ringing and dervishlike repetition of monotonous catchwords, until everybody foams at the mouth. Fanaticism turns into a means of salvation, enthusiasm into epileptic ecstasy, politics become an opiate for the masses, a proletarian eschatology; and reason veils her face.

As Bronnen shouted and gesticulated in the background Thomas demanded:

Is all that German? Is there any deep stratum of the German soul where all that fanaticism, that bacchantic frenzy, that orgiastic denial of reason and human dignity is really at home?

But there in Bronnen, in the carefully planted Nazis screeching in the audience, was his answer. It was a sad truth. Like Heinrich, Thomas found Russian communism "still more foreign to the blood of the German people" then that of Western democracy "against which, to some extent, its hand was raised on 14th September". But Naziism was no answer as a national ideology; as Heinrich had already pointed out it was patently anti-national. "Its hatred," Thomas stated amid cries, "is levelled not so much without as within; yes, actually its fanatical love of the fatherland appears chiefly as hatred not of the foreigner but of all Germans who do not believe in its methods, and whom it promises to destroy root and branch (even today that would be rather a large order); as hatred, in short, of everything which makes for the good report and intellectual renown of Germany today. More and more it looks as though the chief goal were the inner purification of the country, the return of the German to the conception which radical nationalism has of him. But even supposing that such a return was desirable, is it any way possible?" he asked. "Can a people old and ripe and highly cultured . . . can such a people conform, even after ten thousand banishings and purificatory executions, to the wish image of a primitive, pure-blooded, blue-eyed simplicity, artless in mind and heart, that smiles and submits and claps its heels together?"

3

It was not only Thomas' denunciation of the National-Socialists and Bronnen's demonstration in the Beethovensaal, however, which caused headlines, but Thomas' now openly stated personal political stand. "I state my conviction," he declared, "– and I am so convinced that I am ready to set not only my pen but my person upon the issue – that the political place of the German citizen is today with the Social-Democratic Party . . ."

It was, in the context of the traditional aloofness of German literature and art from politics – let alone Party politics – an extraordinary and notable decision which lost Thomas as many friends as it won. Fischer published the speech in book form, and it went into three editions. While the London *Times* blithely explained away the election results ("the Nazis have scored their overwhelming success because they have appealed to something more fundamental and more respectable. Like the Italian Fascists they stand for some national ideal, however nebulous and extravagantly expressed, to which personal and class interests shall be subordinate"[7]), Thomas had descended from Nobel heights and artistic immunity to analyse, to warn, and to indicate his place. Neither the uproar in the audience nor the frightened whispers of Fischer's wife in the front row to "cut it short" had deterred him. Referring to the Leipzig trial where the Supreme Court had unbelievably allowed Hitler to be called as a witness, and to the Nazi disruption of Thomas' Beethovensaal speech, Heinrich wrote for a Paris newspaper:

> Devant les tribunaux ils évoquent les têtes qu'ils feront rouler, et pendant la conférence de l'un des écrivains qui ont fait un peu plus pour leur pays que tous les nationalistes, ils profèrent hautement qu'aucun argument ne préviendra contre les leurs, qui sont à explosion.[8]

The fascist press never forgave Thomas his speech, nor his disparagement of their movement. Already in 1928 they had begun in Munich a campaign to discredit him over the *Reflections of a Non-Political Man,* claiming that Thomas had changed his views and expurgated the new Fischer edition accordingly. After his *Appeal to Reason* this campaign was stepped up.

Yet no one could seriously maintain that Thomas' change of heart was simply opportunism. "I do not propose to dwell on German fascism," Thomas had written as early as January 1925 when he revised his speech *Geothe and Tolstoy* for Fischer's new collection of his essays, *Bemühungen;*

> nor upon the circumstances, the quite comprehensible circumstances, of its origin . . . It is a pagan folk religion, a Wotan cult: it is, to be invidious — and I mean to be invidious — romantic barbarism.

> Now is not the moment for Germany to make anti-humanistic gestures . . . No, on the contrary, it is the time for us to lay all possible stress upon our great human inheritance and to cultivate it with all the means at our command — not only for its own sake, but in order to put visibly in the wrong the claims of Latin civilization. And in particular our socialism, which has all too long allowed its spiritual life to languish in the shallows of a crude economic materialism, has no greater need than to find access to that loftier Germany which has always sought with its spirit the land of the Greeks. It is today, politically speaking, our really national party, but it will not truly rise to the height of its national task until — if I may be allowed the extravagance — Karl Marx has read Friedrich Hölderlin.

Culture and Socialism followed in April 1928.[9] In it Thomas pointed out the sometimes well-meaning misconception abroad about German democracy.

> The sculptors and educators of German humanity, Luther, Goethe, Schopenhauer, Nietzsche, Georg were no democrats — oh no. If people abroad honour them, they ought to take care what they are doing. These

men were the ones who created the idea of *Kultur* with a capital K, the moving force behind German war-ideology. In Paris people applaud the *Meistersingers* — but that is to deny the facts. Nietzsche wrote about this work: "Against Civilization. The German against the French."

Socialism, on the other hand, meant social involvement, and the whole history of German culture cried out against this — as Heinrich had discovered early enough in his life. With great insight Thomas showed how different German conservatism was from that known abroad: for whereas the conservative nations of the West honoured the ideals of Civilization — political freedom above all — German conservatives were still possessed with the fundamentally anti-political notions of *Kultur*.

Culture and Socialism, like most of Thomas' socialist speeches and essays, was excluded from the English translation of his works; yet it was an integral part in the development of Thomas' political thinking that gave rise to his *Appeal to Reason* in October 1930; a development which culminated, still under the Republic, with his *Declaration of Socialism* in 1933.[10]

4

Meanwhile not only the political right attacked Thomas for his stand: even his literary admirers deplored this sally into the political arena as unworthy of a writer of stature.

Their objections, however, showed scant understanding of the nature of Thomas' change. When Ida Herz, Thomas' research aide and a friend of the family since 1924, protested about the speech he gave before a socialist workers' audience in Vienna in 1932, Thomas replied hotly that he was proud to have addressed such an audience for the first time in his life, and that workers after all had as much right to hear him speak as the bourgeoisie — particularly when the theme of his speech was an avowal of socialism.[11]

Admirers such as Ida Herz wished to safeguard the privacy of his genius. What they failed to acknowledge was that genius cannot, must not be unnaturally divorced from the age which determines it. Thomas Mann's pre-war creative impotence had stemmed from just this. Now, despite the pressures of an age far more demanding and threatening than pre-first-war Germany, Thomas' output had increased tenfold and would continue to do so for the rest of his life.

For the urge to be *involved* — to cast aside questions of Nobel dignity or literary reputation — was a sign of courage: and without that courage, that pride, could Thomas have ever survived the years of physical and spiritual deprivation in exile, the envy and sniping that would dog him until death? Thomas' bitter experience in the Great War, his gradual maturing from reactionary war propaganda to the ideals of humanity and social democracy, gave him now a certainty, a faith which neither Hitler nor McCarthy could destroy: a faith which history would confirm, and which rewarded him with the strength, too, to go on writing masterpieces of modern literature into old age.

Where politics had penetrated so deeply into the fabric of life it would have been escapist to remain aloof. To support — with "not only my pen but also my person" — the Social Democrats, to speak before socialist workers, was not a misdirection of creative literary energy but an essentially human response to a nation in crisis. He had come to Berlin in October 1930 originally to read from the manuscript of *Joseph;* "but is it worthwhile," he asked in his *Appeal to Reason,* "to pocket a little praise and a little blame — from an audience which cannot but give me a rather divided attention — and then go home again?"

For a writer so extraordinarily gifted it was not an easy path, despite the claims of some critics who later maintained that Thomas had merely bent according to the wind; just as it had not been simple for Heinrich. When Heinrich's volume of essays, *Sieben Jahre,* appeared in 1929, Thomas congratulated Heinrich (a "rare, complete appreciation" as Heinrich called it in a letter to Felix Bertaux[12]); but to the French literary historian Charles du Bos, Thomas could not withhold his deeper feelings:

How typically my brother's instructional and demonstrative passion differs from the inwardness of yours! There are no more aesthetic or personal moral problems left for him; society, politics, public morality: the idea of Collective is everything. It is the Russian in west-European humanistic form, Germany politicized.[13]

Thomas' judgment here was less than fair; for Heinrich's "collective" message in *Sieben Jahr* was no response, no different from Thomas' *Appeal to Reason,* to the overriding problems of the Republic over the previous seven years — from 1921 to 1928 — covering Constitution, elections, conciliation with France, youth, nationalism, anti-semitism, European unity, Republican justice and Germany's future: a "truly prophetic anticipation of the present, I admit," as Thomas wrote in his letter to du Bos. That the ideas which Heinrich had pioneered and for which he had struggled had been so grossly neglected and even betrayed was scarcely the ideal ground for the investigation of "aesthetic and personal moral problems."

"I was born to write novels in peace and tranquility," Heinrich noted sadly in exile. History had not permitted it.[14]

Meanwhile, in November 1930 Heinrich's latest novel *Die grosse Sache* was published — this time under the celebrated Kiepenheuer imprint — and Thomas consented to write his first review of a book by Heinrich. It appeared in the *Literarische Welt* on 12th December 1930. "If the man would only stick to his beloved politics" Hofmannsthal is reputed to have said once in the 'Twenties about Heinrich. It was time to judge how Heinrich as a novelist had responded to the realities of the Weimar Republic; and without mincing his words, Thomas proceeded to.

5

Heinrich had begun work on *Die grosse Sache* (Onto Something Big) in the summer of 1929. Despite the interruptions of *The Blue Angel*, the September elections and his Rhineland tour, he managed to complete "a sizeable portion" of the novel by December. To Bertaux he wrote on Christmas Day:

I love my characters and have no difficulty with the plot. It seems to me that some of it comes out as more fresh and direct than my earlier writings, before I had such experience. I have more courage to improvise, now, and to allow my characters to take charge of the plot — something I used to do a great deal in earlier days. We will have to wait and see what becomes of it. I cannot be as young as my young characters; and they — or rather their living comrades — take it amiss if one is older than they are. It is extremely curious.

What Heinrich felt was the freedom he had not been granted as a representative Republican in his speeches and essays. Now, for the first time since the war, he allowed himself free rein: and out cascaded a medley of social criticism, parody, fantasy, caricature, political wit, psychology, murder, sport and sheer fun. As with all works of simple honesty, the novel brought forth a series of outraged objections, even before publication. "Now, even before publication of my novel, it has been claimed that it is tendentious, that such a portrayal of modern conditions in fact creates a mood for fundamental change in existing society," Heinrich wrote in an article on his forthcoming book.[15]

But what does "existing society" mean? Society is comprised primarily of people, and I attest firstly that my contemporaries all bear the same stamp and secondly will not cast it off so easily — no matter whether they are right-wingers or left-wingers politically. That would be too simple: one introduces a new political system and immediately one is freed of disquiet or fear, and the aversion to thinking and inclination to violence suddenly cease; the moral code for men and women changes, and from now on there will be no sweet little ones, like my Inge, no corrupt politicians like my Reichschancellor Schattich and no big businessmen who, like my Mr von List, walk over corpses without laying a wreath. What stupidity! All this will not diminish in the so-called Third Reich, but will only really come into its own, for there are those who hadn't got near enough the front and want first to get there properly. That is why they are making such a commotion now. They talk of the "dying system"; but they themselves are in full bloom, and in the meantime it will not help if they change places with the others and alter the name of the system — it will remain.

Imperial Germany, the Weimar Republic — little had changed really in men's hearts, and Heinrich was far too sceptical to imagine that either communism or fascism could suddenly alter them. This was Heinrich at his least programmatic, the other side of his lifelong struggle for justice and social change. *Die grosse Sache* was, if anything, an updating of his first accepted novel, *In the Land of Cockaigne*; even stylistically.

"Heinrich Mann's new novel *Die grosse Sache*," wrote Thomas in the *Literarische Welt*,

is — but was not this always the case with this great artist? — so full of excitement, so overflowing with stimulation, that the pleasure it gives is always on the point of becoming pain; it hurts to read it — all the more so in that it is an extraordinarily readable book. Truly, one returns to any other exceptional modern narration, which one had in his honour interrupted, to Hemingway, Hamsun or even Döblin, and one senses the dying away of that tension and excitement in which, for a while, with fleeting breath, full of laughter, painfully, admiringly, one had lived . . .

From the start, even the tempo of the novel is ruthless and defies one to take a breath; one cannot think of putting it down; excited and bewitched by a style which has no equal in its noble power of attack, a mixture of brilliance and saloperie, of slang and intellectual electricity, one is torn from whirlpool to whirlpool and lands stunned by the hurly-burly of passionate and burlesque adventures and crass travesties, exhausted by laughing over their high-class improbability and brought to tears by the quality of spiritual goodness.

In essence, Thomas' critique had not altered since the days of *Land of Cockaigne*, or *Die Göttinnen* — the unwillingness of the traditional writer of epic to accept a radically different concept of art, narration and "perfection": Only here Thomas *did* accept it, accepted it with all its faults, all its "saloperie" and travesties, just as, in a way, Heinrich had grown to accept the realities of republican life. Thomas continued:

As far as republican society is concerned, no deadly enemy of freedom could pour more contempt upon it or portray it more comically than the way it is done in this novel. Who should do it, however, if not freedom itself? The opposition lacks sufficient talent. But one must not let oneself be deceived: the spirit of self-criticism in freedom lets no water drive the millwheels of its enemies. Its sceptical daredevilry goes to the very limit — in order to say at the very last moment: all this has to be, the corruption, the pitiful comedy; they are much better, much more human and also much more moral than deadly order . . .

Once again, all this is severe, both in humour and in goodness, severe and painful, lonely in its very sociability, knowing and yet unsuspecting, fascinating and yet hard to bear, moving and yet offensive. Like what? Like genius.

6

Within two months of publication of *Die grosse Sache*, Heinrich was finally elected Chairman of the Literary Section of the Prussian Academy of Arts. Several fascists — Kolbenheyer and Schäfer — resigned in protest; but the remaining members, only a few of whom were prepared to support Heinrich's candidature in 1928, now overwhelmingly secured his election. Beneath the storm clouds of Naziism it was considered at last an advantage to have at one's head a man whose incorruptibility and courage had become legendary in Germany, whatever one's response to his literary production.

This was in January 1931. On 27th March 1931 the Academy celebrated Heinrich's sixtieth birthday with a banquet in his honour, and speeches given by Adolf Grimme the Prussian Minister of Education, Max Liebermann the President of the Academy, Lion Feuchtwanger, Gottfried Benn; and Thomas Mann.

It was the counterpart of Thomas' fiftieth birthday banquet in Munich; and in many ways as moving. Something had come full circle, as Thomas felt: the bohemian literary ambitions of two Lübeck schoolboys had miraculously been fulfilled; the "Life's Work" they had once made up in drawings and verse together in Italy in the 1890s had not been so frivolous after all. In the wake of work and struggle, honoured now by their nation, they might still look one another in the eye and utter the astonished, innocent words: "Who would have thought it?"

Against the anti-humanistic pantomime of fascism, Thomas tried — as no one save Felix Bertaux[16] had every really done before — to put into words the contribution Heinrich had made to German letters and to German cultural and political life in general: a "classical representative of German-Mediterranean artistry," a writer who had brought both the sensuous humanity of Italy and the unique intellectual Enlightenment of France to the German mind and literature.

Un-German? Oh yes, the Gallic cultural element which colours the literary timbre of your work is un-German, the accent, the gesture which informs your prose — un-German in the sense of those who would exclude certain qualities once and for all from the notion of German: clarity, brio, the single blow, brilliance, critical spirit, colourfulness, sensual spirituality, psychological instinct, artistic delicatesse; and maintains that such qualities are unbecoming in a German. But what if it is becoming? What if it is so becoming in a German that no Frenchman could do it better, what then? Should it not be a reason for satisfaction, as an extension of national heritage and a cause for pride: "Look, we too have that?" — instead of snapping after it with one's beak and claiming it is national literary treachery? Truly, the question of what is German, what can be German, and the place your work will take in German cultural history, will not be decided by those people who today presume to administer the by no means simple concept of what is German.

It was a human and yet noble speech which, when Heinrich read it in print in a brochure produced by Kiepenheuer after the occasion, "warmed my heart", as he wrote to Thomas in June; and made him ask if they couldn't spend a few days together in the summer.[17]

But if Heinrich's new position in the Academy and the tributes paid on his sixtieth birthday suggested that his life's work — or Thomas' — were accomplished, they were sadly mistaken. Within two years Hitler would be Chancellor, Heinrich dismissed as President of the Literary Senate; and both he and Thomas driven into an exile from which only one would return alive.

7

All this time *Joseph* was growing — in size, depth and a modern, biblical poetry. The years of study Thomas had devoted to early biblical and Egyptian history gave him enormous narrative confidence, and chapters of the book had been appearing in literary periodicals from 1927. Then in the winter of 1930 the Munich publisher, Adalbert Droemer, offered Thomas an advance royalty of 200,000 Marks for a book on Goethe, to be written in time for the official centenary of his death in 1932.

Droemer's offer caught Thomas somewhat off-balance. Thomas had himself suggested such a book the previous spring to Fischer when in Berlin; it belonged "absolutely to my inner programme" as he wrote to Fischer in December;[18] and the money was tempting, if only as a challenge.

Thomas claimed he was "more than three-quarters" resolved to write the book, and felt that Droemer — who had originally suggested the popular edition of *Buddenbrooks* which Fischer then marketed in 1929 and which had sold over a million copies by the following year — should be recompensed with the Goethe book.

Quite how strong Thomas' "three-quarters" resolve really was is difficult to judge, for Fischer had expressed great interest in the idea in spring and felt Droemer had overstepped his mark in approaching a lifelong Fischer author directly. Fischer stepped in, equalled Droemer's offer and sent Thomas a contract. Droemer, whether intentionally or not, had the last word however: he would have to "go elsewhere" then, he informed Thomas; for a Goethe book for 1932 was essential for him. Thomas' scruples about interrupting the Joseph novel for so long, and the bare year in which he would have both to research and write the book had worried him from the beginning; to have now a rival author in another firm competing with him was more than he would accept. Sadly — though perhaps also somewhat relieved — he let the matter drop.

Once again it was Thomas' profound honesty and integrity which really forebade him take a step he might regret, however financially enticing. The figure of Goethe had played too important a role in his life for him to be able to write a full biography to order, particularly under the pressure of time and competition.

Thus Thomas returned to *Joseph;* and in St Moritz in January and February 1931 to a new political tract, *The Rebirth of Decency.*[19] It was in part a defence of his *Appeal to Reason* speech, words almost of desperation. It was as though the small minds who had once taken umbrage at *Buddenbrooks* had now turned fascist and would destroy the very ideals which Thomas himself had only reached by way of great digression and humility. That such opponents took up the now jaded antitheses of his reactionary *Reflections* — such as Kultur and Civilization — had a kind of excruciating and debilitating logic; just as the works of Wagner, Houston Chamberlain and Neitzsche had gained posthumous disciples far more terrifying than their authors could ever have imagined. Referring to the current mystique concerning torture in the Middle Ages Thomas wrote:

We have not become better, we have simply changed; and what was once a grave weapon of the law, whose justice all concerned concurred in, would today in our state of nerves, of imagination, of insight into the body and the soul of man be nothing more than a stinking scandal.

In the light of history, of the systematic torture and extermination of a whole people — and the cry of "innocence" and ignorance afterwards — these sound tragically prophetic warnings.

But who would listen? In March 1931 came Heinrich's sixtieth birthday celebration in Berlin, in May a lecture-tour by Thomas to Strasbourg and Paris, in June a speech before the Republican Students Union at Erlangen (*Europe as a Cultural Unity*[20]), and in July a series of meetings in Geneva of the "Comité des Lettres et des Arts". In September came a further round of lectures and readings, in Königsberg, Elbing and Lübeck.

It was in Lübeck that Thomas addressed his old school, the Katherineum, with *An Address to Youth*.[21] However it was not as Nobel Prizewinner, as the author of *Buddenbrooks, The Magic Mountain* or even his current *Joseph* that Thomas addressed the school, but as a European who would not part from his European heritage lightly. In an age of surging nationalism it was no mean stand.

Yet Goethe, too, had not been forgotten. The next year would see two essays on the master; following which — in mid-exile and beneath the storm-clouds of war — a Goethe novel no one had ever expected, a unique and sidelong insight into greatness: *Lotte in Weimar*.

8

"The master who created us all," declared Gottfried Benn in the Berlin Academy on Heinrich's sixtieth birthday — the same Benn who would welcome the Nazi triumph, support the dismissal of Heinrich as Chairman of the Literary Academy, and take his place as Acting Chairman.

What Benn adulated, and Liebermann and Thomas referred to in admiration, was Heinrich's *Göttinnen*, or *Duchess of Assy* novels — works whose stylistic brilliance still had the power to influence Benn's poetry in the 1920s, nearly three decades after they were written. Heinrich, however, did not care to be reminded of this period of youthful individualism. One hundred and thirty foreign and German writers and artists had signed the "Tribute to Heinrich Mann" that appeared in the *Berliner Tageblatt* on 27th March 1931; and it was this unity of writers which Heinrich felt was important in modern times. His concern that writers and intellectuals should not be afraid to act as leaders of society had not changed since his celebrated *Geist und Tat* essay of 1911 — the title which Kiepenheuer used in republishing that year a collection of Heinrich's essays on French masters between 1780 and 1930.

Society had changed radically since the days of the Empire; now it was only in unity that writers could hope to exercise an influence which once individuals might have held. If the freedom won by centuries of humanitarian struggle were to survive, they would have to be defended in modern times — collectively. This was Heinrich's message to the "Schutzverband deutscher Schriftsteller" on 23rd March 1931 and to the German PEN Club afterwards. If writers believed in reconciliation with France they must press for it; and to be effective in modern times required not only individual courage, but also solidarity. Before a meeting of the German League of Human Rights Heinrich had raised the question of *All Quiet on the Western Front* — a faithful American film of Erich Remarque's record-breaking German novel about the war. All over the Western world the film had been greeted as a shattering plea for peace: except in Germany, where, because of Nazi demonstrations outside the cinemas showing the film, and their release of white mice in the auditorium, the civil authorities banned any further showing, on the grounds that "it would tend to endanger Germany's national prestige". Only solidarity among writers and artists could here have forced the Nazis' hand: and there was none.

"Ne tirez pas!" a Frenchwoman had cried out at the end of the film's première in Paris, when the French sniper takes aim at his German foe. "All of us, without exception — as soon as we listen to our better emotions, join with her in that cry," Heinrich testified.[22]

But *All Quiet on the Western Front* remained banned, the legend of the "Stab in the Back" gained still further credence. Restrictions on the Stahlhelm were lifted, unemployment rose to almost five million; and at every state election the Nazi poll soared.

On 3rd June 1931 Heinrich had an interview with the French Foreign Minister, Aristide Briand. It was a sad meeting following news of the Breslau Stahlhelm rally. "Comrades," the Stahlhelm leader Seldte had been reported as saying, "there is the German East," pointing to the Polish border; "there lies Germany's future and Germany's destiny!" A German-Austrian plan for customs union — in defiance of the Treaty of Versailles and a further Austrian-French agreement in 1922 — had shocked the statesmen of Europe; and in the wake of French withdrawals of short-term loans, bank after Austrian bank failed — while in Germany only government backing saved them from ruin.

What Germany was doing was calculated to bring disaster; for to depart from Stresemann's policy of European peace and agreement was bound to affect the vital monetary loans which Germany needed to survive. Amid Hugenberg's and Hitler's cries for the abolition of the Versailles Treaty and all reparation agreements, more private money flowed out of Germany in 1931 than was saved by Hoover's one-year moratorium on reparations.

Yet a worsening financial and economic crisis was all Hitler could hope for if he were to achieve power legitimately: and by constantly alarming Germany's creditors and trading partners with his threats about the future, he effectively achieved this. Only later, when in power, would he do everything to simulate peace and order to reverse the outflow of money.

In the meantime Heinrich attended the first meeting of the International Federation of Writers' Associations in Paris in June 1931; and in October gave his celebrated appeal for Franco-German understanding in the Admiralspalast in Berlin. But to Felix Bertaux he confided his surprise at finding "even the least degree of honesty now in others". When he left Berlin in October it was "completely pessimistic."[23]

Yet despite the Nazi success at state and provincial polls, Brüning still managed to hold the Government reins, having sacked his Foreign Minister Curtius after the failure of the projected Austro-German Customs Unions. "A Berlin, maintenant, on est optimiste, malgré les faillites, fuites, suicides et le reste," Heinrich wrote in November;[24] and in December, after the disclosure of the Nazi "Boxheim Papers" it seemed still possible the country might come to its senses.

One simply mustn't think; and in living in the world of my new novel I shall perhaps be able to forget a reality worse than any I have ever known.

Rest assured I am not pessimistic, however. Germany will not necessarily suffer fascism — what it has already is enough. Simultaneously it has a dictatorship — bourgeois, it is true — as well as permanent civil war. At the moment an army of 290,000 Hitlerites exists, it will have to act: and should it attack, I think fascism will be defeated.

But Hitler was not going to act prematurely — why should he when matters were moving inexorably his way?

"It is not very relaxing to live in insecurity and among hatred," Heinrich continued his letter to Bertaux:

Spiritual work loses its attraction, even its point. In fact I have retired to Nice to build up my resistance. In 1919 I went on writing my chapter of *Der Kopf* on the day Eisner, the revolutionary Prime Minister of Munich, was assassinated. This time I have decided not to treat of serious things .and to write a light work of little significance. I shall put in songs even, I think. Either way it doesn't make much difference, those of my generation won't have much luck for the final years of their lives.[25]

It was a considerable understatement; but with the death of his friend Arthur Schnitzler on 31st October one that was certainly on Heinrich's mind. In Berlin, at the Staatstheater, Heinrich had given the memorial speech, as once he had for Wedekind. "We are witnessing the disappearance of the best survivors of the 19th century," he wrote to Bertaux, "and one feels very isolated."

9

So the year 1931 came to an end, Heinrich suffering from the "forte dépression que mon dernier séjour de Berlin m'avait infligée",[26] and Thomas confined to bed with "infectious catarrh with concomitant stomach and liver ailment". To "encourage the economy" the Poschingerstrasse house now boasted a superior new radiogram with "dynamo loudspeaker" transmitting the sound of the records.[27]

No Christmas gift, however, could draw attention away from the continual worsening economic and political crisis — as Thomas' letter to Bertram showed. "If one could ignore it all contemptuously!" he wrote. "But what is in store for us? What will break over Germany in more than one bloody wave, and over us all? Believe me, the days of your 'Universities' are also numbered — and in the end it is just as well," he added, referring to the way in which teachers and professors were propagating German nationalism once more. "In the end it serves the whole state right, but what will we have to put up with in its place! . . . Forgive these un-Christmaslike forebodings! But they are hard to suppress."[28]

But Bertram, like so many others, had no forebodings — only an unshakable hostility to the French and blind faith in Germany's national destiny. "An intellectual who attaches himself to the power-clique betrays the intellect," Heinrich had written exactly twenty years before, in his essay *Geist und Tat* — an essay which had gained, not lost, its relevance since the fall of the Empire.

Why one commits suicide was the title of an essay Heinrich had written as early as 1925, and reprinted in his *Sieben Jahre* in 1929. "People usually kill themselves for love, need, or the avoidance of a worse catastrophe than death," he wrote:

Rarely has self-expression been so hard for the sceptical intellect as today. He must be creative, must have an unfailing raison d'être in what he does; then he is safe. To be able to achieve, no hesitation is possible; to achieve is to be completely in command of oneself. Otherwise of course the doubter will lose courage in the face of new contemporaries who have doubts about nothing. They are backed by society, they are its saviours. Not having expected this, the doubter's own way of mind now appears to him as anarchistic. He begins to feel alienated from the world, he, the man who had once mastered it. He withdraws, his house becomes an island, around it a moat. The activity and gestures of life continue for a while, but they are really only for the past's sake, are already dust before he has effected them. What further motive does he need, what further loss?

From Nice in March 1932 Heinrich returned to Berlin for the official celebrations of the centenary of Goethe's death.

He wished neither the limitations of patriotism nor national democracy; for he foresaw that the freedom which had been given to him to live out his life would be diminished for everyone. And it happened. We cannot imagine a Goethe today, and this goes too for a Napoleon. Dependence and ties have grown for everyone in our times, till they have become fear and terror. Where people believe blindly in blind laws of economy, individual personality disappears, and the masses who cannot do without it invent their so-called Führer.

But these are but early, immature conditions of democracy, which throw up such rubbish as fascism. Today we may, however, look forward to the day when, at the end of democracy's difficult coming-of-age, the spiritual man will again come to the fore — the combined spirit of the age in towering personalities.

We celebrate Goethe in all the confusion of our souls — which would be very understandable to him, for he could hate quite well himself, had always to struggle. We celebrate him too because it is essential to hope that one day he will return.[29]

It was a hope Thomas echoed in his two wise and profound contributions to the Geothe year. In *Goethe as representative of the bourgeois age*, delivered before the Berlin Academy in March and all over Germany, Austria and Switzerland in these months, Thomas tried to distinguish between the reactionary and the visionary, to give a genuine and unretouched portrait of the man who had made the international reputation of German intellect and culture. Unless, Thomas declared, the traditional, educated middle class was prepared, in the heritage of Goethe, to challenge the "easy-going ideologies" of the times, it would disappear —

We shall simply yield the stage in favour of a human type free from the assumptions, the commitments, and the outworn prejudice which — one sometimes fears — may prevent the bourgeoisie of Europe from being adequate to the task of guiding state and economy into a new world . . . Not merely by solemn celebration of their own renown can the bourgeoisie show itself worthy of its great sons. The greatest of them, Goethe, issues the challenge:

>Things that are dead let us shake off,
>And love the living ones!

10

But while the Republic celebrated Goethe, Hitler was organizing his bid for the Republic. Tirelessly he flew from city to city in his attempt to take the Presidency. Hindenburg's seven-year term of office expired in April 1932; the Field-Marshal was eighty-four.

Only Hindenburg himself could stop Hitler. "All the combined moral forces of the world are useless against them," Goethe had written of men possessed by the demonic in *Dichtung and Wahrheit* (Poetry and Truth). "The more enlightened member of mankind rails at them in vain, calling them either betrayers or betrayed; but the masses are fatally attracted." Only Hindenburg possessed the prestige and popularity to defeat the self-styled Führer; and it was only Goebbels' uncompromising encouragement which persuaded Hitler to continue his candidacy when Hindenburg announced he would stand again.

Yet the votes for Hitler were uncomfortably large — over 30 per cent of the poll — and a second election was required to give Hindenburg the necessary majority, on 10th April 1932.

"A Nazi President would mean, once and for all: never again peace, never again an atmosphere of honesty, never again a safeguarded existence, never again human happiness," Heinrich had replied to one newspaper questionnaire in March — "but forever hatred, humiliation, catastrophe!"

"If Hindenburg can be a dam against this, then let our votes shore up that dam!" he finished — a stand he reiterated in the *Berliner Tageblatt,* despite the wrath of the Communists, who had put up their own candidate, Ernst Thälmann. Johannes R. Becher delivered a stinging rejoinder to Heinrich's stand in *Die Linkskurve,* claiming that the author of *Man of Straw* had himself become a man of straw.

It had not been an easy decision for Heinrich to take; ironically he himself had been proposed as candidate for the Presidency by a group of socialist littérateurs under the leadership of Kurt Hiller. Pointing to the example of Masaryk (a Professor of philosophy) in Czechoslovakia, Hiller proposed Heinrich in *Die Weltbühne* in February 1932 — though perhaps more in protest at the lack of supra-national idealism than in any hope that Heinrich would stand.

Both the Social Democrats who supported Hindenburg and the Communists who decried him were proved right. Without socialist support Hindenburg would not have beaten Hitler, without Hindenburg not even the combined votes of Social Democrats and Communists for a single candidate would have done so; yet once re-elected the aged Field-Marshal was no match for the political expertise of the Austrian corporal.

Hindenburg had won; yet Hitler was not defeated. Hindenburg was persuaded to issue a Presidential decree dissolving and disbanding the para-military Nazi armies three days after his re-election. Far from giving courage to all republicans in the state, this measure led only to a landslide Nazi victory in the Prussian Landtag elections, held on 24th April. From 6 seats they rocketed to 162; and five weeks later Brüning's government resigned.

It was the fall of Brüning's government, in fact, which rang down the curtain on the Weimar Republic. Hitler had only stood against Hindenburg as President because the old Field-Marshal had rejected his conditions for Nazi endorsement: the dismissal of Brüning and the formation of a rightist Cabinet. Yet by sabotaging the anti-SS decree and denying Brüning any real support Hindenburg effectively complied with Hitler's conditions. Von Papen — an ex-military attaché to the German Embassy in Washington, deported by America for sabotage — became the new Chancellor, von Schleicher the new Defence Minister. Sir Horace Rumbold, the British Ambassador, reported to London on 14th June 1932:

> The present Cabinet is a Cabinet of mutual deception. Herr von Papen thinks he has scored off General von Schleicher, and Hitler, for his part, believes he has scored off both.[30]

Hitler had. By 16th June a new Presidential decree rescinded the SS and SA ban, and von Papen dissolved the Reichstag, setting 31st July for the new elections.

Everything the Social Democrats and moderates had hoped to gain by supporting Hindenburg had evaporated. The General Election provided another sweeping victory for the Nazis, who more than doubled their

Reichstag representation. Their total of 230 seats made the biggest Reichstag delegation any party had won since the creation of the Republic.

Together with Käthe Kollwitz, Heinrich had signed an appeal for the uniting of Social Democrat and Communist parties to fight the election; an appeal which might well have assured enough seats for a new socialist government; but which, when repeated six months later, was to lose Heinrich his post in the Berlin Academy.

As it was, the Communists refused co-operation with the Social Democrats and the struggle for power between Hindenburg's Nationalists and Hitler's Nazis moved into its critical stage.

11

It is hard to imagine, in these circumstances, how any writer could concentrate upon purely literary tasks; yet by July Thomas had completed the second volume of his Joseph work, *Young Joseph,* and Heinrich a new novel which he had only begun in January: *Ein ernstes Leben* (translated into English in 1934 as *The Hill of Lies).*

"J'ai entrepris quelquechose de plus sérieux et qui me touche intimement," Heinrich had written to Felix Bertaux in February 1932 from Nice — for he had discarded the idea of a humorous tale with songs to write a more personal story: a crime story based on the life of the woman he was now living with, Nelly Kroeger.[31]

Heinrich's affair with Trude Hesterberg had ended as impulsively as it had begun; Hesterberg had chosen to go her own way, and while the film of *The Blue Angel* had made Heinrich's story of the schoolmaster and the night-club singer famous, Heinrich now began to live out a tale he had invented almost thirty years before.

Nelly Kroeger came from Lübeck, and was working in a bar on the Kurfürstendamm in Berlin when Heinrich first met her. She was a "red-blond" of striking good looks; and whether she represented the proletarian innocence Heinrich was unconsciously searching for, or simply attracted him as a wilful and handsome woman, they began a relationship which, to outside friends such as Hermann Kesten and Lion Feuchtwanger, had all the unnerving polarity of Professor Unrat and Rosa Fröhlich. From the grand office at the Academy of Arts on the Pariser Platz Heinrich would make his way to the Kurfürstendamm. What Nelly Kroeger told him of her childhood near Lübeck, the hardship, people and poverty, Heinrich now used as the Zola-esque opening for *Ein ernstes Leben:* a tale in which poverty is shown as the crime, not crime itself. "It is my fourteenth," Heinrich wrote of the novel on 1st July 1932 to Felix Bertaux, "not a bad one perhaps, for I have gained a certain experience and am ill-enough advised to recognise it. Moreover in it I have portrayed the innocence of criminals, who are really only human beings, explained and discovered by a commissioner of police." In Berlin Heinrich had witnessed a poor and unemployed passer-by pick up a brick, smash a shop window, take out a coat, which he then put on, and walk away without the slightest murmur of reproach or surprise from those who witnessed the event. "I don't think this has been attempted before, I believe you would have had to have lived in this epoch to imagine it." Other than that he did not think the novel "a work of any importance, and no one will pay it any attention. I even doubt if I shall be paid for it now. No one has any money now, we will have to wait."

But Zsolnay did accept the novel, found it timely and published it in October, only three months later. Thomas wrote to Heinrich after reading it, and on 26th November 1932, Heinrich replied:

> Your letter will remain the best and most beautiful of all that I see about my book, and I thank you. You were always, in every moment of my life, my closest friend, and here again you demonstrate it.
>
> That which you do not like about the novel I do not think I would have done in earlier days. But if I really think out the products of our age, then always I come up against the word crime. It has become a power, humanly and socially, one which we are only just beginning to realize — and the influence on those who are left behind, like the little farmer, proves it best of all. I did write the novel fast, but not unduly so, and when it reached the Berlin part, I was confronted with difficult problems. The self-contained idyll of the first chapters was over, it was impossible to stand above the consequent events — the dissolution as you put it. Only Marie retains her inner firmness and so she survives: that is the message, if the book has one at all . . . But I find it better not to worry myself about the real worth of the book. Like the others, this too has proved imperfect, but it was simply all that I could do.[32]

Against the growing insecurity of the capital, and the Weimar Republic itself it was a praiseworthy effort. "Fortunately you do not know what one suffers in fighting people one despises," Heinrich wrote to Bertaux on his return to Berlin in March from Nice, "and in having to live amid gratuitous hate."[33] Four or five abusive phone calls would come each day, apart from threatening letters. In an interview with a French journalist Heinrich had gone so far as to suggest the French re-occupy the Ruhr if they were ever to contain the threat of resurgent German nationalism — a suggestion which Heinrich then had to "deny with all my might in order not to be called before the Supreme Court in Leipzig" — while every day Hitler referred to the coming end of the Republic with impunity.

"I find so much that is sad in Berlin," Heinrich wrote on 27th March 1932. "But I do not think it is the place, it is more the century we are living in." And in July: "The other day my brother passed through Berlin, and made the observation that in our subconscious we are suffering more than we realize from the hatred that surrounds us."[34]

It was all the more surprising that Thomas, in the midst of this "universal bêtise" as Heinrich called it, should have completed the second volume of his Joseph novel; a novel which in literary terms must be considered among the major accomplishments of the century.

12

On 21st June 1932, Mrs Fischer had written to Thomas: "it is a little like reading 'The History of Humanity', a new kind of Odyssey." Old Samuel Fischer, aged seventy-two, found it no less overwhelming. "I am proud that my publishing house can give people a work of great style again," he wrote on 7th July, after reading both parts.[35]

"As far as I can sense or foresee, this work brings you to your peak, for you were made to become more embracing at each step — from parental home to humanity; I know no reason not to have complete confidence . . . and afterwards will come the great success you deserve, and which each time makes me particularly proud, beside the pleasure I feel at that which you have achieved," Heinrich wrote to Thomas in November 1932.[36]

But Thomas was curiously hesitant in handing over his novel for publication. As Mrs Fischer had noted: "What worries me is what our brown-shirted Nazi youth will say to this history of our ancestors; they want only to hear about blond hero-sons and Thor and Wotan, these idiots!"[37] The anti-semitism of the times scarcely made the moment propitious; and yet it cannot have been this alone which made Thomas hold back publication, for he had waited already almost two years before showing Fischer even the first typescript, *The Tales of Jacob*. It is more likely that Thomas held to the very intimacy and security of his great epic almost as his safeguard against the madness of the times: a comfort, a child almost that he would not allow to go forth until it was full-grown, until the three volumes (as he assumed they would make) were complete.

It was, as time would prove, an error of publishing judgment. Its "post-humous" publication in Germany, after Thomas went into exile, brought Thomas into great dishonour among his fellow emigrants. Had the volumes appeared as they were written, they might well have had the "healing" effect for which Thomas hoped much earlier.

But Thomas remained firm: and it was only the American publisher's insistence that the publication in English begin as soon as the translation of the first volume was ready that forced Thomas' hand: and even then it was to prove too late.

For Hitler would wait for no one, least of all Thomas Mann. As leader of the new majority party in the Reichstag he now claimed his right to be called as Chancellor. Hindenburg refused. Von Papen, any semblance of Reichstag support now lost, attempted to form a new cabinet.

Democracy was at an end. Ten days before the July General Election von Papen had illegally dismissed the Social Democratic government of Prussia and declared himself National Commissioner for the state. All "republican" officers of state — state secretaries, commissioner of police and administrators — were removed from their posts while the army under General von Runstedt surrounded Berlin: and the Prussian Government protested in vain to the Supreme Court.

It was a replay of the post-war nationalist putsches — only this time it was successful. For when Hindenburg refused to appoint Hitler as Chancellor after the election, the Nazis refused all Reichstag support.

Von Papen was thus forced to dissolve the Reichstag, and on 6th November new elections were held. This time, to the astonishment of the Nazis, the myth of their invincible rise to power was broken. Though they retained their Reichstag majority they lost some 2 million votes and 34 seats. It seemed as if Hindenburg's revelation of Hitler's demand for full dictatorial powers when appointed Chancellor, and the hideous Königsberg murders had begun to scare the public at last.

But whatever the reasons for the Nazi set-back on 6th November, the future of the Republic was doomed. A party dedicated to its overthrow had retained a majority of more than 75 over its republican rival, the Social Democrats, and the Communist Party, similarly committed to abolishing parliamentary rule, had leaped to 100 seats. Precedents for government by decree rather than Reichstag coalition had been set: no one believed the parliamentary system could continue.

It was a case now simply of the best dictator: and the republicans, by definition, possessed none. Von Papen and his Minister of Defence von Schleicher might struggle for supremacy: but only Hitler had the undeniable backing of a nationwide party.

In August, after the completion of *Ein ernstes Leben*, Heinrich began to think more carefully about an idea which had possessed him ever since visiting his friend Felix Bertaux at Pau and Lescun in 1927: the idea of a novel based on the life of France's legendary humanitarian ruler, Henri IV. "After your return to Paris I shall ask you for some advice as to what I should read on Henri IV," he wrote to Bertaux on 9th August; the books were promptly sent from Paris, while the situation in Germany deteriorated still further.

"I am also in agreement with your view that open barbarism will not be able to succeed in this country," Heinrich had written to Thomas in May 1932;[38] but now such hopes were steadily losing ground. Towards the end of October Heinrich began what would become a swansong to the democratic, peaceful ideal in Germany: the last major published essay against nationalism and fascism to be published before Hitler became Chancellor, *Das Bekenntnis zum Übernationalen* (The Acceptance of Internationalism).

13

"If only I had the time I too would like to travel in a country I do not know well enough, in France for example. Alas, the moment is not propitious," Heinrich wrote to Felix Bertaux on 31st October 1932. "Nevertheless I have just finished writing a big article for the 'Neue Rundschau' in which I take a decisive position towards the nationalist state. It is time to tell the truth which everyone prefers to keep to himself, without reserve".

The *Neue Rundschau* was prepared to risk *Das Bekenntnis zum*

Übernationalen in its December issue, without alterations; to Bertaux Heinrich confided he might choose to go to Nice then, for safety; and he had already arranged with Paul Zsolnay, his Austrian publisher, to have his royalties transferred to Paris.

"Mankind is being sacrificed to the nationalist lie," Heinrich urged his countrymen to recognize in the essay:

I am sick of listening to the arrogant falsehood that says not the fight for mankind is the higher profession but the fight against it. Those admirers of war and the warlike spirit would best achieve their life's ambition if they were now to commit suicide instead of millions dying unwillingly with them.

Who of all Germans was better equipped to analyse German national-ism than the author of *Der Untertan?* Yet *Das Bekenntnis zum Übernationalen* was not one of Heinrich's best essays, for the same reasons that had worked against his post-war novel *Der Kopf.* Ideals which had once seemed so proud and worthy of struggle — freedom, egality, humanity — had been faith-lessly betrayed during the Republic. The chance for Germany to lead a new social democratic movement in Europe had been eroded by revolution, inflation, penal reparations and resurgent nationalism. The Republic had failed, its constitutional aim "conciliation between peoples" forgotten and rejected.

There was therefore something weary and sorrowful in the essay, in no way resigned and yet prepared for the worst.

"For my part I am now uttering my last word on nationalism — and further, on our national fatherland," Heinrich wrote to Thomas on 1st November 1932. "It has forfeited every right, I cannot hold my tongue any longer. The 'Neue Rundschau', which wants to risk the article in December, has not cut a line from my *Bekenntnis,* but mostly for the reasons I have put down in the article, namely the lack of principles in the outgoing Republic."

To Thomas, Heinrich also confided his plan — "to be kept between us for the moment" — of a union of republican intellectuals to "watch over the coming second Republic from the spiritual side" — a Republic Heinrich would never live to see. What he wanted was an "Upper House, so that the Republic can be stopped from destroying itself ever again through spiritual weakness: this must be worked for and prepared for now." Regarding his own novel *Ein Ernstes Leben* Heinrich added the words: "We must not ask: what value has a novel today? but must put our faith in the hope that the present chaos can be resolved as one resolves a novel."

It needed more than faith, however, to resolve Germany's problem. On 2nd December von Papen's government resigned. Von Schleicher then took the reins: and offered Hitler the post of Vice-Chancellor. Hitler declined; he had only eight weeks to wait before he would take the Chancellorship itself.

In the *Berliner Tageblatt* in August[39] Thomas had also taken his stand on nationalism. "Were it not for the political situation," he wrote to Ida Herz at the end of August about volume 3 of *Joseph,* "I would certainly be further on." "Will the bloody facts of Königsberg at last open the eyes of those who admire the 'movement' that National-Socialism calls itself, those priests, professors, dons and littérateurs who run babbling after it, and open their eyes to the true nature of this folk-disease, this mish-mash of hysteria and fusty romanticism whose megaphone-German character is a caricature and vulgarization of everything really German?" he asked in the *Berliner Tageblatt.*

On 22nd October 1932, Thomas spoke before an audience of Viennese socialist workers — the first time, as he confessed in his speech, he had ever experienced such a situation: and yet remarkable not only for the times which had given rise to such a situation, but also for its "epochal significance in my personal life and in my spiritual development".

"What we have done," wrote Heinrich to Thomas on 26th November 1932, "was right because it befitted our profession; and no one has more, has even as much right to think this as you do while working on your universally significant historical novel."

Few could say as much as the Weimar Republic tottered towards its grave at the end of 1932.

CHAPTER THIRTEEN

Exile

Adolf Hitler was appointed Chancellor of Germany by Hindenburg on Monday, 30th January 1933. Within three weeks both Heinrich and Thomas Mann were in exile.

"The Republic had too much in common with its enemy; the spirit of revenge for Versailles, the fear of communism . . . the dependence on industry . . . But above all the Republic was aware of its own tediousness," Heinrich wrote a decade later.[1] "The people wanted theatre. Public life had disappeared without trace into Nazi theatre. It gripped everyone, everyone."

Heinrich's bitter observation contains a great measure of truth: a truth of which no one was more aware than the propagandist of the Nazi party, Josef Goebbels.

The people wanted theatre; Hitler had promised that "heads would roll". Although his appointment as Chancellor had given him no more than the leadership of a right-wing coalition cabinet in which only 4 Nazis were represented, and still no absolute majority in the Reichstag, the people settled in their seats for the drama to begin: and they did not have long to wait.

A new Reichstag Election was declared for 5th March 1933; but already on 27th February the play had begun, with the burning of the Reichstag building itself. By then Heinrich was already in France, having crossed the frontier with nothing more than an umbrella and a small travelling case, containing his notes on the life of Henri IV, King of France and Navarre.

It was a strange, ominous prelude to the Third Reich: ominous because the situations of both Heinrich and Thomas demonstrated how much support the "people" were prepared to give Hitler — a support they had never accorded to any Republican Chancellor.

Heinrich's act opened on the evening of 15th February. Together with Käthe Kollwitz, Heinrich had again signed the appeal to Social Democrats to unite with the Communist Party in fighting the forthcoming election. It was worded in identical fashion to that of the previous June, and was signed also by Albert Einstein; only this time the new Nazi commissioner at the Prussian Ministry of Culture was able to use it as sufficient grounds for expelling both Heinrich Mann and Käthe Kollwitz from the Academy. The President of the Academy, Max von Schillings, was duly informed. If he declined to expel Mann, the Minister explained, the Prussian government would shut down the Academy.

Von Schillings hastily convened an emergency meeting of the full Academy. The situation was put before the members. Threatened with exclusion from her own studio and work-in-hand in the Academy Käthe Kollwitz had already agreed in advance to resign. But Heinrich Mann could not be found, and the Academy had to decide whether to expel him in his absence. At length Heinrich was located — in a cinema — and the sitting was adjourned while von Schillings spoke to him. In astonishment more than anything else, Heinrich also offered his resignation — without even addressing the assembled members of the Academy.

Only one member resigned in protest; otherwise the ministerial blackmail was accepted without a murmur, and the members even gave an undertaking to reveal nothing to the press. Even Thomas, in a letter to René Schickele, recommended that the Academy, "however deep the shock of the loss of our Chairman may be", should not resign in protest but wait and see whether the authorities would close it by force" — and had written in this vein to Döblin too.[2]

A few evenings later, at a private gathering of republicans, the French Ambassador approached Heinrich. "If you are crossing the Pariser Platz, you are welcome to use my house,"[3] he assured him pointedly. The next morning he telephoned Heinrich.

"I understand you are going to Paris tonight," he began.

Heinrich did not reply. "I wonder if you would be so kind as to visit my mother and to give her my very best wishes."[4]

Under the title "Swansong", the *Völkische Beobachter* had launched a tirade on 19th and 20th February against Heinrich, calling him "national vermin", and demanding that the "disagreeable and now portly Literary President should have a bomb put under him".

This time the warning was unmistakable: and in the light of the hundreds of arrests made less than a week later, it was scarcely too soon. Suspecting he was already being watched Heinrich left that same evening; bought a train ticket to Frankfurt in order to allay suspicion; and from there purchased a further ticket to Strasbourg.

There, on 22nd February he sent a twelve word telegram to Felix Bertaux: "Sain et sauf vous donnerai adresse pour envoi cinq[5] pensées affecteuses Mann."

Thomas' expulsion from Germany, by contrast, took place "in absentia".

In January 1933 Thomas had written a brief political piece entitled *Avowal of Socialism*, his ultimate political stand in the Weimar Republic. It was due to be read at a Convention of Socialist Culture in Berlin on 19th February; but owing to the threat of Nazi demonstrations the Convention was postponed — indefinitely, once Hitler assumed full power.

The personal *Avowal* appeared in the February issue of *Sozialistische Bildung* in Berlin; yet it was not for this anti-Nazi manifesto that Thomas was to be hounded out of Munich and Germany: but for his "slander on our great musical genius", as the protesters of the "Richard-Wagner-Town Munich" put it. Their protest, signed by 45 of the most distinguished officials, professors and artists of Munich — ranging from the Chief Bürgermeister to Richard Strauss and Hans Pfitzner — would become, like the 93-signatory patriotic petition of 1914, a monument to German intellectual humbug in the twentieth century.

Thomas had written about Wagner before, in 1911 and again in his *Reflections of a Non-Political Man* in 1918; but two important perceptions had confirmed his feelings about Wagner since then: and Thomas used them now to devastating advantage. "What is it," Thomas asked in his new essay, *Sufferings and Greatness of Richard Wagner*, written in January 1933, "that raises the works of Wagner to a plane so high, intellectually speaking, above all older musical drama? Two forces contribute, forces and gifts of genius, which one thinks of in general as opposed; indeed, the present day takes pleasure in asserting their essential incompatibility. I mean psychology and myth."

Nothing could have been more profoundly sympathetic, more admiring and respectful while yet preserving its distance ("Wagner as an impassioned man of the theatre — one might call him a theatromaniac . . .") than this tribute to Wagner on the fiftieth anniversary of his death. The essay had been requested by the Goethe Society in Munich, and was to be delivered as a lecture not only there but in Amsterdam, Brussels and Paris. Its writing had occupied Thomas for weeks — to the exclusion even of the *Joseph* novel. "You will understand that for me to have let myself in for the theme of Wagner was dangerous from the beginning," he wrote to his old colleague Walter Opitz on 30th January 1933, "for there is quite a bit to say, especially for me; and it is something of a feat not to write a book." Already at the beginning of January he told Adele Gerhard: "For the moment I have given up work on *Joseph* . . . and am preparing a lecture on Wagner . . . — a tricky, exciting task."[6]

Wagner had dominated the musical horizons of Thomas' youth; had given Thomas something of the feel for grandeur and epic creativity which, with the philosophies of Schopenhauer and Nietzsche, had transformed the precocious dreams of an idle Lübeck schoolboy into the works of a Nobel-Prize-winning novelist. Now, fresh from his appreciation of Freud's work in modern psychology and his years' long labour on biblical myth in *Joseph*, Thomas found himself in a unique position to pay tribute, in all objectivity, to the master of German romanticism. That it could be so misquoted and misconstrued, at five weeks' remove, by the protesters of the "Richard-Wagner-Town Munich" indicated how pathetically little pressure was needed by Hitler to make even the most famous German musicians and composers play his tune.

For the moment, however, they did not dare. Hitler was merely Chancellor, and his predecessors had not lasted long in the post. Smarting from the "insult" to their patriotic pride — and the tumultuous applause it had received at the University of Munich on 10th February — the protesters held their fire until after the March elections. Perhaps they hoped that Thomas would return to be greeted by their now "protected" chorus (the chief signatory to the protest was Max Amman, a director of Hitler's own publishing company).

If so, they were disappointed. Having gone on to deliver the lecture in Amsterdam, in Brussels and Paris (in French), Thomas travelled with Katja for a holiday and a rest to Switzerland; and it was there in Arosa that they heard the baleful news of the burning of the Reichstag, and of Hitler's 288-seat victory at the General Election on 5th March. They packed their bags to try at least to retrieve what they could from the Poschingerstrasse in Munich; but on 12th March Klaus and Erika telephoned from the Bavarian capital. The weather, they said as pointedly as possible, had worsened.

They advised their mother and father not to return for the moment. Thomas' chauffeur was already in the pay of the Munich Brown-House commandant, and it was only out of past loyalty that the man revealed to Klaus the seriousness of the situation. Germany's first and only Nobel Prize-winner for Literature since the war was considered guilty of "pacifistic excesses", of "intellectual high treason" against the new state.[7] And the Commandant of the Brown-House had set his heart on Thomas' car.

So Thomas and Katja — to the relief of their friends — remained in Switzerland. "Moreover the question arises," Thomas wrote to his Italian translator on 13th March 1933, "whether from now on there will be any room at all in Germany for the likes of me, whether I will be able to breathe that air at all. I am much too good a German, far too closely linked with the cultural traditions and the language of my country, for the thought of an exile lasting years, if not a lifetime, not to have a grave, a fateful significance to me."

It was indeed to be an exile lasting unto death; but an exile in which the once "rearguard defendant of a romantic German bourgeoisie" would become one of the acknowledged cultural spokesmen of Western democracy.

2

Almost twenty years before, in his celebrated wartime essay, Heinrich had depicted Zola's exile — the "pain of the outcast who hears news from home only as the echo of madness and terror." It had now become real to him and Thomas.

Wilhelm Herzog had been sufficiently reminded of the relevance of the Dreyfus affair in the last struggling hours of the Weimar Republic to issue a new book on the case: *Fight of a Republic: the Dreyfus Affair, Documents and Facts* in the spring of 1933. To Zsolnay, the publishers, Thomas wrote on 4th March:

> I am reading the book — have almost finished it already — with a degree of violent emotion it would scarcely have aroused in me in my unpolitical middle-class German youth . . . The whole abominable immorality of repression becomes tangible as one reads this book, which along with our own immediate experience can teach us what freedom is, and that it was a stupid, ugly folly of the mind to make a mockery of it.

Yet despite Thomas' private message to Zsolnay in Vienna, and the "envy" which overcame him when reading Zola's polemics, he found himself no less circumscribed than Zola had been when in exile. His house, his possessions, his books, his publisher, his fortune — even his children were in Germany. "It is only be sheer chance that I am outside Germany," he wrote in his letter to Lavinia Mazzuchetti:

> We had counted on Bavaria and expected that, thanks to the strength of its Catholic People's Party, everything would remain pretty much unchanged. Such an electoral outcome as actually occurred there, there of all places, was something that informed people never remotely dreamed of. The news affected me like a senseless natural disaster. We found ourselves deceived in all our hopes, but our very apprehension tugged us to return home, and our bags were already packed. Then from all sides came friendly admonitions and warnings that at present my personal safety could not be guaranteed and that I absolutely must wait out the next few weeks and remain where I fortunately happened to be.

Like Zola, Thomas awaited a signal that the terror was abating, and that he might return home. "It is possible," he added to his letter to Miss Mazzuchetti, "that within the near future some kind of law and order, a tolerably decent way of life, may be restored in Bavaria, so that I can return with my family." Even in December of that year, according to René Schickele, Thomas remained "unbelievably optimistic"[8] about the imminent downfall of the Nazi régime.

Thomas' optimism, as we can see from his diary entries for the years 1933 and 1934, was more an effort of hope than a confidence based on reality. His observation about the way the concentration camps — legalized by Wilhelm Frick, Hitler's Minister of the Interior, on 2nd March 1933 — were a psychological substitute for the prisoner-of-war camps of a successful warrior nation indicates a measure of his still penetrating insight into the Nazi and nationalist phenomenon overtaking Germany.

The March victory for the Nazis at the General Election on 5th March sealed the fate of the Reichstag; for with an absolute majority in coalition with the Nationalists Hitler was able to put forward his "Enabling Act", giving his own Cabinet the power to legislate without reference to the Reichstag — and by June all other political parties — including the Nationalists — were banned.

It was the end of Weimar. The eyes of many fellow émigrés now turned to Thomas in the hope that he would, unequivocally, denounce what was taking place. On 16th April 1933 the *Münchner Neueste Nachrichten* had published the mammoth Wagner-protest, broadcast in part on German radio, which had aroused a storm of controversy.

But Thomas remained silent. As he explained in a letter to A.M. Frey on 12th June,

> I am silent too — simply because I am used to carrying things around inside me for a long time and to working them up, that is, to objectifying them — although in my case there would be many reasons for subjectivity. My situation is difficult and my bitterness great over the decisions I must make, for the only solutions are perilous to life itself.

So far, if there was no prospect of an immediate return to Munich, the freedom to go on publishing in Germany had been given to Thomas. In the great book-burning ceremonies arranged all over the Reich for 10th May 1933, Thomas' work had been spared. Fischer was now preparing to publish the first volume of *Joseph*: why ruin the book's chances — and also the sales of all his other works — for the sake of a public denunciation of the régime?

For the next three years Thomas declined to take a public stand over the Nazi régime, and his readership within Germany was thereby safeguarded. It was left to Heinrich to uphold the honour of German anti-fascism. He did so immediately he arrived in France, without regard to the consequences it might have for himself or his possessions, confirming the consistent moral courage he had shown throughout his lifetime. In the *Dépêche de Toulouse,* one of France's leading newspapers, on 25th February 1933 Heinrich's first public exposure of Hitler's régime appeared, exactly three days after he had crossed the French border. Like the seventy-six pieces that followed it over the ensuing six years, it was written in French and printed as a leading article. Already in March 1933 the German Foreign Office was objecting fiercely to their publication; but since Maurice Sarraut, the proprietor of the paper, was a French government minister, there was little that the Nazis could do.

From Strasbourg, on 22nd February Heinrich had made his way to Nice. The day after Hitler's Reichstag election victory, on 6th March 1933, he wrote to Felix Bertaux's son Pierre: "For my own part I cannot say I am altogether convinced of the future victory of reason: I have seen it fail too many times. But as long as one is alive it would be stupid to give up hope." Already, like Zola before him, he had begun work again. "I am at work again on my *Henri IV* now, as you are on your Hölderlin.[9] On continue, n'est-ce pas?" Ten days later he was quite sure he would never see Germany again. To Felix Bertaux he wrote on 17th March 1933, "In my last letter to Pierre I was still unsure how long my exile would last; now, in contrast, I am disposed to think it will not finish before I do. That is what one gets for devoting oneself to honest but imprudent truth."

In Berlin, he had heard, the Nazis had hoped to arrest him together with other communist sympathizers on the night of the Reichstag fire; they even began announcing his arrest over a public-address system. All they found, however, was Nelly Kroeger. "If they had got me," Heinrich continued his letter to Bertaux:

I would be undergoing the fate of all those whom they put to torture until the poor devils try to commit suicide. I had underestimated by a considerable margin the hate which rages amongst these people, also their pathological minds, the hysteria, their Freudian "complexes". Looked at objectively and as simple phenomena they appear to me like beings who have been plucked of all humanity. Moreover it doesn't date from yesterday; what always exasperated them about the Republic was neither its obvious weakness nor its unpardonable faults; they simply would not accept that it wished, in the final analysis, to render less violent a sentimental people not given to disinterested reason. It seems one becomes "national" in taking on the failings of a nation, and that one remains it in behaving arrogantly within it. Look how they agree among themselves: faked fires, forged elections, the arbitrariness of persecution and vengeance — it is enough for them and for the masses who follow them to justify their accession. For some time yet they will not even attempt to define, either socially or nationally, "National Socialist" power.

Later it might mean war, for I see no one prepared to stop them from arming and even annexing Austria. At the moment they will not dare to give arms to republican workers; but in a year or two things will have changed a great deal, in France as well as elsewhere. Here hundreds of people do not collect in front of posters announcing that the "Republic is finished"; yet at the same time M. Paul-Boncourt claims he will not answer violence with violence. Very well, the day will come when a more or less fascist government will encourage Germany to lash out against "Marxist" Russia. It will then return from it in a worse state than 1918 and the chaos will be even more disastrous. The other way is that of "wise" Mussolini: subjecting permanently the majority of the people while avoiding any international conflict. But then the German character hardly lends itself to that.

Mimi and his daughter Goschi had fled to Prague, and it looked for the moment — until President Masaryk of Czechoslovakia intervened — as if his library and manuscripts in Munich would be confiscated by the Nazis. But "despite everything", Heinrich assured Bertaux, "I am not over-depressed. I consider that I have been very lucky." And when the fate of his colleagues and friends such as Erich Mühsam eventually became known, he could scarcely be said to have been exaggerating.

3

The dissolution of the Weimar Republic and the totalitarianization of the German state took place with frightening speed: and with ominously little opposition. What would have been energetically countered as "Marxist", "bolshevist" and the like only months before, now became the order of the day. Eleven days before even Hitler's "Enabling Act" Goebbels set up his new Ministry of Propaganda and Popular Enlightenment; a day later the President of the Berlin Academy, von Schillings, sent out a questionnaire to all Academy members. In view of the "changed historical situation" members were asked whether they were prepared to give "loyal support" to the new régime, and desist from all criticism. The questionnaire had to be answered Yes or No.

For two years Heinrich had struggled, as Chairman of the Literary Section of the Academy, to introduce a new "republican" history book into the Prussian school curriculum, without the faintest success; now, one day after the creation of Goebbels' new ministry, all Academy members were asked to submit to a totalitarian loyalty. Thomas Mann, Alfred Döblin and Ricarda Huch resigned; ten others — including Franz Werfel, Jakob Wassermann and René Schickele — were subsequently excluded on Ministry orders. But all the remaining members of the Literary Section signed: including Gerhart Hauptmann. It was a distressing moment in the history of twentieth-century German culture.

On 1st April 1933, came Hitler's Boycott Day against the Jews. Heinrich had already determined to make a book out of his articles for the *Dépêche de Toulouse*. Bertaux assured him it would have an enormous market in French, but its author remained sceptical. "As for the great sales you foresee I am afraid it will stop at 8 or 10 thousand as it did with *Professor Unrat*. But one must try everything." It was obvious that such anti-fascist activity would cut down the concentration he could bring to bear on *Henri IV*. "I only hope this new work will not slow down my novel," he wrote to Bertaux. "There is no doubt that one's capacity for work does not increase at my age, and I shall be working on two things at the same time. But it is still my *Henri IV* I put most trust in. It is of international interest and could appear in three languages, assuming that Zsolnay still dares to take me and is permitted to publish it." On 10th April he was writing:

> I am working every day on my novel. However, never before having had to work on unalterable facts, and ones which have been told so many times, I often have the feeling of being a plagiarist. But after all, a book in which one is not permitted too much imagination is probably what I need at the moment.

Henri IV was already turning out to be a far larger undertaking than Heinrich had foreseen. Within months MGM began to show interest in making a film of the novel. But to finish it that year he needed time and peace of mind. "I keep up my daily work in isolation," he wrote to Bertaux at the beginning of May, "and I try to transpose myself mentally to the days of my youth when I still had no great hopes of ever being well-known."[10]

But always events in Germany disturbed him, and *Henri IV* progressed at a snail's pace. Editors in Paris began to ask for articles now, as well as the *Dépêche de Toulouse*. "If only I could remain silent!" he had lamented in March to Bertaux. "But I see I shall not be permitted."[11] Like all the literary and artist exiles who had managed to leave Germany he saw what few foreigners took seriously: that Hitler's war on the intellect was more than simply a clearing of republican political deadwood and left-wing extremists, it was part of a much larger concept, suffused with hate. "The worst thing," Heinrich wrote to Thomas on discovering his address in Switzerland in April, "is that the world, at heart, is inclined to believe it is just an action taken against the communists. Only the persecution of the Jews distorts a picture which would otherwise come to it as quite welcome. I shall try and point out the truth. What has one to lose?"[12]

His articles were models of analysis and compression. Above all he was determined that the Nazi mystique around the Führer and the sham legality of its measures should be exposed. "It is what I call the reign of failures, of misfits," he wrote to Bertaux;[13] their hatred directed in particular towards all excellence except in their own proscribed field of inhumanity. "Their most personal discovery, and that which best unmasks them, is that woodpile on which they burned the books they were incapable of writing, the sum in fact of a whole spiritual culture from which they had been excluded by their own insufficiency. Misfits, failures! And who now take their revenge for blighted hopes," he wrote after the book burning ceremonies of May 1933 in the *Dépêche de Toulouse*.[14]

What augured ill for the future, however, was the popular reactionary tide in which the Nazis had come to the fore. "I believe as you do," Henrich wrote to Bertaux, "that we are unfortunate enough to find ourselves at the start of a mass reaction against the spiritual ambitions and ideals which one calls democracy. Democracy does not assert itself in compact masses, it separates them, penetrates them in small areas, seeks to elevate them. The leaders of uneducated masses only seem to have the ability to make them sink lower. There is nothing more to it than that, and it would have to be the failures, the misfits who succeed. From now on they will hold tight to their country."[15]

Heinrich's articles began to pile up; by June he had had to set aside *Henri IV* in order to complete enough to comprise a book. Querido, the new German émigré publishing house in Amsterdam, had offered a contract for a German edition; but now there seemed some doubt as to whether any French publisher would risk publishing the original: and almost no prospect at all of English or American translation.

Yet there was no other course possible. His conscience, his "pride" even as he put it to Bertaux, demanded that he speak out as he had always done in the past. As he wrote at the end of the year:

> With my past I could hardly have done other than testify to the truth. I was not permitted to keep silent, and even if I had wanted to camouflage my known opinions, I would only have been met with incredulity or worse.[16]

So the summer of 1933 was spent finishing the last essays in French for *La Haine,* as the book was to be called, and then translating them into German. In May Thomas had written to say he was coming to spend the summer on the French Riviera if they could find a house; and delighted, Heinrich arranged to move to Bandol to be nearby. "I am sure I shall meet you in brave spirits," he wrote to Thomas on 12th May "which we must keep up. Sometimes it is hard for me, especially when my working energy suffers. But somehow we must manage."[17]

4

For Thomas, however, exile was to mean something quite different than for Heinrich. "It is true, some very difficult months lie behind us now. It is strange enough, at the end of journey which we undertook in complete innocence, suddenly, to see our return to Germany cut off," Thomas wrote to Robert Faesi in June 1933. "But after shifting from hotel to hotel for many weeks we have found ourselves back in private accommodation, which signifies a sort of substitute for home."

The house they had found was at Sanary-sur-Mer, not far from René Schickele who had suggested they come. Schickele found Thomas looking "unwell . . . very oppressed", he noted however in his diary on 8th May.

For Heinrich Mann exile meant in the end no great change, he was always in opposition . . . In contrast Thomas, however much he had expounded politically in the past few years, has really tumbled from the clouds. Only now does he see the squalid vulgarity of what they call politics in Germany. He did what he thought was right, without considering the consequences; and the consequences appal him. If anyone does not have the stuff of a martyr, it is Thomas Mann.

And on 15th May Schickele recorded:

Thomas said: "How extraordinary! One leaves one's country in order to lecture on Richard Wagner in Amsterdam and Paris, and when one wishes to return, it has run away." It affects him like most Germans of his intellectual kind. They see well enough what is happening and even what is bound to come, but at heart they do not want to acknowledge its reality because it is unbelievably mad; above all, however, because they do not want to admit they have lost their fatherland.[18]

In March Thomas had decided to resign from all official posts and institutional memberships in Germany, and "wherever it may be, to concentrate in seclusion on my own personal tasks," he had written to Ida Herz.[19] Yet it was by no means so easy to find that seclusion, or to ignore what was happening in Germany. Two days later he entered in his journal: "My ears are full of shuddering stories and tales of murder in Munich that accompany regular political acts of violence at every step: wild mishandling of Jews . . . No let up in the violence."[20] The pathetic spectacle of Munich's Richard-Wagner-Town Protest in April had led Thomas to write out a defence for publication in Germany.

It was never to be published. For now, as the Berlin Academy allowed itself to be castrated and Goebbels' Ministry set about the complete "coordination" of all communications in Germany, the true significance of Hitler's totalitarian aims became clear. "One has to admit," Heinrich wrote to Felix Bertaux on 10th April, "that those people over there take more trouble, in their way, over the affairs of the mind than the republicans ever did. Only it is to put an end to them." Believing the *Frankfurter Zeitung* already to have succumbed to Goebbels, Thomas sent his article to Fischer's son-in-law, Gottfried Bermann. "I believe the *Rundschau* could carry it," Thomas wrote, "and it would be good, a sort of triumph, if this tone could once again be raised."[21]

But Bermann was closer to the reality of the new state in Berlin; as a Jewish publishing house not even its international fame could protect it for long, and, most of all, publication of the article would mean the end of any plans to publish *Joseph* in Germany. Despite the biblical theme, Bermann was convinced the Nazis would not dare to ban *The Tales of Jacob* (volume 1 of *Joseph and his Brothers*) without a more political pretext, since they had been careful to exclude all Thomas' previous works from the book burnings in May.

For Bermann it was a calculated risk. There remained a chance that the house of Fischer would escape closure as long as the Nazis could preserve face internationally by leaving it open; and as Nobel Prizewinner Thomas Mann was certainly an international name. It was not perhaps the most farsighted policy for Bermann; but old Sami Fischer would never consent to leave Germany and there was something to be said for preserving the firm intact if Hitler's régime was to be short-lived.

"It is madness," wrote Thomas angrily to Bermann in August. "To put it in a nutshell: *let Querido publish the book.*"[22] He was convinced that in any case *Joseph* would receive no better reception in Germany than the lecture on Wagner. But Bermann was adamant, and pointed out that the publication of *Joseph* inside Germany would be a far greater victory for humanity than the tiny sales it might hope to achieve under Querido outside.

So Thomas allowed himself to be persuaded. "Today the words 'Whichever way you do it is wrong' hold good. But for someone who until now had felt 'blessed' and was used to doing things right, it is at first a somewhat confusing situation."[23] Bermann had won. But in doing so he had in fact tied Thomas' hands behind his back politically: for henceforth any criticism of the Nazi régime, whether inside Germany or outside, would bring an instant ban on the book. The poet had been allowed to speak; but the contemporary moralist, political and cultural, had *de facto* been silenced.

It was an impasse that was to last a further three years, a restriction Thomas can scarcely have foreseen when he gave in to Bermann, and one which would bring him into increasing ill-repute amongst his fellow exiles. It signified the loss of the matrix which had given him the courage to write during even the most difficult days of Weimar. At first it was a release to be away from such turmoil, in the peace of the French riviera. But for a man and a writer as sensitive as Thomas it would not be long before the turmoil was transferred to his own inner self, however he might physically be removed from the Nazi nightmare.

Sanary rapidly became the summer rendez-vous of German Littérateurs, with Brecht, Franz Werfel, Ernst Toller, Lion Feuchtwanger, Arnold Zweig, Hermann Kesten, Erwin Piscator, Ludwig Marcuse and others congregating there. Heinrich and Thomas met regularly: "we have a number of thoughts to exchange. It is a somewhat sad pleasure," Heinrich wrote to Bertaux.[24] "I must work on my articles . . . I have only completed five, I still have 7 to write — and my novel waiting all the time!"

Thomas' presence was a "great consolation" to Heinrich, as he told Bertaux,[25] not only as a friend in the extreme isolation of exile, but in terms of morale too. Thomas read him a chapter of *Joseph,* and all Heinrich's expectations seemed fulfilled. "I foresee a world-wide success for the book," Heinrich wrote to Bertaux, "firstly because of the situation in which the régime de ratés has just placed him, and then thanks to its biblical subject — without mentioning the still more profound understanding of humanity to which the work testifies."[26] Schickele noted in his diary how "obviously contented" Heinrich was to be together and "at one" with his brother. Heinrich read to him and a gathering of emigrés from *La Haine* as it moved towards completion, and Thomas now resumed work on the third volume of *Joseph.* It was once again something of the "division of labour" to which Thomas had referred over a decade before, in the early years of the Republic.

On 4th August Heinrich discovered it was Schickele's fiftieth birthday; a celebration was arranged at Schickele's house. Thomas arrived after lunch with Katja and their two youngest children, and bearing with them a hamper of fresh delicatessen fetched from Toulon. Then in the late afternoon Heinrich appeared, "lightly dressed and perspiring", and behind him "in full summer-toilette", Frau Kröger, recently arrived from Berlin, having escaped from Germany via Copenhagen.

She does not perspire. She sways airily and a little plumply towards us. Her Lübeck-German with its somewhat slow twitter falls neatly into our avian concert which echoes from the garden. We sit in the shade of a tall pine tree. I listen more to the concert than to the conversation. We all feel manifestly well.

A year before, Thomas remarked later in the evening, it would have been an official banquet. But as Katja pointed out, the table of honour was there at least, and they would have to be content with that.

Then on 25th August Hitler's first list of German nationals to be deprived of citizenship under the new law was announced in the *Deutsche Reichsanzeiger.* It was the first of 84 such lists that would be drawn up over the next five years, and it was not unexpected that Heinrich's name should be included in it. In Berlin in June Heinrich had already been sentenced in absentio to a year and a half's imprisonment; *La Haine,* as he wrote to Bertaux on 30th June, "will give them an excuse to condemn me for all perpetuity".

"My task is not to adapt myself but to clarify and correct people's opinions here," he declared. When Bertaux suggested he alter his title

(La Haine: histoire contemporaine d'Allemagne) to "Pourquoi j'ai quitté l'Allemagne", Heinrich pointed out that his polemic was not simply a personal response to Naziism, it was an objection on the grounds of humanity:

I know very well that it [Naziism] responds to the tendencies of the age and that it will lead, through blood and mire, to other epochs more worthy of being lived. Everything which is happening today can be justified by the fact that life goes on. But that doesn't mean it can be legitimized before reason and humanity — which is what one must be concerned with when waging a polemical battle. Victor Hugo little worried about the Empire's right to go on living when he wrote *Napoléon le Petit*. I do not have such far-reaching pretensions myself. I am writing a series of articles, impressions and reflections in which, among other things, I point out that this [Nazi] movement has at least taken upon itself the ordering of chaotic masses hitherto inaccessible to existing political parties. But to what end? To render them more blood-thirsty, more indisciplined at heart, and to fling them in the end into a more or less certain and ultimate war.

The news of his deprivation of German citizenship does not seem to have affected Heinrich unduly; it merely confirmed the extraordinary hatred the Nazis felt for any Germans who did not share their views. The last chapters he had written for *La Haine* were dramatic dialogues: "Scenes from Nazi life". They were the forerunners of Brecht's *The Private Life of the Master Race* (1935–8) and *Arturo Ui* (1941). However it was Heinrich's article *L'Education morale,* published in the *Dépêche de Toulouse* on 21st July, which, when translated into German ("I am sitting down to translate my last small article for an émigré magazine", Heinrich wrote to Bertaux on 16th September), was to raise the first literary scandal of the emigration: and to put, inadvertently, both Schickele and Thomas in the very greatest of personal dilemmas.

5

The first issue of *Die Sammlung* was published in September 1933. It was distributed by Querido, edited by Thomas Mann's son Klaus, and boasted as its three patrons André Gide, Aldous Huxley and Heinrich Mann. Klaus had assured all potential contributors that the magazine's bias would be basically cultural, not political; but from the first issue it was obvious that the two could not be separated. Klaus himself lambasted Gottfried Benn for his "degradation of the spirit", and Heinrich's article had the German Foreign Office ablaze with indignation. In it he gave a masterly account of the so-called Nazi revolution — its unbelievable success achieved by the most obvious deceit: glider-building in order to cover real aircraft production, the cry of "anti-bolshevism" to draw attention away from the régime's own totalitarian measures, its war declared on human reason — "Never yet has such an avalanche of lies descended on a nation, falsified its own recent history and brought about such total oblivion to it," he concluded. "Moral education decides the future of a country and the whole world. To destroy a democracy is nothing; future generations must also be cleansed in their vocabulary from the words peace, justice and truth. Hitler meant what he said when he declared 'We shall take their children from them.'"

The reaction in Germany was immediate. Rosenberg's Reich Office for the Furtherance of German Writing issued on 10th October 1933 a directive to the German book trade not to handle any authors connected with such émigré literary journals. "It goes without question that no German book-seller should sell books by authors who are whipping up a spiritual war against Germany in foreign countries," the directive stated.[27]

For authors like Klaus and Heinrich Mann who had now been deprived of their citizenship and whose books had already been burned in Germany, this was of no consequence. Rather, it showed how seriously Rosenberg (Hitler's party "philosopher" and spokesman) took the threat of such a "spiritual war" abroad against Naziism. Yet for those authors who — for whatever reasons — had managed so far to survive the book burning ceremonies and Nazi black-lists, it meant a new and grave challenge. Dr Bermann and his aide, Professor Samuel Saenger, rushed to Sanary-sur-mer where they managed to persuade Alfred Döblin, René Schickele and Thomas Mann to disclaim all contact with *Die Sammlung*. One by one their telegrams were despatched to Berlin.

CAN ONLY STATE THAT CHARACTER OF FIRST NUMBER SAMMLUNG DOES NOT BEAR OUT ITS ORIGINAL AIMS [Thomas] MANN

AM PAINFULLY SURPRISED BY POLITICAL CHARACTER SAMMLUNG, SINCE OCCASIONAL CONTRIBUTION SOLELY FOR PURELY LITERARY JOURNAL SOLICITED. AM IN NO WAY CONNECTED WITH QUERIDO, DISSOCIATE MYSELF UTTERLY FROM SUCHLIKE. SCHICKELE

DISAVOW ALL LITERARY AND POLITICAL CONNECTION WITH PUBLISHER OF SAMMLUNG. PLEASE ANNOUNCE THIS IN APPROPRIATE FORM SOONEST. WAS NOT AWARE OF JOURNALS LEANINGS. DOBLIN

For Thomas it was perhaps most difficult of all — and all came later to regret it. As Dr Bermann reminded Thomas, the now aged Samuel Fischer would never consent to leave Germany, and his firm already represented the last remaining liberal publishing house in the new Reich. The whole of the first volume of *Joseph* — *The Tales of Jacob* — had been despatched to the book trade on the day of Rosenberg's directive. Not to deny all connection with *Die Sammlung* would inevitably mean the end of *Joseph,* of all future publication for Thomas inside Germany, including the loss of the first 10,000 copy edition. Professor Saenger put the same point to René Schickele — "he spoke for hour after hour, for two days on end. He himself made such a pitiful impression that I was more convinced by his appearance than what he had to say," Schickele excused himself in a letter to Joseph Roth.[28] Heinrich, feeling himself to have been the cause of the whole affair, was quite unequivocal. "Deny it with all your might," he advised.[29]

So Thomas, Schickele, Döblin, Stefan Zweig and others publicly disowned all connection with *Die Sammlung*. For Thomas, however, it meant disowning his own son; and those who did not know the family personally were astonished. The *Arbeiter Zeitung* in Vienna published a bitter article on 19th October 1933, denouncing Thomas. Six days later they carried his explanation:

I was faced, therefore, by the question whether I wished to sacrifice the life of my work, whether I wished to disappoint and take my leave of those people in Germany who listen to me and who in particular had waited for years for this new work of mine, only so that my name might figure on the list of contributors to a magazine . . .

In Prague the *Neue Deutsche Blätter* found the explanation less than satisfactory, however. In their November issue they declared: "Thomas Mann's rejection of his son's journal was a rejection of the anti-fascist struggle — the appearance of his book in Germany will encourage no one, but will simply sugar the lamentable culture-Ersatz with which the Nazis are feeding the population." To be sure, Thomas' decision had indeed played into the hands of the Nazis — who could now claim to have "rid" the country of "bolshevist" and "semitic" work, while continuing to honour their great men of literature, such as Hauptmann and Thomas Mann, whatever their views. Even the following January, in 1934, Thomas could write in all sincerity to his former friend Ernst Bertram:

But one thing I ask you to believe: that my behaviour and my views are in no way formed or influenced by the émigré "front". I stand on my own feet and am not in touch in any way with the German émigrés who have been dispersed around the world. Furthermore, those German émigrés simply do not exist in the sense of a spiritual or political unity. Individual fragmentation is complete; and if one cannot say that your Reich has yet achieved everywhere in the world the correct understanding for its charm and dignity, then it is in no way the fault or service of utterly uninfluential émigrés.[30]

René Schickele had already written in much the same spirit to Thomas in November 1933. "In one year," he asserted, "there will be no trace of a German emigration left, intellectually speaking. All that will be left will be 'single' émigrés with their property."[31]

It was the story of the Weimar Republic repeated: the painful inadequacy of republican spirits to combine their strength into an effective force. The Jewish émigrés remained primarily concerned about the Jewish persecution, Social Democrats and Communists still tore at one another, and the exceptions to the literary black-lists in Germany only served to sow further discord among the exiles. Bermann threatened a law-suit when Schickele tried to transfer his allegiance to Amsterdam,[32] Schickele's diary became — as did Thomas' also at this time — a form of confessional. "Every political entry in the diary costs me self-conquest," Schickele noted on 8th May 1934; but somehow he felt he had to give expression to his conscience, if only privately. Shortly before he had cast doubts on Heinrich's title *La Haine* as a description of Germany under Hitler; he felt it was more a reflection of Heinrich's own bitterness at being cast out of his own country;[33] yet when the news came, in April 1934, of Ludwig Marum's "suicide" in Kislau concentration camp, and the likely end of Erich Mühsam at Oranienburg, he was shattered. "It won't help," he entered on 4th April 1934. "You must. Namely: make a clean breast of it. A small book. Say *everything* in it." By August 1934 Thomas, too, was determined to break his silence. "The time seems ripe," he wrote to Karl Kerenyi on 4th August, "for such a statement as I have in mind, and the moment might soon come when I would repent having delayed too long in silence."

In the meantime, however, a year had passed; the German emigrants had remained in disarray, and the Western powers looked on while with impunity Hitler set up a structure so totalitarian only world war could ever hope to break it.

6

Among the literary émigrés who felt betrayed by Thomas' silence over the Nazi régime was a group of socialist writers who had fled to Moscow and who watched Hitler's elimination of their colleagues with understandable distress. The news that Thomas had now turned his back on political testimony after his progressive championing of socialist ideals under the Republic came as a bitter blow; and an emissary was sent to Heinrich, in France, to ask if he would denounce this betrayal.

Heinrich sent the man packing. "They wanted me to denounce my own brother!" he exclaimed in disbelief to Schickele.[34] He could not do it as a brother, nor as a fellow émigré. No one was more aware of the need for unity and moral courage among the exiles if an effective anti-fascist movement was to be mobilized in Europe; but, despite his ideals, he was and had always been too much of a realist ever to hope for the impossible. He had shown this in 1918 when he declined to join the Spartacist movement; in his private letters to Bertaux at the beginning of the Weimar Republic — "History makes no leaps"; and to Bertaux, in May 1933, he had acknowledged the inevitable nature of fascism as a "mass reaction" to the demands of democracy. Though he was unanimously elected honorary President of the Schutzverband of German Writers in Exile in Paris in October 1933, and became, as Ludwig Marcuse later recalled, a sort of "Hindenburg of the emigration",[35] the "uncrowned President of the 4th Reich",[36] he harboured no illusions about the effectiveness of largely stateless exiles in democracies to whom they were at best a nuisance, at worst a thorn in the flesh. Above all he recognized that in reality the only people who could rid Germany of the Nazis without a European war were the Germans themselves.

"In Paris there are four or five thousand German refugees. It does not encourage me to join them,"[37] Heinrich had written to Bertaux already in

May 1933; and in September, as he neared the end of *La Haine,* "Thank you for saying such consoling things . . . But even supposing that that reign of convicts were to collapse in the near future, I would not be young enough to profit from it. My hopes are quite disinterested. From now on I shall try and detach myself even from the present. I need physical tranquillity, by that I mean distance and oblivion. Here and in Paris too many suspect figures from Berlin come and upset me."[38] Thomas was still in Sanary, but was preparing to leave for Zurich — much to Heinrich's disquiet. "I am not without apprehension," he wrote to Bertaux on 16th September 1933 — though he acknowledged wherever one went there was bound to be some danger. In all the humilation and distress of exile he recognized the émigré's deep-seated need for privacy and protection. "I am very fatigued and no longer find any satisfaction in it," he confessed about the last chapter of *La Haine.* "But one must keep at it and consider this way of life as a sort of special favour which could have been even worse." He believed in Thomas; believed in him not only as a brother but also as a poet of humanity: and, as the publication of *Joseph* in October 1933 would show, he was not mistaken.

On 1st October 1933, Heinrich returned to Nice from Bandol to consult his doctor. On the 4th he wrote to Bertaux: "I still do not know where I shall go for the winter. Now that I walk the familiar streets of Nice I find difficulty in believing it might be dangerous to stay here . . . Of course it would not be very prudent since my book is due out soon, and the winter season will bring many a suspicious figure." Lion Feuchtwanger had suggested they meet in Tunisia; but in the end Heinrich remained in Nice — "I think that in leaving this continent, from which I have never been separated before, I would really have a feeling of emptiness," he explained to Bertaux.[39] Besides, Nice seemed so "harmless" to him as he put it to Thomas;[40] and the danger of German spies and possible assassination perhaps "imaginary."[41] He began to look for a small apartment.

Thomas, meanwhile, had found a house in Küsnacht, outside Zurich and overlooking the lake. On 10th October 1933, *The Tales of Jacob* had been sent out from Leipzig to German booksellers; and within the first week all 10,000 copies of the first impression were sold — a success in no way comparable to the days of *The Magic Mountain* in 1924, but heartwarming against the otherwise disastrous news from Germany. A second, third and fourth impression followed — each of 5,000 copies — and Bermann's confidence was thus vindicated. On 7th November 1933, Thomas wrote to him:

> I am pleased to hear the sales of the book continue to go well. The success of *The Magic Mountain* was always something of a miracle to me. This time even a fifth of that success seems almost more of a wonder. For the moment it will have to make up for the painful confusion my "rescue act" has caused in many hearts I respect.

The Viennese *Arbeiter Zeitung* had used Heinrich's famous phrase "Betrayal of the intellect" from *Geist und Tat* in denouncing Schickele, Döblin, Zweig and Thomas Mann for their emigrant disavowal; and Thomas

had in fact been forced to "join" Goebbels' new Reichschrifttumkammer —
the Reich Writers' Guild — though mercifully avoiding any oath of loyalty to
the new régime by simply referring to his honorary membership of its
predecessor — the Schutverband deutscher Schriftsteller — as a way of
excusing himself from "further formalities".[42]

Heinrich, however, wrote to Thomas on 3rd November 1933:

> In every respect you did the right thing in allowing the book to be
> published in Germany . . . If I were able to do it myself, I would do
> exactly the same — namely, to continue the struggle against the rulers
> of Germany from inside. Unfortunately I am only permitted to do it from
> outside, though of course more directly.

And to A.M. Frey, who had also had qualms about signing the Reich Writers'
Guild membership document, Heinrich wrote simply:

> It is wholly a matter of your own spiritual discretion whether you can do
> it. I understand if in the end one forgets that which one cannot change. It
> is simply not permitted me.[43]

Letters reaching him from inside Germany had proved beyond doubt that
there were still Germans who read his work — whether unburned earlier
books or smuggled articles from France — with "passionate" intensity".[44]
"How much I would like to be able to publish in Germany, if I could," he
exclaimed one day in the following spring to René Schickele. "You see, I
was forced into everything, I have no choice."[45]

It was this separation from their native readership which perhaps most
distressed the exiled German writers in the early years of emigration. To
write for a French newspaper or even in German for an émigré publishing
house was in no way comparable with the freedom to speak to one's own
people. Schickele noted in his diary on 11th December 1933:

> A person like Thomas Mann clings with every thread to Germany, it is a
> part of him. He has to feel the cut in the very tissue of his skin, to feel
> the change right inside his bowels — it is therefore questionable whether
> if severed, he could continue living. The same with Hesse.

Thomas had become a political and cultural voice in Germany, in
Europe. But now his political responsibility and convictions had cut him
away from the very roots through which he had nourished himself, since
childhood, as a writer; and threatened to sever even his readership should he
not renounce all political intentions abroad. When Heinrich came to read
The Tales of Jacob in November 1933, however, he realized how important
a writer Thomas had become in twentieth-century literature. Heinrich wrote
to Thomas on 18th November 1933:

> You have your own exegesis, even your own teaching if I understand
> rightly, it stretches far and deep, and finally comes back to you and to
> us. It is this universality which I honour and admire, and with it of course
> the enormous scholarship with which you "see" the past and bring it to
> life. That eager seriousness in the tone of your dialectic is especially
> attractive to me, behind which appear humour and even parody; and
> behind them again seriousness.

And on Christmas Day 1933:

> Every evening, propped up in bed . . . I read a few pages of your book; for to rush in this case would be pointless. I cannot remember any other book which has given me so much to think about and to marvel at. I do not know where your material comes from, to me it is like a revelation though I presume it is often only a poetic extension of slender sources. Rich poetry, probably your richest; and the most magical thing about it is precisely its derivation from a "known" background, although everyone learns through you that what he knew was in fact nothing and that man's past, when made contemporary, is even more of a fairy-tale than even he himself can have wished it.
>
> Germany today could learn from you that the most extreme intellectualism can change, one knows not how or where, into mysticism — and that mysticism is something about which one must *think*.

But if Germany "were able to learn as much from you", he added, "it would not be the Germany it is today."

7

Germany was the furthest it could possibly be from learning, obsessed with a myth grotesque in its contrast to the rich and wonderful retelling of the story of Jacob and of Joseph. If the book continued to sell well in the bookshops there, its critical acclaim in the press was "miserable". Even Gerhart Hauptmann, in Rapallo, called it a "fifth-rate book" and even an "anti-semitic pamphlet". Naziism was for him an "elementary occurrence".[46]

Meanwhile, in October 1933 Hitler withdrew Germany from the League of Nations, to the subsequent unanimous approval of a national referendum. "Does Germany's withdrawal worry you?" Heinrich wrote to Thomas on 17th October,

> Or the coming unanimous show of national approval? The most extraordinary thing remains that everyone sees through the swindle, only the Germans are not allowed to recognize it — though in fact of course they do. Who is deceiving whom? Enough, the world wishes to be deceived. It obediently follows every dramatic turn of the two dictators, the remaining members will not decide anything more on their own in the League, will not carry out the due sanctions, but on the contrary will tolerate re-armament and even make deals over it.

Heinrich's own book *La Haine* was due out at the end of October. Thomas had said it would penetrate "deep into Germany" and across the world, but Heinrich was himself sceptical. Few copies would ever reach the interior of Germany, and outside the Reich only France seemed to have a "precise and well-formed idea" of what was happening. No English or American publisher had dared touch the book, despite Lion Feuchtwanger's taking it personally to London. "The Anglo-Saxons all look through it until they hit against some detail to which they take objection. Further than that they do not want to know, in order to remain 'agreeable' as you put it."[47] Yet Heinrich could summon no hatred for the Germans as a people, only pity. He had lived too close to the seat of power and known too many politicians to imagine that leaders are only the pawns of their people.

> We must always remember how many of the "inner" Germans — even more than we outside — suffer most directly from the depravity of their country. We would be doing them an injustice if we divorced ourselves from the country, which, to be sure, is wretched and lets itself be made abominable in the eyes of the world by these criminals.

He foresaw that Hitler would not only have to deal with opposition from "better" Germans, for whom he had set up his concentration camps, but even that part of his own following — the SA — who were not getting all they considered due to them. But worst of all was the inevitability of war: the preparation for which was the "raison d'être" of any military régime. "It will first necessitate, without doubt," he wrote, "a long and arduous inner disciplining of the Germans . . . But history knows only two classes of nations: the one which has struggled to achieve freedom and independence, the other which still has much to suffer and to do. It will not be easier for Germany if it continues to diminish its intellectual resources, particularly now with the departure even of 'Aryan' professors."[48] Zsolnay declined further publication of Heinrich's books — but simultaneously refused to release his rights on Heinrich's previous titles. Thus in the period leading up to the Second World War no new German editions of *Man of Straw* or Heinrich's previous political essays were issued.

Nevertheless, after writing an extended essay on emigration — published the following year under the title of *The Meaning of this Emigration* — Heinrich sat down once again to his novel on the life of Henri IV. *La Haine* went into some nine impressions, and Querido's German edition — despite Heinrich's fear that the émigré houses would simply find no market ("It is in no way proved that German books can be sold in sufficient quantities outside Germany," he wrote to Bertaux on 21st November 1933) — met with a "certain amount of success", with a second impression being required within the first fortnight. It was encouraging, but it had left him physically and mentally exhausted. It was not until January 1934 that he was able to take up *Henri IV* where he had left off; and the reading of his brother's *Tales of Jacob* gave him courage, as it did so many other exiles. *Henri IV* was the first "serious" work he had undertaken since finishing *Der Kopf* in 1925 — and it owed much to the lessons of *Der Kopf's* failure. In it Heinrich invested all that he had learned from childhood. He was approaching his sixty-third birthday, and the novel might well turn out to be his last. "In the meantime I go on working, more than used ever to be the case, into the void, though I can remember that as a beginner I promised myself even less of the outside world. But in those days one had a whole lifetime in front of one to be disappointed. Today it is wholly a matter of not leaving anything owing to oneself, of expressing it all," he wrote to Thomas on 5th March 1934; "I would be happy if I succeeded in doing what you have done in Joseph. The tales of Jacob have such serenity, time is suspended for the people who take part as it is for him who writes. That is what most appeals to me in it at present." He decided not to curtail the youth of Henri IV in order to cover the later years, but instead to write the novel in two volumes. As Hitler tightened the noose about European democracy, the brothers Mann seemed determined to uphold the pride of modern civilization in truly epic fashion, and in books that would far outlive the Thousand Year Reich.

8

It was at this moment that a decision arose destined to have a profound bearing on both Heinrich's and Thomas' lives. In December 1933 came an offer to Heinrich for a lecture tour of America. "I am supposed to give lectures in America," he wrote to Schickele on 24th December, "but only if I can speak in English without a text. I must sadly reply that I cannot do it even in German."[49] He was determined to concentrate now on *Henri IV* after the political distractions of 1933; "if I had given in to the eight or ten requests to travel, even to America, this winter, not one sentence of my novel would have been written," he wrote to Thomas on 19th April 1934.

A similar offer came to Thomas only a few days later, this time from his American publisher Alfred Knopf. It was proposed that he and Katja travel to New York to celebrate the publication of the American edition of *The Tales of Jacob*. The whole trip was to take only 4 weeks; and though Dr Bermann had decided to publish the second volume of *Joseph* — *The Young Joseph* — as early as possible in the spring, Thomas had already told Heinrich he did not intend the third — and at this time supposedly last — volume to appear before 1936, thus giving himself time to complete it without undue haste.[50]

So Thomas agreed to make his first journey to the New World — scarcely dreaming he would one day become an American citizen!

They took a Dutch ship, the *RMS Volendam,* from Boulogne: and in New York found that Knopf had prepared a presidential welcome. Journalists swarmed aboard the ship before it docked; and to Heinrich's great pride in Nice the *New York Herald* carried a report on its front page, referring to Thomas as "the most eminent living man of letters". "I thought with pleasure of Shaw's vain old face . . ." Heinrich wrote to Thomas at the end of June.[51]

From the quayside a motor cavalcade with police riders brought Thomas into the city, and banquet after banquet was given in his honour. The climax was a Testimonial Dinner on 6th June 1934, for 300 people, at which Mayor La Guardia gave the welcoming address. Thomas replied in English, obviously deeply moved at finding an appreciation and a following he had not experienced since leaving Germany more than a year before; but when, at the end of his speech, he took the opportunity of thanking Knopf for making it all possible, his knowledge of English failed him. "He is not only a publisher," he turned to Knopf, "he is a creature too." Katja nearly fell off her chair — knowing he meant creator — but fortunately Knopf laughed out loud.

Helen Lowe-Porter's remarkable translation of *Joseph* ensured the book's success in America, and letters of congratulation and appreciation followed Thomas long after his return to Switzerland on 9th June. But while America honoured the most eminent living man of letters, the future of Germany began to look even bleaker. On 30th June Hitler liquidated all remaining threats to his dictatorship — including the previous Reichschancellor Schleicher, von Papen's two secretaries, Röhm and the SA leaders and a host of political opponents dating back to the 1923 Putsch — and on 25th July Nazis murdered the Austrian Chancellor Dollfuss (who had outlawed the Austrian Nazi Party in June) and attempted a coup d'état. Mussolini moved troops up to the Austrian border, however; and Hitler faltered. As far back as December 1933 Heinrich had attempted to point out the "comedian's" love of effect and actual unpreparedness for action. "He aims solely to create an effect, and will collapse in front of any real force, even in front of people capable of unleashing force . . . If there were anything I could wish for, it would be perhaps that the world might take a little more account of this disposition," he wrote to Bertaux on 27th December 1933.

By one of the ironies of literature Heinrich had also begun, in the second week of June 1934, to narrate the story of the Massacre of the French Protestants on the night of St Bartholomew. "How I found myself at home!" he wrote with feeling to Bertaux. "It is something I have witnessed myself, those long preliminaries to a deed which, once it is done, is no longer comprehensible, because one forgets what in fact one had before one's eyes, the state of despair and men being sucked into treachery and murder."[52] Sixteen days later came Hitler's Röhm massacre.

Hindenburg congratulated Hitler on having "nipped treason in the bud"; but a month later he himself was dead, and Hitler merged the titles of both President and Chancellor into one. On 19th August 1934, some thirty-eight million Germans approved this action; four and a quarter million voted against; and more than three quarters of a million spoiled their papers. Germany's history now lay entirely in the hands of one man; and the need for unity among anti-fascist emigrants became paramount. It was at this moment that *La Haine* appeared in German, under the title *Der Hass:* the first and in many ways the most significant anti-fascist work to be written by a German.

"This book reaches near to Zola's *J'accuse*. It is written in flames," the *Prager Montagblatt* declared of *Der Hass;* but Switzerland refused to permit copies to enter the country. The Dutch government itself had the writer Heinz Liepmann arrested for offending the head of a "friendly" state. Liepmann had just escaped from a Nazi concentration camp, and the likelihood of his deportation caused a wave of fear to pass throughout the German émigrés. As Hitler made clear in his later wartime Table Talk,[53] the minimum punishment for returned German émigrés was detention in a concentration camp; if they had previously committed any punishable offence in Germany they were automatically to be shot.

Nor had Heinrich confined his anti-fascist activity to the columns of the *Dépêche de Toulouse* and the pages of *La Haine*. His essay *Tasks of the Emigration* had been published in the *Neue Weltbühne* in Prague in the autumn of 1933 ·and appeared in extended book form as *The Meaning of this Emigration* in Paris in the spring of 1934. He had published his analysis of the Reichstag Arson trial in the *Neue Weltbühne* in October 1933, as well as *Thinking by Subscription* the following March, and *Youth Taken In* in May 1934. He had written the foreword to a Czechoslovakian book of caricatures on the Third Reich which appeared in English, French and German editions; and on the first anniversary of Hitler's book burning ceremonies a German Freedom Library was opened in Paris, founded by André Gide, H.G. Wells, Romain Rolland, Lion Feuchtwanger and others – with Heinrich Mann as its President.

After the news of Liepmann's arrest Heinrich immediately enquired about obtaining a French passport. He had already shaved off the famous pointed beard by which he could be too easily recognized, and made an arrangement whereby all but personal mail was sent to him care of Felix Bertaux outside Paris. "In certain circumstances I can foresee my extradition," he wrote to Bertaux in April 1934. "But if that happens I see no other refuge in the world . . ."[54] Bertaux was concerned lest civil war come to France – a fear confirmed in part by the assassination of Louis Barthou, the anti-fascist French Foreign Minister, at Marseille on 9th October 1934. "None of this is calculated to raise my morale," Heinrich admitted to Bertaux in April; yet the work on *Henri IV* provided a solace, a support. Against the frustrations and anxieties of exile and the fate of Germany, *Henri IV* represented something positive, at once creative and idealistic, a contribution to the future however long it might take for Naziism to burn itself out. "If a later Germany," he wrote in an open greeting to the first Congress of Soviet Writers in August 1934, "should one day improve on its past performance, then I hope this literature will show itself to have been the spiritual antecedent." He was referring to the combined anti-fascist literature of the German emigration; but his conviction stemmed from his work on *Henri IV*; and his reading, among other works, of *Joseph and his Brothers* – the second volume of which had appeared in March 1934. To René Schickele Thomas had expressed himself similarly: "You and I and my brother," he wrote on 16th May 1934, the day before leaving for New York, "from whose *Henri IV* I expect a great deal, must do our jobs very well; then one day people will say that during this period we were the real Germany."

In this respect Heinrich still had no qualms about Thomas' official silence on Hitler's régime. "It is understandable that you would like to digress from your great work," Heinrich wrote to him on 20th September 1934, "to make a personal statement. But in the end, however, you will postpone it. One can also write an obituary to the Third Reich when it is over. Even then I would ask: why? Its true nature is known through and through, and it only continues against the world's better judgment. Once dead, it will be quite dead. Rochefort, having fought for 18 years against him, once said of Napoleon III: Cet imbécile de qui personne ne parle plus. How much more so it will be with Hitler after he has fallen."

But if Thomas permitted himself to be encouraged to continue publishing in Germany and to remain silent on the subject of Naziism even by his brother, he continued to suffer the torments of his own private conscience on the issue. The third volume of Joseph progressed painfully slowly now; and letter after letter testified to his growing need — like Schickele — to "make a clean breast of it".

"My attitude, my plans and my resolves are wavering and ambivalent. As soon as I look up from my curious epic . . . I begin to think about a book-length discussion of German affairs, highly personal and unsparing. One of these days I shall no doubt have to set to work on it, and that, of course, would mean the final breach with Germany until the end of the present régime; which in all probability means to the end of my days," Thomas wrote to Schickele on 2nd April 1934. And on 16th May, thanking Schickele for his appreciation of *Joseph:*

We may as well face the fact that all the things you so kindly note and quote are simply shouted to the wind as far as German ears are concerned. They don't even notice. The Germans want to know nothing; all they have in their heads is "the German people" — at the wrong moment, as usual.

"Unhappy, unhappy nation!" he concluded a letter to Ernst Bertram at the end of July 1934. "I have long ago reached the point of begging the World Spirit to liberate this nation from political life, to dissolve it and disperse it in a new world like the Jews, with whom so much kindred tragic destiny links it." The entries in Thomas' diary became longer and more bitter; they demonstrate the sharpness and clarity both of his analysis and his invective. Those Nazi writers who claimed after the war that Thomas' radio speeches had been messages of rancour from the security of a Californian villa showed not the slightest understanding of Thomas' position from 1933. His house, property, funds and assets had all been sequestered, and the Munich authorities had already applied (vainly), in the autumn of 1933, that he be deprived of his German citizenship. "One has continually to extract the necessary serenity out of the day's grim thoughts," he wrote to Frau Fischer on 8th April 1934; and to Samuel Fischer on 23rd August he confided: "The question of my Munich property I am allowing to go as it will. It concerns me least; whereas public events there continually excite my moral and critical conscience and my journalistic self which is used to reacting, and this has led to the work crisis which my wife has mentioned to yours, and from which I still have not emerged."[55]

On 4th August he wrote to Karl Kerenyi:

When I mention that perplexing "state of Europe" which involves such a complex of problems for the future, I have come to the chief disturbance from which my tranquillity, my peace of mind, my need for concentration, my psychic and even physical health, in short my productivity, have been suffering. I do not know how you as a scholar react to the developments of the day, to political events, so-called "world-history", but I suspect that you know how to keep yourself inwardly freer in regard to them than I can . . . The fate of my country — which also threatens to become the fate of the continent — never ceases to grieve me. Throughout this year and a half I have attempted honestly, though not with consistent success, to carry through my personal tasks in spite of that grief. But I cannot say how much I have been affected by the atrocities of 30th June, the Austrian horrors, and then the coup d'état of that creature, his further elevation, which undoubtedly represents a new consolidation of his tottering régime. I cannot say how much they agitate me and alienate me from the work that, if my heart were firmer and colder, I ought to regard as the only important thing. What concern is "world history" to me, I suppose I ought to think, so long as it lets me live and work? But I cannot think that way.

Therefore I shall probably turn from narration to another profession of beliefs such as I undertook at the time of the *Reflections of a Non-Political Man,* and the completion of my third volume will be postponed to the distant future. So be it. A man and a writer can only do what his fingers are aching to attack. It is logical that the crisis of the world should also be a crisis in life and work for me, and I must regard that as a sign that I am still alive. The time seems ripe for such a statement as I have in mind, and the moment might soon come when I would repent having delayed too long in silence.

To Schickele, on 10th August 1934, he wrote in the same vein:

Of course I am miserable about the novel, which in any case has been delayed, and I know very well how many arguments there are against such an investment of time and energy. Is there even any sense in neglecting finer duties to argue against this rot? On the other hand, isn't it also a duty which the world would thank me for? In short I vacillate and don't know what to put my hand to — a horrible condition. I have long since stopped caring about the breach with "Germany"; I want that breach and would much rather have my books issued outside.

It was a tantalizing moment in Thomas' life. He was well aware that in the writing of *Joseph,* as he had put it in a letter to Karl Kerenyi on 24th February 1934, he had turned from "bourgeois individuality to what is typically and generally human". Yet this very humanity denied the possibly of peace of mind in which to continue his epic. "I am often ashamed of engaging in follies and not doing what is probably my duty: to say some pertinent words on the subject to the world. Or of not doing it yet, at any rate," he wrote to Ferdinand Lion on 3rd September 1934.

Dr Bermann was adamant, however, that Thomas should continue to publish in Germany as long as possible, and had laid plans to publish a new volume of essays, centring on the fateful Wagner lecture. The laudatory essay on Hauptmann Thomas felt, however, he could not include; and thus, in the impasse in which he found himself in the late summer of 1934, he began to write "a light essay called *Voyage with Don Quixote*" based on his voyage to America, "a chatty associative thing which serves to gain me time and, moreover, will complete the volume of essays".

Sufferings and Greatness of the Masters was published the following year. It was the last work by Thomas Mann to appear in Germany until after the war, a tribute to all that Germany was in the act of destroying.

His denunciation of the régime was, as Heinrich predicted in his letter, postponed. But the sufferings continued, the completion of volume three of *Joseph* — *Joseph in Egypt* — required all the determination and discipline Thomas could command. But perhaps too it ensured that when finally Thomas did proclaim his political views, they came with all the conviction of a man who has employed every particle of patience, but who can no longer hold back.

9

Meanwhile, where Thomas was brought near to breakdown by his enforced silence on German affairs, Heinrich, having become perhaps the primary anti-fascist writer of Western Europe, suffered the same situation in reverse. The continual responsibility of providing moral leadership, both privately and in his writings, to the émigré cause made the writing of *Henri IV* seem sometimes an impossible enterprise. In October 1934 he gave way to requests to visit Czechoslovakia to give a series of speeches. As a guest of the Czech PEN Club in Prague on 19th October he delivered his speech to mark the 175th anniversary of Schiller's birth: *Nation and Freedom:* and on 26th October was introduced to the spokesman of the German Marxist émigrés in Russia, Johannes R. Becher. "The Czech police will look after my safety," Heinrich wrote to Bertaux before leaving for Prague. "If, despite everything, I am fired at, I shall perhaps just have time to reflect: it is well done; what was I getting involved in? I was born to write novels in peace and tranquillity. But a tranquil life is no longer accorded to anyone."[56]

The Sudeten Germans did indeed whip up a campaign in protest against Heinrich's anti-fascist speeches; and when, in response to a semi-official offer, Heinrich applied for Czech citizenship in the Reichenberg district, the Sudeten-German Home Front managed to thwart the application with a massive press assault on the whole German emigration.

For the time being, then, Heinrich remained stateless; and was only permitted to return to Nice after French ministerial intervention. It was the worst possible condition in which to write an epic Renaissance novel, and by January 1935 Heinrich too had reached a "crisis" stage, as he confided to Bertaux. Yet undoubtedly, too, the anxiety, threats and deteriorating future for Europe gave insight and actuality to the theme. "I am writing on my great king, whom the people also disliked at heart and in the end got sick and tired of, as with every good man. They cling happily only to 'Führers', of course, and to the bitter end," Heinrich had written to Thomas in

January 1934;[57] and if his portrait of Henry of Navarre was an idealistic one, it was not so much in a personal sense, but in a social and historical context: the struggle of a lonely, hated prince to achieve and to wield power for good in an age of religious incompatibility, of human treachery and continual war. No subject could have proved more actual in the 1930s; and it came as little surprise when the book rights were sold to America, Britain, Italy, Czechoslovakia and even Russia before the first volume was complete.

Henri IV marked the peak of Heinrich's literary career, both linguistically and in its treatment of the subject. Like *Joseph* — and yet how differently — it represented a new summit in German prose, combining the imaginative descriptive power of Heinrich's early writing with the terse, abbreviated thought-structure of his later work. "Happily I have something which gives me courage and which occasionally takes me back to the days when I used to write more colourful things," he wrote to Bertaux in April 1934;[58] and to Thomas at the end of the year, on 17th December: "It is an opportunity to vouchsafe scenes and images which I have preferred to carry within me all my life. In consequence there is a connection with my earliest works, quite an interesting one in fact. The editor at Mondadori's in Milan . . . wrote something to Stefan Zweig about the youthfulness of the narration — encouraging at my age. This much, however, is certain: my novels written during the Republic look old in comparison."

Henri IV had none of the serenity, timeless universality and mythic profundity of *Joseph*. It was written too hurriedly to be perfect; yet undoubtedly it must rank as one of the finest historical novels of twentieth-century Europe. "It moves me as the synthesis of all the gifts of the author," Thomas wrote about it in October 1935 to Schickele, "as a magnificent personal summation of his late and early thought, and also as the intellectual summation of the epoch from Montaigne to Goethe (see the little *Faust* quotations scattered throughout). The conjunction of the German and the French spirit is nothing less than the Faustian spirit of Germany and Greece." Though its style was virtually untranslatable, it was to become a bestseller in America.

For the moment, however, in the autumn of 1934, it was written against time (Querido had begun setting the type in Amsterdam since the summer) and against the responsibilities and expectations of the German emigration. His meeting with J.R. Becher in Prague convinced Heinrich that, despite the Comintern ban on coalition with Social Democrats, a combined anti-fascist front of all republican parties was now both necessary and possible if the spread of Naziism was to be contained. Becher assured him the Russian communists were similarly anxious to preserve German cultural and literary heritage; it was therefore up to the major republican writers of East and West to press for such a front. Thus the seeds of the 1935 Congress of International Writers for the Defence of Culture were sown, in which Heinrich was to take a leading part.

"I have never worked so hard" Heinrich wrote on 22nd May 1935 to Bertaux; "but one has to master oneself and pretend one is only thirty."

Even as the end loomed into view he had feared he might not be able to finish it, with his political articles taking up one out of every four weeks' work.

At last, on 12th June 1935, the first volume of *Henri IV* was ready: "My head is reeling with fatigue," he told Bertaux. "It has been on my hands for two and a half years." Yet even now he was given no time to relax. On condition that he be allowed to refer without let or restriction to the Nazi régime in Germany he had agreed to participate in the International Writers' Congress in Paris, beginning on 21st June. There, on 22nd June, the entire five-thousand strong audience rose to its feet to honour his appearance on the rostrum. Behind him sat André Gide, J.R. Bloch, Robert Musil, André Malraux, Karel Capek, Max Brod, Ilya Ehrenberg, Menno ter Braak and Willi Bredel; and among the other speakers of the Congress were Aldous Huxley, E.M. Forster, William Ellis, Bertolt Brecht, Ernst Toller, Henri Barbusse, Alexei Tolstoi and Louis Aragon. The great writers of European anti-fascism had begun to unite: and they honoured the man who symbolized their spirit, both as writer and campaigner.

While the Old World honoured Heinrich, the New World was again marking its respect for Thomas. Harvard now conferred the title of Honorary Doctor of Letters on Albert Einstein and Thomas Mann, and three days after his sixtieth birthday Thomas left Zurich for America to receive his degree.

The doctoral awards took place at Harvard on 20th June 1935; and when Einstein and Thomas were called forward they received a "mighty ovation" as Thomas wrote to Dr Bermann in July.[59] "I heard that the choice of us — of me in particular — did not come about without some influence on the part of President Roosevelt. He invited my wife and myself privately, without involving the Ambassador, of course, to the White House in Washington."

Roosevelt impressed Thomas deeply:

Completely paralysed for ten years, and yet this energy and experimental, not to say revolutionary, boldness. He has made enemies among the rich, whom he hurts, and among the guardians of the Constitution because of his dictatorial traits. But can one raise much objection nowadays to *enlightened* dictatorship?

It was Roosevelt's New Deal programme as well as his great administrative talent which was to inspire much of Thomas' portrait of Joseph in power; but for the moment he was still only half-way through Joseph's first Egyptian sojourn, as steward to Potiphar. "The third volume is indescribably difficult," he explained to Schickele. "I am now launched on that grand scene between Potiphar and his wife; Klaus commented that it had something of Proust. But then I must once again rework and compress the beginning of the volume; the approach is wrong there."

Thomas' first impulse, in fact, had been to decline the Harvard doctorate in order to concentrate on *Joseph,* and he had only been persuaded to accept by Swiss academics who assured him he would be mad to "throw such an honour to the wind", as he wrote to Ernst Bertram.[60]

Thomas returned to Zurich on 13th July 1935. He had visited Heinrich in Nice in May shortly before his birthday, and Heinrich had written an appreciation of his life's work in *Die Sammlung* in June — covering even Thomas' *Reflections of a Non-Political Man.* He pointed to Thomas' development since *Buddenbrooks,* his extraordinary path from the height of realism to his current mastery of mythological biblical history in *Joseph.*

"Dear brother," Heinrich's article ended, "despite everything it was, as you yourself know best, worth it. Above German heads, their classic authors towered like cranes, as someone once remarked in better days. For this very reason their place and importance, and yours, are more than assured: for they all move beyond the frontiers of nations . . . let us embrace one another now at your sixtieth birthday; we can do so across celebrations and frontiers as long as we live because we are brothers; yes, can even do it after we are dead, for we are writers."

By August *Henri IV* was ready for publication; and Heinrich had travelled to Briançon in the Hautes Alpes, in the hope of resting now that it was finished. However he slept badly ("which in practice means the holiday was useless" as he wrote to Thomas on 2nd September 1935). He had had word from other émigrés that a coup d'état was being prepared in Germany, and put off his intended visit to Thomas in Küsnacht largely for fear of the many Nazi spies said to be operating there. In September 1935 he was invited to join the praesidium of Romain Rolland's World Committee against War and Fascism, and though his lifelong struggle to promote the lessons and examples of French democracy among Germans had never brought the least French official recognition ("By rights he should long ago have received the Légion d'Honneur, not just the ribbon but the rosette," Thomas wrote to Schickele on 31st October 1935), nor his *Henri IV* even a French publisher ("All the world knows Henri IV and we didn't expect a foreign author to make a novel of his life. C'est évident," Heinrich had written sarcastically to Bertaux on 22nd May 1935), he had at last been granted citizenship — and thus a passport — in Czechoslovakia on 21st August.

But the anti-Nazi putsch came to nothing; and though Czech, Austrian and émigré journals welcomed the great novel of humanitarian resistance, there was now the second — and in many ways more important part — of *Henri IV* still to be researched and set down.

"Those madmen over there with their Jews!" he wrote to Thomas on 26th October 1935:

What will they do when there are none left? But they cannot think any further forward than their Jews. The idea that a poverty-stricken, dis-integrating Germany will have to be taken under foreign control and that it will become a colony — instead of the Ukraine — is no longer a fairy-tale. For everything can turn the other way.

10

The "madmen with their Jews" had, in September 1935, convened a special meeting of the Reichstag in Nuremburg to promulgate the infamous *Judengesetze*, depriving German Jews of most civilian rights. In June, as Heinrich had predicted, Hitler had made a naval agreement with Britain, and in March had reintroduced conscription, in defiance of the Versailles Treaty. Laval, the French Foreign Minister, was determined to co-operate with Hitler and sabotage the League of Nations' sanctions against Mussolini, who had launched his Abyssinian campaign. "If Fascism remains unshaken in Europe, only Laval is to blame. He is a thoroughly noisome creature, an incipient Fascist, who is negotiating with Berlin and now has even issued an ordinance for the protection of foreign heads of state and government chiefs." Thomas wrote to Schickele on 31st October 1935. "For my part I hail old Churchill and his golden words in the 'Strand Magazine'. A pure gleam of light." "It would not have been so simple had it not been for that pro-Fascist Laval," Heinrich had written in similar terms to Thomas five days before. "The right man always appears at the opportune moment if there is a chance to hinder any good that might be done."

Yet the International Writers' Congress had not been entirely without consequence. Already the French centre and left-wing parties were beginning to group together in a combined Popular Front to fight the following year's election; and in Paris the German émigrés had finally accepted Heinrich's appeal for unity in exile, constituting a Committee for the Establishment of a German Popular Front — including Social Democrats, Catholics, Communists and Independents — under the chairmanship of Heinrich himself.

The militant humanism, regardless of party, which Thomas had called for earlier in the year in his essay *De La Formation de l'homme Moderne*[61], was starting to show its face: and within months both the French and Spanish Popular Fronts swept to victory at the general elections.

In the meantime, as Dr Bermann now began to make somewhat belated efforts to extricate Fischer Verlag from Nazi Germany, Thomas' own moment of decision was approaching. In June 1934 Heinrich had written to him asking for his help in proposing Carl von Ossietzky, the former editor of the *Weltbühne*, for the Nobel Peace Prize. As Ossietzky had been imprisoned in a concentration camp since 1933 it was a proposal bound to cause political difficulties, and Thomas had not taken the matter further. But now, in the context of the seemingly unopposed slide towards fascism everywhere, Thomas chose to resurrect the proposal; and even to Heinrich's astonishment despatched a magnificent recommendation to the Nobel Peace Prize Committee in Oslo. On 26th October 1935 Heinrich congratulated him:

> Your letter to Oslo is to my mind your finest and most powerful declaration . . . Who knows whether your words will not work wonders; but because it seems unlikely, let us hope so all the more.

They did. To the consternation of Hitler and the Nazis the 1936 Nobel Peace Prize was awarded to Carl von Ossietzky — after which Hitler ordered that no German in future was permitted to receive the Prize.

It was Thomas' first attack on Nazi Germany, and he must have known the letter would be published if Ossietzky received the award. However, with

Bermann's move to leave Germany his last reasons for maintaining silence were in any case coming to an end. Heinemann in London had agreed to support Bermann in rebuilding the firm outside Germany, providing he were able to obtain a base in Switzerland. The Nazis had no objections as long as the old S. Fischer Verlag remained in Germany — under Aryan ownership and direction. Buyers were found and an arrangement made whereby Bermann take with him the books and publishing rights to some twenty-two authors.

But now the Swiss showed how awkward they could be: confronted by the prospect of the most distinguished publisher's literary list in the German language — including Döblin, Hofmannsthal, Wassermann, Zuckmayer, Schnitzler and Thomas Mann — and some 780,000 printed books, they refused permission for him to settle the new firm in Switzerland — and a nightmarish dash to Vienna followed.

Thomas himself was appalled by the small-minded envy and obstructionism on the part of the main Swiss publishers which had led to Bermann's plight. Eduard Korrodi, literary editor of the *Neue Zürcher Zeitung,* had supported the Swiss publishers in their objections to Bermann in December 1935; and when Korrodi published, in January 1936, a further article denying that German literature had "emigrated" — and categorizing what had as Jewish — Thomas decided to take up the cudgels. His letter to the *Neue Zürcher Zeitung* was printed on 3rd February 1936.

Being *völkisch* is not being German. But the German, or the German rulers' hatred of the Jews is in the higher sense not directed against Europe and all loftier Germanism; it is directed, as becomes increasingly apparent, against the Christian and classical foundations of western morality. It is the attempt (symbolized by the withdrawal from the League of Nations) to shake off the ties of civilization. That attempt threatens to bring about a terrible alienation, fraught with evil potentialities, between the land of Goethe and the rest of the world.

In the course of his letter, Thomas had pointed out that those writing in exile from Germany were not solely Jewish. He finished the letter:

Countless human, moral, and aesthetic observations support my profound conviction that no good can possibly come of the present German régime, not for Germany and not for the world. This conviction has made me shun the country in whose spiritual traditions I am more deeply rooted than the present rulers who for three years have vacillated, not quite daring to deny me my Germanism before the eyes of the world. And I am certain down to the bottom of my conscience that I have acted rightly in the eyes of my contemporaries and posterity to join with those to whom the words of a truly noble German poet apply:

> But one who baseness in his heart despises
> From hearth and home by baseness will be banned
> Whenever a servile nation baseness prizes.
> Far wiser to renounce the Fatherland
> Than to endure in all its childish guises
> Blind hatred and the rebel's heavy hand.[62]

It was the declaration all German émigrés had been waiting for, as well as many American, English, French and other European colleagues. Only Hermann Hesse, who had remained with the old S. Fischer Verlag in Berlin, was distressed; and Thomas was quick to set him right. "I believe," he wrote on 9th February 1936,

> I did the right thing at the right moment, "and feel better ever since" as the song has it. Moreover, I am not even sure yet that the gang will strike back. The Olympics, as well as considerations of foreign policy, will hinder them, and I think it quite possible that nothing at all will happen — although I shall never recover my property of course.
>
> Sooner or later I had to declare myself in clear language, both for the sake of the world, in which a good many highly ambiguous, half-and-half notions of my relations to the Third Reich prevail, and for my own sake as well.

Thomas was quite correct about the Nazis' reponse: for the rest of the year, while the Berlin Olympics took place, they declined to respond to his challenge.

In a sense, of course, they had more important preoccupations. Four weeks after Thomas' letter to the *Neue Zürcher Zeitung* Hitler reoccupied the Rhineland.

11

In the autumn of 1935, between preparations for the sequel to the *Youth of Henri IV*, visits to Paris in October and November and his regular *Dépêche de Toulouse* articles, Heinrich had managed to compile another book of essays in the style of *Der Hass: Es kommt der Tag* (The day is coming). It was "something neither serious nor comic, in honour of the Third Reich" as he put it to Bertaux on 20th December 1935, "But in it I have attempted a political psychology of the Germans, a rather curious subject. Moreover I want to interpose quotations from a number of famous authors and make it into a sort of reader — after which I wish to return to Henri IV."

Thomas Mann's son, Golo, helped procure some of the quotations, and the intended publication for 1st March 1936 was thus postponed. Hitler's march into the Rhineland, however, made it perhaps the most important analysis of its time — "a fulminating read" as Thomas wrote to Heinrich later, on 20th August 1936: "I am certain that this manifesto will one day be shown to have played a most honourable historical role — preserving the honour of Germany."

Though the book was translated neither into English nor French it was indeed a work of historical significance in saving Germany's honour: for here a proud and articulate German took apart the Hitlerian myth and demonstrated that the slide towards fascism was, above all, an insult to modern man's intelligence. It was perhaps here that the difference between Heinrich's and Thomas' anti-fascism — as between their great historical novels — was most clearly shown: for Thomas had to bear with him all the accumulated richness and profundity of the German — and European — cultural heritage before he could confront Naziism squarely: whereas Heinrich's response was unencumbered by Schopenhauer, Wagner or the depths of German romantic pessimism. Heinrich believed in the essential simplicity and clarity of the intellect — uncompromisingly — and *Es kommt der Tag* was in many ways the simplest and most powerful of his anti-Fascist manifestos. Almost alone among German bourgeois émigrés he had the imagination and courage to picture a Germany after Hitler. He was in no way a communist; he simply believed in a society of greater social justice, based on constitution and law which political leaders like all others should be subject to, which respected truth. "You see," says the teacher in a projected classroom of 1950:

It would offend our conscience to try and force a community, a nation, through radio broadcasts and denunciations, it would remain superficial like all mass measures. What we want is a genuine acceptance of the true principles of life which do not change, and agreement over which interests do. We do not live for the state and do not have to feed it with human masses. It ought to convince us that it can make us happier and better; and more important, it is up to us to convince ourselves; and that can better be done on our own. Our state will be constructed from hundreds of thousands of such groups as ours here today. It will be formed through knowledge, through the strengthening of character, I am only giving you the old lesson of morality; but at certain times in our history it grew weak, and that is why every decade there came a collapse and the opposite views were taken up. If now, against all expectations, a new world crisis were to hit us, would you, as before, fling all principles to the wind and scream aloud that what is right is what serves the state?

The Nazis in particular smeared Heinrich as a radical communist in the pay of the Jews; but his conception of state and democracy was radical only in its idealist and uncompromising belief in truth and wisdom. Against this he portrayed the deceit and endless lies of Hitler and his followers in merciless and often amusing analytic prose. One had to be mad or to have discarded all claims to rationality to believe in Naziism and in fascism after reading a work such as this.

Yet the rise of fascism was not going entirely unopposed now. Though neither the French nor the British government dared oppose Hitler's bluff in the Rhineland, a Popular Front coalition won the elections in Spain in February 1936, and in France that spring. For a moment it looked as if the menace of fascism would be checked in Europe — until Sanjuro and Franco staged their uprising in July 1936.

"It's war. It's war! O, God's angel protect us — which he had already done, in fact, in stopping us from going to Mallorca, upon which the bombs are now crackling," Heinrich wrote to Thomas on 2nd August 1936. They had arranged, tentatively, to holiday together in Mallorca in the summer after both turning down an invitation to travel to Buenos Aires; and they now agreed to meet together in France, on the south coast.

Franco's war was to develop into the seminal confrontation between fascists and republicans in Europe. Italy sent 100,000 men to assist Franco, and Goering mobilized arms, men and the growing German Luftwaffe to go in too. "If the Spanish Republic wins, it would be an incomparable act of herosim for these times," Thomas answered Heinrich's letter on 4th August. But no one held out much hope.

> The zealousness with which the capitalist press — for instance our own "Neue Zürcher Zeitung" — watches over French neutrality, whereas that of Italy and Germany do not concern it in the least, is of bottomless infamy . . . Your bitter phrase that "Franco will not permit himself to be provoked" epitomizes the whole sad story. The thought that in this way Germany might become *very* strong and Hitler rise to honour and distinction, often robs me of my sleep.

It robbed Heinrich of sleep, too; for with the prospect of a fascist belt stretching from the Baltic to the Mediterranean peninsulas any hope of a peaceable outcome in Europe — let alone the collapse of Hitler's Reich — seemed doomed. With his letter in February to the *Neue Zürcher Zeitung* Thomas had openly entered the anti-fascist arena; time was running out and they both now rose to the occasion — as before they had attempted to rally the sinking spirit of the Weimar Republic. In Vienna, in May 1936 in honour of Sigmund Freud's eightieth birthday, Thomas delivered a carefully-prepared speech, *Freud and the Future;* and in June he travelled to Budapest for a meeting of the Comité de la coopération intellectuelle to which he contributed an updated version of his *De La Formation de l'Homme Moderne* essay entitled *Humaniora and Humanism.* It ended on the same note of appeal for a militant humanism, capable of defending both humanity and Europe's cultural heritage. Yet even this seemed to him, in the circumstances, too indirect; and at the end of a colleague's talk, he seized the opportunity of giving an improvised speech denouncing the "assassins of freedom" — and earning a minute-long burst of applause from the Hungarian audience as well as an "enthusiastic embrace from Karel Capek, the Czech dramatist, who died of a broken heart when the democracies betrayed his country."[63] The Nazis were furious at the press coverage given to Thomas, and the German ambassador rang the Hungarian Home Office to request that less attention be paid to him. "No one took any notice of the threat," Thomas wrote to Heinrich on 2nd July 1936. "But isn't it charming: the German ambassador protests against the interest shown by the press in the only German participant in a meeting of European intellectuals."

Meanwhile Heinrich, now Chairman of the official Committee for the Establishment of a German Popular Front, had assumed the difficult task of uniting Communists, Social Democrats, Catholics and Independents into a single force. At the meeting of the World Committee Against War and Fascism in Paris at the beginning of July, Heinrich strongly argued against inviting Nazi delegates to the forthcoming World Peace Congress, due to take place in England; and with the outbreak of the Spanish Civil War two weeks later and Hitler's intervention, his reasons were justified. It was pointless to talk peace to Hitler: it was essential to unite the minds and forces of anti-fascism.

The World Peace Congress in fact took place in Brussels, between 3rd and 6th September 1936, with more than four thousand delegates present, and Heinrich had to leave Thomas in Le Lavandou in order to be present. On behalf of the German anti-fascists in exile he had already sent a message to the republican government in Spain, declaring their support; and over the next year countless of numbers of addresses to workers in Hitler's Reich, calling on them to sabotage war material intended for Spain, were illegally distributed in Germany.

Yet neither Heinrich nor Thomas stopped work on their great historical novels, despite the many interruptions. "For myself, I write with my memories and my experience, which comes to the same thing," Heinrich wrote to Bertaux on 22nd August 1936. "All this goes into my *Henri IV*. As for the numerous combative articles I have to write, it is a different matter: there I have to act the young man, at which I don't do too badly." Slowly the sequel to *Henri IV* was taking shape; and Heinrich looked forward to the next volume of *Joseph:* "particularly the love-story", Heinrich had written to Thomas on 3rd August 1936.

Joseph in Egypt was finally completed on 23rd August. It had "accompanied" him, as Thomas put it in a letter to Bruno Walter on 25th August, throughout his three and a half years of exile. It was still not the end of the Joseph story, and the erstwhile trilogy would become at least a tetralogy now — if Thomas could go on to finish it. "Once done, the whole will at least be a memorable curiosity, if nothing more," he wrote to Dr Bermann in Vienna, where the new Bermann-Fischer Verlag had been set up.[64]

By setting the type of the main part of the book before Thomas completed the final chapters, Bermann was able to announce publication in October 1936 — a remarkable technical achievement.

But in the meantime Thomas had set his heart on writing an "interlude" before continuing with the fourth volume of *Joseph:* a novella which permitted Thomas to do what he had hankered to attempt since 1930 — and in fact since his earliest days as a writer: a portrait of Germany's greatest man of letters, Johann Wolfgang von Goethe.

It was to be a sidelong, serious, and yet irreverent look at genius. The great *Joseph* saga rested. "I am spending my mornings and actually all my days and nights, spying out the terrain, without having fully clarified the form for myself," he wrote to Bermann.[65]

By the time he had begun writing, however, the German government had acted. and the "most eminent living man of letters" was deprived of German citizenship.

12

Again and again he joined in the pronouncements of international and mostly Jewish manipulated organizations whose hostile attitude to Germany was well-known. In recent months he has repeated his pronouncements openly with *treasonable attacks* on the Reich. On the occasion of a discussion about the merit of emigrant literature in a well-known Zurich newspaper he declared himself unequivocally on the side of the state's enemies and addressed the most serious insults against the Reich, which were widely denounced in the foreign press. His brother Heinrich, his son Klaus, and his daughter Erika have already been deprived of their German citizenship owing to their unworthy activities abroad for some considerable time . . .

The announcement was dated 2nd December 1936, the grounds given were headed: *Traitors of the People and Enemies of the Reich,* and the list published in the *Völkischer Beobachter* on 5th December. Telegrams and messages began to pour in from all over the world. On 19th November 1936, Thomas had been granted citizenship in Czechoslovakia, in the same area (Prosec) as Heinrich the year before, so that he was not left stateless. "It is almost like receiving the Nobel Prize," he wrote to Dr Bermann on 5th December, inundated by congratulations and expressions of support. "It was inevitable," he wrote to Stefan Zweig on 8th December, thanking him for his "soothing" note. "But that does not make it any less nonsensical. There is a truly pretty irony in the fact that I am at the moment writing a novella on Goethe." And in answer to the *Berner Tagwacht's* request for a statement, "I have already on several occasions declared in advance that I am more deeply rooted in German life and heritage than the fleeting figures who rule Germany at the moment."[66]

Yet precisely because of this profound awareness of heritage the news also depressed him. Sigmund Freud had written to him in late November, and in answering his letter Thomas confessed his days had been "somewhat clouded, although I am foolish to let them be so, by the Berlin decree pronouncing me an outcast". He thanked Heinrich for his *Welcome to the Expatriate* in the *Neue Weltbühne* on 10th December — "again one of those small moral poems which have only indirectly to do with 'politics' and which, I believe, will one day be valued very highly by the world, Germany not excepted" — but he was still filled with "rage at all the heartache and suffering that those infamous rulers have caused and continue to cause," as he wrote to Konrad Engelmann on 15th December. "God knows, I was not born for hatred, but I hate those bloodthirsty fools and corrupters from the bottom of my heart and fervently wish them the dreadful end they deserve."

So far, however, he had left the world press to draw its own conclusions from his expatriation. It was a political act which spoke for itself. But then, on 19th December 1936, the Dean of the Philosophical Faculty of the University of Bonn wrote to inform Thomas that "as a consequence of your loss of citizenship the Philosophical Faculty finds itself obliged to strike your name off its roll of honorary doctors". Ten days later Thomas set down his reply: an exchange of letters which was to become a landmark in twentieth-century European cultural history.

A German author accustomed to this responsibility of the Word — a German whose patriotism, perhaps naively, expresses itself in a belief in the infinite moral significance of whatever happens in Germany — should he be silent, wholly silent, in the face of the inexplicable evil that is done daily in my country to bodies, souls and minds, to right and truth, to men and mankind? And should he be silent in the face of the frightful danger to the whole continent presented by this soul-destroying régime, which exists in abysmal ignorance of the hour that has struck today in the world? It was not possible for me to be silent . . .

To what a pass, in less than four years, have they brought Germany! Ruined, sucked dry body and soul by armaments with which they threaten the whole world, holding up the whole world, hindering it in its real task of peace, loved by nobody, regarded with fear and cold aversion by all, it stands on the brink of economic disaster, while its "enemies" stretch out their hands in alarm to snatch back from the abyss so important a member of the future family of nations, to help it, if only it will come to its senses and try to understand the real needs of the world at this hour, instead of dreaming dreams about mythical "sacred necessities". Yes, after all, it must be helped by those whom it hinders and menaces, in order that it may not drag down the rest of the continent with it and unleash the war on which as the *ultimate ratio* it keeps its eyes ever fixed. The mature and cultural states — by which I mean those which understand the fundamental fact that war is no longer permissible — treat this endangered and endangering country, or rather the impossible leaders into whose hands it has fallen, as doctors treat a sick man — with the utmost tact and caution, with inexhaustible if not very flattering patience. But it thinks it must play politics — the politics of power and hegemony — with the doctors. That is an unequal game. If one side plays politics when the other no longer thinks of politics but of peace, then for a time the first side reaps certain advantages. Anachronistic ignorance of the fact that war is no longer permissible results for a while of course in "successes" against those who are aware of the truth. But woe to the people which, not knowing what way to turn, at least actually seeks its way out through the abomination of war, hatred of God and man! Such a people will be lost. It will be so vanquished that it will never rise again.

The meaning and purpose of the National Socialist state is this alone and can be only this: to put the German people in readiness for the "coming war" by ruthless repression, elimination, extirpation of every stirring of opposition; to make of them an instrument of war, infinitely compliant, without a single critical thought, driven by a blind and fanatical ignorance. Any other meaning and purpose, any other excuse this system cannot have; all the sacrifices of freedom, justice, human happiness, including the secret and open crimes for which it has blithely been responsible, can be justified only by the end — absolute fitness for war. If the idea of war as an aim in itself disappeared, the system would mean nothing but the exploitation of the people, it would be utterly senseless and superfluous . . .

So ran Thomas' reply to the Dean. It was soon quoted in almost every newspaper in the Western world and published in book form in Switzerland, England and America. It aroused fury inside Germany where illegal copies circulated quite openly and in foreign newspapers impossible to suppress — so much so that by 26th January 1937, Goebbels gave orders that the German press should "on no account concern itself with Thomas Mann", and forbidding any form of polemical discussion as this would "only make Thomas Mann known in even wider circles and strengthen the inner opposition of those who stayed behind". He was to be "eradicated from all memory and no longer mentioned to German youth".

Heinrich, however, was both delighted and moved. On 19th January 1937, he wrote to Thomas:

I read your exchange of letters with great pleasure. You say everything in one fell swoop, and with the greatest effect. I have to start each time at a different point in my many articles and never come to an end. Rest assured, you missed nothing by your silence; what you say now is the final word.

For a time it was, and Thomas could return both to his work on his novella *Lotte in Weimar* and also to an entirely new project in his life: the founding of a new literary magazine.

13

Heinrich, meanwhile, worked ceaselessly on the second volume of *Henri IV*. His brief visits to Paris on behalf of the German Popular Front Committee and the League of German Writers in Exile as well as his articles became dutiful interruptions to a work which, as he had written to Thomas in March 1934, contained not only the fruits of a lifetime's experience, but represented probably the consummation of his talents as a writer. "My life is becoming almost monastic," he had written then;[67] the effort to complete volume two turned out to be no less demanding. "A complete absence of leisure is one facet of my new life," he wrote to Bertaux on 31st December 1936; and some of the loneliness of the exile he had been able to render in his account of Philippe de Mornay's flight to England — "a country he loves", as Heinrich explained to Bertaux, "but where he only finds, in the end, one friend worthy of the name. When later you read these pages," Heinrich added, "I would like you to see in them a discreet monument to your fidelity and of my gratitude to you."

Sometimes, as he had written to Thomas in March 1935, the news from Germany came like fairy tales, and he returned to his novel "as though to the truth and to real life".[68] Yet it was these "fairy tales" from Germany, the bitter fighting in Spain, and the perilous condition of Europe which made him see in Henri IV such a symbol for modern civilization. The effectiveness of Thomas' exchange of letters had been reported from numerous visitors to Germany; "yet more defeats are being inflicted on these people in Berlin," Heinrich wrote to Thomas on 4th June 1937, "the blows are falling harder. It is hardly comprehensible how they hope to last much longer. Their only chance is dubious England — for war, if they want to take recourse to that, cannot truly be considered a chance." Yet even here, when trying to share a word of optimism with Thomas, Heinrich could not conceal the truth: "I must confess, however," he added, "that for days I have only opened the newspapers with trembling hands; and the danger will only come to an end with that of the régime — whoever doubts it will have to learn the hard way." In the context of Hitler's massive re-armament, the open talk among industrialists in Germany of approaching war, and the increasing measures taken against the Jews, Henri IV's struggle to unite the Catholics and Huguenots in Renaissance France appeared to Heinrich an unparalleled example of courage and humanity within the history of Europe.

"I leave behind me the Edict of Nantes," Heinrich wrote to Bertaux on 21st August 1937, "which already in those days was one of the most perilous undertakings ever assumed by a simple man. In this respect, how is it that history has made of King Henri such a lecherous character, a sort of joker? For he was profoundly serious, possessing an intellectual tenacity bordering both on the tragic and the sublime. The rest is a mask, scrupulously preserved, of the popular hero. I am coming to the death of his Gabrielle, and I tremble at the thought."

In the figure of Gabrielle d'Estrées, Henri's mistress, Heinrich had undoubtedly invested much of his feeling for his own extraordinary mistress, Nelly Kroeger, to whom he clung with both paternal and almost child-like fidelity. For Heinrich, René Schickele noted in his diary, Nelly represented womanhood in its most fundamental essence. "For forty years he has turned to thick-set women with low brows but powerful wrists and who 'know life'," he recorded in March 1934.[69]

> There is no other possibility than that the store of humanity that he brings to bear in these relationships, is itself replenished by them. It is the humanité brute, the raw material of humanity, that attracts him. The type of woman from one's earliest experience is decisive. Lübeck, where it is darkest. Strange mixtures of narrow-minded bourgeoisie and depravity. He sees himself as Professor Unrat, but would like to die as Chief Engineer Birk [Die grosse Sache]. And he will die as that, most certainly. He is both the one and the other. The older he gets the more he longs for the warmth of the *heart*. He seeks it where it is darkest and perhaps most simple . . .

It was indeed one of the strangest relationships among the German émigrés: the most respected and distinguished writer and publicist living with the simple Berlin bar-girl, alcoholic and attractive, a good cook and an impossible guest.

For the moment, though, Heinrich was still living among the characters of his novel when the King's mistress was treated as a Queen; and yet, when the King wished to marry her, must die.

It was in the autumn of 1937 that Heinrich heard rumours he had been put forward as candidate for the Nobel Prize — a prize he did not want, yet which, he felt, would represent a further moral blow against Germany after the award to Ossietzky.

But Ossietzky was dying; and Hitler stronger than he had ever been.

In the meantime in April 1937 Thomas again travelled to America, at the invitation this time of the New School for Social Research in New York. "I indulged somewhat to excess for my age in lectures, dinner speeches and meetings," he confessed to Freud on his return[70] — having spoken not only at the New School, but also to the recently founded American Guild for Cultural Freedom, sponsored a move to found a German Academy in America, and spoken at a memorial service for the victims of fascism. His speech, *The Fight for Freedom*, was published that summer in Moscow;[71] yet it was Thomas' own "freedom of the soul and cheerfulness" which were furthered by the "distancing from Europe" as he put it in a letter to Karl Kerenyi,[72] and he and Katja began seriously to consider spending a proportion of each year in the United States. Almost as though to point a moral he fell ill with neuralgia on his return to Switzerland, and in June he went for a cure to Ragaz. The Goethe novella, however, was "at last moving forward again by a page every day," he wrote to René Schickele at the end of May.

It is only barely going, for I have been limited to an extremely inadequate ration of sleep. Towards midnight I take phenodorm and sleep until three. Then the pains start and I dissolve two anodal tablets in camomile tea. That lasts me until five. Then it's finished, and I can no longer find any position that is endurable even for a few minutes. And what do you do then with a morning that has already started so early?

The new magazine had also to be launched, now that an anonymous patron had set aside sufficient funds for its publication. It was to be called *Mass und Wert* (Measure and Worth), and while internationally it was to be a literary and cultural magazine, unpolemical in nature, Thomas made quite clear in his introductory article that this was not from cowardice. "The craving for human decency, for freedom, reason, and justice, for measure and worth, is not one to be underestimated today," he wrote; there was a growing mood of dissatisfaction with the simplicistic power-ideology of fascism. He was not afraid to be called a socialist either:

Socialists? We are. Not necessarily because we swear by the Marxist philosophy . . . Socialism is nothing other than the duty-prompted resolve not to hide our heads in the sands of metaphysics, in face of the most urgent material demands of the collective social life. Rather let us range ourselves with those who would give meaning, a human meaning to the earth.

Thomas became editor-in-chief with Konrad Falke, while Ferdinand Lion undertook the actual editorship of the journal. The first issue appeared in

September 1937 in Zurich. Simultaneously a postscript by Thomas appeared in a new publication in Zurich published by the Swiss Foundation for the Help of Workers' Children: *Spain — People in Need*:

An insurrection of generals, occurring in the interest of the old exploiters and oppressors, concocted with the help of hopeful foreign interests, blazes up and misfires. When it is already as good as beaten, it is propped up by foreign governments inimical to freedom, in return for promises of strategic and economic advantages in case of victory. It is supported by money, men, and material, fostered and prolonged, until there seems no end to the bloodshed, the tragic, ruthless, obstinate carnage. Against a people desperately fighting for its freedom and its human rights the troops of its own colony are led into battle. Its cities are demolished by foreign bombing planes, women and children are butchered; and all this is called a national movement; this villainy crying out to heaven is called God, order and beauty . . .

It was an uncompromising document, written with passionate intensity; it scarcely seemed possible that against the background of such engagement in the European struggle, interrupted by his "silly triumphal tour" to America (as he had called it to Schickele) and his ill-health, he could manage to create a work which in some ways exceeded even *Joseph* in its artistry. But in the November 1937 issue of *Mass und Wert* appeared Chapter Three of *Lotte in Weimar* — and it dazzled the literary enthusiasts among German émigrés and Swiss readers.

The story, it was becoming evident, would extend far beyond the limits of a small novella. In October Thomas managed to complete Chapter Four; but a new lecture on Wagner's *Niebelungen Ring* had hurriedly to be prepared for the Zurich Stadttheater, as well as a political lecture he had agreed to undertake for a tour in America the following spring. "Please don't make complaints and demands," he wrote to Ida Herz on 8th December 1937; "they add to the nervousness that plagues me anyhow, because I have had to neglect my fictional work for so long that I won't be able to think of it again until May, and even then only continue with *Lotte in Weimar;* Joseph does not even come into question."

In America, to the audience at the New School for Social Research he had explained how difficult it was to lead such a dual life:

These four years past — I say four years, though the process has been going on for twenty — I have had to defend the work that means most to me, the work that is most intimately mine, the work which contains my greatest joy and happiness, against demands upon me which I recognize as duties, noble and urgent duties, but which approach me from the outside, from the civic and political world.

Immersed in the last years of *Henri IV*, Heinrich found himself in an identical position: one day crying "real tears" for Gabrielle d'Estrées; the next, drawing up an appeal to the world democracies to stand firm over Austria. In the face of so much conservative vacillation among the democracies and the suspicion that economic interests in the West preferred

Naziism to communism in Germany, both Thomas and Heinrich emphasized more and more their belief in a socialist future for mankind.

If democracy wishes to make its undoubted moral superiority over fascism effective and challenge its pseudo-socialism, it must adopt in the economic as well as the spiritual domain as much of socialistic morality as the times make imperative and indispensable. Here, likewise, freedom must be restored through social discipline. Democracy must continue to develop the bourgeois revolution not only politically but also economically.

So ran Thomas' speech *The Coming Victory of Democracy* which he took to America in February 1938; and Heinrich's appeals were made in even stronger terms, culminating with his German Popular Front articles published in the *Neue Weltbühne* in April, November and December 1937.

Yet however hard both Thomas and Heinrich tried, neither harboured much hope in their hearts for either Germany or Europe; and Thomas, in fact, now resolved to live in America. "I believe that for the duration of the present European dark age the centre of Western culture will shift to America," Thomas prophesied in his speech. "It is my own intention to make my home in your country, and I am convinced that if Europe continues for a while to pursue the same course as in the last two decades, many good Europeans will meet again on American soil." After Hitler's annexation of Austria in March, it was difficult to doubt.

14

Thomas' fourth visit to America began on 21st February 1938, and his itinerary took him right across the United States, from New York to Chicago, Philadelphia, San Francisco, Los Angeles and back. He was still in New York when German troops crossed the border into Austria on 11th March, and "for weeks we truly believed we would never see Europe again", he wrote to Félix Bertaux.[73] In the circumstances his speech *The Coming Victory of Democracy* gained an extraordinary topicality, and every performance was packed out, as well as winning extensive press coverage. "This was the first piece of work entirely for the American public," Thomas wrote of the speech in his foreword to *Order of the Day,* the collected volume of his political speeches in 1942; "thus it constitutes the bridge in my life, the literary transition from the old world whose ground was slipping from under my feet, to the new . . ."

Eight days after the Austrian Anschluss, Thomas wrote to Agnes Meyer, wife of the publisher of the *Washington Post,* that he had decided to settle in America; and from Illinois, in May, he drove to Canada in order to follow official immigration procedure.

In California in April Thomas had also set down his thoughts in a series of diary entries, part of which — concerning Hitler — would be published the following year under the title *My Brother.* In a letter to Arnold Zweig in December 1935 Heinrich had reflected how in fact he had lived most of his life among foreign peoples — "including Bavarians and Prussians" he had added laconically.[74] Now, in Beverly Hills, California, Thomas expressed the same feelings: "How often," he wrote in his diary, "have the scenes of an earnest game, that cheerful struggle against the passage of time, changed since the schoolroom of my childhood where I first tried to cool my joy and suffering in the framework of the word? Some seemed as though they would last; I would return to them from interim abodes, they were called 'home'. But even they turned out to be temporary . . ."

"What is homelessness?" he asked elsewhere in the diary:

My home is in the works I carry with me. Engrossed in them I experience all the familiarity of home: they are language, German language and thought, a personally developed inheritance from my country and my people. Where *I* am is Germany . . .[75]

And against this pride and certainty he pictured Hitler, his "brother":

Here is a man of a bottomless resentment and a festering desire for revenge; a man ten times a failure, extremely lazy, incapable of steady work; a man who has spent long periods in institutions; a disappointed bohemian artist; a total good-for-nothing. And here is a people obsessed by powerful though far less justifiable feelings of defeat and inferiority, and unable to think of anything save how to retrieve its lost "honour". And then he — who had learned nothing, and in his dreamy, obstinate arrogance would learn nothing; who had neither technical nor physical discipline, could not sit a horse, or drive a car, or fly a plane, or do aught that men do, even to begetting a child — he develops the one thing needful to establish a connection between him and the people: a gift of oratory. He rouses the populace with images of his own insulted grandeur, deafens it with promises, makes out of the people's sufferings a vehicle for its own greatness, his ascent to fantastic heights, to unlimited power, to incredible compensations and overcompensations. He proceeds from the masses of Germany to the masses of Europe, and learns to apply in a larger setting the same technique of hysterical humbug and soul-paralysing ideology which raised him to greatness in the smaller one. With masterly adroitness he exploits the weariness of the continent, its agony of fear, its dread of war. He knows how to stir up the peoples over the heads of their rulers and win large sections of opinion to himself.

Ah, the artist! I spoke of moral self-flagellation. For must I not, however much it hurts, regard the man as an artist-phenomenon? Mortifyingly enough, it is all there: the difficulty, the laziness, the pathetic formlessness in youth, the round peg in the square hole . . . Then the bad conscience, the sense of guilt, the anger at everything, the revolutionary instinct, the unconscious storing up of mines of compensatory wishes; the obstinate need of self-justification, self-proof, the urge to dominate and subdue, the dream of seeing the whole world abased in fear and love, admiration and remorse, at the feet of the once-despised! . . . There is also present the insatiable craving for compensation, the urge of self-glorification, the restless dissatisfaction, the forgetfulness of past achievements, the swift abandonment of the prize once grasped, the emptiness and tedium, the sense of worthlessness so soon as there is nothing to do to take the world's breath away; the sleepless compulsion to make one's mark on something.

A brother — a rather unpleasant and mortifying brother. He makes me nervous, the relationship is painful to a degree. But I will not disclaim it. For I repeat: better, more productive, more honest, more constructive than hatred is recognition, acceptance, the readiness to make oneself one with what is deserving of our hate, even though we run the risk, morally speaking, of forgetting how to say no . . .

Our notion of genius has always been shrouded in a superstitious haze. But I question whether today the haze is thick enough to prevent our calling this man a genius . . . If genius is madness tempered with discretion (and that *is* a definition!), then the man is a genius . . . I will not decide whether history has ever produced a specimen of mental and moral baseness accompanied by the magnetism we call genius, to compare with this one to which we are the amazed witnesses . . .[76]

The "bridge" in Thomas' life had been crossed; and it was as an American immigrant that Thomas returned to Switzerland at the end of June 1938 to arrange his final departure for the United States. In Jamestown, Rhode Island, he had taken up his work on *Lotte in Weimar* once more — his true role, he felt.

Heinrich had hoped to finish volume two of *Henri IV* by the spring of 1938, for by December 1937 the American edition of volume one had sold 17,750 copies and the publisher there was pressing Heinrich for the sequel as soon as possible; but it was August 1938 before the last page was sent off. "I am terribly tired," he wrote to Bertaux on 23rd August; but proud too to have completed a book "in which I have invested my whole self, and beyond which I have no great expectations." Thomas had invited him for a week to Küsnacht. "I hear your great work is finished," he had written to Heinrich on 6th August 1938.

If so that would be glorious — and the time is particularly favourable for a visit . . . We are starting our "homeward" journey to Princeton on 15th September. Would you be our house guest in Küsnacht toward the end of the month and into September? The woods and lake shore, an easy drive, are so beautiful, and you would be coming to a country whose attitude toward *l'infame* has turned into the most gratifying resoluteness since Austria. I have never felt endangered for as much as a moment, and no one need even know that you are here. What do you think?

In Zurich Thomas must have discussed with Heinrich his leaving Europe, the special Professorial post he had been offered at Princeton University lecturing on the German novel; yet despite the rapidly deteriorating prospects for peace Heinrich showed no desire to follow him. He had finally taken an unfurnished apartment in Nice; and, at the risk of losing all, as he had done in Berlin in 1933, he intended to furnish it himself, he wrote to Bertaux from Küsnacht on 29th August. France had been his "home" since leaving Germany: had afforded him not only sanctuary but a living, and the subject of the most important work he had written in his life. "This work," he had written to Bertaux on 1st November 1937, "is, in effect, a serious tribute to the greatest monarch Europe has ever had. The course and destiny of his life teach me, as I write about it, to overcome the sorrows of our own times and to gain some insight into how they might be bettered." From London his English publisher wrote in November 1938 to say he preferred the second volume to the first. "How could it be otherwise," Heinrich wrote to Bertaux on the 4th, "since all the great questions arise only with the coming of maturity of life?"

"As far as I can see at the moment," Heinrich wrote to Klaus Pinkus on 30th November 1938, "I have put pretty well my entire experience into this novel, and have no new one in mind. It would be sad to have to write a historical work again after this one; on the other hand I am not going to let myself in for contemporary novels. What can the convulsive misbehaviour of this race today mean to a writer who is to some degree knowledgeable in human affairs? Too much already, with all my articles — which are to be published soon in book form, collected and futilely. The book is to be called *Courage* . . ."

From the painful assassination of Henri IV, Heinrich turned once more to his moral and political role among the German anti-fasicsts. It was indeed a futile activity. In September, shortly after Heinrich had returned from Zurich, Neville Chamberlain had flown to Berchtesgaden; and at the end of the month Czechoslovakia had been ceded before Hitler's threats. It was obvious the feeble democracies of the West would not confront any threat of war; and Heinrich's bitter experiences in trying to unite the varying political factions of the German Popular Front in Exile had made him lose all hope except in a revolt by the Germans themselves against their Führer.

Chamberlain's sham peace had been secured, transparent to all but the wilfully obtuse. Yet though he held no further illusions about the eventual outcome, Heinrich continued his stream of anti-fascist publications, with his speeches broadcast on short-wave radio into the German interior, as well as hundreds of thousands of copies of his appeals and articles disseminated in the Reich under the guise of advertising brochures: *German workers! You are our hope!, Unity!, United against Hitler!, To the German people!, Defend yourselves!* "I can no longer count the number of my manifestos. My aim in all this is the same as yours," he wrote to Thomas on 25th May 1939: "the German uprising must come before war."

15

Thomas learned of Chamberlain's visit to Berchtesgaden in Paris, shortly before embarking on the *Nieuw Amsterdam.* "I would gladly have written to you long ago" he wrote to Erich von Kahler on 19th October 1938:

But you can imagine how I have been living: first the disturbing days of uncertainty in Paris, then the week of depression along with the painfully inadequate news aboard ship, then the hours of tense hope after arrival here, culminating in a gigantic mass meeting in Madison Square Garden, at which I spoke and witnessed tremendous demonstrations; then Munich, and the realization at last of the filthy play which was being performed all along. The dénouement came when the "democratic" governments transmitted Hitler's blackmail threats of war to their own peoples ... The shame, the disgust, the shattering of all hopes. For days I·was literally sick at heart, and in these circumstances we had to install ourselves here.

"In our New York hotel we got the news of what the Chamberlains and Bonnets had done," Thomas wrote in the foreword to *Order of the Day:*

Never shall I forget how broken Albert Einstein's voice sounded when he spoke to me over the phone on my arrival in Princeton. "I have never in my life been so unhappy" he said. That was the feeling of all good people. The Goethe novel, which I had brought with me from Europe three-quarters finished, had to retire into the background while, in my still unsettled study, I wrote *This Peace.*

The new house at Princeton was large and "very comfortable".

The landscape is parklike, well suited to walks, with amazingly beautiful trees which now, in Indian summer, glow in the most magnificent colours. At night, to be sure, we already hear the leaves trickling down like rain, but people say that the clear, serene autumn often continues until early Christmas . . .[77]

This Peace, however, was far from serene. For the German émigrés, Hitler's actions now were only a repeat performance of what had already taken place once in their lives when the Weimar Republic was felled. For them it was a case of duplication, enacted before an outside world experiencing it for the first time. "Fortunately," Heinrich had written to Bertaux in March 1938, nearing the end of Henri IV's life, "a man's old age is in itself a foreshortening. What happens to him no longer has the freshness and importance of youth; it is the repetition, usually futile, of the déjà vu."[78]

"They have too much inherent consistency, those events," Thomas wrote in *This Peace:*

They were treachery and crime, in the guise of hypocrisy and demoralized pacifism; but however unfortunate and disastrous, they were too positive, they were rooted too deep in the collected will of Europe — employing as its instrument the classic hypocrisy of English statesmanship — not to be regarded as decisive for many decades to come. Those who had hoped for a better, more humane evolution in Germany and Europe have been as much betrayed, sold out, sacrificed, as the brave little land which stood in the path of German fascism on its march towards European hegemony. It is uncanny to see how the wretched figure of von Papen, the conservative who delivered up Germany to Hitler, recurs again in the English Chamberlain. Everything is the same: the treachery, the underlying motives, above all the fundamental self-deception . . . Another Abyssinia was a bitter necessity to the régime — and England gave it to them. There was no room for doubt. England wanted and was working for the preservation and reinforcement of the National-Socialist régime . . . This movement, aided, according to a set play, by the ruling classes of England, won its final triumph in the last days of September 1938 . . . For all those horrors [after the annexation of Austria] England, as the protector of the Nazi invasion, bears the full responsibility . . . It is hard to imagine the mentality of these British statesmen, conscientious only in the service of their own class and their own interests, passing their days in their clubs and their government offices, their weekends in the country — and wholly undisturbed by thoughts of the thousand-fold cases of individual tragedy which were willy-nilly the accompaniment to their astute calculations.

It is one of the foulest pages in history, this story of the betrayal of the Czechoslovak Republic by European democracy . . . The fault is ours — though perhaps it is to our credit that we were not politicians enough to see it through. Despite all that had gone before, including the transparently disingenuous and disgraceful comedy of non-intervention, carried out by England in favour of France, we could not credit the possibility of such heaped-up knavery and manoeuvring. Our simplicity was culpable. What else could it be but hypocrisy, to behave as though one believed in those pulings about "our brothers in Sudetenland" when everybody knew that it was not a question of the brothers, but of the Skoda works, Czech industry, Rumanian oil, Hungarian grain, Germany's economic penetration eastwards, the liquidation of Czechoslovakia as a military and diplomatic factor, the break-up of the French and Russian alliance, the isolation of France?

The essay appeared immediately in book-form in America published by Alfred Knopf, in November 1938. It would not be long, however, before the word peace in the title would have to be replaced by that of war.

In November 1938 came publication too, of the second volume of *Henri IV*, both in America and Holland. It was several months before Thomas obtained a copy in German.

On 2nd March 1939, he wrote to Heinrich:

Your novel arrived at last a few days ago. And I can truly say that I am reading it day and night, by day in every free half-hour, and at night in the quiet before I switch off the lamp — which, thanks to you, happens late. As I read I am never without the sense of an exciting uniqueness, the sense of having to do with the best, the proudest, the highest this age has to offer. Certainly people will someday wonder how our debased times could bring forth anything of this sort — and will realize that all the blatant idiocy and crimes are not so very important after all and that the human spirit, fundamentally undisturbed, meanwhile goes its way and creates its works. It must be said that such growth — such transformation of the static to the dynamic, such perseverance, and such a harvesting — is particularly European. Here in America writers are short-lived; they write one good book, follow it with two poor ones, and then they are finished. "Life" in the Goethean sense belongs to our tradition alone; it is less a matter of vitality than of intelligence and will . . . I can imagine that the German exiles as a group feel proud of this monument! And ultimately, for don't we know how such things go, Germany too will take pride in it. "For he was ours." Well, yes, in a manner of speaking.

Thomas was on the eve of a new transcontinental lecture tour across the United States, this time with a new speech, *The Problem of Freedom.* The American novelist James T. Farrell had sabotaged Thomas' planned anti-fascist manifesto signed by all the most distinguished representatives of the "moral and spiritual world" by publicly attacking the still unpublished version in the columns of the *Herald Tribune;* nevertheless Thomas was rapidly becoming the focus for German-speaking émigrés, particularly of those still trying to leave Austria and Czechoslovakia. "My correspondence, which for years has been very large, has swollen frighteningly, and no fewer than three people have to help me," he had written to Dr Bermann — now established in Stockholm — on 6th December 1938.

On 6th June 1939 Thomas left New York for what was to be his last journey to Europe for another decade. It was his sixty-fourth birthday. On 18th May he had been made an honorary doctor at Princeton University at a special ceremony, and on 2nd June the League of American Writers had appointed him Honorary President of the organization — a unique tribute to a German author still of Czechoslovak nationality. The President of Princeton University had again offered him a guest-professorship for the winter term 1939/40, and to Mrs Meyer Thomas confided he would "probably accept . . . For the present we are looking forward to our European holiday — with plenty of time for work I hope. First Switzerland, then a Swedish seaside resort."[79]

Heinrich met Thomas in Paris, where they were able to spend a few days together. "If it's at all possible we hope to pay you a visit in Nice before our holidays are over," Thomas wrote a few days later on 19th June, "so that we can see your new home and continue our Paris conversations in a domestic atmosphere." Thomas spent the following seven weeks in Noordwijk aan Zee, in Holland, and every morning in his beach-hut he was able to work — first a foreword to a new American edition of *Anna Karenina,* and then the continuation of *Lotte in Weimar,* which Bermann had already begun to set in Stockholm.

On 7th August Thomas left for Zurich, with *Lotte in Weimar* nearing completion; on 18th August 1939 he flew to London to see his daughter Monika, and from there to Stockholm as German representative at the International PEN Club meeting.

However Thomas was unable to deliver his speech to the meeting, for on 1st September 1939 Hitler invaded Poland; and two days later England and France declared war. Thomas and Katja flew back to London immediately, in order to catch the United States Lines liner *Washington* which was due to leave Southampton for New York on 9th September. The Swedish aircraft's route took it over German territory, where new Nazi regulations forced it to fly low. When Katja asked the Stewardess why this was necessary, the Stewardess explained — adding that on the previous day a German aeroplane had forced them to slow down and had inspected the passengers' faces through the windows. Opposite Katja a Jewish-looking man fainted; there was fortunately no cause for alarm though Katja did insist on taking Thomas' usual place by the window. They arrived eventually in England, after stopping in Amsterdam. On the following day, however, the same aircraft was shadowed by a German aircraft and one passenger shot dead in his seat — possibly mistaken for Thomas, it has been said.

"We had a somewhat distressing, perhaps even perilous trip home, first by air to London and then on the overcrowded SS *Washington*," Thomas wrote later.[80] "I carried many papers, lecture notes, and books with me, which were the object of tedious inspection at the remote and camouflaged London airport. The inspecting officers were particularly suspicious of a sketch representing the seating arrangement at a dinner that Goethe gave in his house on the Frauenplan in Weimar in honour of the sweetheart of his youth. It was suspected of being of strategic importance, and I had to deliver a condensed lecture on the novel in order to convince the officials of the complete innocence of the paper." The *Washington* finally left Southampton three days late, with more than 2,000 passengers on board, its lounges crowded with improvised cot-beds.

In Princeton Thomas settled down in solitude to write the last pages of *Lotte in Weimar*. It was then sent to Portugal by way of the Swiss diplomatic bag, and from there to Stockholm by Swedish aircraft. It was somewhat longer than the novella Thomas had characteristically first intended, and so authoritative that at the Nuremberg Trials some seven years later the British prosecutor, Hartley Shawcross, would quote from it under the impression that they were Goethe's own words.

A new "exile" had now begun for Thomas. This time, however, he was unafraid to speak out. Behind him lay a series of works which would ensure his reputation for all time: and before him were even greater achievements: the final volume of his *Joseph* tetralogy, the great twentieth-century version of *Doctor Faustus,* the completion of the first part of his comic masterpiece *Felix Krull,* and a series of some of his finest shorter novels, short-stories and literary essays. Once, much earlier in his life, Thomas had predicted he would only first come into his own in his sixties. That he did so against the background of a new World War and its consequences — including the razing not only of his homeland but the town of his birth and childhood — says much for a man who at heart felt so profoundly German.

For Heinrich the future would be very different.

CHAPTER FOURTEEN

The Second World War

Though Hitler was not to invade France for a further eight months after the outbreak of war, the beginning of hostilities nevertheless marked the end of Heinrich's career as a major writer in the Western world. The end of *Henri IV*, where the king casts his eyes down upon the world from a cloud, was symbolically Heinrich's own end.

The *Last Days of Henri IV* was in fact chosen as the *Times Literary Supplement's* First Choice for Fiction in mid-July 1939: but it was to be the last work of Heinrich's to be translated into English, and was never re-issued. Unlike Thomas, Heinrich had never concerned himself with the Anglo-American world, his heart was in Continental Europe: and with its demise came Heinrich's own as a writer. The times themselves had become, as Heinrich explained in a letter at the end of 1939, the real novel of the age.[1] In May 1940 Hitler invaded France, and German victory followed with alarming speed. The German Popular Front was disbanded and its members were forced to fend for themselves. Some fled to further exile, some committed suicide; the rest were captured by the Nazis and invariably shot.

Heinrich, as their President, ought not to have remained in France: but he was nearing seventy now and his whole being revolted at the notion of leaving the country that had given him refuge for six years, and which represented so deeply the ideals of civilization to which he held firm. "As for me personally, I would be permitted to go to America or Russia," he had written to Bertaux in March 1939, "but it goes without saying that I will undertake nothing without being clear that Goschi is safe. Even if I knew she was out of danger, I revolt at the idea of entering another exile. We are no longer in 1933 when one could take a train to — as one hoped — temporary refuge. Henceforth I know I shall not witness the end of these tribulations. Best to stay put.''

But Heinrich's decision — like that of so many German émigrés — was misguided. Goschi, his daughter, never did get out of Czechoslovakia, and though the Pétain armistice guaranteed a French-controlled southern territory of France, Article 19 agreed to the extradition of all persons wanted by the German government. Once again Heinrich's life was in danger.

On 9th September 1939 Heinrich had married his Berlin mistress, Nelly Kroeger — just as, after the outbreak of the First World War, he had married Mimi. "By marrying her I can help her get well," Heinrich wrote to Thomas — for Nelly had already tried to take her own life. "After ten years, which were not all easy, she has richly deserved it."[2] Yet even here Heinrich was to meet with failure: Nelly made one further unsuccessful attempt at suicide before they left France; in the end, in the wasteland of Hollywood, she did succeed.

Heinrich cabled Thomas in Princeton to ask his help in obtaining an entry visa for the United States, but it was August 1940 before the papers could be got to the American consulate in Marseilles — and by then the French Vichy press had begun a furious campaign denouncing the German émigrés as the primary cause of the catastrophe. Heinrich was listed as the chief public enemy.

Heinrich and Nelly were secretly brought to Marseilles. Police patrols were arresting all foreigners without residential permits and it was only by impersonating the Prefect of the Bouches du Rhône that Heinrich avoided arrest when stopped one night.

There remained, too, the problem of leaving France. Vainly the Czech consul had attempted to get an exit visa for Henrich to leave France, and without such authority each further day spent in Marseilles became more dangerous. "Above all I was concerned with obtaining help from America. I would have no idea where to begin," Heinrich wrote later; "but in the meantime a good friend appeared" — Lion Feuchtwanger.[3]

Feuchtwanger, though largely forgotten today, was the most successful of all the German émigré authors, his historical novels selling in millions all over the world from Russia to America. He proceeded to prepare their escape as if it were the plot for one of his novels, taking into account the people involved and the opportunities open to them.[4] Tunisia offered a temporary haven until they might find a boat to Portugal; but without exit papers they could only hope to persuade a fishing boat to take them across the Mediterranean. Feuchtwanger rejected the idea. "What sort of novel would it have been if on the high seas our rented boat had been stopped by an enemy vessel," Heinrich wrote later, "and the cargo for North Africa had revealed only three mutton carcasses and six still living émigrés? Poorly conceived and weakly composed."[5]

It was decided they would, therefore, have to cross the Franco-Spanish border on foot, avoiding the frontier post — an exhausting and possibly dangerous procedure for a man nearing seventy. A young American

Unitarian promised to act as guide, and at 3 a.m. in the morning the party of émigrés left Marseilles by train for the Pyrenees — Heinrich and Nelly, Lion Feuchtwanger, Franz and Alma Werfel and Golo Mann, Thomas' second son who had escaped from a Vichy internment camp. "I will not easily forget the steep road leading to the station, empty except for our party, with our rucksacks which we let dangle from our arms to look as natural as possible," Heinrich recorded. "They contained everything we possessed at hand. Our baggage was to follow later . . ."[6]

In the foothills of the Pyrenees they lost their guide and had to make their own way up the 2,000 metre goat-paths, Heinrich stumbling and falling amongst the thorn-bushes, supported by his wife. Finally a second American guide found them and directed them to the path which led down into Spain. From Barcelona they travelled fifteen hours by train to Madrid; and then, ironically, they flew to Lisbon by German Lufthansa.

All air flights from Lisbon to America were booked up, but eventually, after weeks of waiting, they managed to get on board a Greek steamship, the *Nea Hellas*. It was during their passage from Lisbon to New York that Mussolini invaded Greece.

"The view towards Lisbon presented the harbour — the last image as Europe faded. It seemed indescribably beautiful. A lost lover is not more beautiful. Everything life had given us had come from this continent, the joy and suffering of one of her ages that was mine . . . It was a parting of exceeding sadness," Heinrich wrote.

"The sea was monotonous, as ever . . ." wrote Alma Mahler-Werfel in her notebook.[7] "Heinrich Mann stayed in his cabin as he was sick. He was also feeling angry with the world. When his nephew went to see him he was in bed. He was drawing women with large breasts; sometimes just the latter."

The *Nea Hellas* docked safely in New York harbour on 13th October 1940. Thomas and Katja were there on the quayside to greet them. "Cheerful and full of hope we disembarked on the 13th — yes, unfortunately on 13th October," Alma Mahler-Werfel noted. "To our misfortune the ominous number would be justified." Neither Werfel nor Heinrich would leave America alive.

But more ominous for Heinrich's literary future in the "golden land" were the newspaper reports. The *New York Times*, recording the arrival of the Greek steamship, informed its readers that Golo Mann, celebrated German author (he had yet to write a book!) and son of the famous novelist Thomas Mann, had arrived on American soil, "accompanied by his uncle Heinrich".

2

Meanwhile, having finished *Lotte in Weimar* in the winter of 1939 Thomas had written a sequel to his speech *This Peace: This War*. It was something "energetically pro-British" as Thomas wrote to Stefan Zweig on 4th January

1940, something which "came from the heart and with utter conviction." It was also filled with "pain and anger," as Thomas admitted in his Foreword to *Order of the Day,* the English volume of his political essays and speeches published in 1942; and it was this bitterness which would make his return to Germany after the war impossible.

What Hitler had done in 1936 in the Rhineland, even the Austrian Anschluss and the rape of Czechoslovakia in 1938, could still be viewed as the frightening behaviour of a mad dictator and his clique of supporters. However the declaration of war, the invasion of Poland forced Thomas at last to consider the responsibility of the German people itself for the crimes they were committing. "Is it possible that any German, in full possession of his senses, who witnessed this spectacle believed even for an hour that this régime wanted peace, that the war was forced upon it and the German nation by malignant foes?" he asked in *This War.*

Did not the Germans know this? Had they so little vision that they did not realize they were confronting the catastrophe which the National-Socialist régime made unavoidable from the very outset, even indeed from before its birth, if the phrase may be permissible, and that nothing else could come of it but this catastrophe?

Thomas concluded they had known; but looking in all honesty at the country, at Hitler's fantastic popular success, Thomas felt they would endure the consequences too:

They will suffer privation, shed their blood, and stand fast year after year; for a hysterical mountebank has restored Germany her honour.

At the end of the war, in an article written for Thomas' seventieth birthday, Heinrich gave perhaps the most perceptive account of Thomas' development in relation to Germany. Thomas was, he said, born "to represent − not to reject. He defended Germany as it was in earlier days against the anger of the world and his own doubts. His conscience had a hard journey before it decided against his own country . . . Today my brother is the one who is deeply stirred. More than most people his country disappointed him. What Germany has made of itself since − or how it permitted itself to be seen − enemy of reason, of thought, of the human: an anathema − all this affected him the more personally, the later it did so. He felt betrayed . . . He believed Germany was ethically safeguarded − hence his anger which shows no compromise."

This War marked the final crystallization of Thomas' feelings towards his own nation, his own people. Though he became an American citizen and came to speak German at home only, his sense of final betrayal stayed with him; the once silent émigré now became Germany's bitterest foe. *This War* was followed in 1940 with his essay-speeches *The War and the Future* and *War and Democracy;* and in October of that year the first of his fifty-five BBC radio broadcasts to Germany: *Listen, Germany!*

3

"I feel that it is my duty to write and tell you that I believe you grossly underestimate the terrible danger of Naziism," Thomas wrote to Edward Edwards on 23rd June 1940:

When you tell me that our enemy is not Hitler but war hysteria, and that the Allies incite alarm to encourage intervention, then I — as a German who knows what this vile thing, Hitlerism, is — must in all sincerity protest against such views.

You say that wars and depressions are but dream manifestations of alarm and that the remedy lies in more optimistic and less pessimistic views. Today there is room neither for optimism nor pessimism but only for courage and action.

It was not easy, however, for Thomas to set aside his creative work. Three days after the above letter he was writing to the Editor of *Foreign Affairs,* Hamilton Armstrong, to apologize for not keeping his promise to contribute a political article. "I am sixty-five years old now," he explained, "have not spared myself during this time, and world history has not done so either. I will not be granted all that long to complete my own creative works. I believe I would do better to concentrate on them rather than spending the rest of my days filling the political pithos of the Danaids."

Yet the perilous situation of England after the fall of France, the helplessness of the German émigrés stranded by the Vichy settlement, and above all the growing danger of American appeasement forced Thomas to continue his public campaign against German fascism. Personal misfortune, too, added to his conviction, for on 23rd September 1940 a German U-Boat sank the British evacuation ship *City of Benares,* crowded with women, children and men unfit for military service on their way to Canada. Among them were his daughter Monika, her husband Jayö Lányi and their baby. Monika and the child were saved and brought back to Scotland after twenty-four hours in the sea, but Lányi drowned before her eyes. News, too, began to arrive of the suicide of Thomas' revered Dutch friend Menno ter Braak and the German execution of Dutch and French anti-fascists. "I cannot say how shocked and embittered I am," Thomas wrote to Agnes Meyer on 24th September 1940. "When will America's Flying Fortresses join with the RAF to put an end to this bestiality?"

Yet when Thomas spoke out in uninhibited political terms, as in *War and Democracy,* Mrs Meyer was deeply offended. It was a speech which, as Thomas confided to Ida Herz on 4th October 1940, "could not have been more pro-British, and whose open criticism of America's conduct since September 1939 was not only swallowed" (at a dinner for 400 "friends" of the Colleges of Claremont, California) "but repeatedly greeted with long applause. That is only a symptom. Whether Wilkie or Roosevelt, I believe we shall have this country at war by the spring." In January 1941, however, Thomas learned how much the lecture had "pained" his patron.

Je fais la guerre — and you want to see me au dessus de la mêlée — in your kindness. But this mêlée is a decisive battle of mankind, and everything will be decided in it, including the fate of my life's work. For decades, at least, my books will not be allowed to return to Germany, into the tradition where they belong, if the wretched rabble should triumph, collecting those dividends of victory prepared for them over eight long years by a sluggish, craven, oblivious world. You don't know what I have suffered in these eight years, and how intensely I wish that the most repulsive baseness that has ever made "history" will be destroyed — and that I will live to see it happen.

A few weeks before, Thomas had written to the American writer Joseph Campbell, regarding the latter's anti-political lecture *Permanent Human Values*.

The question as I see it is this: What will become of the five good things which you are defending, or think you are defending; what will become of the sociologist's critical objectivity, of the scientist's and historian's freedom, of the poet's and artist's independence; what will become of religion and humanistic education, if Hitler wins? I know from experience exactly what would become of all these things everywhere in the world for the next generation, but a good many Americans do not know it yet, and therefore they believe that they must defend these good things by the method and in the spirit that you do.

It is curious: Since you are a friend of my books, you must think that they have something to do with "permanent human values." Now these books are banned in Germany and in all the countries Germany at present dominates, and anyone who reads them, anyone who offers them for sale, anyone who speaks well of me in public, would end in a concentration camp, and his teeth would be knocked out, his kidneys bashed.

"It is said, 'Who is not for me is against me'," Thomas wrote to Agnes Meyer. "But who is not against evil, passionately and with his whole soul, *is more or less for it.*"

Both personally, through Frank Kingdom's "Emergency Rescue Committee", and in his political speeches and statements Thomas had now taken over from Heinrich the mantle of champion of the German democratic, anti-fascist cause. After arranging Heinrich's entry visa for America and helping to bring him from Europe, Thomas also fixed up a Warner Brothers post in Hollywood for a year for Heinrich, at a generous salary of $6,000 per annum. It was there, at the house of Salka Viertel, that Heinrich celebrated his seventieth birthday (several weeks late, owing to Thomas' doctoral honours at Berkeley) on 2nd May 1941; and Thomas paid tribute to the one who had "perceived and comprehended" the modern duties of the writer "earlier than us all":[8]

You, dear Heinrich, you perceived and comprehended this new condition of the spirit earlier than us all; you spoke the word "democracy" when all of us were helpless to know where to begin with it, and you proclaimed the totality of all that is human, including politics, in works which are both the highest art and prophecy in one. Do we not feel books like

Man of Straw, Professor Unrat, The Little Town today as fulfilled prophecy? If genius is the power of anticipation, the passionate portrayal of things to come, then your work carries the mark of genius and over and above its artistic ventures it is a moral phenomenon. I spoke of a simplification and rejuvenation of the spirit, of the mind — your fighting manifestos against the infamy which now raises its foamlike head, these fighting broadsides in their mixture of literary splendour and . . . I would almost say: fairy-tale simplicity, popular humanity, they are the magnificent example of this . . .

A whole generation ago, dear brother, you gave us the myth of Professor Unrat. Hitler is no professor — far from it. But Unrat [excrement] he is, nothing more, and will soon be but the rubbish of history. If you have, as I trust you have, the organic patience to persevere, your old eyes will yet come to see what you described in your youth: the end of a tyrant.[9]

However, before the assembled guests could rise for the toast to Heinrich's health, Heinrich also rose, also put on his glasses and also brought forth a thick manuscript. "First he thanked me for the evening," Salka Viertel remembered:

Then, turning to his brother, paid him high praise for his continuous fight against fascism. To that he added a meticulous literary analysis of Thomas Mann's oeuvre in its relevance to the Third Reich. I no longer remember all the moving and profound thoughts expressed in both speeches. It gave one some hope and comfort at a time when the lights of freedom seemed extinguished in Europe, and everything we had loved and valued in ruins. At the open door to the pantry the "back entrance" guests were listening, crowding each other and wiping their tears . . .

I said to Bruno Frank how touched I was by the wonderful homage the brothers had paid each other.

"Yes," said Bruno. "They write and read such ceremonial evaluations of each other, every ten years."[10]

4

Thomas' political stand before fascism, however anguished, however demanding, had seen not stagnation or paralysis in his creativity but a continuing abundance. No sooner had he finished his Goethe novel in the autumn of 1939 than he conceived a new novella — as removed from the world of Goethe or even Joseph as could be imagined: *The Transposed Heads*. "I am writing something Indian now," he wrote to Agnes Meyer on 5th January 1940, "a grotesque Maya tale belonging to the cult of the Great Mother, in whose honour people decapitate themselves — a play on disunity and identity, not very serious, at most a curiosity, and I still don't know if I shall complete it."

It was finished in August 1940, one of the finest of Thomas' shorter works.

The material for the story Thomas had found in Heinrich Zimmer's book on Indian mythology; nevertheless Thomas was pleased when *The Transposed Heads* appeared in English in the spring of 1941, and a Hindu critic accepted not only his "improvised India" — as Thomas wrote to Mrs Meyer on 11th June 1941 — but also his sensual hermit Kamadamane, whom the three protagonists of the tale consult in their dilemma. Once again Thomas had shown his mastery of myth and legend — not, as *The Times Literary Supplement* claimed, in weighing them down with complexity, but rather the reverse: in penetrating the complexity of myth and legend with all the accumulated insight and techniques of a twentieth-century writer; with psychological depth, humour and humanity. In this respect *The Transposed Heads* was indeed, as Thomas had written to Mrs Meyer on 27th July 1940, shortly before finishing it, "a divertissement and intermezzo", in the larger task of his *Joseph* tetralogy, which he had meant to continue after finishing *Lotte in Weimar,* itself an interlude. "Working with themes invented long before, transforming and elaborating them, carrying them all to a crowning climax, I now had to add a cheerful *'Götterdämmerung'* to my three existing fairy-tale operas. I looked forward to it — and yet I was reluctant to go to work," he wrote in his Foreword to *Joseph.*

It was not because the clay had become dry in the many turbulent years. With tooth and nail I had clung to the old task amid all distractions, and it was alive within me. The reason for my reluctance was simply this: that I feared an anti-climax, a falling off of the fourth volume from the third. The latter, *Joseph in Egypt,* seemed to me unquestionably the artistic zenith of the work, if only on account of the humane vindication that I had undertaken in it, the humanization of the figure of Potiphar's wife, the mournful story of her passionate love for the Canaanite major-domo of her pro forma husband . . .

It was at ·this stage that *The Transposed Heads* was written; and "in Brentwood, California, where I spent the spring and part of the summer of 1940, I found the long-silent tone of the biblical saga again, and the opening chapters of *Joseph the Provider* were written."

Writing to Agnes Meyer he disputed that his political concern had influenced his writing for the bad.

Have I behaved badly during these years and permitted hatred to degrade and paralyse me? I have written *Joseph in Egypt, Lotte in Weimar,* and *The Transposed Heads,* works of freedom and gaiety and, if you will of distinction. I am a bit proud that I have brought all that off, instead of joining the ranks of the melancholics, and I feel my friends should regard the fact that I go on fighting as a sign of strength, not of weakness and humiliation.

In January 1941 both Thomas and Katja had been guests again at the White House — "where we were granted astonishing honours," Thomas informed Mrs Meyer.[11]

The dizzying height was the cocktail in the study — while the other guests had to cool their heels below. And yet we had already had early breakfast with "him"! "He" once again made a strong impression upon me, or shall I say, again aroused my sympathetic interest: this mixture of craft, good nature, self-indulgence, desire to please, and sincere faith is hard to characterize. But there is something like a blessing upon him, and I am drawn to him, so it seems to me, as the born opponent of the creature that must be toppled . . . Why should I not take his part? I felt strengthened afterwards.

Roosevelt's impact on Thomas went deep into *Joseph the Provider* — whose hero, as he wrote in his Foreword, wore a distinctly American "god-mask" for this last volume, "For it is the mask of an American Hermes, a brilliant messenger of shrewdness, whose New Deal is unmistakably reflected in Joseph's magic administration of national economy."

Thomas had in fact begun work on *Joseph the Provider* only a few days after completing *The Transposed Heads* in August 1940. He had already decided not to teach again at Princeton — "I don't think, even if we stay here, that I shall let myself in for such amusements again. I must be free for the 4th volume of Joseph, which must be ready by my 70th birthday (if possible a few years before)," he wrote to Agnes Meyer, and throughout the autumn of 1940 and the whole of 1941 he dedicated himself to this task, as well as continuing his political speeches and BBC broadcasts. In September 1940 he had bought a plot of land near Los Angeles — "with 7 palms and a host of lemon trees," he wrote to Ida Herz — and after some hesitation and a Federal loan work began on a new villa. While the house was being built they rented a "nice, rural, practical little house" in Pacific Palisades, not far from the new site.[12] "In this my favourite season of the year it is also lovely here, although I liked it better in Küsnacht and even in Princeton. Here everything blooms in violet and grape colours that look rather as though made of paper . . ."

However the news from Europe reached its lowest ebb that year. German panzer troops had left for North Africa in December 1940, and on 6th April 1941, Hitler's forces invaded Yugoslavia and Greece. In May a German airborne attack on Crete was launched; and on 22nd June Operation Barbarossa opened along the whole length of Russia's European frontier. Smolensk fell within four weeks: and still America remained neutral. "For the present England can expect only further defeats, and if America cannot be roused, we may well come to the point of asking ourselves whether we are not going to lose this campaign," Thomas wrote to Erich von Kahler on 1st June 1941.

Heinrich meanwhile was becoming more and more unhappy in Hollywood, where "loneliness and ingratitude" had begun to bite.[13] The Warner Brothers contracts, like those of MGM Studios, were basically honorary arrangements guaranteeing distinguished European refugees — among them Döblin, Werfel, Walter Mehring, Leonhard Frank — at least a financially secure first year in the United States. Nevertheless such authors were expected to work eight hours a day preparing scenarios — none of which were taken seriously. "Naturally everyone who has made a film would like me to see it," Heinrich wrote to Thomas on 16th November 1940. "I see it and say something. Actually I could say something without having seen it." Like Brecht he rarely spoke in English, though his linguistic skill had enabled him to pick up the language, especially when written, quite quickly. Yet no one asked Heinrich either to speak publicly or contribute newspaper articles, and in the Hollywood studios he was remembered only as the author of *The Blue Angel*. He had never been gregarious, and did not now seek company outside the small circle of emigrant writers living in and around Los Angeles. That America should have passed up this champion of European democracy, perhaps the most lucid and perceptive of all Hitler's opponents among European intellectuals, was undoubtedly a tragedy; yet to a large extent it was one of Heinrich's own making: he was simply too old to respond to the youthful demands of the New World. When for instance Knopf accepted the manuscript of his 1939 war diary for publication under a number of editorial conditions in the summer of 1941 Heinrich simply refused to comply: "Heinrich Mann declined, he thought he was writer enough to decide *for himself* what *HE* ought to write!" Nelly Mann reported to a friend in September 1941.[14]

It was now that Heinrich's error in not having visited America in the 1930s on the publication of *Henri IV* came home. Already Thomas had more than six honorary doctorates in America, had twice held the post of visiting professor of Literature, had toured almost every major town and university in the United States, and had even broadcast on radio, in the framework of the Emigration and Naturalization Service of the US Department of Justice, under the title *I am an American.*[15] When Warner Brothers — like MGM — failed to renew their émigré scriptwriter contracts after a year, Heinrich was left destitute. By the end of September Nelly had sold all her jewelry and it became imperative to find a cheaper house or flat. In March 1941 Heinrich and Nelly had had to travel to Mexico to conform to official immigration rules, and Thomas had signed an affidavit agreeing to take care of or finance his brother should he fail to be able to support himself ever. "I ask you unwillingly," Heinrich wrote to Thomas on 23rd February 1941, "since I do not know whether it is merely a question of form or entails serious contractual responsibilities for you." By the end of 1941 Thomas was, in fact, having to help. The story of Joseph had come true.

Yet if Heinrich was entering a critical phase of his life, so too was America. On 7th December 1941, the Japanese attacked Pearl Harbour, and the United States, belatedly as in 1917, finally entered the war.

5

"The attack on Pearl Harbour affected me deeply," Thomas wrote to Mrs Meyer on 16th December 1941.

How could the base have been caught so much off guard at this juncture? And things will be harder still. I don't imagine that the Far Eastern and

Pacific theaters of war will provide much cause for rejoicing for months and perhaps for years.

For a while the state of hostilities looked grim. At the beginning of June 1942 Rommel launched his great armoured offensive in North Africa and was soon nearing Cairo; on 28th June the second German offensive opened on the Russian Front, this time bringing them to the suburbs of Stalingrad and almost to the Caspian Sea. On 26th May Hitler's notorious SS-Chief Reinhardt Heydrich had been assassinated; two weeks later, to the horror of the Allied world, the village of Lidice was razed to the ground.

Thomas' monthly broadcast to the European continent was devoted to the infamy of what had happened at Lidice: but the hurt, the shame at German cruelty and bestiality, and the culpable negligence of the civilized world for having allowed it to happen went much deeper.

I am not otherwise hostile to man and can say with Joseph that we, mankind and I, "mostly smiled at each other". But that the civilized world allowed *this* to grow, no, *nurtured* it to fruition, that is my great and bitter disappointment with humanity, and I shall take the grudge I bear about it to my grave.[16]

It was now, if at any time, that *Doctor Faustus* was born. Other writers like Brecht had confronted the problem of Naziism earlier in their fictional, creative work; Heinrich, using notes he had been making since 1940, began a new attempt, a cinematic novel entitled *Lidice* that was published in Mexico the following year.[17] But as in all his work, Thomas needed time to gestate. "I spoke first, but he was the one who was prepared," Heinrich wrote later of the very first novel they had planned together in Italy in the dying years of the 19th century.[18] *Lidice* was completed within a few months, but it was not a success and led to great embarrassment later with the Czech authorities. As once in his comic scenes between Hitler and Hindenburg in *La Haine* in 1933, Heinrich found the fascist mentality *could* only be rendered in grotesque comedy, for it simply defied civilized credibility. "The latest novel *Lidice* you didn't like," Heinrich wrote to his friend F.C. Weiskopf later:

And I understand: only, nothing else was really to be expected from me in view of the circumstances. I made a point of showing evil in its comic aspect — for the nth time in my life. These fatal Germans violate a country which is dear to me . . . there they exaggerate even themselves . . . They become dangerous fools; against them the simple folk in the country scenes attain something almost holy. Their humour, their cunning show the evil ones, no less than like dance or song: what is it you are struggling for? The best is the simple.[19]

Lidice, unfortunately, was too infamous a case to be used in such a way; all over the world it became a symbol — as later the opening of the German concentration camps — of something far too serious for mankind to mock. Yet in Heinrich's case it was understandable. "I had very early had grave doubts about Germany, to the natural indignation of my brother," he wrote in his memoirs. "But what can one do against one's own spontaneous impressions?"[20] Since the early years of the twentieth century he had "perceived and understood" what was happening in Germany: and warned. In *Henri IV,* taking place four centuries previously, he had identified so many of the ailments that had accompanied Hitler's rise to power: political infirmity, assassination, religious intolerance, mob violence, the unwillingness to compromise in the furtherance of higher ideals. He had reached the point at which Henri surveys present time from the clouds, mixing wisdom with extreme simplicity. His very style, in German, reflected this development: and like his first writings, as works of art his fiction now became inaccessible to most readers. Heinrich himself was aware of the parallel with his youth:

As for myself I still struggle to satisfy my profession. Literally I write for myself at the moment, as once I did in my first, obscure beginnings.

That he was forging a style and language of the future, not even Thomas doubted; and the development of post-war German literature was to demonstrate the fact. In the meantime, however, there was neither a German market for his books, nor in translation a readership capable of responding to the masterly sagacity, sardonic humour and intellectual firmness of his writing. It was a problem confronting many of the German émigré authors — including even Brecht who had to distribute typescript copies of his poems to his friends in Hollywood in the absence of a publisher for his work.

Thomas found himself in the opposite situation. Just as he had once conquered Germany with his *Buddenbrooks* and novellas, so now — with all the intellectuality, wisdom and human concern of his age — he had conquered America. In 1939 *Life* magazine had devoted a main feature article on his life and work; by 1942 even the *New Yorker* had commissioned a series of articles on perhaps the greatest man of letters living in the United States. Towards the end of 1942 he was offered 1,000 dollars for a foreword to a new book on the Ten Commandments; the Library of Congress (thanks to the energetic efforts of Mrs Meyer) had appointed him a Consultant in Germanic Literature at a salary of almost 5,000 dollars a year, and he had to ward off requests for lecture tours and speeches. However the day was approaching when, after all the publicity, propaganda and journalistic work he had dedicated to the anti-fascist cause, he would be drawn, like Heinrich, to write about contemporary Germany in his fiction.

First, however, *Joseph the Provider* had to be finished. He had hoped he might finish in the late spring of 1942 after several bouts of inspired narration ("you should hear the second half, it is perhaps the strangest and best narrated of all that I have done," he noted in a letter to his daughter Erika,[21]) after the move, in February 1942, into the new house in San Remo Drive.

However, like so many of Thomas' literary timetables and projections, the work demanded otherwise; and it was only on 4th January 1943, that he was able to complete the "beautiful story and God-invention of JOSEPH AND HIS BROTHERS," as the last line of the book ran.

He was still to write the introduction to *The Ten Commandments* to which he had committed himself; but for some time the idea of *Doctor Faustus* had been passing through his mind: a final confrontation with the problems of Germany, of music, art and genius, which had occupied him throughout his life.

"The year of 1943 was only a few days old when I set down the last lines of the fourth Joseph novel and therewith brought the whole work to an end," Thomas wrote later.[22]

> It was a curious day for me, that fourth of January, but certainly not one marked by high spirits. This great narrative work which had accompanied me through all these years of exile, ensuring me the unity of my life, was done, was finished with, and I was unburdened . . . Why I should have been "suffering, sorrowful, deeply perturbed and weary" during the next few days is something known only to God, to whose knowledge — even about Himself — we must consign so much.[23]

He set to work titling the chapters of *Joseph the Provider* and dividing it into seven parts; meanwhile he began to read up what he could about Moses for the brief Foreword to the book on the Ten Commandments he had been commissioned to write.

> I had long been asking myself why I should contribute only a foreword to the book of stories by distinguished writers — why not rather an "organ prelude" as Werfel later put it? Why not a tale of the issuance of the Commandments, a Sinai novella?

Thus *Tables of the Law,* his novella on Moses, was written — in "not quite two months" and "almost without corrections." It enabled him to use up some of the epic narrative flow which was still "warm" in him, and, after the happy ending of *Joseph and his Brothers,* to declare something more "militant" on the part of humanity, at man's wanton disregard for life and human values: a curse directed "against the present day-wretches" profaning the Ten Commandments. With Moses' curse Thomas bridged biblical times and modernity.

> The morning after completing this story I cleared away all the mythological and Oriental material that had accumulated in the course of *Joseph* — pictures, excerpts, drafts. The stuff was all packed away. The books I had read for the purpose remained on their shelves, a little library in themselves. Only one day later — 15th March, to be exact — my evening notes contained the curt jotting: "Dr Faust".[24]

6

Unlike Thomas' previous works, *Doctor Faustus* did not grow out of an intended novella of limited size. From the very beginning Thomas was aware — as were his fellow émigrés — of the significance of the work. At first he was tempted to "try something else first", such as the fragmentary comic novel he had begun before the First World War, *Felix Krull;* but the very seriousness of the moment in world history forbade such a light-hearted and individual-istic course. The "thorn was in my flesh. This one time I knew what I was setting out to do and what task I was imposing upon myself: to write nothing else than the novel of my era, disguised as the story of an artist's life, a terribly imperilled and sinful artist."[25]

In a sense Thomas stood where Heinrich had once stood in Imperial Germany. "The novel of the German must be written, the time is more than ripe for it," Heinrich had written to René Schickele in 1907;[26] yet as Heinrich himself had found, it was not easy. Only after six years of gestation had he been able to set down *Man of Straw* — and even then he had clutched at outside projects, such as his play *Madame Legros*.

"For all my curiosity and eagerness, I was not at ease about the business," Thomas recorded:

> To propose that a work be big in every sense, to plan it so from the start, was probably not right — neither for the work nor for the state of mind of the author. Therefore I must introduce as much jesting, as much ridicule of the biographer, as much anti-self-important mockery as possible.[27]

The story of Faust had intrigued Thomas since youth, and in 1901 he had even written a three-line outline of the tale. The destiny of modern Germany stood so clearly reflected in the legend, it cried out for a twentieth-century version. To dress it in the costume of a composer reflected also Thomas' life-long concern with music.

> Forty-two years had passed since I set down something about an artist's pact with the devil as a possible subject for a piece of writing, and the seeking and finding of these notes was accompanied by a degree of emotion, not to say inner tumult, which made one thing very clear to me: that the meagre and vague nucleus had been surrounded from the beginning by a belt of personal concern, a density of biographical feeling, which from the first destined the long short story for a novel — though this was far from my mind. To myself I had called this work, which might some day have to be done, my "Parsifal".[28]

Richard Strauss and Hans Pfitzner were the obvious examples of composers who had married their creativity to Hitler's nationalist dream. Yet strangely Thomas did not use them as his models; instead he chose, in principle, the more dramatic example of Nietzsche — whose syphilitic degeneration had long fascinated him — and set him within the more appropriate development of musical genius: that of the Viennese school culminating in Schoenberg's work in the 12-tone system. He would be called Adrian Leverkühn, his roots would lie in the Lutheran period of German history; and his story — the story of modern Germany too — would be told by a "friend": a self-parody of Thomas bearing the humorous name of Serenus Zeitblom.

Whether Thomas was right to intercalate the figure of Zeitblom has concerned critics ever since; and Thomas' daughter Erika did much to improve the readability of the work by suggesting heavy cuts in the incidental narration. "To make the demonic strain through an undemonic medium, to entrust a harmless and simple soul, well-meaning and timid, with the recital of the story, was in itself a comic idea," Thomas later wrote in *The Genesis of a Novel*.

It removed some of the burden, for it enabled me to escape the turbulence of everything direct, personal, and confessional which underlay the baneful conception, to steer it into indirection and to travesty it as I depicted it though the eyes of this good, unheroic soul, who could only wring his hands and shake his head at these events.[29]

It also enabled Thomas to avoid the danger of creating "a new German myth, flattering the Germans with their 'demonism'," as Thomas recalled, comparing his own work with Bruno Frank's *Deutsche Novelle* — for Serenus Zeitblom is a humanist chronicling his fateful story amid the gradual destruction of a Germany whose fellow states will no longer tolerate its evil. Yet Zeitblom cannot help but become an impediment to the story as well as a help. Hitherto Thomas had always been able to achieve Zeitblom's function himself, ridiculing and travestying, altering past focus into present, but allowing the formidable narrative talent he had first revealed in *Buddenbrooks* to take over whenever the occasion demanded. Now, having begun the story of *Doctor Faustus* through the medium of Zeitblom, he was stuck with him. Unlike Dostoievsky's narrator in *The Brothers Karamazov,* Zeitblom had been cast from the beginning as a "friend", as someone intimately involved in Leverkühn's life and therefore inseparably tied to it. What Thomas gained in authenticity he was thus bound to sacrifice in narrative strength and imagination — which in the case of a legend such as that of Faust and the devil was to prove the most damaging feature to the future success of the book.

Yet at the time of its writing, Thomas claimed not to have been concerned with an eventual public: "As long as I was working on the book," he recorded in the *Genesis,* "the concept of its public existence did not enter my mind." It was a personal exploration into the world of modern music and history, arising out of a "strange and licentious spiritual relaxation"; "arcanum and confession", a "montage" of fascinating and extraordinary complexity.[30]

Doctor Faustus was thus begun barely eight weeks after the completion of the *Tables of the Law,* on Sunday 23rd May 1943. Already the tide of military success which had swept Hitler's troops across Europe, Russia and the Mediterranean had begun to ebb. Stalingrad had held out, Montgomery marched from victory to victory in North Africa. What had been at heart a moral faith in history which both Heinrich and Thomas held was now being confirmed in reality.

Thomas had covered over two hundred pages of preparatory notes for the new novel, had borrowed the Faust chapbook and the letters of Hugo Wolf from the Library of Congress and had a "fairly good over-all view" of the work when, with "overbrimming eagerness" he set pen to paper. "I shall have to study music," Thomas had told Heinrich. Here he was to be profoundly helped by the musical philosopher Theodor Adorno, also living in exile in America, and his meeting with Stravinsky and Schoenberg. "Technical musical studies frighten and bore me," he confided to his diary; yet he did not shirk the necessary research which was to give *Doctor Faustus* its great documentary weight. By September 1943 he had completed the first eight chapters of the novel, more than one-seventh of the projected work.

Yet his mood of optimism was not to last, and the problem of matching musical depth and accuracy with narrative proved more difficult than he had imagined. He had begun quite early to read chapters of the manuscript aloud to friends; and in his concern to give a convincing portrayal of modern musical development he perhaps overlooked the need to give a convincing portrait of the Faust figure Leverkühn himself. Over the next three years Thomas was to fill his work with music, history, theology, occultism and even family portraits — of his mother, his two sisters, close friends, admirers: almost as if to make up for this singular and simple omission. Yet at the time it was not so clear, for the symbol and representation of German destiny lay so heavy upon both author and listeners that this seemed a welcome relief. "To depict Adrian's outer appearance was instantly to threaten him with spiritual downfall," Thomas wrote later, "to undermine his symbolic dignity, to diminish and render banal his representativeness."

The pace of work began to slow down; and by the spring of 1944 the novel had barely advanced another four chapters. "Little satisfaction in the work," Thomas recorded in his diary, "which seems to be dissolving under my hands . . ." Throughout this time he continued his political work and lecturing on behalf of the anti-fascist struggle, writing articles for the Office of War Information, and recording his talks for the BBC. A "Free Germany" movement had begun among the German emigrants in America, supported by many Americans of German descent. "The idea was to prepare a democratic German government that would be ready to take over after Hitler's inevitable collapse," Thomas later wrote. "Theologians, writers, socialist and Catholic statesmen belonged to the group, and it was suggested that I be placed at the head of it."[31] Though he was reluctant to assume any political role other than that of writer and moralist, Thomas did agree to sound out the US State Department on its feelings about possible support for such a movement. Not unexpectedly the result was negative, and Thomas was unwilling to insist, as he explained to Bertolt Brecht on 10th December 1943:

> I have become convinced that the formation of such a body would be premature. I have come to this conclusion not only because members of the State Department think it premature and do not want it now, but also out of my own reflections and experiences. The fact is — and if I remember it rightly, it was discussed at our last meeting — that as soon as the public hears rumours of such a German group, uneasiness and mistrust arise among the representatives of the different European nations, and the word immediately goes out that any such German ring must be squashed. It is not only possible but probable that our union would be viewed as nothing but a patriotic effort to shield Germany from the consequences of her crimes. If we come forward now to excuse and defend Germany and call for a "strong German democracy", we would seem to be affronting the feelings of the nations which are groaning and almost crushed under the Nazi yoke. It is too soon to pose German

demands and to appeal to the world's emotions in favour of a country which still has Europe in her power and whose capability for crime has by no means been shattered. Horrors can and probably still will take place, and they in turn will arouse the world's horror of this nation. Where will we be, if we have prematurely vouched for the victory of the better and higher impulses within Germany?

When Allied troops reached the German concentration camps more than a year later these warnings were proved profoundly valid. In the meantime, on 5th January 1944 Thomas and Katja were formally examined and became citizens of the United States of America.

Thus Thomas and Katja gave up their Czech citizenship for that of the United States — the country in which, like Joseph in Egypt, Thomas had prospered. When *Joseph the Provider* appeared in English in the spring of 1944 it was chosen by the Book of the Month Club, guaranteeing Thomas at least 12,000 dollars; by the autumn some 200,000 copies had been sold — exceeding even the sales of *The Magic Mountain* when it was first published in Germany.

7

Sadly, while Thomas' fortunes steadily improved in America, those of Heinrich ebbed into penury and occasional despair. Apart for one lump sum of 750 dollars which the Soviet Ambassador had managed to procure in 1942 from Moscow against the many hundreds of thousands of copies of Heinrich's work sold in Russia (by the time of Heinrich's death the figure had reached nearly 700,000) — which was used mainly to pay outstanding rent, medical and dental bills, and the cost of a car Nelly had purchased — Heinrich now had no source of income. The initial, helping-hand cheques which Thomas had sent Heinrich at the termination of the Warner Brothers Contract became a matter almost of life and death to Heinrich. When one cheque went astray in April 1942, Heinrich had written to Katja: "Perhaps you will find it best to cancel the cheque at your bank . . . In the meantime we owe the rent and only open the door if there is no creditor behind it. Such is fate, and would be even worse were it not for your goodness."[32] Slowly Nelly began to go mad, attempting suicide again, and drinking heavily. "She drank secretly," Salka Viertel later recorded, "slipping out into the bathroom or kitchen, coyly refusing the drinks offered at parties; then insisted on driving Heinrich home, to which he heroically consented."[33] Even later Golo Mann recalled Ludwig Marcuse's experience of being invited to a dinner party at Heinrich's. Nelly had opened the door completely naked, and at table had yowled "Oh, I've got such an old husband!" so often that eventually Heinrich had got up and retired to his room; whereupon the guests all dispersed.[34] She began to buy cars on credit to be resold immediately for cash, Golo remembered, and her behaviour at Thomas' house, where they were invited regularly (about half an hour's drive distant) made the fraternal relationship more and more difficult.

Yet to this "voluptuous, blond, blue-eyed Teutonic beauty with red lips and sparkling teeth", as Salka Viertel called her,[35] Heinrich clung now with a profound and simple gratitude. Under her erratic care he had begun to write again seriously. *Lidice* was finished on 27th September 1942, and in the following two years he set down a sort of autobiography, the story of his life and his time seen with extraordinary clarity, told in a style which later struck Thomas as the "language of the future," a "model" of German prose composition for schoolbooks of the coming century, a mixture of "unbelievably rigorous and clear lustre, of naive wisdom and moral dignity".[36] It was completed a fortnight after the D-Day landing in Normandy, on 23rd June 1944. No publisher, however, had been prepared to pay an advance royalty on the work, and Nelly was forced to go out to work. "My good wife is working as a nurse in the hospital," wrote Heinrich to Eva Lips on 14th December 1944. "It overtaxes her, and shames me. What can I do?"[37] Heinrich was nearing his seventy-fourth birthday. Two days later, on 16th December 1944, Nelly took an overdose of sleeping tablets — her fifth attempt at suicide. This time she was successful, and she died on the way to hospital.

Nelly's death was apparently greeted with some relief in San Remo Drive — "a blessing" as Golo Mann "regretfully" recalled.[38] Thomas' feelings about Nelly had grown worse over the past year as her behaviour had become less and less tolerable to him — and he had on one occasion written to Heinrich that he would not be prepared to see him again for several weeks. Katja paid off the outstanding bills for Heinrich, and it was hoped his life might now be simplified. Katja offered to find a smaller flat for him.

But Heinrich was far from relieved by Nelly's suicide. He was overtaken by a mood of complete desolation and refused to leave the flat. For all her faults he had loved Nelly perhaps more deeply than he had loved any other woman in his life. To him she symbolized the world of woman as magnetically as Künstlerin Fröhlich in the novel he had written forty years before: elemental, candid, unpredictable. Her affairs with other men, her drunkenness and insensitivity to etiquette were bound to outrage Thomas' household; to Heinrich they were merely quintessential womanhood.

"People who know nothing try to assure me it is 'better like this,' " Heinrich wrote on 7th January 1945 to Eva Lips. "No. Her suffering face of the days when she came through the door with bewildered eyes, white — not only her uniform white: even if it all came back I would still hope that things would get better again, for her and for us."[40] Apparently Nelly had been stopped while on probation for drunken driving and was due to appear in court; and this had finally made her put an end to her "constant tussle with the police, her struggle with a language she could never learn, her fear of aging, and her losing battle with liquor," as Salka Viertel summarized.[41]

Heinrich never ceased to grieve for her in the remaining years of his life. "In Bandol-sur-mer, at the beginning of the summer I found my wife standing unexpectedly in my room, having come from Berlin via Denmark, the greatest proof of loyalty ever shown to me in my life. The eight years in France were, despite the worst prospects for the future, a happy time. Since 1940 and our flight to America, everything I had preserved, cheerfulness, the late lustre of youth, shrivelled, above all my wife's health," Heinrich wrote in a résumé of his exile to F.C. Weiskopf in 1947.[42] "Her arrival in France and her parting here, before she committed suicide, are two days by which I measure both my existence and my writing." He counted his life, after her suicide, literally by years and days since her death.

After Nelly's death Heinrich accepted the utter solitude — and wisdom — of age: "in writing and in life," as Heinrich wrote to Weiskopf. "What one calls wisdom is as good as unavoidable; mingles moreover with the traces of life-long intensity. My last novels may be curious affairs."

But for Thomas, still in the public limelight throughout the world as writer, broadcaster and publicist, solitude was not possible. Whatever he wrote was picked over by critics, academic, ignorant or appreciative, and already his attitude towards Germany, particularly a post-war Germany, was causing concern among the more patriotic of the German émigrés in America. In Montevideo and London, Erik Erikson, the psychoanalyst, had published a vitriolic book aimed against Thomas: *Thomas Mann Neueste Wandlung* (Thomas Mann's Latest Turn) with a front cover cartoon ridiculing Teacher Thomas — "Thomas Mann, this deified absolute zero of the 'German intellect', this foul-tasting paper soup of German sub-mediocrity, whose insipid fragrance intoxicates the world the less it produces . . ." Brecht's diaries were full of negative remarks about Thomas; and as the end of the war came nearer, Thomas' position as undoubted spokesman for the German émigrés came more and more under fire.

Hitherto Thomas had had to wrestle with his own conscience and the sometimes defeatist or even pro-fascist opinions of Americans. Throughout the war he had led the forces of militant democracy and anti-fascism. Now that the war was almost won, the vexed question of the future of Germany arose again: and with it Thomas' own exposure to the country which had banished him. The envious diatribes of the "patriotic" German émigrés were only a foretaste of what was to come from within Germany itself.

8

In February 1945 the General Secretary of the Latin-American Committee of Free Germans asked Heinrich (the Honorary President of the Committee since March 1943) if he would prepare an article for a special issue of the magazine *Freies Deutschland* to greet the imminent liberation of Berlin. By 16th March 1945, Heinrich's text was ready, signed by sixty-six authors and émigrés and published seven weeks later. *To the People of Berlin* was addressed to the working people of Berlin, calling upon them to recognize their liberation from Hitler and the Nazis, and to carry out the revolution which in two world wars they had avoided: the creation of a genuine egalitarian society in which large private industrialists would no longer be able to finance and back a madman like Hitler.

Understand fully: only a revolutionary Germany will find regard among the foreigners who have freed you from your oppressors till now. But from future ones you must save yourselves. Love of freedom alone brings true self-reliance, makes all nations of the world equal. Berliners, we know you to be the most aware and clear-headed of Germans. Watch out for your country! Not in war but in the German revolution it is a question of being or not-being. If you win through to life, you will become the capital of a free Germany![43]

In their concept of a new, socialist-inspired Europe Heinrich and Thomas were together. "German Listeners," Thomas had concluded his BBC broadcast of 28th March 1944, "Europe *will* be socialist as soon as it is free. *Social humanism* was already on the order of the day, the vision of the best, when fascism raised its grotesquely squinting head over the world. It will give Europe its outer and inner form, for it is truly new, youthful and revolutionary, if once the lying snake is decapitated." Beveridge's report in England and his plan for a new egalitarian society in particular had impressed both Heinrich and Thomas: yet their attitude towards Germany itself, as Heinrich had noted in the chapter of his autobiography devoted to Thomas, differed greatly in its emotional quality. At a moment when German soldiers, far from the mood of 1918, were fighting every inch of their retreat into Germany Heinrich could still find it possible to address the working people of Berlin as compatriots who, in their heart of hearts, abhorred the monstrous cruelties and nihilism of their Nazi "oppressors". Thomas, too, in all his broadcasts attempted to evoke the remnants of humanitarian feelings left among his German listeners. Yet far more than Heinrich, Thomas was involved and implicated in Germany's tragic destiny. The German break-out in the Ardennes and the sudden fear of military renascence, followed by news reports of the German concentration camps, affected him deeply. With the successful invasion of Normandy in 1944 he had stopped broadcasting to Germany via the BBC, for he had felt no wish to inflict gratuitous humiliation in the moment of German defeat. The Ardennes offensive caused the BBC now to ask him for fortnightly broadcasts, and he was not able to escape the question of the future. "This country is lost for a decent, liberal-democratic republic," he had recorded in his diary in 1943. "What revolutionized, proletarianized, naked and stripped, shattered masses believing in nothing we shall have to deal with after this war." The *Evening Standard* had asked him for an article on "What to Do with Germany?" He had not written it. Now, as the Allies forced their way across the Rhine and the battle for Berlin began, Thomas was filled with ambivalent feelings. The Office of War Information asked him to write an article on "The Camps". "We, who had early understood the nature of what in Germany was called the 'Nation State', found nothing surprising and incredible," he later wrote: it was terribly, overwhelmingly predictable. The absence of any sign of weakening, of "better thoughts" from inside Germany was one distressing omen for the future; but the growing tensions between Russia and America augured badly too. "Victorious but hopeless," he noted in his diary. "I seem to have disbelieved in the capacity of the victors to win the peace after the war," he wrote, looking back. "The victory will be squandered worse than the last time," he said to two Swiss visitors to Pacific Palisades.

President Roosevelt had died on 12th April; it seemed unlikely that without him America would be quite the same. "An era is ending," Thomas noted in his diary. "The America to which we came will no longer exist."[44] Heinrich is said to have burst into tears when he heard the news.

In the chapter of his memoirs devoted to Thomas, Heinrich had warned against taking too vengeful a view of Germany: "One must be careful, in one's surprise and anger, not to reject a nation because of a few villains, or temporary generation of evil-doers."

But in a speech written for the Library of Congress, and delivered in Washington on 29th May 1945, Thomas took the question further. "My statements," wrote Heinrich of his own chapter, "must have been more than presentiments; they were shown to be true" when he came to read the text.[45] For Thomas' speech, entitled *Germany and the Germans*, was certainly no bitter, outright condemnation of Germany.

> To play the judge out of compliance with the immeasurable hatred which its people have aroused, to curse and condemn it and to put oneself forward as the "good Germany" in contrast to the evil, guilty ones over there with whom one has nothing to do, that seems to someone like me to be somewhat inappropriate. One *does* have something to do with German destiny and German guilt if one is born German. Critical distance should not be seen as disloyalty. Truths which one attempts to tell about one's people can only be the product of self-inquiry . . .
>
> What I have sketched for you in great brevity, ladies and gentlemen, is the history of German "inwardness". It is a melancholy tale — I call it so and do not speak of "tragedy" because misfortune should not boast. But one thing this story should make clear: that there are not two Germanies, a good one and an evil one, but only a single one, which turned its best by devilry into bad. Evil Germany, that is the good which has festered, the good in misfortune, in guilt and decline. For this reason it is so impossible for a German-born mind to disown the evil, guilt-laden Germany and to declare: "I am the good, the noble, the righteous Germany in white, the evil I leave to your extermination." Nothing of that which I have said to you about Germany or tried fleetingly to point out, came from knowledge dissociated, cool or uninvolved; I have it also in me, I have experienced it in my own body.

For Heinrich — and many other German émigrés — this was the most profound, significant and courageous confrontation with the problem that Thomas had ever made: and in his letter of 19th May 1945, after seeing the German typescript, Heinrich welcomed it with astonishment and deep admiration:

> Evil Germany, that is the good which has festered, the good in misfortune, in guilt and decline" — this fundamental conception, to have

discovered it in its unforgettable epitome, would justify any other author's whole life.

On 4th May 1945 all German armed forces in Holland, Northwest Germany and in Denmark surrendered unconditionally; and on 7th May the Second World War came to an end in Europe. Yet something told Thomas it was not entirely over. "Capitulation of Germany declared," he noted in his diary:

Unconditional surrender signed with appeal to the generosity of the victors . . . Is this now the day, corresponding with that of twelve years ago, when I began this series of daily notes — a day of fulfilment and triumph? What I feel now is not exactly high spirits. This and that will happen to Germany — but nothing *in* Germany.

CHAPTER FIFTEEN

Doctor Faustus, "Inner Emigration" and Heinrich's Death

On 18th May 1945 the *Bayerische Landeszeitung,* a newspaper issued under American military control, printed an article, *Thomas Mann and the German Guilt.* A young German writer, J.F.G. Grosser, saw it, visited Walter von Molo, Heinrich's predecessor as President of the Literary Section of the Berlin Academy of Arts, and suggested von Molo send an open letter to Thomas Mann. It was published on 13th August 1945 in the *Münchener Zeitung,* also under US military control. It described the conditions of a devastated, defeated country; and begged Thomas to return, like "a good doctor", to help in the reconstruction.

How the American military authorities permitted such a letter to be printed at a time of full censorship remains obscure. Thomas Mann had just celebrated his seventieth birthday. He was an American citizen and would have required special authority to travel to Germany, let alone to live in the country during military occupation. But worst of all, the suggestion that a seventy-year-old internationally renowned German emigrant to America should return, during military occupation, to share the suffering of a people who had done nothing to cast off the dictator responsible for their misfortunes had something painfully thoughtless about it.

Von Molo showed his letter to American pressmen, and within weeks it had reached Thomas. Instead of making a simple statement in the American press that von Molo was one of the unfortunate number of German nationalist writers who had elected to stay in Germany under Hitler, and that he would consider visiting Germany at a time when military occupation was over, Thomas replied at length to von Molo. He could not resist – though at first he postponed the task — because, as once at the time of his exchange of letters with the University of Bonn, "many things came to the fore, demanding to be expressed; I felt that here was my chance to set these matters forth in substantial and documentary form." The piece was despatched to Germany, to the "Aufbau" in New York, and to the Office of War Information.[1]

It was a mistake, and one of far-reaching significance for Thomas' popularity in Germany. Because it was so long (more than seven printed pages) it was bound to be abbreviated when quoted in other newspapers there. To recite the monstrous story of the support von Molo and so many other thinking men had given to Hitler was to rub sore wounds; to set out the bitterness and tragedy of Thomas' own exile at a time when Germany itself lay in ruins was courting disaster. It did not take long to come. "I am nonplussed and saddened by the unbelievable bitterness which my open letter of apology to Herr von Molo — actually a considerate and humanly trusting letter — seems to have aroused in Germany," he wrote the following spring.[2]

Today I am an American citizen . . . To put it bluntly, I do not see why I should not enjoy the advantages of my strange lot, after tasting the disadvantages of the dregs. I especially do not see it because I cannot understand what service I can render the German people which I could not also render from the State of California . . .

In the course of all these years Germany has truly become alien to me. You must grant that it is a frightening country. I admit that I fear the sight of German ruins — both stone and human . . .

It may be superstition, but in my eyes any books that could be printed in Germany from 1933 to 1945 are worse than worthless, and I am reluctant to touch them. A stench of blood and disgrace clings to them; they ought all to be pulped.

Thomas' words were bound to be taken amiss; and even before they appeared in Germany another German writer who had remained in Hitler's Reich, Frank Thiess, had added to von Molo's "brave" letter, advancing now the thesis of "Inner Emigration": a somewhat spurious defence of "all" those writers who had remained in Nazi Germany, and "suffered" the régime in silence. To this Thiess added yet another rehabilitating doctrine: that of the courage of writers who "stayed at their posts" rather than running away. "I believe it was harder to preserve one's personality here than to broadcast messages to the German people from over there," Thiess claimed:

We expect no reward for not having left Germany. It was natural for us to remain. But it would seem very unnatural to us if the sons who have suffered so deeply and honorably as Thomas Mann were not to return today, but just wished to wait and see whether their country's misery results in death or in new life.

Thiess' article appeared also in the *Münchener Zeitung,* printed (with a forenote disclaiming agreement with Thiess' views by the editor) on 18th August. It was a sorry reflection on the German passion for self-righteousness, a further example of the total disregard for the havoc Germany had wreaked on other nations.

Thiess' article, however, found widespread acclaim within Germany, and thus the "great controversy" began — the question of who were morally superior, those who had remained in "shattered" Germany, or those who had left. Thiess became a sort of national hero; and Thomas' reputation, already severely tainted by his wartime broadcasts, sank still further.[3] It was not surprising therefore that Thomas should decline even his agent's proposal for a tour of Europe outside Germany in the coming year. His health was deteriorating — for months he had been losing weight and had been prone to colds and catarrh, and his work on *Doctor Faustus* exhausted him. Thiess' article was forwarded to him by the OWI. "Presumably these 'exiles within' were a community of intellectuals who had 'kept faith with Germany', not 'left her in the lurch in her misfortune', not looked upon her fate 'from comfortable box seats abroad', but honestly shared in it. They would honestly have shared it even if Hitler had won," was Thomas' laconic summary in *The Genesis of a Novel* later on. Despite the new campaign to discredit Thomas in Germany, his mail was swollen with letters from ex-colleagues requesting letters of recommendation or absolution with which to evade the military classification system then in operation. By 14th December 1945, he was writing to Mrs Meyer:

> To be sure, I don't wonder that my life is coming to its lowest ebb this year, as I reach the age in which my mother died — from which it may however yet raise itself again. I prophesied my death for this year, you see — a prophecy which doesn't have to, and seems unlikely to be literally fulfilled. But intimations, at least, it has given.

Thomas' health, in fact, was in even more precarious a condition than even he himself realized. Within four months he was to undergo the most serious operation of his life.

2

On 30th December 1945 the BBC transmitted Thomas' New Year's greeting to Germany, in which he had been asked to repeat his reasons for not returning to Germany. Barely sixty-seven minutes later Frank Thiess was at the microphone of the Northwest German radio. Already, in answer to Thomas' "apology" to Walter von Molo, Thiess had written a second article *Farewell to Thomas Mann* in which he claimed that Thomas' twelve years of exile had lost him the right to consider himself a German writer; a matter which could only be determined by the "German people" itself, Thiess added. Now, in response to Thomas' broadcast, Thiess repeated his *Farewell*. Thomas' hatred for Naziism was, Thiess claimed, in fact a hatred for Germany. To witness the devastation of German cities would be something Thomas "would never get over in his whole life. He would painfully regret having condemned completely a people which now lies helpless on the ground as never before in its 1,000-year-old history." What Thomas had missed, Thiess pointed out, was the "blessing" of the inner-emigrants, the "intimacy of mind, opinion and speech" which this "tightly closed circle" had enjoyed in Nazi Germany. Thomas was speaking, Thiess surmised, from the "infinite distance, which was able only to transmit words whose bitterness and arrogance do not even hurt us any more, because they are dishonourable and behind them the heart of a poet no longer beats."[4]

Thiess was soon discredited when certain adulatory pro-Nazi speeches were discovered from 1933: but the damage was done, and Thomas' reputation in Germany can be said never to have recovered. Worse still, the "vast free country" he had extolled to von Molo, and which had received him with "nothing but open, uncowed, outspoken friendliness, joyous without reservations" was itself moving in a dangerously fascist direction following Roosevelt's death.[5] On 6th August 1945, the United States unleashed the first atomic bomb on Hiroshima, and three days later the second on Nagasaki. "It was a political exploitation of the 'innards of nature' to use Goethe's phrase," Thomas afterwards wrote. "I say 'political' because the victory over Japan could have been achieved entirely without the uncanny weapon. It had been used only to prevent Russia's participation in this victory."[6] He could not fail to be aware of the growing American distrust of all things foreign, the rising tide of anti-communism and even anti-semitism; and by December, out of "fear for the state of democracy in this country," as he wrote to Mrs Meyer, he had joined the "Independent Citizens Committee".

> Why should the Germans in particular have learned from the catastrophe — when nobody else seems to have done so? The peace — if the word be permitted — already looks so bad that one begins to feel the war to have been an elevating interlude.[7]

Bruno Frank, Franz Werfel, Béla Bartok, Richard Beer-Hofmann and Alexander Roda-Roda all died in 1945. The "glorious, future-orientated coast" Thomas had described to von Molo was becoming "deserted all around me," he wrote to Mrs Meyer.[8]

The only thing which seemed to prosper was the novel: and even here Thomas' deteriorating health and his own moods of despair sometimes threatened to leave the work unfinished. Yet the feeling that *Doctor Faustus* contained not only a record and symbol of modern German history but was also a personal testimony kept him going. "How much *Faustus* contains of the atmosphere of my life! A radical confession, at bottom. From the very beginning that has been the shattering thing about the book," he noted in his diary.[9] Into its weave he had brought his own mother and two sisters: for in their unfortunate destiny, again, the fate of Germany itself was reflected. The "story" he had once left "to a later narrative in a larger frame"[10] had now found its place. Even the choice of location for Adrian Leverkühn's pact with the devil was not fortuitous. It was set in Palestrina, in the house where Thomas and Heinrich had begun working on their first novels — for Thomas perhaps the most important moment in his career as a writer. Perhaps, in this choice, there was even a deep-seated awareness of the devilry in his own art, its playing with life, its very temptation in terms of the ego.

Adorno helped him with the difficult task of creating the masterpiece which should issue from Leverkühn's pact. The oratorio chapters took six weeks to write; then there was a tribute for Heinrich's seventy-fifth birthday to be prepared for the German émigré journal in Mexico, *Freies Deutschland: Report on my Brother.* Still Thomas felt unwell, and Heinrich urged him to consult his own doctor, Friedrich Rosenthal. Rosenthal tried injections to bring down Thomas' constant fever, and finally insisted on bringing in a consultant. It was agreed a bronchoscopy would be necessary, with an operation to follow if their diagnosis was proved correct: the removal of an "abscess" of the right lower lung lobe.

"I was more surprised than alarmed, for I had never thought that danger would ever threaten me from my organs of respiration;" wrote the author of *Tristan* and *The Magic Mountain.* The doctors, moreover, agreed that the trouble was not tubercular in character. "Much about my state of health during recent months is explained by this discovery," he wrote. "Under what unfavourable circumstances I have worked! On the other hand, the terrible novel together with the vexations over Germany are certainly responsible for this illness, which the *grippe* has only activated."[11] His planned lecture tour to Europe was postponed at least until October.

In mid-April Thomas set off by rail and road ambulance for the Billings Hospital, Chicago, where the noted pneumonomist, Dr William Elias Adams, was waiting to receive him. Thomas was not unduly worried; but Heinrich was. The two brothers had become "even closer" after the death of Nelly, as Thomas noted:[12] and Heinrich now insisted he come with his brother. Life had come full circle: the elder, pioneering brother, grown old and isolated, wished to protect his younger brother as once he had in their early Munich and Italian days, before their rift.

Katja, quite naturally, would not hear of it. From Santa Monica Heinrich now cabled — in English:

Doctor Rosenthal gave me exact report stop I fight to have confidence and I ask Tommy to retain his admirable courage stop my beloved brother you must have the strength to live and you will stop you are indispensable to your great purposes and to all persons who love you stop there is one who would feel vain to continue without you stop this is the moment for confessing you my absolute attachment stop may my ardent wishes help you to support the danger and to recover health stop Faithfully yours Heinrich

The telegram was never shown to Thomas: but Thomas certainly needed all the strength to live that he could muster. For the bronchopsy had revealed that Thomas was suffering from cancer of the lung: and the chances of survival — let alone of full recovery — were slim indeed.

3

The operation, fortunately, was a complete success. Whether Thomas realized he was suffering from cancer of the lung is not known. Fundamentally, though, Thomas had no wish to know. His recovery was considered unique for a man of his age.

"Just as the operation had proceeded classically and uneventfully, in the clinical sense, so the convalescence progressed speedily and without complications. A man of thirty, the doctors assured me, could not have responded better," Thomas wrote later.[13]

I was looked upon as a kind of prize patient. Of course I could still feel the shock that every operation of that sort imposes upon the nervous system and the whole organism. And a weakness in the chest had remained. Along with a strong tendency towards swallowing the wrong way it made clearing my throat and coughing up phlegm alarmingly difficult. Codeine was used to counter the unavoidable healing pains in the back. And the changes that had been undertaken in my interior, including removal of the seventh rib, upper displacement of the diaphragm, and similar re-arrangements, created a certain shortness of breath when I moved too fast.

On 20th May Thomas left hospital — a week before the prescribed six weeks post-operative term — and two days after returning to Pacific Palisades he was back at work on *Doctor Faustus* — "which seemed to me in its essentials already 'closed in', as workmen say of a building."[14] He had ceased to fret whether it was in fact a novel, and if one, whether it was successful. A year before he had noted in his diary: "Am troubled by dissatisfaction and vexation. I rather think there is no longer any doubt that the work is a failure. Nevertheless I am going to finish it."[15] It was here that Cyril Connolly's remark that one must not be too vain to do a thing badly, and not too craven to admit it, proved a blessing; as did Harry Levin's book *James Joyce*. "The best writing of our contemporaries is not an act of creation," Levin had written, "but an act of evocation, peculiarly saturated with reminiscences." T.S. Eliot's question "whether the novel had not out-lived its function since Flaubert and James" seemed to parallel Thomas' own question "whether in the field of the novel nowadays the only thing that counted was what was no longer a novel".

These were strange thoughts and feelings from someone so closely identified with the traditional novel in German, an author who had chided his brother so vehemently in the first decade of the century for going to "extremes" and denying the traditional exigencies of the form! Thomas himself was aware of the change. "During this particular phase of my life, under the sign of Faustus," he wrote later, "I was greatly drawn to Dostoievsky's grotesque, apocalyptic realm of suffering, in contrast with my usual preference for Tolstoy's Homeric, primal strength":[16] and he had even written a new preface to a volume of Dostoievsky's short novels, *Dostojewski mit Maasen,* for the Dial Press. When Franz Werfel, not long before his death, wrote to Thomas telling him he had just re-read *Budden-*

brooks, and calling it an "immortal masterpiece", Thomas was both moved and puzzled. "I am wondering," he noted in his diary, "whether this book may not be the very one among all my works which is destined to survive. Perhaps my 'mission' was fulfilled in the writing of it, and it has been my lot only to fill the rest of a long life in a tolerably dignified and interesting manner. I do not want to be ungrateful and denigrate the course of my life after that youthful cast of the die, as it developed through *The Magic Mountain, Joseph* and *Lotte in Weimar.* But this might be a case like that of the *Freischütz* — that opera alone has remained alive among the people, although the composer followed it up by a good deal of music that was even better, nobler."[17] And to Mrs Meyer Thomas confided,

> There is something dangerous, however, about the creative. With every work that is left behind one, life becomes more difficult and in the end impossible, since a certain kind of self-plundering drives one in the end to disintegration, to the impossible, the un-executable. How do I keep myself in the realm of what is possible?[18]

Doctor Faustus, then, was perhaps Thomas' greatest struggle with the "impossible". "I strongly feel that in this book you will have given your utmost to the German people," Helen Lowe-Porter, his translator, wrote, and Thomas was aware of it himself. "What else can we ever do but give our utmost?" Thomas wrote in *The Genesis of a Novel.* "All art which deserves the name testifies to this determination to reach the ultimate, this resolve to go to the limits; all art bears the sign, the scar, of the utmost." "Let others cut them out" he wrote in his diary of the "infernally long passages and liberties" he recognized in looking through the manuscript. What was important was the completion of the novel. Even an outbreak of a skin disease he had once suffered before in Zurich — erysipelas — failed to halt him, despite the intense pain. "Even without sleep I will work," he noted in his diary. On the day of his seventy-first birthday Gerhart Hauptmann had died in Germany, after having been given a requisition order by the Poles compelling him to leave his house. The news affected Thomas deeply, for it was Hauptmann who had partly been responsible for Thomas' Nobel Prize in 1929, who had provided the key figure for the latter part of *The Magic Mountain,* and who had chosen, in his old age, the parallel role of representing Nazi Germany.

> He remained in Germany, raised the swastika flag, wrote *I say Yes!* and even went so far as to have an audience with Hitler . . . Isolated, embittered, and on top of all despised by the Nazis themselves for his willingness to capitulate, he must have suffered unspeakably in the stifling air, the bloody vapours, of the Third Reich, must have sorrowed unspeakably over the ruin of the country and the people he loved. His last photographs show the features of a martyr; he became what he had wished not to be. Those pictures floated painfully before my mind at the news of his passing, and I felt his death the harder because of the perception that for all the difference in our natures, and for all that life and events had led us far apart, we had been friends after a fashion.

The last portion of *Doctor Faustus* was itself imbued with death — the death of Clarissa (the story of the suicide of Thomas' own sister Carla), the murder of Rudi Schwerdtfeger by Clarissa's sister Inez, the death of the child who to Leverkühn is like his own son, Nepomuk; and finally the madness and death of Leverkühn himself. Owing to the more narrative character of these latter chapters *Doctor Faustus* sped forwards, so that by Christmas 1946, Emil Oprecht, the Zurich bookseller, was already announcing its impending publication. "There, in clear print, was an announcement of *Faustus* — with its full title and even the probable price for the clothbound edition! I cannot describe the feelings with which I read this announcement — feelings of incredulity, anguish, sheer fright, as at a well meant but embarrassing indiscretion," Thomas wrote in his *Genesis*. But such qualms soon vanished, however, for on 29th January 1947 *Doctor Faustus* was completed.

4

In the meantime Heinrich emerged only slowly from the sense of desolation with which the death of Nelly left him. "I only half-live, and in a thickening shadow," he had written to Felix Bertaux in April 1945, after the Liberation of France. "My dear companion was everything to me, the living past, the eight years we spent in France, all that remained of my youth."[19] He had ruled out returning to France, as he did the possible return to Germany, feeling that he had been completely forgotten. He had continued to write "as of old, but without seeing any further purpose in it. Besides, I am 74," he wrote, "and am tubercular in the manner of old people who do not die of it. They only die from having lived." There was the possibility of his book of memoirs appearing in English, but Heinrich seemed little concerned. "All that scarely interests me. One becomes distant before leaving this earth."[20]

Yet as Nelly's suicide receded in his memory, Heinrich settled into a pattern of quiet and not discontented old age. "Ancien Ecrivain de première classe, retraité. Esprit toujours clairvoyant, mais dont la sérenité tourne à l'indifférence," he described himself in a letter to an old acquaintance in France from the days of the Café de l'univers;[21] and even this indifference turned to fierce European pride as the question of the post-war world loomed larger and larger in the news. Europe's future lay, as he felt sure, in a European federation of states and the socialist-democratic course which only the advent of European fascism had held up. To blame Germany alone, as Thomas had noted in his *Report on My Brother* for *Freies Deutschland*, would have struck Heinrich "as a form of nationalism". Russia must be treated as a European power, he felt, not an Asiatic one; and unless France preserved her relationship with Russia she would never be free to exercise her commanding role in Europe, owing to the "reactionary powers" of Britain and America.[22]

Little, however, of Heinrich's European vision was to be fulfilled; ironically, it was Hitler's prophecy in his last *Testament*, written in the spring of 1945, which came true:

> With the defeat of the Reich and the pending emergence of the Asiatic, the African, and perhaps the South American nationalisms, there will remain in the world only two Great Powers capable of confronting each other — the United States and Soviet Russia. The laws of both history and geography will compel these two powers to a trial of strength, either military or in the field of economics and ideology. These same laws make it inevitable that both Powers should become enemies of Europe. And it is equally certain that both these Powers will sooner or later find it desirable to seek the support of the sole surviving great nation in Europe, the German people.[23]

At times the course of post-war European history brought Heinrich to despair, as it did Thomas, however historically inevitable. Although the Russians printed Heinrich's article on the future of Europe, no French editor could be found to accept it. "Trop spécial" was the reply from one journal, *Europe*.[24]

"Once a week without fail he likes us to bring him out into the country and spend the hours from lunch until dusk at our house," Thomas wrote in his *Report* to Mexico.

> One day, on the way home from our house, he said to his niece Erika, my eldest child: "Politically I am really in very close agreement with your father now. He is somewhat more radical than I am." This sounded infinitely amusing, but what he meant was our relation to our beloved Germany, with whom he is less angry than I for the simple reason that he knew earlier than I what to expect and was spared disappointment . . .

> If the saving revolution had broken out in Germany in time one would have had to appoint him as President of the Second Republic, him and no other. And even now — how ridiculous that this mad fuss had been made about whether I should return or not — whereas no one seemed to ask him. Which of us two showed the mettle of our latin-political heredity from the beginning? Who was the social visionary? Who wrote *Der Untertan*, who introduced the word democracy to Germany at a time when others were satisfied to conduct a melancholy defense of protestant-romantic-anti-political German spiritual bourgeoisie? I had to bite my lips when finally in all gentleness he asked: "Why actually do they leave me completely alone?"

Thomas mentioned the various works which Heinrich was writing, including his autobiography currently being printed in Sweden, whose style seemed to Thomas "the language of the future".

> For my part I can barely wait to see it being read at home in Germany. Of course, they will be offended — when were they not? They always feel offended and misunderstood, at any price, and if one understands them only too well, then they are doubly offended. But all that is childishness. The objective fact that this man, now seventy-five years old, was one of their most talented writers will prove itself stronger than their bad mood, and sooner or later be appreciated even by their negative consciousness.

The article appeared in *Freies Deutschland* in March 1946. Despite his political anxieties regarding the outcome of the defeat of Germany, Heinrich has been working since November 1945 on a new novel, deeply auto-biographical, entitled *Der Atem*. Like *Doctor Faustus* it symbolized the decline of European civilization, traced in the last hours and reflections of an Austrian noblewoman before the fall of France in 1940. Every figure was taken from real life, and within the novel was a mirror of Heinrich's own relationship with Thomas, portrayed as two sisters. In style it followed its unsuccessful predecessor, *Empfang bei der Welt*;[25] but this time there was no attempt at satire. In a sense it was the most serious of all Heinrich's works because it was so profoundly personal. Like *Doctor Faustus* it would be widely condemned for being "difficult" to read; but like *Doctor Faustus* it was the very seriousness of its theme, the reconstruction of a civilization which had passed, which made it so; and it was not till 25th October 1947, nine months after *Doctor Faustus* was finished, that Heinrich completed the manuscript, after two years of uninterrupted application.

5

Celebration of the completion of *Doctor Faustus* took place in the house of Alfred Neumann on 7th February 1947; and two days later Thomas began the lecture which he had arranged to give in Washington, New York, London, Zurich, Bern, Basel and Amsterdam: *Nietzsche's Philosophy in the Light of Contemporary Events* — an "essayistic postlude" to the Neitzsche-novel itself, as Thomas expressed it in his *Genesis*. It took four weeks to write and the lecture tour began on 22nd April. On 16th May Thomas and Katja arrived in Southampton aboard the *Queen Elizabeth*, nearly eight years after they had departed in haste from Sweden.

Yet, though the Nietzsche lecture proved entirely successful in both America and London, Thomas' real concern was with Germany and the reception of *Doctor Faustus* itself. Seeing the enormous devastation caused by bombing in London made him wonder "whether any other nation would have endured it without screaming for peace at any price", as he wrote to Heinrich on 22nd May. After warnings from friends in both Europe and America he had decided not to visit Germany.

"Am I to go around Munich with an M.P. bodyguard?" Thomas asked in a letter to Viko.

Inevitably I would be speaking publicly; let's say I should have to deliver a lecture at the university. Very well then: police cordon, check-up of members of the audience, tension, fear of riot. And what should I, what can I say to the Germans, sensitive plants that they are today, sore, thin-skinned, overwrought? They obviously don't see that Germany is in precisely the straits her leaders wanted her to be in if they were going to lose the war.

Even the interviews Thomas did give to the press were "mutilated and distorted" when reproduced, giving an alarming and sensational impression in Germany itself. Statements like "Germans appear full of self-pity, unable to see the chaos in the neighbouring countries. Only when Europe recovers as a whole, will Germany recover," (to Reuters, May 1947) were bitterly resented in Germany itself; and the decision not to visit the country was received as an added insult. Finally, four days after they landed in Zurich, on 28th May 1947, Manfred Hausmann dropped his bombshell. Under the title *Thomas Mann should keep quiet* Hausmann published an article in the North German *Weser-Zeitung.* In it he claimed to have seen a letter written by Thomas Mann to the notorious and now executed Wilhelm Frick, Minister of the Interior under Hitler, begging that he be allowed to return to the Third Reich. It was all the German press needed, and the savage campaign of vengeance for his decision not to visit the war-scarred fatherland began.

On 4th June 1947, at an international meeting of the PEN Club, Thomas spoke warmly for the recreation of a German branch, citing among others, Riarda Huch, Johannes R. Becher, Erich Kästner, Anna Seghers, Karl Jaspers, Hans Reisiger and even Manfred Hausmann as authors for whom he would be willing to "put his hand in the fire," as the *Neue Zürcher Zeitung* reported the following day. For those who had remained in Germany it was a distinct atonement for Thomas' earlier remarks about German books published under Hitler, contained in his letter to von Molo.

Such atonement, however, came too late to halt the campaign Hausmann had set in motion to discredit him. By June every newspaper in Germany carried the story of Thomas' vain request to the fatherland in 1933, and Thomas was forced to deny the allegation:

> Why he attacks me from the rear with this senseless slander, what I have done to him to deserve this I do not know. Is he enraged because today I "will not" do what I then supposedly "could not" do?

On the other hand Thomas neither had a copy of the alleged letter (if it existed), nor did he remember its contents; and his denial could only be a counter-challenge:

> In my agony at that time I wrote a good many "letters into the night" [such was René Schickele's phrase for them]. If among those appeals addressed to a Germany being rapidly swept away towards its destruction there should also be a letter to Frick, and if Manfred Hausmann has contrived to obtain possession of this letter, he ought to publish it in its entirety instead of peddling an obviously falsified summary of its contents.[26]

But Hausmann would not be drawn. He swore he had had a copy of the letter until 1942, and that its contents were unforgettable. "It was a question of a letter from the great Thomas Mann!" he remembered clearly, and it had confirmed Hausmann's own decision to remain in Germany, "for Thomas Mann also wants to come back." This identification had been offended by Thomas Mann's most recent remarks about Germany and, above all, by his decision not to visit the country, Hausmann declared in his reply in the

Weser-Kurier on 11th June 1947; and in another interview he claimed he had brought up the whole matter only out of a sense of "duty" towards those who had formed Germany's "Inner Emigration".

But Hausmann was not the only German author still intent on discrediting Thomas. Frank Thiess had been exposed by the *Hamburger Volkszeitung*, but Alfred Döblin, equipped with the rank of Colonel in the French military occupation, had restarted his own campaign begun in New York in 1945. "There is such a thing as a Thomas Mann Complex," Thomas had written to Otto Basler in September 1946, "which has already given me a few irksome hours . . . But why Döblin — only since quite recently — hates me and systematically persecutes me is incomprehensible. It suggests he is simply ill. I have never done anything against him, have never crossed his path, on the contrary I have always treated him with the greatest care, bearing in mind Bulwer's words: 'The fool flatters himself, the wise man flatters the fool.' But it did no good, he would like to kill me — for that is really the sense behind his claim that I *am* dead."[27]

Undoubtedly Döblin's star had fallen, as had that of many a popular German author, in American exile; and Thomas' apparent prosperity made Döblin sick with envy and ill-will. Now, under the French occupation, Döblin launched a new literary periodical *Das goldene Tor* in Germany (The Golden Gate); and began schooling younger German writers to take a knock at current literary reputations, under the ominous heading of *Revising Literary Judgement*. Its second issue was devoted to Thomas Mann.

After the strenuous weeks of lectures and readings in Zurich, Bern and Basel, Thomas and Katja retired to Flims in Gräubunden: "glorious, still pine forests with picturesque cliffs and gorges out of Doré, and the sight of the ledges, pinnacles, and high meadows of the surrounding mountains is also a change from the eternal Pacific," he wrote to Alfred Neumann and his wife.[28] "Yet even here one cannot really speak of rest," Thomas wrote to Mrs Meyer, "for there is an Augean stable of unfinished work to be cleared, and the proofs of *Faustus* are pouring in. It is very shaking for me, having rapidly to go through the work of years with the blue pencil. And all the time the dear Germans hack, whack and pester me so that I have already had to send a long letter to the American 'Neue Zeitung' in Munich when it became too disagreeable. And one calls this recuperation!"[29] "Official and unofficial" invitations came by post and by messenger from the grieved fatherland, "but I have been unable to bring myself to go," he wrote to the Neumanns, "and am doing my best to lessen the rancor; have written to German newspapers, done a reading in St Gall for the benefit of the Munich orphanage, etc." In the end, the following year, he even donated all accumulated royalties from his works published in Germany to Lübeck. But the campaign did not cease.

In the circumstances it was more than natural that Thomas should become anxious as to the fate of *Doctor Faustus*. Owing to copyright problems Bermann-Fischer's Stockholm edition of 14,000 copies was limited to Switzerland and extra-German territories for the moment. "My first act,"

Thomas wrote to Hermann Hesse from California in the autumn after the Stockholm edition had been published, "when the mail comes, is to rummage through it to see whether there are any comments from Sweden or Switzerland about the book."[30] Although he was currently preparing a Goethe selection for the Dial Press and writing an Introduction to the volume (later published separately in German as *Phantasie über Goethe*) he was "anxiously awaiting the echo, the 'effect' — if one can speak of it thus — of *Doctor Faustus* as never before — the German edition that is, for the English one scarcely interests me any more and is a long way off," he wrote to Ida Herz on 26th October 1947. Seventy-five thousand copies of Heinrich's Wilhelmenian satire had been sold once published in 1918; but how would an embittered, post-Nazi Germany react to this, the most profoundly investigative account of Germany's twentieth-century slide into barbarism? The months went by, but it was not until the spring of 1948 that *Doctor Faustus* finally reached the "sensitive plants" whose history Thomas had chronicled.

6

In America, meanwhile, the political atmosphere too had darkened — and the wave of anti-European feeling had even led to a considerable drop in Thomas' book royalties. Knopf, his publisher, was "gloomy". "Erika is coming soon, which is cheering," Thomas wrote to Klaus, who was helping him with his Goethe selection, "but not for cheering reasons, for she has hardly any bookings because no-one wants to know about Europe."

"At one time my faith in America's humanitarian vision was very strong," Thomas wrote in the draft of a letter to a Mr Gray:

In the last few years it has been exposed to slight strains. Instead of leading the world, America appears to have resolved to buy it — which is also a very grandiose thing after its fashion, but does inspire less enthusiasm, you know. But even under these circumstances I still remain an American patriot, a fact which is confirmed to me by the grief I feel as I observe the growing unpopularity of America in the rest of the world. The American people are not responsible for this development and do not comprehend it. Those who try to explain the reasons for it are more and more reduced to silence. We can already see the first signs of terrorism, talebearing, political inquisition, and suspension of law, all of which are excused by an alleged state of emergency. As a German I can only say: That is the way it began among us, too.[31]

The activities of the Committee for Un-American Activities were indeed enough to make émigré liberals lose heart in the future of American democracy. Having been since before the war the chief spokesman for the exiled liberal cause in America, Thomas was now inundated by requests for help and support. With such ill-disguised hostility still emanating from Germany, however, Thomas felt "little desire to play the martyr once again," as he wrote to Mrs Meyer.

I myself am no longer signing any of the multitudinous appeals with which the desperate Left is making a nuisance of itself . . . I still would rather think that what is taking place is a certain moral relaxation of the country after the strains of the Roosevelt period of genius.[32]

Heinrich was even more disconsolate — though there was little chance, given the isolation in which he now lived, that he would be called before the Committee itself. The "Inquisition's" concentration on Hollywood made the Committee's sinister work even more close-to-hand, and Brecht's sudden flight from the United States to Switzerland came as a bitter reminder of the first few months of Hitler's chancellorship in Germany; the "conviction" of Brecht's musical collaborator, Hanns Eisler, hit Thomas especially hard, for Eisler had been a stimulating and amusing friend throughout the arduous composition of *Doctor Faustus*. "I know the man very well," Thomas wrote in his letter to Mrs Meyer:

He is highly cultivated, brilliant, very amusing in conversation, and I have often had splendid talks with him, particularly about Wagner. As a musician, he is, in the opinion of his colleagues, first class. Since the Inquisition has turned him over to the "secular area" for deportation, there is danger that he will land in a German camp. I hear that Stravinsky (a White Russian!) means to start a demonstration in his favour. But I have a wife and children and am not inquiring further into the matter.

Yet four days later Heinrich and Thomas had both signed a telegram to President Benes asking whether Eisler could be given entry papers to Czechoslovakia, and were asking if Einstein and William L. Shirer would add their signatures.

Heinrich's health also began to fail, he was complaining of poor nights and fits of fear. Rosenthal his doctor, "speaks behind his back of angina pectoris and vague worries," Thomas informed Klaus. For a while Heinrich was forbidden to climb stairs, and Thomas feared for the worst — "serious problems and shocks" seemed bound to come from that direction too, Thomas concluded.[33]

Nevertheless Heinrich was determined to bring his new novel to a close — "one of the last" as he called it in a letter to Felix Bertaux, both for himself and for the genre.[34] He was contemptuous of the new existentialist movement in literature, its "affected indifference".[35] "Literature as we know it, which exalts life, is a great consolation," he wrote to Bertaux after hearing of the death of his first wife, Mimi, in Prague in April 1947, broken by her years in Theresienstadt. "In contrast existentialism only abases life. The new glory of Heidegger and Kafka proclaims the complete success — if only temporary — of neo-fascism."[36]

Der Atem was completed on 25th October 1947. It was indeed Heinrich's last novel, though it was to be a further two years until it was published in Germany, and it never found an English translator. Even Luise Servicen, the faithful French translator of *Lotte in Weimar,* had declined to take on *Doctor Faustus,* as Thomas reported sympathetically to Helen Lowe-Porter.[37] It was time to leave the snares and complexity of such work, Thomas felt; and while Mrs Lowe-Porter battled with the stylistic vagaries of *Doctor Faustus* Thomas now turned, as he had done after *The Magic Mountain,* to something lighter. "Comedy, laughter, humour seem to me more and more the soul's salvation;" he wrote to Mrs Meyer, "I long for them after the minimum portion of these in *Faustus,* and promise to find a plethora of gaiety despite the gloomiest of world situations. One who wrote the *Joseph* at the time of Hitler's victories will not let whatever is coming get him down, insofar as he lives to experience it."

Thus arose the strange medieval novella whose plot Thomas had found while working on *Doctor Faustus*: the story of the birth of the sainted Pope Gregory and his oedipal fate. "I knew nothing of the multitudinous forms the legend had taken, had scarcely heard of Hartmann von Aue's Middle High German poem. But I liked it so well that even at that time I toyed with the thought of stealing the subject from my hero and making a little archaic novel of it," Thomas wrote in *The Genesis of a Novel.* And to Samuel Singer on 17th February, 1948: "I would like to retell an oft-told medieval legend *Gregorius auf dem Steine* in modern prose, a variation of the Oedipus-story, the choice of a terrible incestuous sinner by God Himself to become the Pope in Rome. It is a pious piece of grotesqueness, the conception of which makes me laugh a great deal, but which deals really with grace":[38] *The Holy Sinner.* By the end of May, having decided to spend the year in California, he had completed the first fifty pages.

7

Yet if Thomas considered his *Joseph* novels to have been misunderstood, worse was to take place with *Doctor Faustus,* finally published under licence in Germany in the spring of 1948.

"I pay heed to every utterance on this book as with none of my previous works," Thomas wrote to Katherine Seiler.[39] "This work in particular" was written with "my innermost feelings", he wrote to his English publisher Fredric Warburg, who had just read the typescript, "I can almost say with my heart's blood, and I am glad to note that you too seem to understand this." The *Times Literary Supplement's* by now almost obsessive campaign to discredit Thomas' works (the reviewer was found not to have read *Lotte in Weimar* after a malicious review of the book) had not halted when it came to *Doctor Faustus.* It was "the first English-language echo to reach me," Thomas told Warburg, and could only hope that "warmer and deeper utterances will follow. I was especially surpised that at the end the author speaks of a 'loosely woven net of ironically glittering prose'. I should like to say that I was never less ironical than in this very serious, confession-like tome, and as concerns the 'loosely woven net', this is in truth an extremely tight-knit composition in which, musically speaking, 'no note is free', and in which all elements are interrelated."[40]

It was in fact the very seriousness of *Doctor Faustus* which confused the critics. Here Thomas' conventional narrative distance, his masterly feel for the organic and epic growth of creative work, was cast aside. *The Magic Mountain,* as Thomas himself acknowledged, had been saved from polemical disintegration by its slow genesis, by the clarity he had previously obtained in the writing of *Reflections of a Non-Political Man. Doctor Faustus,* in contrast, had been written without such years of gestation and preparation, was written both in time of war and the confrontation with disease and — albeit unwittingly — death. That he had failed to write a perfect work of art, Thomas was aware — "It is a work whose rank and value will remain un-determined for some time. Only posterity will be able to decide these questions," he wrote in his letter to Warburg. But that it was, at the time, the most important and disturbing of all his work was for him demonstrated not simply by his unusual concern with its critical reception but by his decision, in July of 1948, to interrupt the new medieval novella with an account, an extended essay, describing the origins and creation of *Doctor Faustus* in the context of both diary entries and the personal and world-historical events of the time when it was written: *The Genesis of a Novel.* "The more such works recede into the past, the more ineffective they become," Thomas quoted Goethe as his justification, "in measure to their effectiveness at the moment . . . Therefore it is meet and fitting to win for them their historical value by discussing their origins with men of understanding and good will."[41]

The Genesis of a Novel was completed on 21st October 1948; in November *Doctor Faustus* was selected by the Book of the Month Club in America, and appeared in an edition of over 100,000 copies.

Critical response to *Doctor Faustus* in America, however, was no more welcoming than in Germany. Thomas had tried to warn Knopf against printing Helen Lowe-Porter's Translator's Note at the beginning of the book:

> It is an intelligent utterance, and I can well understand that Mrs Lowe feels the need to point out the enormous difficulties of her task. I am only afraid that her characterization of the book might have too dis-couraging an effect and might give the impression that the book is terribly highbrow and accessible only to the highest developed intellect . . . The book is, in fact, no insurmountably difficult treatise but, at least in part, an entertaining, even exciting novel. It would certainly not be desirable to make the public scared of it.[42]

But though Knopf did indeed cut the offending passage the book opened to a "largely miserable press ('New Yorker'! The ultimate!)" as Thomas reported to his son Klaus.[43] "For a few days I was thoroughly depressed by the dreariness of the American *Faustus* reviews," he wrote to Erika on 6th November 1948: there seemed a wholesale unwillingness to consider the book's implications for the cultural, artistic and even political state of modern man — "They all place such dreadful stress on the G-e-r-m-a-n allegory," Thomas complained.

It was perhaps not entirely unforeseeable, and it could be argued that Thomas' unwillingness to give Leverkühn "physical body", his insistence on maintaining his "representativeness", had in some ways obtained the opposite effect, a cardboard figure who thus places too much weight on the style of the writing itself — and that not even Helen Lowe-Porter's powers as a translator could give it the necessary brilliance to sustain the interest of all but the "highest developed intellects" in America. "My own fault I know it," Thomas confessed to Erika. "If I live and keep my strength I'll throw them *Felix Krull*, which consists of nothing but pranks, so that at last they'll stop regarding me as a 'ponderous philosopher'."

But not only the American press took exception to *Doctor Faustus*. If Leverkühn was a synthetic, representative figure in the book there were a score who were not — cameos of friends and individuals whose uninhibited portraits had helped to give Thomas some of the sense of documentary truth he needed: for who could be more typical of the intellectual climate in which Germany — and Europe — had been swept into the abyss than Thomas' own wide-ranging circle of friends and acquaintances? One by one they had taken their places in the apocalyptic tragedy: and not all were satisfied by their likenesses. Letters of explanation were rushed off. Some — like Hans Reisiger and Emil Preetorius — were mollified; others could not be brought to forgive such licence (Annette Kolb broke off all relations with Thomas and never spoke to him again in her life).

Yet perhaps the most humorous consequence of *Doctor Faustus* was the reaction of Arnold Schoenberg. It was Alma Mahler-Werfel who first mentioned to Schoenberg that by "stealing" the invention of the twelve-tone system for his novel, Thomas might well detract from Schoenberg's place in the future annals of musical history; but instead of approaching Thomas directly with this fear, Schoenberg — a near-neighbour of Thomas' in Los Angeles — first concocted a mythical contribution to the *Encyclopedia Americana* of 1988, written by a Hugo Triebsamen, in which the credit for the invention of the twelve-tone system was accredited to Thomas Mann. In this way, Schoenberg hoped, Thomas might be brought to see the gravity of what he had done, and Schoenberg forwarded the mythical article with a bitter note.

Ever since beginning *Doctor Faustus* Thomas had been aware how much the novel took him back "after many intellectual wanderings" as he put it to Walter Kolb in 1948, "to the German urban world of my first book *Budden-brooks*"; and how similar now was the response! Schoenberg's sally must indeed have reminded Thomas of the days, almost half a century before, when the citizens of Lübeck rose on their high horses and Friedrich Mann launched into print against his nephew, "the sorry bird who defiles his own nest".

"Instead of accepting my book with a satisfied smile as a piece of contemporary literature that testifies to his tremendous influence upon the musical culture of the era," Thomas replied to the *Saturday Review of Literature*, "Schoenberg regards it as an act of rape and insult. It is a sad spectacle to see a man of great worth, whose all-too-understandable hyper-sensitivity grows out of a life suspended between glorification and neglect, almost wilfully yield to delusions of persecution and of being robbed, and involve himself in rancorous bickering. It is my sincere hope that he may rise above bitterness and suspicion and that he may find peace in the assurance of his greatness and glory!"

8

In October 1948 Katja managed to find Heinrich a new apartment within walking distance of San Remo Drive, in Santa Monica; but Heinrich was loath to leave the old flat in which Nelly had died, in which "every inch of floor preserved the steps of my departed wife," as he wrote to Karl Lemke on 26th October. "Here I want for nothing, expect nothing," he wrote of his new home. Katja arranged for a nurse (also an émigrée) to live in with him, and did everything she could to help Heinrich settle. A letter of Thomas' in December 1948 relates that "forever busy and overworked" Katja was now also having to "visit and look after the needs of my old brother".[44] It was not always easy; though still in perfect mental health Heinrich had undoubtedly become frail, and often demanding in the manner of the elderly.

Nevertheless Thomas continued to look after Heinrich financially, they continued to meet at least once a week; and to her credit, despite a personal coolness that dated back to their first meeting (until the end of Heinrich's life they addressed each other in the polite "Sie"), Katja continued to look after Heinrich as if he were her own father.

By the spring of 1949, however, the pressure for Heinrich to return to the Soviet sector of Germany — first mooted in 1945 — became official. He was offered the post of President of the German Academy of Arts in Berlin, which was to be reconstituted, and everything would be done in advance to fulfil his wishes concerning living and working facilities. On 25th April 1949 he had been awarded the German National Prize for Art and Literature, and his books had achieved among the largest sales of post-war publications in the Soviet sector. In Russia, too, his popularity had not dimmed: in 1949 he was one of only four foreign authors to be published in the USSR. The editor of the Aufbau Verlag had assured him that on his return he would become a millionaire immediately — a promise Heinrich took with quiet humour — "a millionaire in East-Marks, still it's very nice to die a millionaire," he wrote to Alphonse Sondheimer.[45]

Did he wish to go? He was now in his seventy-ninth year, and given the state the cold war was reaching it was inevitable that his departure to East Germany would be used for propaganda purposes. Could he really face the strenuous round of conferences and public appearances that would be demanded of him, after eight years of total isolation in America? And how confront the necessity of dealing with men like Walter Ulbricht who had done more to wreck Heinrich's efforts of building the German People's Front in the 1930s than any other? In the autumn of 1937, Heinrich had confided to Alfred Kantorowicz and Max Braun that he would not consent to sit at the same table with Ulbricht again, he found the man so untrustworthy. "You see, I can't sit at a table with a man who suddenly claims that the table we are sitting at is not a table but a duckpond, and who wants to force me to agree with him."[46] Ulbricht's slave-like deference to the Comintern had earned him nothing but mistrust among European intellectuals, the last straw coming when on 9th February 1940, Ulbricht denounced Britain and France for not accepting Hitler's latest peace offer — "which the USSR supported", as he wrote in *Die Welt*.

Yet the wave of fascism sweeping America, "the ignorance which surrounds me" as Heinrich wrote to one correspondent,[47] the very determination of the West to revitalize the Ruhr under the same private ownership which had once led to Hitler, the necessity perhaps to rise above personal qualms and serve the reconstruction of a new Germany based on egalitarian principles made it a difficult decision to make — the choice between a country which bought his books in terms of thousands, and a nation which had not published a single work of his since 1939 and which forced him to live on his younger brother's charity. As for West Germany, the cold war had led to a complete embargo on his name and his past career — as though he had never existed, never served the first Republic, never fought against Hitler. "In fifty years I have not been so completely disregarded as now," Heinrich wrote of the West in a letter to Karl Lemke in July 1949.[48] "If one had no need of dollars one would laugh. At least let me smile."

So for the moment Heinrich hesitated, while the pleas from East Germany became more urgent. Yet curiously, amid the hesitations about whether he ought to accept his call to Berlin or not, it was to be Thomas and Katja who were the first to visit the Soviet sector of Germany — unexpectedly in the summer of 1949, and to the consternation of American and Western observers.

9

To begin with, Thomas had no intention of visiting Germany in 1949, but only of repeating his 1947 tour, this time lecturing about Goethe on the 200th anniversary of his birth. Even this trip depended on the cold war "remaining cold" as Thomas wrote to Richard Schweizer in October 1948[49] for the Russian blockade of Berlin had begun on 24th June and anti-communist warmongering in America was reaching its height. The visit to Europe, anyway, would be a "change of air" after the year's sojourn in California which Thomas likened to the life of a "toadstool". "Germany?" he wrote to Hans Reisiger on 19th December 1948. "I think I would rather not, even this time. It is difficult to foresee anything but confusion, pain, most unwholesome shock, and very divided reception. Emigrés are not well regarded. They didn't remain loyal to Germany," he paraphrased Thiess and

Hausmann sarcastically.

> Under Hitler, you see, one had to stay loyal to Germany, and afterwards one can go, like Wiechert and Jaspers, to Switzerland, or like Furtwängler to Chicago. It's laughable. The situation is also so bad that German newspapers, in cool misuse of their licence, are permitted to denounce British and American citizens as "Communists" against their governments — that is what Munich papers are doing to my own children.

But if Thomas imagined he could travel a second time to Europe without visiting Germany he was being optimistic. Though he had become a symbol of the "good Germany" in the war among democratic nations he was now an unhappy reminder of virtue and conscience to a people bitter with shame and savage in their self-righteousness. "Why can't those who are receptive to what I have to offer take pleasure in it and the others not bother with me? But they continue to bother themselves ceaselessly, report on me, hatefully and yet at the same time fascinated, never stop busying themselves with me, spitting gall and stupidity at me," Thomas wrote to Otto Basler in March 1949.[50] "And why must I come in person to Germany?" he asked Wilhelm Buller. " 'Where I am, is Germany', and where my books are, there I am too. They are after all the distilled best of me, and the Germans should read them, as if I were already a departed spirit. I'm not so very far from the end anyway."

But Germany *did* want Thomas in the flesh; and with accustomed zeal they pressed until they had him. Thomas had decided to decline membership of the newly reconstituted Bavarian Academy of Arts in Munich when in February 1949 — despite some opposition and one walk-out (in protest against his erstwhile speech *Germany and the Germans)* — he was elected Honorary Chairman of the Literary Section. No sooner had he accepted this honour — which he balanced by accepting the Weimar Goethe Prize for 1949 in the Eastern sector — than it was insisted he should come to Munich in June for the proposed Goethe ceremonies and "speak at a solemn public occasion", as Thomas put it to Reisiger on 19th March 1949. "I have not yet consented," he added, "but I shall probably have to, and my peace is gone." It promised to be "a ghostly adventure" after sixteen years, "a veritable trial. For so very long, being taken to Germany", "falling into the hands of the Germans", had been a nightmare.

> And what am I to say? It is all so terribly complicated. So I must put everything aside and embark on inward efforts to put together a speech — and then again I cannot do it, for there is a block. The awareness of how much we and they have drifted apart in all these years prevents me from finding the right tone . . .

Yet this was only the beginning of an historic trip that would be shadowed by death within the family. On the eve of their departure for Chicago and Washington news arrived that Thomas' younger brother Viktor had died in Munich. Although relations between the two elder brothers and Viktor had always been distant, his death came as an unexpected blow. After the suicide of both Carla and Julia it now left Heinrich and Thomas as the only survivors of the once patrician household from the Mengstrasse in Lübeck. Viktor had only recently completed the manuscript of his family recollections, *Wir waren fünf,* had diligently researched the origins of the Manns, the Martys and the Bruhns, and was looking forward to seeing Thomas in Switzerland.

But this was only the first blow. On 10th May 1949, Thomas, Katja and their daughter Erika left by plane for London and Oxford, where Thomas was to be invested at a special ceremony as an Honorary Doctor of the University. His lecture — *Goethe and Democracy* — was delivered in German in the Taylorian Institute in Oxford, and in English in London. Then on 19th May they flew on to Sweden; and it was there, on 21st May, that the news of Klaus Mann's suicide in Cannes first reached them. He was forty-three.

Klaus had already made an attempt on his life in the summer of 1948. "The situation remains dangerous," Thomas had written to Theodor Adorno shortly afterwards. "Both my sisters killed themselves, and Klaus has much of the elder one in him."[51] It cannot have been easy — as Thomas was deeply aware — for Klaus to establish his own identity as a writer and even as a man in view of the renown his father enjoyed. "My relationship to him was difficult and not without feelings of guilt, for my very existence cast a shadow over him from the start," Thomas wrote to Hermann Hesse after the tragedy.[52] Thomas' immediate impulse was to return to America, and to cancel the rest of the European visit, as he wrote to Alfred Knopf.[53] Or was it?

It remains one of the ironic aspects of Thomas' genius that, given the love he lavished on his work, he should sometimes have failed to show it in real life. Konrad Kellen, his secretary for several years, has remarked on his curious relationship with his children, his "impersonal manner in dealing with them", the way he wrote about "their books or articles as though he were criticizing the work of some author entirely unknown to him".[54]

Thus Klaus was buried at Cannes without a single member of his family present — not even Erika left her parents — and only at the last moment did his younger brother Michael, on tour with Monteux's San Francisco Symphony Orchestra, appear at the graveside. Heinrich, in Santa Monica, was deeply moved when he heard of the event. "Perhaps you too have read of the scene at Klaus' grave," he wrote to Karl Lemke on 15th June 1949.

His younger brother Michael appeared in the funeral procession quite unexpectedly . . . On the way to the cemetery he carried a small case, out of which, when they arrived, he took a viola or viola d'amore. Over the coffin which had been lowered into the grave he played a largo; then silently the gathering broke up.[55]

After considering the alternative carefully Thomas decided to go ahead with his European schedule — to Sweden to receive an Honorary Doctorate from the University of Lund, then to Switzerland where he was due to give lectures and readings in Zurich, Küsnacht, Bern, and Basel: to be followed by his final and long-awaited return to Germany — after sixteen years.

In Washington in April 1949 Thomas had been honoured with the quinquennial award of the American Academy of Arts and Letters; and there on behalf of the Oberburgermeister of Frankfurt, Walter Hallstein had informed Thomas he was to be awarded the 1949 German Goethe Prize. It was thus Frankfurt which became the destination for Thomas' symbolic return to the father-land, and throughout the early part of the summer preparations were made for his arrival. In June the BBC broadcast a talk by Thomas on Geothe, *Goethe, the German miracle* which he had recorded in London — "the best contribution I made to the Goethe celebrations", as Thomas afterwards called it, "a three fold portrait of the Great Men of the German nation: Luther, Goethe, Bismarck; Goethe placed at the end with honour".[56] His remarks about Luther as the cause of so much bloodshed and barbarity in Germany were not new — they had already been put forward in *Doctor Faustus* — but they now called down upon their author the outraged con-demnation of the German Protestant Church — and a special press-conference was called in Oxford where the Lutheran World League was meeting, as well as a public meeting in London to "reject" such "insults" to the great reformer.

This, however, was only to be a minor combustion point in Thomas' progress through Europe in 1949. Word had reached Thomas that, apart from their own award of a Goethe Prize, the town of Weimar wished to honour Thomas with the Freedom of the city. Thomas decided not only to accept, but to receive the honour in person in the Soviet zone.

In the midst of the so-called cold war, only weeks after the Russians had been forced to end their unsuccessful Berlin blockade, the news was received with disbelief. It was announced at a press-conference in Frankfurt on 25th July, two days after his arrival in the city; and in his Goethe speech in the packed cathedral of St Paul later that day Thomas explained his decision.

I am surrounded by the ruins which the national catastrophe has left behind, I find the country torn and divided into zones of the victorious powers, and I understand all too well the patriotic grief, the bitter impatience from which, whether loudly or quietly, the words "foreign rule" burst out. Let us accept that the rule of barbarism which lay over Germany for twelve years, and which led to this situation, was even worse. But what is happening now hurts and upsets and weighs heavily enough and the longing for it to end would not be strange to any people on earth. One day it must and will end. But for me, as I stand here, it is already over. I know no zones. My visit applies to Germany itself, to the whole of Germany, not to any one area of occupation. Who should guarantee and represent the unity of Germany if not an independent writer whose true homeland is, as I have said, the German language, free and untouched by occupation . . .

"Is he a communist, then?" Katja could hear people murmuring in the audience — and the next day the West German press erupted in a storm of comment and protest. The American Consulate told them that as American citizens they could not be stopped from going to Weimar, but that the matter was not well regarded. In the context of the increasing witch-hunt in America and the pressure for anti-communist legislation in Congress, this was an understatement. Even liberals in the West saw a danger of re-awakening the nationalist beast that had been laid low after so much slaughter.

But Thomas did not stay to defend himself. On 27th July he arrived in Munich, gave his *Goethe and Democracy* lecture in the great hall of the Ministry of Economics, and on 30th July was collected by Johannes R. Becher in a Soviet military car from Bayreuth and accompanied in state across the border to Weimar. The visit to East and West Germany lasted barely ten days: yet its reverberations were to last almost to the end of Thomas' life. The East Germans were profoundly moved and heartened that, on the bicentenary of Goethe's birth, the greatest novelist of the Western world should have had the courage to set aside all ideological conflicts between East and West and visit them on his first post-war return to Germany. Contrary to the vitriolic denunciations made in the Western press, Thomas' visit was not made into a massive propaganda exercise by the East German communists, but was treated throughout as a deeply human gesture by an old and distinguished "bourgeois" German writer, now an American citizen. If the route was lined with schoolchildren and villagers and be-decked with flags it was not to pretend that the Eastern zone was better than the Western, but as a way of showing him the pride they felt in their new and growing socialist state, despite the ravages of the war and the criminal reparations exacted by the Russians.

Though he was not "duped" by the somewhat artificial nature of his reception in East Germany — as his account of his trip was to show[57] — he found the spirit of denazification, of honest endeavour to rebuild the country on egalitarian lines, both genuine and admirable — a recognition which neither made him a communist nor blinded him to the perils or disadvantages of such a totalitarian system — as his letter to Walter Ulbricht on the fate of the post-war inmates of Buchenwald also demonstrated. "Among the Communist functionaries of the German East Zone there are of course some lick-spittle, self-serving and power-hungry despots," Thomas wrote in his reply to Paul Olberg's Open Letter[58] condemning his visit. "But I have looked into other faces and seen resolute good will and pure idealism — the face of people who work eighteen hours a day and sacrifice themselves to make a reality of what they believe to be truth, and to create those social conditions inside their country which, as they say, will prevent a relapse into war and barbarism." To Erich von Kahler Thomas was even more specific: not only did he foresee that the social democrats would be "swept away" in West Germany, but found renazification "running at full speed under our kindly protection, and I should think," he added sarcastically, "that in a couple of years the German honour will have been completely restored. You have no idea of the shamelessness of the press there . . ."[59] He had been denounced, sent threatening letters, and it was with some relief that he boarded the *Nieuw Amsterdam* in Le Havre on 5th August 1949. "Never again," he wrote in his letter to Albrecht Goes on 3rd September.

In Pacific Palisades Thomas sat down in August 1949 to write an account of his German visit which the *New York Times* had requested for its magazine — though his account of East Germany made Thomas wonder whether, in the current anti-communist climate, the *New York Times* would dare to print the article.[60]

> My abhorrence of Fascist vileness has never succeeded in making me a Communist. That much is known. I am a stranger to the totalitarian state, to its Jacobin virtue, its secret-police methods, the humorless optimism, its scorn of bourgeois refinement and all it describes as decadent, formalistic, remote from the common touch.
>
> Yet it is known too that I am a non-Communist rather than an anti-Communist; that I disdain to bring into play, against something that is still under trial, ideals that have so often become hyper-critical pretexts for ulterior interests; and the simple fact, finally, that I refuse to take part in the rampant hysteria of Communist persecutions, that I speak on behalf of peace in a world whose future has long since become unimaginable without Communist traits — that fact is apparently sufficient to earn me a certain confidence among the devout of that social creed.

Thomas explained in the article — though it was unlikely to stem the current tide in America. "I am no fellow-traveller," Thomas made the point neatly in his reply to Paul Olberg. "But it appears that I can count some clever Communists among my fellow-travellers."

Nevertheless the visit to Weimar had convinced Thomas that Heinrich would be treated in East Germany with respect and veneration. Though it would probably mean they would not see each other again, Thomas felt it was better than Heinrich ending his days in the total obscurity and anti-socialist hostility of America. Johannes Becher wrote to say that a villa in Berlin, together with a chauffeur and an office in the Academy, were standing ready; but the news, in September and October 1949, that Germany was to become two separate states, a Federal Republic and a Democratic Republic respectively, meant that the Academy would not now become the all-German institution the East Germans had hoped in their official invitation of 23rd May 1949.[61] "Might be that it turns out to be the only genuine measure to preserve peace," Heinrich wrote to Karl Lemke on 25th December 1949; but the division of Germany increased the very irrevocability of the step he would be taking. He hesitated, and for the moment Thomas declined on his behalf, "at least until the following spring," as Thomas wrote to Alfred Neumann in October 1949.[62]

In the event fortune took the matter out of their hands. In December 1949 it was announced that all Czech passports were to be recalled and new ones would be issued. "The latest is that I am without a passport," Heinrich wrote in his letter to Lemke. "Will it take until Christmas 1950 until I can travel?" Though representations were made and the matter expedited, it was only by the spring of 1950 that, with his new passport, a passage could be booked on the Polish ship *Batory,* bound for Gdynia and due to leave on 28th April 1950.

He had ceased to work after finishing the proof-corrections of *Der Atem* in March 1949. He had considered continuing the fragment of his play on Frederick the Great which he had begun in the early 1940s. He completed an outline of the whole play, and in 1948 wrote a short essay, *The King of Prussia;*[63] but he was aware, as he wrote to Maximilian Brantl, that the undertaking would be no less demanding than *Henri IV* had been — and would take as long. "What I am still undertaking, a *Frederick*, can scarcely be finished now," he had written in October 1947. "It would be counterpart to my *Henri,* but I spent six years on that. Well, fragments are also worthwhile. One never does reach the end, as little in one's own efforts as with the contemplation of the world."[64]

"Productivity is a curious thing," Thomas wrote in his only public statement upon Heinrich's death. "When one becomes, in the end, too tired for it, one finds one no longer misses it either; I never heard him complain about his capacity for work failing him, it left him seemingly quite indifferent." He continued to read, if only the great masters of French Literature he so loved — Flaubert, Stendhal, Anatole France, Voltaire, and in German, Goethe and Fontane — and listened to music. "The world settled into a difficult sleep as in the nights of ungovernable catastrophes, when we too are tired and lay down the word," were the last lines of *Der Atem.* On 11th March 1950, Heinrich spent a long evening listening to a Puccini opera on the radio and it was only with difficulty that his nurse persuaded him to go to bed. In sleep came a brain haemorrhage, and in the morning he could not be woken. Though his heart continued to beat faintly until nightfall, it was the end. "It was, at bottom, the most merciful solution," wrote Thomas.

The funeral was worthy. Feuchtwanger and Reverend Stephen Fritschman of the Unitarian Church spoke, and the Temianka-Quartet played a slow and beautiful movement from Debussy. It was how he would have wished it. Then I followed the coffin over the warm grass of the Santa Monica cemetery.

May he rest in peace after a full life whose traces can only vanish, as I believe, with culture itself and the self-respect of humanity.[65]

CHAPTER SIXTEEN

The Last Exile

Thus Heinrich died in California, in the same obscurity in which he had first set foot on American soil almost ten years before. In his last novel *Der Atem* he had depicted the death of his autobiographical heroine Lydia, the last message she dictates to her successful and beloved sister Marie-Louise, and finally Marie-Louise's own arrival in the room in which her dead sister lies. Marie-Louise takes powder and lipstick and proceeds to make up the face of the corpse so that it should look presentable to the world. She is the last of the Traun family alive, and involuntarily she finds herself blaming her sister for this, for leaving her alone, for making her lose her composure for a moment.

Though Thomas confined himself to a single public statement on Heinrich's death, it affected him profoundly; and in his private letters he gave vent both to his grief and his bitter, bitter shame that no word of condolence, of sympathy or recognition of Heinrich's life's contribution came from Western Germany. "I feel shaken to the marrow by so many deaths in one year," Thomas wrote to Dr Pfeiffer-Belli in April 1950 — "first our son, then in Germany my youngest brother, and now my elder brother . . . Moreover I am hurt and angry that from Munich as from the rest of West Germany (Bonn, Frankfurt, his hometown Lübeck) no single word of official sympathy (Academy! Town Council!) has reached me concerning the death of my brother Heinrich. It seems they have no idea in the West German federal state who it is that has died."[1]

"Miserable!" Thomas wrote to the West German newspaper-editor Emil

Belzner, *"Not one word!"*[2]

It was indeed a sad ending to life of the shy, proud champion of European democracy, of justice and social progress. "Recently I have been writing a novel the publication of which seems unlikely to me," Heinrich had written to Thea Sternheim in 1945. "No matter. The world we have known will not survive our works, which have every chance of slumbering with it."[3] He was prepared for personal eclipse, though he found the post-war political reaction galling for those who, like himself, had sacrificed everything for an anti-fascist future. "Will Pierre permit me an opinion?" he asked in his penultimate letter to Felix Bertaux in 1947 on hearing that Bertaux's son was entering politics. "It would be this: that at present one is not practising politics, but mendacity — and throughout 'free' Europe."[4]

America was no different. "Please understand that I am not on the point of becoming a martyr for a cause which is not mine," Thomas explained his political position to Walter H. Perl on 25th March 1950; "I can never endorse the totalitarian state. But a good many people here are on their way to becoming martyrs — namely, all those who oppose the destruction of democracy, a process which is in full swing under the guise of protecting that democracy. Doesn't it all strike you as dreadfully familiar, dreadfully like Germany?" and he quoted from his celebrated *Exchange of Letters* with the Dean of Bonn University:

> "Something very wrong must have happened . . ." — oh yes, things are happening and things are building up which were previously inconceivable in a country before the coming of Fascism. The "cold war" is bringing physical and moral ruin upon America; that is why I am against it — and not "against America". If the Mundt-Nixon Bill should be passed, I shall *flee* — head over heels, together with my seven honorary doctorates.

It was Thomas' first indication that he might leave America — the country which had once fêted and rewarded him for his exemplary stand against Hitler, and was now branding him as a communist. The Library of Congress which had once made him a Consultant was itself now implicated, since the House Committee on Un-American Activities had declared it "infested with communists"; Thomas' planned speech there, in the spring of 1950, was cancelled in haste, and Thomas reduced to the title of Fellow. He was never to speak in the institution again. "Let me hope, at any rate," Thomas wrote to Mrs Meyer, "that I shall be able to deliver the lecture in Chicago and New York; for I would be reluctant to admit in Europe that I am no longer allowed to speak in America. That would be shaming."[5]

The matter was hushed up; but the reception in Sweden, in Paris, and finally in Switzerland that summer was to have a lasting effect, despite all the loyalty Thomas still felt for his adopted country. In Sweden, in May, he was received by Prince Michael, President of the Swedish PEN Club; in Paris the reception at the Ritz was a veritable "tumult", as Thomas reported to Mrs Meyer; "for three hours I had to sign books in a *librairie* while people stood *queuing* on the street under police supervision; and the lecture had to be transferred to the large *amphi-théâtre*. Two thousand people came — it is a long time since anything like that has occurred, I was told — and the conduct of this crowd too was extraordinary."[6]

His lecture was entitled *The Years of My Life,* and its elucidation of America's "mindless hysteria", the American attempt to buy out the non-communist world, the very *similarity* between Americans and Russians — their lack of reserve, their openness, their "cheerful primitiveness" — was not calculated to appeal to hysterical American anti-communists. It was, as Thomas noted to Emil Belzner, an updated version of his own *Appeal to Reason* speech of 1930, a "prayer for peace".[7] Mrs Meyer was "grieved" by the text when she read it; but its honesty, its faith in a progressive, not regressive, future for mankind aroused sympathy throughout Europe. Even the South German Radio insisted on broadcasting the lecture in its entirety on Thomas' birthday.

"May America, great and good and only badly overwrought, not mis-understand me!" Thomas appealed to Mrs Meyer. "I am attached to her and truly mean very well by her. I tell nobody that I was not allowed to speak in Washington, and only stress that I lectured in Chicago and New York."[8]

But when Ida Herz wrote from London asking whether she ought to accept the post of custodian of the Thomas Mann Collection at Yale, he advised her against emigrating — "you would feel extremely alienated over there . . . I am afraid you would inevitably feel homesick for a less malignant atmosphere."[9] "But how do things look in America?" Thomas wrote from Zurich to Theodor W. Adorno. "Often enough we find ourselves considering the idea of *leaving* it. Who would have thought a second emigration possible even three years ago?"[10] "I keep repeating: the Upper Engadin is the finest abode in the world," he wrote to Otto Basler from St Moritz. "I do not speak lightly of happiness, but I almost believe I am happy here." And two weeks later:

Who knows whether we shall see one another, whether we shall see Europe itself and all that it conceals, ever again if we go back now. I say "if", for we really are in two minds about it, and will probably be so until the last moment. It is an agonizing situation, for whichever way I choose will be considered wrong.

When finally he arrived "home" in Pacific Palisades at the end of August 1950. Thomas found Mrs Meyer's aggrieved letter about his lecture. "I do not want to 'abandon America to socialism' (which may be an inevitable necessity for Europe) any more than you do; but it grieves me," Thomas replied, "that this land of pioneers and liberty is at present supporting the old, worn-out, rotten and corrupt forces throughout the world, and that America in a time of inexorable change plays the 'policeman' of the status quo . . ."

Though he had no intention of ever resettling in Germany, Thomas had now begun to long for the neutral, German-speaking freedom and surround-ings of Switzerland, as once he had enjoyed them in the 1930s, while working on the now impossibly serene-seeming idyll *Joseph and his Brothers.*

"I would really be glad to have *The Holy Sinner* appear only in German," he wrote to Mrs Meyer, "for I am already shuddering at the stupidities of the critics who will be going by the English version. The Germans are a thoroughly unbearable people, but I am after all a German writer through and through and a devotee of the German language, and I do frequently dream of ending my life in a German-language area, in Switzerland."

As more and more of his friends began to leave America to return to Europe, and now that Heinrich was no longer alive, there was less and less reason to stay in the "hostile" climate of post-war America. *The Holy Sinner* was finished on 26th October 1950. Thomas was now seventy-five. It remained only to be decided what new literary project — if any — he should undertake: and where.

2

The Holy Sinner was Thomas' seventh novel, and his shortest. Its unusual theme took Thomas back to the days of *Wälsungenblut — Blood of the Walsings* — to the erotic nature of twin siblings. This time, however, instead of sublimating their urges, the twins unite: and it is the fruit of their union, the child Gregorius, who is the central figure of the tale. The novel was published in German in the spring of 1951; and although the book received a mixture of critical reviews, it was paradoxically in America, the country currently doing its utmost to alienate the distinguished immigrant, that it took the public by storm, and was, in September 1951, chosen as Book of the Month with a minimum edition of 100,000 copies.

By then Thomas had chosen to continue the fragment of his humorous novel *Confessions of Felix Krull* which he had set aside in 1911 to write *Death in Venice*. He had begun, on 8th January 1951, on the same page of the actual manuscript where he had left off — yet how much lay between! Despite the seemingly insuperable problem of the interval, of bridging a gap of forty years in style and experience, Thomas was unruffled, he had looked forward to the moment for so many years. After all, though a bogus auto-biography, *Confessions of Felix Krull* was, at a deeper level, a distinctly personal projection, the autobiography of what might have been (together with many real episodes from Thomas' life); and the intervening years between 1911 and 1951 were themselves rich in humour and anecdote — his own servant caught stealing after the First World War, the scandal of the confidence trickster Heinrich's daughter married . . . And there was the lure of demonstrating "life's unity", as Thomas had put it in *The Genesis of a Novel*.

But although the first pages flowed easily, it was only by closing eyes and ears to the outside world that Thomas could pick up the lightness and gaiety of the *Confessions*. He declined to join the American Peace Crusade, issued a statement to the United Press Agency that he was refusing to subscribe to any collective movement, and wrote in confidence to Philip Morrison, one of the physicists involved in the development of the Atom bomb:

This decision is not based so much on fear and the desire for security . . .
it is due to a true inner withdrawal of my interest from the destinies of
this country which, in my opinion, has embarked on a wrong and
ruinous course.[11]

By now, however, it was too late to withdraw. The witch-hunt had begun
in earnest as the Korean War blossomed into the inevitable East-West confrontation. First the right-wing magazine *The Freeman* published an article
by Eugene Tillinger on 26th March 1951, using photo-montage techniques
and an extract from a private letter to denounce Thomas for "communist-
front activities," and the accusations were soon syndicated by UP to every
newspaper in America. In great bitterness Thomas wrote an open letter to the
New York German-language newspaper *Aufbau*:

I am not a Communist and never have been one. Neither am I a "fellow-
traveller", nor could I ever be one where the destination was totalitarian-
ism. I felt it an honour and a joy to become a citizen of this country. But
hysterical, irrational, and blind hatred of communism represents a danger
to America far more terrible than native communism. Indeed, the
persecution mania and the mania to persecute that we have succumbed to
and that we seem on the point of surrendering ourselves to, body and
soul — these cannot lead to anything good. Unless we change our course
immediately they will surely lead from bad to worse.[12]

It was of no avail. "Obstinately and inexorably the nemesis takes its course,
following the vilest laws," Thomas had already written to Erich von Kahler
in February, "and sometimes I catch myself thinking: just as well; let it come
the way they insist on having it. Human wickedness deserves a visitation
such as the earth has not yet seen — and this civilization of grabbers, fools
and gangsters deserves to perish."[13]

It was only weeks before the next "denunciation". Again it was by Eugene
Tillinger, though this time in the ominous-sounding (to an émigré) newspaper
New Leader. It was called *Thomas Mann and the Commissar*, an "exposé" of
Thomas' birthday message to the East Berlin magazine *Aufbau* on the
occasion of Johannes R. Becher's sixtieth birthday. How this innocent
tribute to a German colleague could have been so misconstrued can only be
understood in the context of fear, hypocrisy, and ill-will then sweeping the
United States as once it had swept Germany. In the House of Representatives
Congressman Donald L. Jackson rose on 18th June to ask that the *New Leader*
article be put on the "appendix record" of the House, and to accuse Thomas
of having become "one of the world's foremost apologists for Stalin and
company".

"On 22nd May 1951," Jackson informed the House:

Mr Mann sent warm and cordial birthday greetings to an East German
Stalinist literary hack by the name of Becher. Mr Becher's chief claim to
fame would appear to be his consistent ability to tongue the boots of his
political superiors . . . While none will deny that Mr Mann is a literary
giant, many will question his good judgement and his political wisdom.
Some may even go so far as to question his loyalty to the principles of

personal freedom of action under the law . . . Thousands of lives have already been lost in the mortal struggle against international communism and the leaders of that godless crusade. Mr Becher is an artist whose devotion to Stalin and to communism is unquestioned and universally accepted. The American people do not share Mr Mann's high regard for Mr Becher and the way of life to which he pays such high tribute. Our eminent guest within the gates of what we Americans consider to be a land of liberty and justice will do well to lard his obvious sympathies for communism and communists with a few strips of common sense and common gratitude. Mr Mann should remember that guests who complain about the fare at the table of their host are seldom invited to another meal.[14]

"For some time I have been engaged on the continuation of the Memoirs of Felix Krull. But the sick, tense atmosphere of this country oppresses me and I have to steel myself, despite trembly nerves, to ward off detestable and mortally dangerous attacks on me," Thomas wrote to Peter de Mendelssohn.[15] "The world is sliding irrevocably into darkness, catastrophe and barbarism," he wrote to his Italian translator Lavinia Mazzucchetti. "The poisoned, sick, tense atmosphere, burdened with mischief, weighs upon me, and my productive mood is shattered — without which I am lost. This time there is no way out. The world's coffin has been nailed — in every sense."[16]

"Your words encounter a yearning which, the shorter the time that is left me, grows stronger and stronger within me: the urge to go back to the old earth," Thomas wrote to Hans Carossa in Switzerland. "I have no desire to rest my bones in this soulless soil which I owe nothing, and which knows nothing of me. Where George, Rilke and Mombert returned, that is where I would have my gravestone. The question is only whether it will be possible."[17]

After the speech in Congress it was with infinite relief that Thomas and Katja set out once again for Europe on the French steamship *De Grasse*. This time the entire summer was spent in Switzerland and Austria — where at Bad Gastein, once Heinrich's favourite spa, Thomas sought treatment for arthritic and rheumatic pains torturing his hip and arm. They had hoped to spend at least a year in Europe this time, but they had not been able to find a ready buyer for the house in Pacific Palisades and in October they returned once more to the "poisoned atmosphere" of America for the winter. Inwardly, however, the decision was made.

3

It was an exaggeration for Thomas to maintain he owed America nothing, for he owed her probably more than any other émigré from Hitler's Germany: his freedom, even his life, a new public, honours, and the sunshine climate of California. Like Joseph, his own literary child, Thomas had been accepted and "raised to high office" in a foreign country — which made it all the more galling that the country should now turn hysterically against him. He had no wish to leave like an outcast a second time in his life, and the move to Europe, therefore, was arranged with the utmost circumspection and avoidance of publicity. He left Pacific Palisades on 24th June 1952, and boarded the aeroplane for Switzerland on 29th June, with only a briefcase and travelling luggage.

The last winter in America had been fruitful, however, and almost three-quarters of *Felix Krull* lay completed when the time came to depart. Indeed, the work had so preoccupied Thomas that in May he had decided to interrupt the story with a novella which, as he wrote to Ida Herz, would provide a "refreshing distraction" from the lengthy confidence novel — *The Black Swan,* the last of Thomas' distinguished line of short stories and novellas.[18]

The subject of *The Black Swan* was no less tabu than *The Holy Sinner,* a tragic insight into the deceit of life, which stemmed from a chance conversation with Katja. They had been talking of an ageing friend when Katja said she was worried, she felt the lady's complaints of sickness might be pathological in origin. When Thomas asked what she meant, Katja told him the story of a woman she had once known who, in middle age, had suddenly fallen in love with a much younger man. Triumphantly she had come one day to announce to Katja a miracle had happened, and that her periods had re-started. It was cancer of the womb. "Victory, Anna, victory," exclaims the unfortunate heroine of *The Black Swan* to her daughter one day: "it has come back to me, come back to me after such a long interruption, absolutely naturally and just as it should be for a mature, vigorous woman! Dear child, what a miracle! What a miracle great, beneficent Nature has wrought in me, how she has blessed my faith!"

It was a cruel story, and was to upset many of Thomas' staunchest admirers. With its self-exiled American as the object of Frau von Tümmler's affections, its harsh indictment of Nature's treacherous deceit, it was indeed a swansong to the wonders of California and the Pacific. By the time it was finished, Thomas had become an expatriate American residing in Switzerland. "Passing of the evening of life and literary activity," ran the permit he had obtained. "To be welcome does make one feel good after all," he wrote to Hans Reisiger.[19]

4

The "second exile" as Thomas called it, was in many ways similar to the first, not least in the decision, to begin with, not to make public or political statements about the country from which he had "fled". When the *New York Times* asked him to give his opinions "on the realities and dangers in the current trend of American policy towards restriction of entry and investigation (and castigation) of non-conformist opinion in all walks of life — everything, in short, that will be suggested to you by the names McCarthy and McCarran," Thomas declined.[20] Yet the "craving for headlines," as he termed the

American passion, was not to be satisfied by Thomas' silent withdrawal to Switzerland. Despite the innocuous lecture with which Thomas toured Europe in the summer and autumn of 1952 *(The Artist and Society)* and his refusal to give interviews "on America", the American press finally caught him at a press-conference he had been forced to hold in Vienna in November. "Pressed by newspapermen what political system he preferred, Mann declined to answer" flashed the AP-report to America; and once again Thomas was forced to defend himself, both to the Associated Press agency and in America in the columns of the New York *Aufbau*. "If I knew a 'system' preferable to our sadly abused and deeply endangered democracy — I would be off today to offer my services," Thomas declared in what came to be known as his "Declaration of loyalty to the Western world".

I am an American citizen. Never, as such — even if there were no such thing as a "press" — would it occur to me abroad to speak unsympathetically or even deprecatingly of a country to which I belong now and in the future. However the older I get, the more I desire to renew physical contact with the "old earth" — and if this passes for disgrace, then I must have been ignorant of the true meaning of the word until now.

But of course in our bloodily-divided world there is no end to misunderstanding, of spying, of insinuation and denunciation; and so I suppose I shall not be left in peace to the end of my days.[21]

After the defeat of Adlai Stevenson in the American Presidential Election in November 1952 even the prospect of a visit back to America was ruled out in Thomas' mind. "An invitation has come from America, a joint one from three large Quaker colleges, to lecture to them in the autumn," Thomas wrote to his publisher, Bermann-Fischer, in May 1953. "Good people! But in the words of Ludwig Thoma's rapscallion: 'I'm not that dumb.' "[22]

In the summer of 1952 the Accademia dei Lincei in Rome awarded Thomas the 1952 International Literature Prize, with a special commendation not only for his "gigantic" literary contribution to modern letters, but "the real example of a living humanism which transcends the divisions of our times and thus provides guidance to all creative spirits."[23] In December 1952 the French government awarded him the Officer's Cross of the *Légion d'Honneur,* with the citation: "Cette distinction est un hommage rendu par la France à l'exceptionelle valeur et à la signification mondiale de votre oeuvre littéraire ainsi qu'à la lutte que vous n'avez cessé de mener dans l'intérêt de la liberté et de la dignité humaine" — "the finest words of welcome Europe could offer me on my return," as Thomas wrote to Mrs Meyer on 8th February 1953. Finally in June 1953 he was awarded an Honorary Doctorate of the University of Cambridge.

Despite such tributes, however, Thomas maintained his ironical, if grateful, stance of old towards success. "I go about with the *rosette* of the Legion of Honour in my buttonhole. I am excessively vain about it, just like a Frenchy," he concluded one letter to Ida Herz in April 1953. It was impossible not to be aware of the more farcical elements of life and "achievement" when writing a book as irreverent as *Felix Krull* undoubtedly was. Though the work exhausted him and he was becoming increasingly frail, he had recommenced the novel as soon as he put paid to the savage Nature-novella in April 1953; and two weeks later in Rome, where he was to receive his International Literature Prize, he was granted an audience with Pope Pius XII. At the end of his brief audience he was given a small silver medal with the Pope's portrait as a memento, genuflected once more, "Which I found was very easy and natural to do. I think back on the episode with a certain tenderness."[24]

Katja had found a house to let in Erlenbach near Zurich into which they had moved in December 1952, followed closely by their furniture and possessions from Pacific Palisades. It was too small, however, and by the summer of 1953 they were looking for a house on Lake Geneva. Thomas was now seventy-eight. "I feel my strength ebbing slowly away, and think about death a great deal," he wrote to Lavinia Mazzucchetti from Erlenbach.[25] His problematic relationship with Germany had improved since his return to Europe, and he had spent more than a month in Munich and Frankfurt with Erika in the autumn of 1952, followed by his first visit to Hamburg since the 1920s, in June 1953. Everywhere — and particularly with university students in Frankfurt and Hamburg — his readings from the manuscript of *Felix Krull* brought tremendous applause. It was indeed remarkable that, nearing eighty, the "ponderous philosopher," as he had been called in America, should manage to convey such youth and satirical gaiety in his work.

From Hamburg Thomas had made a brief excursion to the town of his birth and to Travemünde where as a child he had been so contented. "The memory of having once more breathed the air of Travemünde, that children's paradise, 'sits smiling to my heart' as the line runs in *Hamlet*," he wrote in an open letter in the *Lübecker Freie Presse* on 4th June 1953.

His life was coming full circle. He continued working on *Felix Krull* throughout the autumn in Erlenbach, and completed it — or what was intended to be the first volume of Felix Krull's Confessions — at the end of January 1954. It was his last novel, and the last of his fictional work; for although Thomas had harboured plans for a Renaissance novella portraying Erasmus, Hutten and Luther — no doubt ironically — and even prepared some fifty pages of notes for a play to be called *Luther's Wedding*, he no longer had the strength or the time. The last year-and-a-half of his life was to be devoted to the honouring of literary forebears — of Fontane, Kleist, Chekhov; and finally the 150th anniversary of Schiller's death: a departing tribute to Germany's greatest playwright.

5

When he completed the manuscript of *Felix Krull* Thomas had no idea what a world-wide success the novel would be; and as the German publication loomed nearer in the summer of 1954 he grew more and more wary. "I am steeling myself for its publication with some embarrassment," he wrote to his daughter Erika on 7th June. "Often I can't help thinking that it would have been better if I had departed from this earth after the *Faustus*. That, after all, was a book of seriousness and a certain power . . ." He was afraid even to send a copy of *Felix Krull* to Agnes Meyer in Washington. "I fear you would not approve of these partly very loose amusements, not find them appropriate to the seriousness of the times." But seriousness, he warned her, was an understatement of the world situation, and "all humour today must be understood as grim humour" — a humour which, as he explained in his letter to Erika, was "extracted from ill-humour" in the case of *Felix Krull*. "I am always pleased when people see in me less an ironist than a humourist," Thomas had said in a radio-discussion in September 1953:

Irony, it seems to me, is the artistry with which a smile, an intellectual smile I should say, is evinced from the reader or audience, whereas humour brings heartfelt laughter, which I rate higher artistically and which I am happier with in my own work than the Erasmian smile that comes from irony.

He need not have worried. The jubilant applause his own readings from *Krull* had evoked was now reflected in the runaway success of the book. Bermann-Fischer's cautious first edition of 20,000 copies immediately went out of print, and printing after printing followed in quick succession. If the structure of the book was "loose", no one minded, for besides the humour something of Thomas' feel for the European novel came through in his easy, open-eyed manner. At heart it was little more than a transposition of Thomas' own theories about the essentially suspect nature of artistic creation (Thomas made no bones of the fact that he knew nothing more than he managed to put into his books and promptly discarded and forgot any research he did for them) into the adventures of a young confidence man; but its recreation of *fin de siècle* nineteenth-century society made it also an illuminating social portrait, a satire in the vein of Heinrich's novel *In the Land of Cockaigne* of 1900, but much more deftly modulated and perfectly constructed. It was this feeling for perfection in art which Heinrich had felt to be the deciding issue in any comparison between them; and in his book of memoirs *Ein Zeitalter wird besichtigt* Heinrich had confronted this issue:

"If I interpret correctly," he wrote, "what stands to my brother's credit, even more than his talents, is that what he chose to do, he fulfilled. Complete perfection would be beyond human possibility; to strive ceaselessly to come near to it is the highest one can hope to achieve." To Katja, at the end of his life, Heinrich is said to have declared: "You know, of the two of us, Tommy is the greater, of that I am certain, I am quite clear about it."

If Thomas felt so, he never said it aloud. Like Goethe in his relations towards Schiller, Thomas refused to be drawn into any dispute about their comparative merit. To Alfred Kantorowicz, Professor of German Literature in East Berlin, Thomas wrote: "The stupid Germans are always squabbling over which one of us is really the greater; but the 'really' great one would be the one nature would have made had she taken from us both."[26] To Guido Devescovi, Professor of German at Trieste, however, Thomas showed a little of his own shame at the way Heinrich was currently forgotten in the West. "The figure of Heinrich Mann, obscured by the great shadow of his brother for such a long time, is today appearing more and more in its true light and greatness," Devescovi had written in an essay on *Doctor Faustus*. "May that be true!" Thomas replied.

His status is officially very high in the Communist part of Germany; but with few exceptions, one of which you cite, the West is silent about him. Even his beloved Italy and his still more beloved France show little receptivity to his life work, entirely Latin in schooling and character though it was, for all the peaks of sheer genius in it, such as *Die kleine Stadt, Professor Unrat, Henri IV,* and the late masterpiece, *Ein Zeitalter wird besichtigt.* I can assure you that a chariness concerning the obscuring "grande ombra" has marked my whole life since *Buddenbrooks.* Granted, I too have contributed to the Europeanization of the German novel, but my way of doing it was more traditionally German and closer to music, sounding a more ironic note than his — a dubious advantage, but a real one precisely in the eyes of the Germans and of Latin students of German literature. At the same time, my basic attitude toward him and his somewhat formidably intellectual work was always that of the little brother looking up at the elder. It is expressed autobiographically in *Royal Highness,* where Klaus Heinrich says to his brother, the Grand Duke: "I have always looked up to you because I always felt and knew that you were the more distinguished and superior of us two and I am only a plebeian compared with you. But if you deem me worthy to stand at your side and bear your title, *and represent you to the people,* although I do not consider myself so very presentable and have this hindrance here with my left hand, which I must always hide — then I thank you and am yours to command . . .

It was an indescribable shock to me, and seemed like a dream, when shortly before his death Heinrich dedicated one of his books to me with the words: "To my great brother, who wrote *Doctor Faustus".* What? How? *He* had always been the great, the big brother. And I puffed out my chest and thought of Goethe's remark about the Germans' silly bickering over who was the greater, he or Schiller: "They ought to be glad they have two such sons."[27]

The parallel between the brothers' relationship and Goethe's celebrated friendship with Schiller was indeed a close one, and had already provided much of the insight and perception behind Thomas' earlier essay *Goethe and Tolstoy* in 1922. And if Thomas, invited by both East and West German governments to deliver a speech to mark the 150th anniversary of Schiller's death in 1955, was moved to overcome his natural diffidence before the "mountains of literary-historical writing on the subject, each of whose thousand and one authors would be individually worthier, more qualified, more professionally able by vocation than me", as he wrote to Emil Preetorius,[28] it was in part this same brotherly insight, the desire to do justice to an artist with whom he had little in common but much in sympathy and respect, which enabled him to do so.

A new house had been found, in January 1954, on the hills above the Lake of Zurich at Kilchberg; and Thomas and Katja moved in in April — "my definitive and final address" as Thomas wrote to Georges Motschan.[29] With gladness, having settled in his "comfortable and roomy" quarters on the hillside, he set aside the difficult and as yet formless concept for his Reformation novella, and began, in August 1954, the festival speech on Schiller. Interrupted by one lecture trip to the Rhineland, the Schiller essay was to take until Christmas 1954 to complete. It was over 100 pages long, and Erika was asked to assume the near-impossible task of reducing it by five-sixths for the actual speech. But once completed, Thomas was proud of the work. The climax, at the end, was Goethe's own opinion of Schiller. With masterly navigation and tact Thomas weighed Goethe's feelings towards his eminent colleague and rival. Like Heinrich, Schiller's genius had been the more poetic in character, in contrast to the profounder, more inward and organic creativity of Goethe. As in Heinrich's and Thomas' case, the relationship between Schiller and Goethe had begun with some hostility; yet they had then settled down to create in their very distinct and individual manners.

His [Schiller's] method was not at all to spin a work of art silently out of his inner self. Rather, he put his hand boldly upon some great subject, observed it, turned it this way and that. He saw his subjects only from outside, so to speak, that was how he did it, that was his way . . .

Thomas' essay, subtitled: "On the 150th anniversary of the poet's death — dedicated in love to his memory," was a last attempt to honour the "other side" of literature, those writers who, without the blessing from Nature enjoyed by Goethe or Tolstoy, nevertheless had striven in the written word to extract from life the true ideals of humanity. Schiller was the subject of the essay, but beyond him in the ranks of world literature were figures such as Dostoievsky — and Heinrich, his brother.

"Goethe in his old age, when his daughter-in-law had said something deprecating about Schiller, answered her: 'You are all far too wretchedly earthbound for him,'" Thomas wrote to Agnes Meyer in February 1955. He had only six months to live.

"The capacity to admire and to look up appears to me as a prerequisite of any kind of learning and political growth," Thomas had written to an American sailor who had sought advice from him in 1951.[30] "You should study the great works of world literature, and study them with intense admiration in order to be able to create something yourself . . ."

It was this faculty, above all, which had enabled Thomas to travel the difficult road from self-concern to representative greatness; and which provided his strongest intellectual tie with Heinrich. "Admiration is an endowment, a gift, to keep the mind from complacency, to keep it awake.

It is a moral gift, capable of distinguishing both above and below," Heinrich had written in *Ein Zeitalter wird besichtigt.* "I have surrendered my life to a kind of festive dissolution," Thomas wrote to Herman Hesse in the midst of his series of Schiller speeches in 1955; and while Thomas paid tribute to the genius of Schiller, the world paid homage to its greatest living novelist on his eightieth birthday. Two hundred of the most distinguished writers, thinkers, artists and politicians of France had contributed to a birthday volume *Hommage de la France à Thomas Mann* — from the French President, Vincent Auriol, to Picasso, Camus, Malraux and Albert Schweitzer. "Thomas Mann a maintenu durant la traversée la gloire intacte du génie allemand. Sa vie illustre son oeuvre. Sa grandeur n'appartient pas seulement aux lettres. Il a su, au temps de l'asservissement, demeurer un esprit libre. Il a préservé l'honneur de l'Allemagne," wrote François Mauriac.

But Germany — or West Germany — was less sure of the honour Thomas had preserved on its behalf. Once again, as in 1949, he had insisted on giving his speech not only in West Germany, in Stuttgart, close to Schiller's birthplace, but also in Weimar, in East Germany, where Schiller, more appropriately from the point of the 150th anniversary, had died. Schiller's University at Jena awarded Thomas an Honorary Doctorate on 15th May, and again he was received and fêted in the Democratic Republic by the "Stalinist" poet Johannes R. Becher (by this time Minister of Culture in the Republic). The West German press was in uproar — the more so because of Thomas' consistent willingness to grant interviews, provide recordings of his literary readings, and even accept "criminal" financial conditions to allow his works to be published under licence in the East. The result was that only after a walkout of half the members of the *Bürgerschaft* in Lübeck was the town able to honour Thomas with the Freedom of the city for his eightieth birthday; Konrad Adenauer refused to send his own greeting as Chancellor of the Federal Republic, and thus only a "temperate telegram" came, from the Minister of the Interior, Gerhard Schröder. "He must have wrung permission for that from Adenauer in a difficult conversation," Thomas remarked laconically in his letter to Hesse. Even worse, the members of the German order *Pour le Mérite,* the highest decoration the country can offer, were unable to agree to his election to the order in time for Thomas' birthday, and when finally, under the influence of Theodor Heuss, agreement was reached, it was too late. The news was sent by telegram on 10th August, but neither the medal nor the official notification arrived in time. On 12th August 1955 Thomas was dead.

Not that Thomas would have minded. From Holland, where he had just been awarded the Commander Cross of the Order of Orange-Nassau by Queen Juliana, he wrote to Henry W. Braun in Washington:

Life is becoming more and more curious and unpredictable. Commander Crosses, Pour-le-Mérites, Freedom of cities and all that stuff are coming in now, and it is a good thing that admidst all the virgin honey refreshing, sobering outbreaks of poison and gall, of enraged denials, negations of my life come too. Who knows what delusions one might suffer from without them![31]

Since childhood he had struggled to "assert" his own identity, both against Heinrich, and against the envy real or imagined, of the outside world; and if his last months of life were not free of it, the goodwill and the tribute of those he respected were there as well. His Schiller speech was received with genuine and overwhelming applause in Stuttgart (where the entire audience stood up at the end to applaud), in Weimar, and in Amsterdam; and in Lübeck, on his way back to Switzerland from Weimar, Thomas accepted his Freedom with profound emotion. He wished, he declared in his acceptance speech, that Dr Baethcke, the schoolmaster who had once impressed upon his class the immortal greatness of Schiller, could have witnessed his indolent pupil giving the memorial speech on the 150th anniversary of Schiller's death; wished that his father, the Senator, could have witnessed the sight of his son that day, "in this historic hall, in this house where as Senator he would come and go", and "see that, against all expectation, I was able to prove myself a true son in my own way after all . . ."

I still see him raising his top-hat and coming out from the *Rathaus* between the sentries presenting arms when he left a sitting of the Senate, see him with elegant irony acknowledging the respect of his fellow citizens. I think I can say that his example has stood behind me all my life, through all my work, and I have always regretted that in his own lifetime I gave him such little hope that I would one day achieve anything in the world . . .[32]

Yet curiously Thomas expressed no desire to visit the family grave in the Ehrenfriedhof. He, for whom death had been such an integral theme in his conception of life and art, had never liked its physical presence. "I never come to these things," Alma Mahler-Werfel had excused her absence from the funeral of her husband Franz Werfel in 1945 — a remark which had struck Thomas as incredibly comic at the time.[33] Yet, as once Katja had refused to allow the doctor to let Thomas know the true nature of his illness in 1946, so now too, on the beloved coast of Noordwijk in Holland in July 1955, resting from the gruelling months of speech-making and celebration, Katja withheld the true nature of his sudden disability. He had begun to complain of extreme pain in his left leg, which at first he thought must be rheumatic. A doctor from the nearby Institute for gout, arthritis and related diseases disagreed. Thomas was ordered to bed, and a telephone call from Professor Mulder at Leiden informed Katja it was thrombosis. Two days later he was flown to the Kantonsspital hospital in Zurich. For a while the swelling in his leg seemed to be healing, but the thrombosis was in fact only a secondary manifestation of advanced arteriosclerosis, and there could be no hope of recovery.

Among the last things Thomas had done was a preface to a new volume of *The Finest Stories of the World,* and the preparation for a play he would never write — *Luther's Wedding.* He had sent Erika to England to obtain the signatures of Bertrand Russell, E.M. Forster and Arnold Toynbee to a new document he intended to write, a manifesto of the leading world intellects which called for practical efforts to achieve peace in the world.

But the manifesto was never published. On the evening of 12th August 1955, heavily sedated with morphine injections, Thomas managed to joke with the doctor, and even speak English and French with him. Then he asked Katja for his spectacles, and when he had them, fell asleep for the last time.

He was buried in the village cemetery at Kilchberg on 16th August 1955.

The President of the Swiss confederation had attended his birthday, and arrangements were being made to offer him Swiss citizenship "on an altogether exceptional basis" as Thomas had noted in his letter to Hermann Hesse. It was too late, however, and two of Germany's greatest twentieth-century men of letters, Heinrich and Thomas Mann, died as, respectively, Czechoslovak and American citizens.

NOTES

The following abbreviations are used throughout the notes:
TMA: Thomas Mann Archiv, Zurich
HMA: Heinrich Mann Archiv, East Berlin
PBA: Pierre Bertaux Archive, Sèvres
SNM: Schiller-Nationalmuseum, Marbach a. Neckar

Chapter One
1. Preserved in HMA. Extracts published in *Aus den Familienpapieren der Manns*, Berlin 1965, from which these quotations are drawn.
2. *As Johann Siegmund Mann sen. in de oole Hansastadt Lübeck fyvuntwintig Jahr lang, mit synen Söhn Johann Siegmund Mann jun. herumwirtschaft un Handel dreeben hett . . .* printed 1848. Stadtbibliothek, Lübeck.
3. *Aus den Familienpapieren der Manns*, op. cit.
4. *Erinnerungen aus meinem Leben, geschrieben im Winter 1908*, Elizabeth Mann (manuscript), Kaufmannschaft zu Lübeck Collection.
5. *Die Strassentumulte in Lübeck 1843 und 1848*, M. Funck, Verein für Lübeckische Geschichte und Alterthumskunde, Band 8, Heft 2, 1901.
6. *Aus Dodo's Kindheit*, Julia Mann, Constance 1958.
7. *Aus Dodo's Kindheit*, op. cit.

Chapter Two
1. *Das Kind*, Heinrich Mann in *Sie sind jung*, Paul Zsolnay Verlag 1929.
2. *Erinnerungen an das Haus Mann, von einem alten Lübecker* in *Lübecker Anzeiger*, 1925.
3. *A Sketch of My Life*, Thomas Mann, Paris 1930 and London 1961.
4. *Kinderspiele*, Thomas Mann in *Das Spielzeug im Leben des Kindes*, Berlin 1904.
5. *Ein Zeitalter wird besichtigt*, Heinrich Mann, Stockholm 1945.
6. *Das Verlorene Buch*, Heinrich Mann in *Das Kind*, op. cit.

7. *Zwei gute Lehren,* Heinrich Mann in *Das Kind,* loc. cit.
8. In *The Dilettante,* 1897, republished in *Extract* under the title *Das Bild der Mutter* in *Hannoversche Neueste Nachrichten.*
9. *Lebenslauf,* Thomas Mann in *Les prix Nobel en 1929,* Stockholm 1930.
10. Preface to *Autobiographisches* (Thomas Mann), Erika Mann, Frankfurt 1968.
11. *A Sketch of My Life,* op. cit.
12. *Fantasien über meine Vaterstadt L,* Heinrich Mann, dated May 1891, published in *Sinn und Form,* January 1963.
13. *The Masked Ball,* Heinrich Mann in *Das Kind,* op. cit.
14. *Lübeck als geistige Lebensform,* Thomas Mann, Lübeck 1926.
15. Letter to Ludwig Ewers, 9.2.1890, HMA.
16. Ibid.
17. *Ein Zeitalter wird besichtigt,* Heinrich Mann, op. cit.
18. *Ein Zeitalter wird besichtigt,* Heinrich Mann, op. cit.
19. Letter from Heinrich to Ludwig Ewers, 9.2.1890, HMA.
20. Letter to Frieda Hartenstein, 14.10.1889.
21. Letter to Frieda Hartenstein, 2.1.1890.
22. *Lebensabriss,* Thomas Mann, *Die Neue Rundschau,* June 1930, translated as *A Sketch of My Life,* op. cit.
23. Letter to Hermann Lange, dated 19.3.1955, from Kilchberg, Switzerland.
24. HMA. Extracts in *Aus den Familienpapieren der Manns,* op. cit.
25. Ibid.
26. Letter of 22.5.1891, HMA.
27. Letter to Karl Lemke, 27.10.1948.
28. *Fragment über das Religiöse,* Thomas Mann in *Dichterglaube,* Berlin 1931.
29. *Die beiden Gesichter* in *Das Kind,* op. cit.

Chapter Three
1. Letter of 24.8.1892, HMA.
2. Letter to Karl Lemke, 29.1.1947.
3. Ibid.
4. *A Sketch of My Life,* op. cit.
5. *Im Spiegel,* first published in *Literarisches Echo,* 15.12.1907.
6. *Vom Beruf des deutschen Schriftstellers in unserer Zeit* in *Die Neue Rundschau,* June 1930.
7. *A Sketch of My Life,* op. cit.
8. *A Sketch of My Life,* op. cit.
9. Ibid.
10. *Das Bild der Mutter,* op. cit.
11. *Erinnerungen ans Lübecker Stadttheater* in *Jahrbuch des Lübecker Stadttheaters,* Lübeck 1930.
12. Klaus Mann, *The Turning Point,* New York 1942.
13. M.J. Bonn, *The Wandering Scholar,* London 1947.
14. Unpublished MSS, HMA.

15. Unpublished MSS, HMA.
16. Letter to Ludwig Ewers, HMA.
17. c.f. Thomas Mann: *Eine Chronik seines Lebens,* Bürgin & Mayer, Frankfurt a.M. 1965.
18. Letter to Mrs Lehmann, 29.5.1898, HMA.
19. *Simplicissimus,* Eugen Roth, Hannover 1954.
20. Letter to Korfiz Holm, 6.11.1896.
21. Letter to Korfiz Holm, 6.11.1896.
22. Letter to Erwin Gerzymisch, 12.5.1947, HMA.
23. *A Sketch of My Life,* op. cit.
24. HMA.
25. The *Picture Book for Good Little Children* became a treasured possession at home in Munich. Many years later, after Thomas had given Viktor a "princely" gift, Viktor returned the book to Thomas, whose children were thus also brought up on it. It came to grief, unfortunately, in 1933, when the Nazis took possession of his house in the Poschingerstrasse, and was never seen again.
26. Foreword to a chapter from *Buddenbrooks* in *The World's Best,* New York 1947.
27. Ibid.
28. *A Sketch of My Life,* op. cit.
29. Ibid.
30. Ibid.
31. Ibid.
32. *Ein Zeitalter wird besichtigt,* op. cit.
33. *A Sketch of My Life,* op. cit.
34. Unsent letter, 5.1.1918.
35. *A Sketch of My Life,* op. cit.
36. Letter to Karl Lemke, 29.1.1947.
37. *Ein Zeitalter wird besichtigt,* op. cit.
38. Letter to Albert Langen, 24.2.1901.
39. *A Sketch of My Life,* op. cit.
40. Letter of 1.5.1898.
41. *A Sketch of My Life,* op. cit.
42. *Wir waren fünf,* Viktor Mann, Constance 1949.
43. *A Sketch of My Life,* op. cit.
44. *Erinnerungen ans Münchner Residenztheater,* Thomas Mann, first published in *Zweihundert Jahre Residenztheater in Wort und Bild,* Munich 1951.
45. *Ein Zeitalter wird besichtigt,* op. cit.
46. HMA.
47. *Wir waren fünf,* op. cit.
48. Book III of *Buddenbrooks* with the relevant chapters was nevertheless dedicated to Julia in the original edition.
49. *Wir waren fünf,* op. cit.
50. Letter of 29.6.1900.
51. *A Sketch of My Life,* op. cit.

52. *Schonungslose Lebenschronik*, Kurt Martens, Vienna and Munich 1921.
53. Letter of 4.8.1899.
54. *A Sketch of My Life*, op. cit.
55. *Reflections of a Non-Political Man*, first published in Berlin 1918.
56. *A Sketch of My Life*, op. cit.
57. Ibid.
58. Ibid.

Chapter Four
1. Letter of 29.6.1900.
2. *A Sketch of My Life*, op. cit.
3. Letter dated November 1900.
4. *A Sketch of My Life*, op. cit.
5. Letter to Paul Ehrenberg, 29.6.1900.
6. Letter to Heinrich, 25.11.1900.
7. Letter to Heinrich, 27.4.1912.
8. *Lebensgeschichte eines Rebellen*, Arthur Holitscher, Berlin 1924.
9. Letter of 26.10.1900. Quoted in *S. Fischer und sein Verlag*, Peter de Mendelssohn, Frankfurt 1971.
10. *Wir waren fünf*, op. cit.
11. *Lübeck als geistige Lebensform*, Lübeck 1926.
12. Letter of 2.11.1900.
13. Letter to Heinrich, 17.12.1900.
14. *Hamburger Nachrichten*, 27.3.1921.
15. Letter of 8.1.1901.
16. Letter of 24.2.1901 (draft), HMA.
17. In *Velhagen und Klasings Monatshefte*, Bielefeld und Leipzig, January 1901.
18. Letter of 29.12.1900.
19. *Ein Zeitalter wird besichtigt*, op. cit.
20. Letter to Heinrich, 29.12.1900.
21. Letter to Heinrich, 8.1.1901.
22. Ibid.
23. Letter to Heinrich, 21.1.1901.
24. Ibid.
25. Ibid.
26. Quoted in *S. Fischer und sein Verlag*, op. cit.
27. Letter of 13.2.1901.
28. Letter of 27.3.1901.
29. Letter of 7.3.1901.
30. Letter of 28.2.1901.
31. Letter of 7.3.1901.
32. Letter of 1.4.1901.
33. In *Das Blaubuch*, Berlin 8.8.1907.

34. Letter to Lou Albert-Lasard, circa 1916, in *Wege mit Rilke,* Frankfurt 1952.
35. Letter to Heinrich, 7.5.1901.
36. *A Sketch of My Life,* op. cit.
37. Ibid.
38. Letter of 30.12.1917.
39. *A Sketch of My Life,* op. cit.
40. Letter to Heinrich, 13.2.1901.
41. *A Sketch of My Life,* op. cit.
42. Ibid.
43. W. Fred in *Die Zukunft,* Berlin 27.6.1903.
44. *Wir waren fünf,* op. cit.
45. Letter of 15.9.1903.
46. Letter of 30.12.1903.

Chapter Five
1. Letter of 29.6.1903.
2. *A Sketch of My Life,* op. cit.
3. G. Keller, 1819-90: Swiss-German story-teller and poet, a failed painter who became one of the finest 19th-century authors writing in German.
4. Letter of 29.10.1903.
5. Ibid.
6. Letter of 5.12.1903.
7. Letter of 23.12.1903.
8. Letter of 30.12.1903.
9. Letter of 23.12.1903.
10. Letter of 27.2.1904.
11. c.f. Hans Andersen, *The Pine Tree.*
12. Letter of 27.3.1904.
13. Ibid.
14. Letter of early April 1904.
15. Not published until 1914 in *Das Wunderkind.*
16. Letter to Kurt Martens, 13.6.1904.
17. Letter of 27.2.1904.
18. *Ein Zeitalter wird besichtigt,* op. cit.
19. Notebook no. 7, 1905, TMA.
20. c.f. *Ansprache zu Heinrich Manns siebzigstem Geburtstag,* speech delivered 2.5.1941.
21. Notebook no. 7, 1905, TMA.
22. Letter to Katja Pringsheim, early June 1904.
23. Letter of late June 1904.
24. Letter also of late June 1904.
25. Letter of 14.7.1904.
26. Ibid.
27. Letter of late August 1904.
28. Letter of end of August 1904.

29. Heinrich was now working on the first German translation of Laclos' *Les liaisons dangereuses,* published by Rothbart, Leipzig 1905.
30. Letter of 20.11.1904, HMA.
31. Letter of 4.1.1905, HMA.

Chapter Six
1. Letter to Heinrich, 18.2.1905.
2. Ibid.
3. Preface in *Frankreich. Aus einem Essay* in *Freiheit und Arbeit, Kunst und Literatur Sammlung,* Leipzig 1910.
4. Letter of 19.1.1905.
5. op. cit.
6. Letter of 14.6.1905, HMA.
7. HMA.
8. Letter of 14.6.1905, HMA.
9. Ibid.
10. In *Stürmische Morgen,* Albert Langen 1906.
11. Letter of 9.6.1905, HMA.
12. Letter of 30.6.1905, HMA.
13. Letter of 1.7.1905, HMA.
14. Letter of 25.7.1905, HMA.
15. Introduction to new English edition of *Royal Highness,* 1940.
16. Letter to Heinrich, 22.10.1905.
17. Letter of 22.1.1906.
18. Letter of 14.11.1906.

Chapter Seven
1. i.e. marriage.
2. *Thomas Mann und die Renaissance, Berliner Tageblatt,* 5.3.1906.
3. Letter of 13.3.1906.
4. Letter of 21.3.1906.
5. Ibid.
6. *Die Gebrüder Mann,* 21.3.1906.
7. Letter of 15.1.1906.
8. Letter of 28.3.1906.
9. Letter of 7.6.1906.
10. Ibid.
11. Letter to Heinrich, 5.12.1905.
12. Letter of 17.1.1906.
13. Letter to Heinrich, 27.5.1907.
14. Ibid.
15. In *Velhagen und Klasings Monatshaften,* November 1906.
16. Quoted in Thomas' letter to Heinrich, 22.6.1907.
17. Letter of 6.2.1907.

18. Letter of 22.9.1907, HMA.
19. Quoted in letter from Adalberto Schmied to Heinrich, 2.11.1907, HMA.
20. Ibid.
21. Letter of 10.8.1905.
22. Letter to Heinrich, 26.8.1905.
23. Letter to Heinrich, 22.12.1908, HMA.
24. Quoted in letter from Adalberto Schmied to Heinrich, 22.9.1907, HMA.
25. Letter of 23.10.1907, HMA.
26. Letter of 3.8.1906, HMA.
27. Letter of 31.10.1906, HMA.
28. Letter of 12.6.1907, HMA.
29. Letter to Heinrich, 30.7.1909.
30. Letter of 20.4.1908, HMA.
31. Letter of 6.4.1908, HMA.
32. Letter of 29.4.1908.
33. Letter to Heinrich, 12.6.1908, HMA.
34. Letter of 29.6.1908, HMA.
35. Letter of 6.1.1909.
36. Letter of 22.7.1908.
37. Letter of 12.9.1908, HMA.
38. Letter of 7.12.1908.
39. Letter from Thomas to Heinrich, 7.12.1908.
40. Letter of 7.12.1908.
41. Letter of 25.3.1909.
42. Letter of 22.12.1908, HMA.
43. Letter of 6.1.1909, HMA.

Chapter Eight
1. Letter of 11.1.1910, HMA.
2. Letter of 19.2.1910, HMA.
3. Letter of 7.2.1910, SNM.
4. Letter of 2.12.1909, HMA.
5. Letter to Ludwig Ewers, 20.2.1910, HMA.
6. Letter of 10.1.1910.
7. Ibid.
8. Letter of 17.2.1910.
9. Letter to Walter Opitz, 26.8.1909.
10. Letter to Heinrich, 26.1.1910.
11. Letter of 10.1.1910.
12. Letter of 20.3.1910.
13. Letter of 16.3.1910.
14. Letter to Kurt Martens, 11.1.1910.
15. In *Ein Zeitalter wird besichtigt,* op. cit.
16. Letter of 27.12.1909, SNM.
17. Letter of 1.3.1910.

18. Letter of 26.8.1909.
19. Letter of 18.12.1909.
20. *A Sketch of My Life,* op. cit.
21. Ibid.
22. Letter of 17.2.1910.
23. 500 Marks per month, or 6000 Marks per year.
24. Letter to Ernst Bertram, 11.8.1911.
25. *A Sketch of My Life,* op. cit.
26. Ibid.
27. Ibid.
28. Hyperion Verlag had published a limited 1300-copy edition in 1912.
29. In the *Neue Rundschau,* April 1913.
30. Letter of 8.11.1913.
31. Letter of 11.11.1913.
32. Letter to Heinrich, 8.11.1913.
33. Letter of 8.1.1907, HMA.
34. Sylvia von Harden, *Erinnerungen.* The verse was by John Höxter — painter and drug addict.
35. In *Ein Zeitalter wird besichtigt,* op. cit.
36. *A Sketch of My Life,* op. cit.

Chapter Nine
1. Letter of 7.8.1914.
2. Letter of 18.11.1914.
3. Erich Mühsam, *Tagebuch,* HMA.
4. *A Sketch of My Life,* op. cit.
5. Ibid.
6. HMA.
7. HMA.
8. Letter of 4.5.1915.
9. Letter of 31.5.1915, HMA.
10. In *Les Nouvelles Littéraires,* Paris 14.1.1939.
11. Letter to Heinrich, 3.1.1918.
12. It is claimed that Heinrich and Thomas did not in fact speak to one another in person throughout the war.
13. *Wir waren fünf,* op. cit.
14. Klaus Mann, *The Turning Point,* New York 1942.
15. Ibid.
16. c.f. Letter to Paul Amman, 30.6.1917.
17. c.f. Draft of letter to Kurt Wolff, 29.10.1916.
18. c.f. Letter of Thomas Mann to Ernst Bertram, 2.2.1922.

PART TWO

Chapter Ten
1. *A Sketch of My Life*, op. cit.
2. Quotation from Goethe, *Epigrammatical Collection.*
3. *A Sketch of My Life*, op. cit.
4. Letter to Amman, 25.3.1917.
5. *A Sketch of My Life*, op. cit.
6. Letter to Ernst Bertram of 25.12.1917; to Ehrenberg of 20.12.1917.
7. Letter of 11.9.1918.
8. Paul Amman, *Politik und Moral in Thomas Manns Betrachtungen eines Unpolitischen* in *Münchner Blätter für Dichtung und Graphik*, 1919.
9. *A Sketch of My Life*, op. cit.
10. Letter of 27.8.1917.
11. Quoted in M.J. Bonn, *The Wandering Scholar*, London 1947.
12. Ibid.
13. *Ein Zeitalter wird besichtigt*, op. cit.
14. *A Sketch of My Life*, op. cit.
15. Letter of 26.6.1919.
16. "Brief an den Dekan der philosophischen Fakultät zu Bonn", 3.8.1919.
17. Letter to Philipp Witkop, 12.5.1919.
18. c.f. *The German Republic*, op. cit.
19. *A Sketch of My Life*, op. cit.
20. c.f. Letter to Ernst Bertram, 13.4.1918.
21. *A Sketch of My Life*, op. cit.
22. Cable from Munich correspondent of the *Leipziger Tageblatt.*

Chapter Eleven
1. Letter to Felix Bertaux, 16.3.1923. PBA.
2. In *Vossische Zeitung*, 11.10.1923.
3. Letter of 16.3.1924 to his Hungarian translator.
4. *A Sketch of My Life*, op. cit.
5. Samuel Fischer to Gerhart Hauptmann, letter of 31.12.1924. Quoted in *S. Fischer und sein Verlag*, op. cit.
6. G. Bermann-Fischer, *Bedroht-Bewahrt*, Frankfurt 1967.
7. Letter of 11.4.1925.
8. *Der Sohn*, 1919; *Die Ehrgeizige*, 1920; *Die Tote und andere Novellen*, 1921; *Der Jüngling*, 1924; *Abrechnungen*, 1925.
9. *Macht und Mensch*, 1919; *Diktatur der Vernunft*, 1923.
10. *Der Weg zur Macht*, 1919; *Das gastliche Haus*, 1924.
11. Essay on *Der Kopf*, first published in *Kulturaufbau* no. 6, 1950.
12. Letter of 24.11.1924.
13. In *Der Bücherwurm*, Christmas 1926.
14. In *Ansprache an den Brüder*, speech given by Thomas Mann, 27.3.1931.
15. Hitler to Burgerbräukeller crowd, 8.11.1923.

16. Letter to his daughter Erika, 7.5.1925.
17. Letter to Ernst Bertram, 4.2.1925.
18. Letter of 17.9.1926.
19. *Dial*, November 1924.
20. Thomas Mann, letter to Ernst Bertram.
21. "Patrioteer" was the first translated title of *Der Untertan*, later altered to *Man of Straw*.
22. Letter of 8.10.1925.
23. Letter of 18.3.1925.
24. Ibid.
25. Letter to Kurt Tucholsky, 12.5.1925, HMA.
26. *A Sketch of My Life*, op. cit.
27. *Unterwegs*, 12.4.1925.
28. *A Sketch of My Life*, op. cit.
29. Ibid.
30. *Dial*, October 1925.
31. c.f. *Briefe ins ferne Ausland*, 1925, in *Sieben Jahre*, Leipzig 1929.
32. *Ein Zeitalter wird besichtigt*, op. cit.
33. Letter to Felix Bertaux, published in *Neue Deutsche Literatur*, Vol. 19, no. 3.
34. *The Turning Point*, op. cit.
35. Letter of 3.2.1926.
36. *Die neuen Gebote*, 1926, published in *Sieben Jahre*, op. cit.
37. Letter of 14.8.1926.
38. Letter of 23.8.1927, TMA.
39. Ibid.
40. Letter of 29.8.1927.
41. *Hamburger Fremdenblatt*, 6.6.1925.
42. Reprinted frequently in the 1920s, and in book form in *Geist und Tat*, Berlin 1931.
43. Letter of 21.1.1910, HMA.
44. Quoted in *A Sketch of My Life*, op. cit.
45. Letter of 2.5.1925, HMA.
46. Letter to Felix Bertaux, 8.12.1926.
47. Thomas Mann, letter to Rudolf Goldschmidt-Jentner, 1.12.1926.
48. Ibid.
49. In *Sieben Jahre*, op. cit.
50. Letter of 14.5.1927.
51. Letter of 8.6.1927.
52. Letter of 3.7.1927.
53. Letter to Felix Bertaux, 13.2.1928.
54. Letter to Felix Bertaux, 11.6.1923.
55. In *Literarische Welt*, edition of 24.2.1928.
56. Letter of 11.3.1928.
57. i.e. The trans-oceanic aviators Köhl and Hünefeld. Letter to Arthur Hübscher, 27.6.1928.

58. Letter to Stefan Grassmann, 5.8.1928.
59. Letter of 31.12.1928.
60. Letter of 21.6.1929.
61. In Heinrich Mann, *Das öffentliche Leben (Public Life)* essays and speeches, Paul Zsolnay Verlag 1932.
62. Letter of 7.1.1930.
63. Letter of 20.1.1930.

Chapter Twelve
1. Letter of 10.3.1930.
2. *I am shown the Blue Angel* in *Das öffentliche Leben,* op. cit.
3. Postcard of 29.4.1930.
4. February 1948.
5. Ibid.
6. In *A Sketch of My Life,* op. cit.
7. *The Times,* 16.9.1930.
8. *Situation de l'Allemagne* reprinted in *Das öffentliche Leben,* op. cit.
9. In *Preussische Jahrbücher,* April 1928.
10. *Bekenntnis zum Sozialismus:* also excluded from the English versions of Thomas Mann's essays.
11. Unpublished letter, Ida Herz Collection, TMA.
12. Letter of 26.6.1929.
13. Letter of 3.5.1929.
14. Letter to Felix Bertaux, 7.10.1934.
15. *Mein Roman* in *Das öffentliche Leben,* op. cit.
16. In his extraordinarily perceptive and intelligent, but sadly little read *Panorama de la littérature allemande,* Paris 1927.
17. Letter of 15.6.1931, TMA.
18. Letter of 9.12.1930, Letter Archive of G.B. Fischer, Camaiore.
19. *Die Wiedergeburt der Anständigkeit* in *Der Staat seid Ihr,* Berlin 2–23 March 1931.
20. *Europa als Kulturgemeinschaft,* retitling of *Die Bäume im Garten,* published in *Vossische Zeitung,* 20.5.1930.
21. Published in *Vossische Zeitung,* 8.9.1931.
22. In *Die Zensur,* published in *Das öffentliche Leben,* op. cit.
23. Letter of 23.11.1931.
24. Ibid.
25. Letter of 24.12.1931.
26. Letter to Felix Bertaux, 12.1.1932.
27. Letter to Ernst Bertram, 27.12.1931.
28. Ibid.
29. Published in the *Berliner Tageblatt,* 22.3.1932, reprinted in *Das öffentliche Leben,* op. cit.
30. *Documents on British Foreign Policy,* III, 167.
31. Letter to Felix Bertaux, 10.2.1932, PBA.

32. TMA.
33. Letter of 12.3.1932, PBA.
34. Letter of 31.7.1932, PBA.
35. Quoted in *S. Fischer und sein Verlag,* Peter de Mendelssohn, Frankfurt 1971.
36. Op. cit.
37. Letter of 21.6.1932, ibid.
38. Letter of 31.5.1932, TMA.
39. *Was wir verlangen müssen* (What we must demand) in the *Berliner Tageblatt,* 8.8.1932.

Chapter Thirteen
1. *Ein Zeitalter wird besichtigt,* op. cit.
2. Letter to René Schickele, 27.2.1933, SNM.
3. *Ein Zeitalter wird besichtigt,* op. cit.
4. Related to Charlotte Bloch-Zavrel later that day.
5. i.e. 5000 francs, PBA.
6. Letter of 2.1.1933.
7. Thomas Mann, letter to Lavinia Mazzuchetti, 13.3.1933.
8. René Schickele, *Tagebücher,* December 1933.
9. Pierre Bertaux, *Hölderlin: essai de biographie intérieure,* Paris 1936.
10. Letter of 2.5.1933, PBA.
11. Letter of 24.3.1933, PBA.
12. Letter of 15.4.1933, TMA.
13. Letter of 2.5.1933, PBA.
14. *A quoi cela aboutit?* in *Dépêche de Toulouse,* 23.6.1933.
15. Letter of 2.5.1933, PBA.
16. Letter to Felix Bertaux, 27.12.1933, PBA.
17. TMA.
18. Entry for 11.5.1933. All in Réne Schickele, *Tagebücher* in *Werke in drei Bänden,* Cologne 1959.
19. Letter of 22.3.1933, TMA.
20. In *Leiden an Deutschland* (1933 and 1934) Pazifische Presse, Los Angeles 1946.
21. Letter of 18.7.1933.
22. Letter of circa 21.8.1933.
23. Letter of 31.8.1933.
24. Letter of 17.5.1933, PBA.
25. Letter of 16.6.1933.
26. Ibid.
27. In *Börsenblatt für den deutschen Buchhandel,* 10.10.1933.
28. Letter to Roth, 28.1.1934, in R. Schickele's *Werke in drei Bänden,* op. cit.
29. Ibid.
30. Letter of 9.1.1934.

31. Letter of 18.11.1933, loc. cit.
32. Diary entry of 14.4.1934, loc. cit.
33. Diary entry of 21.3.1934, loc. cit.
34. Ibid.
35. Ludwig Marcuse, *Mein zwanzigstes Jahrhundert,* Munich 1960.
36. Ludwig Marcuse, *Wahrheit und Dichtung um Heinrich Mann* in *Der Aufbau,* New York 15.4.1960.
37. Letter of 2.5.1933, PBA.
38. Letter of 1.9.1933, PBA.
39. Letter of 4.10.1933, PBA.
40. Letter of 8.10.1933, TMA.
41. Letter to Felix Bertaux, 21.11.1933, PBA.
42. Letter to A.M. Frey, 1.1.1934.
43. Letter of 23.8.1933, SNM.
44. Letter to Thomas Mann of 3.11.1933, TMA.
45. Schickele, letter to Julius Meier-Graefe, 6.4.1934, loc. cit.
46. Reported by Meier-Graefe and entered in Schickele's diary 14.4.1934, loc. cit.
47. Letter to Thomas, 3.11.1933, TMA.
48. Ibid.
49. Letter 24.12.1933, SNM.
50. c.f. Letter from Heinrich to Thomas Mann, 5.3.1934, TMA.
51. Letter of 27.6.1934, TMA.
52. Letter of 14.6.1934.
53. *Hitler's Table Talk,* London 1953.
54. Letter of 26.4.1934, PBA.
55. *S. Fischer und sein Verlag,* op. cit.
56. Letter of 7.10.1934, PBA.
57. Letter of 25.1.1934, TMA.
58. Letter of 26.4.1934, PBA.
59. Letter of 10.7.1935.
60. Letter of 14.6.1935.
61. Reprinted as *Achtung Europa!,* Vienna 1938.
62. August von Platen, 1796–1835.
63. Foreword to the American edition of *Joseph and his Brothers,* op. cit.
64. Letter of 31.10.1936.
65. Ibid.
66. *Berner Tagwacht,* 10.12.1936.
67. Letter of 5.3.1934, TMA.
68. Letter of 30.3.1935, TMA.
69. Entry of 21.3.1934, loc. cit.
70. Letter of 4.5.1937.
71. *Bekenntnis zum Kampf für die Freiheit* in *Das Wort,* Moscow July 1937.
72. Letter of 4.5.1937.
73. Letter 1934, TMA.
74. Letter of 26.12.1935, HMA.

75. *Tagebuchblätter*, Lowe-Porter Collection, Yale University.
76. *My Brother* published in *Esquire*, March 1939, as *This Man is My Brother* and in book form in *Order of the Day*, New York and London 1942.
77. Letter to von Kahler, 19.10.1938.
78. Letter of 1.3.1938, PBA.
79. Letter of 2.5.1939.
80. Foreword to *Joseph and his Brothers*, op. cit.

Chapter Fourteen
1. Letter to Eva and Julius Lips, 2.12.1939. In *Zwischen Lehrstuhl und Indianerzeit*, Berlin 1965.
2. Letter of 25.5.1939.
3. *Ein Zeitalter wird besichtigt*, op. cit.
4. Ibid.
5. Ibid.
6. Ibid.
7. Alma Mahler-Werfel, *Mein Leben*, Frankfurt 1960.
8. *Ansprache zu Heinrich Mann siebzigsten Gerburtstag* of 2.5.1941, published in *Thomas Mann, Heinrich Mann: Briefwechsel*, Frankfurt 1969.
9. Op. cit.
10. Op. cit.
11. Letter of 24.1.1941.
12. Letter to Joseph Angell, 19.4.1941.
13. Letter to Thomas, 2.1.1942.
14. Letter to Salomea Rottenberg, 25.9.1941, HMA.
15. Published in 1941 in New York by Alliance Book Corporation in a volume entitled *I am an American* by Famous Naturalized Americans, edited by Robert Spiers.
16. Letter to Agnes Meyer, 26.6.1942.
17. *"Lidice"*, editorial *El Libro Libre*, Mexico 1943.
18. In *Ein Zeitalter wird besichtigt*, op. cit.
19. Letter of 9.1944, F.C. Weiskopf Archive, East Berlin.
20. *Ein Zeitalter wird besichtigt*, op. cit.
21. Letter of 24.2.1942.
22. *The Genesis of a Novel*, London and New York 1961.
23. Ibid.
24. Ibid.
25. Ibid.
26. Letter of 31.12.1907, SNM.
27. *The Genesis of a Novel*, loc. cit.
28. Ibid.
29. Ibid.
30. Ibid.

31. Ibid.
32. Letter of 4.4.1942.
33. *The Kindness of Strangers*, New York 1969.
34. *Die Brüder Mann und Bertolt Brecht* in *Die Zeit*, 23.2.1973.
35. Loc. cit.
36. *Brief über das Hinscheiden meines Bruders Heinrich* in *German Review* No. 25, 1950.
37. *Zwischen Lehrstuhl und Indianerzeit*, Eva Lips, Berlin 1965.
38. Letter of 10.10.1947.
39. Op. cit.
40. Op. cit.
41. Letter of 10.7.1947, F.C. Weiskopf Archive.
42. *An das Volk von Berlin* in *Freies Deutschland*, Special No. 9, May 1945; also distributed in Berlin in pamphlet form.
43. *The Genesis of a Novel*, op. cit.
44. Letter to Thomas, 3.6.1945.

Chapter Fifteen
1. *The Genesis of a Novel*, op. cit.
2. Letter to Dolf Sternberger, 19.3.1946.
3. Even in 1973, some twenty-seven years later, letters were still being published in German newspapers condemning Thomas Mann's wartime broadcasts as disloyal and dishonourable: c.f. *Die Zeit* (Leserbriefe), March 1973.
4. Published in *Ruhr-Zeitung*, 5.1.1946.
5. *The Genesis of a Novel*, op. cit.
6. Ibid.
7. Letter of 14.12.1945.
8. Letter of 25.10.1945.
9. *The Genesis of a Novel*, op. cit.
10. *A Sketch of My Life*, op. cit.
11. *The Genesis of a Novel*, op. cit.
12. Ibid.
13. Ibid.
14. Ibid.
15. Ibid.
16. Ibid.
17. Ibid.
18. Letter of 25.10.1945.
19. Letter of 3.4.1945, PBA.
20. Ibid.
21. Letter to Klaus Pinkus, 28.12.1945.
22. Letter to Klaus Pinkus, 31.8.1946.
23. *The Testament of Adolf Hitler*, London 1961.
24. Quoted in a letter from Heinrich to Klaus Pinkus, 31.8.1946.

25. Published posthumously in 1956.
26. In *Neue Zeitung*, 28.5.1947.
27. Letter of 23.9.1946.
28. Letter of 14.7.1947.
29. Letter of 27.7.1947.
30. Letter of 25.11.1947.
31. Draft letter dated 12.10.1947.
32. Letter of 10.10.1947.
33. Letter of 19.9.1947.
34. Letter of 26.4.1947.
35. Letter to Félix Bertaux, 4.12.1946.
36. Letter of 3.6.1947.
37. Letter of 7.11.1947.
38. Extract of letter published in *Thomas Mann: Eine Chronik seines Lebens*, op. cit.
39. Letter of 29.2.1948.
40. Letter of 4.3.1948.
41. Quoted from Goethe's *Poetry and Truth* on second title page, *The Genesis of a Novel*.
42. Letter to Blanche Knopf, 10.3.1948.
43. Letter of 12.11.1948.
44. Letter to Hans Reisiger, 19.12.1948.
45. Letter of 2.4.1949.
46. Alfred Kantorowicz, *Exile in Frankreich*, Bremen 1971.
47. Letter to Erwin Gerzymisch, 3.2.1949, published in *Aufbau* No. 6, 1950.
48. Letter of 2.7.1949.
49. Letter of 12.10.1948.
50. Letter of 13.3.1949.
51. Letter of 12.7.1948.
52. Letter of 6.7.1949.
53. Letter of 20.6.1949.
54. Konrad Kellen, *Reminiscences of Thomas Mann* in *Yale Review*, 1965.
55. Letter of 15.6.1949.
56. Letter to Albrecht Goes. 3.9.1949.
57. *Germany Today* published unabridged in the *New York Times Magazine*, 25.9.1949.
58. Open Letter to Thomas Mann in *Volksrecht*, Zurich 9.9.1949.
59. Letter of 10.9.1949.
60. *Germany Today* in *New York Times Magazine*, 25.9.1949.
61. Letter from Paul Wandel, HMA.
62. Letter of 20.10.1949, SNM.
63. Published in *Die Neue Rundschau*, Spring Number, 1949.
64. Letter of 31.10.1947, HMA.
65. *Brief über das Hinscheiden meines Bruders*, op. cit.

Chapter Sixteen

1. Letter of 5.4.1950, SNM.
2. Letter of 21.3.1950.
3. Letter of 11.8.1945, SNM.
4. Letter of 15.12.1947, PBA.
5. Letter of 27.3.1950.
6. Letter of 21.5.1950.
7. Letter of 24.5.1950.
8. Ibid.
9. Letter of 4.7.1950.
10. Letter of 30.8.1950.
11. Letter of 18.2.1951.
12. Letter of 3.4.1951.
13. Letter of 1.2.1951.
14. *Congressional Record* for 18.6.1951.
15. Letter of 21.4.1951.
16. Letter of 28.4.1951.
17. Letter of 7.5.1951.
18. Letter of 16.3.1952 quoted in Bürgin and Mayer, op. cit.
19. Letter of 1.11.1952.
20. Quoted in letter to Agnes Meyer, 8.2.1953.
21. *Aufbau,* 19.12.1952.
22. Letter of 27.5.1953.
23. Quoted in letter to Agnes Meyer, 20.6.1952.
24. Letter of 27.5.1953.
25. Letter of 19.4.1953.
26. Quoted in *Heinrich und Thomas Mann,* Alfred Kantorowicz, Berlin 1956.
27. Letter of 1.5.1955.
28. Letter of 6.9.1954.
29. Letter of 3.2.1954.
30. Letter to Gordon T. Wick, 4.6.1951.
31. Letter of 16.7.1955.
32. *Ansprache in Lübeck* delivered on 20.5.1955, and published in the *Lübecker Nachrichten* and *Lübecker Freie Press* the following day.
33. Quoted in *The Genesis of a Novel,* op. cit.

Note on the Bibliography

Except where otherwise stated, all correspondence relating to Heinrich Mann has been drawn from his published letters (see bibliography) and by permission from the collections of the Heinrich Mann Archiv, Berlin, and Professor Pierre Bertaux, Sèvres. Much of this latter material can be found in the Berlin Academy of Arts 600-page handbook to the Heinrich Mann Centenary Exhibition held in East Berlin in 1971, entitled: *Heinrich Mann 1871–1950. Werk und Leben in Dokumenten und Bildern*, Berlin 1971 – perhaps the most important sourcebook available to the biographer of Heinrich Mann, though sadly not accessible in Great Britain or the USA.

Letters between the brothers Mann are drawn from their published correspondence (see bibliography) except for a number of newly discovered letters from Heinrich to Thomas not yet published, shown to me at the Thomas Mann Archiv in Zurich in 1972. All Thomas Mann letters, except where otherwise stated, are quoted from his published correspondence (see bibliography).

The number of secondary works relating to Heinrich and Thomas Mann now fills four volumes of bibliography, to which the specialist must address himself (Zenker, E. *Heinrich-Mann-Bibliographie*, 2 volumes, Berlin 1968f; Matter, H. *Die Literatur über Thomas Mann; eine Bibliographie 1898 – 1969*, 2 volumes, Berlin 1972); however the following works have proved invaluable to me in the writing of this book and provide a basic groundwork for all biographical enquiry:

Heinrich Mann 1871–1950 (quoted above)
Bürgin & Mayer: *Thomas Mann. Eine Chronik seines Lebens*, Frankfurt a. Main 1965
Mann, Viktor: *Wir waren fünf*, Constance 1949
Kantorowicz, Alfred: *Heinrich und Thomas Mann. Die persönlichen, literarischen und weltanschaulichen Beziehungen der Brüder*, Berlin 1956.
Schröter, Klaus: *Heinrich Mann in Selbstzeugnissen und Bilddokumenten*, Reinbek 1967
Schröter, Klaus: *Thomas Mann in Selbstzeugnissen und Bilddokumenten*, Reinbek 1964
Banuls, André: *Heinrich Mann. Le poète et la politique*, Paris 1966

BIBLIOGRAPHY

HEINRICH MANN

FIRST EDITIONS IN GERMAN

In einer Familie (Novel), Munich: Verlag von Dr E. Albert   1894
Das Wunderbare und andere Novellen (Stories), Paris, Leipzig,
    Munich: Verlag Albert Langen   1897
Ein Verbrechen und andere Geschichten (Stories), Leipzig: Verlag
    von Robert Baum   1898
Im Schlaraffenland. Ein Roman unter feinen Leuten (Novel),
    Munich: Verlag Albert Langen   1900
Die Göttinnen oder die drei Romane der Herzogin von Assy
    (Trilogy of novels), Munich: Verlag Albert Langen   1903
      Diana, Roman der Herzogin von Assy
      Minerva, Roman der Herzogin von Assy
      Venus, Roman der Herzogin von Assy
Die Jagd nach Liebe (Novel), Munich: Verlag Albert Langen   1903
Flöten und Dolche (Stories), Munich: Verlag Albert Langen   1905
Professor Unrat oder das Ende eines Tyrannen (Novel), Munich:
    Verlag Albert Langen   1905
Eine Freundschaft. Gustave Flaubert und George Sand (Essay),
    Munich: E.W. Bonsels   1905/6
Schauspielerin (Short novel), Vienna and Leipzig: Wiener Verlag   1906
Stürmische Morgen (Stories), Munich: Verlag Albert Langen   1906
Mnais und Ginevra (Stories), Munich: Leipzig: R. Piper Verlag   1906
Zwischen den Rassen (Novel), Munich: Verlag Albert Langen   1907
Die Bösen (Stories), Leipzig: Insel-Verlag   1908
Die kleine Stadt (Novel), Leipzig: Insel-Verlag   1909
Das Herz (Stories), Leipzig: Insel-Verlag   1910
Variété (Drama), Berlin: Paul Cassirer Verlag   1910

Die Rückkehr vom Hades (Stories), Leipzig: Insel-Verlag   1911
Schauspielerin (Drama in 3 Acts), Berlin: Paul Cassirer Verlag   1911
Die grosse Liebe (Drama in 4 Acts), Berlin: Paul Cassirer Verlag   1912
Madame Legros (Drama in 3 Acts), Berlin: Paul Cassirer Verlag   1913
Der Untertan (Novel), privately printed. (Leipzig, Munich: Kurt
     Wolff Verlag)   1916
Drei Akte: Der Tyrann, Die Unschuldige, Variété (Drama), Leipzig:
     Kurt Wolff Verlag   1917
Brabach (Drama in 3 Acts), Leipzig: Kurt Wolff Verlag   1917
Die Armen (Novel), Leipzeig: Kurt Wolff Verlag   1917
Bunte Gesellschaft (Stories), Munich: Verlag Albert Langen
     (Langens Mark-Bücher, 18)   1917
Der Untertan (Novel), Leipzig, Munich: Kurt Wolff Verlag   1918
Der Weg zur Macht (Drama in 3 Acts), Leipzig: Kurt Wolff Verlag   1919
Macht und Mensch (Essays), Munich: Kurt Wolff Verlag   1919
Der Sohn (Short novel), Hannover: Paul Steegemann Verlag   1919
Die Ehrgeizige (Stories), Munich: Roland-Verlag, Dr Albert Mundt
     (Die neue Reihe, 19)   1920
Die Tote und andere Novelle (Stories), Munich: O, C, Recht
     Verlag (Novellen in Gelb, 3)   1921
Diktatur der Vernunft (Essays and Lectures), Berlin: Verlag Die
     Schmiede   1923
Das gastliche Haus (Comedy in 3 Acts), Munich: Gunther Langes   1924
Der Jüngling (Stories), Munich: Gunther Langes   1924
Abrechnungen (Stories), Berlin: Propyläen-Verlag (Das kleine
     Propyläen-Buch)   1925
Der Kopf (Novel), Berlin, Vienna, Leipzig: Paul Zsolnay Verlag   1925
Kobes (Short novel), with ten lithographs by George Grosz, Berlin:
     Propyläen-Verlag   1925
Liliane und Paul (Short novel), Berlin, Vienna, Leipzig: Paul
     Zsolnay Verlag   1926
Mutter Marie (Novel), Berlin, Vienna, Leipzig: Paul Zsolnay
     Verlag (Collected Works)   1927
Eugénie oder die Bürgerzeit (Novel), Berlin, Vienna, Leipzig:
     Paul Zsolnay Verlag (Collected Works)   1928
Bibi. Seine Jugend in 3 Akten (Drama), Berlin: S. Fischer Verlag   1928
Sieben Jahre. Chronik der Gedanken und Vorgänge (Essays),
     Berlin, Vienna, Leipzig: Paul Zsolnay Verlag   1929
Sie sind jung (Stories), Berlin, Vienna, Leipzig: Paul Zsolnay Verlag   1929
Die grosse Sache (Novel), Berlin: Gustav Kiepenheuer Verlag   1930
Geist und Tat. Franzosen 1780–1930 (Essays), Berlin: Gustav
     Kiepenheuer Verlag   1931
Ein ernstes Leben (Novel), Berlin, Vienna, Leipzig: Paul Zsolnay
     Verlag   1932
Das öffentliche Leben (Essays), Berlin, Vienna, Leipzig: Paul
     Zsolnay Verlag (Collected Works)   1932

Das Bekenntnis zum Übernationalen (Essay), Berlin, Vienna,
    Leipzig: Paul Zsolnay Verlag   1933
Der Hass. Deutsche Zeitgeschichte (Essays), Amsterdam: Querido
    Verlag   1933
*Heinrich Mann und ein junger Deutscher: Der Sinn dieser
    Emigration,* Paris: Europäischer Merkur (Die Streitschriften
    des Europäischen Merkur)   1934
Die Jugend des Königs Henri Quatre (Novel), Amsterdam: Querido
    Verlag   1935
Es kommt der Tag (German Reader), Zurich: Europa-Verlag   1936
Die Vollendung des Königs Henri Quatre (Novel), Amsterdam:
    Querido Verlag   1938
Mut (Essays), Paris: Editions du 10 mai   1939
Lidice (Novel), Amsterdam: Editorial "El Libro Libre"   1943
Ein Zeitalter wird besichtigt (Autobiography), Stockholm: Neuer
    Verlag   1945
Der Atem (Novel), Amsterdam: Querido Verlag   1949
Empfang bei der Welt (Novel), Berlin: Aufbau-Verlag   1956
Die traurige Geschichte von Friedrich dem Grossen (Fragment of
    a novel), Berlin: Deutsche Akademie der Künste, special
    printing from the review *Sinn und Form,* Vol. 10, Nos 2
    and 3   1958
Das Strumpfband (Comedy in 3 Acts), Berlin: Henschelverlag   1965
*Verteidigung der Kultur. Antifaschistische Streitschriften und
    Essays,* Berlin: Aufbau-Verlag   1971

LETTERS

Briefe an Karl Lemke 1917—1949, Berlin: Aufbau-Verlag   1936
Briefe an Karl Lemke und Klaus Pinkus, Hamburg: Claasen Verlag   1965
Thomas Mann—Heinrich Mann, Briefwechsel, Berlin: Aufbau-
    Verlag   1965
Thomas Mann—Heinrich Mann, Briefwechsel, Frankfurt:
    S. Fischer Verlag   1969

FIRST EDITIONS IN ENGLISH

Berlin: The Land of Cockaigne (Im Schlaraffenland), translated by
    Axton D.B. Clark, London: Gollancz   1929
The Little Town (Die kleine Stadt), translated by Winifred Ray,
    London: Martin Secker   1930
The Blue Angel (Das blaue Engel), London: Readers Library
    Publishing Co.   1931

The Royal Woman (Eugénie oder die Bürgerzeit), translated by
    Arthur J. Ashton, London: E. Mathews & Marrot   1931
The Hill of Lies (Ein ernstes Leben), translated by Edwin and
    Willa Muir, London: Jarrolds   1934
Henri Quatre, translated by Eric Sutton in 3 volumes, London: 1937,
    Secker & Warburg   1938, 1939
Man of Straw (Der Untertan), translated by Ernest Boyd, London:
    Hutchinson   1947

TRANSLATIONS BY HEINRICH MANN

Wer zuletzt lacht . . . translation of *Qui perd gagne* by Alfred
    Capus, Munich: Verlag Albert Langen   1901
Komödiantengeschichte, translation of *L'histoire comique* by
    Anatole France, Munich: Verlag Albert Langen   1904
Schlimme Liebschaften, translation of *Les Liaisons dangereuses*
    by Pierre Ambroise François Choderlos de Laclos; with an
    introduction by Heinrich Mann, Leipzig: Insel-Verlag   1905

THOMAS MANN

FIRST EDITIONS IN GERMAN

Der kleine Herr Friedemann (Stories), Berlin: S. Fischer Verlag   1898
Buddenbrooks (Novel), Berlin: S. Fischer Verlag.   1901
Tristan (Stories: contains *Tonio Kröger*), Berlin: S. Fischer Verlag   1903
Fiorenza (Drama), Berlin: S. Fischer Verlag   1905
Königliche Hoheit (Novel), Berlin: S. Fischer Verlag   1909
Der Tod in Venedig (Short novel), Berlin: S. Fischer Verlag   1913
Das Wunderkind (Stories), Berlin: S. Fischer Verlag   1914
Betrachtungen eines Unpolitischen (Autobiographical Reflections),
    Berlin: S. Fischer Verlag   1918
Herr und Hund. Idyll (Contains also *Gesang vom Kindchen*, an
    idyll in verse) Berlin: S. Fischer Verlag   1919
Wälsungenblut (Story), Munich: Phantasus Verlag   1921
Bemühungen (Essays), Berlin: S. Fischer Verlag   1922
Rede und Antwort (Essays), Berlin: S. Fischer Verlag   1922
Bekenntnisse des Hochstaplers Felix Krull: Buch der Kindheit
    (Fragment of a novel), Stuttgart: Deutsche Verlags-Anstalt   1923
Der Zauberberg (Novel), Berlin: S. Fischer Verlag   1924
Unordnung und frühes Leid (Short novel), Berlin: S. Fischer Verlag   1926
Kino (Fragment of a novel), Berlin: S. Fischer Verlag   1926
Pariser Rechenschaft (Travelogue), Berlin: S. Fischer Verlag   1926
Deutsche Ansprache: Ein Appell an die Vernunft (Lecture),
    Berlin: S. Fischer Verlag   1930
Die Forderung des Tages (Essays), Berlin: S. Fischer Verlag   1930

Mario und der Zauberer (Short novel), Berlin: S. Fischer Verlag	1930
Goethe als Repräsentant des bürgerlichen Zeitalters (Lecture), Berlin: S. Fischer Verlag	1932
Joseph und seine Brüder (Tetralogy),	
I *Die Geschichten Jaakobs*, Berlin: S. Fischer Verlag	1933
II *Der junge Joseph*, Berlin: S. Fischer Verlag	1934
III *Joseph in Ägypten*, Vienna: Bermann-Fischer Verlag	1936
IV *Joseph, der Ernährer*, Stockholm: Bermann-Fischer Verlag	1943
Leiden und Grösse der Meister (Essays), Berlin: S. Fischer Verlag	1935
Freud und die Zukunft (Lecture), Vienna: Bermann-Fischer Verlag	
Ein Briefwechsel Zurich: Dr Oprecht & Helbling AG	1937
Schopenhauer (Essay), Stockholm: Bermann-Fischer Verlag	1938
Achtung, Europa! (Manifesto), Stockholm, Bermann-Fischer Verlag	1938
Die schönsten Erzählungen (Stories: contains *Tonio Kröger, Der Tod in Venedig, Unordnung und frühes Leid, Mario und der Zauberer*), Stockholm: Bermann-Fischer Verlag	1938
Das Problem der Freiheit (Essay), Stockholm: Bermann-Fischer Verlag	1939
Lotte in Weimar (Novel), Stockholm: Bermann-Fischer Verlag	1939
Die vertauschten Köpfe: Eine indische Legende (Short novel), Stockholm: Bermann-Fischer Verlag	1940
Deutsche Hörer! (Broadcasts), Stockholm: Bermann-Fischer Verlag	1942
Das Gesetz (Story), Stockholm: Bermann-Fischer Verlag	1944
Doktor Faustus: Das Leben des deutschen Tonsetzers Adrian Leverkühn, erzählt von einem Freunde (Novel), Stockholm: Bermann-Fischer Verlag	1947
Der Erwählte (Novel), Frankfurt am Main: S. Fischer Verlag	1951
Die Betrogene (Short novel), Frankfurt am Main: S. Fischer Verlag	1953
Altes und Neues: Kleine Prosa aus fünf Jahrzehnten (Essays), Frankfurt am Main: S. Fischer Verlag	1953
Bekenntnisse des Hochstaplers Felix Krull. Der Memoiren erster Teil (Novel), Frankfurt am Main: S. Fischer Verlag	1954
Die Enstehung des Doktor Faustus (Novel), Berlin: Aufbau Verlag	1955
Lebensabriss (Autobiography), Berlin: Aufbau Verlag	1955
Nachlese: Prosa 1951–55 (Essays), Frankfurt am Main: S. Fischer Verlag	1956

LETTERS

Thomas Mann, Briefe 1889–1936
Thomas Mann, Briefe 1937–1947
Thomas Mann, Briefe 1948–1955 und Nachlese, Frankfurt: 1961,
   S. Fischer Verlag   1963, 1965

Thomas Mann, Briefe an Paul Amman 1915–1952, Lübeck:
Stadtbibliothek   1959
*Thomas Mann an Ernst Bertram, Briefe aus den Jahren 1910–
1955*, Pfullingen: Neske Verlag   1960
Thomas Mann–Robert Faesi, Briefwechsel, Zurich: Atlantis
Verlag   1962
Thomas Mann–Karl Kerenyi, Gespräch in Briefen, Zurich: Rhein-
Verlag   1960
Thomas Mann–Heinrich Mann, (see under Heinrich Mann)
*Thomas Mann, Briefwechsel mit seinem Verleger Gottfried Bermann-
Fischer 1932–1955*, Frankfurt: S. Fischer Verlag   1973

FIRST EDITIONS IN ENGLISH (published by Secker & Warburg, London, unless
otherwise stated)

Royal Highness: A novel of German Court Life (Königliche Hoheit),
translated by A. Cecil Curtiss, London:
Sidgwick & Jackson   1916
Secker & Warburg   1940
Bashan and I (Herr und Hund) translated by Herman George
Scheffauer, London: Collins   1923
Buddenbrooks translated by H.T. Lowe-Porter   1924
The Magic Mountain (Der Zauberberg), translated by H.T. Lowe-
Porter, two volumes   1927
Death in Venice (Der Tod in Venedig), translated by H.T. Lowe-
Porter (contains *Death in Venice, Tristan*, and *Tonio Kröger*) 1928
Early Sorrow (Unordnung und frühes Leid), translated by H.T.
Lowe-Porter   1929
Mario and the Magician (Mario und der Zauberer), translated
by H.T. Lowe-Porter   1930
A Sketch of My Life (Lebensabriss), translated by H.T. Lowe-
Porter,
Paris: Harrison   1930
London: Secker & Warburg   1931
Three Essays, translated by H.T. Lowe-Porter (contains trans-
lations of *Friedrich und die grosse Koalition* from *Rede und
Antwort*, and of *Goethe und Tolstoi* and *Okkulte Erlebnisse*
from *Bemühungen)*   1932
Past Masters and Other Papers, (Leiden und Grösse der Meister),
translated by H.T. Lowe-Porter   1933
Joseph and His Brothers (Joseph und seine Brüder),
I   *The Tales of Jacob*   1934
II *Young Joseph*   1935
III *Joseph in Egypt*   1938

IV *Joseph the Provider*   1944
    (the complete work in 1 volume), translated by H.T. Lowe-
    Porter   1948
Stories of Three Decades, translated by H.T. Lowe-Porter, (contains
    all of Thomas Mann's fiction prior to 1940 except the long
    novels)   1936
The Coming Victory of Democracy, translated by Agnes E. Meyer
    (includes *An Exchange of Letters*, translated by H.T. Lowe-
    Porter)   1938
This War (Dieser Krieg), translated by Eric Sutton   1940
Lotte in Weimar, translated by H.T. Lowe-Porter   1940
*The Transposed Heads: A Legend of India (Die vertauschten
    Köpfe)*, translated by H.T. Lowe-Porter   1941
Order of the Day: Political Essays and Speeches of Two Decades
    translated by H.T. Lowe-Porter, Agnes E. Meyer, and Eric
    Sutton   1943
The Tables of the Law (Das Gesetz), translated by H.T. Lowe-Porter   1945
Essays of Three Decades translated by H.T. Lowe-Porter   1947
*Doctor Faustus: The Life of the German Composer Adrian Lever-
    kühn as Told by a Friend*, translated by H.T. Lowe-Porter   1948
The Holy Sinner (Der Erwählte), translated by H.T. Lowe-Porter   1951
The Black Swan (Die Betrogene), translated by Williard R. Trask   1954
*Confessions of Felix Krull, Confidence Man: The Early Years,
    (Bekenntnisse des Hochstaplers Felix Krull)*, translated by
    Denver Lindley   1955
Last Essays translated by Richard and Clara Winston and Tania
    and James Stern   1959
Stories of a Lifetime (Two volumes: the collected stories, includ-
    ing *Stories of Three Decades, The Transposed Heads, Tables
    of the Law, The Black Swan*)   1961
The Genesis of a Novel (Die Entstehung des Doktor Faustus),
    translated by Richard and Clara Winston   1961

LETTERS

The Letters of Thomas Mann 1889—1955, Volume 1: 1889—
    1942, Volume 2: 1943—1945, translated by R. and C.
    Winston, London: Secker & Warburg   1970
Thomas Mann. Letters to Paul Amman, translated by R. and C.
    Winston, London: Secker & Warburg   1961

INDEX